UNITED NATIONS FORCES

AUSTRALIA
The Law Book Co. of Australasia Pty. Ltd.
Sydney : Melbourne : Brisbane

GREAT BRITAIN
Stevens & Sons
London

INDIA
N. M. Tripathi Private Ltd.
Bombay

ISRAEL
Steimatzky's Agency Ltd.
Tel Aviv

NEW ZEALAND
Sweet & Maxwell (N.Z.) Ltd.
Wellington

PAKISTAN
Pakistan Law House
Karachi

U.S.A. AND CANADA
Frederick A. Praeger, Inc.
New York

UNITED NATIONS FORCES

A Legal Study

BY

D. W. BOWETT

With the Assistance and Collaboration of

G. P. BARTON
HENRY CARTER CARNEGIE
WING-COMMANDER A. E. COBUS
J. G. COLLIER
MICHAEL HARDY
ROSALYN HIGGINS
LOUIS B. SOHN

Published under the Auspices of
The David Davies Memorial Institute

FREDERICK A. PRAEGER, *Publishers*

NEW YORK · WASHINGTON

BOOKS THAT MATTER

Published in the United States of America in 1964
by Frederick A. Praeger, Inc., Publishers
111 Fourth Avenue, New York 3, N.Y.

© David Davies Memorial Institute 1964
Library of Congress Catalog Card Number : 64-22489
Printed in Great Britain

FOREWORD

by

Lord McNair, Q.C.

THIS is an important and very topical book. It is a history of the creation of international forces during the last two decades; a handbook for those responsible for their future organisation and administration; and a text-book for the lawyer called upon to advise on the many legal questions to which they give rise.

It has long been obvious that, if the United Nations is to become effective in its peace-keeping role, a permanent Force of one kind or another must be placed at its disposal or be made available for use under its authority. So far, the use of force for the purposes of the Charter of the United Nations has taken a variety of forms, and it is unlikely for some time that a single and regular form will emerge. The operations required of it may vary from something approaching a full-scale war, as in Korea, to the duty of putting out " bush-fires " or supervising a truce or armistice or arranging an exchange of populations.

Equally varied are the legal problems to which these operations can give rise; for instance, which of the organs of the United Nations has power under the Charter to create a Force or to appoint its commander? Should the Force be formed by the enlistment of individuals or by the contribution of contingents by member States? How far, if at all, is a Member State responsible for the action of its own contingent? What is the status of the Force? Where does responsibility for military discipline reside? Do the laws and customs of war and any of the Hague Conventions of 1899 or 1907 apply? Who has the right to sue for compensation upon the unlawful killing or injury of a member of a United Nations Force—his Government or the United

v

Nations? What is the liability of member States to contribute to the cost of United Nations Forces? And so on.

I wish to make it clear that a United Nations Force discharging the tasks mentioned above is not the kind of Force which will be required for the control of gradual and parallel disarmament. It may well be that a United Nations peace-keeping Force as hitherto envisaged and actually seen in operation may prove to be the precursor of a disarmament Force, and there is no doubt that many lessons will be learnt from the existence of a permanent peace-keeping Force which will be helpful in the creation of a Force for the control of disarmament; but it is a profound mistake to think that the establishment of a permanent Force for peace-keeping purposes can await the progress or conclusion of the disarmament negotiations. This has long been my personal view, and it is a view which I am glad to see Dr. Bowett shares.

Dr. Bowett is an experienced international lawyer who has had the great advantage of spending two years on the staff of the Secretariat of the United Nations and has thus acquired some insight into the extreme complications of international administration. After a careful investigation of the vast documentation to which the creation of United Nations Forces in the past has given rise, he has elaborated in this book a scheme which is moderate, gradual and practical. I sincerely hope that it will be carefully examined by all those who regard the establishment of a permanent peace-keeping Force under the control of the United Nations as a prime objective, and that the work sponsored by the David Davies Memorial Institute, and undertaken by Dr. Bowett in this book will focus public opinion upon the achievement of this objective.

The plan of the book is an examination of the actual experience of United Nations Forces since 1950, a discussion of the principles governing their creation and functions, the relationship of such a Force to disarmament, and the outline of a scheme for the gradual creation of a permanent peace-keeping Force. After a brief mention of some of the *ad hoc* international Forces which preceded the establishment of the United Nations, for instance, for the purpose of the Saar plebiscite in 1935, he describes the scheme embodied in Chapter VII of the Charter of the United Nations and the failure to implement it. He then examines the action of the United Nations in regard to Korea from 1950 onwards, the composition and character of the Force, its command structure, its strategic and political control, and the legal status of the operations. There were sixteen participating States, of which one—the United States—was " the executive agent of the United Nations Forces in Korea." In Dr. Bowett's words the Korean operations " marked the first attempt by an international organisation to check an act of aggression," and, though these operations were anomalous in several respects, certain lessons, military, political and legal, can be learned from them.

He then considers a number of *ad hoc* field missions appointed by the United Nations for the purposes of conciliation, good offices and mediation between States involved in a dispute, and, as one of the main functions of these missions is to obtain impartial information, he classifies them as " United Nations Observer Groups." One instance is the despatch to Israel in 1948 of a Truce Commission and Count Bernadotte as Mediator. His assassination in Jerusalem was followed in 1949 by the Advisory Opinion of the International Court of Justice—known as the *Reparation for Injuries Suffered in the Service of the United Nations* Opinion, which is of general application and in which Count Bernadotte is not mentioned. The Opinion contains some important remarks upon the international personality of the United Nations and affirms its capacity to bring international claims for the protection of its agents. Other instances of an Observer Group occur in the Lebanon in 1958 when the Security Council decided to " dispatch urgently an observation group to proceed to the Lebanon so as to ensure that there is no illegal infiltration of personnel or supply of arms or other war material across the Lebanese border "; in West

New Guinea in 1962 where the Netherlands and Indonesia were involved in a dispute; and in the Yemen in 1963.

We now come to more serious operations. The *United Nations Emergency Force* (UNEF) was formed in November 1956 as a result of the Suez crisis. It was created under the authority of Resolutions of the General Assembly, and its legality and constitutionality have been the subject of much controversy. Dr. Bowett devotes sixty pages to the purpose, structure and operations of this Force. Its main function was to " supervise the voluntary acceptance of the recommendations of the General Assembly by the State concerned." The relations between the United Nations and the ten participating Member States, and between the United Nations and the host State (Egypt), the command structure, the strategic and political control, its privileges and immunities, and the budgetary arrangements are fully discussed. " One of the fundamental characteristics of UNEF is that it is a United Nations Force, and is neither a Force representing the interests of the national States contributing members to it, nor one which can be used as an instrument of its policies by the host State " (p. 121). In the Status Agreement the Force is described as an " organ of the General Assembly." It is significant that no units of the Force were drawn from any of the Big Five Powers having permanent seats in the Security Council. It was formed not by the enlistment of individuals but by the contribution of contingents by the participating States, which did not include any of the Big Five Powers. The cost has given rise to certain grave questions which have not yet been settled.

The next major operation was the organisation and despatch of the *United Nations Force in the Congo* (ONUC) to that country in 1960, to which 100 pages of this book are devoted. Constitutionally it was based on Resolutions of the Security Council and of the General Assembly. As in the case of UNEF, ONUC consisted of contingents supplied by Members of the United Nations, not by individual enlistment. As in the case of UNEF, it was impossible to include contingents from the Big Five Powers. In the light of this fact—common to both UNEF and ONUC—it is significant, if one may say so with all respect for the ability, courage and resourcefulness of the officers and men of these Forces in the face of great and novel difficulties, that in the composition and command of these armies it was not possible to draw upon the great reservoir of military talent and experience which those Big Five Powers possess.

The creation of the United Nations Force in Cyprus was too late for detailed treatment in this book, but it contains a postscript of seven pages upon the subject.

In 1962 the General Assembly requested an Advisory Opinion of the International Court on the subject of certain expenditure incurred upon UNEF and ONUC and was advised that it was "expenses of the Organisation" within the meaning of Article 17, paragraph 2, of the Charter. The application of this Opinion is still under consideration by the General Assembly.

Part I of the book concludes with a few pages on the United Nations Temporary Executive Authority (UNTEA) established in 1949 for the purpose of enabling the Secretary-General to carry out certain tasks resulting from the Agreement between the Netherlands and the Indonesians concerning West New Guinea (West Irian).

From Part I, which is mainly historical and specific in its treatment, we turn to Part II (pp. 265 to 516) which forms the substance of the book. In it the author, while continually illustrating his argument by reference to the actual experience described in Part I, sets himself the task of fundamental thinking upon the political difficulties which surround any proposal for a United Nations Force and the constitutional and other legal problems which must be solved, once the decision to create a Force has been taken. This is the very heart of the matter, and the reader cannot fail to be greatly impressed by the courage with which Dr. Bowett faces the problems and the honesty that he exhibits in a field where realism wages war with enthusiasm, optimism and wishful thinking. This Part is devoted to the consideration of questions of principle, many of which have already been raised by actual experience, while others are bound to arise in attempting to create something systematic instead of improvising every time the need of an international Force arises. He discusses the various possible functions of a United Nations Force and distinguishes between the " enforcement functions " contemplated by the hitherto abortive Chapter VII of the Charter and the " peace-keeping functions " with which this book is primarily concerned. The constitutional bases of the Force, its structure and control, the agreements between the United Nations and participating States, the logistical support of the Force, the relevance of the consent of the " host " State in the presence of a Force, agreements with the " host " State, the financing of the Force, the application of the laws and customs of war, and many other factors, are examined with great care and knowledge.

Part III (pp. 519–551) deals with Disarmament and an International Force, and the Conclusions contains the scheme for the creation of a Permanent Force in four stages spread over ten years.

The documentation which it has been necessary for Dr. Bowett to examine and assess for the purposes of this book is truly immense. But I am sure that his labour has not been in vain. Nearly every step in the process of creating any of the international Forces described above has been marked by acute conflict. His approach is that of the lawyer, and the reader will be grateful for the clarity and objectivity with which he has steered his course through a mass of controversial material.

The characteristic of the past fourteen years has been hurried improvisation in an atmosphere of conflict and suspicion every time a crisis arises. What is now needed is to equip the United Nations with a strong Headquarters Military Staff whose duty it will be to prepare in advance the framework of an international Force of moderate size which can be rapidly deployed in accordance with pre-existing negotiations with the Governments of Member States for the supply of military units, and to plan for contingencies likely to arise as a national Military Staff would do. That is the essence of Dr. Bowett's proposal based on a well-documented argument and marked by clear and practical thinking.

PREFACE

In July 1962 I was invited by a Study Group, set up by The David Davies Memorial Institute, to undertake a Study on United Nations Forces. The Study Group consisted of the following:

> Sir Frank Soskice (Chairman)
> Professor Norman Bentwich
> Professor N. C. H. Dunbar
> Mr. J. B. S. Edwards
> Mr. Michael Hardy
> Lord McNair
> Mr. Michael Mann
> Dr. Andrew Martin
> Professor Sir Humphrey Waldock

Having approved a general plan for the Study, the Study Group left me entirely free to formulate my own views and, whilst I have benefited considerably from suggestions made by individual members of the Group, the Study has evolved as an expression of my personal opinions and not those of members of the Group, either individually or collectively. Hence the Study, as it is now published in this book, is a work for which I assume sole responsibility. The book will, in due course, form the basis—but not the exclusive basis— upon which the Group as a whole will examine the problems arising from the creation and employment of United Nations Forces and it is hoped that a collective report may eventually be published by the Group as such.

The Institute, the Group and I shared a common belief that a study of United Nations Forces was both opportune and, indeed, urgent. Thus I began my own work convinced not only of its importance but also of the need for expedition in bringing it to an early conclusion.

This same need for expedition suggested that completion of the Study would be advanced if the preparation of some parts of it, in the form of first drafts, could be entrusted to persons who were known to be interested in the subject. Accordingly, I asked the following to assist in this way: Dr. G. P. Barton, Victoria University of Wellington, New Zealand; Mr. Henry Carter Carnegie, Institute of Advanced Legal Studies, London; Wing-Commander A. E. Cobus; Mr. J. G. Collier, King's College, London; Mr. Michael Hardy; Dr. Rosalyn Higgins, The Royal Institute of International Affairs, Chatham House, London, S.W.1; Professor Louis B. Sohn, Harvard Law School, Cambridge, Mass., U.S.A.

It is fitting that I record my very real appreciation of the generosity of these contributors who, by undertaking to help in this way, have assisted in bringing the Study to an early completion. However, their generosity can best be illustrated by recording also the basis upon which they agreed to assist, for that included my own freedom to integrate, revise and rewrite any of the drafts so submitted. The extent to which this has had to be done has varied, but it has meant that the Study as it is now published is, again, something for which I must accept sole responsibility.

In addition to the advice and assistance received from the Study Group and the seven contributors named above, I have greatly valued the help of Dr. Oscar Schachter of the United Nations Secretariat in providing me with current United Nations documents; of Professor R. R. Baxter of the Harvard Law School and the Hon. Alastair Buchan of the Institute for Strategic Studies in offering advice and criticism on certain parts of the Study; and of Lt.-Colonel T. Randers, Air and Army Attaché of the Royal Norwegian Embassy, London, in providing factual information.

It is a pleasure to record my own appreciation of the constant help and encouragement which I have received from The David Davies Memorial Institute and, in particular, from Miss M. M. Sibthorp, but for whose enthusiasm and determination this Study would probably not have been written. Finally, I should wish to express my gratitude to Messrs. Stevens & Sons, who have contrived to make yet another contribution to the study of problems of international law by undertaking the publication of the Study.

The scope of the Study is apparent from the Table of Contents. Part One sets out what may be termed the " precedents ": it is a series of brief case-studies of the attempts to establish international forces, and it is on the basis of an examination of these precedents that, in Part Two, an attempt has been made to examine some of the problems common to any United Nations Force which may be established. The entirety of Part Two, and in particular the proposals which it embodies for development of a United Nations Force within the framework of the Charter of the United Nations, is concerned with the immediate future. The proposals relate to what it is believed can and should be done *now*: they do not presuppose any general agreement on disarmament or revision of the United Nations Charter. Part Three alone is devoted to plans for a United Nations Force under a disarming or disarmed world, and, in so far as this part constitutes but a small part of the entire Study, this is done intentionally so as to reflect the view that the development of a permanent United Nations Force ought to begin now, and not await general and complete disarmament.

The decision of the Security Council to authorise the establishment of a United Nations Force in Cyprus was reached after the typescript had been submitted to the Press, and it was therefore impossible to do more than to cover this latest example of a United Nations Force in a postscript at the end of the book.

Much of the Study, and of the proposals which it contains —and these are summarised in the Conclusions—is not new. Yet it is believed that, in its entirety, it is the first attempt to examine comprehensively the problems of United Nations Forces, to state the case for the formation of a permanent United Nations Force and to suggest steps which may be taken towards creating a permanent United Nations Force. I am deeply conscious of the inadequacies of the Study as a comprehensive examination of so large, and so important, a problem; and certainly not all of these inadequacies are explained by the attempt to produce it as quickly as possible. However, the conviction that such a Study might assist in the understanding of the problems involved in creating a more effective machinery for maintaining the peace and security of the world is most sincerely held, and it is hoped that it will help to spread and strengthen the will to create such machinery.

D. W. BOWETT.

QUEENS' COLLEGE,
    CAMBRIDGE.

March, 1964

CONTENTS

Foreword by Lord McNair, Q.C.   *page*   v
Preface   xiii
Table of Abbreviations   xxi
Table of Maps and Diagrams   xxiv

PART ONE

1. INTERNATIONAL FORCES PRIOR TO THE ESTABLISHMENT OF
THE UNITED NATIONS   3
    I. Permanent "international" police forces   4
    II. *Ad hoc* international forces   5

2. THE MILITARY STAFF COMMITTEE, THE COLLECTIVE MEASURES
COMMITTEE AND THE PROPOSALS OF THE SECRETARY-
GENERAL IN 1948 AND 1952   12
    I. The Military Staff Committee   12
    II. The Secretary-General's proposals for a United Nations
      Guard   18
    III. The Collective Measures Committee   21

3. THE UNITED NATIONS ACTION IN KOREA   29
    I. The action taken by the Security Council   30
    II. The United Nations Forces in Korea   36
    III. The Armistice and truce negotiations   47
    IV. The legal status of the conflict and the application of
      the laws of war   53
    V. Status of Forces Agreements   57
    VI. Civilian relief operations   58
    VII. Conclusions   59

4. UNITED NATIONS OBSERVER GROUPS   61
    I. Constitutional basis of Observer Groups   61
    II. Composition and equipment   68
    III. Functions   71
    IV. The obligations assumed by States   79
    V. Claims   85
    VI. Conclusions   86

5. THE UNITED NATIONS EMERGENCY FORCE (UNEF)   90
    I. The establishment of UNEF   90
    II. The constitutional basis of UNEF   93
    III. The role of the Secretary-General   99
    IV. Functions of UNEF   105

Contents

5. THE UNITED NATIONS EMERGENCY FORCE (UNEF)—*continued*
  V. Relations between the United Nations and participating
     States   109
  VI. Command Structure   115
  VII. Strategic and political control   117
  VIII. Administrative arrangements   118
  IX. The Regulations for UNEF   119
  X. UNEF as a United Nations international Force   121
  XI. Relations between the United Nations and the host State   124
  XII. Relations between the United Nations and other States   136
  XIII. Financial arrangements   139
  XIV. Claims   149

6. THE UNITED NATIONS FORCE IN THE CONGO (ONUC)   153
  I. The basic Resolutions adopted by the Security Council
     and General Assembly   154
  II. The constitutional basis of the Resolutions adopted   174
  III. The role of the Secretary-General   183
  IV. The functions of the Force   186
  V. The restrictions on ONUC inherent in the principle of
     non-intervention and in the principle that ONUC
     should act only in self-defence   196
  VI. Relations between the United Nations and contributing
     States   205
  VII. Relations between the United Nations and Member
     States generally   224
  VIII. Relations between the United Nations and the "host"
     State   230
  IX. Claims and responsibility   242
  X. Civilian relief operations   248
  XI. Financing of ONUC   249

7. THE UNITED NATIONS TEMPORARY EXECUTIVE AUTHORITY
  (UNTEA)   255
  I. The action of the General Assembly   255
  II. The functions of UNTEA generally, and of the UNSF in
     particular   257
  III. Composition of the Force   259
  IV. Privileges and Immunities   260
  V. Finance   260

PART TWO

INTRODUCTION   265
8. THE FUNCTIONS AND CONSTITUTIONAL BASES OF UNITED
  NATIONS FORCES   266
  I. Enforcement functions   267
  II. "Peace-keeping operations" for the maintenance of
     international peace and security   267
  III. Constitutional bases   274

9. STRUCTURE AND CONTROL OF UNITED NATIONS FORCES   313
    I. Types of Force   313
    II. Methods of raising United Nations Forces   330
    III. Command Structure   337
    IV. Political control of United Nations Forces   353

10. AGREEMENTS BETWEEN THE UNITED NATIONS AND PARTICI-
    PATING STATES FOR THE PROVISION OF FORCES   361
    I. " *Ad hoc* " Agreements   361
    II. " Stand-by " Agreements   371
    III. Agreements for a permanent Force   377
    IV. Withdrawal of national contingents   379

11. LOGISTICAL SUPPORT AND MOVEMENT OF UNITED NATIONS
    FORCES   387
    I. Arrangements between the United Nations and Member
        States for logistical support   387
    II. Movement and supplies   394
    III. Financial arrangements between the United Nations
        and Member States   406

12. THE RELEVANCE OF CONSENT TO THE PRESENCE OF A UNITED
    NATIONS FORCE   412
    I. The question whether the consent of a State is required
        for the presence of a United Nations Force upon its
        territory   412
    II. The effect of withdrawal of consent to the presence of
        the Force by the host State   420
    III. Consent and the rule of non-intervention   422

13. AGREEMENTS WITH " HOST " STATES   428
    I. The basic Agreement   428
    II. United Nations Status of Forces Agreements   432
    III. Transit Agreements   455
    IV. Bases Agreements   458

14. FINANCING OF UNITED NATIONS MILITARY OPERATIONS   468
    I. Sources of funds   468
    II. Prospects of future financing   481

15. THE APPLICATION OF THE LAWS OF WAR TO OPERATIONS BY
    UNITED NATIONS FORCES   484
    I. Classification of United Nations Forces in terms of their
        function   484
    II. Classification of United Nations Forces in terms of their
        Command Structure   487
    III. Areas of the law of war relevant to United Nations
        operations   488
    IV. Extent to which the areas of the law of war are applic-
        able to United Nations Forces   492

Contents

PART THREE

16. Disarmament and an International Force   519
    I. The relationship of disarmament to peacekeeping   519
    II. The relationship of an international Force to other
         peacekeeping arrangements   523
    III. The United Nations, the International Disarmament
         Organisation (IDO) and an international Peace Force   531
    IV. The constitutional basis of an international Force   538
    V. Financial arrangements   543
    VI. The functions of an international Force and the Peace
         Observation Corps   545

Postscript: The United Nations Force in Cyprus (UNFICYP)   552
    I. The Resolution adopted by the Security Council   552
    II. The role of the Secretary-General   554
    III. The functions of the Force   555
    IV. Relations with the host State   558

Conclusions   561
    I. Stage One (to be completed within three years)   563
    II. Stage Two (to be completed within two years)   565
    III. Stage Three (to be completed within two years)   566
    IV. Stage Four (to be completed within three years)   566

Index   571

TABLE OF ABBREVIATIONS

ADL	Armistice Demarcation Line
A.J.	*American Journal of International Law* (1907–)
ANC	Armée nationale congolaise
Ann.Fr.D.I.	*Annuaire Français de Droit International* (1955–)
B.F.S.P.	*British and Foreign State Papers* (1812–)
Blueprint	Blueprint for the Peace Race: Outline of Basic Provisions of a Treaty on General and Complete Disarmament in a Peaceful World, US Arms Control and Disarmament Agency, Publication 4 (May, 1962)
BYBIL	*British Year Book of International Law* (1920–)
Cmd.	United Kingdom Command Papers (1919–56)
Cmnd.	United Kingdom Command Papers (1956–)
Columbia L.R.	*Columbia Law Review*
C.M.R.	Courts Martial Reports of the United States
Dept.State Bulletin	*United States Department of State Bulletin* (1939–)
F. 2d.	Federal Reporter Second Series (United States)
G.L.J.	*Georgetown Law Journal*
H.C. Deb.	Parliamentary Debates (Hansard), House of Commons, Official Report
H.L. Deb.	Parliamentary Debates (Hansard), House of Lords, Official Report
I.C.J. Reports	Reports of the International Court of Justice
I.C.L.Q.	*International and Comparative Law Quarterly*
IDO	International Disarmament Organisation
I.L.A.	International Law Association
I.L.Q.	*International Law Quarterly*
I.L.R.	International Law Reports (1950–)
I.M.T.	International Military Tribunal
Int.Organisation	International Organisation (1947–)
K.B.	King's Bench (Division of English High Court)
L.N.T.S.	League of Nations Treaty Series
MAC	Mixed Armistice Commission
Martens N.R.G.	G. F. de Martens, Nouveau recueil général de traités
Michigan L.R.	*Michigan Law Review*
NATO	North Atlantic Treaty Organisation
Ned.Tijd.Int.Recht	*Nederlands Tijdschrift voor international recht* (1953–)
N.Z.L.J.	*New Zealand Law Journal*
N.Z.T.S.	New Zealand Treaty Series

Off.Rec.G.A.   Official Records of the General Assembly of the
                    United Nations
Off.Rec.S.C.   Official Records of the Security Council of the
                    United Nations
ONUC   United Nations Operations in the Congo
Pa.   Pennsylvania Law Reports
P.A.S.I.L.   *Proceedings of the American Society of Inter-*
                    national Law (1907–   )
P.C.I.J.   Permanent Court of International Justice
Repertory   Repertory of Practice of United Nations Organs,
                    vols. 1–5 and Supplements
R.C.   *Recueil des cours de l'Academie de la Haye de*
                    droit international (1923–   )
R.D.I.P.   *Revue de droit international public* (1927–38)
R.G.D.I.P.   *Revue Générale de droit international public*
                    (1894–   )
R.I.I.A.   Royal Institute of International Affairs
S.D.Cal.   South Dakota Reports, California
S.D. Indiana   South Dakota Reports, Indiana
SOFA   Status of Forces Agreement
S.R.   Summary Records
S.R. (N.S.W.)   State Reports, New South Wales (Australia)
Summary Study, etc. Summary Study of the Experience derived from
                    the establishment and operation of the Force
                    (UNEF).   Report of the Secretary-General
                    (A/3943)
Tex.   Texas Supreme Court Reports
U.K. Treaty Series United Kingdom Treaty Series
UNCIO Docs.   Documents of the United Nations Conference
                    on International Organisation, San Francisco,
                    1945, 16 vols.
UNCIP   United Nations Commission in India and
                    Pakistan
UNCOK   United Nations Commission on Korea
UNCURK   United Nations Commission for the Unification
                    and Rehabilitation of Korea
UNEF   United Nations Emergency Force
UNFICYP   United Nations Force in Cyprus
UNKRA   United Nations Korea Reconstruction Agency
UNMOGIP   United Nations Military Observer Group in
                    India and Pakistan
UNOGIL   United Nations Observer Group in the Lebanon
UNSCOB   United Nations Special Committee on the
                    Balkans
UNSF   United Nations Security Force (attached to
                    UNTEA)
UNTEA   United Nations Temporary Executive Authority
U.N.T.S.   United Nations Treaty Series

UNTSO	United Nations Truce Supervision Organisation
UNYOM	United Nations Observer Group in the Yemen
U.S.T.	United Nations Treaty and other International Acts Series (1946–)
Yale L.J.	*Yale Law Journal* (1891–)

TABLE OF MAPS AND DIAGRAMS

	PAGE
Jammu and Kashmir—Cease-fire Line	72–73
Lebanon—Operations of UNOGIL	72
The Congo—Deployment of ONUC	152
Command Structure of ONUC	210
Structure of proposed United Nations Headquarters Military Staff	350

Part One

1

International Forces Prior to the Establishment of the United Nations

WHILST it is the intention in this book to study the legal problems arising from the creation and operation of international forces within the context of the United Nations Charter, it is important that these problems should be seen in their historical context, and not least because a good deal of opposition to the idea of an international force springs from the quite unwarranted assumption that the idea is completely novel.

Admittedly the relevance of historical precedents may depend upon one's definition of an " international force." However, whilst today such a definition would stress the fact of creation by and responsibility to an organ of the international community to which the requisite powers had been delegated by the States, this is to assume a stage of development in international institutions which is very recent indeed. There may well be advantages in examining the use of " international forces" at an earlier stage of development when, lacking comparable institutions, the States would rely upon collective, voluntary action to establish such a force. A definition appropriate to this earlier stage may well have to abandon the criteria of establishment by and responsibility to an organ of the international community and concentrate, instead, on the international composition and international purpose of the force.

One advantage of adopting this wider definition of an international force, at least for the purposes of this chapter, is that, with the aid of historical precedents,[1] a fuller appreciation of the variety of roles of a force is possible. It will become apparent from the following pages that an armed force capable of dealing with threats to international peace and security is by no means the only possible type of international force. Forces ranging from an army in the field to a simple police force are possible in a whole variety of situations, and the role of the force will determine its character. Yet another advantage of a brief review of the historical precedents is to demonstrate the dangers inherent in a system whereby a group of States

[1] The precedents to be used are those from actual State practice: space does not permit any detailed treatment of the views of writers, philosophers and statesmen who, from the Middle Ages onwards, have advocated an " international " force of one kind or another. A summary of these views can be found in Rosner, *The United Nations Emergency Force* (1963), Historical Appendix; Possony, " Peace Enforcement " (1946) 55 Yale L.J. 910; Davies, *The Problem of the Twentieth Century* (1930), Chap. 2.

are left free to take collective action of an " international " character; more than one of the precedents will demonstrate the difficulty of distinguishing the true " international " purpose from the pursuit of purely national interests. The variety of roles which forces have played in the past will, therefore, be examined briefly.

I. PERMANENT " INTERNATIONAL " POLICE FORCES

It would be surprising if many examples of permanent forces were found, but certainly a few examples do exist of police forces being established with a reasonable degree of permanence for a purpose which is more international than national.

In some cases the only " international " element is the direction of a purely national police force by an international body for international purposes. Thus the "Sanitary Police" serving the international sanitary commissions at Constantinople,[2] Alexandria [3] and Tangiers [4] were simply the local police attached to the international commissions or councils for the purpose of enforcing the sanitary regulations. Similarly the police attached to the European Commission of the Danube were the local, Rumanian police, although under the control of the Commission; in addition, the Commission could call upon one of the warships of the signatory Powers to the Paris Treaty of 1856 [5] stationed in the estuary. The Danzig Port and Waterways Board provided for in Chapter III of the Paris Treaty of 9 November 1920 [6] between Danzig and Poland also relied on Danzig police until, in 1934, a special Harbour and River Guard of twenty-four officials was created, exclusively under the authority of the Port Board although, in their appointment, subject to the approval of the Danzig Chief of Police.[7] The Memel Harbour Board, established by Article 5 of the Convention of 8 May 1924,[8] also had its special force of police, but these always remained part of the local police of the Memel Territory.

The more striking examples of permanent international police forces are those of the forces of international composition recruited for service in the international concessions of Shanghai and in the international zone of Tangier. Here the international character of the force, in terms of its composition, is added to the fact of control by an international body for an international purpose. In Shanghai the International Settlement [9] was like an international city state,

---

[2] Wehberg, *International Policing* (1935) p. 37; Vitta, " Le droit sanitaire international " 33 R.C. 583.
[3] *Ibid.*, pp. 585–588.
[4] *Ibid.*, pp. 588–589.
[5] Martens, *N.R.G.*, 1st Ser., 15, p. 770, Art. 19.
[6] L.N.T.S., 6, p. 190.
[7] Wehberg, *op. cit.*, p. 33.
[8] L.N.T.S., 29, p. 95. See generally Ydit, *International Territories* (1961) pp. 48–50; Wehberg, *op. cit.*, p. 35.
[9] See Escarra, *Droits et Intérêts Etrangers en Chine* (1928) p. 60 *et seq.*; Wehberg, *op. cit.*, pp. 11–12; Davidson-Houston, *Yellow Creek* (1962). The right of the Municipal Council to have its own defence force had been

4

governed by a Municipal Council of international composition and subject only to the somewhat tenuous jurisdiction of the Consular Body consisting of the consuls of the fourteen foreign powers with extraterritorial rights. The Municipal Council had at its disposal not only an internationally composed municipal police but also a small army, the Shanghai Volunteer Corps (SVC) with British, American, Chinese, Portuguese, Russian, Filipino and, later, even Jewish companies. Moreover, in 1927, because of the advance of the Chinese Nationalist Armies, the United States, France, Great Britain, Italy, Netherlands, Spain, Portugal and Japan gathered together in Shanghai an *ad hoc* force of 40,000 to protect the settlement and reinforce the SVC. The system collapsed when Japan entered the war in 1941 and occupied the International Settlement.

The international administration of Tangier, as carried out under the revised Statutes of 18 December 1923 and 25 July 1928, had at its disposal a force of 250 police of which the European contingent was half French and half Spanish, but officers might be of other nationalities.[10]

These then, are the examples of rudimentary international forces permanently attached to international commissions or other bodies with administrative functions.

II. AD HOC INTERNATIONAL FORCES

The variety of types of international forces constituted *ad hoc* far exceeds that of the permanent forces and is by no means confined to forces assisting administrative organs.

Many examples are really little more than collective action taken by States for the promotion of their national interests, either by way of joint military action or joint naval blockade. Hence the action by Great Britain, France and Spain against Mexico in 1861 was military action " taken in the name and on account of the High Contracting Parties, without reference to the particular nationality of the forces employed to execute (it)." [11] The naval blockade of the Greek coast in 1886 by five European Powers was designed to maintain the balance of power and force Greece to accept the union of

---

conceded in the "Land Regulations" of 1856: see Ydit, *op. cit.,* pp. 127–153. An international police force also remained in the diplomatic quarter of Peking under Art. 7 of the Final Protocol of 7 September 1901, after the Boxer rebellion had been quelled and the international forces withdrawn.

[10] See Ydit, *op. cit.,* pp. 156–157; Wehberg, *op. cit.,* pp. 12–14; Stuart, *The International City of Tangier* (1931) pp. 31–39. The U.S. in 1896 had suggested having international officers and N.C.O.s to lead the local police force: *Archives of the Department of State, Consular Letters, Tangier,* Vol. 21, 28 December 1896.

[11] Convention of 31 October 1861; the text is given in *Moore's Digest,* Vol. 6, p. 485. The British and Spanish forces withdrew in April 1862 after satisfaction of their claims had been tendered, leaving the French to march on Mexico City alone.

Eastern Roumelia with Bulgaria.[12]   The naval blockade and military invasion of Crete in 1897 by the European Powers was effective in preventing union with Greece and substituting, until 1909, government by a "Commission of the Consuls" of the Powers backed by international forces but subject to Turkish suzerainty.[13]   The three-power blockade of Venezuela in 1902 by Great Britain, Italy and Germany was designed, principally, to enforce claims for debt.   An international squadron, drawn from five States, forced the Sultan of Turkey to introduce financial reform in Macedonia in 1905 and to accept a reorganisation of the gendarmerie, with officers nominated by the five Powers being attached to it.

In some cases the collective action had an aim which could be acknowledged to be somewhat more "international" and less blatantly "national" than those just mentioned.   Hence Great Britain and Germany blockaded Zanzibar in 1888 to secure concessions concerning slavery.   Indeed the anti-slavery provisions in the General Act of the Berlin Conference of 1885 and the Brussels Anti-Slavery Act of 1890 introduced agreement on a very rudimentary form of policing of the high seas in so far as they conceded the right of visit and search of vessels belonging to the signatories.[14]

The intervention in China in 1900, after the Boxer rebellion had revealed a general threat to the lives and property of the foreign community in Peking, affords a remarkable example of military action by international forces drawn from seven States.[15]   The forces were referred to by Lord Salisbury as "international troops"[16] and, in the advance on Peking from Tientsin, whilst no unified command was set up, military direction was assumed by a council of war meeting as necessary and taking decisions by majority.   Following the relief of Peking a German Commander-in-Chief was appointed, Count von Waldersee, and after the evacuation of the main force an

---

[12] B.F.S.P., 1886, Greece, No. 1, p. 7; a full account is given in Hogan, *Pacific Blockade* (1908) pp. 126–130.

[13] Ydit, *op. cit.*, pp. 109–128.   The "Commission of the Consuls" was technically subordinate to the "Board of European Ambassadors" at Istanbul, but was in fact the effective governmental organ except for the period when Prince George governed on behalf of the European Powers between 1899 and 1906; the revolt against him brought the Commission of the Consuls back into control.   The main forces had been withdrawn, only to be brought back to quell this revolt; otherwise only small units of 200 men were left in the territory which was divided up into 4 zones (British, French, Italian, Russian) and the one "international" zone at Canea where the garrison was a mixed one: Dutkowski, *L'occupation de la Crète* (1952) pp. 78, 99.

[14] A similar rudimentary form of policing, simply by conceding rights of visit and search, was introduced by the Convention for the Regulation of the Police of the Fisheries of the North Sea of 1882 and the Convention concerning the Abolition of the Liquor Traffic among the Fishermen in the North Sea of 1887: Martens, *N.R.G.*, 2nd Ser., 9, p. 556, and 14, p. 540.

[15] The forces were approximately 8,000 Japanese, 4,800 Russian, 3,000 British, 2,000 American, 800 French, 100 Austro-Italian and perhaps 200 Germans. See generally B.F.S.P., Vol. XCIV, pp. 1050–1299, Vol XCV, pp. 1136–1352, Vol. XCVI, pp. 864–1126.   For a general account of this incident see Clements, *The Boxer Rebellion* (1915).

[16] Salisbury to Macdonald, 22 June 1900.

international police force remained. This pattern of leaving an international police force once the strictly military contingents had been withdrawn had been adopted previously in Crete in 1897. It was an obvious pattern once the decision had been taken to leave behind an international body with administrative powers, for these could well have to be supported by police action.

The relative success of these embryonic international forces was sufficient to create advocates of a permanent military or naval force. At the Third Hague Peace Conference in September 1910 van Vollenhaven advocated an international navy to enforce arbitral awards and protect the rights of neutral powers,[17] and by 1919, at the Paris Peace Conference, the French Delegation moved an amendment to the Hurst-Miller draft that "The Executive Council shall determine the conditions which are necessary for assuring the permanent existence and the organisation of an international force." [18] The idea was both ambitious and, it turned out, premature. However, the immediate post-First World War years produced a number of opportunities for the use of *ad hoc* international forces in connection with a recurrent problem, that of determining the future of disputed territories, in particular where a plebiscite under international supervision was required.

A situation in which a dispute exists over territory affords an obvious opportunity for the use of an international, and presumably "neutral," force so as to occupy the territory temporarily pending a peaceful solution to the dispute: it may well be the only effective means of preventing war within the territory by the two rival claimant States. In a sense the occupation of Scutari in 1913 [19] by the troops of Great Britain, Italy, Austria, France and Germany pending the creation of an Albanian administration provides an example of this, although the forces were there to enforce a settlement dictated by the European powers to the Montenegrins rather than to ensure either the acceptance of a judicial determination as to title or a political determination of the wishes of the people by plebiscite.

When, however, the international force is used to assist in a plebiscite its "neutral," or perhaps more truly "international," function becomes clearer. The use of the plebiscite was certainly known before the First World War.[20] First employed by the revolutionary Government of France after 1789, it fell into disuse until the wave of revolutions in 1848 called for its revival, and then again fell into comparative neglect, being scarcely used after 1870 except for

---

[17] Wehberg, *op. cit.*, p. 57.
[18] Miller, *The Drafting of the Covenant* (1928) Vol. 1, p. 207, Vol. 2, pp. 241–246, 460; Brück, *Les sanctions en droit international public* (1933) pp. 262–265; Davies, *op. cit.*, p. 127. The French envisaged a general staff at the League's Headquarters which would control the national quotas contributed by each member.
[19] B.F.S.P., 1913, Vol. 106, pp. 448–449.
[20] See Wambaugh, *A Monograph on Plebiscites* (1920).

the dissolution of the Norway-Sweden Union in 1905. However, the many experiences with the plebiscite indicated certain broad conclusions which were relevant to the question of the desirability of an international force. First, the "neutralisation" of the area by the evacuation of troops of the interested States was essential: this much had become clear ever since the evidence of duress by French troops in the Rhine Valley plebiscite in 1793.[21] However, the consequent "power vacuum" carried its own dangers, and evidence of tampering with the returns, for example, in Moldavia and Wallachia in 1857 [22] or in Savoy and Nice in 1860,[23] or of the outbreak of disorder, as in Sicily and Naples in 1860,[24] sufficed to demonstrate the need for international and "neutral" supervision of the actual conduct of the plebiscite, backed up by an international force adequate to maintain order.

The recognition of this need came only after the First World War. The spate of plebiscites made necessary by the territorial readjustments envisaged in the various Peace Treaties marked the first real experiment with an internationally supervised plebiscite. The principle of evacuation by the troops of the contending parties was written as a matter of course into the provisions for every plebiscite in the Treaties of Versailles and Saint-Germain. In fact the only plebiscite attempted between the wars which did not adopt this principle, that in Tacna-Arica in 1925–1926, failed in large measure because of this.[25]

The administration of the plebiscites demanded both a "civil" side, namely, a plebiscite commission in some form which would possibly both administer the territory and supervise the plebiscite, and a "military" side which could range from a police force to a full military force according to circumstances and which would maintain order and ensure the execution of the orders of the "civil" side.

On the "civil" side, the German, Austrian and Hungarian delegations at the Paris Conference had demanded a neutral authority composed of the nationals of neutral States.[26] Of the commissions established, the two most nearly approaching neutrality were those for Schleswig in 1920 and for Vilna, also in 1920. The former held two neutral members (*i.e.*, neither Allies nor nationals of the contending parties), the latter, being a Commission established by the League of Nations and not by the Allied Powers, not unnaturally contained a stronger neutral element of three neutral members; the Vilna plebiscite did not, in fact, take place, since Poland and Lithuania agreed on a solution. For the rest, the plebiscites resulting from the

---

[21] Wambaugh, *op. cit.*, p. 51.
[22] *Ibid.*, p. 117.
[23] *Ibid.*, p. 83.
[24] *Ibid.*, p. 92.
[25] Wambaugh, *Plebiscites since the World War* (1933) Vol. 1, Chap. 9; this was a plebiscite organised by the U.S., not the League.
[26] See Comments by the German Delegation on the Conditions of Peace, *International Conciliation*, No. 143, p. 1228.

Peace Treaties and held under Allied auspices were all supervised by an entirely Allied Commission.

On the "military" side the demand by the Central Powers for neutral troops to fill the vacuum consequent upon evacuation by their own forces proved impracticable and Allied troops only were used. In Schleswig (1920), with an area of approximately 2,000 square miles, the force consisted of one British battalion, one French, and two cruisers and three destroyers from the fleets of the two countries—a force of 3,000 men in all. This international military force was in fact never used, but it lay ready to assist the newly established but locally recruited police force of 250 men controlled by the Police Director of the Plebiscite.[27] Allenstein (1920)[28] had one British and one French battalion, Marienwerder (1920)[29] had a combined Italian and French force of only 700 and Teschen (1920)[30] a similar force of 1,200 whose smallness proved one cause of the failure of the attempt to hold the plebiscite. Klagenfurt (1920)[31] had no Allied troops other than some fifty-eight Allied officers present at the polling booths, although the plebiscite was a success. In Sopron (1921)[32] the attempt to transfer the territory to Austria had first been frustrated by a Hungarian uprising and the Allied Commission actually ousted from part of the territory; hence the plebiscite, which emerged as a solution advocated by Italy as mediator, clearly called for Allied troops although, in the event, only 450 Italian troops supervised the polls: the dissatisfaction with the results suggests both insufficient time for checking the registrations and insufficient troops for checking intimidation.

In Upper Silesia (1921)[33] a history of disturbances made a large force essential and 20,000 Allied troops were put at the disposal of the Commission in addition to the Allied officers who were attached to the local police. Three-quarters of the troops were French and, with only two Italian and four British battalions, criticism has been made of the partisan character of the force, for the French clearly favoured the Poles[34]: the result was a somewhat unruly plebiscite.

All these examples of plebiscites conducted under Allied auspices show the wisdom of the principle of "neutralisation," but they equally show the necessity for a force to fill the vacuum and, preferably, a force of a "neutral" character. The fact that the troops were confined to those of the Allied Powers necessarily reduced the

[27] Wambaugh, *op. cit.*, p. 67.
[28] *Ibid.*, Chap. 3 and p. 448.
[29] *Ibid.*
[30] *Ibid.*, Chap. 4 and p. 448.
[31] *Ibid.*, Chap. 5 and p. 448.
[32] *Ibid.*, Chap. 7 and p. 449.
[33] *Ibid.*, Chap. 6 and p. 448.
[34] *Ibid.*, p. 261. Note the interesting observation quoted by Wambaugh that whereas the British and Italian technique was not to interfere until the local police were in difficulties, the French technique was to have the troops very much in evidence at normal times but to confine them to barracks if serious disturbances developed: *ibid.*, p. 448, note 1.

neutral character of the force and indicated the likely superiority, in terms of acceptance by the population, of a truly international force.

Hence one would expect to find that a similar plebiscite conducted under the auspices of the League of Nations would have decided advantages, both on the civil and the military side. The proposed plebiscite at Vilna in 1920 [35] was suggested by the Council of the League on 28 October 1920, and, to assist the International Commission, a force of 1,000 men drawn from nine States was requested by the Secretary-General. Provision was made for the payment by the League of all expenses additional to the normal charges of maintaining the troops [36] and Sweden, Norway and Denmark, all States which had specially constituted contingents in readiness for the task, were in fact compensated by the Assembly [37] when the plebiscite was cancelled and, therefore, the troops not required. Thus the first attempt by the League to control by an international force a plebiscite organised under its own auspices never came to fruition. It did, however, as a plan, provide a precedent for the great opportunity offered by the Saar plebiscite in 1935.

In the case of the Saar the territory was already under the administration of the League, through the Governing Commission of the Saar, an international body comprising one French national, one Saarlander not a French national and three other nationals of neither France nor Germany: this Commission was the effective government of the Saar.[38] Whilst it had always controlled the local police force, between 1927 and 1930 a special force of international composition had been put at its disposal as a Railway Guard Force: this enjoyed extra-territorial status and consisted of 630 French troops, 100 English and 68 Belgian.[39] When, however, at the expiration of this fifteen years' experiment, the time for the plebiscite arrived it became clear that the Governing Commission and the Plebiscite Commission would need the backing of sizeable troops. The political antagonism between the Socialists and the " German Front " not only carried a potential threat of internal disorder but, far more serious, created a risk of intervention by French and German troops. Hence, upon a French proposal, the decision was taken to constitute a special force.

On the " civil " side the Plebiscite Commission, which was not concerned with the actual government of the territory since that remained the task of the Governing Commission, had at its disposal an " inspectorate " of forty-four persons from ten different nationalities, all " neutral," and an equally neutral body of 960 persons to act as presidents of the voting bureaux. On the " military " side an international force of 3,200 troops drawn from Great Britain, Italy, the Netherlands and Sweden was deployed throughout the territory,

---

[35] Wambaugh, *op. cit.*, Chap. 8.
[36] League of Nations, Council Minutes, 11th Sess., Annex 129a.
[37] The intention that the Assembly would recoup the cost from Poland and Lithuania was never realised.
[38] For the " Saar Statute," see the Treaty of Versailles of 1919, Pt. III, s. IV.
[39] *Off. Journal of the League of Nations*, 8th yr., p. 403 *et seq.*, p. 1045.

the heaviest concentration being in the highly industrialised area of Saarbrucken. The national contingents retained their separate identity and each had their own " zones." The cost of the force, over and above normal maintenance costs, was borne by the League. However, the Council of the League had decided on 4 June 1934 that Germany and France would each contribute to the League 5 million francs and the Governing Commission of the Saar a further million francs as immediate expenses to cover the cost of the plebiscite.[40] The principle of contribution, therefore, represents something of a precedent for those States which currently argue in relation to United Nations costs for forces like UNEF and ONUC that the major contributions should come from the States directly concerned.[41] The whole operation proved remarkably successful and, when on 1 March 1936 the German troops entered the Saar, not a single member of the international force remained on the territory; the contingents had been withdrawn by stages since the end of January.[42]

The Saar experience is important in that it constitutes the only occasion on which the League really established an international force.[43] Clearly the fact that government already lay in the hands of a League Commission greatly facilitated the operation, but apart from that the secret of its success lay in the fact that the force represented a " neutral " or truly international force which was able to remain aloof from the political issues of the plebiscite and thus obtain the respect and confidence of the population. In addition, the force appeared to be adequate in size for the operation and well disciplined, although it was fortunately never tested by serious outbreaks of disorder. The conclusion which suggests itself is that an international force possesses clear advantages over a force such as the Allied forces in the Peace Treaty plebiscites where, on occasions, the Allied forces were regarded as partisan.

[40] Rosner, *op. cit.*, p. 214. The future government of the Saar was to assume the obligations of compensation for loss or damage to material belonging to contingents of the Force, and for death or injury pensions payable to members of these contingents (*Off. Journal, ibid.*, p. 1763).

[41] *Post*, pp. 475–476.

[42] For details of the preparation for the plebiscite, see Wambaugh, *op. cit.*, Chap. 10. For details of the actual conduct of the plebiscite, see " Policing the Saar," *The New Commonwealth*, Ser. A, No. 8, 1936; Walters, *History of the League of Nations* (1952), Vol. II, Chap. 49; R.I.I.A. Information Dept. Papers No. 14, " The Saar Plebiscite " (1935). Note that, whilst no unified command was created, a general headquarters was established with which each contingent had liaison officers. The League Council had authorised the Governing Commission to enact legislation necessary to exempt the international force from responsibility for acts done in the performance of its mission and to confer on itself powers to requisition any accommodation, supplies and transport necessary for the force (*Off. Journal of the League,* 15th yr., No. 12, Part II, Seventh Meeting, p. 1763). The Supreme Plebiscite Tribunal was competent to punish Saar inhabitants for offences committed against the Force or its members, but not to assume jurisdiction over the Force or its members.

[43] The League did have a Commission administering Leticia for a year in 1933 during the dispute between Colombia and Peru, but this Commission used Colombian troops with special armbands : see Wehberg, *op. cit.*, p. 17.

2

The Military Staff Committee, the Collective Measures Committee and the Proposals of the Secretary-General in 1948 and 1952

THE Forces actually created by the United Nations are dealt with in the subsequent, substantive chapters of Part One of the present study. The purpose of this present chapter is to survey the main discussions and proposals which have been made within the United Nations for the establishment of United Nations Forces and which have proved abortive in the sense that they have not led to the actual creation of a Force.

The scheme for establishing United Nations Forces laid down in the Charter, and now forming part of Chapter VII of the Charter, owes its origin to proposals made by the United States at Dumbarton Oaks [1] : these, in turn, owed a good deal of their origin to the French proposals at the Disarmament Conference in 1932.[2] The implementation of the Charter scheme called for agreements between the Security Council and Member States under Article 43 of the Charter, and it was the task of the Military Staff Committee to elaborate the principles on which these agreements should be based, so that an examination of the discussions in that Committee, and of the discussions in the Security Council upon the basis of the report presented by the Committee, is essential to an understanding of the reasons why it proved impossible to implement the Charter scheme.

I. THE MILITARY STAFF COMMITTEE

Article 47 of the Charter provided for the establishment of a Military Staff Committee " to advise and assist the Security Council on all questions relating to the Security Council's military requirements for the maintenance of international peace and security, the employment and command of forces placed at its disposal, the regulation of armaments, and possible disarmament." The Committee was to

---

[1] U.S. Dept. of State, *Postwar Foreign Policy Preparation, 1939–1945*, Publication 3580 (Washington, D.C., Government Printing Office, 1949) pp. 602–603.
[2] Conference for the Reduction and Limitation of Armaments, " Proposals of the French Delegation," *Conference Documents*, Vol. I, pp. 113–116. For a discussion of these proposals see Walters, *A History of the League of Nations* (1952) Vol. II, p. 502.

consist of the Chiefs of Staff of the Permanent Members of the Security Council or their representatives. It was to this body that " strategic direction of any armed forces placed at the disposal of the Security Council " was to be entrusted.

However, the first task was to provide for such forces and Article 43 [3] anticipated that agreements would be concluded, on the initiative of the Security Council, between the Council and all Members of the United Nations so as to make forces available to the Council upon its call. Hence, at its twenty-third meeting on 16 February 1946, the Security Council directed the Committee, as its first task, " to examine from the military point of view the provisions contained in Article 43 of the Charter, and to submit the results of the Study and any recommendations to the Council in due course." [4]

Thus it was that the Committee attempted to formulate the basic principles which would be embodied in the agreements to be concluded under Article 43. It was a task of considerable difficulty under any circumstances, and in the circumstance that the political unanimity of the five Permanent Members had collapsed it proved impossible to fulfil; the effort was virtually abandoned in August 1948. The Committee did, however, present to the Council, in its Report of 30 April 1947,[5] a set of " General Principles governing the organisation of the armed forces made available to the Security Council by Member Nations of the United Nations." These were not in all cases agreed principles, and on certain articles two or more alternative texts were given, recording the extent and nature of the disagreement; they were

---

[3] *Article 43.* (1) " All Members of the United Nations, in order to contribute to the maintenance of international peace and security, undertake to make available to the Security Council, on its call and in accordance with a special agreement or agreements, armed forces, assistance, and facilities, including rights of passage, necessary for the purpose of maintaining international peace and security.

(2) Such agreement or agreements shall govern the numbers and types of forces, their degree of readiness and general location, and the nature of the facilities and assistance to be provided.

(3) The agreement or agreements shall be negotiated as soon as possible on the initiative of the Security Council. They shall be concluded between the Security Council and Members or between the Security Council and groups of Members and shall be subject to ratification by the signatory states in accordance with their respective constitutional processes."

[4] *Off. Rec. S.C.*, 1st yr., 1st Ser., No. 1, 23rd Mtg., p. 369.

[5] *Off. Rec. S.C.*, 2nd yr., Spec. Suppl. No. 1 (S/336) pp. 1–32. Note that the Report did not attempt to deal with financial obligations which might arise in connection with the fulfilment of obligations under Art. 42 of the Charter. The Report contains as Annex A the statements of position of the delegations of the Committee on articles on which unanimity had not been reached, and as Annex B some general comments by the French delegation. For a general commentary on the Report see Attia, *Les Forces armées des Nations Unies en Corée et au Moyen-Orient* (1962) pp. 32–48; Rosner, *The United Nations Emergency Force* (1963) pp. 217–219; Ruth B. Russell, *United Nations Experience with Military Forces*, Institute for Defence Analyses, Research Paper P-27, May 1963, pp. 15–23. This last work analyses the reasons behind the U.S. policy in the discussions in the Committee.

discussed [6] and amended by the Security Council in June and July 1947. The texts of these " General Principles " [7] are perhaps of more than historical significance, for they indicate not only a large area of agreement between the five Powers but also the areas where disagreement exists and, therefore, where the major difficulties in the way of implementing the Charter scheme for the provision of international forces lie. What now follows is a brief commentary on the salient features of these " General Principles."

Dealing first with the area of agreement, it may be noted that under Article 1 the purpose of the armed forces, not unnaturally, was defined entirely in terms of Article 39 of the Charter, namely to maintain or restore international peace and security in cases of a threat or breach of international peace or any act of aggression. This does not suggest that it is only for such purposes that international forces may be used, but rather that the Committee had been concerned solely with the problem of providing forces for enforcement action under Chapter VII of the Charter. It was agreed (Art. 2) that the armed forces made available should be composed of units of national armed forces and that the overall strength of the armed Force would be assessed by the Council on the advice of the Military Staff Committee (Arts. 5 and 8). It was also agreed that contributions by Members were a matter of opportunity and obligation (Art. 9), but that in the early stages the major portion would have to come from the Permanent Members (Art. 10). The size and composition of contributions of individual Member nations would be determined on the initiative of the Council in the process of negotiating with each Member (Art. 12), although contributions by Members other than the Permanent Members might be by way of facilities or other assistance rather than armed forces (Art. 14). Any change in the size or composition of a given contribution would be by agreement between the Member concerned and the Security Council (Art. 15). Employment of armed forces made available would be solely by the decision of the Council and for the fulfilment of the tasks envisaged in Article 42 of the Charter (Art. 18) and their degree of readiness would be fixed by the Council (Art. 22). Each Member would be responsible for the logistical support of its own forces and would maintain levels of reserves and replacements adequate to maintain these forces (Arts. 29, 30). Pending call, the armed forces would remain under the exclusive command of the contributing Member, but upon call would operate under the authority of the Security Council (Art. 36) and the Military Staff Committee would be responsible for their strategic direction (Art. 38). Command of national contingents would be exercised by their respective commanders and the contingents would retain their national character and be subject to their own military discipline

[6] The Security Council adopted provisionally the articles agreed by the Committee and then turned to those not agreed; after the failure to agree on Article 11 the remaining articles were not discussed.
[7] *Repertory*, Vol. II, p. 396.

(Art. 39); commanders would be entitled to communicate directly with their national authorities (Art. 40).

Turning to the areas of disagreement, the first and insurmountable problem proved to be that of reaching agreement on both the total size of the forces and on the relative sizes of the contributions of the five Permanent Members. There was disagreement over the overall, optimum size of the armed forces required: the U.S.S.R. apparently contemplated something of the order of 12 ground divisions (say 125,000 men), 600 bombers, 300 fighters, 5–6 cruisers, 24 destroyers and 12 submarines. The United States wanted 20 ground divisions (say 300,000 men), 1,250 bombers, 2,250 fighters, 3 battleships, 6 carriers, 15 cruisers, 84 destroyers and 90 submarines.[8] However ludicrous in retrospect this disagreement seems, for today one would tend to welcome an agreement at far lower figures than the U.S.S.R. then suggested, it represented a difference in conception as to the nature of the force[9] and, since the Permanent Members were to contribute the largest portion, it directly affected the question of their individual contributions. On this particular question the disagreement is reflected in the alternative texts for Article 11. The U.S.S.R. insisted on "the principle of equality" both in size and composition for all Permanent Members, and would allow deviation from this principle only by a special decision of the Council.[10] The text proposed by the other four spoke of "comparable" contributions; as explained by the United States delegate, the contributions would be "properly balanced and rendered roughly comparable without prejudice to the interests of individual nations."[11] The same disagreements spread to the article on air forces (Art. 16)[12] and to the question

---

[8] *Off. Rec. S.C.*, 2nd yr., Suppl. No. 13, pp. 133–135.

[9] The U.S.A. wanted "a mobile force able to strike quickly at long range and to bring to bear, upon any given point in the world, where trouble may occur, the maximum armed force in the minimum time": *Off. Rec. S.C.*, 2nd yr., No. 43, 138th Mtg., June 4 1947, p. 956. The U.S.S.R. aimed at relatively small forces on the assumption that they would never be used against a Permanent Member, if only because of the veto; the U.K., France and China tended to share this desire for smaller forces. See the table of proposed figures given by Attia, *loc. cit.*, p. 38.

[10] One disadvantage of this view would be that if, at that time, one member such as China had been unable to contribute many aircraft, for example, the contribution of every other Permanent Member would be scaled down in proportion. The Soviet position was based on the assumption of fact that "the five States *can* make armed forces available on the principle of equality"; this assumption was described by the French as "utopian" and by the others as impractical. The deviations from the principle of equality which the Soviet draft would admit as exceptional cases the U.S.A. stated would "of necessity become the rule": Annex A, pp. 9–13.

[11] Cited in Frye, *A United Nations Peace Force* (1957) p. 53.

[12] Not discussed in the Security Council, but only in the Military Staff Committee. This article concerned the relationship between the forces to be made available under Art. 43 and the air-forces to be made immediately available in order to enable the UN to take urgent military measures under Art. 45. The Soviet position really aimed at postponement of action under Art. 45 until the agreements under Art. 43 had been concluded: Annex A, pp. 13–14.

of additional contributions to be supplied by Permanent Members (Art. 28).[13]

The second basic disagreement was as to the location of the forces pending or after their use by the Security Council under Article 42 of the Charter and to the period after use within which the forces must be withdrawn to their agreed location. The U.S.S.R. proposed that the forces should be based on their own national territories, and withdrawn back to such bases within thirty to ninety days after having fulfilled the measures envisaged in Article 42, unless the Security Council decided otherwise (Arts. 20 and 32). The alternative proposed by the West was to allow the location generally of the armed forces in any territory to which they have a legal right of access and, after use, withdrawal to the " general locations " governed by the special agreements under Article 43, and within a time-limit to be specified by the Security Council in the light of the prevailing circumstances. The Soviet position is more familiar today in the form of its opposition to " foreign bases " and its suspicion of possible political pressure by means of such bases. Also linked with this problem was that of Article 34, the Western proposal calling for notification to the Security Council of any displacement of forces likely to modify their availability: the Soviet Union wanted the full right to change the areas of garrisoning at the discretion of the Member, and without informing the Council.

The third basic disagreement related to the provision of assistance and facilities, including rights of passage, for armed forces. The Western proposal[14] for Article 26 was that the agreements under Article 43 should include both " a general guarantee of rights of passage and of the use of such of the Member nation's available bases as are required. . . ." and " specific provisions covering details " to be included either in the original agreements or in subsequent agreements under Article 43 of the Charter to be concluded at the appropriate time. In contrast, the Soviet proposal avoided all reference to general guarantees and made the provision of assistance and facilities subject to the special agreements under Article 43 and provided for specific agreements, made at the appropriate time, as to the " duration and the other conditions involved in the exercise of rights thus extended . . ." In particular, the Soviet Union objected

---

[13] Not discussed in the Security Council.

[14] France submitted a different text which simply provided that the agreements under Art. 43 would indicate the bases, assistance and facilities to be placed at the disposal of the Council, and additional agreements could be made as necessary: it was therefore something of a compromise between the two extremes of the Western and Soviet views. If this text were supplemented by a reference to " good faith " and the general obligation of Art. 9 it might well be that the gulf between the two extremes could be bridged. The U.K.'s objection to the French proposal was that it was impossible to foresee in advance when particular bases might be required. The objection is not an impressive one since States normally establish bases long in advance of particular situations.

to any provision obliging States to make bases available. The difference is obviously one over the extent to which a Member should be committed in advance in respect of the use of its territory by the armed forces operating under the Security Council. This crucial article was not discussed in the Security Council, but only in the Committee.

The fourth disagreement was over the extent to which a Member, unable to meet the obligation in Article 29 to provide full logistical support for the forces it has contributed, may seek assistance from another Member. The proposal by China, the United Kingdom and the United States in Article 31 would have allowed this when the Security Council negotiated with appropriate Members for the provision of this assistance; it excluded any simple bilateral negotiation between the two States concerned. The French and Soviet text provided for deviations from the principle of Article 29 only in individual instances and by special decision of the Security Council. Given that in both texts the decision to allow aid rested with the Security Council, it would appear that the disagreement is scarcely a basic one; it was not discussed in the Council.

Whilst the above may be characterised as the major disagreements between East and West, it should not be assumed that the West presented a united front on all matters. France submitted a separate text on Article 26 (provision of assistance and facilities, including rights of passage) and on Article 32 (general location of armed forces). She joined China in a separate text on Article 17 which would have allowed the Member to make use of the armed forces it had made available to the Security Council in case of self-defence and of national emergencies.[15] She joined with the U.S.S.R. in a common text for Article 31, allowing deviations from the principle of independent logistical support only by special decision of the Council. She joined with the United Kingdom in a common text for Article 41, providing for the possibility of appointing a Supreme Commander and Commanders-in-Chief of land, sea and air forces by the Security Council for the period of employment of the forces, as against the combined Soviet, Chinese, American text which spoke merely of an " overall commander." [16] The difference appears to be one as to the extent to which the appointment of commanders-in-chief of the different kinds of forces—the second level of command—should be a matter for the " Supreme " or " overall " commander or for the Security Council : the additional paragraph to Article 41 in the Franco/British text reflects the latter view.

This work by the Military Staff Committee is of very great

---

[15] Both countries were, of course, to experience after this date a " national emergency " which called for the large-scale commitment of their armed forces; this is much the wider reservation since, presumably, action in self-defence under Art. 51 of the Charter would in any event be merged into measures ordered by the Security Council. The other delegations thought that Art. 51 adequately covered all reasonable requirements.

[16] Not discussed by the Security Council.

significance because it indicates a general conclusion, namely, that the obstacles in the way of agreements under Article 43 are not, fundamentally, military or strategic ones but rather political ones. The major disagreements as to relative size of contributions, location of forces and bases, and assistance to Members unable to meet their obligations under Article 29 are all explicable in terms of the political suspicion with which East and West regarded each other's actions. The Soviet Union was, in political terms, in a minority of one and evidently feared the advantages which might have accrued to the West under the Western proposals. It is, therefore, a trite but evidently true statement that further progress cannot really be made until this political distrust has been allayed.

II. THE SECRETARY-GENERAL'S PROPOSALS FOR A UNITED NATIONS GUARD

On 28 September 1948, and significantly only eleven days after the assassination of Count Bernadotte in Palestine, the Secretary-General presented a report to the General Assembly [17] calling for the establishment of a United Nations Guard. The Report recited the need for protection of United Nations Missions in the field, a need demonstrated by the difficulties already encountered by Missions in Greece, the Balkans, Indonesia, Korea, Palestine, India and Pakistan and suggested that such a Guard would obviate the suspicion of partiality which the use of local police or national militia engenders.[18] Furthermore, the Secretary-General suggested that, whilst Missions had so far been charged with responsibilities ranging from investigation and mediation to observation and supervisory duties in connection with such matters as the cessation of hostilities, future functions might well include supervision of referendums and assisting in security measures incidental to the demilitarisation of specified areas: in all such functions a Guard able to offer the minimum protective services as well as limited technical services would be desirable.

The legal basis of the Guard [19] would be Articles 97 and 98 of the Charter under which the Secretariat shall comprise " such staff as the Organisation may require . . ." and the Secretary-General shall perform " such other functions as are entrusted to him by these (the main) organs . . ." The Guard would, therefore, be integrated into the Secretariat and be subject to Articles 100 and 101 of the Charter.

The functions of the Guard [20] would include protection of the archives, officers and personnel of Missions,[21] the protection of neutralised areas or supply lines under a truce arrangement or the supervision of a plebiscite under United Nations auspices. That the

[17] Document A/656: *Off. Rec. G.A.*, 3rd Sess., Pt. 2, 1949, Plen. Mtgs.
[18] *Ibid.*, para. 2.
[19] Appendix A of the Report.
[20] Given in detail in Appendix 3.
[21] A Headquarters Guard already existed for this purpose in New York.

Guard would not be used for functions comparable to the military enforcement measures contemplated in Article 42 (with which the Military Staff Committee had been solely concerned) was vigorously stressed. The Guard was to be " entirely non-military " in character, its equipment limited to " personal emergency defence weapons " and to " emergency technical equipment "; its size would exclude any possibility of use as an aggressive force. It would not have the powers of a civilian or military police force. So far as the relationship with the State on whose territory it was to operate is concerned, the Guard would function " only with the consent, express or implied, of the territorial sovereign." [22] For simple protective functions in relation to a Mission the consent of the State to the entry of the Mission would be enough, but where additional functions are envisaged a specific consent would be necessary.

The organisation of the Guard [23] would be in the form of a nucleus of 800 men made up of a permanent establishment of 300 men recruited under Articles 97, 98, and 100 (therefore " international " recruits) and a " reserve cadre " of 500 men in national sections available upon call for utilisation as a " multi-national unit." These reserve cadres would be paid a small retainer fee when not on active duty and would receive periodic training in their own States. Except when on active duty the permanent force would be located at United Nations Headquarters or at locations to be arranged whereas the reserve would be located at their normal place of residence. Arms would be limited to light, personal defence weapons; tanks, artillery, aircraft, vessels or " major offensive weapons " would not form part of the Guards' equipment. The estimated cost of the plan was $4,000,000 per annum.

The discussion of the Secretary-General's proposals in the *Ad hoc* Political Committee in April 1949 [24] quickly revealed a considerable amount of opposition, but resulted in the proposal to refer the problem to a special committee, a proposal which the General Assembly adopted.[25] Prior to the meeting of the Special Committee on a United Nations Guard the Secretary-General attempted to meet the objections advanced by a radical revision of his plans. The plan, as revised, envisaged two units rather than one, namely a Field Service and a Field Reserve Panel (later termed " Panel of Field Observers ").

The Field Service was to consist of 300 men, seconded from national governments but integrated into the Secretariat; it would be a uniformed force, not regularly supplied with arms, capable of exercising guard duties and of providing transport and communications services, but not intended for truce supervision or plebiscite

[22] Appendix A, para. 3.
[23] Appendix C.
[24] *Off. Rec. G.A.*, 3rd Sess. Pt. 2, *Ad hoc* Pol. Committee, S.R. of Mtgs., 6–11 April 1949.
[25] Resol. 270 (III).

functions. These latter functions would be entrusted to the Field Reserve Panel, a list of, say, 2,000 men in national service recommended by national governments and able to be called into service by the General Assembly or the Security Council or a subsidiary organ of those two main organs. The legal basis for the Panel would be the same as for any Secretariat unit, and the total cost would be approximately $1,000,000 per annum. The plan envisaged not so much an implement for collective security as an instrument of peaceful settlement.

The report of the Special Committee [26] disclosed a majority support for the establishment of both units. The separate minority statement [27] of the representatives of the U.S.S.R. Czechoslovakia and Poland regarded the whole scheme as *ultra vires* the Secretary-General and, despite the clear attempt in the revised plan to eliminate the "military" character of the units, as a usurpation of the Security Council's monopoly over the creation of armed forces or units of a military type. The function of guarding United Nations Missions should, in their view, be confined to the forces of the territorial State, and the use of United Nations units to supervise plebiscites or truces would serve as a pretext for intervention in the domestic affairs of the State and lead to friction between the parties. It need only be said of these minority objections that, historically, the evidence was against them [28] and that the future was to show that they were in principle ill-founded.[29]

When resumed in the *Ad hoc* Political Committee these objections were repeated, together with certain other doubts by other States, and in the outcome a somewhat lukewarm approval of the plan for a Field Service was adopted in the form of a draft Resolution: the vote was thirty-eight votes to five with eight abstentions. The draft Resolution on the Panel of Field Observers, similarly lukewarm, was adopted by twenty-eight votes to seven with eighteen abstentions.[30] The Resolutions were adopted by the General Assembly on 22 November 1949 by forty-six to five, with three abstentions and thirty-eight to six with eleven abstentions respectively.[31]

The comparative apathy of the Member States is striking; it has been said that "the will to construe the legalities, and to overcome the financial and other practicalities, so as to realise the Secretary-General's plan, was present neither among the great powers nor among the great voting *blocs*." [32] No doubt, equipped with hindsight,

[26] *Off. Rec. G.A.*, 4th Sess. Suppl. No. 13, 10 October 1949.
[27] A/959.
[28] See *ante*, pp. 7–11.
[29] *Post*, pp. 95–99, 288–290, on the Opinion of the I.C.J. in the *Expenses Case*.
[30] The United Kingdom abstained on the ground that the functions of the observers were not sufficiently precise and that this would make it difficult in practice to select members of the Panel.
[31] Resols. 297 (IV) A and B: the estimated cost was reduced to $71,000 in the Report of the Fifth Committee (A/1122).
[32] Schwebel, "A United Nations 'Guard' and a United Nations 'Legion'," in Frye, *A United Nations Peace Force* (1957) p. 207.

many of the Members would now take a somewhat different view from that to which they adhered in 1949. The events in Korea in 1950 were soon to shake Members out of their apathy.

The creation of the United Nations Command in Korea, and the way in which that Command operated, form the subject-matter of the next chapter. During the course of the Korean operations, however, the General Assembly adopted the celebrated Resolution on Uniting for Peace of 3 November 1950 [33] and this established a Collective Measures Committee which dealt with those same problems which the Military Staff Committee had dealt with, although from the point of view of the operation of that Resolution rather than Chapter VII of the Charter.

III. THE COLLECTIVE MEASURES COMMITTEE

The Collective Measures Committee was established by General Assembly Resolution 377A (v) of 3 November 1950, the " Resolution on Uniting for Peace." [34] Consisting of fourteen States, it was directed " to study and make a report on . . . methods, including those in section C of the present Resolution, which might be used to maintain and strengthen international peace and security. . . ." It will be recalled that it was in section C that, *inter alia*, each Member was invited to survey its resources in order to determine " the nature and scope of the assistance it may be in a position to render in support of any recommendations of the Security Council or of the General Assembly . . ." and was recommended to " maintain within its national armed forces elements so trained, organised and equipped that they could promptly be made available, in accordance with its constitutional processes, for service as a United Nations unit or units. . . ." The Committee presented three reports [35] of considerable interest in the context of the present study for, as was said in the First Report, it constituted " the first systematic attempt by the United Nations to study the whole field of collective action." [36] It must be said at the outset, however, that

---

[33] Resol. 377 (V). For further discussion of this Resolution see *post*, pp. 290–298.

[34] No Member of the Communist *bloc* participated; their attitude, throughout, was that the Resolution, and therefore the Committee, was *ultra vires* the Assembly and envisaged an assumption of powers which were conferred exclusively upon the Security Council by the UN Charter.

[35] First Report, *Off. Rec. G.A.*, 6th Sess., Suppl. No. 13 (A/1891); Second Report, *ibid.*, 7th Sess., Suppl. No. 17 (A/2215); Third Report, *ibid.*, 9th Sess., Annexes, Agenda item 19 (A/2713–S/3283). For a commentary on these reports see Attia, *Les Forces Armées des Nations Unies en Corée et au Moyen-Orient* (1962) pp. 92–97; Rossignol, " Des tentatives effectuées en vue de mettre un nouveau mécanisme de sécurité collective à la disposition de l'A.G. des N.U. et de leur constitutionalité," (1954) R.D.I.P. 94–129; Katzin, " Collective Security : The Work of the Collective Measures Committee " in *Annual Review of United Nations Affairs*, 1952 (1953) p. 206; Ruth B. Russell, *op. cit.*, pp. 23–28.

[36] A/1891, para. 36.

this study produced a set of "guiding principles" for future action and nowhere proposed actual steps to be taken so as to constitute in advance an embryonic United Nations Force.

The measures examined by the Committee fell into three main categories: political measures, economic and financial measures, and military measures. Whilst, for our purposes, it is the work of the Committee within this last category which merits attention, it should not be forgotten that the measures envisaged in the first two categories could constitute sanctions powerful enough to render unnecessary, in a great number of cases, resort to military measures.[37]

Turning to the military measures, it was stressed from the outset that the Committee was concerned to devise measures which could be used pending the conclusion of the agreements provided for in Article 43 of the Charter.[38] The measures are therefore conceived as a substitution for those which should have been devised under Chapter VII of the Charter.

1. *Organisation of United Nations resources*

The Committee was, at the time of its First Report, already in possession of thirty-eight replies to the invitation in para. 9 of the Resolution to inform it of measures taken to implement the recommendation to Members to "maintain within their national armed forces elements so trained, organised and equipped etc. . . ."[39] Of these thirty-eight, four were negative, five were simple acknowledgments, and the others to a large extent referred to the measures already taken in relation to Korea. Hence the Committee found it necessary to reaffirm the importance of Member States maintaining this nucleus of an international force and to state that when maintenance of specific units was impossible it might be possible nevertheless for States to pay special attention to the organising and training of units in their forces so that such units could be more efficiently integrated into combined United Nations Forces.[40] The Committee also stressed the desirability of a survey of resources so as to determine what "ancillary support" could be provided, in the nature of assistance and facilities, and to make whatever constitutional arrangements are necessary *in advance* so as to be able to grant promptly "rights of passage and related rights" to United Nations Forces.[41]

---

[37] In the Second Report the Committee compiled a list of arms, ammunition and implements of war to be applied *in toto* as part of an arms embargo against any aggressor and a list of strategic items of which the first part would be regarded as a logical supplement to any arms embargo and the second part could be regarded as of vital importance in specific cases of aggression; A/2215, Chap. 2, and Annexes H and I.

[38] A/1891, para. 167.

[39] The replies are summarised in Annex II to the Report.

[40] Para. 178.   [41] Para. 181.

The Committee also noted the terms of the Resolution, which provided that units would be maintained by Members "without prejudice to the use of such elements in exercise of the right of individual or collective self-defence recognised in Article 51 of the Charter" and that the Committee should take into account "collective self-defence and regional arrangements." In fact several of the replies had indicated the possibility that forces committed under such arrangements might be used as United Nations units, and the Committee therefore stressed that "there should be a mutual supporting relationship between the activities of such arrangements or agencies and the collective measures taken by the United Nations." [42]

So far as the Panel of Military Experts envisaged under para. 10 of the Resolution was concerned the Committee adopted the Report submitted by a Working Group [43] which specified that their function would be to give technical advice to Members regarding the organisation, training and equipment of the units maintained by Members and that the members of the Panel would be of high rank, nominated by the Secretary-General, and selected from active or retired officers from the national military services of Members on the basis of their individual qualifications. It is not known that any Member State has ever requested the services of this Panel.

2. Co-ordination of efforts of States in a United Nations collective military action

Under this head the Committee dealt with the many problems which the Korean experiment had revealed.[44] The necessity for an "executive military authority" was obvious[45]; it was equally obvious that, since the arrangements contemplated were in substitution for those in Chapter VII of the Charter, the Military Staff Committee could not be that authority. Accordingly the Committee concluded that the United Nations should nominate a State or group of States as such an authority either contemporaneously with the decision to use United Nations Forces, or as soon as possible thereafter. Special consideration would be given to the inclusion of States in geographical proximity to the actual victim, and the victim State itself could be included, although not necessarily so. The

---

[42] Para. 187. The Committee did not, however, indicate how the relationship could be achieved: on the dangers of action under such arrangements before any determination of the aggressor by the Security Council or the General Assembly see Bowett, *Self-Defence in International Law* (1958) pp. 234–248.

[43] Annex III to the Report. The Second Report, A/2215, para. 77, notes the appointment by the Secretary-General of members of the Panel. There is no record of the services of this Panel ever being used.

[44] A summary of the co-ordinating procedures used in Korea was appended to the First Report as Annex IV.

[45] Paras. 200–210.

authority would be empowered to co-ordinate the efforts of individual States and to organise the contribution of forces, assistance and
facilities; this would include the conclusion of agreements with
contributing States relating to size and supply of units contributed.[46]
Whilst the original request for contributions would be made by the
Assembly or Security Council, the offers would be made to the
executive military authority. It would be for the authority to
designate a Commander-in-Chief who would be subject to the
directions of the authority. The Commander-in-Chief would have
sole operational control of United Nations Forces, although national
contingents would be under their own commander and the senior
military representative of each State contributing forces would have
direct access to the Commander-in-Chief on national matters and
matters of major policy affecting the operational capacity of the
forces concerned. The importance of liaison arrangements in the
theatre of operations was particularly stressed, and a normal liaison
between national contingents and the United Nations Command was
assumed in addition to this right of direct access. The senior
military representatives would also have direct access to their own
government.

Whilst the immediate need would be for air, sea and land forces,
the Committee emphasised the importance of different types of
assistance [47] such as transportation, armaments, communications
facilities, medical and other non-combatant units, rights of passage,
etc. Moreover, supplies and technical aid might be needed for the
civilian relief and assistance programme which the Committee
envisaged as an essential part of the overall United Nations action.[48]

The relationship of the executive military authority to the
political organs of the United Nations, to the contributing States and
to the victim State (assuming it was not part of the "authority")
was clearly, after the Korean experiment, a crucial issue. The
Committee had no hesitation in confining the authority's responsibility for co-ordination and strategic direction and control of forces
"within the framework of the policies and objectives as expressed
through such Resolutions as the United Nations may adopt at any
stage of the collective action." [49] The United Nations would also
have to be kept regularly informed of the course of the military
operations by the "military authority." Moreover, in the event of
a failure by the authority to carry out its responsibilities to the
satisfaction of the United Nations, the appropriate organ could

---

[46] The Second Report suggested that an *ad hoc* committee of UN Members
might best negotiate the details of the forces, manpower, assistance facilities, services and funds required for the effective conduct of the military
operations.

[47] Paras. 211–216.

[48] The Korean experiment had clearly shown this. Indeed, ever since the
Allied invasion of Italy in 1943 the heavy responsibility of an army in the
field for the relief of civilians had to be accepted as part of the burden
of war.

[49] Para. 208.

terminate the mandate.[50] Hence the Committee envisaged the authority as completely under the political control of either the Assembly or the Security Council.

With regard to contributing States the Korean experience suggested that a far more effective system of liaison was necessary. The initial arrangements to be concluded between the "authority" and the contributing States would comprise such matters as size, nature and logistical support for forces made available. Thereafter the authority would "arrange for and maintain, close consultation with participating States . . . both at its seat of government and in the theatre" (an obligation also existing towards the Secretary-General and the victim State).[51] These consultations would be on a regular basis so as to ensure "joint consideration of matters of common interest." [52]

With regard to the victim State, this might well be one of the group of States composing the "authority." In any event, the Committee considered that "the United Nations should . . . pay special attention to the interests of the victim State at all stages of the operation." [53] Whilst the exact relationship could not be determined in advance, special arrangements would be necessary to ensure co-ordination between that State's own defence effort and the United Nations military measures and, as we have seen, regular consultation was deemed essential. Moreover, the civilian relief measures would be directed principally towards the victim State, necessitating co-ordination in this sphere, quite apart from the military sphere. The Committee did not, it may be noted, determine that it was essential for the forces of the victim State to be integrated into the United Nations Command.

A further problem was that of ensuring the identification of the operations as United Nations operations. The political control to be exercised by the United Nations political organs has already been mentioned. Further measures towards this end would be the designation of the forces as "United Nations Forces," and of the command as a "United Nations Command." All orders and instructions from the Commander-in-Chief would be issued in the name of the United Nations Command. Use of the United Nations flag, marking of equipment with the United Nations insignia, and even the award of a United Nations medal would also promote this identification.

3. The Secretary-General's proposals for a United Nations Volunteer Reserve

Amongst the proposals made to the Collective Measures Committee were proposals by the Secretary-General for a "Volunteer Reserve." In contrast with his earlier proposals for a Field Service and Field

---

[50] Para. 205.
[52] Para. 226.

[51] Para. 210.
[53] Para. 198.

Reserve Panel [54] the Secretary-General proposed the creation of a " United Nations Legion " which would be, decidedly, an instrument for collective security rather than for peaceful settlement. This plan [55] rested on the premise that, lacking international or supra-national forces organised in advance, resistance to aggression would depend upon the use of national forces contributed by Members. In order to add to the strength of forces likely to be made available to a United Nations Executive Military Authority he suggested that States whose resources would not permit the contribution of the kind of self-contained units envisaged in para. 8 of the Resolution on Uniting for Peace should consult on the possibility of establishing a United Nations Volunteer Reserve.[56] This would assure the organisa-tion in advance of combatant or auxiliary units which could be speedily integrated into a United Nations Command. The advantage would be that the international character of any United Nations Force would be maximised by securing contributions from the smaller States unable to contribute self-contained units.

Additionally, he proposed that a Volunteer Reserve could comprise individuals who volunteered for service under a United Nations Command but who would be recruited and trained to that end by the national military establishments of Members (*e.g.*, as part of the British Territorial Army or the United States National Guard). The cost of recruiting, training and equipping the reservists would be borne by each Member and agreements between the Members and the United Nations would specify the conditions under which reser-vists could be used as part of the normal national forces of the Members as opposed to a United Nations Force. There would be no separate Command Staff or structure but, upon mobilisation, the reserve units would be placed under command staffs of national military establishments or else under the command provided by the Executive Military Authority, depending on the circumstances. The Reserve would be in the region of 50,000 to 60,000 strong and would have a recognised international character.

The reactions of the Collective Measures Committee were, to say the least, lukewarm. In its Second Report it stated that it " was able to give only preliminary consideration to the Secretary-General's proposals for a United Nations Volunteer Reserve and was not able to take any decision on the merits, in terms either of their political possibilities or of their military feasibility." [57] The Third Report noted that " the Secretary-General did not wish, for the time being, to proceed with the proposals." [58] Presumably the Members doubted the practicability of the proposals, although the grounds for such doubts nowhere appear. It was thus that the only proposals which

---

[54] *Ante*, pp. 19–20.
[55] See Second Report, A/2215, pp. 12–13.
[56] The name " Legion " was rejected by the Committee as misleading.
[57] A/2215, para. 91.
[58] A/2713–S/3283, para. 5.

envisaged positive action, as opposed to the formulation of principles, were discarded.

4. *The Committee's reactions to the major problems revealed in the discussions within the Military Staff Committee*

The way in which the Committee dealt with those same problems which had proved insurmountable within the Military Staff Committee and the Security Council between the years 1946 to 1948 is not without interest. In general the Committee's viewpoint was that of the Western Powers, a fact not altogether surprising in view of the fact that the Eastern *bloc* boycotted the work of the Committee.[59] It may be noted that in respect of the size of national contributions the Committee never contemplated strict equality of contributions but emphasised "the equitable sharing of military, financial and other assistance."[60] No question of location of forces really arose since the forces envisaged were essentially national forces and it was assumed throughout that their location, when not in action, would be on their own national territory. The third major disagreement in the Military Staff Committee over the provision of assistance and facilities including rights of passage, was certainly settled in the Collective Measures Committee in favour of the Western view: the Committee strongly emphasised the necessity for States to make such assistance available as a matter of obligation rather than as one for negotiation in each particular case.[61] Again, on the fourth major disagreement, the Committee regarded it as right and proper for States to provide additional assistance and logistic support "so as to help States able to furnish armed forces but lacking the means necessary to bring their full contribution to bear."[62] Arrangements for such assistance would, of course, be made through the Executive Military Authority, or possibly the proposed *ad hoc* Committee; but such arrangements were, as in the Western view, conceived as perfectly normal and not exceptional deviations from the obligation to provide independent logistical support, as in the Soviet view.[63] Indeed the Committee seems to have been thinking in terms of a kind of logistical "pool."[64]

5. *Limitations of the Reports*

Quite apart from the failure of the Committee to propose concrete steps for the development of a system whereby national units could be made available to the United Nations, otherwise than in the form

[59] *Ante*, p. 21.
[60] Second Report, A/2215, para. 78; and see First Report, A/1891, paras. 211–222.
[61] A/1891, para. 214; A/2215, paras. 79 and 80. [62] A/1891, para. 213.
[63] *Ante*, p. 17. [64] A/1891, paras. 231–234.

of " guiding principles," the Reports may be said to suffer from over-concentration on the lessons of the Korean experiment. Hence little is to be found within the Reports on the many problems which were subsequently to be faced in 1956 with UNEF and in 1960 with ONUC. For example, the problems of financing the operations received scant attention as did the problems of privileges and immunities (and jurisdictional control generally), of withdrawal of contingents, of withdrawal of consent by the victim State to the presence of United Nations forces, and so forth. The general impression left by these Reports (an opinion fortified by the dis-interest in the Secretary-General's proposals for a Volunteer Reserve) is that the Committee was concerned to elaborate on the principles contained in the Resolution on Uniting for Peace but was not really concerned to set in motion steps leading to the establishment of an embryonic international force. Hence, as we shall see, despite all the efforts revealed by these Reports, when in 1956 the time came for a United Nations Force to be summoned into being the task became one of sheer improvisation and not of the putting into motion of an existing practical scheme which would have ensured an effective and efficient United Nations Force.

3

The United Nations Action in Korea

It may be recalled that on 14 November 1947 the General Assembly had established the United Nations Temporary Commission on Korea to facilitate the establishment of a national Government of Korea by means of nation-wide elections.[1] Having been barred from North Korea, the Commission was authorised to organise and observe elections in South Korea and these took place on 10 May 1948, a Government being formed by President Rhee; at its third session, in December 1948, the General Assembly in Resolution 195 (111) declared this Government a lawful Government and the only such Government in Korea. Thus it was that instead of a unified Korea being established, as the Moscow Agreement had contemplated, the 38th parallel (which had been no more than the demarcation line between the zones of United States and U.S.S.R. military occupations) became a frontier between a State with a recognised Government and an area of territory recognised as Korean but under the control of authorities who had received no kind of recognition from the United Nations. The development of security forces by the lawful Government of Korea enabled the complete withdrawal of United States military forces to be effected by 29 June 1949. The development of strong military forces in North Korea and the likelihood of clashes between these forces and the newly-established security forces of South Korea had been stressed by the Commission in its report to the fourth session of the General Assembly.[2] By January 1950 comparative estimates of the strength of the North and South Korean forces were 175,000 men (including 130 tanks, 60 armoured cars and 102 planes) in North Korea and 100,000 men (with no tanks and no planes) in South Korea.[3] On 25 June 1950 the United States informed the Secretary-General of the United Nations that North Korean forces had invaded the territory of the

---

[1] See *Yearbook of the UN 1947-8*, pp. 81-88; States from the Communist *bloc* took no part in the vote. For a summary of the attitude adopted by the Communist States, and of the work of the Commission generally, see Annual Report of the Secretary-General, *Off. Rec. G.A.*, 5th Sess., Suppl. No. 1 (A/1287), pp. 18-21.

[2] A/936 and Add. 1. The Commission had been established anew by Resolution 195 (111) on 12 December 1948 on a permanent basis, consisting of Australia, China, El Salvador, France, India, the Philippines and Syria.

[3] Report of the UN Commission on Korea (A/1350); the report was not, however, based on independent evidence but on the statement of the Chief of Staff of the Republic of Korea.

Republic of Korea at several points in the early morning of that day, and requested an immediate meeting of the Security Council.[4] On the same day the United Nations Commission on Korea informed the Secretary-General that according to a statement by the Government of the Republic of Korea, attacks in strength had been launched against it all along the 38th parallel.[5]

I. THE ACTION TAKEN BY THE SECURITY COUNCIL

1. *The Resolutions adopted*

The Security Council met at 2 p.m. on 25 June 1950 and the Secretary-General, acting on his powers under Article 99 of the Charter,[6] characterised the situation as a "threat to international peace" and called on the Council to "take steps necessary to re-establish peace in that area."[7] The Council then adopted a Resolution in the following terms:

". . . *Noting* with grave concern the armed attack upon the Republic of Korea by forces from North Korea,
Determines that this action constitutes a breach of the peace.

I. *Calls for* the immediate cessation of hostilities; and *calls upon* the authorities of North Korea to withdraw forthwith their armed forces to the 38th parallel;

II. *Requests* the United Nations Commission on Korea
    (a) To communicate its fully considered recommendations on the situation with the least possible delay,
    (b) To observe the withdrawal of the North Korean forces to the 38th parallel, and
    (c) To keep the Security Council informed on the execution of this Resolution;

III. *Calls upon* all Members to render every assistance to the United Nations in the execution of this Resolution and to refrain from giving assistance to the North Korean authorities."[8]

At its next meeting on 27 June the Council had before it a number of telegrams from the United Nations Commission on Korea, including a summary report of the background events prior to the outbreak of hostilities; the report concluded that the evidence pointed to a calculated, co-ordinated attack by the North Korean authorities. The representative of the United States noted that the North Korean authorities had neither ceased hostilities nor withdrawn their armed forces and informed the Council that United States air and sea forces had been ordered to give the troops of the Korean Government cover

---

[4] S/1495.
[5] S/1496.
[6] See Secretary-General's statement to the General Assembly, *Off. Rec. G.A.*, 5th Sess., Plen. Mtgs., Vol. 1, 289th Mtg., para. 40.
[7] *Off. Rec. S.C.*, 5th Sess., No. 15, 473rd Mtg., p. 3.
[8] S/1501, adopted by 9 votes with 1 abstention (Yugoslavia) and 1 member absent (U.S.S.R.).

and support; he then proposed a further Resolution, which the Council adopted, in the following terms:

" . . .

Having determined that the armed attack upon the Republic of Korea by forces from North Korea constitutes a breach of the peace,

. . .

Having noted the appeal from the Republic of Korea to the United Nations for immediate and effective steps to secure peace and security,
Recommends that the Members of the United Nations furnish such assistance to the Republic of Korea as may be necessary to repel the armed attack and to restore international peace and security in the area." [9]

The reaction of Member governments to these recommendations, and the assistance in fact provided, are matters which will be dealt with later. In so far as military assistance was provided by sixteen Members, there arose the practical necessity for co-ordinating this assistance and at the 476th meeting on 7 July a United Kingdom/ France draft Resolution was adopted which, in its terms:

" . . .

Recommends that all Members providing military forces and other assistance pursuant to the aforesaid Security Council Resolutions make such forces and other assistance available to a unified command under the United States;
Requests the United States to designate the commander of such forces;
Authorises the unified command at its discretion to use the United Nations flag in the course of operations against North Korean forces concurrently with the flags of the various nations participating,
Requests the United States to provide the Security Council with reports as appropriate on the course of action taken under the unified command." [10]

These Resolutions represent the total Security Council contribution to the Korean action. With the return to the Council of the Soviet representative in August the veto frustrated any further action by that organ. The initiative passed to the Assembly, acting under the Resolution on Uniting for Peace of 3 November 1950.[11] Thus, it was by virtue of the " approval " of the Assembly in its Resolution of 7 October 1950 that action north of the 38th parallel was continued, and it likewise fell to the Assembly to condemn the People's Republic of China as an aggressor and to recommend an arms embargo against the People's Republic and the North Korean authorities.[12] When, in due course, the problem of exchanging prisoners-of-war arose as part of the general Armistice Agreement, it was the General Assembly which affirmed the principle of " non-forcible " repatriation which the Unified Command had adopted.[13] However, since the initiation of military action was by Security Council Resolutions, it is the constitutional validity of these Resolutions which is now our primary concern.

[9] S/1511, adopted by 7 votes to 1 (Yugoslavia) with 1 member absent (U.S.S.R.) and 2 abstaining (Egypt, India); India subsequently accepted the Resolution (S/1520).
[10] S/1588, adopted by 7 votes, with 3 abstentions (Yugoslavia, Egypt, India) and 1 member absent (U.S.S.R.). [11] *Post*, pp. 290–298.
[12] *Post*, p. 47. [13] *Post*, p. 50.

2. *Constitutional basis*

The constitutional basis of these three vital Resolutions of the Security Council is a matter of some complexity. There is no reference to specific articles of the Charter in the Resolutions themselves so that one is forced to deduce the basis of the Resolutions in the Charter by an analysis of the actual wording used.

In the Resolution of 25 June there is the specific determination of a " breach of the peace " so that the Security Council would seem to have been acting under Article 39 of the Charter [14]; operative paragraph I, calling for the immediate cessation of hostilities, and calling upon the authorities of North Korea to withdraw, is more in the nature of a call for provisional measures under Article 40,[15] although such measures would normally be expected prior to a determination by the Council of the party actually responsible, whereas in this Resolution the Council had virtually determined the North Korean authorities to be responsible for the "armed attack." Operative paragraph III, on the other hand, suggests that the Council is invoking the obligations of Members under Article 2 (5), although at this stage no "action" had been taken in which they could render assistance.

The Resolution of 27 June was the crucial one in so far as it contained the recommendation to Members to furnish assistance to the Republic of Korea. This recommendation was probably based upon the power under Article 39 to "make recommendations . . . to maintain international peace and security"; there is no limitation in the Charter as to what these recommendations may be, for they are simply envisaged in Article 39 by way of contrast with the decisions in accordance with Articles 41 and 42.[16] Hence, as a mere recommendation, the assistance rendered by Members was purely voluntary [17]; the recommendation operated as an authorisation to Members to take action which, without such authorisation, might have been illegal. It should be added that one State, the United States, in fact instructed its sea and air forces to render assistance to South Korea on the 27 June 1950 *before* the Resolution of that date was passed. It is extremely doubtful whether, in fact, the Resolution of 25 June can be regarded as justifying such action,[18]

---

[14] Kunz, "Legality of the S.C. Resolutions of June 25 and 27, 1950," (1951) 45 A.J. 139; Kelsen, *Recent Trends in the Law of the UN* (1951) p. 931 doubts this because the Resolution did not go on to make a recommendation or to decide upon enforcement measures.

[15] Stone, *Legal Controls of International Conflict* (1959) p. 229.

[16] Kelsen, *op. cit.*, pp. 932–933 does not share this view and regards recommendations under Art. 39 as confined to pacific settlement of disputes; Stone, *op. cit.*, p. 230 is of the same opinion.

[17] Indeed, even had the Security Council attempted to take a *decision*, this would not have imposed any legal obligation to take armed action in the absence of agreement under Art. 43 : see U.K. representative, *Off. Rec. S.C.*, 5th yr., No. 17, p. 8.

[18] It was in fact so justified by the Statement of the U.S. President, June 27, 1950, *United States Policy in the Korean Crisis*, Dept. State Publication

although it may have been possible to justify it on the basis of collective self-defence.[19]

The Resolution of 7 July, having welcomed the support given by Members to the Resolutions of 25[20] and 27 June, proceeded to establish (again by recommendation) a Unified Command for which the United States was requested to appoint a commander; the Command was to be authorised to fly the United Nations flag and the United States was requested to report to the Security Council on the course of action taken by the Unified Command. It is believed that this Resolution may be regarded as merely an implementation of the two previous Resolutions, so that its legality stands or falls with them. The excess of technicality with which Kelsen opposed the legality of establishing a United Nations Command, or of authorising the use of the United Nations flag[21] stems from a basic premise that nothing is lawful unless expressly authorised by the Charter: this view is contrary to the whole development of *implied* powers, which are lawful so long as they are consistent with the general and *express* powers conferred upon particular organs.[22] It is because of their excessive technicality that writers like Kelsen and Stone have denied that the Korean action was enforcement action under Chapter VII or even United Nations action at all.[23] For Kelsen this results from the fact that the Security Council made recommendations and did not take decisions in accordance with Articles 41 and 42; yet, as we have seen, Article 39 does speak of "recommendations" which do not necessarily have to relate to Chapter VI rather than Chapter VII. In any event, why should not the Council, especially when agreements under Article 43 are lacking, act by way of recommendation rather than decision? It may be noted that in the Advisory Opinion on *Certain Expenses of the United Nations*[24] the criteria adopted for enforcement action by the Court are that it should be directed *against* a State (or, presumably, any other "aggressor") and should not be based on the consent of the State; the International Court of Justice did not make

---

3922, Far Eastern Series 34 (1950), p. 18. Goodrich, *Korea: A Study of U.S. Policy in the United Nations* (1956) at p. 110 takes the other point that the "neutralisation" of Formosa by the same Presidential instructions involved the UN indirectly in the consequences of an action with regard to which they had not been consulted and of which many of them did not approve: this certainly went beyond the Resolution of 25 June.

[19] Stone, *op. cit.*, p. 231, note 13.

[20] Since the Resolution of 25 June did not call for assistance, Kelsen, *op. cit.*, p. 935 suggests this was an *ex post facto* justification of the premature U.S. action on 27 June.

[21] Kelsen suggests that a "United Nations Command" could only be established by a *decision* of the Security Council, that the action was not a United Nations action (for the same reason) and that the authorisation of the use of the flag was contrary to the Flag Code issued by the Secretary-General on 19 December 1947: *op. cit.*, pp. 936–938.

[22] See Advisory Opinion on *Reparations for Injuries*, I.C.J. Reports, 1949, at p. 182.

[23] Kelsen, *op. cit.*, pp. 936–937; Stone, *op. cit.*, p. 232.

[24] *I.C.J. Reports*, 1962, at pp. 164, 165, 177.

33

the concept turn on whether it was authorised by a decision or a recommendation. The Korean action was directed against the North Korean authorities and the Council had determined them to be responsible for a breach of the peace; the action therefore conforms to the concept of "enforcement action" adopted by the Court.

For Stone an additional and substantial defect is that the Resolutions adopted were not in conformity with Article 27 (3) and this leads him to conclude that the legal basis for the whole Korean action was either the right of individual or collective self-defence under Article 51 or simply voluntary action by Member States not prohibited by the Charter, in particular by Article 2 (4).[25] There is considerable doubt whether some assisting States could possibly be said to have any right to "collective self-defence,"[26] and the references in the Resolutions to an "armed attack" have no significance other than indicating that, as between the North and South Korean authorities, it was the former which was responsible for the breach of the peace and it was the latter which was engaged in self-defence. Even more important, as we shall see, the participating States regarded their action as essentially United Nations action under the authority of the Security Council, and not unilateral action in the absence of any prohibition: it may also be recalled that at San Francisco a French proposal to give Members such a licence to act was rejected.[27]

The better view is to regard the Korean action as enforcement action authorised by recommendations under Article 39. In terms of the actual content of the Resolutions, their validity rests on the broader basis that the action taken by Members was fully consistent with the Purposes and Principles of the Charter and was authorised by Resolutions of a competent organ of the United Nations.[28] It is this approach, rather than a discussion of the minutiae of the wording of each paragraph of each Resolution (in practice simply a result of political compromise) in relation to specific Charter provisions, which is suggested as the only realistic approach to what is, after all, a dynamic *political* organisation. Moreover, given that the Korean action had as its purpose the restoration of international peace and security, the action taken by the Security Council must be deemed to be within its powers. As the Court stated in the *Expenses Case*:

"But when the Organisation takes action which warrants the assertion that it was appropriate for the fulfilment of one of the stated purposes of the United Nations, the presumption is that such action is not *ultra vires* the Organisation."[29]

[25] *Op. cit.,* p. 234.
[26] Bowett, *Self-Defence in International Law* (1958) pp. 215–218.
[27] UNCIO, Docs., Vol. 9, p. 696.
[28] See Potter, "Legal Aspects of the Situation in Korea," (1950) 44 A.J. 709, 712.
[29] *Loc. cit.,* p. 168.

This same presumption must also apply to the other objections to the constitutionality of the Resolutions which have been raised: these objections are distinct from the ones previously examined in that they do not turn on the compatibility of the wording of the Resolutions with the Charter provisions, but on more fundamental limitations on the power of the Security Council and on the voting procedure by which the Council acts. These are all, significantly, objections raised by the Soviet Union in the August debates after the return of its delegate to the Council meetings.

There is, first, the question whether the situation in Korea fell within the province of the United Nations at all since, to do so, there must be a threat to or breach of "*international*" peace. It was argued, initially in a Polish note to the Secretary-General of 30 June [30] and later by the Soviet Union [31] that the situation was simply one of civil war in which intervention by the United Nations was illegal. Of course the prohibition of Article 2 (7) does not in any event apply to enforcement action under Chapter VII because of the express proviso in paragraph 7. Even apart from this (since it may be suggested that the Security Council did not take "enforcement action"), this argument must be rejected since it cannot be suggested that a civil war is inevitably *not* a threat to international peace and security; whether it is or not depends on the facts and, as a question of fact, the Council had determined a "breach of the peace" which clearly means, within the context of Chapter VII, a breach of *international* peace. The Resolution of 27 June placed this beyond any doubt by referring specifically to assistance necessary "to restore *international* peace and security." In any event the Soviet Union's assumption that Korea was but one State can hardly be accepted. The recognition of statehood, implicit in the General Assembly's Resolution 195 (III), cannot obscure the fact that the recognised Government had no control over the territory north of the 38th parallel and under the control of the North Korean authorities. Moreover, the very use of the term "armed attack" signifies that the Security Council was dealing with an *external* threat to the territory over which the recognised Government had control. The Security Council's attitude was consistent with treating the North Korean authorities as having belligerent status [32]; no further recognition as a government or State was necessary in order to define the situation accurately as one constituting a threat to international peace. Similarly, the fact that the Republic of Korea was not a Member of the United Nations is also irrelevant to the notion of a threat to "international" peace, for the Charter nowhere limits this situation to attacks upon Members.

Second there is the question of whether the Security Council, as

---

[30] UN Doc. S/1545.   [31] *Off. Rec. S.C.*, 5th yr., 482nd Mtg., pp. 6–8.
[32] Stone, *op. cit.*, p. 230; Kelsen, *op. cit.*, p. 731; Kunz, *loc. cit.*, p. 139; Attia, *Les Forces Armées des Nations Unies en Corée et au Moyen-Orient* (1962) pp. 120–122.

it was composed at the time of the adoption of the Resolutions, was a lawfully constituted organ competent to make the Resolutions in question. The objections here are twofold. Firstly there is the objection [33] that the seat of China was occupied by the " representative of the Kuomintang group." This has been a perennial objection in the Security Council and, however paradoxical the representation of China may be, the fact is that it is the representation accepted by the Security Council according to its own rules of procedure; the objection could equally be applied to every Security Council Resolution over the past fifteen years, so that its relevance here is negligible. The second, and the only substantial, objection which was made [34] related to the absence of the Soviet Union from the Council when the three Resolutions were passed. This raises the whole question of whether absence can be equated with abstention and whether a non-procedural vote under Article 27 (3) can be adopted in the absence of a Permanent Member. The literature on this is voluminous [35] and the question is too complex to be treated in detail here. Suffice it to say that the Soviet Union, in absenting itself, was in breach of Article 28 of the Charter, and the action of the majority of the Council was inspired by a determination to carry out its " primary responsibility " for the maintenance of international peace and security despite the attempt by one Permanent Member to prevent it. It is, indeed, difficult to reconcile the action with the literal wording of Article 27 (3); it is not in the least difficult to reconcile it with the overriding Purposes and Principles of the Charter. The Resolutions indicated a political will to succeed which was never present under the League of Nations: the fact that they involved action of questionable legality by reference to the specific Charter provisions is, of course, a matter of great concern. In due course it will be seen how that concern was reflected in the assumption of powers by the General Assembly, under the Resolution on Uniting for Peace of 3 November 1950.[36]

II. THE UNITED NATIONS FORCES IN KOREA

1. *Negotiations with States for contributions to the Force*

On 29 June the Secretary-General transmitted to all Member States the Resolution of 27 June and asked what assistance they would be

---

[33] S/1545, S/1523, and the statement by the Soviet Union's representative, *Off. Rec. S.C.*, 5th yr., 480th Mtg., p. 2. See generally Stone, *op. cit.*, Chap. 8, Discourse Eleven, and the authorities there cited; Attia, *op. cit.*, pp. 122–123.

[34] *Off. Rec. S.C.*, 5th yr., 480th Mtg., p. 20, statement by the U.S.S.R.

[35] Gross, " Voting in the Security Council," (1951) 60 Yale L.J. 210; McDougal and Gardner, " The Veto and the Charter: an interpretation for survival," *ibid.*, p. 258; Kelsen, *op. cit.*, pp. 927–949; Stone, *op. cit.*, Chap. VIII; Kunz, *loc. cit.*, p. 141; Green, " Korea and the United Nations," (1950) 4 *World Affairs* 427; Brugière, *Droit de Veto* (1952) pp. 82–90, 107–145; Attia, *op. cit.*, pp. 124–132; Day, *Le droit de Veto dans l'O.N.U.* (1952) pp. 136–138.

[36] *Post*, pp. 290–298.

prepared to give to the Republic of Korea. The replies ranged from specific support of the Resolution and offers of armed forces or other assistance (foodstuffs, medical supplies, air and sea transport, finance, etc.) to general support but with no firm offer of assistance; from the Soviet *bloc* the replies all challenged the legality of the Resolution.[37]

The Secretary-General communicated all offers of assistance to the United States Government and, after the Unified Command had been created by the Resolution of 7 July, a standing procedure developed whereby the Secretary-General communicated offers to the United States permanent representative at United Nations Headquarters who in turn passed them on to Washington. Preliminary, informal discussions were held so as to ensure that offers corresponded to actual needs.[38] By a cable dated 14 July (S/1619) the Secretary-General informed those States which had responded affirmatively to his earlier communication that the United States was prepared to enter into " direct consultation with governments with regard to the co-ordination of assistance," and offers of assistance were to be communicated to the Secretary-General " in general terms, leaving detailed arrangements for . . . an agreement between the Government and the Unified Command." The United States thus entered into bilateral negotiations with the contributing State and, in many cases, the agreement was formalised in treaty form[39]; when this was done the United States always purported to act as " the executive agent of the United Nations Forces in Korea."

It is clear that the United States did not accept every offer made, and two central problems arose. The first was that of the minimum strength of individual military contributions; in general the United States insisted that a national contingent should be of battalion strength (1200 men) with supporting artillery, that engineers or ordnance units should be able to function as independent units, and that the contributing State should provide reinforcements so as to maintain the initial strength. Hence some offers of volunteers and officers were declined as inadequate. The second problem was the logistical problem of supplies, and, with the exception of Commonwealth countries and States using British equipment for which a separate logistical line of supply was established, the United States

---

[37] A complete table of assistance offered up to 1 January 1951 is given in the *UN Yearbook*, 1950, pp. 226–228. It may be noted that assistance was offered by one non-Member State (Italy) and by nine organisations. A second table giving the different assistance proffered by Members as of 15 January 1952 is given in the *UN Yearbook*, 1951, p. 249. A third table, giving a table of assistance as of 15 February 1953 is given in *UN Yearbook*, 1952, p. 213.

[38] Frye, *A United Nations Peace Force* (1957) p. 187; Weissberg, *International Status of the United Nations* (1961), pp. 82–83. Some States, such as Colombia and Argentina, seem to have made offers direct to the Unified Command.

[39] See, for example, the agreements with S. Africa (3 U.S.T. 3990); Netherlands (*ibid.*, 3987); Belgium (*ibid.*, 6, 2829); Sweden (*ibid.*, 2, 1209); Norway (*ibid.*, 2, 1903).

insisted that a single line of supply, using United States materials, should be established.

The financial arrangements between the United States and the other contributing States were complicated and, of course, proceeded on the basis that no part of the necessary finance would be forthcoming from the United Nations. In the various agreements entered into between the United States and States providing assistance, arrangements were made for the United States to furnish " materials, supplies, services and facilities" which the other contributing government was unable to supply, against reimbursement in dollars.[40] It was provided that classified items, and those in short supply, might be returned in certain circumstances and credited against the cost of materials furnished earlier.[41] No claims were permitted between the two governments in respect of death or injury incurred by their personnel, or of loss, damage or destruction of the other's property.[42] The various contributing States were required to maintain accounts of materials received from other governments, either directly or through the Commander of the Unified Command, and to settle any claims directly with the government concerned.[43] In the case of Belgium, a supplementary Agreement was entered into dealing expressly with the financial arrangements for logistical support furnished by the United States Department of Army to the Belgian contingent.[44] This listed the various headings, such as supplies and transportation services, for which payment was to be made. Broadly speaking, in the case of supplies, equipment and transportation services, a sum representing the cost price was paid; as regards ammunition and maintenance costs, it was agreed that reimbursement should be made on a fixed-sum basis.

Agreements were also necessary to deal with the problem of the local currency needs of the United Nations Forces in Korea. The basic agreement in this respect was that between the United States and the Republic of Korea " regarding expenditures by forces under the command of the Commanding General, Armed Forces of the Member States of the United Nations," dated 28 July 1950,[45] under which Korea provided local currency to the Commanding General, who was responsible for any transfers made to the forces of other countries participating under his command. It was specified that

---

[40] See *e.g.* Article 1 of the Agreement between the United States and Norway, concerning the participation of a Norwegian Mobile Surgical Hospital in the United Nations Operations in Korea, U.N.T.S., Vol. 140, No. 1895, p. 313 at p. 314. Norway offered to pay all the expenses of the Field Hospital and its operation for half a year. S/2038, *Off. Rec. S.C.*, 6th yr., Suppl. January–December 1951.

[41] *Ibid.*, Article 3.   [42] *Ibid.*, Article 4.

[43] *Ibid.*, Article 5.

[44] U.N.T.S., Vol. 223, No. 3041, p. 11.

[45] U.N.T.S., Vol. 140, No. 1883, p. 56. See also the Agreement relating to economic co-ordination between the Unified Command of the United Nations and the Republic of Korea, *ibid.*, Vol. 179, No. 2353, p. 23, esp. Article 4.

claims in respect of the currency transferred were to be settled directly between Korea and the governments of the countries concerned. A provision to this effect was therefore included in the agreements between the United States and contributing States.[46] By an exchange of notes between Korea and Australia, New Zealand and the United Kingdom, detailed arrangements were made for an appropriate form of settlement of advances of Korean currency supplied in order to meet the local needs of the forces of the three latter States.[47] It may also be noted that, under an exchange of notes between the United States and Japan " relating to the assistance to be given by Japan in support of United Nations actions " [48] following the entry into force of the Peace Treaty with Japan, it was provided that the expenses involved in the use of Japanese facilities should continue to be met in the same way as previously, or as otherwise mutually agreed between Japan and the United Nations Member concerned. In so far as the United States was concerned, it agreed to continue to pay the expenses incurred in respect of the use of facilities and services by its own troops, over and above those furnished pursuant to the pre-existing Security Treaty. This agreement was later modified by the entry into force of the Agreement on the Status of United Nations Forces in Japan, dated 19 February 1954, between Japan and the States participating in the United Nations action.[49] However, except in so far as that Agreement was negotiated by the United States and opened for signature by other States, and entailed certain financial consequences by reason of the exemption from Japanese taxes of purchases and disbursements made in connection with the operation of the Force, it did not touch upon the major issue of the apportionment of expenses.

2. *The composition of the Force*

The Force was essentially composed of national contingents and volunteers or individual recruits were not accepted. The Secretary-General's own informal proposals to the United States that the Unified Command should find a means to utilise all capable volunteers from foreign countries, possibly in the form of an international brigade, were rejected.[50] In part due to the geographical proximity of United States forces in Japan, the initial forces sent to the aid of the Republic of Korea were entirely United States forces: United Kingdom forces, the next to arrive, entered Korea only in August. Thereafter the dominance of United States forces remained marked, and whilst fifteen other Member States eventually contributed military

---

[46] See *e.g.* Article 6 of the Agreement between the United States and Norway, *ibid.*, Vol. 140, No. 1895, p. 313.
[47] *Ibid.*, Vol. 207, No. 2812, p. 293.
[48] *Ibid.*, Vol. 136, No. 1834, p. 203.
[49] *Ibid.*, Vol. 214, No. 2899, p. 51.
[50] Trygve Lie, *In the Cause of Peace* (1954) p. 339.

forces, it has been estimated [51] that, numerically, the United States contributed 50.32 per cent. of the ground forces, 85.89 per cent. of the naval forces and 93.38 per cent. of the air forces. The Republic of Korea contributed 40.10 per cent., 7.45 per cent. and 5.65 per cent. respectively, the fifteen other United Nations Members contributing the remainder. These figures do not, however, include other kinds of assistance such as transportation facilities, medical supplies, hospital units, etc.

It is clear that, at least in the case of Nationalist China who offered three infantry divisions, a decision was taken on political grounds not to accept the offer; the offer was in fact made on 3 July 1950, long before the intervention by Chinese Communist forces.

3. *Command structure*

The existence of a comprehensive United States Far East Command under General MacArthur, coupled with the predominance of United States military assistance, made the establishment of a Unified Command under the United States a logical step; this was taken by the Resolution of 7 July and the United States was requested to designate the commander for all United Nations Forces. President Truman's appointment of General MacArthur followed on 8 July.[52] The Republic of Korea, though not directly affected by this Resolution (as a non-Member) also assigned to General MacArthur command authority over all its armed forces on 15 July.[53] Supreme command was thus vested in the United States and General MacArthur was replaced by successive United States officers, Generals Ridgeway and Clark.

The United Nations Command was in practice fully integrated with the United States Far East Command, with headquarters in Tokyo. From here General MacArthur commanded the United States Eighth Army, which included the ground forces of all participating Members and of the Republic of Korea, the United States Far Eastern Air Force and the United States Seventh Fleet, which had attached to it naval units contributed by Members. The integration of national military units of Members into United States Divisions, except in the case of the separate Commonwealth Division, formed on 27 July 1951, was considered justified not only by reason of the effectiveness of command thereby assured, but also by reason of

---

[51] Frye, *op. cit.*, p. 188; Goodrich, *op. cit.*, pp. 114–119. The figures are based on the U.S. Dept. of State publication, *United States Participation in the United Nations, Report of the President to Congress for the Year 1951*, Publication No. 4583 (Washington: U.S. Govt. Printing Office, 1952), pp. 273–288. The U.S. contribution of land forces was 3 Army Corps and 1 Marine Division, as compared with the U.K.'s next largest contribution of 2 Brigades.
[52] Dept. State Bulletin 23 (1950), p. 83.
[53] S/1267.

the necessity for a single logistical supply line and similar military procedures.[54]

The chain of command in effect, therefore, began with the President of the United States and came down through the Secretary of Defense, the Joint Chiefs of Staff, the Chief of Staff of the Army, General MacArthur, and Divisional Commanders.[55]

Liaison was dealt with as a normal, military procedure, but two unusual features distinguished the Korean action as a United Nations action. One was the multi-national character of the Command at lower levels, especially at the Eighth Army Headquarters in Tokyo, and the other was the conferment on the senior military representative of each Member State contributing forces of a right of direct access to the United Nations Commander " on matters of major policy affecting the operational capabilities of the forces concerned." [56]

4. *Strategic and political control of United Nations Forces*

It was obvious that the Security Council could not utilise the Military Staff Committee, envisaged in Article 47 of the Charter, as a means of obtaining the military advice upon which the broad, political decisions of policy had to be based : the presence in that Committee of Major General Ivan A. Skliarov of the U.S.S.R. ensured that. Nor, indeed, could the Security Council, complete with a representative of the U.S.S.R., be expected to discuss even those broad policy questions which pre-supposed an intimate knowledge of the military situation and advance military planning, so that true political control could not be exercised by United Nations organs and some kind of substitute organ seemed desirable.[57] Hence as early as 3 July the Secretary-General proposed informally a " Committee on co-ordination of Assistance for Korea " to be composed of contributing States and the Republic of Korea; of this Committee he has written :

" Its deeper purpose was to keep the United Nations ' in the picture,' to promote continuing United Nations participation in and supervision of the military security action in Korea of a more intimate and undistracted character than the Security Council could be expected to provide. The delegates of the United Kingdom, France and Norway liked the idea of such a committee; the United States Mission promptly turned thumbs down. The Pentagon was much opposed to such United Nations activity." [58]

[54] U.S. House of Representatives, 80th Cong., 1st Sess., *Contributing to the Effective Maintenance of International Peace and Security*, House Report 996 : cited in Frye, *op. cit.*, p. 190.
[55] See " *Military Situation in the Far East*," *Hearings before the Committee on Armed Services and the Committee on Foreign Relations of the U.S. Senate*, 82nd Cong., 1st Sess., Part 1, pp. 150-151, testimony of General MacArthur.
[56] *Off. Rec. G.A.*, 6th Sess., Suppl. No. 13, Report of the Collective Measures Committee (A/1891), p. 46.
[57] See " *Military Situation in the Far East*," *loc. cit.*, Part 3, p. 1724, where Secretary of State Acheson testified that, because of the presence of the Soviet Union's representative, it was impossible to discuss within the Security Council the policy question of whether " hot pursuit " of enemy planes should be continued over the Manchurian border.
[58] Trygve Lie, *op. cit.*, p. 334.

The Security Council had, of course, by its Resolution of 7 July, requested reports on action taken from the United States, and bi-weekly reports were in fact transmitted to the Council by the United States Government.[59]   But these were factual statements of events that had occurred and were not of the character to allow the Council to know in advance of the military planning of the United Nations Command.   There seems to have been not only a reluctance on the part of the United States to take the Security Council into its confidence (understandable enough in the circumstances) but an equal reluctance to consult with the participating States, and it was only later, after the Chinese intervention had revealed marked divergencies of view as to the political desirability of certain military measures, that, belatedly, weekly conferences of the " Committee of Sixteen " began in Washington : this was a committee of representatives of participating States, but with purely advisory functions and it " was not a true substitute for overall directives by an organ of the [United Nations]." [60]

Thus it was that political and strategic control of the United Nations Command vested, effectively, in the United States Joint Chiefs of Staff in Washington, rather than in a United Nations organ or even in a body representative of the contributing States.   It has been suggested that, because of MacArthur's great prestige, Washington was reluctant " to prescribe in detail what the Commander in the field could or could not do." [61]   There is, however, the testimony of MacArthur himself before the United States Senate that :

"The Agreement that was . . . made between the United Nations and the United States Government was that the . . . Government should be the agent for the United Nations in the campaign in Korea. The orders that came to me were from the American Government, but they had under that basis the validity of both the United States Government and the United Nations . . . My instructions from the Joint Chiefs of Staff acting as the agency for the United Nations, ha[d] modified the military conditions under which I operate[d]." [62]

On the other hand, as General MacArthur also testified, " my connection with the United Nations was largely nominal . . . I had no direct connection with the United Nations whatsoever." [63]   It is

[59] The Secretary-General apparently had difficulty in ensuring that the Council received these before they were released to the Press by American attachés in Tokyo : *ibid.*   General MacArthur testified in the Hearings before the U.S. Senate Committee that his reports were subjected to a certain censorship in Washington before transmission to the UN : " *Military Situation* " etc., *loc. cit.*, Part 1, p. 11. The Secretary-General did appoint his own liaison officer to the UN Command. A summary of the reports of the UN Command is given in the Yearbooks of the UN; the full texts are also given in the Dept. of State Bulletin.

[60] Frye, *op. cit.*, p. 57; he actually says " of the General Assembly," but this is because he discusses the defects of the Committee of Sixteen in the context of the later shift of control to the Assembly.

[61] *Ibid.*, p. 193.

[62] " *Military Situation in the Far East*," *Hearings before the Senate Committee on Armed Services and Foreign Relations*, 82nd Cong., 1st Sess. (1951), Part 3, p. 1937.   [63] " *Military Situation* " etc., Part 1, p. 10.

clear from this testimony that he believed the United Nations had given to the United States a mandate to "run the campaign," and that no continuing direction of the campaign could be expected from the United Nations.

The actual degree of control exercised by the United Nations, or even by the contributing States, is extremely difficult to assess on the basis of available information.[64]   What is clear is that dissatisfaction arose after the Inchon landing of 15 September 1950 and the decision to cross the 38th parallel and advance to the Yalu river after the North Korean authorities had rejected MacArthur's call to surrender on 1 October 1950 (S/1829).   The problem posed was the funda-mental one of how far the United Nations was entitled to restore the *status quo ante*, or to take all necessary measures to destroy the aggressor.   In principle the latter solution was the only proper solu-tion, especially since there was no evidence of any intention on the part of the North Korean authorities to cease fighting once pushed back over the 38th parallel.   The General Assembly's Resolution of 7 October 1950, reiterating the necessity for a " unified " Korea, was taken as an endorsement of the decision already taken by the Unified Command to proceed beyond the 38th parallel.[65]   How far this decision motivated the intervention of Chinese Communist military units may never be known, but it is clear that by 5 November 1950 the United Nations Command was reporting contact with such units [66]

[64] It is clear that prior discussion of the political wisdom of authorising "hot pursuit " of aircraft across the Manchurian border took place with 6 of the 13 contributing States, via the U.S. embassies, and that the U.S. Govern-ment accepted the negative views of those six States: testimony of Secretary of State Acheson, "*Military Situation*" etc., Part 3, p. 1723. Postponement of bombing of the Yalu bridges appears to have been due to a commitment to the British: Truman's *Memoirs*, Vol. 2, pp. 374–375.

[65] Disapproval of MacArthur's political views had been expressed in the House of Commons even prior to the Chinese intervention (H.C.D. Vol. 478, cols. 1341–1342); this disapproval and distrust became even more evident when on 16 November specific questions were asked of the Minister of Defence on whether instructions had been given to cross the 38th parallel; these received only the vague reply that " instructions are issued from time to time " (*ibid.*, Vol. 480, cols. 1908, 1912).   In the general debate on foreign policy on 29 and 30 November this issue was again taken up by several members and the Foreign Secretary replied: " I wish to assure the House that the objectives of General MacArthur are no more and no less than the objectives of the United Nations . . .   It has . . . been necessary to leave the control of the operations very much in the hands of the United Nations Commander, provided always that when his plans might involve questions of general policy there must be appropriate consultation on such matters.   I can assure the House that this is in fact what has happened." (*Ibid.*, Vol. 481, col. 1164).   Trygve Lie suggests that the General Assembly Resolution of 7 October 1950 (Resol. 376 (V)) in referring to the objective of a " unified " Korea expressed the general approval of the Assembly for the continued advance: *op. cit.*, p. 345.   Goodrich, *Korea: A Study of U.S. Policy in the United Nations* (1956) pp. 133–134, 142–143, takes the same view and so did General MacArthur ("*Military Situation*" etc., Part 1, p. 245) and Secretary of State Acheson (*ibid.*, Part 3, p. 1735). However, Goodrich, *op. cit.*, p. 143 has clear reservations about the wisdom of this policy, as does Attia, *op. cit.*, pp. 163–167.

[66] S/1884.   The original contention by the People's Republic that these were " volunteers " was belied by the size and armaments of the units; it was not a contention which was seriously persisted in.

and that earlier, on 28 August (S/1772), the People's Republic of China had complained of bombing raids on North East China.[67] The fear of a threat to the security of China was in fact attempted to be allayed by the draft Resolution of the Security Council of 10 November:
" . . .

Affirming that United Nations forces should not remain in any part of Korea otherwise than so far as necessary for achieving the objectives of stability throughout Korea and the establishment of a unified independent and democratic government in the sovereign State of Korea.
Insistent that no action be taken which might lead to the spread of the Korean conflict to other areas and thereby further endanger international peace and security.
. . .
Affirms that it is the policy of the United Nations to hold the Chinese frontier with Korea inviolate and fully to protect legitimate Chinese and Korean interests in the frontier zone.
. . ." [68]

This draft Resolution was vetoed by the U.S.S.R. and the invitation of the Council to the Peking Government to be present during the Council's discussion of the report of Chinese intervention by the United Nations Command, made two days earlier, was declined on 11 November. There was, in fact, little evidence of any desire to be "placated." It fell to the General Assembly, by Resolution 498 (V) of 1 February 1951 to affirm that the Central Government of the People's Republic of China had, in opening hostilities against the United Nations Forces in Korea, itself engaged in aggression in Korea.

The eventual dismissal of General MacArthur by President Truman in April 1951 does not, however, appear to have been based on any allegation that he took action beyond what was authorised, but rather on the ground that his public statements on the broad question of policy of whether to fight a restricted or unrestricted war against Communist China were improper. It also seems clear that the contributing States did not in any way influence the President's decision.[69]

However, it is generally clear that MacArthur felt there was an absence of a clear, political policy: he stated " I was operating in what I call a vacuum . . . there is no policy—there is nothing, I tell you, no plan, nor anything." [70] Even allowing for a certain over-statement due to the fact that his own policy had not been accepted,

[67] This complaint was first placed on the Security Council agenda by the U.S.S.R. on 31 August; it was repeated in a statement by the Ministry of Foreign Affairs of the Chinese People's Republic dated 11 November (S/1902). The complaint was denied by the U.S. representative, 526th Mtg., 28 November. The U.S. proposal for an investigation of these complaints on the spot (S/1727) was rejected by the U.S.S.R.   [68] S/1894.
[69] " *Military Situation* " etc., Part 1, pp. 39 (testimony of General MacArthur) 341, 417, 427 (testimony of Secretary Marshall). Attia, *loc. cit.*, pp. 191–194 develops a thesis that MacArthur surpassed his instructions, but the declarations and letters of MacArthur on which he relies really only show indiscretion and too forceful an expression of his own views on policy.
[70] *Ibid.*, pp. 30, 68.

it is tolerably clear that the essential issue of whether to fight a limited war, designed simply to restore the status quo at the 38th parallel (leaving the rest of the problem for a pacific settlement) or whether to concentrate on the annihilation of aggressor forces was not squarely faced. Moreover, the situation in which the United Nations Forces were authorised to act by the Security Council, were commanded by the United States military authorities, and were subject to political and strategic direction vested largely in the United States Government (although subject to inhibitions stemming from the views of the United Nations and the contributing States) was not an ideal situation by any means.[71] Hence the successive political crisis involved in the decisions on whether to cross the 38th parallel, to take up hot pursuit of aircraft across the Manchurian border, to bomb the bridges on the Yalu, to enlist the support of Chinese nationalist troops, or to impose an economic and arms blockade on China, were not solved in a satisfactory manner. The weakness of strategic and political control is perhaps the most significant fact that emerges in so far as, within this study, the Korean action is examined for the purpose of drawing conclusions about the use of United Nations Forces.

5. The character of the forces as United Nations Forces

The fact that the forces available to the Unified Command were predominantly United States forces, and that only fifteen other States contributed forces, must be viewed with considerable regret; but that fact does not really affect the character of the Force as a matter of law. There is ample evidence that the Security Council and the General Assembly, the United States and other contributing States, and even the People's Republic of China were all of the view that this was a United Nations action and that the forces involved were United Nations Forces. It is to this evidence that we now turn.

The Korean action originated from Resolutions of the Security Council and was in the nature of enforcement action under Chapter VII of the Charter; as already explained,[72] it is impossible to accept the view that this was not United Nations action but merely the action of certain Members under their residual liberty of action. The subsequent General Assembly Resolutions of 7 October 1950,[73] with its specific reference to " United Nations armed forces," of 12 December 1950,[74] with its reference to " men and women who

---

[71] See the strong criticisms of Goodrich, *op. cit.*, pp. 146–148 about the inadequacy of the system for consultation with the UN and the contributing States and the laxity of control over MacArthur.

[72] *Ante*, pp. 33–36. For a detailed discussion of the nature of the Korean action see Weissberg, *op. cit.*, pp. 78–105; Attia, *loc. cit.*, pp. 141–159.

[73] Resol. 376 (V).

[74] Resol. 483 (V); and see the later Resol. 906 (IX) requesting the Secretary-General to seek the release of the eleven personnel of the UN.

have served on behalf of the United Nations in repelling aggression in Korea," and of 18 January 1951,[75] which called upon the People's Republic of China to " cease hostilities against the United Nations Forces" and affirmed "the determination of the United Nations to continue its action . . ." are all symptomatic of the generally-held view that this was, indeed, a United Nations action.

The United States, it will be recalled, concluded agreements with contributing States as "the executive agent of the United Nations Forces in Korea." It rejected claims submitted against it by the U.S.S.R. and the People's Republic on the ground that these should be submitted to the United Nations, whose agent the United States was.[76] Subsequently, in hearings before the United States Senate, Secretary of State Acheson described the Korean operations as " under the aegis of the United Nations and . . . not a question of the whole series of nations acting independently to the same result." [77] General MacArthur called for the cessation of hostilities by the North Koreans as " the United Nations Commander-in-Chief " and on 9 October threatened that otherwise he would " proceed to take such military action as may be necessary to enforce the decrees of the United Nations." [78] The reports transmitted to the Security Council from the Unified Command, via the United States Government, referred consistently to "United Nations Forces," "United Nations prisoners," "United Nations Commander," etc.

The contributing States such as Australia,[79] Canada,[80] France, Bolivia, Thailand, Turkey, New Zealand, Union of South Africa, Denmark and Philippines were equally clear that their offers of assistance were to the United Nations. Their acceptance and support of the Security Council's authorisation to use the United Nations flag [81] and of the General Assembly's Resolution 483 (V) authorising the Secretary-General to arrange with the Unified Command for the award of a " distinguishing ribbon or other insignia for personnel which has participated in Korea in the defence of the Principles of the Charter of the United Nations " is equally evidence of their view that the forces could be regarded as United Nations Forces.

Whilst the Soviet Union persisted in her view that this was not a United Nations action, the People's Republic of China took a more realistic view. Complaints about the violation of her territory were addressed to the United Nations.[82] Moreover, when later the truce

[75] Resol. 498 (V).
[76] *Post*, p. 57.
[77] " *Military Situation in the Far East* " : *loc. cit.*, p. 1937.
[78] UN Docs. S/1829, S/1883.
[79] UN Docs. S/1524, S/1530, S/1646.
[80] UN Docs. S/1538, S/1602, S/1617.
[81] Resol. of 7 July 1950 (S/1588). The original flag code, based on General Assembly Resol. 167 (II) of 20 October 1947 did not envisage the use of the flag in military operations, but the Secretary-General issued a new flag code with a new Part 6 headed " Use of Flag in Military Operations."
[82] UN Docs. S/1722, S/1743, S/1808, S/1857, S/1870, S/1876.

negotiations began, the Commander of the North Korean Army and the Commander of the "Chinese Volunteer Units" addressed their reply to the "Commander-in-Chief of the United Nations Forces"[83]; the armistice of 27 July 1953 was also signed by General Clark under the same title.[84] Even the Chinese political representatives were prepared to concede that they were dealing with United Nations Forces: Chou En-lai, in a message to the President of the General Assembly concerning the exchange of prisoners of war, referred to the proposals of the "Commander-in-Chief of the United Nations Command."[85]

There can be no doubt that, in practice, the overwhelming majority of States involved in the Korean action were fully prepared to regard it as a United Nations action involving United Nations Forces. It was only subsequently, because of extraneous political considerations, that in the course of the negotiations for a political conference to follow up the Armistice Agreement the United States chose to minimise the character of the action as United Nations action and to stress the interests of the participating States as such.

III. THE ARMISTICE AND TRUCE NEGOTIATIONS

The initial attempts to arrange a cease-fire came from the General Assembly which on 14 December 1950[86] established a Three-Man Committee for this purpose. Its efforts to meet and negotiate with the representatives of the Central People's Government failed entirely.[87] The reason soon became apparent for another large-scale offensive by the Communist Chinese and North Korean forces began on 1 January 1951, an offensive initially so successful as to threaten the United Nations action once again. Hence it was only after very clear evidence that the People's Republic of China had no intention of complying with the Assembly's call for a cease-fire that the General Assembly proceeded, under the Resolution on Uniting for Peace, to find that

"the Central People's Government of the People's Republic of China, by giving direct aid and assistance to those who were already committing aggression in Korea and by engaging in hostilities against United Nations Forces there, has itself engaged in aggression in Korea."[88]

It was as a result of the report of the Collective Measures Committee, submitted at the request of the Assembly in paragraph 6 of this same Resolution, that the Assembly subsequently recommended the application of an embargo on shipments of war materials to Communist China and North Korea.[89]

---

[83] *UN Bulletin*, 11 (1951) pp. 49–50. [84] UN Doc. S/3079, pp. 1, 26.
[85] UN Doc. A/2378, pp. 2–3; see also the cablegram of 25 August 1953 from Chou En-lai referring to "United Nations Forces" (A/2466, p. 3).
[86] Resol. 384 (V).
[87] See the narrative of Lie, *op. cit.*, pp. 354–357; representatives were actually in New York at that time.
[88] Resol. 498 (V), 1 February 1951.
[89] Resol. 500 (V), 18 May 1951.

By 20 May 1951 the impetus of this offensive had been lost and the tide of battle again changed in favour of the United Nations Forces.[90]   No doubt because of this change of fortune, in a broadcast on 23 June the Soviet representative, Mr. Malik, suggested that cease-fire negotiations were possible on the basis of mutual with-drawal behind the 38th parallel—in effect a restoration of the status quo.   It also became apparent, after conferences between the United States Ambassador and the Soviet Foreign Minister, that any cease-fire was to be arranged between the respective military commanders and not between the Communist representatives and a General Assembly Committee.[91]   The authority of the Unified Command to negotiate a cease-fire was not seriously in doubt; it normally lay within the province of military commanders in the field and the Secretary-General had circulated a memorandum from the United Nations Legal Department supporting this view.[92]   The authority of the United Nations Command did not, however, extend to political questions.[93]

The ensuing truce meetings, beginning on board a Danish hospital ship in Wonsan harbour and later transferred to Panmunjon, dragged on for two years until the final truce was concluded on 27 July 1953. It may be useful to summarise the principal problems involved since they are likely to be recurrent problems whenever a United Nations Force is faced with the task of concluding an armistice agreement. These problems, as listed on the agreed agenda,[94] were four in number.   Without going into the detailed steps of the protracted negotiations, the agreement eventually reached on these different problems, and embodied in the Armistice Agreement of 27 July 1953,[95] can be summarised as follows.

First, the fixing of the military demarcation line had given rise to difficulty because the United Nations Command rejected the 38th parallel in part because it meant abandoning strong defensive

---

[90] The details can be gathered from the reports of the UN Command, sum-marised in *UN Yearbook*, 1951, pp. 237–241.
[91] This may well have been due to the Assembly's action in adopting Resol. 500 (V) on 18 May 1951.
[92] Lie, *op. cit.*, p. 364.
[93] See the statements by the Secretary-General (*UN Bulletin*, 11 (1951) p. 50 at p. 86) and by Secretary of State Acheson ("*Military Situation*" etc., *loc. cit.*, Part 3, p. 1941).
[94] The agenda for the negotiations, agreed upon on 26 July 1951, is given in "Korea No. 1" (1952) Cmd. 8596, p. 16 and in *UN Yearbook*, 1951, p. 242. The heads were:
" 1. Adoption of the agenda.
  2. Fixing a military demarcation line between both sides so as to establish a demilitarised zone as a basic condition for a cessation of hostilities in Korea.
  3. Concrete arrangements for the realisation of a cease-fire and armistice, including the composition, authority and functions of a supervising organisation for carrying out the terms of a cease-fire and armistice.
  4. Arrangements relating to prisoners-of-war.
  5. Recommendations to the governments of the countries concerned on both sides."
[95] Text in *UN Yearbook*, 1953, pp. 136–146.

positions north of that line and, it may be surmised, in part because of a reluctance to give that line an importance which might later support an argument for its adoption as a definitive, political boundary. The agreement eventually reached was to adopt the " line of contact " between the opposing forces at the armistice date as the demarcation line and for both sides to withdraw two kilometres from this line so as to establish a " demilitarised zone "—a " buffer " zone. No hostile acts were to be permitted within the zone, and no person was to be permitted to enter the zone except by permission of the Military Armistice Commission.[96]

Second, agreement on concrete arrangements for a cease-fire and armistice involved an undertaking to withdraw forces to behind the demilitarised zone, to withdraw forces from the " rear and coastal islands and waters " of the other side, and to cease the introduction of military personnel into Korea save for " rotation " personnel and equipment, *i.e.*, replacements as opposed to reinforcements. The United Nations Neutral Nations Supervisory Commission, through its inspection teams at specified ports, was to guarantee this undertaking. This body was to include officers appointed by Sweden, Switzerland, Poland and Czechoslovakia. The Military Armistice Commission, in contrast, was composed equally of officers from the United Nations Command and the Korean People's Army and Chinese People's Volunteers; its function was to supervise the armistice and settle any violations. To some extent, necessarily, its functions overlapped with those of the United Nations Neutral Nations Supervisory Commission; a clash in competence was, however, avoided by broadly restricting its functions to the area of the " demilitarised zone," whereas, outside the zone, the Neutral Nations Commission would be primarily responsible for investigation. However, in so far as the reports of the Neutral Nations Commission were to be transmitted to the Military Armistice Commission,[97] the ultimate responsibility for dealing with any violation clearly lay with the Military Armistice Commission and not the Neutral Nations Commission.

Third, the arrangements relating to the exchange of prisoners of war proved to be the most difficult on which to agree. Whilst agreement on all other major items had been reached by the end of 1952, this particular item remained intractable. Essentially, the problem was whether the United Nations Command was under a duty to repatriate all prisoners of war in its hands, regardless of their personal preferences, or whether the United Nations Command was entitled not to repatriate prisoners of war who were prepared to forcibly resist repatriation. The intricacies of the legal arguments for both sides go beyond the limits of the present study,[98] and are

---

[96] Art. I.
[97] Art. II, para. 47.
[98] See Mayda, "The Korean Repatriation Problem and International Law," (1953) 47 A.J. 414; Charmatz and Wit, "Repatriation of Prisoners of War and the 1949 Geneva Convention," (1953) 62 Yale L.J. 391.

more a question of the law of war generally than of a special problem for United Nations Forces, but it may be recalled that the draft agreement of 29 August 1952 stated simply that:

" All prisoners of war in the custody of each side . . . shall be released and repatriated as soon as possible."

The Geneva Convention on Prisoners of War of 1949 had been "recognised" as applicable to the conflict by the People's Republic of China,[99] the Republic of Korea, the Democratic People's Republic of Korea,[1] and by the United Nations Command.[2] That Convention provided in Article 118 (1) that:

" Prisoners of war shall be released and repatriated without delay after the cessation of active hostilities."

and, further, according to Article 7:

" Prisoners of war may in no circumstances renounce in part or in entirety the rights secured to them by the present Convention."

Thus, whilst a literal interpretation favoured the Communist argument,[3] the United Nations Command was forced to argue more on moral and humanitarian grounds, although fortified by General Assembly Resolution 610 (VII) to the effect that:

" Force shall not be used against the Prisoners of War to prevent or effect their return to their homelands and no violence to their persons or affront to their dignity or self-respect shall be permitted . . ."[4]

The impasse over prisoners of war was partially broken by the agreement of 11 April 1953 to repatriate the sick and wounded as a matter of priority, and this was followed by a general Prisoners of War Agreement of 8 June 1953 which was to be incorporated into the Armistice Agreement. The signing of the Armistice Agreement was, however, delayed by the action of the authorities of the Republic of Korea on 18 June in bringing about a break-out of some 27,000 prisoners who dispersed amongst the civilian population and proved impossible to recapture. This extraordinary lapse was

---

[99] *New York Times*, 17 July 1952, p. 1.

[1] *Ibid.*, 14 July 1950, p. 1.

[2] Cmnd. 8596, p. 26, and see Fifth Report to the Security Council of the UN Command, S/1834, p. 5.

[3] This argument can be seen in detail in the exchange of letters between the Senior Delegates and the Supreme Commander, 11–20 October 1952: Dept. State Bulletin, Vol. 27, pp. 752–753.

[4] Proposal III, 3 December 1952, adopted by 54 votes to 5 with 1 abstention. There was a further legal argument that the word "released," used in the Geneva Convention, could scarcely be applicable to prisoners-of-war who had to be repatriated forcibly. At the Geneva Diplomatic Conference of 1949 an Austrian amendment to Art. 118, providing that a prisoner-of-war should not be repatriated against his will, was rejected, although statements of various representatives indicated that the detaining Power had a right to afford asylum: see the very clear exposition of Kunz, "Treatment of Prisoners of War," (1953) P.A.S.I.L. 69, at p. 108. The questions put to prisoners by the UN Command in interviews designed to determine the wishes of the prisoners are given in *UN Yearbook*, 1952, p. 157. As a result of these interviews the UN Command estimated that of 121,000 prisoners 83,000 would not oppose repatriation.

admitted by the United Nations Command[5] to be a breach of the Agreement of 8 June.

The final Armistice provisions on prisoners of war involved an exchange of lists of prisoners of war held by both sides, the choice of an exchange site at Panmunjon, the acceptance of the principle of no forcible repatriation, and, whilst a Committee for Repatriation composed equally of representatives of the United Nations Command and the Communist forces dealt with general repatriation (under the authority and control of the Military Armistice Commission), a special Neutral Nations Repatriation Commission (composed of Sweden, Switzerland, Poland, Czechoslovakia and India) was to assume custody of those prisoners who initially declined to be repatriated. This Neutral Nations Repatriation Commission was then to explain to the prisoners their rights and arrange for either repatriation, release to civilian status or transport to a neutral State, according to choice. The Commission was also to make use of joint Red Cross teams (equally composed of representatives from both sides) to provide "humanitarian services." A separate Committee for Assisting the Return of Displaced Civilians (similarly equally composed) dealt with the problems of displaced civilians, under the authority of the Military Armistice Commission.

It may be said, in conclusion, that, quite apart from this central problem of compulsory or non-compulsory repatriation, the whole system for the custody of prisoners of war by both sides left much to be desired. The attacks upon prisoner-of-war camps, the rioting within those camps, and reports of large-scale murder of prisoners of war lead to the conclusion that too lax a system of custody was permitted.[6]

Fourth, it was necessary to make "recommendations to the governments of the countries concerned on both sides." Initially the Communist delegation had proposed a political conference ranging over the whole Far Eastern situation, but the United Nations Command insisted on confining itself to recommendations on the Korean situation. Agreement was reached as early as 19 February 1952 and, as embodied in the final Armistice Agreement, this contained a recommendation " to the governments of the countries concerned on both sides that, within three months after the Armistice Agreement is signed and becomes effective, a political conference of a higher level of both sides be held by representatives appointed respectively to settle through negotiation the questions of the withdrawal of all

---

[5] UN Doc. S/3079, p. 17.
[6] See the section on "Incidents relating to prisoners of war," in *UN Yearbook*, 1952, pp. 159–161; for example, in one compound, Compound 76, the UN Command reported the discovery of 3,000 spears, 1,000 gasoline grenades, 4,500 knives and innumerable other weapons. The UN Command prepared a special penal code for the disciplinary control of prisoners, together with regulations governing their trial by a UN Military Commission for offences committed after capture (*ibid.*, p. 248).

foreign forces from Korea, the peaceful settlement of the Korean question etc." The necessity for a political conference had never really been in doubt since it had been accepted that the authority of the military commands to negotiate lay only in respect of matters arising from the military truce; the broader political issues of the future of Korea lay outside their competence.

This, then, was the final Armistice which came into effect on 27 July 1953 and which brought to an end the Korean hostilities. The General Assembly, in Resolution 711 (VII) of 28 August 1953, approved the Armistice Agreement, which it described as a "major step . . . towards the full restoration of international peace and security in the area," noted the recommendation as to a political conference and recommended that:

"The side contributing armed forces under the Unified Command in Korea shall have as participants in the conference those among the Member States contributing armed forces pursuant to the call of the United Nations which desire to be represented, together with the Republic of Korea. The participating governments shall act independently at the conference with full freedom of action and shall be bound only by decisions or agreements to which they adhere;" [7]

The terms of this Resolution are striking in that they signify the adoption of a position essentially inconsistent with the position hitherto maintained.[8] The whole emphasis hitherto had been on the fact that, despite all its shortcomings as a truly international action, the action in Korea was nevertheless a United Nations action. At the stage of arranging the political conference, however, the United States and all other contributing States (with the exception of South Africa) performed a "*volte-face*" and, with the intention of excluding any representation by other United Nations Members, arrogated to themselves the right to be designated as one "side" to the conflict. The misgivings of other United Nations Members over this position, quite apart from rigorous Soviet opposition, are apparent in the records.[9] The details of this particular problem of the composition of "both sides" at the political conference, with the

---

[7] Para. 5; the paragraph contained the further obligation to inform the UN of any agreement reached and to keep the UN informed "at other appropriate times." The Resolution was adopted by 43 to 5 with 10 abstentions. It was sponsored by the United States and 14 of the other 15 States contributing forces to the UN Command in Korea and, whilst the original draft proposal would have excluded the U.S.S.R. from participation, an amendment was adopted recommending participation by the U.S.S.R. "provided the other side desires it."

[8] Frye, *op. cit.*, p. 57, states: "The new Administration which took power in Washington in 1953 . . . agree[d] to hold peace negotiations outside the UN . . . even though that meant accepting what had been, until then, a communist contention, namely, that the 16 nations—not the UN as a whole—constituted the non-communist side in the struggle." And see generally the account by Weissberg, *op. cit.*, pp. 94–103.

[9] See *Off. Rec. G.A.*, 7th Sess., First Committee, 622nd Mtg., p. 746 (Indian delegate); 624th Mtg., p. 760 (Guatemalan delegate). The Soviet proposal was for a "neutral" element of 9 States.

eventual agreement as to composition reached at the Berlin Conference in 1954 [10] and the failure of the subsequent Geneva Conference,[11] go beyond the scope of the present study. What is clear, however, is that the conclusion of an armistice after hostilities by United Nations Forces will scarcely end all difficulties: the difficulties of a final political settlement, and above all the difficulty of determining who are to be the parties to that settlement, will remain.

IV. THE LEGAL STATUS OF THE CONFLICT AND THE APPLICATION OF THE LAWS OF WAR

1. *The legal status of the conflict*

The Charter does not, except in the preambular reference to the "scourge of war," refer to war or belligerency or neutrality; the terms "collective measures," "enforcement measures" or "preventive or enforcement action" are to be found instead, suggesting that military action to be taken by the United Nations (or by States acting under its authority) is not to be regarded as "war." This was certainly the commonly-accepted view of the United Nations action in Korea.

Statements by various heads of States and governments were adamant in their rejection of the idea that forces contributed by those States to the action were involved in a "war." [12] The general tendency of municipal courts, when faced with the issue of whether "war" existed in Korea, was to say that it did not, although there was no consistency over this issue.[13] However, it is believed that

---

[10] See UN Doc. A/2640, p. 1: the composition agreed upon was U.S.A., France, U.K., U.S.S.R., Chinese People's Republic, Republic of Korea, People's Democratic Republic of Korea and the other contributing States (although S. Africa did not attend in fact).

[11] See *The Korean problem at the Geneva Conference, 26 April–15 June 1954*, Dept. of State Bulletin 5609.

[12] See the U.K. Secretary of State for Foreign affairs, in H.C. Debates, Vol. 502, col. 292; President Truman of the U.S.A. described it as "police action" and not war (*New York Times*, 30 June 1950, p. 1); Canadian Prime Minister, 30 June 1950 (UN Doc. S/1538).

[13] Decisions of U.S. courts dealt primarily with the question of the application of double indemnity clauses in life insurance policies: *Beley v. Pa. Mut. Life Ins. Co.*, 373 Pa. 231 (1953); *Harding v. Pa. Mut. Life Ins. Co.*, 373 Pa. 270 (1953) held it was not a war. Decisions holding it was are *Western Reserve Life Ins. Co. v. Meadows*, 152 Tex. 559 (1953); *Weissman v. Metro. Life Ins. Co.*, 112 F.Suppl. 420 (S.D. Cal. 1953); *Christiansen v. Sterling Ins. Co.*, U.S. Sup.Ct. of Washington (1955) I.L.R. 1955, p. 893. All the decisions of the U.S. Military Court of Military Appeals held the hostilities were "war" within the meaning of the code: see Pye, "The Legal Status of the Korean hostilities," (1956) 45 G.L.J. 45 and especially *U.S. v. Bancroft* (1953) 11 C.M.R. 3; *U.S. v. Gann et al.* (1953) 11 C.M.R. 12.

Decisions of Australian courts accepted that there was no "war": *Burns v. The King*, I.L.R. (1953) p. 596; *Australian Communist Party v. The Commonwealth*, ibid., p. 592, and *Marcus Clark & Co., Ltd. v. The Commonwealth*, ibid., p. 594. See Green, "The Nature of the 'War' in Korea," (1951) 4 I.L.Q. 462 for a discussion of these cases. For a similar New Zealand decision, see *In re Berry*, I.L.R. (1955) p. 898 (construing "actual military service ").

the issues facing the municipal courts is generally quite distinct from that with which we are now concerned. A municipal court will face this issue incidentally in a prosecution for treason [14] or sedition, or in a civil suit involving the construction of a contract of insurance or a charterparty; a military court may face this issue for the purposes of construing its own disciplinary codes or perhaps the regulations affecting entitlement to service pensions. In all cases such as these the municipal court is really concerned with the construction of statutes, codes or contracts by parties and is essentially seeking to ascertain the intent of the legislature or the parties. It is perfectly proper, therefore, for a municipal court to decide as a matter of construction that, *so far as the scope of the statute or the intention of the parties to a contract is concerned*, the action by United Nations Forces constitutes "war," without this in any way determining the character of the action *for purposes of international law*. This is not, of course, a problem newly arisen under the Charter; it had always been accepted that there was no necessary identity between the concept of "war" for municipal law purposes and the concept of "war" for international law purposes.[15]

It is believed, therefore, that it is both improper under the Charter and inconsistent with the attitude adopted by the contributing States to regard the Korean action as "war" waged by the United Nations. As Lauterpacht has said:

"The dignity and the purpose of the collective enforcement of the rule of law in international society may require that it should rank in a category different from war as traditionally understood in international law." [16]

This view is justified not only by the necessity of avoiding the implication of the historic definition of war that both sides are in complete parity—and their "causes" legally indistinguishable—but also by the necessity of emphasising that the scope of a sanction is more limited than that of traditional war. Whereas, traditionally, a State waging war was entitled to do so to the stage of complete annihilation and subjugation of the other side, it can scarcely be maintained that United Nations action can be pursued so far. Such "collective" or "enforcement" action, as distinct from war, is limited to the measures necessary to resist aggression and to maintain and restore international peace and security. To this extent the United Nations can only wage a "limited" war, and it is evident that it is this precise question of the constitutional limits on United

---

[14] The Attorney-General in the British House of Commons on 20 November 1950 distinguished the Korean action from war but went on to say that the law of treason "is as applicable to such a conflict as it is to an ordinary war between State and State": H.C. Debates, Vol. 481, col. 13.

[15] See *Kawasaki Case* [1939] 2 K.B. 544 and, generally, McNair, *Legal Effects of War* (1948) pp. 6–9.

[16] "The Limits of the Operation of the Law of War," (1953) 30 B.Y.I.L. 206 at p. 221; see also the Report of the Committee on Study of Legal Problems of the UN "Should the Laws of War apply to UN Enforcement Action," (1952) P.A.S.I.L. at p. 220; and, for a general discussion in relation to the Korean conflict, Weissberg, *op. cit.*, pp. 103–105.

Nations action which weighed heavily in the doubts of some United Nations Members over the propriety of crossing the 38th parallel—quite apart from the political desirability of that course. The ends of war and of United Nations action thus differ. Hence, whilst in the Korean case it is believed that, as a matter of constitutional propriety, the United Nations was justified in pursuing across the 38th parallel an army which showed no signs of desisting from aggression, one can envisage certain action which would have gone beyond the necessities and the purposes of the United Nations action : for example, the wholesale destruction of every major town in North Korea by an all-out aerial attack.[17]

This conclusion, that United Nations action in Korea was not war, does not, however, affect the separate question of how far the laws of war apply to the actual conduct of hostilities by United Nations Forces, and it is to this separate question that we now turn.

2. *The application of the laws of war*

It is in the sense of attributing to the United Nations the obligations and rights of a belligerent under the laws of war that the United Nations may be described as a belligerent in Korea. The United Nations Forces certainly were so described, both by the Soviet Union and the People's Republic of China.[18] Indeed, the whole conduct of the Armistice negotiations by the Unified Command implied that the United Nations Command was a " belligerent."

It is equally clear that, whatever the arguments for maintaining that as a belligerent the United Nations is not bound by the totality of the rules of law normally applicable to a belligerent [19] (and this is a matter discussed later in Chapter 15), in practice the United Nations Forces claimed no exemption from or special privileges in relation to the laws of war. The entire action was conducted on the basis of their full subjection to the laws of war. Evidence of this is only too apparent. The acceptance of the Geneva Conventions of 1949 by both sides—and the subsequent argument on the repatriation

---

[17] It may be recalled that an immediate and hostile reaction occurred to the rumour that the U.S.A. was prepared to use the atomic bomb in Korea.

[18] UN Doc. A/2786, pp. 4, 8.

[19] See the Committee Report referred to above at p. 54, n. 16, (1952) P.A.S.I.L. p. 220 which implies that the UN can " select " those rules to which it will conform. The sounder view is that of Baxter, (1953) P.A.S.I.L. at p. 95; Lauterpacht, *loc. cit.*, pp. 242–243; and Taubenfeld, " International Armed Forces and the Rules of War," (1951) 45 A.J., 670 at p. 674. The difficulty of such a unilateral selection is, as both Baxter and Lauterpacht point out, that the other belligerent will simply not accept this selection and will retaliate. If certain rules are not to apply to UN action they will have to be determined by general agreement and after the kind of exhaustive analysis of the rules of war which has not yet been attempted for this purpose. Certainly those rules which are based on humanitarian motives will bind the UN; there may, however, be rules on the right to acquire or requisition property in occupied territory or a liability for reparations, for example, which can be adjusted so as to discriminate between the UN as a belligerent and an " aggressor " State as a belligerent.

provisions in the 1949 Prisoner of War Convention—has already been referred to.[20] The Soviet charges against the United States of illegal bombing specifically cited Article 25 of the Hague Regulations of 1907 and Hague Convention IX [21]; complaints by the People's Democratic Republic of Korea did likewise.[22] The allegations against United Nations Forces of engaging in bacteriological warfare were based on a similar assumption of the complete applicability of the laws of war, as were the complaints of maltreatment of prisoners.[23] The instructions to United Nations Forces promulgated by the United Nations Command with regard to the treatment of prisoners of war [24] and the reports of the Command to the Security Council reflect the same assumption. For example, the Third Report stated:

"United Nations Forces are urgently endeavouring to restrict destruction to the established military forces of the invader . . . Civilians are warned daily (by radio, leaflets, etc.) to move away from military targets that must be bombed." [25]

There is, in fact, no known case in which the United Nations Command ever claimed exemption from any of the accepted rules of the laws of war, customary or conventional.

---

[20] *Ante*, pp. 49–50; and see General Assembly Resol. 610 (VII) of 3 December 1952 affirming that release and repatriation "shall be effected in accordance with the Geneva Convention . . . [and] the well-established principles and practices of international law . . ."

[21] See statement by Soviet representative in the Security Council, 497th Mtg., 7 September 1950, p. 9 (S/1679), and see the later draft Resolution (S/1812).

[22] S/1778/Rev. 1 and S/1800.

[23] Allegations of atrocities against prisoners were made against the U.S.A. by the U.S.S.R. (A/2355, 20 December 1952), the People's Democratic Republic of N. Korea (S/2012, 11 February 1951; S/2092, 15 April 1951; A/2359, 21 December 1952) and the People's Republic of China (A/2358, 21 December 1952): these were denied by the UN Command which stressed that the camps were open to inspection by the International Committee of the Red Cross, which the Communist camps were not. The counter-allegation of the U.S.A. (A/2531, 30 October 1953) led to General Assembly Resolution 804 (VIII) of 3 December 1953 condemning such acts by any governments or authorities. The allegations against the U.S.A. of bacteriological warfare (S/2142/Rev. 2, 8 May 1951) were eventually considered by the Assembly at its seventh session at the request of the U.S.A. (A/2231); the Geneva Protocol of 1925 was specifically invoked. The U.S.A., had invited impartial investigation by the International Committee of the Red Cross since March 1952 without response. The General Assembly Resolution of 23 April 1953 (Resol. 706 (VII)) set up a Commission of 5 "neutral" States but no reply was received from the N. Korean authorities or the People's Republic of China to the request for facilities to enter their territory and investigate. This entire record suggests that the minimum of truth should be attached to the allegations against UN Forces.

[24] See statement by MacArthur of 4 July 1950: *New York Times*, 5 July 1950, p. 2, col. 7. On the difficulties of a United Nations Force acting as a detaining power under the Geneva Prisoner-of-War Convention see *post*, Chap. 15.

[25] S/1756, pp. 6–7; see also in regard to observance of the Geneva Prisoner-of-War Convention of 1949, Fifth Report, S/1834, p. 5, Sixth Report, S/1860, p. 9.

3. *Responsibility for breaches*

Given the existence of large-scale hostilities by United Nations Forces, it was inevitable that certain breaches of the laws of war would occur; indeed, human nature and its capacity for error being what it is, it is unlikely that any army, national or international, can fight on such a scale without breaches being committed.

Complaints of the strafing of airfields on Soviet territory were made by the U.S.S.R. against the United States in October 1950, and there were other allegations of infringements of her airspace. The United States rightly insisted that the proper recipient of such complaints was the United Nations[26]; however, the United States admitted the strafing by error and apologies were tendered through the Secretary-General, together with an offer of payment of damages to be " determined by a United Nations Commission or other procedure." [27] Similar complaints by the People's Republic of China were addressed directly to the United Nations[28] and, again, the United States accepted the obligation to pay compensation determined by an appropriate United Nations Commission after investigation of the charges.[29]

The insistence that the charges were a matter for the United Nations to consider, and the insistence on the necessity for an impartial fact-finding Commission, was undoubtedly right. Whether it was equally right for the United States to offer compensation is less sure, for there is much to be said for the view that compensation ought normally to be a matter for the United Nations[30]—as part of the operational budget of actions by United Nations Forces—and not for individual contributing States. Of course, the difficulty in Korea, as opposed to the later UNEF and ONUC experiments, was that there was no operational budget of the United Nations: each contributing State paid its own costs for its forces and no budgetary item for the cost of the Korean military action ever appeared on the United Nations budget.

V. STATUS OF FORCES AGREEMENTS

There appears to have been no specific agreement with the Republic of Korea over the status of the United Nations Forces in Korea. The agreement between the United Nations and Korea embodied in the exchange of letters of 21 September 1951[31] was concerned solely

---

[26] *New York Times*, 11 October 1950, p. 8.
[27] UN Doc. S/1856.
[28] UN Docs. S/1722, S/1743, S/1808, S/1857, S/1870, S/1876.
[29] *Off. Rec. S.C.*, 5th yr., 493rd Mtg., 31 August 1950, p. 26; 497th Mtg., p. 19, 499th Mtg., p. 11.
[30] This would not affect the duty of the individual States to punish for breaches of the law of war those members of its own contingent found to be responsible for committing such breaches.
[31] U.N.T.S., Vol. 104, p. 323. The only other agreement between the UN and Korea was the Agreement for the Establishment and Maintenance of a UN Memorial Cemetery in Korea of 6 November 1959: *ibid.*, Vol. 346, p. 289.

with the privileges and immunities of the Organisation and its organs, representatives of Member States and officials, experts and locally recruited personnel: it did not cover the United Nations Forces. The United States/Korean Mutual Security Pact of 7 January 1952 [32] contained a very general undertaking by Korea to "take appropriate steps to insure the effective utilisation of the economic and military assistance provided by the United States," and further agreements between the two States dealt with expenditures by United Nations Forces [33] and with the settlement of claims arising from the provision of utilities services by the United Nations Members contributing military forces or field hospitals [34]; but no comprehensive status of forces agreement was ever concluded.

Similarly with Japan, the agreement on privileges and immunities concluded between Japan and the United Nations on 25 July 1952 [35] covered the Organisation and its civilian representatives but not United Nations Forces in Japan. Subsequently, by a Protocol of 26 October 1953 [36] (which was replaced by a Protocol of 19 February 1954 [37]), a comprehensive status of forces agreement was concluded to cover United Nations Forces, modelled on the NATO Status of Forces Agreement of 1952 in so far as it accepted the principle of concurrent jurisdiction but with "primary" rights to exercise jurisdiction vesting in Japan or the sending State according to the circumstances. However, this was concluded not by the United Nations as such but by the United States acting as the Unified Command and by the Governments of Canada, New Zealand, United Kingdom, Union of South Africa, Australia, Philippines, France and Italy. The details of this agreement will be dealt with at a later stage.[38]

VI. CIVILIAN RELIEF OPERATIONS

Whilst the purpose of the present study is to concentrate on lessons to be drawn from the Korean action relating to international armed forces it is necessary to emphasise the extent to which the military operations had to be paralleled by civilian relief operations: this clearly indicates that the United Nations will have to regard any involvement in military action as carrying with it the probability of heavy involvement in civilian relief.

UNCURK (United Nations Commission for the Unification and

---

[32] *Ibid.*, Vol. 179, p. 105.
[33] See Agreement of 28 July 1950 which the U.S.A. concluded on behalf of all the forces under the Unified Command: U.N.T.S., Vol. 140, p. 57.
[34] Utilities Claims Settlement Agreement of 18 December 1958, concluded on behalf of the States furnishing military forces or field hospitals: U.N.T.S., Vol. 325, p. 240. And see the U.K., Australia, New Zealand/Korean Agreement on settlement of advances of Korean currency of 28 September 1954: U.N.T.S., Vol. 207, p. 294.
[35] U.N.T.S., Vol. 135, p. 305.
[36] U.N.T.S., Vol. 207, p. 237.
[37] *Ibid.*, Vol. 214, p. 51.
[38] *Post*, pp. 439–440, 456.

Rehabilitation of Korea) was established by the General Assembly on 6 October 1950 [39] as a Commission of seven States which would proceed to the area and there consult with and advise the Unified Command on relief and rehabilitation. The Security Council had earlier requested the Unified Command "to exercise responsibility for determining the requirements for the relief and support of the civilian population of Korea." [40] The relief operations in due course involved a complex system of co-ordination between UNCURK and the Unified Command, the Korean Government,[41] the Secretary-General, the specialised agencies and even non-governmental organisations, and Member States.[42] In due course the Assembly established a special authority to plan and supervise rehabilitation and relief— the United Nations Korea Reconstruction Agency (UNKRA)—under the direction of the Secretary-General, but also with an advisory committee of five States to advise the administrative head of the Agency, the Agent-General.[43] The financing of these operations was not by the ordinary budget of the United Nations, as a matter of legal obligation, but by way of voluntary contributions from Member States negotiated by a special Negotiating Committee.[44] The details of the programme undertaken by UNKRA are given in the successive Yearbooks of the United Nations and, of course, in the reports of the Agent-General.

VII. CONCLUSIONS

The conclusion which emerges from this survey of the United Nations action in Korea is, firstly, that it was United Nations action designed to prevent a clear case of aggression and to restore international peace and security. It marked the first attempt by an international organisation to check an act of aggression, and it still stands as the only occasion on which enforcement action has been taken against aggressor States or other authorities. This alone justifies a full examination of both the merits and the defects of the action. The Korean action may not have been a military victory according to the textbooks, for the outcome in military terms was by no means conclusive: but the action was certainly a political victory for the purposes and principles of the Charter. It may well be that, had the League of Nations taken a similar stand against Japan in 1931, the successive acts of international banditry and aggression by Germany, Italy and the Soviet Union, which in due course led to the Second World War, would never have been attempted. It is impossible to estimate how far similar acts have been deterred by the determination of some of the United Nations Members in taking positive enforcement action in Korea.

[39] Resol. 376 (V).
[40] Resol. S/1657, adopted at 479th Mtg. on 31 July 1950.
[41] On 24 May 1952 the UN Command signed an agreement with the Republic of Korea setting up a Combined Economic Board (S/2768).
[42] See *UN Yearbook*, 1950, pp. 268–270.
[43] Resol. A/1567.   [44] *Ibid.*, Part B.

The action in Korea remains, in many respects, unsatisfactory as a model of United Nations action, and this survey has been deliberately critical so that the "lessons" of Korea may be emphasised. The principal defects were:

1. The uncertainty as to the legal basis for the Security Council Resolutions.

2. The dominant role of one Member, the United States, by virtue of its assumption of the major military burden. This, it is believed, reflects credit on the United States and discredit on those many other United Nations Members which, at this crucial time of trial, sought refuge from their obligation—even though of an imperfect legal character—"to maintain international peace and security, and to that end: to take effective collective measures for the prevention and removal of threats to the peace, and for the suppression of acts of aggression etc. . . ." (Art. 1, Charter).

3. The inadequacy of the system of political control over the military command. Again, this was no doubt in part due to the impossibility of utilising the Charter machinery, the Security Council and the Military Staff Committee; yet there was too little real indication of a will to vest control even in a body representative of the contributing States.

4

United Nations Observer Groups

ONE of the techniques developed by the Security Council, and to a lesser extent the Assembly, for handling disputes which have deteriorated into actual armed conflict has been the appointment of field missions, operating under the authority of the Council or Assembly, which have carried the United Nations machinery closer to the scene of conflict and, at the same time, provided the Council or Assembly with impartial, first-hand information. Whilst the primary purpose of these field missions has generally been one of political negotiation—conciliation, good offices, mediation—there has also been the essential function of " observation " for which special units of military personnel have proved necessary. This " observer " function is certainly one of the functions capable of being assumed by a United Nations Force and it is therefore useful to examine, briefly, these various missions on which a United Nations observer group of military personnel has been employed.

I. CONSTITUTIONAL BASIS OF OBSERVER GROUPS

The first occasion on which military observers were attached to a field mission was when, by Resolution of 19 December 1946,[1] the Security Council established a Commission of Investigation under Article 34 of the Charter to investigate the Greek allegations of illegal border incursions from Albania, Bulgaria and Yugoslavia. However, with the transfer of authority over the matter to the General Assembly, the Special Committee of the Assembly (UNSCOB) established its own observation group. The constitutional basis for the observer groups thus shifted; it remained unspecified by the Assembly and, if a guess has to be made, it is probable that Articles 11 and 22 constitute the basis for the Assembly's action.[2] The second occasion

---

[1] S/339. The Security Council was unable to reach any decision on the problem and removed the matter from its agenda on 15 September 1947, so that thenceforth the Assembly took it up and established the UN Special Committee on the Balkans (UNSCOB) by Resolution 109 (II) of 21 October 1947. For the Report of UNSCOB see Off. Rec. G.A., 3rd Sess., Suppl. No. 8 (A/574); the earlier Report of the Commission of Investigation can be found in Off. Rec. S.C., 2nd yr., Spec. Suppl. No. 2.

[2] The Repertory, Vol. 1, treats the Assembly's action under Art. 11. The Resolution in question was Resol. 109 (II), adopted on 21 October 1947. The Special Committee was discontinued by the Assembly on 7 December 1951 by Resolution 508 (VI) and replaced by the Balkan Sub-Commission of the Peace Observation Commission. This consisted of but six observers, as State representatives, later reduced to three, so that it ceased to be a military force within the scope of the present study.

was on 25 August 1947 [3] when, at the request of the Republic of Indonesia, the Security Council requested the establishment of a Consular Commission at Batavia to observe and report on the action by the Governments of the Netherlands and of Indonesia in compliance with the call for a cessation of hostilities in the Council's earlier Resolution of 1 August 1947.[4] The Council's own Committee of Good Offices [5] subsequently utilised the "military assistants" of the Consular Commission at the request of the Council.[6] The Council on this occasion appears to have been acting under Article 40 of Chapter VII of the Charter,[7] although no specific reference to this Article appears in any of the Resolutions adopted. However, it is clear that in principle the Council has power to institute an "observer" corps or force to report on compliance with any provisional measures ordered under Article 40.

In the Palestine situation, the Security Council, having called for a truce on 1 April 1948,[8] on 23 April established a Truce Commission composed of representatives of members of the Security Council having career consular officers in Jerusalem (following the Indonesian precedent), but it quickly became apparent that the observer personnel they were able to muster were totally inadequate to the size of the task confronting them. Hence the Commission itself requested the United Nations to send out the officers necessary for control and supervision of the truce.[9] The subsequent call for a cease-fire of 22 May 1948 [10] appears to have been adopted under Article 40, although again not explicitly, and called upon all parties to facilitate the task of the United Nations Mediator, Count Bernadotte, who had been appointed by the Assembly on 14 May. By 29 May the Council had instructed the Mediator and the Truce Commission to act in concert in supervising the injunctions listed in the Resolution of that

---

[3] S/525, 194th Mtg.
[4] S/459, 178th Mtg., p. 1839.
[5] Established on 25 August 1947, Resol. S/525 and reconstituted as the UN Commission for Indonesia by Resol. S/1234 of 28 January 1949.
[6] S/597.
[7] See *Repertory*, Vol. 11, paras. 40–48.
[8] S/704. The Special Committee on Palestine was created by the General Assembly Resolution 106 (S–1) of 15 May 1947, and this was succeeded by the Palestine Commission established on 29 November 1947 by General Assembly Resolution 181 (11) and it was this Commission which reported in April 1948 that the fact that the Security Council had failed to provide the necessary armed assistance to the Commission was one of the factors responsible for the Commission's failure to implement the Assembly's Resolution (A/532, p. 36, para. 5). The Palestine Commission was terminated by Security Council Resolution on 14 May and replaced by the Mediator in Palestine, appointed by the Assembly by Resolution 186 (S–2) of 14 May, or rather by the Committee established for that purpose. For the general background to the Palestine problem and the work of the Conciliation Commission see Hurewitz, "The UN Conciliation Commission for Palestine," (1953) *International Organisation* p. 482, and Burns, *Between Arab and Israeli* (1962) Chap. 2.
[9] *Off. Rec. S.C.*, 3rd yr., 291st Mtg., p. 21 (statement by President of the Security Council).
[10] S/773.

date,[11] and decided that "they shall be provided with a sufficient number of military observers." The proposal of the Soviet Union [12] to attach from thirty to fifty observers to the Mediator, drawn from and appointed by the members of the Security Council, was not adopted and, in view of the truce then in effect, a certain lack of a sense of urgency was understandable. With the expiry of the truce on 9 July the situation clearly deteriorated and the decision of 15 July 1948,[13] ordering the cessation of military action, was expressly made under Article 40.

The observer force remained an instrument in the control of the United Nations Mediator and, after the death by assassination of Count Bernadotte on 17 September 1948, of the Acting Mediator. However, with the conclusion of the first armistice agreement in February 1949 in response to Security Council Resolutions of 4 and 16 November 1948,[14] the functions of the Mediator were regarded as having been discharged and the United Nations Truce Supervision Organisation (UNTSO) achieved formal and separate recognition by the Security Council, in its Resolution of 11 August.[15] This step really achieved a separation between the function of conciliation, which was surrendered by the Acting Mediator to the Conciliation Commission (a General Assembly body established by the Assembly on 11 December 1948), and that of observation and supervision of the Armistice Agreements. The coincidence of these two functions had, according to the evidence of the Acting Mediator, seriously impeded the task of political conciliation.[16] Hence, UNTSO, whilst organised and developed by the Mediator, acting in consultation with the Secretary-General, became a separate organ of the Security Council based essentially on Article 40 of the Charter.

In the Kashmir dispute between India and Pakistan the appointment of the United Nations Commission by Security Council Resolution of 20 January 1948 was, at least so far as its powers of investigation were concerned, expressly based on Article 34.[17] That Resolution made no reference to observers but rather to "its members, alternate members, their assistants and its personnel." By 21 April 1948 [18] the Council appeared to have switched from

---

[11] S/801.
[12] S/841, 320th Mtg., p. 8. The Mediator had already recruited some observers under his mandate from the Security Council expressed in the Resolutions of 29 May and 15 July.
[13] S/902.
[14] S/1070, S/1080.
[15] S/1376–1.
[16] See *Off. Rec. S.C.*, 4th yr., No. 36, p. 7 where Bunche describes how the Armistice Agreement had supplemented the Truce and General Assembly Resol. 194 (III) of 11 December 1948 had provided for the transfer of the Mediator's conciliation functions to the Conciliation Commission.
[17] S/654. See Lourié, "The UN Military Observer Group in India and Pakistan," (1955) *International Organisation* p. 19.
[18] S/726. This Resolution, in its third section, envisaged a UN Plebiscite, so that supervision of this would have become part of the task of UNCIP: this proposal for a plebiscite was not accepted by either Government.

Chapter VI to Chapter VII, and the Resolution of that date, which instructed the Commission to " establish in Jammu and Kashmir such observers as it may require," may fairly be regarded as being based on Article 40. The United Nations Commission, but not its observers, ceased its functions when on 14 March 1950 [19] the Security Council appointed a single United Nations Representative, evidently on the basis that the kind of United Nations action appropriate was political mediation by a single person, but that the cease-fire must be maintained as a necessary condition for any political mediation.

The United Nations Commission on Korea (UNCOK) was established by the General Assembly on 12 December 1948 [20] with the task of lending its good offices so as to bring about the unification of Korea and also of observing and verifying the withdrawal of the occupying forces; for this purpose it was empowered to " request the assistance of military experts of the two occupying Powers." The additional task of observing and reporting on developments which might lead to or otherwise involve military conflict in Korea was conferred by a later Assembly Resolution of 21 October 1949,[21] and this gave a general discretion to appoint observers. The reliance on impartial observers, rather than the military experts of the occupying Powers, was clearly desirable, but the " military " element of this observer function remained very small, consisting of eight observers with the necessary military staff and equipment, later supplemented by two additional observers.[22] It was the report of the Commission which was despatched to the Secretary-General on 25 June, revealing the responsibility of the North Korean authorities for the armed invasion across the 38th parallel.[23] No clear constitutional basis was specified for the Assembly's action in constituting this Commission, but it would seem that it must lie in Articles 10, 11, or 14, coupled with Article 22.

The United Nations Commission for the Unification and Rehabilitation of Korea (UNCURK), replacing UNCOK, continued to use this small group of observers to supply information on the military situation, to examine prisoners of war, and to investigate particular problems such as the refugee problem : this continued until the team of observers was disbanded in January 1951 with the Commission's evacuation to Pusan, and the Commission thereafter relied on a single senior officer of the Royal Australian Air Force.

The establishment of the United Nations Observer Group in the

---

[19] S/1469. The later Resolution of the Security Council of 30 March 1951 expressly decided to continue the Military Observer Group to supervise the cease-fire : S/2017/Rev. 1. The Group remains in being at the time of writing.

[20] Resol. 195 (III).

[21] Resol. 293 (IV).

[22] UNCOK's Report, *Off. Rec. G.A.*, 5th Sess. Suppl. 16 (A/3150); and see the same Report as S/1518, dated 29 June 1950.

[23] S/1496. This was later supplemented by the Observers' Report (S/1518) on 29 June. See *ante*, Chap. 3, for the subsequent UN action in Korea.

Lebanon (UNOGIL) came as a result of Lebanon's complaint of intervention by the United Arab Republic in its internal affairs. The Security Council, by its Resolution of 11 June 1958 [24]:

"*Decides* to dispatch urgently an observation group to proceed to the Lebanon so as to ensure that there is no illegal infiltration of personnel or supply of arms or other *matériel* across the Lebanese borders;
Authorises the Secretary-General to take the necessary steps to that end."

Thus, whilst the organisation and operation of the Group was left to the Secretary-General, he acted under a Security Council mandate issued under Chapter VI of the Charter. The Secretary-General was later to describe UNOGIL, like UNEF, as " an instrument of efforts at mediation and conciliation." He continued:

"It may be noted in this context that UNOGIL has not given rise to any constitutional objections; the fact that the Group was created by the Security Council is in this case irrelevant, as the Council acted entirely within the limits of Chapter VI of the Charter, and as a similar action obviously could have been taken by the General Assembly under Article 22." [25]

On 21 September 1962 the General Assembly authorised the Secretary-General to assume certain tasks entrusted to him under the Agreement of 15 August 1962 between the Netherlands and Indonesia, relating to the territory of West New Guinea. It may be presumed that the Assembly acted under Article 14 of the Charter in granting this authorisation. One of the effects of this was to enable the Secretary-General to establish, as part of the United Nations Temporary Executive Authority for West New Guinea (UNTEA), an Observer Group to supervise the implementation of the Agreement, including the withdrawal of Netherlands forces. However, since this Group was but a part of a larger operation, it may be briefly mentioned at this juncture and dealt with in greater detail in Chapter 7.

The latest example [26] of a United Nations observer group is to be found in the establishment of a United Nations observer group in the Yemen (UNYOM). After a period of hostilities in the Yemen which involved not only the two rival Yemeni factions but also troops from Saudi Arabia and the United Arab Republic (on opposite sides) the Secretary-General, assisted by United States Ambassador

---

[24] S/4023. The origins and development of the operations in the Lebanon are described in Ruth B. Russell, *United Nations Experience with Military Forces : Political and Legal Agents*, Institute for Defence Analysis, Research Paper P–27, May 1963. pp. 84–94; Burns and Heathcote, *Peace-Keeping by UN Forces* (1963) pp. 9–15.

[25] *Summary Study of the experience derived from the establishment and operation of the Force (UNEF)*: Report of the Secretary-General (A/3943), *Off. Rec. G.A.*, 13th Sess., Annexes, Agenda Item 65, para. 180.

[26] The designation of Lt.-General Gyani of India on 16 January 1964 as the Secretary-General's Personal Representative in Cyprus " to observe the progress of the peace-keeping operation for an initial period extending to the end of February 1964 " is scarcely an observer group in the sense of this Chapter and is more akin to the kind of UN " presence " used in Jordan in 1958.

65

Bunker, mediated between the parties with such success that they reached agreement on the terms of a disengagement.[27] A demilitarised zone of twenty kilometres on each side of the demarcated Saudi-Arabian-Yemen frontier was established and supervision of the observance of the terms of the disengagement was to be entrusted to " impartial observers " which, in the context of the undertaking to co-operate with the Secretary-General, suggested a United Nations Group to be appropriate. Accordingly, the Secretary-General took the initiative of sending out to the three countries concerned General Von Horn, the Chief of Staff of UNTSO, and it appeared as though he was prepared to establish a Group on his own initiative. However, in a letter dated 8 June 1963 [28] the Permanent Representative of the U.S.S.R. requested a meeting of the Security Council " since the reports contain proposals concerning possible measures by the United Nations to maintain international peace and security, on which, under the Charter, decisions are to be taken by the Security Council." This, by now, traditional distrust of the U.S.S.R. of the claim by the Secretary-General to establish anything resembling a military force resulted in the passing of a formal Resolution by the Security Council on 11 June 1963 [29] in which it:

" 1. *Requests* the Secretary-General to establish the observation operation as defined by him;
2. *Urges* the parties concerned to observe fully the terms of disengagement reported in document S/5298 and to refrain from any action which would increase tension in the area
. . ."

No indication of the Charter provisions under which the Council was acting is given, but, bearing in mind the absence of any finding under Article 39 and the fact that para. 2 does not appear to be mandatory, it looks rather as though it is Chapter VI rather than Chapter VII, even though Article 40 is a possible alternative basis. In the request to the Secretary-General to establish the operation there is a reliance on Article 98, but this is really only a variation in the *means* by which the operation is established, for the Council could have done so itself rather than via the Secretary-General: the constitutional basis of the power to do so lies either in Chapter VI or Article 40.

It thus appears that the Security Council can establish an Observer Group either under Chapter VI or Chapter VII of the Charter and in practice has often failed to indicate which. In the former case this will be either under the specific powers of Article 34 or the more general power under Article 29 to establish a subsidiary

---

[27] The terms of this agreement are reported, in substance, in the Report by the Secretary-General to the Security Council, dated 29 April 1963 (S/5298). The mediation technique, even to the use of Ambassador Bunker, is very similar to that used in settling the Indonesian/Netherlands dispute over West New Guinea: see *post*, p. 255.
[28] S/5326. The reports referred to are the Secretary-General's Reports of 29 April (S/5298), 27 May (S/5321), 3 June (S/5323) and 7 June (S/5325).
[29] S/5331. The U.S.S.R. abstained on the vote.

organ necessary to enable the Council to carry out its functions under Chapter VI. Whatever the distinction between the power to establish subsidiary organs under Article 29 and the power to investigate under Article 34,[30] it seems reasonably clear that an observation group of the kind we have been considering ought not to be established by a simple procedural vote under Article 29. The important part of the Council's decision is the decision to act under Chapter VI, and that requires a non-procedural vote. The decision to establish a subsidiary organ through which to act is really secondary, and could, as a separate decision, be regarded as procedural under Article 29. If, however, the vote is taken as a single step rather than by distinguishing between the two stages of deciding to act and establishing an organ through which to act, the vote ought to be a non-procedural vote.

The further difficulty is that it has been doubted whether Article 34 is an entirely satisfactory basis for an observation group, for it has been argued that there is a very real distinction between an investigation of past events and the observation of future developments.[31] Whilst this may be true, it is believed that this is too narrow a view of Article 34 if it purports to show that this Article cannot be the constitutional basis of an observer group. A more real difficulty is not so much whether Article 34 can be the basis for observer functions under Chapter VI, but rather what the obligations of Member States are once the group has been established, in particular does this involve an obligation on States to admit the group to its territory? Kerley has argued persuasively that, provided the group is established and instructed to proceed to a State's territory by a *decision* of the Council, this is obligatory on all Members under Article 25.[32] However, in practice the Resolutions of the Security Council under Chapter VI have been regarded as recommendatory rather than obligatory, and both in the Greek and Lebanese cases the States to the north of Greece and the States to the north and east of the Lebanon refused permission for the United Nations Observer Groups to operate on their territory, without any formal condemnation ensuing from the Council. Similarly Jordan refused to allow an observer group comparable to UNOGIL to be established on her territory.[33]

---

[30] See generally the excellent discussion by Kerley, "The powers of investigation of the UN Security Council," (1961) 55 A.J. 892. And see the Report of the Sub-Committee of the Security Council established under Resolution S/4216 of 7 September 1959 (S/4236), paras. 13–19: this had been set up under Art. 29 to go to Laos after the Laotian complaint of 4 September 1959 (S/4212).

[31] See statement of the representative of Panama in the Lebanon debate: *Off. Rec. S.C.*, 13th yr., 825th Mtg., p. 3; Kerley has similar doubts, *loc. cit.* p. 899.

[32] *Loc. cit.*, pp. 895–897.

[33] *Off. Rec. G.A.*, 3rd Emergency Sess., 1958, 735th Mtg., para. 51. And note that the Secretary-General, in answer to the Netherlands request to send observers to West Irian, replied that this would not be "appropriate" unless Indonesia agreed (S/5124).

It would, of course, always be possible for the Council to switch from Chapter VI to Chapter VII, as indeed it did in Kashmir. Once under Chapter VII there is no doubt as to the power of the Council under Article 40 to take binding decisions to which Articles 25 and 49 would be applicable and neglect to comply could, when necessary, be met with enforcement procedures. Whilst Article 40 has been the basis of Observer Groups in Indonesia, Kashmir, and Palestine, it would perhaps be possible also to utilise Article 39 [34]; once in Chapter VII the Council would be free to take binding decisions.

So far as the General Assembly is concerned, the very wide powers under Articles 11–12, 14 and 22, could always permit the Assembly to establish an observer group, and, indeed, the Assembly has done so by its authorisation to the Secretary-General to establish UNTEA and probably this was the basis of UNCOK also. However, the Assembly could not impose legal obligations upon States other than the obligation to meet the cost of its operations if these were determined to be part of the "expenses of the Organisation" under Article 17 (2).

II. COMPOSITION AND EQUIPMENT

In the case of the Commission of Investigation on the Greek Frontier Incidents the technique used was to authorise each member of the Commission (composed of a representative of each of the members of the Security Council for 1947) "to select the personnel necessary to assist him" [35]; hence the military observers were really aides to the political representatives and not directly appointed by or responsible to the Security Council. UNSCOB, the General Assembly Committee replacing the Council's Commission of Investigation, formed four groups of observers "under the authority of the Committee and composed of personnel supplied by the nations represented on the Committee." [36] The plan to establish a fifth group and a reserve group was abandoned for lack of personnel. Similarly, the "military assistants" used for observation in the Indonesian affair were in fact personnel appointed by the Consular Commission in Batavia, that is to say, by the six States with consuls there; they were not recruited as United Nations personnel. An approximate

---

[34] Kerley, *loc. cit.*, p. 901.
[35] Resol. S/339, para. 7.
[36] Report of UNSCOB (A/574), para. 11. At para. 15 it states: "the international character of the Observation Groups was ensured by the provision of observers by the delegations of Brazil, China, France, Mexico, Netherlands, U.K. and the U.S.A., and by the attachment of one member of the UN Secretariat as secretary to each Group." See also the later report of UNSCOB (A/935) which sets out the subsequent modifications of the system of organisation of the Observer Groups. By 1 August 1949 there were 34 observers and the 1949 Budget had provided for partial finance, *i.e.*, a daily allowance for observers and the entire pay of the ancillary staff of interpreters, mechanics, drivers, typists as well as the maintenance of the Group's equipment. UNSCOB later produced a "Handbook for Observers" (A/AC.16/SC.1/56 and 57).

strength of sixty-eight observers was small enough to supervise the withdrawal of 30,000 troops.

In the Palestine affair the problem was so large as to make this solution impracticable. Following the rejection of the Soviet proposal to enable the members of the Security Council to appoint observers, the Mediator was forced to continue to rely upon a few Swedish officers and such other officers as were chosen in consultation with their Governments from the United States, Belgium and France, totalling sixty-eight observers.[37] The exclusion of British personnel was due to Britain's stake in Palestine. The peak strength reached in Palestine was 300 officers (out of a total mission strength of 600).[38]

In Kashmir, when in September 1949 the Military Observer Group (UNMOGIP) was at its largest, it consisted of forty-two officers drawn from the United States, Canada, Belgium, Mexico and Norway. The group in Korea (UNCOK) was a bare ten military observers, regarded very much as ancillary to the political representatives on the Commission, following the Balkan and Indonesian precedents.

UNOGIL achieved a strength of 200 by 17 July 1958 [39] and was increased to 591 (469 ground observers and 32 N.C.O.s and an air section of 90) by 14 November 1958.[40] It may be noted that the Secretary-General increased the strength of UNOGIL in July 1958 on his own initiative after a Resolution which, *inter alia*, recommended an increase had been vetoed on 22 July by the U.S.S.R. However, since the objections of the U.S.S.R. were not directed to that part of the Resolution the Secretary-General was simply falling back on his residuary powers in order to give effect to a general wish of the Council and on the basis of the very wide mandate of 11 June.[41] UNOGIL was withdrawn upon the completion of its task (and having found little evidence of infiltration) on 9 December.

The Observer Group in UNTEA numbered a mere twenty-one members, drawn from the existing personnel of UNTSO, although

---

[37] Bernadotte requested 5 Swedish Colonels, 21 officers from each of the three States and later 10 more from these three States. He also obtained 10 U.S. auxiliary personnel—pilots, maintenance men, radio-operators, etc. and 51 guards recruited from the UN Headquarters Staff to assist the military observers: see Mediator's Progress Report, dated 16 September 1948, *Off. Rec. G.A.*, 3rd Sess., Suppl. No. 1 (A/648), Pt. 2, paras. 2–4. The initial practice of assigning personnel due for home leave after service in Germany was not, apparently, a success; these were later replaced by volunteers from the United States, a policy which improved morale: see Mohn, "Problems of Truce Supervision," (1952) *International Conciliation* 51, at p. 67.

[38] This increase resulted from Bernadotte's visit to Lake Success. The 300 were appointed as follows: Belgium, 50; France, 125; U.S.A., 125. The additional 300 were enlisted men and not officers.

[39] Second Interim Report of UNOGIL, S/4052, para. 4.

[40] Fifth Report, S/4114, para. 7.

[41] A/4132, p. 18 and *Off. Rec. S.C.*, 837th Mtg., paras. 10–17. Note that this enlargement was carried out after the Lebanon had called for the formation of a UN police force to seal the border (*ibid.*, 827th Mtg., para. 76) and the U.S.A. had landed troops on the assumption that more than the team of UN observers was required (Statement of President Eisenhower, in *Keesing's Contemporary Archives*, 1958, p. 16295).

the main Security Force consisting of a Pakistani battalion could, no doubt, have been called upon had the situation become difficult.[42] Both the Observer Group and the Security Force withdrew on 1 May 1963 upon the transfer of administration from UNTEA to Indonesia. The Observer Group in the Yemen similarly relied for its nucleus on existing personnel in UNTSO, UNEF and possibly UNMOGIP and totalled 200 officers and men, out of which a ground patrol unit numbered 100 men.[43]   Of these the largest component was the Yugoslav reconnaissance unit of 110 officers and men, detached from UNEF with the agreement of Yugoslavia (and replaced there by another Yugoslav unit); Canada provided an air unit of some fifty officers and men.[44] The estimated duration of the mission was four months.

The very nature of the observers' function which, as we shall see, consists of far more than simple observation, demands that the observer have an authority (and indeed personality) which will ensure respect; they have no armed forces on which to rely for authority.   Hence the observers have been almost entirely commissioned officers, and the Group in the Yemen marked the first experiment with a majority of ordinary ranks as opposed to officers. However, the functions expected of the Yugoslav ground patrol unit were very different from those expected of the UNTSO officers.

UNTSO and UNOGIL both experienced the need for helicopters, observation aircraft and crews and for other personnel such as drivers, radio-operators, maintenance staff and a number of other ranks which, even unarmed, could constitute patrols for simple observation duties.[45] The need for guards, particularly of United Nations premises and equipment, was severely felt in Palestine and it was for this purpose that forty-nine members of the United Nations Headquarters Guard were despatched from New York on 19 June 1948, although subsequently replaced.   Interpreters, too, were badly needed.   The task of UNTSO observers was seriously impeded by their having to rely upon the liaison-officers from the forces of the opposing parties to interpret the evidence given to the observers when interviewing local commanders in the field.   The Yemen Group to some extent reflected past experience, for the Secretary-General made specific provision for aircraft, including helicopters,

[42] *Post*, pp. 257–260.
[43] S/5321.
[44] UN Information Bulletin (London News Summary), 25 June 1963. From early December 1963, however, the Yugoslav ground patrol had been withdrawn and the Group was restricted to 25 military observers from Denmark, Ghana, India, Italy, Netherlands, Norway, Pakistan, Sweden and Yugoslavia, supplemented by a Canadian Air Transport Unit capable of carrying out patrol duties as well as providing logistic support.   Moreover, both parties agreed to finance the extension of the mandate for a further two months until 4 March 1964: *ibid.*, Release 1/64.
[45] See Second Interim Report of UNOGIL, S/4052, para. 7; Cablegram of 28 July 1948 from Chairman of Committee of Good Offices in Indonesia, S/929.

and their crews in addition to personnel for "such essential supporting services as communications, logistics, medical aid, transportation
and administration." [46]

So far as equipment is concerned, prior to the Yemen Group, only
in Indonesia were any of the observers armed, and this for their own
protection against guerrillas and not as a means of enforcing their
demands or their freedom of movement. The Yemen ground patrol
unit was to be armed "for self-defence only." [47] The real needs
were for jeeps, aircraft,[48] radio equipment and the other necessities
for rapid movement and communications.

III. FUNCTIONS

The functions of "observers" have not, in practice, been limited
simply to observation. Observers are, of course, limited by their
terms of reference which may stem directly from the Resolutions of
the United Nations organ under whose authority they operate or,
especially where these are in very general terms, from the instructions of the Mediator or Chief of Staff controlling the observers.[49]
In Palestine the Security Council repeatedly directed the Mediator,
and through him the observers, to assume specific tasks.[50] The
terms of reference may also stem from agreements between the
parties. Hence the Truce or Armistice Agreements constituted a
consent by them to certain functions being assumed by the UNTSO
observers. In Kashmir, the role of the military observers was defined
in terms of the cease-fire agreement between the parties.[51] The
observers in UNTEA and in the Yemen were there by reference to
agreements between the parties and their functions were accordingly
defined in those agreements rather than in the Resolutions authorising
the establishment of the Groups. Whilst the functions necessarily
vary somewhat, according to the particular nature of the situation
with which the observers are confronted, the following are all
functions which have in fact been assumed under the United Nations.

1. *Border control*

In the Balkan situation the function of the military observers was,
essentially, that of reporting on violations of the frontier of Northern

[46] S/5321, para. c.
[47] *Ibid.*
[48] S/4052, para. 9. Apparently in Kashmir the parties supplied the UN
with jeeps and drivers: see Lourié, *loc. cit.*, p. 26. When complaints were
made by Egypt that British and French forces were not observing the
cease-fire in Port Said UNTSO decided to send observers there and in fact a
British warship, *H.M.S. Striker*, conveyed them from Haifa to Port Said on
13 November 1946: see Burns, *op. cit.*, p. 195.
[49] See the instructions given to the military observers in Indonesia by the
Committee of Good Offices (S/1193).
[50] *e.g.*, Resolutions S/801 of 29 May 1948; S/902 of 15 July 1948; S/1376–II of
11 August 1949.
[51] See Doc. S/AC.12/MA/1, Instructions and General Information for Military
Observers of the UNCIP. The terms of the cease-fire are given in the
UNCIP Third Interim Report, S/1430.

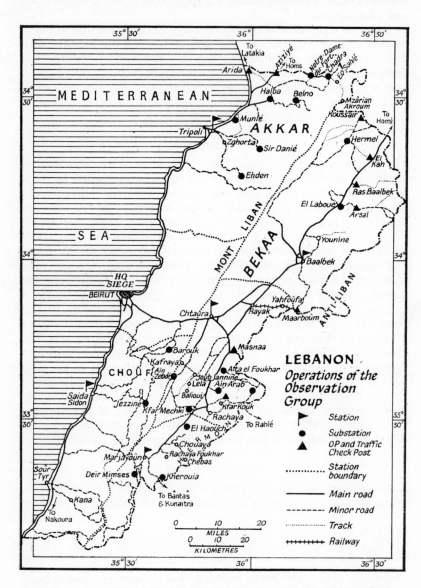

Reproduced from Official Records of the Security Council, Thirteenth Year, Suppl. p. 156, Document S/4100.

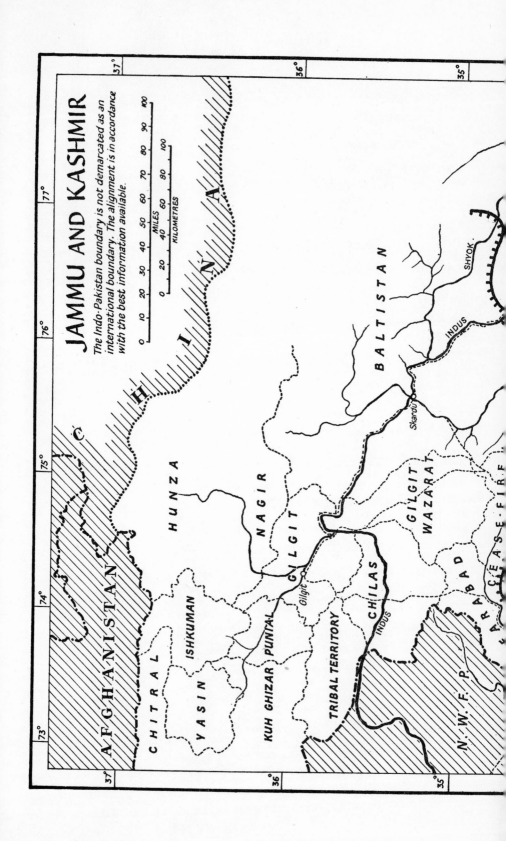

JAMMU AND KASHMIR

The Indo-Pakistan boundary is not demarcated as an international boundary. The alignment is in accordance with the best information available.

MILES
0 10 20 30 40 50 60 70 80 90 100

KILOMETRES
0 20 40 60 80 100

C H I N A

A F G H A N I S T A N

CHITRAL

ISHKUMAN

YASIN

KUH GHIZAR PUNIAL

HUNZA

NAGIR

GILGIT

Gilgit

TRIBAL TERRITORY

CHILAS

INDUS

BALTISTAN

Skardu

SHYOK.

INDUS

GILGIT WAZARAT

N. W. F. P.

GARABAD

CEASE-FIRE

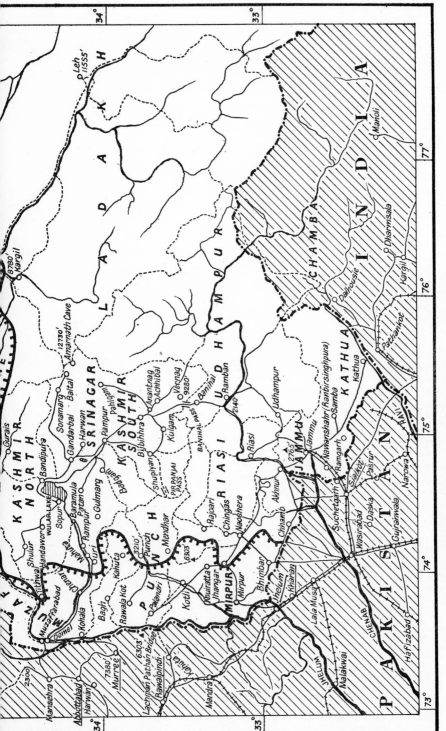

Reproduced from Official Records of the Security Council, Twelfth Year, Supplement, p. 42.

Greece; similarly, in Korea, the military observers attached to the United Nations Commission on Korea [52] were able to concentrate on observing the 38th parallel. In Palestine the international borders became less important than the truce or armistice lines, but the true borders never became irrelevant, for the Security Council entrusted the Mediator and his observers with the task of reporting on compliance with its injunctions to the parties not to "introduce fighting personnel into Palestine, Egypt, Iraq, Lebanon, Saudi Arabia, Syria, Transjordan and Yemen during the cease-fire," and "to refrain from importing war material" into the same areas.[53] The task was a gigantic one and simply could not be effectively carried out by an observer force of the size which the Mediator had at his disposal.[54] It was for this reason that the observers were largely concentrated in Palestine.

UNOGIL was, as the terms of the Security Council Resolution of 11 June 1958 suggested, essentially entrusted with the task of border control. In relation to this function the use of fixed border posts was increased, additional to roving patrols, and considerable emphasis was placed on aerial reconnaissance.[55] It may be noted that, whilst in fact a situation of civil strife existed in the Lebanon, UNOGIL observed strict impartiality on this internal, constitutional issue and limited its activities to checking infiltration from external sources. This attitude of impartiality—the adoption of a principle of "non-intervention"—was in due course to be cited by the Secretary-General as a precedent when, in the Congo, he emphasised the necessity for a similar attitude by the United Nations Forces there.[56] The Yemen Observer Group assumed a function which was in part that of border control, or, more strictly, that of observing that no forces belonging to any of the parties entered the demilitarised zone of twenty kilometres from either side of the demarcated border between Saudi Arabia and the Yemen.[57]

2. *Supervision of cease-fire, truce and armistice agreements*

In Indonesia, Kashmir and, more particularly, Palestine, this became the primary function of the observers. The distinctions between a "cease-fire," a "truce" and an "armistice agreement" are not entirely clear, and, even in the practice of the Security Council, the first two terms tend to be used interchangeably. However, there is something to be said for the view that a "truce," as opposed to a

---

[52] *Ante*, p. 29.
[53] Resol. S/801 of 20 May 1948.
[54] See the account of Mohn, *loc. cit.*, pp. 74–75 of the very limited supervision which the observers attempted. The Mediator reported that "it was not possible within the limits of personnel and equipment available to establish observation posts to cover all the ports, airfields, boundaries and coastlines of all seven Arab States as well as Palestine," *loc. cit.* (A/648), Pt. 2, para. 4.
[55] Second Interim Report of UNOGIL, Doc. S/4052, para. 12.
[56] Second Report by the Secretary-General, S/4417/Add.6, 12 August 1960; and see *post*, pp. 196–200.
[57] S/5298, para. 4.

" cease-fire," is normally more than a simple cessation of hostilities and incorporates a complex of mutual undertakings and conditions : it is, however, a temporary state of affairs as opposed to an " armistice." In West New Guinea and the Yemen the notion of a " disengagement " agreement came into operation. It involved an agreement to cease fire but, in addition, the further principle of withdrawal of forces from the territory. When completed, in West New Guinea there were simply no forces left opposing each other, but in the Yemen the United Arab Republic troops only were intended to withdraw and the Saudi-Arabian and Yemen forces remained on their respective sides of the demilitarised zone surrounding the territorial border. Wherever forces remained in positions facing each other the importance of the line of demarcation became acute, and even more acute where this line was either uncertain or uncontinuous.

In Indonesia there were no continuous front lines, so that a " status quo " line was delineated on the ground with the assistance of United Nations observers and " demilitarised zones " were established on both sides of this line. Often the lines would surround large pockets of Indonesian-held territory behind the Netherlands' positions. In Kashmir a single cease-fire line was established by mutual agreement of the parties and verified on the ground by local commanders from both sides with the assistance of observers; after verification identical maps showing the cease-fire line were issued to both High Commands. Troops were to withdraw to 500 yards from the line.[58]

In Palestine the situation was more confused and no single truce line was ever established, so that the problem became one of agreeing on lines to which each side would withdraw, leaving a " no-man's land " between them.[59] The eventual Armistice Agreements [60] fixed a Demarcation Line beyond which the respective forces could not proceed. The extremely comprehensive formula used was :

" No element of the land, sea or air military or para-military forces of either party, including non-regular forces, shall commit any warlike or hostile act against the military or para-military forces of the other party, or against civilians in territory under the control of that party; or shall advance beyond or pass over for any purpose whatsoever the Armistice Demarcation Line . . ."

They also provided for certain Demilitarised Zones and even Defensive Areas in which only limited defensive forces, as defined in an

[58] For a detailed description of how the Observer Group operated, see Lourié, *loc. cit.*, pp. 27–30.
[59] For a detailed description of the techniques of supervision of the two truces in Palestine, see Part Two of the Mediator's Progress Report of 16 September 1948 : *Off. Rec. G.A.*, 3rd Sess., Suppl. No. 11 (A/648). The Truce Commission itself assumed responsibility for the supervision of the City of Jerusalem.
[60] See Israel/Egyptian Agreement of 24 February 1949 (*Off. Rec. S.C.*, 4th yr., Spec. Suppl. No. 3); Israel/Lebanon Agreement of 23 March 1949 (*ibid.*, Suppl. No. 4).

Annex to the Agreements, could be maintained. Special arrangements had to be made for the supply of "pockets" such as Mount Scopus, held by Israeli forces in the middle of Jordanian-held territory.[61] The execution of the Armistice Agreements was entrusted to the Mixed Armistice Commissions (MACS) under Article X and these commissions were empowered to employ observers either from the military organisations of the parties or from UNTSO, the latter observers remaining under the command of the Chief of Staff of UNTSO.

Whatever the manner by which and in which the demarcation lines are agreed, such lines constitute an essential element in the supervision system; for violations of the cease-fire, truce or armistice will in many cases, although not entirely, consist of transgressions of these lines. To take, by way of illustration, the Progress Report of the Mediator in Palestine of 16 September 1948,[62] the complaints of breaches of the cease-fire included: troop movements, traffic in war materials, military training, attacks on positions, abductions, seizure of positions, firing on United Nations personnel, harvesting incidents, work on fortifications, minelaying, and illegal aircraft flights.

The function of the observers is really twofold: it consists firstly in the checking of violations and secondly in the prevention of violations.[63] The checking of violations, sometimes involving hundreds of infractions a month, is in itself no mean task. The test to be applied in order to determine whether or not a violation had occurred, in the absence of a clear provision in the truce or armistice agreement, is of necessity a somewhat subjective test. In supervising the Armistice Agreements in Palestine the test adopted was that specified in Article IV of the Agreements:

"The principle that no military or political advantage should be gained under the truce ordered by the Security Council is recognised."

Hence, on the basis of this test, the Mediator determined that Arab non-compliance in restoring the water supply to Jerusalem was a violation since the action resulted in a disadvantage to the Israeli

---

[61] On the problems of implementing the special agreement on Mount Scopus of 7 July 1948, see *UN Yearbook*, 1958, pp. 59–60. The UN observers assumed responsibility for checking that the convoys permitted access to Mount Scopus did not contain war materials.

[62] *Off. Rec. G.A.*, 3rd Sess., Suppl. No. 11, p. 39.

[63] For the instructions given to the observers, see *ibid.*, p. 33: "In addition to investigating alleged breaches of the truce, they were charged with the task of carrying on routine observation and with dealing with incidents and complaints on the spot. They had no power to prevent a violation of the truce or to enforce their decisions." In the case of the UNTEA Observer Group the "Memorandum of Understanding on Cessation of Hostilities," which constituted an agreement between Indonesia and the Netherlands, specified the tasks of the observers as being "(i) to observe the implementation of this agreement and (ii) in particular to take necessary steps for the prevention of any acts endangering the security of forces of both parties to this agreement" (A/5170, Annex A to the letter to the Acting Secretary-General of 13 August 1962, para. 1 (c)). Here the function of *prevention* was even given primary emphasis.

side which became aggravated day by day.[64]   However, in the main, the difficulty is simply one of ascertaining the facts, so that the freedom of movement of observers to the *locus in quo* is absolutely essential; the denial of freedom of movement is, as we shall see,[65] one of the main obstacles to the observers.

Prevention of violations clearly involves more positive action than mere checking of violations. To some extent the Israelis in Palestine denied that the observers had a preventive function, and attempted to restrict the observers to investigating an incident once it had occurred and had been reported to them for investigation by the MAC.[66] The observers in Palestine, being unarmed, had to rely for their " preventive " effect on the fact of their presence and on the fear of the parties that, should they violate the truce or armistice, action would be taken by the Security Council. In other words, especially in a somewhat tense military and political situation, the preventive effect of unarmed men will be minimal once the parties believe that no sanctions will ensue upon a violation of the truce or armistice. The Security Council had, of course, by its Resolution of 15 July 1948,[67] determined that the situation constituted a threat to the peace within the meaning of Article 39 and declared specifically that:

". . . failure by any of the Governments or authorities concerned to comply with the [cease-fire order] would demonstrate the existence of a breach of the peace within the meaning of Article 39 of the Charter requiring immediate consideration by the Security Council with a view to such further action under Chapter VII of the Charter as may be decided upon by the Council; "

However, this threat of ultimate sanctions had little effect on irregular forces and its effect on regular forces diminished as, with the passage of time, it became clear that the Council would not initiate any coercive action against either party. The result is, necessarily, a weakening of the authority of the observers to prevent truce or armistice violations.

The absence of effective United Nations sanctions for a breach of the truce led to action being taken by the other party by way of " reprisals "; so serious a threat to the whole truce did this practice become that on 19 August 1948 the Security Council issued a warning that:

" (a) Each party is responsible for the actions of both regular and irregular forces operating under its authority or in territory under its control;

(b) Each party has the obligation to use all means at its disposal to prevent action violating the Truce by individuals or groups who are subject to its authority or who are in territory under its control;

---

[64] A similar, and very difficult, problem arose from the Israeli plans for the division of the River Jordan in the Israel-Syrian Demilitarised Zone. General Bennike, as Chief of Staff of UNTSO, ordered the work to stop, and his decision was endorsed by the Security Council. However, the only effective sanction which had any effect on the Israelis seems to have been the United States' threat to cease economic aid : see Burns, *op. cit.*, p. 111.
[65] *Post*, pp. 79-81.   [66] See Mohn, *loc. cit.*, p. 61; Burns, *op. cit.*, p. 54.
[67] S/902; and see even the earlier Resolution S/801 of 29 May 1948.

(c) Each party has the obligation to bring to speedy trial and in case of conviction to punishment, any and all persons within their jurisdiction who are involved in a breach of the Truce;

(d) No party is permitted to violate the Truce on the ground that it is undertaking reprisals or retaliations against the other party;

(e) No party is entitled to gain military or political advantage through violation of the Truce." [68]

These warnings were of no avail and "reprisal" actions continued to occur; the Qibya "reprisal" raid of 14–15 October 1953, the Gaza raid of 28 February 1955 and the attack at Lake Tiberias in December 1955, were but a few of the incidents which were later to occur and to receive condemnation by the Security Council. The Gaza raid has been regarded by one writer as having destroyed any possibility of negotiating a peace settlement. [69]

3. *Supervision of withdrawal of forces*

Closely linked with supervision of the observance of cease-fire, truce or armistice agreements is the function of supervising the withdrawal of forces agreed to by the parties. In Indonesia the Renville Truce Agreement of 17 January 1949 involved the evacuation of 35,000 Republican combatants from behind the forward positions of Netherlands troops, and under the supervision of the observers of the Consular Commission. [70] Under the Armistice Agreements in Palestine withdrawal of forces was specifically made subject to United Nations supervision [71]; the special annex to the Israeli/Egyptian Agreement, containing the plan for withdrawal from Al Faluja, provided for the UNTSO Chief of Staff to define the order of priority of withdrawal operations and for heavy equipment to be handed over to the United Nations for custody. The observers attached to UNCOK were specifically entrusted with the task of reporting on the withdrawal of the occupying forces from Korea. The Observer Group attached to UNTEA was to observe the withdrawal of Netherlands forces from West New Guinea [72] and the Yemen Group had the specific function of certifying "the outward movement of the United Arab Republic forces and equipment from the airports and seaports of Yemen." [73]

UNOGIL had a function which was not so much to supervise the withdrawal of United States forces from the Lebanon as to "facilitate" that withdrawal. The Resolution of the Third Emergency Assembly, passed unanimously on 21 August, [74] called on the

---

[68] Resol. S/983. [69] Burns, *op. cit.*, p. 21.

[70] See Third Interim Report to the Security Council of the Committee of Good Offices (S/848/Add. 1): *Off. Rec. S.C.*, 3rd yr. Suppl., Spec. Suppl., p. 122.

[71] See Israel/Egypt Agreement (*loc. cit.*, S/1264/Rev. 1), Arts. III (3), VII and Annex I.

[72] A/5170, *Aide-Mémoire* from Acting Secretary-General to Representatives of Indonesia and Netherlands, para. 2. [73] S/5298, para. 4.

[74] A/3893/Rev. 1; Resol. 1237 (ES–III). No observer group operated in Jordan since Jordan had refused its consent, and a UN Special Representative became the only UN "presence." *Off. Rec. G.A.*, 735th Mtg., para. 51.

Secretary-General to make "practical arrangements" which would "facilitate the early withdrawal of the foreign troops" from both the Lebanon and Jordan. UNOGIL was, of course, only a part of these arrangements, but its final report did note the evacuation of the last United States troops.

4. Supervision of exchange of prisoners of war

A somewhat similar, and very useful, function can be assumed by an observer group in that it can supervise the exchange of prisoners of war. In Palestine, with the conclusion of the Armistice Agreements, such an exchange became possible. Article IX (1) of the Israeli/Egyptian Agreement provided that "the exchange of prisoners of war shall be under United Nations supervision and control throughout." By Resolution of 19 January 1956 the Security Council called on the Chief of Staff to arrange the immediate exchange of prisoners of war.[75]

5. Quasi-judicial functions

Quite apart from the specific functions which the Chief of Staff of UNTSO assumed as Chairman of the Mixed Armistice Commissions,[76] it is clear that, on occasions, he assumed the quasi-judicial function of determining disputes between the parties. Examples can be found in his decision that attempts to harvest crops made by civilians in no-man's-land should be permitted only up to the halfway line and no nearer to the Israeli positions,[77] or in the decisions taken to determine the truce lines, both in Palestine [78] and in Kashmir. Even the individual observers occasionally assumed such functions: under the withdrawal plan for Al Faluja inspections of the withdrawal were to "be made exclusively by United Nations Military Observers, and their decisions in all such cases shall be accepted as final." [79] By Resolution of 22 January 1958 the Security Council directed the Chief of Staff to conduct a survey of property records in the area surrounding Government House, Jerusalem, "with a view to determining property ownership in the zone." [80] The supervisory functions of UNTSO in relation to the convoys to Mount Scopus, whereby the observers determined whether items in the cargo manifest were

---

[75] Resol. S/3538. For an account of earlier UNTSO good offices in arranging exchanges of prisoners of war, see Burns, *op. cit.*, Chap. 3.

[76] These were Commissions of 3 from each side with the Chief of Staff of UNTSO or a senior officer from the observer personnel acting as Chairman and having the casting vote. These Commissions, with the exception of the successful Israel/Lebanon MAC, functioned only irregularly after 1951: see *UN Yearbook*, 1958, p. 58. The reasons for their non-operation and the type of problems faced by the Commissions are well illustrated in General Burns' book, *Between Arab and Israeli*.

[77] A/648, pp. 43–44.

[78] See Chief of Staff's Report S/2833 and Add. 1.

[79] Doc. S/1264/Rev. 1, Annex I, para. 7.

[80] Doc. S/3942.

properly to be included in the convoy are, similarly, quasi-judicial functions.[81]

IV. THE OBLIGATIONS ASSUMED BY STATES

Apart from actual decisions by the Security Council binding on Member States, obligations will only be assumed by States involved in the dispute or conflict under agreements made *inter se*, as in the Truce or Armistice Agreements, or in special undertakings entered into with the United Nations. Whilst, at least in relation to decisions of the Security Council, a general duty to give every assistance to the observer groups established by the Council may be stated,[82] the principal obligations which must be assumed by States as the necessary precondition to the proper functioning of the observer groups are the following.

1. *The obligation to accord freedom of movement*

The initial obligation upon a State to admit observers into its territory is one which could only stem from an agreement between the States concerned, as in West New Guinea or the Yemen, or from a decision of the Security Council under Chapter VII of the Charter; it is clear that an observer group formed under Article 34 of Chapter VI, for example, has no right of entry into a State's territory without consent.[83] But the Security Council could always order a State to admit such a group under Chapter VII, probably as part of mandatory provisional measures under Article 40, and that order could, if necessary, be enforced by enforcement action. However, in practice, the States or authorities involved have generally been prepared to admit observers, and to concede " freedom of movement " to them. This is obviously essential to the proper functioning of the observer group, and, by and large, the most frequent cause for complaint by the observer groups has been that they were not in fact accorded the freedom of movement which had been promised.

In the Balkans, apart from one occasion,[84] the Security Council's Commission and, later, UNSCOB were never permitted into the territories of States other than Greece; however, neither body was established under Chapter VII, so that there was no obligation on States to admit them. In Indonesia the observers were initially able to observe only in the regions newly occupied by Netherlands forces; this restriction appears to have stemmed more from the fact that

---

[81] See *UN Yearbook*, 1958, p. 59.
[82] As one illustration it may be noted that the UN was not prepared to accept the contention by the Lebanon that Lebanese law did not permit UN interrogation of prisoners : see Third Report of UNOGIL, S/4085, para. 13.
[83] *Ante*, p. 67.
[84] The UNSCOB Report (A/574), para. 12, disclosed that, except for one occasion, its observers were never allowed access to the territory of Greece's northern neighbours.

elsewhere the observers were in constant danger from guerrilla forces than from positive refusal to permit access by the Netherlands or Republican forces.[85]   After the Renville Truce Agreement movement became more free.

In Palestine complaints of restrictions upon freedom of movement were numerous, hence on 19 October 1948 the Security Council reminded all parties of their duty—

"(a) to allow duly accredited United Nations Observers and other Truce Supervision personnel bearing proper credentials, on official notification, ready access to all places where their duties require them to go including airfields, ports, truce lines and strategic points and areas;
   (b) to facilitate the freedom of movement of Truce Supervision personnel and transport by simplifying procedures on United Nations aircraft now in effect, and by assurance of safe-conduct for all United Nations aircraft and other means of transport;
   (c) to co-operate fully with the Truce Supervision personnel in their conduct of investigations into incidents involving breaches of the truce, including the making available of witnesses, testimony and other evidence on request;
   (d) to implement fully by appropriate and prompt instructions to the Commanders in the field all agreements entered into through the good offices of the Mediator or his representatives;
   (e) to take all reasonable measures to ensure the safety and safe-conduct of the Truce Supervision personnel and the representatives of the Mediator, their aircraft and vehicles, while in territory under their control;
   (f) to make every effort to apprehend and promptly punish any and all persons within their jurisdictions guilty of any assault upon or other aggressive act against the Truce Supervision personnel or the representatives of the Mediator." [86]

The safety of observers was to some extent ensured by the system whereby they moved in company with liaison-officers from the respective Army Commands of the parties whenever they entered the territory under the control of a particular party.[87]   The disadvantage of this system was that the liaison-officers "managed" the observers so as to ensure that they went where it was desired they should go and, to the extent that they relied upon the officers as interpreters, heard what it was intended they should hear.

The Armistice Agreements eventually embodied a formal agreement to freedom of movement; Article X (10) of the Israeli/Egyptian Agreement provided:

"Members of the Commission and its Observers shall be accorded such freedom of movement and access in the areas covered by this Agreement as the Commission may determine to be necessary, provided that when such decisions are reached by a majority vote United Nations Observers only shall be employed."

[85] See Report dated 24 January 1949 from the Committee of Good Offices (S/1223): *Off. Rec. S.C.*, 4th yr., Suppl., p. 60.
[86] S/1045. This Resolution reiterated the Resolutions of 15 July and 19 August 1948 (S/902, S/983). Further admonitions on freedom of movement were made by the Council on 29 December 1948 (S/1169), 18 May 1951 (S/2157).
[87] Mohn, *loc. cit.*, p. 80, says: "The observers were severely restricted as to their movements and could hardly take a step outside their quarters without being escorted by an obliging liaison-officer."

Problems of freedom of movement continued to occur long after the Armistice Agreements; as late as 4 June 1956 the Security Council was still passing Resolutions declaring that full freedom of movement of United Nations observers must be respected in all areas along the Demarcation Lines, in the Demilitarised Zones and in the Defensive Areas.[88] Despite this United Nations observers were expelled from El Auja by the Israeli Army on the eve of the attack against Sinai.[89] On 20 April 1957 the Chief of Staff was still reporting Israel's refusal to allow observers to enter the Demilitarised Area.[90] The Israeli practice of issuing identity cards which would alone permit freedom of movement was clearly wrong; in principle the United Nations identity card should be a sufficient guarantee of the status of the individual.

The attempt by Israel in November 1956 to force UNTSO's withdrawal from the Gaza area by informing the Chief of Staff that the Armistice Agreements were no longer valid was promptly met by the General Assembly's Resolution of 2 November 1956 reaffirming the validity of the Armistice Agreements.[91]

In the Lebanon, UNOGIL reported that the Group had been assured of freedom of movement within and access to the areas under Government control; but constant difficulty was experienced (and considerable danger) in gaining access to areas of Lebanese territory under the control of opposition forces.[92] This in part accounted for the use by UNOGIL of the new technique of supervision by aerial reconnaissance.[93] Full freedom of access to all parts of the Lebanese frontier was only gained on 15 July 1958.[94]

The withdrawal of UNOGIL on 9 December 1958 followed the request by the Lebanese Government of 16 November 1958 for deletion of its complaint from the agenda of the Security Council.[95] However, the Group itself, in its Fifth Report of 14 November, had previously indicated that its mission had been accomplished.[96]

The Observer Group attached to UNTEA may be mentioned as unique in having the advantage that UNTEA was itself the effective government of the territory during the period of the Group's activities: there were no State authorities exercising powers of government or administration in a position to deny freedom of movement.[97]

---

[88] Resol. S/3605. See *UN Yearbook*, 1956, pp. 9–11; and see at p. 13 the acceptance of the Chief of Staff's proposals for certain fixed observation posts.
[89] Burns, *op. cit.*, p. 179.
[90] *UN Yearbook*, 1957, pp. 33–34.
[91] Resol. 997 (ES–I).
[92] First Report of UNOGIL, Doc. S/4040 and Add. 1: *Off. Rec. S.C.*, 13th yr.. Suppl., paras. 4–12.
[93] *Ibid.*, para. 14 (e).
[94] Interim Report of UNOGIL, Doc. S/4051, *ibid.*
[95] S/4113.
[96] S/4114.
[97] See *post*, pp. 257–260.

2. *The obligation to control both regular and irregular forces so as to ensure the safety of observers and the implementation of Security Council Resolutions or Truce and Armistice Agreements*

Practice of the Security Council has made it clear that it will regard the State as under a duty to control both its regular and irregular forces, operating either under its authority or in territory under its control, so as to preserve observers against attack and to maintain any truce or armistice. The inability of the observers in Indonesia to move in many areas because of fear of guerrilla activities has already been mentioned. In Palestine, on 19 August 1948, the Council reminded parties that

" (a) Each party is responsible for the actions of both regular and irregular forces operating under its authority or in territory under its control;

(b) Each party has the obligation to use all means at its disposal to prevent action violating the Truce by individuals or groups who are subject to its authority or who are in territory under its control;

(c) Each party has the obligation to bring to speedy trial and in case of conviction to punishment, any and all persons within their jurisdiction who are involved in a breach of the Truce." [98]

The assassination of Count Bernadotte on 17 September 1948 was believed to have been committed by a group of Israeli terrorists [99] and the United Nations took the view that Israel was responsible internationally for this act.[1] The specific bases of responsibility alleged were three: failure to exercise due diligence and to take all reasonable measures for the prevention of the murder; liability of the Government for actions committed by irregular forces in territory under the control of the Israeli authorities; and failure to take all the measures required by international law and by the Security Council Resolution of 19 October 1948 to bring the culprits to justice.

It may be noted that this obligation is, in conformity with the general principles of State responsibility, limited to the areas of territory under the effective control of the government assuming the obligation. The Lebanese Government assumed no obligations towards UNOGIL in areas under the control of the opposition forces.

The importance of effective control over guerrilla forces can best be illustrated by noting, simply, that the abandonment of the Armistice in the Israeli invasion of Sinai in October 1956 came in response to a campaign, which had lasted for a year, whereby the " fedayeen "—groups of guerrillas recruited amongst the Arab refugees and other civilians but not officially part of the Egyptian forces—

---

[98] S/983.
[99] See Resol. S/1006 of 18 September 1948.
[1] See Annual Report of the Secretary-General, *Off. Rec. G.A.*, 5th Sess., Suppl. No. 1 (A/1287), p. 125. See also *Off. Rec. G.A.*, 6th Sess., Suppl. No. 1 (A/1844), p. 189, when the claim for the death of a UN guard, Bakke, was based upon violation of the Mount Scopus Agreement of 7 July 1948, violation of the obligation to co-operate in carrying out the Mediator's mandate and to furnish adequate protection to the Mediator's staff, and failure to bring the culprits to justice.

carried out marauding raids into Israeli territory. The annihilation of these groups and their bases was the avowed aim of the Israeli attack.

3. *The obligation to control civilians in areas under the control of the parties so as to prevent breaches of the Security Council Resolutions, Truce and Armistice Agreements*

One of the recurring problems, particularly in Palestine, was the absence of any United Nations authority over civilians. Yet, as we have seen, the crossing of the truce or armistice lines by civilians, especially in order to harvest crops or cultivate land, posed a constant threat to the security of the truce.[2]   The control of civilians remained, however, a matter for the civil police of the parties and Article V (4) of the Israel/Egypt Armistice recognised the duty of the parties to control civilians:

"Rules and regulations of the armed forces of the Parties, which prohibit civilians from crossing the fighting lines or entering the area between the lines, still remain in effect after the signing of this Agreement . . ."

The United Nations' concern was that supervision of civilians ought to be handled by civil police and not by armed forces, for the latter course heightened the risk of a clash between opposing armed forces.[3] As late as 1957 the Acting Chief of Staff of UNTSO was reporting difficulties in the areas of Government House and Mount Scopus due to civilian activities and arising from the lack of any specific authority over civilian activities.[4]   Indeed, the control of civilian activities was one of the problems specifically referred to the Mixed Armistice Commission by the Security Council.[5]   The principle seems clear, that the parties bound either by Resolutions of the Security Council or by the terms of Truce or Armistice Agreements are under a duty to ensure that all persons within the areas subject to their control so conduct themselves as to maintain the validity of the Resolutions or Agreements.

4. *The obligation to accord the privileges and immunities necessary for the effective performance of the functions of the observers*

The grant of privileges and jurisdictional immunities to observers was not a matter over which overmuch concern seems to have been expressed in the Balkans, in Indonesia, in Kashmir, in West New Guinea,[6] in the Yemen or, initially, in Palestine.   In the Balkans the

---

[2] See Burns, *op. cit.*, Chap. 7.
[3] And see Lourié, *loc. cit.*, p. 30, on the similar problem in Kashmir.   It may be noted that civilians crossing the ADL were sentenced to imprisonment by the Israeli authorities—soldiers doing so were also punished and had no status as prisoners of war: see Burns, *op. cit.*, p. 109.   But see the *British Manual of Military Law*, Part III, s. 457: "Soldiers captured in the act of breaking an armistice must be treated as prisoners of war."
[4] See *UN Yearbook*, 1957, pp. 36, 38.
[5] Resol. S/3942, para. 3 (a), 22 January 1958.   [6] *Post*, p. 260.

Security Council's Commission of Investigation would presumably benefit from Articles 104 and 105 of the Charter, but Greece did not become a party to the Convention on Privileges and Immunities of the United Nations until 29 December 1947. Moreover, whether the observer personnel supplied by the nations represented on the Commission and, later, the General Assembly's Committee (UNSCOB) fell within Article IV (16) [7] of the Convention is not clear. A similar problem would have existed in Indonesia, where the Netherlands became a party to the Convention only on 19 April 1948 and Indonesia was not a party at all.[8] One distinct advantage of utilising United Nations observers as opposed to military assistants of representatives of Member States is that the former, as United Nations personnel, will benefit from the Charter and the General Convention on Privileges and Immunities of 1946, at least in relation to a Member State which has accepted the Convention.[9] UNTSO, UNOGIL and the Yemen Group became subsidiary organs of the Security Council and therefore entitled to benefit both from the General Convention and Articles 104 and 105 of the United Nations Charter, as did the UNTEA Group as an Assembly subsidiary organ. However, at the beginning of the Palestine operation Israel was not even a member of the United Nations and the Arab States were not at that time parties to the Convention.[10] In relation to UNOGIL it was evidently felt by the Secretary-General that even greater privileges and immunities were needed. An agreement was concluded by an exchange of letters dated 13 June 1958 [11] conferring full diplomatic status on the three senior members of the Group, the military observers and the United Nations Secretariat. Additionally, the Lebanese Government agreed to grant:

". . . freedom of entry, without delay or hindrance, of property, equipment, and spare parts; freedom of movement of personnel, equipment and transport; the use of United Nations vehicle registration plates; the right to fly the United Nations flag on premises, observation posts and vehicles; and the right of unrestricted communication by radio, both within the area of operations and to connect with the United Nations radio network, as well as by telephone, telegraph or other means."

---

[7] This section refers to "all delegates, deputy delegates, advisers, technical experts and secretaries of delegations."

[8] An agreement by an exchange of letters was effected between the Principal Secretary of the UN Commission and the Prime Minister of Indonesia on 23 May 1950, conferring diplomatic privileges and immunities, but this could not have benefited the observers in 1947–48.

[9] But see *post*, p. 260, on the curiously restrictive use of the term "officials" of the UN in the UNTEA Agreement. It may be doubted whether the observers were "officials" in this sense.

[10] Egypt became so on 17 September 1948, the Lebanon on 10 March 1949, Syria on 29 September 1953; Israel acceded on 21 September 1949. Thereafter the UNTSO observers became entitled to the privileges of "experts" under Art. VI, s. 22 of the 1946 Convention.

[11] *U.N. Legislative Series* (ST/LEG./SER.B/10), "Legislative Texts and Treaty Provisions concerning the Legal Status, Privileges and Immunities of International Organisations," pp. 330–332.

5. The obligation to contribute towards the financing
of the observer group

The question of the obligation of the States directly affected by the functions of the observer groups (in the sense of the States on whose territories they operate, or whose cease-fire agreements they supervise) is best postponed until the larger question of the financing of United Nations Forces is dealt with in Chapter 14.

However, it may be useful at this juncture to point out that UNTEA—of which only a part was the Observer Group—and the Group in the Yemen are distinguishable from the other United Nations observer groups in that, in both cases, the States directly affected agreed to share the costs of the operations. This was done, on an equal basis, by Indonesia and the Netherlands by virtue of Article XXIV of their Agreement of 15 August 1962.[12] In the case of the Yemen there was no such initial agreement, but the Secretary-General had, on 27 May 1963, expressed the hope that the two parties principally involved, Saudi Arabia and the United Arab Republic, would undertake to bear the costs of the mission (estimated at $1 million for a mission designed to last four months).[13] In his subsequent report of 7 June 1963 [14] the Secretary-General reported that the parties had agreed to assume the entire financial burden for at least the first two months, without precluding the possibility of further financial assistance beyond that time. The parties have since extended their agreement until 4 March 1964.

V. CLAIMS

The Advisory Opinion of the International Court of Justice of 11 April 1949 on *Reparations for Injuries suffered in the service of the United Nations* [15] stemmed directly from the assassination of the United Nations Mediator, Count Bernadotte, and the desire of the General Assembly to have clarified the legal position of the United Nations in bringing a claim for damages both to the United Nations and to the agent of the United Nations or to persons entitled through him.[16] Acting on the opinion of the Court and of General Assembly Resolution 365 (IV) of 1 December 1949, to the effect that the United Nations could espouse a claim, both against Member and non-Members of the United Nations, by a letter of 21 April 1950 [17] the Secretary-General claimed from Israel $54,628 as " reparation for

[12] *Post*, p. 260.
[13] S/5321, and see the breakdown of costs in S/5323.
[14] S/5325.
[15] *I.C.J. Reports*, 1949, p. 188.
[16] For a review of opinions expressed in the Sixth Committee prior to the request for an advisory opinion, see Weissberg, *The International Status of the UN* (1961) Chap. VII.
[17] UN Doc. A/1287; Sweden, whose national Bernadotte was, had previously informed the Secretary-General that the widow did not wish to present any claim and that Sweden would claim independently.

monetary damage borne by the United Nations." Israel met the claim, without admitting the validity of all the legal contentions put forward on behalf of the Secretary-General.[18] The Government of Israel also met in full the claim for $25,233 and 200,000 francs submitted by the United Nations as a result of the death of Colonel Sérot, a French observer assassinated at the same time; the latter sum covered a claim by Colonel Sérot's father.

Other governments proved less amenable to settlement. Claims submitted against Egypt for the deaths of two French observers shot whilst leaving a United Nations plane have not been met. Jordan, similarly, refused to meet a claim for the death of Bakke, a United Nations guard, and refused a suggestion that the matter should be submitted to arbitration or to a board of inquiry.[19] The General Assembly, after consideration by the Sixth Committee in 1952, re-affirmed that such claims should be settled by the procedures envisaged in Resolution 365 (IV).[20]

It is not known that any claims were presented on behalf of members of the United Nations Special Committee on the Balkans killed or wounded in the performance of their duty, or on behalf of the observers in Indonesia. Perhaps one explanation is that these observers were never United Nations observers in the strict sense of United Nations personnel; hence claims would be more appropriately submitted by the States whose nationals they were.

VI. CONCLUSIONS

The various observer groups so far established by the United Nations have not, of course, been fighting forces; they have, apart from certain exceptions in Indonesia and the Yemen, not even been armed. In the main they have operated simultaneously with conciliation efforts by the United Nations and often, as in Palestine until the termination of the Mediator's role on 11 August 1948, they have been commanded by the same person as conducted the conciliation effort. Experience suggests that a separation of the conciliatory or mediatory function from the observer function is far preferable, for a mediator who has on one day determined a party to be guilty of a violation of a truce is apt to find conciliation with that party difficult on the next day. As Bunche has stated:

---

[18] See Annual Report of the Secretary-General, *Off. Rec. G.A.*, 5th Sess., Suppl. No. 1 (A/1287), pp. 124–125.

[19] Weissberg, *op. cit.*, pp. 184–189.

[20] Resol. 690 (VII), 21 December 1952. In the Sixth Committee Egypt, Iran, Mexico, Syria and the U.S.S.R. opposed arbitration on the ground that it involved the UN in being both judge and party, that proceedings should be before national courts, and that the submission to arbitration involved an admission of responsibility of the State. The first of these depends entirely on how the arbitral tribunal is constituted, the second is in principle wrong, and the third is sheer nonsense. See *Off. Rec. G.A.*, 7th Sess., Sixth Committee, 357th Mtg., 19 December 1952.

" . . . the separation of the functions of mediation or conciliation from the functions of supervision and enforcement, whether of cease-fire, or truce or armistice, is a very sound and practical principle . . . Our experience in Palestine with the mediation and truce supervision was that the duties of truce supervision and enforcement often conflicted with the functions of mediation . . ." [21]

The truce " observer " function obviously becomes the easier to fulfil as the situation, in military terms, becomes less tense; hence Kashmir or the Lebanon proved far easier to handle than Palestine and, where forces are actually withdrawn from the territory, as was intended in the Yemen and as actually occurred in West New Guinea, little difficulty is experienced by the observers. In contrast, when the Israeli attack on Sinai developed in October 1956 the situation of the observers and their dependants became so precarious (and to some extent their presence useless since the Armistice was no longer being applied) that all observers bar eight were evacuated by the United States Sixth Fleet. [22] Moreover, the task of supervising a truce becomes more and more difficult as time passes, for it is essentially a precarious state of affairs, a temporary suspension of hostilities, and even an armistice leaves a situation of great potential danger; the authority and efficacy of supervision by observers is likely to be greater when there is a prospect of a permanent peace settlement reasonably soon.

In general, all the observer groups have been understaffed and under-equipped; they have also suffered from all the drawbacks of *ad hoc* constitution, and the creation of a permanent United Nations Force which could provide ready-trained observer personnel would be a decided advantage. Not only would the personnel be more truly international, but they would be already trained to such tasks. It is not without significance that, as each United Nations military force or observer group has been established, it has tended to be formed around a nucleus drawn from an existing United Nations unit. UNTSO provided a nucleus for UNEF and UNOGIL, UNEF and UNTSO for ONUC, and later for UNTEA and the Yemen Group. A United Nations Force or observer group has been in continuous existence for almost the whole of the life of the United Nations. The desirability of a multi-purpose, permanent United Nations Force can be strongly argued, and this is an argument to which, in Part Two of the present study, we shall have to return.

The use of military assistants serving State representatives, as in the Balkans and Indonesia, is not as good a system as using a properly constituted United Nations organ. As the Secretary-General has stated :

[21] See the testimony of Bunche before the Security Council, *Off. Rec. S.C.*, 4th yr., No. 36, pp. 27–28. Similarly, Lourié, *loc. cit.*, p. 24 describes the separation of function in Kashmir by appointing a Chief Military Observer with no responsibility for advising UNCIP on the conditions necessary for holding a plebiscite.
[22] Burns, *op. cit.*, p. 184. The UN personnel attached to the Egyptian/Israeli MAC, however, remained in the Gaza strip.

"Thus, a United Nations operation should always be under a leadership established by the General Assembly or the Security Council, or on the basis of delegated authority by the Secretary-General, so as to make it directly responsible to one of the main organs of the United Nations, while integrated with the Secretariat in an appropriate form." [23]

The decision not to arm observers is understandable, for their task necessitates their non-involvement in military action against one of the parties. The decision not to provide them with their own United Nations guards, who could be armed, is more open to question, especially since most of the claims submitted against States for the death of observers alleged specifically the failure of these States to accord to observers the necessary protection. Admittedly an observer group should not in general become a para-military force, but in situations like Palestine, or Indonesia, protection against guerrillas and uncontrolled bands may simply not be forthcoming from the parties themselves. Moreover the distinction between observers and a military group is often a question of degree: it is worth noting that, once UNEF entered the Gaza strip in March 1957 and took up positions on the Armistice Demarcation Line, UNEF assumed the observer functions on that line hitherto exercised by UNTSO.[24] In retrospect, Palestine would appear as a situation which needed a force like UNEF from the outset, rather than an observer force. The Palestine Commission had, as early as February 1948, warned the Security Council of the dangerous vacuum likely to ensue from the withdrawal of the mandatory's force and asked the Security Council to establish " an adequate non-Palestinian force." [25] It is regrettable that the Security Council did not see fit to comply with this request, and equally regrettable that the Secretary-General's proposals for a United Nations Guard Force in 1948 received such scant regard.[26] The approval of his revised plan for a Field Service and a Panel of Observers did, of course, meet many of the criticisms centring on the inadequacies of auxiliary personnel to be attached to an observer group and the problems of *ad hoc* recruitment of observers.

One final conclusion may be noted from the work of UNOGIL. This Group reported a distinct set-back to its operations as a result of the landing of United States troops on 15 July 1958 (these being withdrawn on 25 October); apparently this intervention caused a

---

[23] *Summary study of experience, etc.* (A/3943), para. 172.

[24] For an account of the political negotiation which preceded this final withdrawal of Israeli forces, see Burns, *op. cit.*, pp. 246–254. The General Assembly, by Resolution 1125 (XI) of 2 February 1957 considered that the placing of UNEF on the ADL was necessary.

[25] *Off. Rec. S.C.*, 3rd yr., Suppl. No. 2, Doc.A/AC.21/7 and 9. And see Trygve Lie's statement ". . . acutely conscious of how different things in Palestine could have been had the United Nations had an international force at its disposal," in *In the Cause of Peace* (1954) p. 192.

[26] *Ante*, pp. 18–21.

general loss of confidence in the United Nations observers by the
local inhabitants, which took some time to regain.[27]   The conclusion
would seem to be that unilateral armed intervention by a Member
State is likely to increase the difficulties of a United Nations observer
operation, at least in what is virtually a domestic strife.

[27] Second Report of UNOGIL (S/4069), para. 2; Third Report (S/4085), para. 3.
Perhaps a comparable "intervention" was the Czechoslovakian supply of
arms to Egypt in September 1955 which clearly heightened the tension
between Israel and Egypt and increased the difficulties of UNTSO'S task:
see Burns, *op. cit.*, p. 99.

5

The United Nations Emergency Force

I. THE ESTABLISHMENT OF UNEF [1]

On the night of 29 October 1956, units of the Israeli armed forces crossed the Armistice Demarcation Line, entered the territory of Egypt and advanced across the Sinai Peninsula towards the Suez Canal. On 31 October, military action against objectives on Egyptian territory was also undertaken by the United Kingdom and France. Egypt referred the matter to the Security Council, where two Resolutions were proposed, by the United States and by the U.S.S.R.,[2] both of which failed of acceptance because of the negative votes of two of the Permanent Members, the United Kingdom and France. The United States draft Resolution called upon all parties " to refrain from the use of force or the threat of force in the area in any manner inconsistent with the principles of the United Nations," and " to assist the United Nations in ensuring the integrity of the armistice agreement " between Egypt and Israel.[3]

The inability of the Security Council to act led to a proposal from Yugoslavia [4] to call an extraordinary session of the General Assembly, under the provisions of the " Uniting for Peace Resolution." [5] A

---

[1] There is now an extensive bibliography on UNEF of which the following is a selection: Poirier, *La Force Internationale d'Urgence* (1962); Burns and Heathcote, *Peace-Keeping by UN Forces—from Suez to the Congo* (1963); Chaumont, *La Situation juridique des Etats Membres à l'Egard de la Force d'Urgence des Nations Unies*, Ann. Fr. de D.I. (1958) p. 399; Rosner, *The United Nations Emergency Force* (1963). The last named gives a bibliography with references to most of the periodical literature.

[2] The Soviet Union contemplated members providing military assistance to the Security Council under Art. 42 of the Charter in order to " halt the aggression," and suggested that the Soviet Union and the U.S.A. should provide the core of this military assistance. See the exchange of messages between the two Governments in *Docs. on American Foreign Relations* (1957) ed. by Paul Zinner, pp. 355–358.

[3] S/3710.   [4] S/3719.

[5] General Assembly Resol. No. 377 A (V) of 1950. This provides in part: " That if the Security Council, because of lack of unanimity of the Permanent Members, fails to exercise its primary responsibility for the maintenance of international peace and security in any case where there appears to be a threat to the peace, breach of the peace, or act of aggression, the General Assembly shall consider the matter immediately with a view to making appropriate recommendations to Members for collective measures, including in the case of a breach of the peace or act of aggression the use of armed force where necessary, to maintain or restore international peace and security. If not in session at the time, the General Assembly may meet in an emergency special session within twenty-four hours of the request therefor. Such emergency special session shall be called if requested by the Security Council on the vote of any seven members."

counter-proposal by the United Kingdom and France which would have declared the proposal to call the General Assembly into emergency session out of order, since the grounds for invoking the "Uniting for Peace Resolutions" did not exist,[6] was lost, and the Yugoslavian proposal received the necessary seven affirmative votes.[7]

On first being seised of the matter, the General Assembly passed, on 2 November 1956, Resolution 997 (ES–1), which was based on a United States draft,[8] and was adopted by sixty-four votes to five with six abstentions. This called upon the parties to cease fire, to withdraw to their previous positions, and to refrain from the introduction of military *matériel* into the area of conflict. It called upon the parties to make a full observance of the armistice agreements, and generally to reopen the Suez Canal, which had then been blocked for some days.

The next day, the Secretary-General reported that France and the United Kingdom were willing to stop their military action if the Governments of Egypt and Israel agreed to accept a United Nations Force to keep the peace, if the United Nations itself decided to constitute and maintain such a Force until peace were agreed between Israel and Egypt and until satisfactory arrangements had been made with regard to the reopening of the Suez Canal, and on the understanding that the United Nations would guarantee such arrangements.[9]

The question of setting up a United Nations Force had already begun to occupy the minds of Member States; for they realised that extraordinary measures had to be taken to achieve all the objectives sought by the General Assembly's first Resolution.[10] A leading part in the discussion was played by Canada and in particular by Mr. Pearson, the Canadian Minister for External Affairs; his first idea was that the United Kingdom and France should be asked to act as a United Nations Force and should, for this purpose, be furnished with the United Nations flag. In view of the political difficulties involved in this proposition, however, the Canadians put forward an alternative proposal[11] which was accepted by the General Assembly on 4 November, by fifty-seven votes to nil, with nineteen abstentions,[12] and became Resolution 998 (ES–1).[13]

The General Assembly, " Bearing in mind the urgent necessity of facilitating compliance with its Resolution 997 (ES–1)," requested

---

[6] See S/PV 751; *United Nations Review*, November 1956, 14–15; for a criticism of the British arguments, see Macdonald, (1957) *Canadian Bar Review* 53.

[7] S/3721.

[8] *Off. Rec. G.A.*, 1st Emergency Special Sess.; doc. A/3256.

[9] *Off. Rec. G.A.*, 1st Emergency Special Sess.; docs. A/3268; A/3269.

[10] *Summary Study of the experience derived from the establishment and operation of the Force : Report of the Secretary-General*, 9 October 1958; *Off. Rec. G.A.*, 13th Sess., Annex I : doc. A/3943, para. 6.

[11] For an account of the Canadian activities, see Frye, *A United Nations Police Force* (London. 1957) pp. 1–7; Spry, " Canada, The UNEF and the Commonwealth," (July 1957) *International Affairs* 289–300.

[12] Including the Soviet *bloc* and Egypt.

[13] *Off. Rec. G.A.*, 1st Emergency Special Sess., Suppl. No. 1 (A/3354), p. 2.

the Secretary-General, as a matter of priority, " to submit to it within forty-eight hours a plan for the setting up, with the consent of the nations concerned, of an emergency international United Nations Force to secure and supervise the cessation of hostilities in accordance with all the terms of the aforementioned Resolution."

Having received such a plan from the Secretary-General,[14] the General Assembly, again by fifty-seven votes to nil, with nineteen abstentions, proceeded to adopt a Resolution on the basis of a draft submitted by Canada, Colombia, and Norway.[15] In this, the Assembly noted with satisfaction the plan produced by the Secretary-General, and made the following dispositions :

"The General Assembly :

1. *Establishes* a United Nations Command for an Emergency international Force to secure and supervise the cessation of hostilities in accordance with all the terms of General Assembly Resolution 997 (ES–1) of 2 November 1956;

2. *Appoints*, on an emergency basis, the Chief of Staff of the United Nations Truce Supervision Organisation, Major-General E. L. M. Burns, as Chief of the Command;

3. *Authorises* the Chief of Command immediately to recruit, from the observer corps of the United Nations Truce Supervision Organisation, a limited number of officers who shall be nationals of countries other than those having permanent membership in the Security Council, and further authorises him, in consultation with the Secretary-General, to undertake the recruitment directly, from various Member States other than the Permanent Members of the Security Council, of the additional number of officers needed;

4. *Invites* the Secretary-General to take such administrative measures as may be necessary for the prompt execution of the actions envisaged in the present Resolution." [16]

Following the receipt, on 6 November, of the Secretary-General's Second and Final Report on the Plan for an Emergency Force,[17] the General Assembly passed its Resolution 1001 (ES–1) of 7 November, the operative part of which reads :

"*The General Assembly* . . .

1. Expresses its approval of the guiding principles for the organisation and functioning of the emergency international United Nations Force as expounded in paragraphs 6 to 9 of the Secretary-General's report;

2. Concurs in the definition of the functions of the Force as stated in paragraph 12 of the Secretary-General's report;

3. Invites the Secretary-General to continue discussions with governments of Member States concerning offers of participation in the Force, toward the objective of its balanced composition;

4. Requests the Chief of Command, in consultation with the Secretary-General as regards size and composition, to proceed forthwith with the full organisation of the Force;

5. *Approves* provisionally the basic rule concerning the financing of the Force laid down in paragraph 15 of the Secretary-General's report;

6. *Establishes* an Advisory Committee composed of one representative from each of the following countries : Brazil, Canada, Ceylon, Colombia, India,

[14] *Off. Rec. G.A.*, Agenda item 5, doc. A/3289.
[15] *Off. Rec. G.A.*, Agenda item 5, doc. A/3290.
[16] Resol. 1000 (ES–1), *Off. Rec. G.A.*, Suppl. No. 1 (A/3354), p. 2.
[17] *Ibid.*, agenda item 5, doc. A/3302.

Norway and Pakistan, and requests this Committee, whose Chairman shall be the Secretary-General, to undertake the development of those aspects of the planning for the Force and its operation not already dealt with by the General Assembly and which do not fall within the area of the direct responsibility of the Chief of Command.

7. *Authorises* the Secretary-General to issue all regulations and instructions which may be essential to the effective functioning of the Force, following consultation with the Committee aforementioned, and to take all other necessary administrative and executive action;

8. *Determines* that, following the fulfilment of the immediate responsibilities defined for it in operative paragraphs 6 and 7 above, the Advisory Committee shall continue to assist the Secretary-General in the responsibilities falling to him under the present and other relevant Resolutions;

9. Decides that the Advisory Committee, in the performance of its duties, shall be empowered to request, through the usual procedures, the convening of the General Assembly and to report to the Assembly whenever matters arise which, in its opinion, are of such urgency and importance as to require consideration by the General Assembly itself;

10. Requests all Member States to afford assistance as necessary to the United Nations Command in the performance of its functions, including arrangements for passage to and from the area involved."

These were the constituent documents with which the General Assembly created the Force; following the Secretary-General's consultations with Member States and others, and following the acceptance by Egypt of the presence of UNEF on its territory, the first units of the Force reached the staging area at the Capodichino airport, Naples, Italy, on 10 November, and its first elements, which consisted of officers recruited from UNTSO, arrived in Egypt on 12 November, followed by advance units of troops on 15 November.

II. THE CONSTITUTIONAL BASIS OF UNEF

From the start, the legality or constitutionality of the creation of UNEF by the General Assembly has been challenged by some Member States, notably the Soviet Union and other members of the Soviet *bloc*. In explaining his attitude towards Resolution 1001, in the vote upon which the Soviet Union abstained, the delegate of that State declared that the creation of UNEF constituted a violation of the Charter of the United Nations, for only the Security Council could, under Chapter VII of the Charter, create an international armed force. The only reason for a Soviet abstention, rather than a negative vote, was that Egypt, the victim of aggression,[18] had accepted the presence of the Force on its territory.[19]

This attitude was adopted in spite of the fact that the Soviet Union had voted for the transfer of the question to the General

---

[18] It may be noted that none of the three States, Israel, France, or the United Kingdom was ever qualified by any organ of the UN as an "aggressor."

[19] *Off. Rec. G.A.*, 1st Emergency Special Sess., paras. 291–297. That the Soviet Union was not prepared to abandon its view that only the Security Council could establish an international armed force is clear from the statement of the Soviet delegate, Kuznetsov; *ibid.*, 567 Mtg., 7 November 1956, pp. 127–128.

Assembly in the first place, and has since been maintained although several of the Eastern European States offered contingents for the Force in the early days of its creation. The result has been a refusal to pay assessed contributions to the cost of the Force, which led the General Assembly ultimately to request an Advisory Opinion from the International Court of Justice.

It was never contended that the creation of a Force such as UNEF is beyond the competence of the United Nations as a whole; what was in issue was whether or not the Organisation's acts were undertaken by the proper organ; if not, it was contended that the acts must be taken to be unconstitutional.

There are two possible methods of testing the legality of the creation and operation of UNEF, and they start from diametrically opposed points of view. Nevertheless, it is thought that, whatever method is followed, the result will be to vindicate the constitutionality of the proceedings.

The first method is to take the Charter, as the basic constitutional document of the United Nations, and ask whether there is anything contained therein which would prohibit the line of action taken by the General Assembly. This has commended itself to certain governments. For instance, when asked in the House of Commons under which article of the Charter the Force was created, the Joint Parliamentary Under-Secretary of State for Foreign Affairs replied that no specific article supplied the basis of the creation of UNEF, but that it was set up as a result of General Assembly Resolutions, and that no article of the Charter prevented this.[20] The opponents of UNEF have also used this approach, but they have affected to discover in the Charter, particularly in Chapter VII, prohibitions upon the ability of the General Assembly to set up forces of the type exemplified by UNEF.

The opposite method is to attempt to discover some provision in the Charter which would expressly authorise the General Assembly to act, rather than looking for a provision which would prevent it from doing so. This is perhaps the more satisfying approach both from a legal and from a political point of view. For if a body is created with certain powers, as the United Nations and its principal organs were, the existence of a power which justifies any particular course of action is conclusive upon its constitutionality.

The difficulties in applying this method to the creation and operation of UNEF are increased by two factors. First, although Article 22 of the Charter permits the General Assembly to set up subsidiary organs which it deems necessary for the performance of its functions,[21] there is no Article which expressly permits the

---

[20] Hansard, Parliamentary Debates, Vol. 562, cols. 456–457, 12 December 1956; see E. Lauterpacht in (1957) 6 *International and Comparative Law Quarterly* 322.

[21] For earlier actions by the General Assembly in setting up subsidiary organs, see the Special Commission in the Balkans and the Commission in Korea: pp. 61, 64, *ante*.

creation by that body of a military or even a "para-military" force, whose purpose is to secure the maintenance of international peace and security. The only mention in the Charter of such matters is contained in Chapter VII of the Charter, under whose provisions only the Security Council is permitted to act. Second, none of the Resolutions under which the Force was created or operated referred in any way to any specific article of the Charter in justification.

In fact, the first time that the Charter was seriously discussed and reference was made to a specific article which would support the General Assembly's action under Article 22 for the purposes for which UNEF was created, was on the occasion of the examination of the General Assembly Resolutions by the International Court of Justice in the *Case concerning Certain Expenses of the United Nations (Article 17, paragraph 2 of the Charter)*.[22] The case took the form of a request from the General Assembly to the Court for an Advisory Opinion on the question whether the expenditures authorised by the various Resolutions of the General Assembly relating to the financing of UNEF and the United Nations operations in the Congo[23] constituted "expenses of the organisation" within the meaning of Article 17, paragraph 2 of the Charter. By nine votes to five, the Court agreed that the expenditure was covered by the terms of the Article in question. In its Opinion, the Court first dealt with the interpretation of the term "expenses" within Article 17 (2),[24] and then turned to a consideration of whether the budgetary powers of the General Assembly contained in that Article are limited in any way by other provisions of the Charter, and this led the Court into a discussion of the respective competences of the Security Council and the General Assembly in the maintenance of international peace and security.

Various arguments were adduced in support of the contention that the Assembly's action was *ultra vires*, and they took the form of an attempt to show that there *were* provisions of the Charter which legally prevented the General Assembly from establishing UNEF. The Court in its Opinion held that the supposed obstacles to the Assembly's freedom of action did not exist, and further, based the constitutionality of the Assembly's proceedings upon specific provisions of the Charter, thus combining both of the methods of approach outlined above.

The main arguments put forward against the constitutionality of the creation of UNEF were the following: First, it was said that the intention of the framers of the Charter was that enforcement action should only be undertaken by reliance on Article 43 of the Charter and the special agreements contained therein, that is, by the Security

---

[22] *I.C.J. Reports*, 1962, p. 151. For an examination of the various opinions given in this case, see R. Y. Jennings, (1962) 11 *International and Comparative Law Quarterly*, 1170 *et seq.*

[23] See Chap. 6.

[24] *I.C.J. Reports*, 1962, pp. 157–161.

Council.   The whole field was outside the competence of the General
Assembly.   Only the Security Council may act when international
peace and security are in issue, and the General Assembly's powers
are limited to discussion, consideration, study, and recommendation;
it cannot therefore impose any obligation upon Member States to
contribute towards expenses.[25]   Two things may be noted about this
argument; it depends upon the assumption that the action undertaken
in the case of UNEF was "enforcement action" within the meaning
of the Charter, and it accepts the result that the veto will probably
operate so as to stultify any action taken to maintain international
peace and security, in view of the impasse into which the Permanent
Members of the Security Council have fallen since the United Nations
came into being.[26]   Moreover, the proposition that the General
Assembly can never do anything but consider, discuss, study or
recommend (although it is admitted that coercive and enforcement
action may only be ordered by the Security Council under Chapter
VII) is untrue.   Article 18 refers to voting in the General Assembly
on "decisions"; whilst some of these might be merely the decision
to make recommendations, some, such as decisions under Article 5
dealing with the suspension of members, entail action.   An extremely
important and relevant sphere in which the Assembly alone, and
not the Security Council, might act is budgetary questions, for
Article 17 (1) provides that ". . . the General Assembly shall consider
and *approve* the budget of the organisation."

Further it was argued that the field of international peace and
security was altogether outside the purview of the General Assembly
since Article 24 of the Charter gives "primary responsibility" to the
Security Council in such matters.   Moreover, it was said, Article 11
(2) emphasises this primacy in that it requires that any question on
which "action," within the meaning of the Charter, is necessary
should be referred by the General Assembly to the Security Council.
This again depends upon whether the General Assembly actions can
be called "action" for this purpose.

Apart from requiring that the General Assembly's proceedings
constitute "action" and more specifically "enforcement action"
within the Charter, these arguments rest also upon the contention
that the giving of "primary responsibility" to the Security Council
entails the total incompetence of the General Assembly in the
maintenance of international peace and security.

The argument based upon the primacy of the Security Council
contains an inherent weakness, for the very fact that this was given
must imply that there is a secondary responsibility; the functions of
the Security Council are not, therefore, exclusive, and the General
Assembly, therefore, possesses the residuum of authority.   The
argument from Article 11 (2) would lead to the conclusion that, in

[25] *Ibid.*, p. 162.
[26] This argument has been castigated as "cynical": Jennings, *op. cit.*, p. 1170.

the case of the situation in Egypt in October and November 1956, the United Nations would have been powerless to do anything, and a reference of the case from the General Assembly to the Security Council, which had already passed on the matter to the General Assembly, would involve acting in a circular motion of a particularly futile character.

Later in its Opinion the Court faced the argument that, whatever the other provisions of the Charter might permit, Article 43 is in the nature of a *lex specialis* derogating from the general rule laid down in Article 17 (1), so that expenditure for the maintenance of international peace and security could only, and in all circumstances, be provided for by means of voluntary agreements made with Member States under Article 43. Since only the Security Council could enter into these agreements, the General Assembly was precluded from exercising its general budgetary power. This argument was rejected because Article 43, if applied in the way suggested, would confine the actions even of the Security Council within its limits; there was, however, nothing to prevent the Security Council from providing forces for the maintenance of international peace and security from sources not contemplated in Article 43 as indeed had been the case with ONUC; moreover, this was scarcely relevant to the General Assembly's powers, for Article 43 only applies to "enforcement action."

Turning to the Articles of the Charter which might be prayed in aid of justification of the General Assembly's proceedings, it seems that three Articles require to be examined.

Article 10 provides that:

"The General Assembly may discuss any questions or any matters within the scope of the present Charter or relating to the powers and functions of any organs provided for in the present Charter, and except as provided in Article 12 may make recommendations to the Members of the United Nations or to the Security Council or to both on any such questions or matters."

Article 11 (2) reads:

"The General Assembly may discuss any questions relating to the maintenance of international peace and security brought before it by any Member of the United Nations, or by the Security Council, or by a State which is not a Member of the United Nations . . . and, except as provided in Article 12, may make recommendations with regard to any such questions to the State or States concerned or to the Security Council or to both. Any such question on which action is necessary shall be referred to the Security Council by the General Assembly either before or after discussion."

According to Article 14:

"Subject to the provisions of Article 12, the General Assembly may recommend measures for the peaceful adjustment of any situation regardless of origin, which it deems likely to impair the general welfare or friendly relations among nations, including situations resulting from a violation of the provisions of the present Charter setting forth the Purposes and Principles of the United Nations."

97

All three Articles are subject to Article 12, which provides that:

"While the Security Council is exercising in respect of any dispute or situation the functions assigned to it in the present Charter, the General Assembly shall not make any recommendation with regard to that dispute or situation unless the Security Council so requests."

In the case of UNEF, it is clear that Article 12 cannot be a fetter on the actions of the General Assembly, since the Security Council was not at the time the General Assembly recommendations were made exercising its Charter functions in respect of the situation; indeed, it had itself referred the matter to the General Assembly.

Therefore, it seems the General Assembly action could be based on either Articles 10, 11 (2) or 14. In the case of Article 11 (2) the provisions of Article 12 are again inapplicable in a case such as UNEF; the only other limitation is implicit in Article 11 (2) itself; that is, if the decision of the General Assembly in the case of UNEF amounted to "action," the Assembly was incompetent to act.

The main point clearly before the Court was whether the "action" referred to in Article 11 (2) meant "enforcement action" and, if so, whether the action undertaken by the General Assembly was "enforcement action," since, if it was not, there was no legal restriction upon the General Assembly's action, either through Chapter VII of the Charter or through Article 11 (2). As to this, in a factual sense, the actions actually undertaken by the Force could not be said to be in the nature of "enforcement," since everything that was done was done with the consent of the parties involved.

The Court examined the Resolutions by which the Force was created, and those which provided for its financing. The crucial Resolution is Resolution 1000 (ES–1), whose first paragraph states that the Force is established "to secure and supervise the cessation of hostilities in accordance with the terms of General Assembly Resolution 997 (ES–1) . . ." Although the word "secure" in the Resolution might be taken to imply some enforcement, this meaning disappears when the terms of the Resolution are considered together with the requirement of the consent of the States concerned.

The Court concluded, on this point, that the "action" of Article 11 (2) did in fact refer to "enforcement action," that the General Assembly's action was not of this character and that the action taken by the General Assembly constituted "measures" within Article 14. Thus, the constitutional basis of the Force was found by the Court in that Article. Article 11 (2) was not regarded by the Court as excluded as a possible constitutional basis but, significantly, the Court did not rest the constitutionality of UNEF on the Resolution on Uniting for Peace of 3 November 1950.[27]

The remaining question was whether the expenditure incurred in

[27] *I.C.J. Reports*, 1962, pp. 164–165, 172. See *post*, pp. 288–296. The Secretary-General, in his Report on UNEF of 6 November 1956 had in fact done so (A/3302, p. 20); also Sohn, (1958) 52 A.J.I.L. 235.

the operation of UNEF was in accordance with the provisions of Article 1 of the Charter, that is, within the purposes of the Organisation; when this Article is examined it is clear that it was, for the operations were undertaken to promote and maintain international peace and security, and the Court so found.

III. THE ROLE OF THE SECRETARY-GENERAL

While UNEF was, from a legal point of view, the creation of the General Assembly, the major single contribution to the creation and direction of the Force was made by the Secretary-General. The tasks entrusted to the Secretary-General and the powers delegated to him by the General Assembly were multifarious, and they may be seen in the three stages in the history of the Force.

Before the creation of UNEF, in connection with the hostilities on Egyptian soil, the General Assembly requested the Secretary-General to observe and report upon compliance with its Resolutions, and authorised him to arrange with the parties to the conflict for the cease-fire to be implemented, and for the halting of the movement of military forces and arms into the area.[28] He was further requested, in conjunction with the United Nations Truce Supervision Organisation, to obtain the withdrawal of all forces behind the armistice lines [29]; later, he was requested to continue his efforts in this direction and to report on the completion of the withdrawal within five days.[30]

In the actual creation of the Force, the Secretary-General played a role of vital importance. He was requested by the General Assembly to submit to it a plan for the creation of an international Force to secure and supervise the cessation of hostilities in accordance with all the terms of the General Assembly's Resolutions.[31] It was on the basis of the two reports submitted by the Secretary-General,[32] and approved by the General Assembly,[33] that the Force was in fact modelled. The Second and Final Report is the document in which the Secretary-General discussed the principles behind a force of the type required to deal with the situation which had arisen in the Middle East, its functions, its essential characteristics, its size and organisation, and basic questions of finance and recruiting.

As to the type of Force which might be required, the Secretary-General observed that one of three different plans might be adopted.[34]

First, a force could be set up on the basis of the Charter principles. From this it would follow that its chief responsible officer should be

---

[28] Resol. 997 (ES–1), *Off. Rec. G.A.*, 1st Emergency Special Sess.
[29] Resol. 999 (ES–1).
[30] Resol. 1123 (XI): *Off. Rec. G.A.*, 11th Sess.
[31] Resol. 999 (ES–1): *ibid.*, 1st Emergency Special Sess., Suppl. No. 1 (A/3354), p. 2.
[32] First Report, *ibid.*, agenda item 5, doc. A/3289; Second Report, *ibid.*, A/3302.
[33] Resols. 1000 (ES–1); 1001 (ES–1).
[34] A/3302, para. 4.

appointed by, and be responsible to, one of the organs of the United Nations; his authority should make him independent of the policies of any one nation, particularly, of course, his own.

A second possibility would be to follow the policy which had been employed in the case of the United Nations Command in Korea.[35] This would mean that one country or a group of countries should be asked to provide an independent force to be used by the United Nations. The objection to this method was clearly that "it would be impossible to achieve the same independence in relation to national policies as would be established through the first approach."

A third possibility was to set up an international force by agreement among a group of countries which would later be brought under a proper relationship with the United Nations. This was an idea which was canvassed at one time, for there were forces which, being in Egypt, might be used in this way; that is, the Anglo-French armed forces, who were purportedly there for "police purposes," purposes for which an international force was required.

In fact, the General Assembly had already chosen the first of these alternatives, and the Secretary-General's further proposals consisted of ideas stemming from this choice. He pointed out that the terms of the Resolution on the United Nations Command, which authorised the Commander (or Chief of Command, as he was then entitled) to recruit officers from UNTSO or from Member States other than the Permanent Members of the Security Council, already demonstrated two main characteristics of the Force. They are, the independence of the Commander in the recruitment of officers, and the exclusion of the Five Great Powers from the composition of the Force.

Then follow several matters of principle which are derived from the previous acts of the General Assembly, and which have great significance in connection with the characteristics of the Force, its functions, and, when that was challenged, its constitutionality.

First, the Force is set up on an "emergency" basis; it is to be of a temporary nature and the length of its assignment is uncertain. Therefore, there is no intent in the creation of the Force to influence the military balance in the conflict, and, thereby, the political balance affecting efforts to settle the conflict.

Second, since the Force was to function on the basis of decisions reached by the General Assembly under the "Uniting for Peace" Resolution, there could be no *obligation* placed upon any Member State to take any action in connection with it. Its creation would be contingent upon the voluntary consent of States to contribute to it, but this would not authorise its employment in any State's territory. "While the General Assembly is enabled to *establish* the Force with the consent of those parties which contribute units to the Force, it would not request the Force to be *stationed* or operate on

[35] See Chap. 3, p. 40.

the territory of a given country without the consent of the government of that territory," for it was not an enforcement action.

It was for the Secretary-General to obtain the necessary consents from the contributing States,[36] from the States through which transit must be made,[37] and from the host States.[38]

As a further corollary to the fact that the Force was established by the General Assembly, and not by the Security Council acting under the provisions of Chapter VII of the Charter, the needs of the Force and its character need not be the same as those in which enforcement action was taken. Whilst the Force would need to be something different from a mere observation corps, like UNTSO, its nature would not be that of a force with military objectives, although it would be " para-military " in nature.[39]

Having approved the report, the General Assembly requested the Secretary-General to undertake appropriate measures to implement his plan. He was also invited to continue his discussions with Member States concerning offers of participation in the Force.[40]

The third period covered the activities of the Secretary-General in the operation of UNEF. The General Assembly delegated to him almost all its powers and responsibilities in the administrative and executive spheres,[41] contenting itself, when occasion demanded, with approving his actions. In some Resolutions, the Secretary-General was expressly asked to discuss with and to communicate with certain Members of the Organisation on particular matters. Further, he sometimes performed the task of interpreting the General Assembly Resolutions to governments. As a prime example of this, before the consent of Egypt to the entry of the Force, an exchange of views took place with its Government in which the Secretary-General gave his interpretation of the Resolutions of the Assembly concerning the character and functions of the Force, which explanations were accepted, and which led to an agreement with Egypt on the presence and the functioning of UNEF in Egypt.[42]

A most important function performed by the Secretary-General was the conclusion of agreements with States and other authorities. Not only did he enter into the agreements with the participating States and the host State, but the agreements regarding the withdrawal of the armed forces of the United Kingdom, France and Israel from Egypt, although actually entered into by the Commander of the Force, were made on the authority of the Secretary-General.

---

[36] *Post,* p. 111.
[37] *Post,* p. 136.
[38] *Post,* p. 124; and see *Summary Study, etc.* (A/3943), Annex 1.
[39] A/3302, paras. 6–10. For criticism of this term, see *post,* p. 328.
[40] Resol. 1001 (ES–1), para. 3; see *post,* p. 111.
[41] See further *post,* p. 118.
[42] *Report of the Secretary-General on Basic Points for the Presence and Functioning in Egypt of the United Nations Emergency Force.* November 20, 1956; A/3375; Annex: *Aide-mémoire on the Basis for Presence and Functioning of UNEF in Egypt.*

With regard to the host State, the Secretary-General concluded, by exchanges of letters, the Agreement on the presence and functioning of UNEF in Egypt,[43] and the subsequent and more formal Agreement on the Status of UNEF in Egypt.[44]

The legal arrangements made with the participating governments were also entered into by means of an exchange of letters between the Secretary-General (21 June 1957) and these governments.[45]

Arrangements were also made with other Member States concerning such matters as the air-lift of the Force to Egypt, supplies and equipment, and the right of air passage over national territories.[46]

The Agreement with Egypt on the Status of the Force was registered by the United Nations as a treaty, under the provisions of Article 102 of the Charter. The Secretary-General stated that the bilateral agreements which he entered into did not require ratification; nevertheless, the *Aide-mémoire* on the presence and functioning of UNEF in Egypt constituted an understanding with Egypt " when noted with approval " by the General Assembly.[47] Further, the Status Agreement was contained in a report of the Secretary-General to the General Assembly, which " noted with approval " the report.[48]

The Secretary-General has wide powers in relation to the internal affairs of the Force. In its Resolution 1001 (ES–1), the General Assembly authorised the Secretary-General to issue all regulations and instructions which may be essential to the effective functioning of the Force, in consultation with the Advisory Committee, and to take all other necessary administrative and executive action.[49]

In pursuance of this provision, the Secretary-General issued the Regulations for UNEF in February 1957.[50] The very fact that such authority is placed in the Secretary-General is illustrative of his superiority over the Commander, whose responsibility is, indeed, to the Secretary-General. The Regulations themselves underline this fact, as do the Resolutions of the General Assembly.

The latter body provided that the authority given to the Commander should be exercised in consultation with the Secretary-General; for example, his authority to undertake direct recruitment of officers for the United Nations Command,[51] and his authority to proceed to full organisation of the Force.[52]

The Regulations provide that the Commander has the power to issue command orders, but these are subject to review by the

[43] *Ibid.*
[44] *Report of the Secretary-General on Arrangements concerning the Status of the United Nations Emergency Force in Egypt*, 8 February 1957; A/3526, Annex. The agreements with the Lebanon on various matters were concluded by the Commander, see *post*, p. 138.
[45] Letter of 21 June 1957; A/3943, Annex 1.
[46] A/3943, para. 131.
[47] Resol. 1121 (X); and see A/3943, para. 133.
[48] A/3943, para. 134.
[49] Para. 7.
[50] ST/SGB/UNEF.1.
[51] Resol. 1000 (ES–1), para. 3.
[52] Resol. 1001 (ES–1), para. 4.

Secretary-General.[53] They also ordain that the Commander is to consult the Secretary-General in the prescription of uniform and insignia,[54] in the entire operation of the Force, and the provision of facilities, supplies and auxiliary services.[55] The Commander is to arrange with the Secretary-General for the recruitment of personnel from the United Nations Secretariat for service with the Force; during their service, although these persons are responsible to the Commander for the performance of their functions, they are still under the Secretary-General's authority.[56] The public information activities and relations with the Press and other media are under the responsibility of the Commander, but it is his duty to act in accordance with the policy laid down by the Secretary-General.[57] Finally, his authority to issue identity cards to members of the Force is exercisable under the authority of the Secretary-General.[58]

The Regulations specifically grant the Secretary-General authority for all administrative, executive, and financial matters.[59] In connection with the last, the Secretary-General was authorised by the General Assembly to establish a Special Account for the Force and to advance funds to it; he was also requested to establish rules and procedures for the Account and to make the necessary arrangements for its effective administration and control.[60]

The Advisory Committee

The Secretary-General's authority in its turn was made subject in some respects to consultation with the Advisory Committee. However, the Secretary-General was himself made Chairman of the Committee, which itself possessed no executive powers, but whose functions were purely advisory as its name indicates. More particularly, the Advisory Committee, which like UNEF was given the status of a subsidiary organ of the General Assembly, has the task of developing those aspects of the planning of the Force and its operation not dealt with by the General Assembly and which were not placed under the direct responsibility of the Commander, and the Secretary-General was obliged to consult the Committee when issuing regulations for the Force.[61] The Committee was empowered to request the convening of the General Assembly if matters should arise which, in its opinion, were of such importance and urgency as to require consideration by the Assembly.[62]

[53] Reg. 4.
[54] Reg. 8.
[55] Regs. 16, 21.
[56] Reg. 19 (b).
[57] Reg. 28.
[58] Reg. 36.
[59] Reg. 15.
[60] Resol. 1001 (ES–1), paras. 6 and 7. For details of financial administration, see A/3943, paras. 103–107. The financial Resolutions of the General Assembly in connection with UNEF all contain the grants of authority to the Secretary-General. See *post*, p. 142.
[61] Resol. 1001 (ES–1), paras. 6–8.   [62] *Ibid.*, para. 9.

In fact, this authority has never been invoked. The Committee has only met when matters have arisen which required discussion, or when the Secretary-General has required advice, or when he believed that it should receive information about the Force. The Committee was consulted more particularly on the questions indicated by the General Assembly, such as the Regulations for the Force, its policy with regard to self-defence, and the issue of medals for members.[63] It was also consulted on, and approved, the interpretation of the Assembly Resolutions which Egypt had required before agreeing to the entry of the Force and which the Secretary-General subsequently gave to Egypt.[64]

With the experience of the conduct of UNEF behind him, the Secretary-General was able to say that: " The Advisory Committee is fully informed. . . . There is a free exchange of views in closed meetings where advice can be sought and given. . . . Dissenting views are not registered by vote, but are put on record in the proceedings of the Committee." Nevertheless, he emphasised that " ultimate decisions rest with the Secretary-General, as the executive in charge of carrying out the operation." [65]

The powers expressly conferred upon him by the General Assembly gave the Secretary-General wide scope for the exercise of his administrative functions. This must needs be so, since it was obviously impossible for the General Assembly, or even a Committee thereof, to undertake the organisation and operation of such an exercise as UNEF; the Secretary-General is the chief administrative officer of the United Nations, and was the only functionary who could be entrusted with the job.[66] Once this was done, the Secretary-General's duties were to perform all the functions entrusted to him. But merely to brandish his powers would have availed the Secretary-General little in the case of UNEF, and the performance of his tasks called for the exercise of political acumen and diplomatic skill of a rare sort. The tasks placed within his responsibility by the General Assembly were essentially political, and his performance of them was the high watermark of Mr. Hammarskjold's political prestige.

But it must be emphasised, as the Secretary-General himself insisted, that the exceedingly wide trust reposed in him was, after all, a trust, with the limitation of scope that that concept implies. In other words, whatever the breadth of the field in which he could operate, legally his powers were circumscribed by the terms of his authority given by the General Assembly, whose powers are founded in the Charter and the " Uniting for Peace " Resolution; there could not be a total delegation of the Assembly's powers to the Secretary-General.[67]

---

[63] A/3943, para. 22.
[64] Rosner, *op. cit.*, p. 52.
[65] A/3943, para. 181.
[66] Charter, Arts. 97, 98.
[67] A/3943, para. 174.

IV. FUNCTIONS OF UNEF

Just as UNEF was a Force of a different type from the United Nations Command in Korea, so were its functions different. In the case of Korea, the main purpose was to drive the aggressor out of the invaded State and to restore the *status quo ante bellum*, but in the Middle East, although the restoration of the position before the Israeli attack on Egypt was the ultimate objective, the function of UNEF was to supervise the voluntary acceptance of the recommendations of the General Assembly by the States concerned. In this it was more akin to the United Nations Truce Supervision Organisation in Palestine than to the United Nations Command in Korea.

Yet, although UNEF was not a " belligerent " Force, it differed in both character and functions from UNTSO. When it first established the Force, the General Assembly stated that its objective in doing so was the " securing and supervising the cessation of hostilities in accordance with all the terms of Resolution 997 (ES–1) of 2 November 1956." [68] This Resolution called for a cease-fire, withdrawal of non-Egyptian forces from Egyptian territory, and the restoration of the observance of the Armistice Agreement between Egypt and Israel. As the Secretary-General stated later: " These objectives could not be achieved through an organisation similar in kind to UNTSO or to the Egyptian-Israel Mixed Armistice Commission, which had been established in other and different circumstances and were designed to meet different and narrower needs. The role of UNTSO is to observe and maintain the cease-fire in Palestine ordered by the Security Council. The Mixed Armistice Commission, serviced by UNTSO, is the bilateral machinery established under the Egyptian-Israel General Armistice Agreement in connection with the execution of the provisions of that Agreement, exercising such functions as the investigation of incidents and complaints." [69]

An attempt was made by the Secretary-General to give more precision to the stated objectives of the General Assembly in his Second and Final Report of 6 November 1956, although he stated that " It is difficult in the present situation and without further study to discuss [the question of functions] with any degree of precision." [70] However, he thought that Resolutions 1000 (ES–1) and 997 (ES–1) combined indicated that " the functions of the United Nations Force would be, when a cease-fire is being established, to enter Egyptian territory with the consent of the Egyptian Government, in order to help maintain quiet during and after the withdrawal of non-Egyptian troops, and to secure compliance with the other terms established in the Resolution of 2 November 1956." [71] Two years later, the Secretary-General emphasised that the Force had not been a fully military force, exercising " through force of arms, even temporary

[68] Resol. 1000 (ES–1), 5 November 1956.
[69] *Summary study, etc.* A/3943, para. 8.
[70] A/3302, para. 11.
[71] *Ibid.*, para. 12.

control over the territory in which it is stationed." It did not have military objectives, or military functions exceeding those necessary to secure peaceful conditions on the assumption that the parties to the conflict would take all the necessary steps for compliance with the General Assembly's recommendations.[72] The Force, as a subsidiary organ of the United Nations created by the General Assembly, in a sense was an extension of the functions of the General Assembly with respect to the pacific settlement of disputes, and not an instrument of enforcement.

The scope of the actual tasks undertaken by the Force in the field was determined by these principles; the purpose of UNEF was to see that the States concerned should abide by their undertakings to carry out the recommendations of the General Assembly. This was so in spite of the fact that in Resolution 997 (ES–1) the General Assembly had used the word " secure " as well as " supervise " in the statement of the basic purpose of the Force.[73] There was no intent, in using the Force, to influence the military balance in the conflict, and thereby the solution of the underlying political problems which bedevilled relations between Egypt and Israel and Egypt and the United Kingdom and France.[74]

It was, however, felt that the creation of peaceful conditions in the area required an avoidance of any repetition of the state of affairs into which conditions had deteriorated in previous years as a result of the failure by Egypt and Israel to implement the clauses of the Armistice Agreement.

It was difficult, of course, to foresee exactly what UNEF's employment might be until it had reached Egypt, for no one could have any prevision of how the respective parties to the conflict would implement their acceptance of the recommendations of the General Assembly. The initial function was to secure and supervise the cease-fire and the withdrawal of armed forces; Israel had agreed to disengage its armed forces and to withdraw them behind the Armistice Line and the International frontier, so here the Force had to follow the withdrawal of the Israeli forces. The United Kingdom and France had agreed to withdraw from the areas occupied by them in the neighbourhood of the Suez Canal. This meant that UNEF had to co-operate with those two States in securing an orderly withdrawal of their troops, and that it had to maintain order and security whilst the troops were leaving. It may be noted that the Force had no responsibility as regards the clearance of the Suez Canal, for this was an entirely separate United Nations operation.[75] After the fulfilment of its initial tasks, UNEF would have to maintain peaceful conditions

---

[72] A/3943, para. 15.
[73] The International Court of Justice was of opinion that this usage did not lead to the necessary conclusion that the General Assembly's establishment of the Force was " enforcement " action within the meaning of the Charter. *I.C.J. Reports* 1962, p. 170.
[74] A/3302, para. 8. See also A/3512, para. 29.
[75] Frye, *A United Nations Peace Force* (1957) p. 16; Rosner, *op. cit.*, pp. 73–76.

in the area by its deployment along the lines separating Egyptian and Israeli forces.

In the first phase of its operations,[76] the Force was placed between the Anglo-French and the Egyptian armed forces. It entered Port Said and Suez and undertook responsibility for the maintenance of order in co-operation with the local authorities. Guard duty was operated, but all administration and police functions were left to the responsibility of the Egyptian authorities the day after the Anglo-French withdrawal. Before the withdrawal was completed, the Force undertook all essential administrative functions with respect to the protection of civilian life and property, public services and utilities; it also investigated alleged breaches of the cease-fire, the whereabouts of missing persons, and allegations of smuggling. Mine-fields in the area about the Suez Canal were cleared, and the Force arranged for the exchange of prisoners and detainees between the opposing authorities.

In the Sinai peninsula the Force separated the Egyptian and Israeli armies. The Israelis withdrew in three stages ending on 22 January 1957, and the Sharm el Sheikh and Aqaba areas were evacuated in early March.[77] The Force performed similar functions in the wake of the Israeli forces in the Sinai area to those which it performed in the Suez Canal area.

The most problematical area was the Gaza Strip,[78] since it was here that most of the incidents leading up to the Israeli invasion in October 1956 had taken place, and it was here that a large number of Palestinian Arab refugees had been living since the war of 1948; the Strip was still a large source of contention between Egypt and Israel, and the Force might take no action which might affect the juridical status of the Armistice Agreement.

Within the Gaza Strip, the action took place in two stages; the first consisted of the withdrawal of Israeli troops and the simultaneous entry of the Force. After this, pending the re-establishment of civilian authority in the area, many of the local responsibilities were borne by UNEF.[79] However, the plan that the United Nations should assume the responsibility for civil administration of the Gaza Strip (which was the assumption on which the Israeli forces had been withdrawn) was not fulfilled. The population of the Strip was organised into an opposition to any United Nations administration and Egypt actively opposed it by appointing an Egyptian Governor of

[76] A/3943, para. 53–59.
[77] The history of these problems, and of the negotiations which led to eventual Israeli withdrawal, is described in detail by Rosner, *op. cit.*, pp. 92–97.
[78] *Ibid.*, pp. 76–92.
[79] Much of the opposition to UNEF'S entry into the Gaza Strip was based on the notion that the UN should not, and could not, become the actual administrator of territory: see *Off. Rec. G.A.*, 11th Sess., Plen. 638th Mtg., pp. 892–893. But see post, pp. 255–261 for the establishment of UNTEA with precisely this function.

Gaza, so that the plan for a temporary civil administration never became operative.[80]

This particular phase of the operations is particularly instructive in that it indicates the inherent deficiencies of the United Nations machinery in a situation of this kind. Clear instructions on exactly what administrative measures were to be taken were not apparently given (had they been there would probably have been intense opposition by Egypt and the Soviets); moreover the Force had no power to assume a police role and imprison the instigators of the opposition to United Nations administration, for its use of force was confined to self-defence and UNEF's reaction to rioters was therefore hesitant and ineffective. Moreover the United Nations had no jurisdiction over these civilians and could neither detain nor punish them. The plan might have been feasible had the United Nations received the full co-operation of the Egyptian Government and the local populace: in the face of their opposition it was doomed to failure. It affords an interesting contrast with the successful administration of UNTEA dealt with in Chapter 7.

The second phase [81] of the operation consisted in the re-establishment of the lines behind which the two sides had been positioned before the conflict broke out. The General Assembly had resolved that " the scrupulous maintenance of the Armistice Agreement requires the placing of the United Nations Emergency Force on the Egyptian-Israel armistice demarcation line and the implementation of other measures as proposed in the Secretary-General's report,[82] with due regard to the considerations set out therein with a view to assist in achieving situations conducive to the maintenance of peaceful conditions in the area." [83] So the Force was deployed along the Armistice Demarcation Line around the Gaza Strip, and, further to the south, along the International boundary. The Force, which was mainly concerned with the prevention of infiltrations through the lines, was used in patrol and reconnaissance work to avoid such incidents and generally to maintain quiet.

Throughout the entire operation troops serving with UNEF had the right to fire, but only in self-defence; they were instructed never to take the initiative in the use of arms, but they might respond with fire to an armed attack upon themselves from any quarter.[84]

One question which arose once the Force had taken up its

---

[80] For a full account of the events in Gaza during the period of the Israeli evacuation and the entry of UNEF, see Rosner, *op. cit.*, pp. 85–92; Burns, *op. cit.*, Chaps. 17, 18; Ruth Russell, *UN Experience with Military Forces: Political and Legal Aspects*, Institute for Defence Analyses, Research Paper P. 27, May 1963, pp. 73–84.

[81] A/3943, paras. 60–74.

[82] A/3512.

[83] Resol. 1125 (XI), 2 February 1957. The vague terms of this Resolution concealed a wide margin of disagreement on the actual functions which UNEF was to assume and the duration of these functions; it was left to the Secretary-General to proceed on the basis of his own discretion.

[84] A/3943, p. 31.

positions along the Armistice Demarcation Line was the scope of its responsibilities vis-à-vis those of the Mixed Armistice Commission and UNTSO. The Israeli Government took the view that their own actions had deprived the Armistice Agreement of any effect, but the United Nations refused to accept this argument, and the Chairman of the Egyptian-Israel Mixed Armistice Commission and the UNTSO military observers continued at their posts throughout. When the Israeli forces had been withdrawn, arrangements were made for the placing of the Mixed Armistice Commission under the operational control of the Commander of UNEF, who was, of course, Chief of Staff of UNTSO. Upon the appointment in March 1958 of a new Chief of Staff for UNTSO, it was decided that the Commander of UNEF would continue to exercise his functions as Chief of Staff in respect of the Armistice Agreement, that is, as Chairman of the Mixed Commission. The Israel Government, in view of its thesis that the Armistice had lapsed, continued thereafter to lodge its complaints with UNEF, but UNEF maintained in its turn that official investigations of incidents could only be carried out through the Mixed Armistice Commission.[85]

V. RELATIONS BETWEEN THE UNITED NATIONS AND PARTICIPATING STATES

1. *Composition and recruitment of the Force*

Although it was the General Assembly which ordained the creation of the Force, this could not be implemented without the consent and co-operation of Member States. The difficulties which had to be overcome in the case of UNEF were not encountered in the securing of this consent, for many Member States did in fact make offers of contingents for employment by the United Nations; rather did they lie in the selection of States whose offers might be acceptable. It was essential, if the character of UNEF as an international force was to be secured, that the ultimate power of recruitment should lie with the United Nations itself, or with one of its officials.

In the field of recruitment this principle was established in the terms by which the General Assembly appointed the Chief of Command (later, Commander) of the Force, for he was authorised to recruit his staff from the officers serving with UNTSO or from Member States directly.[86] Subsequently, recruitment of contingents from amongst Member States was undertaken by the Secretary-General by means of direct negotiation with the governments of Member States.

In the same Resolution the General Assembly also established the rule that the Force should not contain any members of the nationality of any of the five States having permanent representation on the

[85] A/3943, paras. 72–74; and A/3512, p. 48.
[86] Resol. 1000 (ES–1), paras. 2, 3.

Security Council. This was necessary not only because two of them, the United Kingdom and France, were implicated in the events which had made the establishment of UNEF expedient, but also to prevent the Force being dogged by "Cold War" politics. This principle the Secretary-General observed when asking for offers of contingents from Member States.

The Secretary-General's entire freedom of choice in the matter might be further circumscribed by other factors. A prime influence would be the agreement or otherwise of Egypt to the inclusion of contingents from particular States. Since Egypt had given her consent to the entry of the Force upon its territory, it might be thought that this would be sufficient to leave the matter entirely in the hands of the Secretary-General; nevertheless, the whole operation was limited by the requirement of Egypt's consent, and, in the event of an Egyptian objection, her representations must, for reasons of prudence, be taken into account lest Egypt should withdraw her consent to the entire enterprise. Thus, the Secretary-General said later:

"The choice of contingents for the Force, while subject to the decision of the United Nations alone, is nevertheless of major concern also to the country in which the Force operates. Thus, the United Nations must give most serious consideration to the views of the host government on such matters without, however, surrendering its right to take a serious difference, should one develop, to the political level for resolution. In the experience of UNEF, this latter course has not been necessary, since no impasse has ever developed in this area." [87]

Objections were raised by the Egyptians (which were deferred to by the Secretary-General) to only three of the States which volunteered contingents, all three members of the Commonwealth. In the case of Canada, which had offered both a contingent and several supporting units, the latter were accepted, but it was requested that the former should be kept in reserve, as a consequence of the representation by the Egyptians that the resemblance of Canadians to British soldiers might be taken amiss by the Egyptian populace; and the offer of Pakistan to provide a contingent was refused on the ground that certain statements made by Pakistani leaders *à propos* of the Suez Canal dispute might make Pakistani contingents unacceptable to the government of the host State.[88] New Zealand's offer was declined for a similar reason.

In addition to the principle that members of the Force should not be drawn from the Big Five Powers—a principle described by the Secretary-General as "both sound and practical" [89]—other considerations taken into account in the selection of national contingents were the need for an operationally balanced Force with adequate supporting units, and, on political grounds, a well-distributed geographical representation.[90] Here it was necessary to avoid recruiting from

[87] A/3943, para. 16.
[88] Goodrich and Rosner, "The United Nations Emergency Force" (1957) 11 *International Organisation* 424.
[89] A/3943, para. 44.   [90] *Ibid.*

States either having too close an affiliation with the leading antagonists in the Cold War, or from too many States having a close political alliance, since a combination between them leading to the withdrawal of their forces might ruin the whole enterprise. Further consideration was given to contingents in terms of their availability, especially the extent to which they would be self-contained, equipped, and could be conveniently transported to Egypt.

Before the General Assembly passed the Resolution which established UNEF, the Secretary-General had entered into informal consultation with several governments for contributions to a possible United Nations Force, and, in his First Report to the General Assembly on a plan for such a Force,[91] he was able to report a favourable response from three States. Between November and December 1956, offers of assistance, mostly of infantry units, were received from twenty-four States, some of whom offered other forms of assistance, as did other Member States who did not offer contingents.[92]

In the result, contingents for the Force and supporting units were provided by ten States: Brazil, Canada, Colombia, Denmark, Finland, India, Indonesia, Norway, Sweden and Yugoslavia.

In the interest of efficiency, supporting units were each composed of troops of a single nationality. The Supply Depot and the Service Institute were provided by the Indians, who with Canada also supplied the Provost Marshal and the Signals Units. Norway contributed Medical Units, and Canada Dental and Medical Units, the Ordnance Depot and Workshop, the Base Post Office, Engineers, Movement Control and Air Support.[93]

Within the national contingents rather frequent periodic rotation of troops was the practice. This was dictated by national terms of military service, the nature of the mission, conditions of weather and terrain, and considerations of morale and efficiency, since it was impossible at the outset to determine or foresee the duration of the mission of UNEF. Schedules of rotation were fixed by the participating governments in consultation with the Commander, so as to ensure continuity and to protect the Force from being undermanned.[94]

At the peak of its strength the Force consisted of about 6,000 officers and men.[95]

2. Agreements with the participating States

In the middle of 1957, in order to put the relations between the United Nations and the participating States on a more formal footing, most of the participating States entered into basic agreements with

[91] A/3298, para. 2.
[92] A/3302 and Annexes; A/3943, para. 45. The States offering contributions were: Afghanistan, Brazil, Burma, Canada, Ceylon, Chile, Colombia, Czecho-slovakia, Denmark, Ecuador, Ethiopia, Finland, Indonesia, Iran, India, Laos, New Zealand, Norway, Pakistan, Peru, Philippines, Roumania, Sweden, Yugoslavia.   [93] A/3943, para. 47.
[94] Ibid., paras. 48–49.   [95] Ibid., para. 45.

the Organisation through the medium of the Secretary-General. These agreements were constituted by exchanges of letters; the Secretary-General transmitted identical letters to each of the States, and these, with their replies, were deemed to constitute Agreements.[96]

With the Secretary-General's letter were enclosed copies of the Agreement with Egypt on the Status of the Force,[97] and the Regulations issued for the Force by the Secretary-General after consultation with the Advisory Committee.[98] The Agreements must therefore be read in conjunction with these two documents, since acceptance of them is a requisite of acceptance of the Agreements.

The Secretary-General's letter recalls [99] the guiding principles for the organisation and functioning of the Force set out in his Second and Final Report to the General Assembly,[1] and the definition of the functions of the Force as approved by the General Assembly.[2] The participating States are reminded of the affirmation in the Force's regulations of its character as an international Force, and that their contingents serve with the Force in that character.[3]

Particular reference is made to the question of the exercise of criminal jurisdiction over the Force. This, as will be seen,[4] is taken out of the competence of the host State on the understanding that the participating States will undertake to exercise their own criminal jurisdiction over members of their own national contingents. It is assumed that the participating governments will act accordingly.[5]

Further, in view of the provision in the UNEF regulations concerning the maintenance of good order and discipline within the national contingents,[6] under the general responsibility of the Commander of the Force for good order, the commanders of the national contingents are to have direct responsibility for members of the force serving under them. Participating States are required to ensure that their commanders have the necessary disciplinary powers, and the governments are to intimate that they are prepared to exercise the necessary jurisdiction.[7]

---

[96] For the text of the Secretary-General's letter, see A/3943, Annex 1. For the replies, see U.N.T.S., No. 3966, Vol. 274, p. 199 (Brazil); No. 3957, Vol. 274, p. 41 (Canada); No. 3959, Vol. 274, p. 81 (Denmark); No. 3913, Vol. 271, p. 135 (Finland); No. 3968, Vol. 274, p. 233 (India); No. 3917, Vol. 271, p. 223 (Norway); No. 3914, Vol. 271, p. 187 (Sweden); No. 4006, Vol. 277, p. 191 (Yugoslavia); Colombia and Indonesia sent no reply, and later withdrew their contingents.
[97] A/3526; see *post*, p. 125.
[98] ST/SGB./UNEF.1 : see *post*, p. 119.
[99] Para. 2.
[1] A/3302, paras. 6–10 : see *ante*, p. 100.
[2] *Ibid.*, paras. 11, 12, and see *ante*, p. 105; the approval of the General Assembly was given in Resol. 1001 (ES–1).
[3] See *post*, p. 122.
[4] See *post*, p. 132.
[5] Para. 5.
[6] Reg. 13.
[7] Para. 7.

A most important clause in the Agreements is that which concerns the withdrawal of contingents by participating governments. One of the dangers which the United Nations had to guard against was that any one State might be able to exercise an untoward control of the employment of the Force as a whole by threats to withdraw its contingent altogether. This was partially avoided by the principle of having the different national contingents of a similar size, so that there could be no disproportionate contingents from any one State whose withdrawal might effectively paralyse any action by the remaining contingents, and by drawing the national contingents from various States not in the same complex of political interests, so far as this was possible. Nevertheless, the danger remained that a group of States might withdraw their contingents suddenly, or that one State might do so without notice, so impeding the ability of the Commander in his freedom to plan the course of operations.

Therefore, the participating States agree that they will not withdraw their contingents without prior notification, and the United Nations, for its part, agrees that if any particular national contingent is not required further, notification to the State concerned will be given, and consultation between it and the Secretary-General will be undertaken.[8] However, certain of the governments contributing contingents had made clear that they did not regard the Force as being constituted indefinitely,[9] so that it remained open how far it remained possible for a participating State to make its own determination that the Force had completed its task and to decide to withdraw its contingent.

Whilst the contingents are serving with UNEF, any changes in their contingents must be made in consultation between the Commander of UNEF and the appropriate authorities of the participating States.[10]

In the event of any dispute between the parties arising out of the interpretation or application of the Agreement, it is to be referred to a tribunal of three members, one to be appointed by each of the parties, and an umpire by both parties jointly. In the event of disagreement and failure to appoint the umpire within three months, the President of the International Court of Justice may be asked by either party to undertake the task of appointment. Vacancies in the tribunal are to be filled by the method laid down for the original appointments. A quorum is constituted by two members, and the concurring votes of two members on a particular matter are sufficient for a majority. Whereas the rest of the Agreement terminates upon the departure of the national contingents, the provisions regarding the

---

[8] Para. 8. Indonesia withdrew its contingent on 12 September 1957, Finland on 5 December 1957, and Colombia on 28 October 1958.
[9] See the Swedish letter of 5 November 1956 (A/3302, Annex 7, p. 23) and the Indonesian reservation in *Off. Rec. G.A.*, 11th Sess., Plen. Mtg., 649th Mtg., 1 February 1957.
[10] Para. 9.

settlement of disputes are to continue in force until after all outstanding disputes have been settled.[11]

Questions concerning the allocation of expenses between the participating States and the United Nations were left to be dealt with in a supplementary agreement.[12]

No provision is made in the letter for ratification of the Agreements. They were registered with the United Nations, pursuant to Article 102 of the Charter.[13] Since the Agreements were not entered into until some considerable time after the departure of the national contingents for Egypt, they are made to operate retrospectively to that time. They remain in force until the date of the departure of the contingents from Egypt for their own States.[14]

3. *Powers of the participating States*

So long as their contingents remain under United Nations Command, the powers of the participating States are limited. They have no say in the political or strategic direction of the operation, nor in the command of their troops in the field, for their contingents may only take orders from the General Assembly, which are channelled via the Secretary-General and the Chain of Command.[15]

The powers of the States are, in sum, confined to the area of personnel matters. The recruitment of members of their contingents is in their hands; they may place regular units of their armies or special volunteer units at the disposal of the United Nations. They may withdraw a particular unit or replace the commanders of their units, although they may only do so by giving notice to the Commander and in consultation with him.[16] During their service with UNEF, the members of the Force remain in the service of their home States,[17] and commanders of contingents may communicate with their governments in personnel matters affecting their units. Promotions in rank for members of the Force remain the responsibility of the participating governments,[18] as does responsibility for pay,[19] and benefits and compensation payable under municipal laws for death, injury or illness suffered by members of the Force on service with UNEF.[20]

In respect of disciplinary matters, members of the Force are subject to their own military laws and regulations,[21] and the national contingents have the power of arrest over their members.[22] And, of

[11] Para. 12.
[12] Para. 10. *Post*, p. 139.
[13] *Ante*, p. 102.
[14] Para. 11.
[15] ST/SGB/UNEF.1. Reg. 12.
[16] *Ibid.* Agreement with participating States, para. 9.
[17] Reg. 6.
[18] Reg. 43.
[19] Reg. 38.
[20] Reg. 40. And see *post*, pp. 141, 369.
[21] Reg. 34 (c).
[22] Reg. 14.

course, criminal jurisdiction resides entirely with the participating States, to the exclusion of any other authority.

VI. COMMAND STRUCTURE

In its Resolution of 5 November 1956, the General Assembly appointed as the Chief of Command (later, Commander) of the Force, the Chief of Staff of the United Nations Truce Supervision Organisation, Major- (later Lieut.-) General E. L. M. Burns of Canada, who was authorised to recruit, in consultation with the Secretary-General, officers to serve in the Force.[23] The General Assembly soon afterwards requested the Commander to proceed forthwith to the full organisation of the Force.[24]

Unlike the procedure adopted in Korea,[25] this early established the principle that the Commander of UNEF should be appointed by, and therefore be responsible to, the General Assembly, and not be appointed by and answerable to any one Member State. This principle was stated by the Secretary-General in the following terms: "The authority of the Commander should be so defined as to make him fully independent of the policies of any one nation." [26]

The Commander is not only the leader of the Force, responsible, under the Secretary-General, for the day-to-day administration of the Force, but he is also a representative of the United Nations and is the principal agent of the Secretary-General within the area of his command.[27] He enjoys the privileges and immunities of a diplomatic agent.[28]

The functions of the Commander are the supervision of the operations of UNEF and the oversight of its other activities.[29] To this end he is given the power to issue orders not inconsistent with the Resolutions of the General Assembly, which are the foundation of his powers, and these orders may be subject to review by the Secretary-General.[30]

The authority of the Commander over the Force is of the widest kind: it is stated in Chapter III of the Regulations for the Force.[31] Generally, he possesses "full command authority over the Force," with full operational responsibility for the performance of all functions assigned to it by the United Nations, and for the deployment and assignment of the troops at his disposal.[32] He is

---

[23] Resol. 1000 (ES–1) A/3289. In 1959 Lieut.-Gen. Burns was succeeded by Major-General P. S. Gyani of India: Resol. 1442 (XIV).
[24] Resol. 1001 (ES–1), 7 November 1956, A/3354, para. 4.
[25] See *ante*, Chap. 3, p. 40.
[26] *Second and Final Report, etc.*, 6 November 1956, A/3302, para. 4.
[27] *Summary Study, etc.*, A/3943, paras. 76, 77.
[28] *Post*, p. 119.
[29] A/3943, para. 75.
[30] Regulations for the United Nations Emergency Force: ST/SGB/UNEF.1, Reg. 4.
[31] *Ibid.*
[32] Reg. 11.

responsible for good order and discipline throughout the Force, and reports on disciplinary action are to be communicated to him.[33] He is responsible for seeing that members of the Force observe due respect for the local law.[34] The Commander provides for military police in the premises occupied by the Force, and for areas where the Force is deployed in the performance of its functions. In their turn, the military police possess the power of arrest over all members of the Force.[35]

In the performance of his duties the Commander is assisted by the Military Staff Organisation. This originally consisted of officers recruited by the Commander from the staff of UNTSO and those recruited by him direct from Member States. Later, it was composed of officers selected from each of the contingents serving with UNEF. It is headed by the Chief of Staff, who acts for the Commander in the latter's absence. There are three sections of this Headquarters Staff: (1) Personnel; (2) Operations; and (3) Logistics, and a special staff of specialised officers to advise and assist the Commander.[36]

Beneath the Commander extends the chain of command. The regulations provide that the Commander:

". . . shall designate the chain of command for the Force, making use of the officers of the United Nations Command and the commanders of the national contingents made available by participating governments. He may delegate his authority through the chain of command. He has authority with respect to all assignments of members of the United Nations Command, and of members of the Force through the chain of command." [37]

The Commander and his chain of command alone have the power to issue instructions to members of the Force concerning the performance of their functions as a Force.[38]

The other end of the chain of command is provided by the national contingents, whose commanders themselves are members of the designated chain of command. The national contingents retain their separate national identities and organisational unities; each contingent is under the command of its own officers.

The commanders of the national contingents have disciplinary powers over members of their contingents,[39] and each contingent's military police has the power to arrest its own members.[40] The disciplinary power is subordinate to the general responsibility of the Commander for good order, and the power of arrest is shared with the military police created by the Commander. But the national

---

[33] Reg. 13.
[34] Reg. 6.
[35] Reg. 14. This refers to the Military Police established by the Commander, as distinct from the Military Police of any one particular contingent whose rights of arrest are confined to their own contingent.
[36] *Summary Study, etc.,* A/3943, para. 70.
[37] Reg. 12.
[38] Reg. 31.
[39] Reg. 13. In the Agreements between the participating States and the UN, the former guarantee their willingness to exercise their disciplinary powers over their own contingents: A/3943, Annex 1, paras. 6, 7.
[40] Reg. 14.

commanders have powers of punishment which are not available to the Commander of the Force. For " to confer such authority upon the Commander would probably require specific legislation in most participating States." [41]

Although, within their spheres of command, the commanders of the contingents may give orders, and although they are free to communicate with their own governments in personnel matters, they must, in turn, take their orders from the Commander, through whom they may be transmitted from the Secretary-General and from the General Assembly, and they may not receive instructions from their governments in matters falling within the domain of the Commander of the Force.[42]

On occasion a particular national contingent may undertake more than one task, and when this happens the different sections of the contingent will have their own commander.[43]

It has been the practice of some participating States to appoint " liaison officers " at UNEF Headquarters. These officers do not form part of UNEF, nor are they placed under the authority of the Commander. The difficulties arising from the existence of these persons are summarised by the Secretary-General in his Summary Study of October 1958.[44]

VII. STRATEGIC AND POLITICAL CONTROL

The ultimate strategic and political control over UNEF lies with the General Assembly, which has the ultimate power of dissolution of the Force. The host State has no powers over the Force, except in the sense that its consent was required to its entry and its wishes were taken into account in the selection of the States who were invited by the Secretary-General to provide contingents.[45] In Korea, the main control over the Force was vested by the United Nations in one State, and, whereas the President of the United States of America was able to dismiss the Commander of the United Nations Force, in the case of UNEF only the General Assembly could do so,[46] the participating States having no powers in this respect.

In fact, the General Assembly has delegated many of its powers in this respect to the Secretary-General, who is really responsible for the military planning.[47] In the sphere of strategic control, he was assisted by a group of military representatives of countries which contributed troops to the Force, and who sat as a military advisory committee at United Nations Headquarters at the start of the operation. The group was chaired by a Major-General appointed as

[41] A/3943, para. 139
[42] *Ibid.*, para. 79.
[43] *Ibid.*, para. 80.
[44] *Ibid.*, para. 82.
[45] See *ante*, p. 110.
[46] See Chap. 3, p. 44.
[47] For an account of the Secretary-General's duties, see *ante*, p. 99.

personal adviser to the Secretary-General, and provided assistance and expert planning on all military matters connected with UNEF.[48] Once the operation was established, these arrangements were reduced and simplified.

In the sphere of political control, apart from the direction of the Assembly itself, the Secretary-General was assisted by the Advisory Committee created by General Assembly Resolution 1001 (ES–1).[49] Hence, subject to the overriding control of the Assembly, the Secretary-General was in effect both the political and the strategic directorate of the Force, for the military planning group and the Advisory Committee were no more than advisory.

VIII. ADMINISTRATIVE ARRANGEMENTS

1. *Functions of the Secretariat*

The Secretary-General has full overall authority for the administrative, executive and financial matters affecting the Force,[50] and although direct operational responsibility and the day-to-day administration of the Force lies with the Commander, there are certain matters within his province in which he has to work in consultation with the Secretary-General.[51]

Administrative responsibility was given to the Secretary-General in order to ensure that the operation would be carried out in a manner consistent with the established practices of the United Nations. He assigned senior Secretariat officials to assist the Commander in the discharge of his administrative responsibilities, and three categories of Secretariat Staff have served with the Force: (1) Officers, such as the Chief Administrative Officer, who had responsibility for the application of United Nations rules and procedures. This officer reported directly to the Commander, but has had contact directly with United Nations Headquarters. He is assisted by a Chief Procurement Officer, Finance Officer and Personnel Officer; (2) Officials like the Legal Adviser, and the Public Information Officer, both of them on the staff of the Chief Administrative Officer, but working with the Commander; (3) Persons who provide services not readily available from military sources, or requiring special training or knowledge; for instance, the Field Operations Service provides communications and security officials.[52]

2. *Functions of the Commander*

As stated above, actual day-to-day administration is in the hands of the Commander.[53] In the performance of his functions he " operates under the instructions and guidance of the Secretary-General on the

[48] *Summary Study, etc.*, A/3943, paras. 31, 182.
[49] See *ante*, p. 103.
[50] ST/SGB/UNEF.1. Reg. 15.
[51] *Ante*, p. 102.
[52] *Summary Study, etc.*, A/3943, paras. 84–85.
[53] Reg. 16.

basis of executive responsibility for the operation entrusted to him by the Assembly.   In practice, from the inception of the Force, the Commander has functioned as the principal agent of the Secretary-General, in the area of operation, within the limits of his post." [54] In particular, the Regulations give the Commander certain powers which he must only exercise in consultation with the Secretary-General.[55]

The Regulations state that the Commander is to establish the Force Headquarters, operational centres and liaison offices,[56] to recruit officers for the Command from Member States, and local personnel as required.[57]   He is also responsible for the provision of food, accommodation and amenities, transportation, supplies, equipment, communications, maintenance, and medical, dental and sanitary services.[58]   In the performance of his functions the Commander may enter into contracts and make commitments binding on the United Nations.[59]

3. *Joint civilian-military organisation*

Thus, the administrative arrangements for UNEF are in the hands of a joint military and civilian administration.

The two sides of the activities of the Force are each represented in the person of the Commander, who is the only officer who operates essentially in each of the capacities, military and civil. Direction of operations is in the hands of the military officers, and the civilian officers, who are not, strictly speaking, " members of the Force," run the purely administrative activities of the Force. Occasionally there has been friction, because the areas of respective responsibility cannot always be rigidly demarcated, and in some of the tasks the two aspects are inextricably mixed.   Thus, slight difficulties have arisen in matters of personnel, maintenance and construction, welfare programmes, rotation of contingents, and relations with the various interested governments.   More likely sources of dispute are the fields of logistics, finance and accounting, radio communication and so on.   The Secretary-General has stated that " with regard to senior officers on the civilian side and staff officers on the military side, it may be said that too frequent rotation has been a hindrance to the development and consolidation of maximum efficiency in administration." [60]

IX. THE REGULATIONS FOR UNEF

The internal regulations for UNEF were drawn up by the Secretary-General, acting in consultation with the Advisory Committee, under

---

[54] A/3943, para. 76.
[55] *Ante*, p. 102.
[57] Reg. 19 (a) (c).
[59] Reg. 27.

[56] Reg. 17.
[58] Regs. 20–26.
[60] A/3943, para. 87.

powers conferred on him by the General Assembly,[61] and were promulgated on 21 February 1957,[62] to be effective from 1 March 1957.[63] They were accepted by the participating States in their Agreements with the United Nations from the following June onwards,[64] as regulating the conduct of their own nationals serving with the Force in Egypt.

The Regulations provide that they may be amended or revised in the same way as they were made, and that with respect to matters not delegated to the Commander the Secretary-General may issue supplementary regulations.[65] It is also provided that, subject to review by the Secretary-General, the Commander may issue command orders to the Force not inconsistent with General Assembly Resolutions or the Regulations themselves, either in the discharge of his duties as Commander of the Force, or in implementation or explanation of the Regulations.[66]

Many of the provisions of the Regulations are similar to the terms of the Status Agreement with Egypt,[67] for instance, the Regulation regarding respect for the local law and conduct befitting the international status of members of the Force whilst in Egypt,[68] and the arrangements with regard to jurisdiction and settlement of claims contained in the Agreement appear in abbreviated form in the Regulations.[69] So, also, there are parallel provisions regarding the United Nations flag, uniform and insignia and the markings to be carried by equipment used by the Force.[70]

The other provisions are those which are of purely domestic concern to the Force and its relationship with the United Nations and the participating States. Examples of such provisions are those dealing with the administrative, executive and financial arrangements,[71] those concerned with the international legal protection of the United Nations,[72] the reception of instructions and their non-communication,[73] pay,[74] the proscription of the attendance without permission of dependants of members of the Force,[75] leave and promotion.[76]

---

[61] Resol. 1001 (ES–1), para. 7.
[62] ST/SGB/UNEF.1.
[63] Reg. 1.
[64] *Ante*, p. 102.
[65] Regs. 2, 3.
[66] Reg. 4.
[67] A/3526, *post*, p. 125.
[68] Reg. 29; Status Agreement, para. 6.
[69] Reg. 34; Status Agreement, paras. 10-12
[70] Regs. 7–9; Status Agreement, paras. 19–21.
[71] Chapter VI of the Regulations, 15–28.
[72] Reg. 30.
[73] Regs. 31–32.
[74] Reg. 38.
[75] Reg. 41.
[76] Regs. 42, 43.

Most of the provisions of the Regulations are discussed elsewhere, but one important provision of the Regulations which requires mention here is Regulation 44 which reads:

"The Force shall observe the principles and spirit of the general international Conventions applicable to the conduct of military personnel."

The rules of customary international law on the laws of war can scarcely be applied to the operations of UNEF since the Force, although it is composed of military persons, is not an instrument of war and its functions and operations are the reverse of warlike; and although its members bear arms, these are solely for use in self-defence, not attack. Nor, it is thought, would the Geneva Conventions of 1949 be applicable *eo nomine* in the present case, since the conditions under which they come into operation do not exist.[77] This Regulation may, therefore, be considered as an *ad hoc* extension of the appropriate provisions of the Conventions to the situation and a reminder of the basic characteristics of the laws of war and the Conventions, namely, that action by military persons should be carried out according to the dictates of chivalry and humanity.

X. UNEF AS A UNITED NATIONS INTERNATIONAL FORCE

One of the fundamental characteristics of UNEF is that it is a United Nations Force, and is neither a Force representing the interests of the national States contributing members to it, nor one which can be used as an instrument of its policies by the host State. This principle is reflected throughout the Status Agreement with Egypt [78] and the Regulations for the Force,[79] both of which documents have been accepted by the participating States.[80] It is also reflected in the relationship between the Force and the General Assembly, which created it, and the Secretary-General, as the Chief Administrative Officer of the United Nations.[81]

The Force is a subsidiary organ of the United Nations, in particular of the General Assembly. This appears to be the best way of describing the situation, for the Force is stated in the Status Agreement to be an "organ of the General Assembly," [82] and in the Regulations to be "a subsidiary organ of the United Nations . . . established by General Assembly Resolution 1000 (ES–1). . . ." [83] The Force consists of the United Nations Command and all military personnel placed under the Command by Member States.

---

[77] See generally *post*, pp. 507–511.
[78] A/3526, *post*, p. 125.
[79] ST/SGB/UNEF.1.
[80] See *ante*, p. 112.
[81] Charter, Art. 97.
[82] A/3526: see the 1st paragraph of the letter from the Secretary-General to the Foreign Minister of Egypt which precedes the terms of the Agreement.
[83] Reg. 6. The UN may establish such subsidiary organs as may be found necessary in accordance with the Charter: Charter, Art. 7. The General Assembly's power is contained in Art. 22.

The Force enjoys the privileges and immunities of the Organisation in accordance with the Charter [84] and the Convention on the Privileges and Immunities of the United Nations [85]; the members of the Command are, for that purpose, considered as experts on mission for the Organisation.[86] Further, for the purpose of international legal protection, all the members of the Force are entitled to the international legal protection of the United Nations, which means that for this purpose they are assimilated to agents of the Organisation.[87]

International control and international responsibility in respect of the Force as against the possible rival claims of the host State or the participating States are secured in the various Agreements and Regulations. As far as operational control is concerned, it is clear that the host State is in no position to give orders to the members of the Force and cannot dictate to the Commander the tasks upon which the Force is to be employed. It is in the Regulations of the Force that its independence of the participating States is most clearly affirmed, and these are supported by the Agreement with the participating States, paragraph 4 of which expressly states:

"The Regulations . . . affirm the international character of the Force, a subsidiary organ of the General Assembly, and define the conditions of service for the members of the Force. National contingents provided for UNEF serve under these Regulations."

Chapter II of the Regulations contains the provision dealing with the international character of the Force, and its uniform, insignia, and privileges and immunities. In the provision dealing with "international character" [88] it is asserted that:

"The members of the Force, although remaining in their national service are, during the period of their assignment to the Force, international personnel under the authority of the United Nations and subject to the instructions of the Commander through the chain of command. The functions of the Force are exclusively international and members of the Force shall discharge these functions and regulate their conduct with the interest of the United Nations only in view."

This statement is supplemented by those provisions of the Regulations dealing with the chain of command and the giving of instructions. The Commander has full command authority over the Force and is responsible for the performance of all the functions assigned to the Force by the United Nations, and for the deployment and assignment of the troops making up the national contingents.[89] In two most important Regulations it is secured that:

[84] Art. 105.
[85] U.N.T.S., Vol. I, p. 15.
[86] See further *post*, p. 130.
[87] Reg. 30; for the right of international protection of its agents vested in the UN, see the *Advisory Opinion of the I.C.J. concerning Reparation for Injuries Suffered in the Service of the United Nations, I.C.J. Reports, 1949,* p. 185.
[88] Reg. 6.
[89] Reg. 11.

" In the performance of their duties for the Force the members of the Force shall receive their instructions only from the Commander and the chain of command designated by him " [90]

and that :

" Members of the Force shall exercise the utmost discretion in regard to all matters relating to their duties and functions. They shall not communicate to any person any information known to them by reason of their position with the Force which has not been made public, except in the course of their duties or by authorisation of the Commander."

The latter duty of discretion and non-communication of information does not cease upon the termination of the members' assignment to the Force, that is, upon their return home. [91]

In order to prevent the seduction from their international loyalties of the members of the Force by worldly gifts from such sources as their own States or the host State, no member of the Force is allowed to accept any honour, decoration, favour, gift or remuneration incompatible with the individual's status and functions as a member of the Force. [92] The only exceptions are ordinary pay from their home States, [93] and promotion, which is likewise in the hands of the participating governments. [94]

The Regulations prescribe that the flag to be flown by the Force shall be the United Nations flag, this being a right recognised by the Egyptian Government. [95] The flag is to be displayed upon the Headquarters, posts and vehicles used by the Force and otherwise as decided by the Commander. Other flags or pennants, including those of the participating States, may only be displayed in exceptional cases and in accordance with conditions prescribed by the Commander. This right presumably includes the right to fly the flag on ships used by the United Nations. [96] The Regulations go on to provide that a distinctive mark and licence of the United Nations is to be borne by all UNEF's means of transport, " including vehicles, vessels and aircraft, and all other equipment specifically designated by the Commander." [97] It appears that vessels chartered to UNEF or made available by governments have sometimes flown their national flags, sometimes the United Nations flag and sometimes both. In Egyptian ports all ships used by UNEF have flown the Egyptian flag. [98]

With respect to the uniform of members of the Force, it was at

[90] Reg. 31.
[91] Reg. 32.
[92] Reg. 33.
[93] Reg. 38.
[94] Reg. 43.
[95] Reg. 7; Status Agreement, para. 26.
[96] The Geneva Convention on the High Seas, 1958, Art. 7, recognised that the provisions of that Convention (Arts. 4–6) did not prejudice the question of ships employed on the official service of an intergovernmental organisation flying the flag of the organisation : Cmnd. 584 (1958), Annex II.
[97] Reg. 9.
[98] Seyersted, " Some Legal Problems of the UN Force " (1961) 37 B.Y.B.I.L. 379, citing *United Nations Conference on the Law of the Sea, Official Records.* Vol. 4, p. 139.

first envisaged that there should be a distinctive uniform, and it is prescribed that "Members of the Force shall wear such uniform and distinctive insignia as the Commander, in consultation with the Secretary-General, may prescribe." [99]   However, this was impracticable at the start of the operation, and as it later came to be appreciated that a new uniform would be unwarrantably expensive, the idea was dropped.   Nevertheless, the clear identification of members of UNEF beyond wearing the customary United Nations armbands was a necessity for security and other practical reasons. So light blue helmets with United Nations markings were adopted, later supplemented by blue berets and desert caps and UNEF badges and insignia.[1]   The troops wore the uniforms of their own armies; the only member of the Force to have a uniform made for him which was not that of his own army was the Commander.[2]

XI. RELATIONS BETWEEN THE UNITED NATIONS AND THE
HOST STATE

1. *The principle of consent*

Throughout the history of the establishment and operation of UNEF, the principle that the Force could only be used on the territory of a Member State with its consent has governed the relations between UNEF and Egypt.   It was this principle which caused the United Nations to send the Force to Egypt only; for Israel objected to the presence of any international force within its borders.

The General Assembly Resolutions which established the Force, Resolutions 998 (ES–1) and 1001 (ES–1), approved the principle when the Secretary-General was asked to submit a plan for the setting up of an emergency international force " with the consent of the nations concerned " [3] and when the Assembly approved the principles outlined in the Secretary-General's Second and Final Report.[4]   In that report, the Secretary-General was at pains to point out that the General Assembly could not request the Force " to be stationed or operate on the territory of a given country without the consent of the government of that country." [5]

The consent of Egypt was secured in the early stages of the proceedings, after the Secretary-General had given his interpretation of the General Assembly's Resolutions to the satisfaction of the Egyptian Government.   Thereafter, the Secretary-General travelled to Cairo and conducted negotiations with the President and the Foreign Minister of Egypt, concerning the bases for the presence and functioning of the Force in Egypt.   The discussions resulted in an agreement, summarised by the Secretary-General in a report to the

---

[99] Reg. 8.   [1] *Summary Study, etc.,* A/3943, para. 43.
[2] Major-General E. L. M. Burns : *Between Arab and Israeli,* p. 237.
[3] A/3354, p. 2.
[4] *Ibid.,* p. 3.
[5] A/3276, para. 9.   How far this conclusion is necessarily correct as a principle of law is discussed *post,* at pp. 412–417.

General Assembly on 20 November 1956.[6] The *Aide-mémoire*, annexed to the report, which had the approval of the Egyptian Government, commences by reiterating the principle of consent, and notes that the Government of Egypt accepted the General Assembly Resolution which established the Force " in exercise of its sovereign rights." The basic points for the presence and functioning of the Force were stated to be: an undertaking by the Government of Egypt to be guided in good faith by its acceptance of the General Assembly's Resolution when exercising its sovereign rights; an undertaking by the United Nations to be similarly guided by the task established for the Force, and to maintain UNEF until its task be completed; and a declaration of mutual intention to explore the various aspects of the stationing and functioning of the Force in Egypt. The General Assembly noted the contents of the *Aide-mémoire* with approval on 24 November 1956.[7]

In addition to seeking the consent of Egypt for the presence of the Force in Egypt in principle, the Secretary-General also consulted the Egyptian Government from time to time as regards its wishes in the matter of its composition.[8]

2. Agreement on the Status of UNEF in Egypt

By an exchange of letters dated 8 February 1957, the Secretary-General, acting on behalf of the United Nations, and the Minister for Foreign Affairs of Egypt, acting on behalf of his country, signed an Agreement on the Status of UNEF in Egypt.[9] This Agreement was approved by the General Assembly by its Resolution 1126 (XI) of 22 February 1957.[10]

Two fundamental points underlie this Agreement; the first is the recognition of the sovereign rights of Egypt, a corollary of the principle of consent, and the second is that the Force is an organ of the United Nations, created by the General Assembly. The recognition of Egypt's sovereignty is reflected throughout almost all the provisions of the Agreement, and more particularly in those dealing with entry and exit, the premises of the Force, freedom of movement and communication, and the flag, uniform, and the carrying of arms. The second point is the basis for most of the provisions dealing with jurisdiction over the Force and its members. These will be discussed in turn.

The Agreement begins with five definition paragraphs.[11] The Force

---

[6] A/3375.
[7] Resol. 1121 (XI): *Off. Rec. G.A.*, 11th Sess., Suppl. No. 17 (A/3572), p. 61.
[8] *Ante*, p. 110. Note that Egypt never expressly consented to UNEF's operations in the Gaza Strip; this was assumed by the Secretary-General in his statement in *Off. Rec. G.A.*, 11th Sess., Plen., 659th Mtg., 22 February 1957, Vol. II–III, pp. 1192–1193.
[9] Report of the Secretary-General, 8 February 1957, A/3526. U.N.T.S., Vol. 260, p. 61.
[10] A/3572, p. 62.
[11] Paras. 1–5.

is stated " to consist of the United Nations Command . . . and all military personnel placed under the United Nations Command by a State Member of the United Nations." A " member of the Force " is " any person, other than a person resident in Egypt, belonging to the military service of a State serving under the Commander of the United Nations Emergency Force either on the United Nations Command (Headquarters Staff) or with a national contingent " and " any civilian placed under the Commander by the State to which such civilian belongs."

The " Commander " includes the Commander of the United Nations Emergency Force and other authorities of the Force designated by him. An " Egyptian citizen " is a person of Egyptian citizenship and " a person resident or present in the territory of Egypt other than one associated with the Force." " Participating State " means " a Member of the United Nations that contributes military personnel to the Force."

The term " Area of operations " includes areas where the Force is deployed in the performance of its functions, military installations, and lines of communication and supply utilised by the Force.

The definitions are followed by a paragraph of fundamental importance, in which the sovereignty of Egypt is fully recognised. It is stated that :

" Members of the Force and United Nations officials serving with the Force shall respect the laws and regulations of Egypt and shall refrain from any activity of a political character and from any action incompatible with the international nature of their duties or inconsistent with the spirit of the present arrangements. The Commander shall take all appropriate measures to ensure the observance of these obligations." [12]

This also ensures the character of the Force as an international organ of the United Nations, and the paragraph is repeated in the Regulations for the Force.[13]

(a) ENTRY AND EXIT

Members of the Force are exempt from passport and visa regulations and immigration inspection and from restrictions on entry or departure from Egyptian territory. They are also exempt from restrictions placed upon the residence of aliens, but at the same time they are under no circumstances to be considered as having acquired any residence or domicile in Egypt. For identification by the Egyptian authorities upon their entry and exit, members are required to have merely a movement order issued by the appropriate authority of the Force and a personal identity card.[14]

There is no provision in the Agreement either granting or denying to Egypt the right to object to or to prevent the entry into Egypt of any particular individual member of the Force. It has been argued

[12] Para. 6.
[13] ST/SGB/UNEF.1, Reg. 29; see *post*, p. 132.
[14] Para. 7.

that even in the absence of any such provision, Egypt would continue to possess the right of all States, under customary international law, of excluding an individual on the ground that his personal presence constituted a potential danger to the State's internal security.[15]

Nor is it stated whether Egypt has or has not the right to expel an individual member if, for instance, he was deemed to be a menace to its security. The Commander of UNEF has this right, and if the Commander knows that a member of the Force has left the service of his home State, and is not repatriated, he must inform the Egyptian authorities immediately. If an expulsion order is made, the Commander is responsible for ensuring that the person concerned shall be received by his home State.[16] This, presumably, refers to an expulsion order made by Egypt; but it only refers to ex-members of the Force. In the case of serving members, disciplinary sanctions are in the hands of the Commander and the commanders of the national contingents, and the participating States have sole jurisdiction over the commission of criminal offences.[17] It does not appear, therefore, that the host State would itself have any power of expulsion over serving members of the Force, though, should Egypt desire the withdrawal of such a member, doubtless the Commander or the Secretary-General would view such a request favourably.

(b) THE PREMISES OF THE FORCE

The Egyptian Government agrees to provide, in agreement with the Commander, such areas for headquarters, camps, or other premises as may be necessary for the accommodation and fulfilment of the functions of the Force.

The sovereignty of Egypt is specifically stated by the provision that such premises are to remain Egyptian territory, but they remain inviolable and subject to the control and authority of the Commander alone, and his consent is required for the entry of local officials to perform their duties on such premises.[18]

The provision clearly bases the immunity of the premises on the functional test,[19] which is clearly the foundation for all the privileges and immunities enjoyed by the Force and its members in the Agreement,[20] and just as clearly rejects the doctrine of " exterritoriality " as an explanation of the rationale of international immunities.

(c) FLAG, UNIFORM, ARMS

The Egyptian Government recognises the right of the Force to display its flag in appropriate places; and agrees that the Force shall

---

[15] See Attia, *Les Forces Armées des Nations Unies en Corée et au Moyen Orient* (1963), p. 391.
[16] Para. 9.
[17] Paras. 6, 11, 13.
[18] Para. 19.
[19] See Bowett, *The Law of International Institutions* (1963), p. 295.
[20] See *post*, pp. 129–136.

wear the prescribed uniform; conditions under which civilian dress may be worn by members of the Force are to be notified by the Commander to the Egyptian authorities, and it is provided that those authorities are to be notified as to identification marks used by vehicles, vessels, and aircraft.[21]

Members of the Force are permitted to possess and carry arms whilst on duty, in accordance with their orders. In this matter, as in the others, the Commander is to give sympathetic consideration to requests from the Egyptian authorities.[22]

(d) FREEDOM OF MOVEMENT AND COMMUNICATION

The Force and its members are to enjoy freedom of movement between the Force Headquarters, camps, and other premises within the area of operations, and to and from points of access to Egyptian territory agreed upon or to be agreed upon between the Government of Egypt and the Commander. With respect to large movements, the Commander is to consult with the Egyptian authorities. The Egyptian Government recognises the right of the Force and its members to freedom of movement across armistice demarcation lines in the performance of the functions of the Force and of the official duties of its members.[23]

The freedom of movement is accompanied by guarantees of the use of roads and waterways, port facilities and airfields, without payment of fees except for charges for services rendered.[24] The Force also has the right, in its area of operations, to unrestricted communication by means of radio, telegraph and telephone, and the right to make its own postal arrangements free of charge.[25]

Thus the right of freedom of movement enjoyed by the Force is enjoyed only within the limits set by its functional requirements, and the Force is not free to spread itself at will throughout the rest of Egypt where the Egyptian Government retains the right to interdict its movements. The situation of UNEF in this regard may be compared with that of the United Nations Force in the Congo, where there is freedom to operate throughout the whole territory of the Congo Republic.[26] This difference between the rights of the two Forces is a reflection of the different functions they have to perform.

Locally recruited persons are required to obtain permits to cross the frontier between Sinai and the Gaza Strip, and sometimes these permits have been withdrawn by the Egyptian authorities for reasons of security.[27]

---

[21] Paras. 20, 21.
[22] Para. 22. For a discussion of these provisions, see further *ante*, p. 120.
[23] Para. 32.
[24] Para. 33.
[25] Paras. 29–31.
[26] See Chap. 6, p. 203.
[27] A/3943, para. 146.

(e) MISCELLANEOUS RIGHTS

The Force may use water, electricity and other public utilities at a rate not less favourable than those granted to comparable customers. It may also generate its own electricity.

The Government of Egypt is to make available against reimbursement in acceptable foreign currency such Egyptian currency as the Force requires at a most favourable rate of exchange.

The Egyptian Government will assist in obtaining provisions, supplies and other services. Members of the Force may purchase goods for their consumption locally at a rate not less favourable than that available to Egyptian citizens, and the Government and the Force are to co-operate in health matters.[28]

The Commander of the Force and the Egyptian authorities are to take the appropriate measures to ensure liaison between themselves.[29]

As to the body and the personal effects of a deceased member of the Force, the Commander may take charge of and dispose of these after the member's debts incurred whilst in Egyptian territory have been discharged.[30]

(f) PRIVILEGES AND IMMUNITIES

UNEF is not an army of military occupation, and its nonsubjection to the local law is not, therefore, dependent upon the principles which apply to that type of army. It is a subsidiary organ of the United Nations, created by the General Assembly, and any status which it enjoys in the host State is dependent, therefore, upon the Charter of the United Nations,[31] and, in so far as the provisions of the Charter are inapplicable, upon special agreement with the host State.

In the case of UNEF, the provisions of the Charter and of the Convention on the Privileges and Immunities of the United Nations adopted by the General Assembly on 13 February 1946,[32] and acceded to by Egypt on 17 September 1948, are applicable to the Force itself, and to members of the staff of the United Nations operating in Egypt with the Force. With respect to the latter, the Status Agreement incorporates the relevant provisions of the Convention of 1946. Special provision had to be made to cover members of the Force who remained in their national service, since their duties with UNEF did

---

[28] Paras. 34-36.
[29] Para. 41.
[30] Para. 42.
[31] Art. 105 states that: " 1. The Organisation shall enjoy in the territory of each of its Members such privileges and immunities as are necessary for the fulfilment of its purposes. 2. Representatives of the Members of the United Nations and officials of the Organisation shall similarly enjoy such privileges and immunities as are necessary for the independent exercise of their functions in connection with the Organisation. 3. The General Assembly may make recommendations with a view to determining the details of the application of paragraphs 1 and 2 of this Article or may propose conventions to the Members of the United Nations for this purpose."
[32] U.N.T.S., Vol. I, p. 15, referred to hereafter as the " Convention of 1946."

not entail that they were to be regarded as officials of the United Nations.

(i) *The Force*

As a subsidiary organ of the United Nations and, in particular, the General Assembly, the Force enjoys the status, privileges and immunities of the Convention of 1946. This is expressly recognised by the Government of Egypt in the Status Agreement, which especially recognises the right of the Force to import, duty free, equipment, provisions and supplies for the exclusive use of the Force, and for members of the Secretariat of the United Nations detailed for work with the Force, including the right to establish for those persons amenities in service institutes.[33]

Other rights granted to the Force have been discussed previously.[34]

(ii) *The Commander, and the Headquarters Staff*

The Commander (a term which includes other authorities designated by him) [35] is entitled to the privileges and immunities set out in sections 19 and 27 of the Convention of 1946. This means that, in addition to the privileges enjoyed by all officials of the United Nations, he is entitled to the same treatment as States have contracted to accord to the Secretary-General and the Under-Secretaries, that is he is regarded as entitled to the privileges accorded by public international law to diplomatic agents.

Officials of the United Nations Command, that is, the Commander's Headquarters Staff, are entitled to the privileges and immunities of Article VI of the Convention of 1946. This means that they are entitled to the status of experts on mission for the Organisation, immunity from personal arrest or detention of their persons or their luggage, and from local jurisdiction in respect of their acts done in the course of their missions. They are entitled to the inviolability of their papers and documents, and various consequential immunities. They are accorded these privileges and immunities in the interests of the United Nations and not in their personal interests. The Secretary-General may, therefore, waive their immunity if that would not prejudice the interests of the United Nations.[36]

(iii) *Members of the United Nations Secretariat*

Members of the United Nations Secretariat detailed by the Secretary-General to serve with the Force are entitled to the benefit of the provisions of Articles V and VII of the Convention of 1946.[37]

---

[33] Para. 23. A mutually satisfactory procedure, including documentation, is to be arranged between the Force and the Egyptian customs authorities, to effect duty-free importation with the least possible delay. The Commander is to take measures to prevent abuse, including resale to outsiders.

[34] See *ante*, pp. 126–129.

[35] Para. 2.

[36] Para. 25.

[37] Para. 24.

That is to say they are entitled to immunity from jurisdiction over their official acts, from taxation of their salaries, and from national military service and other immunities. Again, the Secretary-General may waive, and must waive, their immunities if not to do so would hinder the course of justice, and to do so would not prejudice the interests of the Organisation. They may also carry the United Nations laissez-passer.

The provision as to waiver of immunities distinguishes these persons, and the members of the Headquarters Staff, from members of the Force serving with their national contingents.[38]

(iv) *Locally recruited personnel*

The Force may recruit persons locally, in Egypt, and the Egyptian authorities, on the request of the Commander, will assist in such recruitment. It seems to be assumed that such persons would be citizens of Egypt, but there does not appear to be anything in the terms of the Status Agreement to exclude the possibility of recruiting non-Egyptian nationals. The terms and the conditions of service of persons recruited locally are prescribed by the Commander.[39]

In respect of this category of persons, the immunities applicable are very restricted, and in fact they may only have immunity from the local jurisdiction in respect of their official acts, as provided in Article V, Section 18, of the Convention of 1946.[40] They are expressly excluded from the benefit of Article 23 of the Status Agreement with regard to fiscal privileges.

(v) *The participating States*

The participating States enjoy, of course, the normal privileges and immunities from suit accorded to States by customary international law. However, with respect to the property, funds and assets of the participating States used in Egypt in connection with the national contingents of UNEF, the Convention of 1946 is to apply.[41] This means that the United Nations is entitled to claim the immunities and privileges contained in that Convention for the property of the States.

The participating States may not, without the agreement of the Government of Egypt, acquire immovable property in that country. Although the Status Agreement is made between the Government of Egypt and the United Nations, not the participating States, the last named have accepted the provisions of the Status Agreement.[42]

(vi) *Members of the Force*

The members of the Force who are at the same time members of the national contingents serving with UNEF in Egypt are not entitled

---

[38] See *post*, p. 132.
[39] Para. 37.
[40] Para. 24.
[41] Para. 23.
[42] A/3943 Annex 1; see *ante*, p. 112.

to the privileges and immunities from jurisdiction contained in the Charter of the United Nations, since, although they are, for the purposes of the Regulations of the Force, " international personnel under the authority of the United Nations and subject to the instructions of the Commander through the chain of command," [43] they are not agents or officials of the Organisation.

The position of Members of the Force is, therefore, specifically regulated in the Status Agreement. It is expressly declared that the arrangements with regard to civil and criminal jurisdiction contained therein " are made having regard to the special functions of the Force and to the interests of the United Nations, and not for the personal benefit of members of the Force." [44]

Nevertheless, as will be seen, in the case of criminal jurisdiction at any rate, this limitation would seem to have little practical effect in so far as the Egyptian courts are concerned, for there is no provision for waiver of immunity in the case of this category of persons.

Criminal jurisdiction. In regard to criminal jurisdiction, the Secretary-General has stated:

" The question . . . raised a number of points of basic policy in the establishment of UNEF. It is essential to the preservation of the independent exercise of the functions of such a force that its members should be immune from the criminal jurisdiction of the host State."

A policy like this, " obviously, makes easier the decision of States to contribute troops from their armed forces." [45] Members of the Force are subject exclusively to the jurisdiction of their own home States in respect of any criminal offences committed by them in Egypt.[46] A provision of this sort in the Status Agreement would, by itself, lead to what the Secretary-General called a " jurisdictional vacuum," for it might mean that a member of the Force might not be subject to prosecution by the laws of his own State, and would thus be able to escape the legal consequences of his act. The Agreements between the United Nations and the participating States, therefore, contain a provision to the effect that the " immunity from the jurisdiction of Egypt is based on the understanding that the authorities of the participating States would exercise such jurisdiction as might be necessary with respect to crimes or offences committed in Egypt by any members of the Force provided from their own military services." [47] The participating States were asked to assure the Secretary-General that they were prepared to exercise such jurisdiction.[48]

Though the States' agreement to this was made a condition of the acceptance of their contingents for service with UNEF, not all

[43] ST/SGB/UNEF.1, Reg. 6.
[44] Para. 10 of the Status Agreement.
[45] *Summary Study, etc.,* A/3943, para. 136.
[46] Status Agreement, para. 11. See also Regulations for the Force, Reg. 34 (a).
[47] A/3943, Annex 1, para. 5.
[48] *Ibid.,* para. 7.

the possible legal problems which might arise were solved, and the Secretary-General thought it expedient to request the governments of participating States to review the position under their respective municipal laws.[49] Examples of problems which might arise were given by the Secretary-General. The treatment of offenders might differ as between the Forces of different nationalities. Municipal laws differ in the extent to which they confer on courts-martial in peacetime jurisdiction over civil, as opposed to military, offences, and the jurisdiction which they confer on their courts, whether military or civil, over offences committed by their nationals abroad. It may be added that, despite the provisions of the Agreements with the participating States, the act in question could be deemed to be criminal by the law of the host State but not by the law of the relevant participating State, and the laws of the different participating States might differ amongst themselves in a similar manner.[50]

As to this type of problem, the Secretary-General could only state the situation without attempting to offer any solutions in the abstract. Comfort may be gleaned from the fact that the commission of offences of the type under discussion was extremely rare.

It has already been noted that there is no provision in the Status Agreement for the waiver of jurisdictional immunities of the Members of the Force by the Secretary-General, the Commander, or the governments of the participating States, and that this distinguishes the status of Members of the Force with national contingents from that of the international officials.[51] Three possible reasons have been given [52] for the omission of a similar provision in the Status Agreement to that of the Convention of 1946 with regard to waiver: the urgent entry of the Force into Egypt rendering it more akin to the type of force entering a foreign State in time of war than to a force stationed in a foreign country in time of peace; the temporary character of the Force; and the fact that the Force is an international organ of the United Nations, and does not represent national interests. It can scarcely be said that any of these is convincing. By February 1957 the Force's entry had been accomplished, and it was clearly there for some time to come, and the third reason reads somewhat oddly, since officials of the Organisation are international officials and do not represent their national interests. In the result, the members of the Force possess a more absolute immunity from the criminal

---

[49] A/3943, para. 137.
[50] See the statement by the Philippine representative in *Off. Rec. G.A.*, 11th Sess. Plen., 659th Mtg., 23 February 1957, Vol. II–III, p. 1192, where he raised these problems, in particular the problem of an offence being treated as civil by Egyptian law but criminal by the law of the contributing State and the problem of the member having a right in criminal prosecutions under his own law to confront any witnesses whose evidence was brought against him: the question is how this right could be exercised if he were tried in his home country, thousands of miles from the *locus in quo* where the witnesses were available.
[51] See *ante*, p. 130.
[52] Chapman, 57 *Michigan Law Review*, November 1958, p. 72.

jurisdiction of the host State than is usual for members of Visiting Forces, for instance, under the NATO Status of Forces Agreement.[53]

In addition to the provisions of the Agreement with regard to criminal jurisdiction, there are several paragraphs devoted to the powers of the military police, arrest, and the transfer of custody, and mutual assistance between the Force and authorities of the host State.

It is provided that the Commander shall take all appropriate measures to ensure the maintenance of discipline and good order among members of the Force, and to this end military police are to police the premises and areas where the Force is deployed in the performance of its functions. Outside such places, military police may only act in liaison with the Egyptian authorities and subject to arrangements with them. The military police are given the power of arrest over all members of the Force.[54]

The military police may also take into custody any person within their areas who is subject to Egyptian criminal jurisdiction preparatory to delivering him to the appropriate Egyptian authorities.[55] The Egyptian authorities may do the same in case of persons who are to be handed over to the authorities of UNEF.[56]

The Commander and the Egyptian authorities are to assist each other in the carrying out of all necessary investigations into offences in respect of which either or both has or have an interest, and each is to notify the other of any case the outcome of which is of interest to the other, or in which there has been a transfer of custody from one authority to the other. The Egyptian Government is to ensure the prosecution of persons subject to its criminal jurisdiction who are accused of acts in relation to the Force or its members, which, if committed in relation to the Egyptian forces or their members, would have rendered them liable to prosecution. The authorities of the Force are to take such measures as are within their power with respect to crimes committed against Egyptian citizens by members of the Force.[57]

Civil jurisdiction. The provisions in the Status Agreement which concern civil jurisdiction differ from those connected with the criminal jurisdiction in the distinction made in the former between immunity in respect of official acts and the absence of it in respect of non-official acts, and in the absence of any reference to the jurisdiction or the law of the member's home State in civil cases.

It is provided that members of the Force shall not be subject to the civil jurisdiction of the Egyptian courts or tribunals in matters relating to their official duties.[58] In those cases in which the local

[53] U.K. Treaty Series, No. 3 (1955), Cmd. 9363.
[54] Status Agreement, para. 14.
[55] Para. 15.
[56] Para. 16.
[57] Para. 18.
[58] Para. 12 (a); see also the Regulations for the Force, Reg. 34 (b).

courts are entitled to exercise their jurisdiction over a member of the Force, they shall grant him sufficient opportunity to safeguard his rights. If the Commander certifies that a member of the Force cannot, on account of his official duties or of his authorised absence, defend his interests, the court is to suspend the proceedings until the disability is eliminated, but in any case for not more than ninety days.

If the Commander certifies that property of the member in question is needed by him for the performance of his official duties, then that property is free from seizure in satisfaction of a judgment, decision or order. Further, the liberty of such a person may not be restrained by an Egyptian court in a civil proceeding, whether to enforce a judgment, decision or order, to compel an oath or disclosure, or for any other reason.[59] There is provision for a special procedure for the settlement of claims in the cases in which the action arises out of the official duties of the member of the Force, or in those cases where it does not so arise, at the option of the claimant.[60]

If a civil proceeding is instituted against a member of the Force in cases in which the Egyptian courts have jurisdiction, the Commander is to be notified, and he is to certify whether or not the proceeding relates exclusively to acts done in the performance of the member's duties. This certificate is presumably conclusively binding on the Egyptian courts.[61]

Privileges other than jurisdictional. Members of the Force are exempt from Egyptian taxation on their incomes, whether these are derived from their own governments or from the United Nations. They are likewise exempt from all other direct taxes except municipal rates for services enjoyed, and from all registration fees and charges.[62]

With respect to customs duties, members may import personal effects duty free when they first take up their posts. Such personal property as is not required by them by the nature of their presence in Egypt is subject to the Egyptian customs and foreign exchange regulations. Special entry and exit facilities are to be arranged by the Egyptian authorities for regularly constituted contingents provided advance notification is given. A reasonable certified residue of members' emoluments may be taken by them out of Egypt on their departure therefrom. Special arrangements are to be made between the Commander and the Egyptian authorities with regard to these provisions.[63]

[59] Para. 12 (b).
[60] Para. 38, and Reg. 34 (d) of the Regulations for the Force. The claims procedure is discussed further *post*, p. 149.
[61] Para. 13. It is believed that the certificate is conclusive.
[62] Para. 26.
[63] Para. 27.

The Commander is to co-operate with the Egyptian customs and fiscal authorities to see that members of the Force comply with the Egyptian customs and fiscal regulations.[64]

(g) EFFECTIVE DATE AND DURATION

The Agreement operates retrospectively, for it is deemed to have been in effect since the date of the arrival of the first elements of the Force in Egypt. Except for the provisions relating to the settlement of disputes, it is to terminate on the departure of the Force from Egypt. The effective date of departure is to be defined by agreement between the Secretary-General and the Egyptian Government.[65] It is to be noted that there is no provision as to who shall decide on the effective date in the event of a dispute, nor is there any provision as to who is to decide when the task of the Force has been completed. This presumably would have to be determined by agreement between the Secretary-General and the Egyptian Government.

XII. RELATIONS BETWEEN THE UNITED NATIONS AND OTHER STATES

Because ancillary services had to be provided for UNEF which necessitated the use of the territory of States other than the participating States and the host State, the United Nations entered into arrangements with two other Member States, and indirectly one non-member State, at the start of the operation, and with one other Member State during the course of the operations.

1. *Transport and transit agreements*

The need for a speedy arrival of UNEF in Egypt meant that the majority of the contingents had to be flown there. The Secretary-General was therefore obliged to arrange for means of transport and for the setting up of a staging point outside Egypt as a rendezvous for the contingents. Three States were concerned in these arrangements, the United States, Italy and Switzerland, the latter indirectly. Of these the first-named State is a Permanent Member of the Security Council and the third is not a member of the United Nations.

The United States of America offered facilities for the transportation of troops to Italy on 4 November 1956,[66] and this offer was confirmed on 13 November. The offer was of free means of transport, by air and sea, to the staging area and thence to the zone of operations.[67] The offer was accepted by the Secretary-General, as it was deemed that the principle of the exclusion from participation in

---

[64] Para. 44.
[65] Para. 44.
[66] *Off. Rec. G.A.*, 1st Emergency Special Sess. A/PV/565, para. 102.
[67] A/3302/Add.20.

the Force of States having permanent representation on the Security Council did not apply to the provision of support for the Force. The General Assembly had called upon Member States to give necessary support to the United Nations, particularly in making arrangement for passage to and from the area involved in the operations.[68]

Arrangements were made with Italy for the provision of a staging post at Capodichino airport, Naples, to which those contingents which did not go to Egypt through the Red Sea could be brought, and where they could be assembled and briefed before being sent on to Suez. The arrangement was confirmed by a letter from the Italian delegate to the United Nations to the Secretary-General on 27 November 1956, in which he stated that as a contribution to the putting into effect of the Resolutions of the General Assembly the Italian Government had furnished, since 10 November, the facilities which had been asked for, and had provided planes and pilots to take troops and equipment from Italy to Egypt.[69]

The initial airlift from Naples to the arrival point at Abu Suweir was carried out by aircraft chartered to the United Nations by the Swiss Air Line, Swissair. The original form of agreement between the Organisation and the Airline had taken the form of a contract of a private law nature between the two parties.

The Swiss observer to the United Nations made an offer to the Secretary-General on 26 November 1956. This contained a statement that Switzerland would pay the cost of transport facilities provided by Swissair, and did this out of a desire to help in the re-establishment of the peace in the Middle East, and added: " Elle n'apporte aucune modification au caractère juridique du transport de la force internationale qui n'implique aucune responsabilité de la Suisse, mais a fait l'objet d'un accord de droit privé entre l'Organisation des Nations Unies et la Swissair." [70]

This indirect manner of supplying aid to the United Nations was doubtless adopted in order to avoid any suspicion that Switzerland had abandoned its neutrality, or had done anything to jeopardise its status of permanent neutralisation. It is doubtful, however, whether a direct agreement by Switzerland to provide support would have imported this conclusion, for the Force was not a belligerent force. It has been suggested that such action by the Swiss Government would have been merely in conformity with the Charter, Article 2 (6) of which states that the Organisation is to ensure that non-member States act in accordance with the principles of the Charter " so far as may be necessary for the maintenance of international peace and security." [71]

Most of the troops sent to Egypt came by way of Naples, though

[68] Resol. 1001 (ES–1), para. 10.
[69] A/3302/Add.30.
[70] A/3302/Add.29.
[71] Poirier, *La Force Internationale d'Urgence*, p. 109.

some were sent by air via Beirut and some came by sea through the Red Sea. The Yugoslav contingent went directly by sea to Port Said, and the main element of the Canadian and Brazilian contingents arrived in national vessels on 11 January and 2 February.[72]

Naples was used as a Post Office, in connection with a franking privilege worked out through the Universal Postal Union; mail for UNEF contingents was flown through Naples, except in the case of Yugoslav and Indian contingents.[73]

2. *UNEF leave centre, postal arrangements, air transit facilities in the Lebanon*

During the course of the operations of UNEF, the Commander of the Force concluded, by means of exchanges of letters with the Lebanese Government, agreements for a Leave Centre in the Lebanon for members of the Force, for a UNEF transit centre at Beirut International Airport, and for a base Post Office at Beirut. The last two were needed because of the closing of the Naples base on 1 February 1958.

The Agreement on the Leave Centre [74] is the most detailed. It provides for the setting up of an Administrative Unit in the Lebanon with an officer who is responsible for the UNEF units, and for entry and exit facilities.[75] The Convention on the Privileges and Immunities of the United Nations of 1946[76] is applied to the Force expressly, and the immunities of the United Nations Secretariat employees and the locally recruited personnel are the same as in the Status Agreement with Egypt.[77] As in the case of that Agreement, jurisdiction in criminal matters is reserved to the participating States to the total exclusion of the Lebanese authorities, and they have no jurisdiction over civil cases arising out of acts committed by members of the Force whilst on official duty. If the member in question should be on leave or off duty, then the local courts may take jurisdiction over him.[78] Claims are to be settled by the procedure set out in Article VIII of the Convention of 1946.[79] In order to help keep discipline amongst UNEF members, UNEF military police are provided; the two parties agree to render mutual assistance to this end.[80] The Lebanese authorities will assist in the apprehension of United Nations troops going absent without leave.[81] The agreement concludes with an agreement for liaison, and provisions as regards the disposition of the body and effects of a deceased member of the Force.[82]

[72] *Summary Study, etc.*, A/3943, paras. 35, 39.
[73] *Ibid.*, para. 93.
[74] U.N.T.S., Vol. 266, p. 125.
[75] Arts. 1–4.
[76] U.N.T.S., Vol. I, p. 15.
[77] *Ibid.*, Vol. 266, p. 125, Arts. 5, 7.
[78] Arts. 14, 15.
[79] Art. 14.
[80] Arts. 16, 17.
[81] Art. 18.
[82] Arts. 19, 20.

The Agreement for a Transit Unit at Beirut International Airport [83] refers to previous discussion between the Commander and the Lebanese Prime Minister. The Convention of 1946 is expressly adverted to, and the provisions of the Leave Centre Agreement are applied here *mutatis mutandis*.

The Agreement with regard to postal arrangements [84] is based upon similar considerations to the original agreement with the Italian Government.

XIII. FINANCIAL ARRANGEMENTS

In any consideration of the financial arrangements adopted by the General Assembly for UNEF, two distinct matters must be examined: (1) the apportionment of expenses between the United Nations as an Organisation on the one hand, and the Member States which provide contingents on the other; and (2) the apportionment of those expenses which are to be borne by the United Nations amongst the Member States.

1. *Apportionment between the United Nations and the participating States*

In his Second and Final Report on the plan for an international United Nations Emergency Force of 6 November 1956, the Secretary-General put forward for the General Assembly's consideration the following basis for the apportionment of expenses between the United Nations and the participating States:

". . . a nation providing a unit would be responsible for all costs of equipment and salaries, while all other costs should be financed outside the normal budget of the United Nations." [85]

Nearly a year later, the Secretary-General, in a report to the General Assembly [86] elaborated on this basic principle, which had secured the approval of the General Assembly.[87] It was now proposed that the method of apportionment should remain that previously suggested, that is, that the expenses in connection with payment of salaries and wages and the cost of the normal equipment of the national contingents should rest upon the participating States, but that the United Nations should make reimbursement to the States for the following items: for the first six months, in respect of any

---

[83] U.N.T.S., Vol. 286, p. 189.
[84] *Ibid.*, p. 199.
[85] A/3302, para. 15.
[86] Report of 9 October 1957; *Off. Rec. G.A.*, 12th Sess., Annexes, agenda item 65, doc. A/3694.
[87] Resol. 1001 (ES-1), 7 November 1956, para. 5; approved *provisionally*. This was followed by Resol. 1089 (XI), on 21 December 1956, in which the Assembly decided that "the expenses of the United Nations Emergency Force, other than for such pay, equipment, supplies and services as may be furnished without charge by governments of Member States shall be borne by the United Nations."

special allowances payable to members of the Force as a result of their service with the Force, provided that these allowances could be considered "reasonable"; if a contingent were to remain with the Force for longer than six months, or if a replacement was sent, the United Nations would repay to the States in question all the extraordinary costs which they incurred by reason of the service of their contingents with the Force; for example, pay and allowances over and above those which the government of the State would be obliged to meet in any event.

With respect to the equipment of the contingents, the United Nations would bear the cost of replacement of equipment destroyed or worn out or for its deterioration beyond what might be envisaged in normal depreciation schedules.

The General Assembly approved these principles and proposals, and authorised the Secretary-General in connection therewith to enter into such agreements as might be necessary.[88]

Although these apportionment rules might be simple to state as a general rule based on equitable principles, in practice difficulties cannot be avoided. The Secretary-General has discussed some of these. It is not always clear what may be regarded as a "special allowance" as distinct from basic pay. Further, although it had been supposed at first that the contingents furnished by States would be drawn from their standing armed forces, in the event some States organised special volunteer contingents, and others went to the length of replacing the contingents sent to serve with UNEF, to keep up the numbers available to their national armies. The extra costs which some governments thus incurred should, they thought, be met by the United Nations. The policy which has been adopted has been for the United Nations to pay the full cost of pay and allowances in the case of volunteers, but only "extra" expenses in the case of conscripts or regular soldiers. Further difficulties arose from the provisions as to reimbursement in respect of equipment. The formula adopted did not say whether the term "equipment" should be interpreted to mean "equipment, *matériel* or supplies," nor did it set any qualification that the items should have been normal and necessary in the circumstances, or that they should have saved the United Nations from expense which it would otherwise have had to incur. Decisions therefore had to be taken, in the Secretary-General's words, "based on interpretations of the formula in the light of the actual circumstances of each particular case." The procedures relating to equipment have been considerably strengthened over the years. A complete record of all contingent-owned equipment has been maintained since October 1958 in the case of UNEF, and contingents were informed that, after 1 January 1959, the United Nations would accept no financial responsibility for any type of equipment,

[88] Resol. 1151 (XII), 22 November 1957, para. 2. *Off. Rec. G.A.*, 12th Sess., Suppl. No. 18 (A/3805), p. 58.

expendable supplies or items of personal issue, unless the United Nations had given approval to the transport to the area of the items in question.[89]

Another matter which raises questions as to possible indemnification of the participating States by the United Nations is compensation in cases of death or accidents arising out of service with the Force. In November 1956 the Secretary-General had suggested that it had been assumed that in such cases the persons concerned or their dependants would qualify for benefits under their own national regulations, and so would not receive such benefits directly from the United Nations.[90] Further, it is provided in the Regulations for the Force which were accepted by the participating States,[91] that in the event of death, injury or illness, the respective State from whose military service the member has come will be responsible for such benefits or compensation awards as may be payable under the laws and regulations applicable to service in the armed forces of that State.

In his Report of 9 October 1957,[92] the Secretary-General drew the attention of the General Assembly to this matter, and pointed out that the Advisory Committee on Administrative and Budgetary questions agreed with the validity of his earlier view. However, the United Nations would accept responsibility for defraying the cost of payment of such benefits by the participating governments. Consultations had taken place with those governments, and the Secretary-General had assured them that the Organisation would accept liability to make reimbursement. In the Secretary-General's view, benefits and awards should first be paid directly by the governments concerned, and they would, in turn, lodge claims with the United Nations.[93]

As to expenses borne directly by the United Nations, these are numerous and detailed, but may be summarised as follows: the cost of provisions and the upkeep of the troops, and a daily overseas allowance, as well as travel and subsistence allowances, the operation of leave centres and the costs of motor transport, barrack stores,

---

[89] *Summary Study, etc.*, 9 October 1958, A/3943, paras. 116–119. 25th Report of the Advisory Committee on Administrative Questions: Budget estimates for the period 1 January to 31 December 1959, paras. 9–10, *Off. Rec. G.A.*, Agenda item 65, 13th Sess., 1958, Annexes.

[90] Report of 21 November, 1956, A/3383, para. 13.

[91] ST/SGB/UNEF.1, Reg. 40; accepted by the States in their Agreements with the United Nations, see further *ante*, p. 120.

[92] A/3694, pp. 32 *et seq.*, paras. 92–98.

[93] The UN had protected itself against such claims for death or injury to members of the Force by taking out commercial insurance: see *Thirty-fifth Report of the Advisory Committee on Administrative and Budgetary Questions*, *Off. Rec. G.A.*, 11th Sess., Annexes, Vol. II–III, Agenda item 66, p. 32. However, this was coverage for one month, on a temporary basis, and the Advisory Committee recommended its termination as being too high in cost in comparison with the actual risk. The Advisory Committee in due course recommended that such claims should be restricted to death or serious injury involving a material cost to the contributing State for medical costs and/or pension benefits and should be arranged so that the UN could commute its liability to a lump sum payment, leaving the State to administer payment: A/3694 and Add. 1, p. 11.

workshop equipment, stationery, etc., and the use of planes of the Royal Canadian Air Force for transportation. Additionally, the Organisation has to meet the salaries and allowances due to United Nations officials detailed to serve with the Force, the costs of communications, the issuing of supplies, and the satisfaction of successful claims against the United Nations.[94]

2. *Apportionment of expenses of the Organisation between Member States*

(a) BUDGETARY ARRANGEMENTS

Before considering the rules which the General Assembly has adopted for the apportionment of the expenses incurred directly or indirectly by the Organisation, the budgetary methods adopted for the financing of the Force require discussion, for not all the bill has to be met by a system of apportionment.

" In financial terms, the expenses caused by UNEF'S formation and operation have had to be considered as extraordinary, according to the definition generally applied by the General Assembly." [95]

The expenses of such an operation as UNEF could not be borne by the normal budget of the Organisation; the funds necessary for its sustenance had to be provided from other sources. One possible source of supply which might have been drawn upon was the amount raised under the authority of annual Resolutions of the General Assembly to meet unforeseen and extraordinary expenses relating to the maintenance of international peace and security,[96] but the amount which the Secretary-General was authorised to raise for this purpose was limited to $2 million, an amount obviously inadequate for the present project.

For several reasons,[97] it was thought preferable to finance the initial expenses of UNEF on an *ad hoc* basis, rather than to seek an increase in the amount authorised in these annual Resolutions; the uncertainty of the scope and duration of the exercise, the receipt of voluntary contributions, and the basic rule for the apportionment of costs between the United Nations and the participating States was still only provisional.[98] Therefore the General Assembly was asked for authority to raise money to pay for the Force, and this has been granted by a series of Resolutions each year.

In November 1956, the General Assembly gave its approval to the recommendations of the Secretary-General as to the financing of the Force,[99] and decided at the same time that an initial amount of $10

---

[94] A/3943, para. 120.
[95] A/3943, para. 108.
[96] See, for instance, General Assembly Resols. 980 (X) of 16 December 1955, for the year 1956; 1084 (X) 21 December 1956, for 1957; 1231 (XII), 14 December 1957, for 1958, and 1339 (XIII), 13 December 1958, for 1959.
[97] A/3943, para. 108.
[98] See *ante*, p. 139.
[99] A/3302, para. 15.

million, outside the regular budget, should be raised.[1]   On 27 February 1957, the Secretary-General was authorised to increase this to $16·5 million in respect of the period ending 31 December 1957,[2] and to $30 million in November 1957.[3]   With respect to the period after December 1957, the General Assembly in its Resolution of November 1957, authorised the Secretary-General to spend another $25 million. This authority has been continued since that time,[4] although the expenses have decreased somewhat as the size of the Force has been reduced.

The General Assembly, by its Resolution of 26 November 1956,[5] gave the Secretary-General authority, for accounting purposes, to set up a Special Account to which all funds received by the United Nations for the purpose of the Force should be credited; all payments made out on account of the Force were to come from the same account.   The Secretary-General was also authorised to advance from the Organisation's Working Capital Fund, pending the receipt of funds for the Special Account, such sums as that Account should require to meet any expenses chargeable to it.[6]   This authority was renewed in February 1957, in the same Resolution as that which gave the Secretary-General the power, in case the Working Capital Fund should not be able to bear such advances, to arrange for loans to the Special Account from appropriate sources, such as governmental and other international agencies, and from other funds under his care or control.[7]   As to these loans, the Secretary-General has said:

"The loan procedure was suggested and adopted as an extraordinary measure, designed to meet serious gaps in standard methods of providing for cash requirements of the Organisation.   The necessity to use this authority has been avoided to date [October 1958], but only narrowly so."[8]

The two main sources of supply for the Special Account have been (1) Voluntary contributions from Member States.   In its Resolution of 27 February 1957, the General Assembly invited Member States to make voluntary contributions to meet the sum of $6·5 million so as to ease the financial burden for 1957 on the United Nations membership as a whole.[9]   The expenditure of $30 million

---

[1] Resol. 1122 (XI) of 26 November 1956; A/3572, p. 61.
[2] Resol. 1090 (XI), A/3572, p. 46.
[3] Resol. 1151 (XI) of 22 November 1957; A/3805, p. 58.
[4] See, for instance, the Resols. 1337 (XIII) of 13 December 1958; 1441 (XIV) of 5 December 1959; 1575 (XV) of 20 December 1960.
    The expenses for the financial year 1962–63 have totalled approximately $7 million.   Because of this, the Secretary-General has forecast another reduction in the strength of UNEF; see *The Times* (London), 17 September 1963.
[5] Resol. 1122 (XI), para. 1.
[6] *Ibid.*, para. 3.
[7] Resol. 1090 (XI), para. 3.
[8] A/3943, para. 110.
[9] Resol. 1090 (XI).   Voluntary contributions pledged as of October 1957 were: Dominican Republic, $3,250; Greece, $6,500; New Zealand, $27,950; Pakistan, $5,000; United Kingdom, $507,650; United States, $3,250,000.   Doubts about the wisdom of relying on voluntary contributions were expressed by the Secretary-General in A/3694, p. 12.

incurred down to the end of 1957 was borne to the extent of $1,841,700 by such voluntary contributions, and as to a further $13,129,312 by grants of special assistance made by some Member States for the purpose of reducing the amount assessable on all [10]; (2) The remainder, consisting of contributions to be assessed on the Organisation's membership as a whole.

The wisdom of establishing a Special Account for UNEF has been questioned on the grounds that:

" It permitted States to default in their contributions to UNEF, without, at the same time, defaulting in their assessments for the regular budget. It permitted nations, in essence, to veto an important activity of the United Nations. Psychologically, the system of separate accounting obstructed any immediate financial benefits which might have been gained at the very start when UNEF was being given near-unanimous approval by the Assembly Members. It opened the way to doubts concerning the application of Article 17 of the Charter. Finally, it made more difficult a possible conversion of the Force into a permanent organ, as had been done with other operations in the past." [11]

Certainly the International Court of Justice rejected the argument that the allocation of the expenses to a Special Account made any difference to the application of Article 17,[12] but there remains a good deal of force in these criticisms. However, they are criticisms based on hindsight, and, at the inception of UNEF, the difficulties which the future held were not anticipated by the Secretary-General. The criticisms apply rather more forcefully to the financing of ONUC by a separate *ad hoc* account [13] for by that time the difficulties were certainly known; presumably it was thought that to abandon separate accounting for ONUC would have had serious repercussions on the position of the UNEF Special Account, almost admitting the validity of the distinction between the regular budget and separate accounts for the purposes of Article 17.

(b) THE METHOD OF APPORTIONMENT ADOPTED

The General Assembly has consistently adopted, as its method of apportionment of the expenses mentioned in (a) (2) above the principle of assessing the Member States according to the scale laid down by the General Assembly for the contributions to the regular Budget of the Organisation.

The Secretary-General first suggested this method of apportionment in his reports to the General Assembly and to the Assembly's Fifth Committee of 21 November [14] and 3 December 1956 [15] respectively, and this was endorsed by the General Assembly and applied to the

[10] A/3943, para. 113.
[11] Rosner, *op. cit.*, p. 182.
[12] *Post*, p. 251.
[13] *Post*, p. 250.
[14] A/3383; see also A/3572, paras. 78–81.
[15] A/C.5/687.

first ten million dollars of expenses " without prejudice to the subsequent apportionment of any expenses in excess of $10 million which may be incurred in connection with the Force." [16]

For the financial year ending 31 December 1957, the General Assembly, after long discussion in the General Assembly itself and in its Fifth Committee, authorised the application of the proposed method in the following terms :

" . . . the expenses . . . shall be borne by the Members of the United Nations in accordance with the scales of assessments adopted by the General Assembly for the financial years 1957 and 1958 respectively." [17]

Two main lines of attack upon this method of allocation between the Member States can be discerned in the assaults which have been made upon it ever since it was adopted, and which have resulted in the refusal of payment by an appreciable number of States. The thesis of the Soviet *bloc* has been that the total expenses of the United Nations in respect of UNEF (and the expenses incurred in the clearing of the blocked Suez Canal between December 1956 and March 1957) should logically be borne only by those States which had committed " aggression " against Egypt; that is, the United Kingdom, France, and Israel.[18] To put the charge on all the Member States would, it was argued, encourage aggressors, who would be able to commit their illegal acts secure in the knowledge that any efforts undertaken to counteract them by the United Nations would have to be paid for by all Member States, including the victims of the aggression. This position was taken in the General Assembly in 1956,[19] and was to be repeated the following year. The Arab States in general shared this view.

Another line of attack was adopted by the Latin-American States, and was more fully developed by them in the debates in 1957. This rested on the argument that, since the Permanent Members were entrusted with primary responsibility for the maintenance of international peace and security, the primary responsibility for financing UNEF should rest with those States.

In view of the divergence of views which had already appeared, the General Assembly, in its Resolution of 21 December 1956, decided that, whilst the expenses up to $10 million might be apportioned in accordance with the regular scale of assessments, the consideration of the apportionment of expenses over $10 million required closer study. To this end, it established a Committee of nine States to examine the apportionment of expenses above that limit.[20] The Committee was

---

[16] Resol. 11089 (XI), 21 December 1956; A/3572, paras. 1 and 2.

[17] Resol. 1151 (XI), para. 4, 27 November 1957.

[18] It should be observed that these States had never been adjudged guilty of aggression by the General Assembly or by any other organ of the UN.

[19] *Off. Rec. G.A.*, Doc. A/PV/632, para. 65. And see, in the Fifth Committee, 544th Mtg., 5 December 1956, p. 67.

[20] Resol. 1089 (XI) A/3572, p. 46, para. 3. The States were Canada, Ceylon, Chile, India, Liberia, Salvador, Sweden, U.S.A., U.S.S.R.

instructed to study the matter in all its aspects, including the possibility of further contributions, the fixing of maximum amounts of expenses which could be established on each occasion, and the possibility of drawing up a scale of contributions different from the one which had been provisionally adopted.

This Committee put forward a report [21] which formed the basis of the Resolution of 27 February 1957, but the latter makes no mention of the question of apportionment other than stating that the General Assembly should, at its twelfth session, consider the basis for financing any costs of the Force in excess of $10 million not covered by voluntary contributions.[22]

During the twelfth session of the General Assembly, the matter was discussed in the Fifth Committee once more. The Soviet delegate repeated the arguments already outlined, and the Latin-American representatives, with the exception of the Brazilian, put forward their own thesis. These States differed, however, from the Soviet *bloc*, in that they agreed that the burden of the expenses should fall upon the membership of the Organisation as a whole. Their disagreement was with the method of apportionment, which was stigmatised as lacking in equity [23]; it was again argued that since, under the Charter, the primary responsibility for the maintenance of international peace and security is placed upon the Security Council,[24] it was the members of the Security Council, and in particular those States having permanent membership, who should bear the brunt of the costs.

A further method of shifting the burden from the shoulders of all States on to those of a few was suggested by the delegate of Guatemala.[25] This was that the "aggressors" should bear the greater part of the cost; those States with particular interests in the maintenance of peace in the Middle East, those responsible for the troubled conditions obtaining there, and the five Permanent Members of the Security Council should pay the rest. Under this plan, of course, some States would pay under more than one category.

During its twelfth session the General Assembly rejected these arguments for the year 1958, and decided once more that the expenses should be carried by the Member States in accordance with the scales established for their contributions to the normal budget for the year 1958.[26]

During its thirteenth session the General Assembly discussed the question once again, and the three main theses were once again before it. The Soviet *bloc* reiterated its often-expressed view that

[21] A/3560, pp. 47–55.
[22] Resol. 1090 (XI), A/3572, p. 46, para. 4.
[23] The Soviet thesis was argued in the General Assembly : A/PV/720, para. 139, and in the Fifth Committee : A/3560, para. 25. The Chilean delegate used these terms in the General Assembly : A/PV/721, para. 93.
[24] Art. 24 of the Charter.
[25] A/PV/721, para. 68–79.
[26] Resol. 1151 (XII), 22 November 1957, para. 4.

the General Assembly's creation of UNEF was illegal, and refused to vote for any decision whereby the Organisation was engaged to pay the expenses of the Force, and, further, refused to pay any amount towards its expenses.

However, the General Assembly again selected the previously-applied method of allocation for the year 1959. At the same time, it suggested to the Secretary-General that he should consult with the governments of Member States concerning the manner of financing UNEF in the future.[27] The Secretary-General acted upon this suggestion, and by October 1959, fifty States had replied to the Secretary-General's inquiries.[28]

Twenty-nine States approved of the method of sharing the cost between Member States in accordance with the scale of assessments for the ordinary budget.[29] Nine others, whilst agreeing that the whole cost should be shared among the Member States and should form part of the budget of the Organisation, requested that some other, unspecified method of allocation be adopted.[30] The Soviet *bloc* States, with one or two others, wished to place the burden on the so-called "aggressor" States; two Members said they could not afford to pay,[31] and one [32] thought that the whole cost should be defrayed out of voluntary contributions.

Further, some States wished to continue the division of the account between the voluntary contributions and the remainder to be borne by all the Member States,[33] whilst others [34] gave as their opinion that the expenses of UNEF should be provided for in the ordinary budget of the Organisation.

Throughout this whole controversy the method of apportionment has remained that first selected, although this has only been autho-rised from time to time, and not as a matter of permanence. The only real departure from this method came on 5 December 1959, when the Assembly agreed to apply the voluntary contributions as a credit to reduce by 50 per cent. the contributions of as many governments as possible, beginning with those with the minimum assessment.[35] Hence this was a concession to those States with the least capacity to pay and, in 1960, this was extended so as to reduce the assessments of States receiving assistance under the Expanded Programme of Technical Assistance.[36] However, in 1960 this whole question of the financing of UNEF became involved with the question

---

[27] Resol. 1337 (XIII), 13 December 1958, para. 5.
[28] Doc. A/4716 and Add. 1 and 2.
[29] Including the United Kingdom, France, U.S.A. and most Commonwealth and West European States.
[30] Burma, Ceylon, China, Cuba, Greece, Guatemala, Mexico, Spain, Venezuela.
[31] Guinea, Jordan.
[32] Chile.
[33] Including the U.S.A.
[34] Australia, Japan, Netherlands, United Kingdom.
[35] Resol. 1441 (XIV), A/4486, 13 September 1960, *Off. Rec. G.A.*, 15th Sess., Annexes, p. 21.
[36] Resol. 1575 (XV).

of financing ONUC, so that the problem of apportionment may best be left, as to UNEF, at this stage and resumed in Chapter 6.

In 1962, the question of the expenses of both UNEF and ONUC was referred by the General Assembly to the International Court of Justice for an Advisory Opinion upon whether they constitute " expenses of the Organisation " within the meaning of Article 17 (2) of the Charter.[37] To a certain extent this depended for an answer upon an interpretation of the terms of Article 17, and, because of the arguments put before the Court, on the legality or otherwise of the actions of the General Assembly in establishing and operating the Force.[38] However, the question of " apportionment " of the expenses by the General Assembly was not directly in issue in the case. The Court distinguished between three questions : (1) the identification of what are " expenses " of the Organisation; (2) the question of apportionment; (3) the interpretation of the phrase " shall be borne by the Members " as used in Article 17.[39] It was only the first question which was actually before the Court, it being one which " has to do with a moment logically anterior to apportionment, just as a question of apportionment would be anterior to a question of Members' obligation to pay." The Court answered the question which it had isolated in the affirmative, and this answer was endorsed by the General Assembly when it " accepted " the opinion in a Resolution of 19 December 1962, by seventy-six votes to seventeen with eight abstentions.[40]

But the Court did not answer the question whether the adopted method of apportionment was the correct one, nor did it decide whether there was a legal obligation upon the Member States to pay, although since the General Assembly is given the power to make mandatory decisions with respect to budgetary matters, it would seem that there is.

It is the case, however, that Member States are not directly bound by the Advisory Opinions of the International Court of Justice, so presumably the legality of the action of the dissenting States in their refusal to pay their assessed contributions may only be tested in the General Assembly itself. The sanction of the General Assembly here is contained in Article 19 of the Charter, whereby a Member State in arrears to the amount equalling or exceeding the amount of the contributions due from it for the preceding two full years shall have no vote, unless the General Assembly is satisfied that failure to pay is due to conditions beyond the control of the member. It was, in fact, a fear of this consequence that led some of the smaller States to protest the legal obligation to pay and the method of assessment of their contributions.

[37] *I.C.J. Reports*, 1962, p. 151.
[38] See *ante*, p. 93.
[39] *I.C.J. Reports*, 1962, p. 158.
[40] Resol. 1854 (XVII).

XIV. CLAIMS

1. *Claims of a private law nature*

The claims of a private law nature which arise during the operation of the Force are dealt with in the Status Agreement with Egypt. The terms of the Agreement cover claims by Egyptian citizens against members of the Force and against the Force itself, by the Government of Egypt against the Force or a member thereof, and by the Force against the Egyptian Government.

In the case of disputes or claims arising out of contract, or otherwise of a private law nature, to which the United Nations is a party, the Organisation is to make provision for the appropriate mode of settlement.[41] It is also provided in the Regulations of the Force that the Secretary-General shall make provision for the settlement of claims against the Force.[42]

However, in respect of claims by an Egyptian citizen for the damages alleged to result from an act or omission of a member of the Force relating to his official duties, and to a claim made by the Government of Egypt against a member of the Force or a claim by the Force against the Government of Egypt or vice versa, a definite mode of settlement by means of a Claims Commission is established.[43] This method of settlement may also be employed at the option of the claimant, where he has a claim against a member of the Force which does not arise out of the defendant's official duties, instead of a resort to the Egyptian courts which is permitted by the Agreement.[44]

The Agreement provides for a Claims Commission of three, of whom one member is to be appointed by the Secretary-General and one by the Egyptian Government, and a jointly appointed chairman. In the event of failure to agree on a chairman, the President of the International Court of Justice may be asked to appoint. An award shall be notified to the Commander or to the Egyptian authorities, as the case may be, with a view to satisfaction. If a claim which is settled in favour of an Egyptian individual is not satisfied, the Egyptian authorities may call upon the Secretary-General to use his good offices to obtain satisfaction.[45]

It appears that these provisions are also applicable to claims by non-Egyptian nationals, provided that they are resident in Egypt when the alleged damage is suffered and not associated with the Force, for the term " Egyptian citizen " as used in the Agreement includes these categories of person.[46]

No mention is made of the system of law which is to be applied

[41] A/3526, para. 38 (a).
[42] ST/SGB/UNEF 1. Reg. 15.
[43] Agreement, para. 38 (b).
[44] *Ibid.*, para. 12 (c).
[45] *Ibid.*
[46] Para. 3.

in the settlement of claims by the Commission. It might be Egyptian law, as the *lex loci*, or it might be the general principles of law.[47]

In practice, claims have been settled by a process of informal negotiation between the parties directly, or between UNEF and the Egyptian liaison office subject to the ratification by the claimant. UNEF has taken into account in settlements the local levels of compensation as evidenced by the systems of diyet used by the Sharia courts, workmen's compensation laws and other local practice.[48]

Disputes concerning the terms of employment of locally recruited persons are to be settled by administrative procedures under the aegis of the Commander.[49]

With respect to claims arising from UNEF'S occupation of privately owned land, a large number of these were presented to UNEF. It was agreed that UNEF should pay for damage to real property arising out of negligence or other causes not related to the necessary functions of the Force, and should pay reasonable rentals for such property used by the Force. With respect to privately owned land taken for operational needs, a procedure agreed with the Egyptian authorities was to survey the sites and on that basis (and on the assumption that the Egyptian Government would have honoured the claim) UNEF makes payment to the owners, reserving its rights under the Agreement and the possibility of making in the future demands for reimbursement from the Government.[50]

So far as the actual procedures for settlement of claims of a public law nature are concerned, differences between the United Nations and Egypt which raise a question of principle regarding the interpretation and application of the Convention on Privileges and Immunities of the United Nations shall be settled in accordance with section 30 of the Convention,[51] and all other disputes concerning the Agreement not settled by negotiation or other agreed method are to be settled by a Tribunal composed in a fashion similar to the method of appointment of the Claims Commission.[52]

2. *Claims of a public law nature*

However, apart from these procedures for settlement, there are a number of substantive problems which would be raised in claims pursued under these procedures. The case of a claim by the United

---

[47] See Statute of International Court of Justice, Art. 38.
[48] *Summary Study, etc.*, A/3943. para. 141.
[49] Para. 38 (c).
[50] A/3943, para. 142.
[51] Para. 30. This procedure has not been used, so that nothing is known of what questions will be regarded as questions " of principle." Presumably the question whether the certificate of the Commander regarding the " official " nature of the acts of a member of the Force is conclusive for the Egyptian authorities would be such a question; it is not specifically dealt with in the Agreement. No doubt the I.C.J. would first determine whether a question " of principle " were involved, as a jurisdictional problem antecedent to its right to give an advisory opinion on the matter.
[52] Para. 40.

Nations for a breach of the Agreement would raise little difficulty. The more difficult case will be that in which the United Nations asserts a right of " functional " protection against Egypt on behalf of a member of the Force. The Force is an organ of the United Nations, and some of the staff are themselves officials thereof; further, in regard to those members of the Force who are members of their national contingents, it is expressly provided in the Regulations that they " are entitled to the legal protection of the United Nations and shall be regarded as agents of the United Nations for the purpose of such protection." [53] In such cases, the United Nations is, therefore, in a position to pursue international claims against Egypt for any injury sustained by any of its agents and caused by a breach of international law by Egypt. This follows from the Advisory Opinion of the International Court of Justice in the *Reparations for Injuries Case*.[54] The type of case in which such a claim could be sustained is one of the subjection of members of the Force to mob violence which the host State did nothing to prevent, or the maltreatment of a member by the Egyptian police.

A further question which arises here is as to the possibility of a claim by a participating State against Egypt for injuries suffered by one of its troops through a breach by Egypt of its obligations owed at international law to aliens generally. No case in which this duality of claims is possible is known to have occurred with UNEF, but it raises a general problem which will be discussed in Chapter 6 of the present study under the head of " Claims and Responsibility." [55]

[53] UNEF Reg. 30.
[54] *I.C.J. Reports*, 1949, 181
[55] See *post*, pp. 242–248.

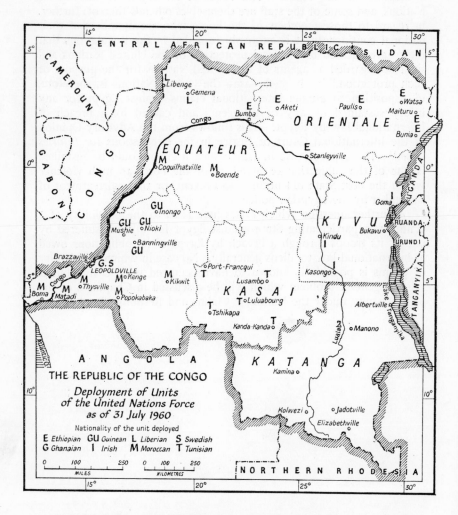

THE REPUBLIC OF THE CONGO

*Deployment of Units
of the United Nations Force
as of 31 July 1960*

Nationality of the unit deployed

E *Ethiopian* GU *Guinean* L *Liberian* S *Swedish*
G *Ghanaian*   I *Irish*   M *Moroccan* T *Tunisian*

0   100   250   0   100   250
    MILES   KILOMETRES

Reproduced, but with additions, from the Official Records of the Security
Council, Fifteenth Year, Suppl. for July, August and September 1960, p. 236.

6

The United Nations Force in the Congo (ONUC)

THE Republic of the Congo, a territory of 2,343,930 square miles, achieved independence from Belgium on 30 June 1960,[1] and on 1 July applied for admission to the United Nations: this was recommended by the Security Council on 7 July, and was voted by the General Assembly on 20 September. Meanwhile, between 7 and 8 July the Force Publique mutinied[2] and Belgian troops were re-introduced into the territory, on 12 July, for the stated purpose of protecting lives and property.[3] On the previous day Moise Tshombé had announced the secession of Katanga from the new Republic.[4] On 12 July the President of the new Republic, Kasavubu, cabled the Secretary-General of the United Nations, alleging a violation of the Treaty of Friendship of 29 June 1960 by Belgium, condemning the Belgian intervention as aggression and requesting the "urgent dispatch of military assistance."[5] A second cable followed by way of clarification on the 13 July,[6] stating additionally that, unless assistance was received, an appeal would be made to the Bandung Treaty powers.

The Secretary-General, acting expressly under Article 99 of the Charter,[7] requested a meeting of the Security Council and the Council

---

[1] For a brief account of the pre-independence history of the Congo, see King Gordon, *UN in the Congo* (1962) pp. 8–13; Colin Legum, *Congo Disaster* (1961); Ruth Slade, *The Belgian Congo* (1961) London Institute of Race Relations; Washington Okumu, *Lumumba's Congo : Roots of Conflict* (1963) Part One.

[2] See the account by Bunche in his Press Conference of 1 September 1960, Note No. 2230; or in Legum, *op. cit.*, Chap. XI; Chomé, J., *La Crise Congolaise* (1960) pp. 101–170. And see *Congo 1960*, Vol. I, "Les Dossiers du C.R.I.S.P.," pp. 371–459 for documentary evidence relating to the mutiny.

[3] The evidence of danger to Belgian life and property is given in a statement by the Belgian Minister of Justice at a press conference on 28 July and published as *Congo, July 1960—Evidence*. Chomé, *op. cit.*, pp. 155–174, after reviewing the reactions in Belgian newspapers and statements by members of the Belgian Cabinet, concludes that "la Belgique . . . était plongée dans le mensonge et la propagande" (p. 174). A series of extracts from Belgian parliamentary statements and Ministerial declarations is given in *Congo, 1960*, Vol. II, pp. 494–517.

[4] *Congo, 1960*, Vol. II, pp. 718–719.

[5] S/4382, I.

[6] S/4382, II. For the telegram from Kasavubu and Lumumba to Mr. Khrushchev on 14 July 1960, and Mr. Khrushchev's reply promising "des mesures résolues pour mettre fin à l'agression" if the UN were unable to take such measures, see *Congo, 1960*, Vol. II, pp. 554–556.

[7] This does not appear in the Secretary-General's letter to the President of the Council (S/4381), but is clearly stated in his statement to the Council on 13 July: *Off. Rec. S.C.*, 15th yr., 873rd Mtg., p. 3.

met in the evening of 13 July. At that meeting the Council initiated the operations which were in due course to present the Organisation with greater problems than it had ever before encountered. It is to the successive Resolutions of the Security Council and of the General Assembly that we now turn. The Resolutions will be presented as part of an historical narrative of the events in the Congo, a narrative which, whilst necessarily brief, is essential to an understanding of the circumstances in which, and the purposes for which, the Resolutions were passed.

I. THE BASIC RESOLUTIONS ADOPTED BY THE SECURITY COUNCIL AND GENERAL ASSEMBLY

On 14 July 1960 at its 873rd Meeting the Security Council adopted [8] the Tunisian proposal which, in its operative part:

" 1. *Calls upon* the Government of Belgium to withdraw their troops from the territory of the Republic of the Congo;

2. *Decides* to authorise the Secretary-General to take the necessary steps, in consultation with the Government of the Republic of the Congo, to provide the Government with such military assistance as may be necessary, until, through the efforts of the Congolese Government with the technical assistance of the United Nations, the national security forces may be able, in the opinion of the Government, to meet fully their tasks;

3. *Requests* the Secretary-General to report to the Security Council as appropriate."

Amendments by the U.S.S.R.[9] which would have had the Council condemn the "armed aggression" by Belgium, which would have called for withdrawal of Belgian troops "immediately" and which would have limited the military assistance to be provided to "African States members of the United Nations" were all rejected.

The dissatisfaction of the Congolese Government with the rate of Belgian withdrawal led to an ultimatum to the United Nations, on 17 July, that unless all Belgian troops were withdrawn in forty-eight hours, the Congo would appeal for aid to the Soviet Union.

On 22 July, having meanwhile received the first report of the Secretary-General,[10] the Security Council adopted [11] a second Resolution unanimously which, in its operative part:

" 1. *Calls* upon the Government of Belgium to implement speedily the Security Council Resolution of 14 July 1960, on the withdrawal of their troops and authorises the Secretary-General to take all necessary action to this effect;

2. *Requests* all States to refrain from any action which might tend to impede the restoration of law and order and the exercise by the Government of the Congo of its authority and also to refrain from any action which might undermine the territorial integrity and the political independence of the Republic of the Congo;

---

[8] S/4387; adopted by 8 in favour—o against—3 abstentions (China, France, U.K.). Belgium was present at this meeting and the Congo was asked to send a representative.

[9] S/4386. The votes on the three amendments were 2-7-2, 2-7-2, 4-5-2.

[10] S/4389 and Add. 1-6: *Off. Rec. S.C.*, 15th yr., Suppl. p. 16.

[11] S/4405; a second Soviet amendment (S/4402) was not proceeded with. Both Belgium and the Congo were represented at this meeting.

3. *Commends* the Secretary-General for the prompt action he has taken to carry out Resolution S/4387 of the Security Council and his first report;

4. *Invites* the specialised agencies of the United Nations to render to the Secretary-General such assistance as he may require;

5. *Requests* the Secretary-General to report further to the Security Council as appropriate."

Whilst the Secretary-General had, at the 877th meeting on 20 July, stated as his interpretation of the Resolution of 14 July that it applied to the territory of the Republic as a whole, and whilst no objection to this interpretation had been raised in the Security Council (indeed the Resolution of 22 July referred to "the territorial integrity" of the Republic) the fact was that United Nations Forces had not entered Katanga. The Congolese Prime Minister, Lumumba, in a letter to the President of the Security Council of 31 July [12] called for evacuation of Belgian troops and United Nations entry into Katanga, and on 2 August the Belgian Government stated that such entry would not be opposed by Belgium.[13] However, on 3 August a message was received by the Secretary-General from the head of the newly-proclaimed Katangese Government, Mr. Tshombé, to the effect that entry would be opposed by force.

In these circumstances the Secretary-General instructed his representative, Bunche, to visit Elisabethville to discuss "with the appropriate Belgian authorities" and through them with Mr. Tshombé and other representatives of the population the preparations for United Nations entry into Katanga.[14] Bunche left on 4 August for Elisabethville [15] and returned on 5 August, reporting to the Secretary-General that the evidence suggested opposition was likely, that the United Nations' plans for the operation did not envisage having to meet such opposition, and recommending that the operations for entry into Katanga should be stopped. The Secretary-General accepted this recommendation and turned to the Security Council asking in his Second Report "for instructions . . . and for such decisions as the Council may find appropriate in order to achieve integrally its aims."[16] The necessity for such further action by the Council stemmed from the principle, which the Secretary-General had throughout treated as fundamental,[17] that the United Nations Force could not take the initiative in any armed action but was restricted

---

[12] S/4414.
[13] Statement by M. Wigny, Minister for Foreign Affairs (S/4417, *ibid.*, p. 47).
[14] The general plan for entry had been outlined in the statement of the Secretary-General of 2 August (Press Release Co/20/Add. 2, pp. 6–7 and S/4417, p. 4). The instructions to Bunche are set out in the Second Report of the Secretary-General, S/4417, para. 8. In a statement on 3 August, released in Leopoldville, the Secretary-General had clarified and restated the principle of non-intervention with specific reference to proposed entry into Katanga (PR.SG/939 and S/4417, para. 6): on the "breakthrough to Elisabethville" see generally Gordon, *op. cit.*, pp. 37–44.
[15] Note that the Secretary-General refused to allow Bunche to be accompanied by representatives of the Central Government and 20 Ghanaian soldiers: S/4417/Add. 2.
[16] *Ibid.*, Second Report, para. 9.
[17] See *post*, p. 200.

to self-defence. Hence, on the assumption that "the entry of United Nations military units into Katanga would have had to be achieved by the use of force," [18] the Secretary-General put the problem to the Security Council in these terms:

". . . the aims of the Resolutions cannot be achieved by the use of the United Nations Force, as its mandate has been defined. If the Council, as it is assumed, wishes to maintain its objectives, the Council must, therefore, either change the character of the Force, which appears to me to be impossible, both for constitutional reasons, and in view of the commitments to the contributing governments, or resort to other methods which would enable me to carry through the implementation of its Resolution without going beyond my instructions as regards the Force." [19]

The "other methods" referred to were not made more explicit, except by a reference to the possibility of laying down "such rules . . . as would serve to separate effectively questions of peaceful and democratic development in the constitutional field from any questions relating to the presence of the United Nations Force." This suggestion of a form of reassurance on the non-intervention by the United Nations in the internal political problems was in due course given.

The Security Council met on 8 August, again at the request of the Secretary-General, to consider the Second Report. After an oral statement by the Secretary-General in amplification of this Report,[20] and a general discussion in which representatives of the Congolese Central Government participated, the joint draft Resolution of Ceylon and Tunisia [21] was adopted in the following terms:

". . . *Noting* however that the United Nations had been prevented from implementing the aforesaid Resolutions in the Province of Katanga although it was ready, and in fact attempted, to do so,

Recognising that the withdrawal of Belgian troops from the Province of Katanga will be a positive contribution to and essential for the proper implementation of the Security Council Resolutions,

1. *Confirms* the authority given to the Secretary-General by the Security Council Resolutions of 14 July and 22 July 1960 and requests him to continue to carry out the responsibility placed on him thereby;

2. *Calls upon* the Government of Belgium to withdraw immediately its troops from the Province of Katanga under speedy modalities determined by the Secretary-General and to assist in every possible way the implementation of the Council's Resolutions;

3. *Declares* that the entry of the United Nations force into the Province of Katanga is necessary for the full implementation of this resolution;

4. *Reaffirms* that the United Nations force in the Congo will not be a party to or in any way intervene in or be used to influence the outcome of any internal conflict, constitutional or otherwise;

5. *Calls upon* all Member States, in accordance with Articles 25 and 49 of the Charter, to accept and carry out the decisions of the Security Council and to afford mutual assistance in carrying out measures decided upon by the Security Council;

[18] *Ibid.*, para. 9.   [19] *Ibid.*, para. 10.
[20] *Off. Rec. S.C.*, 15th yr., 884th Mtg., pp. 2–6.
[21] S/4424; adopted by 9–0–2 (France, Italy). The Soviet Resolution (S/4425) which would have imposed upon the Secretary-General the obligation "to take decisive measures, without hesitating to use any means to that end, to remove Belgian troops from the territory . . ." was not pressed to the vote.

6. *Requests* the Secretary-General to implement this Resolution and to report further to the Security Council as appropriate."

Thus the Resolution did not change the character of the Force, but took the other alternative of declaring the necessity for entry into Katanga and reaffirming the principle of non-intervention [22]; it also, in paragraph 5, by referring to Articles 25 and 49, left no doubt as to the mandatory character of the decisions of the Council. The Secretary-General then returned to Leopoldville on 11 August and, after an exchange of cables with Mr. Tshombé, the President of the Provincial Government of Katanga,[23] arranged to visit Elisabethville on 12 August with a party of advisers and two companies of Swedish troops from the United Nations Force. On 13 August a communiqué was issued by the Secretary-General,[24] following discussions with military representatives of Belgium and with the Katanga authorities, announcing that the two Swedish companies would assume guard duties at Elisabethville airport and that arrangements had been made for the immediate withdrawal of Belgian troops to their bases and the speedy deployment of the United Nations Force which was to begin its arrival on 15 August.[25] It was thus that entry into Katanga was effected.

Immediately prior to the arrival of these United Nations Forces in Katanga, a serious difference of opinion arose between Mr. Lumumba and the Secretary-General. In a letter dated 14 August [26] Mr. Lumumba accused the Secretary-General of failing to carry out the Resolutions of the Security Council in that he had not used United Nations troops to " subdue the rebel Government of Katanga " and, secondly, had " dealt with the rebel Government of Katanga " in violation of the Resolution of July 14. This, the first of an exchange of letters,[27] raised directly in issue the Secretary-General's interpretation of the principle of non-intervention [28] for it demanded the use of United Nations troops to solve the internal constitutional problem of Katangese secession by force. The third letter from Mr. Lumumba [29] declared that the Congolese Government had lost confidence in the Secretary-General and asked for the creation of a group of observers from Afro-Asian countries to ensure the " immediate and entire

---

[22] For the detailed Memorandum on Implementation of the Security Council Resolution of 9 August 1960, operative paragraph 4, prepared by the Secretary-General and given to the Central Government and the provincial government of Katanga, see S/4417/Add. 6, dated 12 August 1960.

[23] *Ibid.*, Add. 4.

[24] Press Release Co/2o/Add. 4, 19 August 1960.

[25] Press Releases Co/49 and Co/52 revealed that 4,000 troops from Ethiopia, Ireland, Mali, Morocco and Sweden would take part in the entry into Katanga, being deployed at Elisabethville, Jadotville, Kolwezi, Kamina, Kabalo, Albertville and Manono.

[26] S/4417/Add. 7 (II). Mr. Lumumba's position was also taken by the Congolese Council of Ministers in a letter to the Secretary-General of 21 August (Press Release Co/2o/Add. 5, p. 6).

[27] S/4417/Add. 7, *passim*.

[28] See *post*, pp. 196–200.

[29] S/4417/Add. 7 (VI).

application" of the three Security Council Resolutions. It was in these circumstances that the Secretary-General requested a meeting of the Council in order to obtain a clarification of his mandate. Addressing the Council on 21 August[30] the Secretary-General reviewed the whole trend of events and dealt with the various objections made by Mr. Lumumba. However, after three meetings (during which a Soviet proposal[31] for the establishment of a group of contributing States to ensure on the spot and without delay "the execution of the Council's Resolutions" was withdrawn) no formal decision was taken: the President of the Council expressed the view that the Secretary-General "will have found in this debate the clarification which he desired . . ."[32] Support for the Secretary-General's interpretation was in fact forthcoming from Tunisia, Argentina, Italy, Ceylon, Ecuador, the United Kingdom, the United States, China and France: the Congolese criticisms found support only from the Soviet Union, Guinea (participating in the debate but not a Council member) and Poland.

By the end of August the withdrawal of Belgian forces from the Congo, which by a letter of 20 August[33] had been promised for 29 August, had not in fact been completed and this led to a formal protest by the Secretary-General.[34] This situation, coupled with evidence of assistance being given to both the Katangese authorities and the Congolese Central Government from outside and "tending to reintroduce elements of the very kind which the Security Council wished to eliminate when it requested the immediate withdrawal of Belgian troops"[35] and also increasing evidence of hostility by Congolese forces to United Nations troops and officials,[36] led the Secretary-General to urge, in his Fourth Report to the Security Council, that it "reaffirm its request to all States to refrain from any action which might tend to impede the restoration of law and order . . . and that it clarify, in appropriate terms, the mandate of the United Nations Force."[37] The Secretary-General referred specifically to the threats to human life which "may necessitate a temporary disarming of military units which . . . are an obstacle to the re-establishment of

---

[30] *Off. Rec. S.C.*, 15th yr., 887th Mtg., p. 2.
[31] S/4453.
[32] 889th Mtg., p. 29.
[33] S/4475 and Add. 1–3, Annex I and II.
[34] The exchanges of communications are given in the Secretary-General's Third Report, S/4475 and Add. 1–3: the Belgian explanation was the lack of transport facilities.
[35] Fourth Report of the Secretary-General, S/4482, para. 11. And see the letters dated 4 and 8 September from the Secretary-General to the Permanent Representative of Belgium complaining of the sending of weapons to the Katangese authorities, S/4482/Add. 1, and of the attachment of Belgian officers to the Katangese forces, S/4482/Add. 3. The letter dated 8 September from the representative of Yugoslavia to the President of the Security Council also protested at "outside interference," S/4485.
[36] See *post*, p. 205.
[37] S/4482, para. 12. And see the Secretary-General's statement to the Security Council on 9 September recounting information about attacks on the Baluba tribes by the Armée Nationale Congolaise.

law." The deterioration in the relations between the Central Government and the United Nations Force, which began during August, had
evidently continued and, indeed, the difficulties of co-operating with
the Central Government had been increased by the internal rift which
began by the dismissal of Mr. Lumumba by President Kasavubu on
5 September and the counter-declaration by Mr. Lumumba that he
had dismissed the President.[38]

Thus, when the Security Council met again on 9 September the
Secretary-General justified the actions so far taken on the basis of
their impartiality and called on the Council to insist that assistance
to the Congo should be channelled exclusively through the United
Nations. This followed on the Secretary-General's communications
with Belgium and, on 5 September, with the Soviet Union, about
unilateral aid to Tshombé and Lumumba respectively. The meetings
on 9, 10 and 12 September were adjourned without any decision
being reached, in part because it had become clear from documents
circulated on 12 September that two delegations from the Congo
were due to arrive in New York, the one accredited by Prime Minister
Lumumba and headed by Mr. Kanza and the other accredited by
President Kasavubu and headed by Mr. Bomboko.[39] The arrest of
Mr. Lumumba on the instructions of the President on 12 September
further obscured the constitutional position.[40] On 14 September
Colonel Mobutu, the Army Chief of Staff, declared that the Army
was assuming power in the country, and on 20 September announced
yet a third Government, the " Collège des Universitaires."

Meeting again on 14 September, the Security Council devoted two
meetings to the question of representation of the two rival delegations
and refrained from taking a decision on the credentials of either so

[38] It was at this stage of the constitutional crisis that the UN first closed the
airports to prevent any influx of pro-Lumumbist troops on Soviet transport
aircraft and the radio station to prevent its use for purposes of inciting the
population to acts of violence : see statement of the Secretary-General to the
Council on 9 September. An attempt by Mr. Lumumba to enter the radio
station accompanied by ANC troops was prevented on 12 September by
UN troops : see message from the Special Representative of the Secretary-
General, Mr. Dayal, S/4505 and Adds. 1 and 2.

[39] S/4504, Annexes I and II, S/4504/Add. 1. For the further communications
on the authority of these two rival delegations, see S/4511, S/4512, S/4514.

[40] See letter from Mr. Kanza to the President of the Security Council dated
14 September, S/4515. The authority of President Kasavubu, resting on the
Loi Fondamentale of 19 May 1960, was challenged in the letter dated 14
September from the Special Delegate of the Congo to the Security Council,
S/4517, who pointed out that the Chamber of Representatives, by 60 votes
to 19, rejected the President's order dismissing Prime Minister Lumumba,
and this was upheld in the Senate by 41 votes to 2. These events are outlined in the First Progress Report to the Secretary-General of his Special
Representative, Mr. Dayal, dated 21 September 1960, S/4531, paras. 20–28.
See also Chomé, *Le gouvernement congolais et l'O.N.U. Un paradoxe
tragique* (1961) pp. 91–123 : at p. 51 he refutes the argument that Kasavubu
had power to dismiss Lumumba. For the protest by President Kasavubu
to the Secretary-General on UN "interference in the Congo's internal
affairs," see S/4520, 16 September 1960. The rupture between Lumumba
and Kasavubu can be followed from the documents reproduced in *Congo
1960*, Vol. II, pp. 815–867.

as to avoid involvement in this delicate constitutional problem.[41] The substantive debate centred on the Secretary-General's Fourth Report and Soviet hostility to the Secretary-General increased further. Whilst both the United States and the U.S.S.R. introduced draft Resolutions, a compromise Resolution emerged in the form of the Ceylon/Tunisian draft Resolution [42] which, *inter alia*, would have specifically reaffirmed the obligations of all States not to interfere in the Congo and to channel all assistance through the United Nations. The Soviet Union did not find this a satisfactory basis for a positive solution and submitted a series of amendments.[43] The original Soviet proposal and the Soviet amendments to the joint Ceylon/Tunisian proposal were rejected and in the vote on this joint proposal the veto of the Soviet Union was cast.[44] The Soviet Union then announced that it had requested the inclusion of the question of " the threat to the political independence and the territorial integrity of the Republic of the Congo" on the agenda of the General Assembly which was due to meet in two days' time. However, a United States proposal to convene an emergency special session under the Resolution on Uniting for Peace was adopted by eight votes to two (U.S.S.R. and Poland) with one abstention (France). Thus it was that, once again, the responsibility for dealing with a matter affecting international peace and security shifted from the Council to the Assembly.

When the Assembly met on 17 September in emergency session the debate revealed the same fundamental divergence of views as to what the United Nations Force should be doing in the Congo as had already emerged in the Security Council. However, a seventeen-power Afro-Asian Resolution was adopted without a single dissenting vote on 20 September, the text of which was as follows:

" The General Assembly, . . .

1. *Fully supports* the Resolutions of July 14 and 22 and of August 9 of the Security Council;

2. *Requests* the Secretary-General to continue to take vigorous action in accordance with the terms of the aforesaid Resolutions and to assist the Central Government of the Congo in the restoration and maintenance of law and order throughout the territory of the Republic of the Congo and to safeguard its unity, territorial integrity and political independence in the interests of international peace and security;

3. *Appeals* to all Congolese within the Republic of the Congo to seek a speedy solution by peaceful means of all their internal conflicts for the unity and integrity of the Congo, with the assistance, as appropriate, of Asian and African representatives appointed by the Advisory Committee on the Congo, in consultation with the Secretary-General, for the purpose of conciliation;

4. *Appeals* to all member governments for urgent voluntary contributions to a United Nations Fund for the Congo to be used under United Nations control and in consultation with the Central Government for the purpose of rendering the fullest possible assistance to achieve the objective mentioned in the preamble;

[41] A Polish proposal to seat the Lumumba delegation received 3 votes (Ceylon, U.S.S.R. and Poland) and 8 abstentions.
[42] S/4523.
[43] S/4524.
[44] The actual vote was 8-0-2 (U.S.S.R. and Poland).

5. *Requests*:

(a) All States to refrain from any action which might tend to impede the restoration of law and order and the exercise by the Government of the Republic of the Congo of its authority and also to refrain from any action which might undermine the unity, territorial integrity and the political independence of the Republic of the Congo;

(b) All Member States, in accordance with Articles 25 and 49 of the Charter, to accept and carry out the decisions of the Security Council and to afford mutual assistance in carrying out measures decided upon by the Security Council.

6. Without prejudice to the sovereign rights of the Republic of the Congo, *calls upon* all States to refrain from the direct and indirect provision of arms or other materials of war and military personnel and other assistance for military purposes in the Congo during the temporary period of military assistance through the United Nations, except upon the request of the United Nations through the Secretary-General for carrying out the purposes of this Resolution and of the Resolutions of July 14 and 22 and of August 9, 1960, of the Security Council." [45]

The significance of the Resolution was twofold. First, paragraph 2, in requesting the Secretary-General "to continue" to take vigorous action in accordance with the Resolutions of the Security Council, virtually amounted to a vote of confidence in the Secretary-General: significantly, the Soviet amendments had been directed to deleting the words "to continue." Second, paragraph 5, in addressing a general request to *all* States, made the demand for non-intervention and the channelling of all aid through the United Nations which the Secretary-General had urged on the Security Council but which had there been blocked by the Soviet veto.

However, the appeal to the Congolese to achieve internal unity, contained in paragraph 3, remained unheeded.[46] Not only were two rival groupings contending for national leadership, each invoking ONUC's aid to confirm its authority, but, to complicate matters further, separatist governments in the provinces refused to recognise *any* central authority. The Collège des Universitaires announced by the ANC Chief of Staff, Colonel Mobutu, on 14 September had indeed been confirmed by a presidential ordinance of 20 September but the status and role of the Ileo Government announced on 12 September remained unclear. Moreover, Mr. Lumumba remained supported by a large group of parliamentarians and various (and conflicting) lists of reshuffled cabinets were published. An attempt to arrest Mr. Lumumba by ANC on 10 October was frustrated by ONUC which regarded the warrant of arrest as prima facie invalid as

---

[45] A/Res/1474/Rev. 1 (ES–IV), adopted by 70–0–11. A Soviet draft Resolution (A/L. 293), which would have condemned Belgian aggression, urged the withdrawal of all troops of NATO powers and noted the "failure" of the Secretary-General and the UN Command to implement the Security Council Resolutions, was not pressed to a vote: nor were a number of Soviet amendments (A/L.292/Rev. 1) to the 17-Power Resolution. For the records of the meeting, see *Off. Rec. G.A.*, 4th Emergency Special Sess., Plen. Mtgs., 858th to 863rd Mtgs.

[46] The description of events which follows is taken from the Second Progress Report to the Secretary-General from Mr. Dayal, dated 2 November 1960 (S/4557).

contrary to the *Loi Fondamentale* and the privileges of parliamentarians; this particular incident led to an ultimatum against ONUC that ANC would attack if Mr. Lumumba was not handed over. A "constitutional decree-law" signed by the Chief of State on 11 October purported to establish a College of Commissioners-General, to adjourn Parliament and to transfer its legislative power to the College and to vest the executive authority of the Prime Minister in the President of the College. The attitude taken by ONUC was to take no position on the legality of this but to decline to give recognition to a régime founded on military force and to limit its relations with the new régime to those which could be pursued informally on the technical plane.[47]

Meanwhile ANC had itself become an increasing threat to the maintenance of law and order. Undisciplined (and often unpaid) bodies of ANC personnel committed acts of lawlessness against members of the administration, the civilian population and ONUC itself. On 26 October, however, Colonel Mobutu agreed to withdraw all ANC troops from Leopoldville and confine them to barracks. In Katanga serious clashes between the Katangese gendarmerie and the Balubas occurred which ONUC attempted to prevent by offering to place certain regions under United Nations protection, an offer accepted by the Katangese authorities. In Kasai province the withdrawal of ANC troops had been followed by an occupation by forces owing allegiance to Mr. Kalonji, these forces taking extreme repressive measures against the Basonga and Kanioka tribes.

Apart from the serious internal disorders the report[48] of the Secretary-General's Special Representative, Mr. Dayal, disclosed another very significant development which had occurred during September and October. Whilst, with the exception of technical personnel at Kamina base, Belgian troops had been withdrawn from Katanga, there was increasing evidence of Belgian "intervention" in another form. On 31 October there remained 231 Belgian nationals in the Katangese gendarmerie and fifty-eight Belgian officers in the police. Moreover, a steady return of Belgian nationals to all parts of the Congo was occurring[49] and, particularly in Katanga and South Kasai, these were increasing their participation in political and administrative activities as advisers, counsellors or executive officials.

---

[47] However, the Kasavubu delegation had its credentials approved as representing the Congo within the General Assembly by Resol. 1498 (XV) on 22 November; the vote was 53–24–19. There was considerable distrust of this by the African States on whose support the Secretary-General depended in the Congo; these States, which either abstained or voted against the Resolution, had wanted a postponement of any decision until the Conciliation Commission returned from the Congo and they regarded the approval of the Kasavubu delegation's credentials as a manoeuvre to ensure a "pro-Western" delegation to represent the Congo: see Gordon, *loc. cit.*, pp. 84–85.

[48] A/4557, 2 November 1960.

[49] The Belgian population of Leopoldville, which had dropped to 4,800 in July, was back to 6,000 in October. See Gordon, *loc. cit.*, pp. 79–82.

Even in the College of Commissioners-General, Belgian Chefs de Cabinet assumed a directive role, with corresponding diminution of the co-operation shown to the United Nations military and civilian authorities. It should be added that Belgium strongly contested this view of the development and considered Mr. Dayal's views as biased and unsupported by the facts.[50] One further disturbing development was the arrest by ANC of Lumumba, who had voluntarily left ONUC's protection on 27 November; this action, backed and defended by Kasavubu, alienated the Afro-Asian States to the extent that five States contributing troops to ONUC—Ceylon, Guinea, Indonesia, the United Arab Republic and Yugoslavia—announced their intention to withdraw their contingents.

It was against this background that the Security Council met from 7–14 December. However, having debated the situation produced by the internal disorder, the uncertain constitutional position of the various factions and the return of the Belgian non-military personnel,[51] the Council was unable to agree on any positive Resolution.[52] Similarly the Assembly, meeting from 16–20 December, failed to adopt either the joint United Kingdom/United States Resolution[53] asking the Secretary-General to continue to discharge his mandate and to continue to ensure that no foreign military or para-military personnel were introduced into the Congo; or the eight-Power (Afro-Asian and Yugoslavian) Resolution[54] urging the liberation of political prisoners, the neutralisation of armed forces, withdrawal of all Belgian military personnel, advisers and technicians and the establishment of a Standing Committee on the Congo. The lack of any dominant will amongst United Nations Member States on what policy should be pursued could not but weaken the Secretary-General's hand and, for the first time, his policy had failed to win specific endorsement from the Assembly.

When the Security Council met again from 12–14 January at the request of the Soviet Union to discuss the Belgian action in allowing Congolese troops from Leopoldville to attack Bukavu through Ruandi-Urundi,[55] no Resolution could be adopted.[56] By the beginning of

---

[50] Note Verbale to the Secretary-General, dated 7 December 1960 (A/4629).

[51] See *post*, pp. 195–196.

[52] A four-Power Resolution (S/4578/Rev.1) was rejected by 7–3 (Ceylon, Poland, U.S.S.R.)–1 (Tunisia), as were the Soviet amendments to this Resolution. The Soviet Resolution (S/4579) was rejected 2–8–1.

[53] A/L. 332; 43–22–32.

[54] A/L 331 and Add. 1; 28–42–27. Whilst no Resolution was adopted the Secretary-General on 21 December communicated with the President of the Congo, emphasising the widespread opinion in the Assembly that Parliament should be reconvened (S/4606).

[55] See *post*, p. 228. Kivu and Orientale provinces had, at the end of December, fallen under the control of Antoine Gizenga, formerly deputy Prime Minister to Lumumba, and the ANC troops of Colonel Mobutu had been ousted. This expedition by the ANC was designed to re-assert the authority of the Central Government in Kivu, but proved a failure.

[56] The three-Power Resolution (Ceylon, Liberia, U.A.R.) S/4625 which, *inter alia*, recommended the Assembly to consider this act a violation of the trusteeship agreement, was not adopted, receiving 4–0–7.

February there had been complaints by President Kasavubu of interference by the United Arab Republic in the domestic affairs of the
Congo,[57] protests by Afro-Asian powers over the treatment and continued detention of Mr. Lumumba,[58] and protests by Belgium about
the treatment of Belgian nationals in Orientale and Kivu provinces[59];
the Security Council therefore met on 1, 2 and 7 February in response
to three separate requests. The Secretary-General, addressing the
Council on 1 February, evidently felt that the prime need was to
ensure the army's withdrawal from politics and its reorganisation so
as to bring about a disciplined force under the control of a constitutional government. Various representatives, however, reverted to
questions such as the necessity for measures to ensure the release of
Mr. Lumumba, the reconvening of Parliament, the withdrawal of
Belgian and foreign military and para-military personnel and the
disarming of Colonel Mobutu's forces. During the adjournment
from 7 to 13 February the Council learnt of the renewal of offensive
action by the Katangese force against the population of Northern
Katanga[60]; it also learnt first of the escape of Mr. Lumumba and, on
13 February, of his death.[61] This tragic development led to a determined attack on the Secretary-General by the Soviet Union and
certain other States, calling for his resignation. An extreme Soviet
draft Resolution[62] was followed by a less extreme three-Power draft
Resolution[63] from Ceylon, Liberia and the United Arab Republic.
During an adjournment from 17–20 February there were circulated
two messages from the Conciliation Commission to the Advisory
Committee (which a covering note from the Committee warned
contained conclusions not necessarily acceptable to all members of
the Committee)[64] and several proposals for a solution of the problem
by the President of Ghana.[65] Meeting again on 20 February the
Council learnt of further political arrests and executions[66] so that a
second three-Power Resolution was introduced, dealing with the
question of arrests, deportations and assassinations.[67] In the voting
on these three Resolutions the Soviet proposal was rejected,[68] the

---

[57] S/4639. The allegation was specifically that a U.A.R. aircraft had landed
with arms for the authorities in Stanleyville.
[58] S/4641.
[59] S/4649.
[60] S/4691 and Add. 1, 12 and 16 February 1961 and, later, Add. 2 on 20
February.
[61] S/4688, Report from Mr. Dayal dated 12 February and S/4688/Add.1, dated
13 February.
[62] S/4706. This would have condemned the actions of Belgium as leading to
the murder of Lumumba, called on Members to apply Art. 41 sanctions
against Belgium and instructed the UN Command to arrest Tshombé and
Mobutu and disarm ANC, remove Belgian troops and personnel and dismiss
the Secretary-General.
[63] S/4722.
[64] Annual Report of the Secretary-General, *Off. Rec. G.A.*, 16th Sess., Suppl.
No. 1 (A/4800), p. 35.
[65] S/4725 and Add. 1.
[66] S/4727 and Add. 1, 2.
[67] S/4733 and Rev. 1.   [68] 8–0–2.

first three-Power Resolution was adopted [69] and the second three-Power Resolution was not adopted.[70] Hence the only Resolution adopted was the important Resolution of 21 February which clarified the mandate without providing a wider legal basis; it provided that:

A.

" The Security Council, . . .

1. *Urges* that the United Nations take immediately all appropriate measures to prevent the occurrence of civil war in the Congo, including arrangements for cease-fires, the halting of all military operations, the prevention of clashes, and the use of force, if necessary, in the last resort;

2. *Urges* that measures be taken for the immediate withdrawal and evacuation from the Congo of all Belgian and other foreign military and para-military personnel and political advisers not under the United Nations Command, and mercenaries;

3. *Calls* upon all States to take immediate and energetic measures to prevent the departure of such personnel for the Congo from their territories, and for the denial of transit and other facilities to them;

4. *Decides* that an immediate and impartial investigation be held in order to ascertain the circumstances of the death of Mr. Lumumba and his colleagues and that the perpetrators of these crimes be punished;

5. *Reaffirms* the Security Council Resolutions of 14 July, 22 July and 9 August 1960 and the General Assembly Resolution 1474 (ES–IV) of 20 September 1960 and reminds all States of their obligations under these Resolutions."

B.

" The Security Council,

Gravely concerned at the continuing deterioration in the Congo, and the prevalence of conditions which seriously imperil peace and order, and the unity and territorial integrity of the Congo, and threaten international peace and security, . . .

1. *Urges* the convening of the Parliament and the taking of necessary protective measures in that connexion;

2. *Urges* that Congolese armed units and personnel should be reorganised and brought under discipline and control, and arrangements be made on impartial and equitable bases to that end and with a view to the elimination of any possibility of interference by such units and personnel in the political life of the Congo;

3. *Calls* upon all States to extend their full co-operation and assistance and take such measures as may be necessary on their part, for the implementation of this Resolution."

Following the adoption of this Resolution the Secretary-General, in consultation with the Advisory Committee, undertook measures designed to implement the Resolution.[71] These involved, first, the

[69] 9–0–2 (France, U.S.S.R.).

[70] As revised, the draft Resolution received 6–0–5 and therefore failed to secure the required majority of 7. The U.S.A. and U.K. representatives explained that, had the amendments calculated to remove the somewhat one-sided preambular paragraph not been vetoed by the U.S.S.R., they would have voted for the Resolution. The Secretary-General announced his regret at this Resolution not being adopted and said he would use its " full moral value " in directing ONUC's efforts in the light of the fact that there had been no difference of opinion over the operative paragraphs.

[71] For successive reports on the implementation of the Resolution, see S/4752, 27 February and Add. 1; S/4771, 20 March 1961; S/4790/Add.1; S/4807 and

substantial increase of the strength of ONUC [72] and approaches to
President Kasavubu and other Congolese leaders [73] to secure their
immediate co-operation. The Congolese President had, on 22 February,[74] informed the Security Council of his apprehension that the
Resolution might be interpreted in a way contrary to his country's
sovereignty and of his intention to resist any violation of Congolese
sovereignty, whether by the United Nations or any other power.
Incidents involving the arrest of and violence against United Nations
personnel occurred in Leopoldville on 26 and 27 February,[75] and on
27 February President Kasavubu in a broadcast charged the United
Nations with "betrayal" and called on Mr. Tshombé to unite with
him in the face of a common danger.[76] A series of attacks against
ONUC occurred, by ANC forces, between 3 and 5 March [77] and by
Katangese gendarmerie in Elisabethville later in April. During late
February and early March what was described in the reports of the
Special Representative of the Secretary-General as the "civil war
situation" deteriorated, and hostilities intensified in the Kasai sector,
especially around Luluabourg, whilst in Katanga the attacks by the
gendarmerie on Baluba villages continued, resulting in the capture of
Manono, which remained in their control until reoccupied by the
United Nations on 6 June; in the Equateur-Orientale sector no
fighting occurred but the arrival of ANC troops led to extreme
tension.[78] Clearly co-operation was not forthcoming.

The second measure was directed to securing the withdrawal of
Belgian and other foreign military and para-military personnel,
political advisers and mercenaries. Notes to all Member States were
dispatched by the Secretary-General on 22 and 23 February, calling
their attention to their obligations under the Resolution of 21 February, and an exchange of correspondence took place with Belgium
during 22 February—4 March 1961 [79] with no satisfactory results.
Parallel negotiations with the Congolese President and Mr. Tshombé
were undertaken, assisted by the dispatch of Messrs. Robert Gardiner
and F. C. Nwokedi to Leopoldville, and on 17 April an agreement
was signed by Congolese and United Nations representatives on the
general principles concerning the implementation of the Resolution
of 21 February.[80]

Add 1, 17 and 18 May 1961; S/4841 and Add. 1–3, 20 June 1961; S/4940 and
Add. 1–12, and Add. 12/Corr.1, 14 September 1961; S/4940/Add.13; S/4940/
Add.14, 15 and Corr. 1, 16–19, 29 November–22 December 1961.

[72] *Post*, pp. 206–207.
[73] S/4752, 27 February, Annex IV.
[74] S/4743. For the Secretary-General's reply, see S/4752, Annex IV; by letter
dated 25 February Kasavubu accused ONUC of opposing ANC forces at Ikela
whilst giving "free passage to the rebels from Stanleyville" (S/4750/Add.2).
For the report of the Special Representative on this incident, see S/4750/
Add. 1, 4, 5.
[75] S/4753.
[76] S/4761, Annex I.
[77] Report of the Special Representative, 8 March 1961, S/4761 and Corr. 1;
see *post*, p. 204.   [78] S/4750/Add. 4, 5, 6, 7 and S/4791.
[79] S/4752, Annex I and Add. 1, 2, 4.   [80] *Post*, p. 195.

When the General Assembly resumed its fifteenth session on 7 March the situation revolved around two central problems: the first was to secure the implementation of the Resolution of 21 February; and the second was to promote the political unity of the Congo without which the efforts of ONUC were largely stultified.

On the 15 April the Assembly was in fact able to pass three separate Resolutions. The first, a twenty-one Power Resolution,[81] recited the Assembly's conviction (which the Secretary-General had long held) that the "central factor" was the continued presence of Belgian and other foreign military and para-military personnel, political advisers and mercenaries and called on Belgium to comply fully and promptly with the will of the Security Council and of the Assembly. It also *decided* that these personnel shall be completely withdrawn and evacuated and called on all States to co-operate in implementing the Resolution. This Resolution therefore dealt with the first of the two central problems.

A second Resolution sponsored by seventeen Powers[82] was adopted which dealt primarily with the second central problem. Having noted the report of the Conciliation Commission,[83] it reaffirmed its own and the Security Council Resolutions, particularly that of 21 February; it called on the Congolese authorities to desist from attempting a military solution and considered control over the influx of arms by the Secretary-General essential; it urged the release of political prisoners and the convening of Parliament; it decided to appoint a Commission of Conciliation of seven members; and it urged the Congolese authorities to co-operate.

The third Resolution adopted, a four-Power Resolution[84] also dealt with the implementation of the Security Council Resolution of

---

[81] Resol. 1599 (XV), adopted 61–5–33. A clause providing for withdrawal within 21 days failed to achieve a two-thirds majority on a separate vote and a Congolese amendment (A/L.346) making withdrawal conditional upon replacement of such personnel by persons recruited with UN assistance was rejected.

[82] Resol. 1600 (XV), adopted 60–16–23. An 8-Power African amendment (A/L. 342 and Corr. 1 and Add. 1) to delete specific reference to the Resolution of 21 February, to amend the provision concerning the convening of Parliament so as to simply call on the Chief of State to make provision for a return to normal parliamentary life, and to provide for a Commission of "assistance" rather than "conciliation" was rejected.

[83] A/4711 and Corr. 1 and Add. 1 and 2. This Commission of 15 members, mainly African, had been established by the Advisory Committee under Resol. 1474 (ES–IV) of 20 September 1960. It was attacked by the Soviet Union and others as not an official UN organ and the members from Guinea, Indonesia, Mali and the U.A.R. had withdrawn from it. The report was not signed by the Ghanaian representative, and the Nigerians had reservations. However, its principal conclusions were that the *Loi Fondamentale* was incomplete and ill-adapted to the situation, that the Army must be isolated from politics and civil war cease, that the principal Congolese political leaders should meet at a neutral place, that all political prisoners should be released and arrests and executions should cease, and that the main cause of the deteriorating situation was the deliberate violation of the decisions of the Security Council and Assembly calling on Members to refrain from assisting either side for military purposes.

[84] Resol. 1601 (XV), adopted 45–3–49.

21 February in that it decided to establish a Commission of Investigation of four members to investigate the circumstances of the death of Mr. Lumumba.

A Soviet draft Resolution,[85] the fourth submitted to the Assembly, was rejected.

It may be seen, therefore, that, apart from establishing the Commissions of Conciliation and Investigation, the effect of these Resolutions was not to inaugurate new policies but to reinforce those already adopted and, in particular, to throw the moral weight of Assembly support behind the Security Council's Resolution of 21 February. The problem of political unity, of effecting a reconciliation between the Congolese political leaders, was clearly the one in which the Assembly considered that it might assist the most. However, the absence of any specific reference to the meeting of eighteen Congolese political leaders [86] at Tananarive in Madagascar on 8 March and to its decisions to establish a confederation, coupled with the specific reference to the convening of Parliament " so that Parliament may take the necessary decisions concerning the formation of a national government and on the future constitutional structure of the Republic of the Congo in accordance with the constitutional processes laid down in the *Loi Fondamentale*," suggest that the Assembly was reluctant to approve of any constitutional solution which was not based upon parliamentary action and sanction.

The solution of the internal constitutional difficulties thus remained an essential precondition of successful ONUC operation, and was far from being realised. A conference at Coquilhatville from 23 April to 28 May 1961 advocated reorganisation on a federal basis, but this met with opposition from Mr. Tshombé who was thereupon detained by the Leopoldville authorities. President Kasavubu's announcement of his intention to convene Parliament in Leopoldville was countered by Mr. Gizenga's announcement of his intention to convene it at Kamina, where he asked for United Nations protection for Parliament. The good offices of the representative of

[85] A/L.341 and Corr.1, rejected by 53–29–17. This Resolution would have declared that no actions violating the unity, political independence and territorial integrity of the Congo should be allowed, that it was deemed necessary for Parliament to convene within 21 days and would have requested the UN Command to ensure the safety of members of Parliament.

[86] These included President Kasavubu, Mr. Ileo (whose " provisional " government had replaced the Council of Commissioners-General on 9 February by decree of the President but had not been approved by Parliament, still adjourned since 11 October), Mr. Tshombé and Mr. Kalonji—but not Mr. Gizenga (heading the " government " established in Stanleyville in December and exercising authority over Orientale and Kivu provinces) who was invited but did not attend. The other decisions, to call for a cessation of the transport of the Indian contingent of ONUC and to request the UN to seek an Advisory Opinion from the I.C.J. on the legality of the Resolution of 21 February, were scarcely calculated to secure the Assembly's support for this meeting.

the Secretary-General assisted in arranging a meeting of delegations from both Leopoldville and Stanleyville on 13 June at United Nations Headquarters in Leopoldville, and from this ensued an agreement to convene Parliament at the University of Louvanium on 19 June— which was to be "neutralised" by the United Nations for that purpose.[87] The authorities in South Kasai, but not the Katangese authorities,[88] subscribed to this agreement. From this meeting of Parliament in July–August, a Government of "national unity and political reconciliation" emerged under Mr. Adoula; yet Katangese secession remained a fact. The Secretary-General on 13 August wrote to Prime Minister Adoula confirming that the United Nations would deal with his Government as the Central Government and would render aid and assistance to it exclusively: thus the United Nations henceforth had a "legal" Government with which to deal.

The problem of Katanga thus remained as the outstanding problem, and, whilst President Kasavubu by Ordinance of 24 August 1961 ordered the immediate expulsion of all non-Congolese elements from the Katangese forces (and called on the United Nations Command to assist in its execution) it became apparent that Mr. Tshombé and his advisers were not prepared to see the withdrawal of these elements upon which the strength of their position so largely depended.[89] By September the resistance offered to the United Nations in its task of apprehending and evacuating these elements, a task assumed on the basis of paragraph A-2 of the Security Council's Resolution of 21 February and the Presidential Ordinance of 24 August, mounted and on 13 September a sizeable military action between ONUC and Katangese forces occurred in Elisabethville and soon spread to Jadotville, Kamina and other areas. It was during his flight to Ndola in Northern Rhodesia for the purpose of negotiating a cease-fire with Mr. Tshombé that the Secretary-General met his death, on 17 September.[90] On 20 September a provisional cease-fire was negotiated by the Chief of the ONUC civilian operations, M. Khiari, and this was further implemented by a protocol of 13 October 1961.[91] A renewal of hostilities, this time between Katangese forces and Central Government forces towards the end of October was regarded by the United Nations Command as a breach of the cease-fire agreement, and early in November acts of disorder

---

[87] See Report of 4 August 1961 on measures taken by UN to assist in implementing this agreement, S/4917.

[88] The action of the Katangese authorities may be regarded as going back on the agreement reached between Mr. Tshombé and President Kasavubu in the protocol signed 24 June 1961 to convene Parliament and integrate Katanga into the Republic. Mr. Tshombé had been released on 22 June.

[89] The details of the attempts to bring about the expulsion of these elements are given *post*, pp. 195–196.

[90] See S/4940/Add. 5 and 9. No satisfactory explanation of the crash, except in the sense of a failure to find evidence of sabotage, was able to be made by the UN Commission of Investigation: see Report of 24 April 1962, A/5069 and Add. 1.   [91] See S/4940/Add. 11.

and attacks on United Nations forces were occurring, by mutinous units of the National Army at Luluabourg, in Kasai province, and at Kindu in Kivu province.[92]

When the Security Council met on 13 November [93] a draft Resolution,[94] submitted by Ceylon, Liberia and the United Arab Republic, proposed that the Acting Secretary-General be authorised to take vigorous action, including the use of force, for the apprehension and deportation of the foreign elements covered by the Resolution of 21 February. Several States, including France, the United Kingdom, China, Sweden and Belgium spoke against such extreme measures, favouring a path of pacification and conciliation, and the United States submitted several amendments to the proposal [95] which were then the subject of sub-amendments by the U.S.S.R.[96] In the voting certain of the amendments of the United States were adopted and the draft Resolution, as amended, was then adopted on 24 November in the following terms [97] :

" The Security Council, . . .

Reaffirming the policies and purposes of the United Nations with respect to the Congo (Leopoldville) as set out in the aforesaid Resolutions, namely :

(a) To maintain the territorial integrity and the political independence of the Republic of the Congo;

(b) To assist the Central Government of the Congo in the restoration and maintenance of law and order;

(c) To prevent the occurrence of civil war in the Congo;

(d) To secure the immediate withdrawal and evacuation from the Congo of all foreign military, paramilitary and advisory personnel not under the United Nations Command, and all mercenaries; and

(e) To render technical assistance, . . .

1. *Strongly deprecates* the secessionist activities illegally carried out by the provincial administration of Katanga, with the aid of external sources and manned by foreign mercenaries;

2. *Further deprecates* the armed action against United Nations forces and personnel in the pursuit of such activities;

3. *Insists* that such activities shall cease forthwith, and *calls upon* all concerned to desist therefrom;

4. *Authorises* the Secretary-General to take vigorous action, including the use of requisite measures of force, if necessary, for the immediate apprehension, detention pending legal action and/or deportation of all foreign military and

---

[92] See Report of Officer-in-Charge of ONUC, dated 16 November, S/4940/Add. 13.

[93] Ethiopia, Nigeria and the Sudan requested the meeting. Prior to the meeting, on 11 November, the report of the Commission of Investigation established by Assembly Resol. 1601 (XV) of 15 April 1961 to investigate the circumstances of Mr. Lumumba's death was published (S/4976): this Commission had not been able to visit the Congo, but, on the evidence, rejected the official Katangese version of his death and accepted the likelihood of the implication of Katangese provincial officials in his death and concluded that President Kasavubu, Mr. Tshombé and the Katangese Minister of the Interior, Mr. Munongo, should not escape responsibility.

[94] S/4985 and Rev. 1.

[95] S/4989 and Corr. 2 and Rev. 1 and 2.

[96] S/4991.

[97] S/5002, adopted 9–0–2 (France, U.K.). Reports on the implementation of this Resolution and the previous Resolution of 21 February can be found in S/5053 and Add. 1–5, 5/Corr. 1, 6, 6/Corr. 1, 7, 8.

paramilitary personnel and political advisers not under the United Nations Command, and mercenaries as laid down in paragraph A-2 of the Security Council Resolution of February 21, 1961;

5. Further *requests* the Secretary-General to take all necessary measures to prevent the entry or return of such elements under whatever guise and also of arms, equipment or other material in support of such activities;

6. *Requests* all States to refrain from the supply of arms, equipment or other material which could be used for warlike purposes, and to take the necessary measures to prevent their nationals from doing the same, and also to deny transportation and transit facilities for such supplies across their territories, except in accordance with the decisions, policies and purposes of the United Nations;

7. *Calls upon* all Member States to refrain from promoting, condoning or giving support by acts of omission or commission, directly or indirectly, to activities against the United Nations often resulting in armed hostilities against the United Nations forces and personnel;

8. *Declares* that all secessionist activities against the Republic of the Congo are contrary to the *Loi Fondamentale* and Security Council decisions and specifically *demands* that such activities which are now taking place in Katanga shall cease forthwith;

9. *Declares* full and firm support for the Central Government of the Congo, and the determination to assist that Government in accordance with the decisions of the United Nations to maintain law and order and national integrity, to provide technical assistance and to implement those decisions;

10. *Urges* all Member States to lend their support, according to their national procedures, to the Central Government of the Republic of the Congo, in conformity with the Charter and the decisions of the United Nations;

11. *Requests* all Member States to refrain from any action which may directly or indirectly impede the policies and purposes of the United Nations in the Congo and is contrary to its decisions and the general purpose of the Charter."

The crucial parts of the Resolution were, of course, the paragraphs 4 and 5 which authorised the Secretary-General to use a degree of force which surpassed the limits of self-defence and involved positive action. This Resolution was in fact regarded by the Katangese authorities as a decision to launch a war on Katanga [98] and a highly inflammatory propaganda campaign was soon followed by repeated incidents of violence against United Nations personnel and road-blocks were erected by Katangese gendarmerie, severing the United Nations line of communications between the Headquarters and the airport.[99] On 5 December these road-blocks were cleared by force by Indian troops and United Nations planes attacked the airports at Jadotville and Kolwezi and disarmed gendarmerie at Manono. A series of direct attacks by the mercenary-led gendarmerie against United Nations positions occurred, necessitating the reinforcement of United Nations troops and allowing the United Nations to take the initiative militarily, so that, once again, the United Nations became involved in serious fighting.[1] That this degree of initiative was not

---

[98] See the speech by Tshombé on 25 November at a public meeting in Elisabethville : S/4950/Add. 15.

[99] S/4940/Add. 15 and Corr. 1 and Add. 16–19.

[1] For a description of these events, see the Secretary-General's Annual Report: *Off. Rec. G.A.*, 17th Sess., Suppl. No. 1 (A/5201), pp. 14–15 and S/4940/Add. 17.

welcomed by all States is clear from the appeals for a cease-fire received by the Secretary-General from the United Kingdom, Belgium, Greece, Madagascar and the Congo (Brazzaville).[2]

A rapprochement between Mr. Tshombé and Prime Minister Adoula occurred, through the good offices of the United States and the United Nations, resulting in a declaration by Mr. Tshombé of 21 December at Kitona accepting the *Loi Fondamentale*, recognising the indissoluble unity of the Republic and the authority of the Central Government, recognising President Kasavubu as head of State and agreeing to place the Katangese gendarmerie under his authority, and agreeing to Katangese participation in the constitutional Commission due to meet in Leopoldville on 3 January and in the national Parliament.[3] With the Kitona declaration a good deal of the tension was lifted, and the Katangese provincial assembly met to discuss its implications. At the same time the United Nations and Mr. Tshombé agreed on new measures to bring about the expulsion of mercenaries.[4] Mutiny amongst ANC personnel continued to occur, with consequent disorder, at Kongolo in North Katanga; and in Kasai Mr. Gizenga's renewed opposition to the Central Government brought about conflict between the provincial gendarmerie supporting Mr. Gizenga and ANC forces in Stanleyville, terminating in the surrender of the gendarmerie and Mr. Gizenga's dismissal from his post as Vice-President by President Kasavubu.[5]

Meeting on 30 January at the request of the U.S.S.R., the Security Council adjourned in deference to the views of the Congolese Prime Minister[6] and the Conference of African and Malagasy States[7] (then meeting at Lagos) who regarded such a meeting as inopportune at a time when conciliation within the Congo was in progress. The Adoula-Tshombé talks in March and April produced certain proposals which, after consideration by the Katangese delegation, drew forth Katangese counter-proposals and a new series of meetings in May were attended by United Nations representatives but by the end of July the Acting Secretary-General was reluctantly forced to inform his Advisory Committee that no agreement between the parties had been reached.[8] The proposals of the Acting Secretary-General for a political settlement[9]—the "Plan of National Reconciliation"—went unheeded.

When the Assembly met in September there had been virtually no

[2] S/5035.
[3] See Report by Secretary-General on the Kitona negotiations, S/5038, 21 December 1961.
[4] *Post*, p. 195.
[5] See generally Gordon, *loc. cit.*, pp. 160–162.
[6] S/5066.
[7] S/5069.
[8] For the Report by the Officer-in-Charge of ONUC on the talks, see S/5053/Add. 10 and Annexes. Prime Minister Adoula openly charged Mr. Tshombé with negotiating solely for the purpose of buying time in which to build up his armed forces: *ibid.*, Annex 2, p. 4.
[9] S/5053/Add. 11 and Add. 1 and Annexes.

change in the political impasse, and by October the Cuban crisis had become the focal point of concern, rather than the Congo. However, the Officer-in-Charge of ONUC reported a build-up of Katangese mercenary strength and frequent incidents between ONUC and Katangese forces occurred throughout September.[10] The Officer-in-Charge of ONUC subsequently reported that these incidents were in part deliberately designed to make the position of ONUC in Elisabethville untenable.

Since the Katangese authorities had given no evidence of their intention to fulfil the Plan of National Reconciliation, on 10 December 1962 the Officer-in-Charge of ONUC informed Mr. Tshombé that phases I–IV of the Plan would henceforth be applied.[11] These envisaged an economic boycott, in particular a concerted boycott by all interested governments of all imports of copper and cobalt into their territory except when these had been exported under licence from the Central Government at Leopoldville. On 11 December the Secretary-General again appealed to Belgium to exert its influence on the Union Minière so as to make it desist from paying revenues to the Katangese authorities.[12]

Renewed fighting against ONUC positions in Elisabethville occurred during 24–28 December and road-blocks were established by the gendarmerie; all attempts to secure Mr. Tshombé's agreement to a cease-fire failed and on 29 December a statement by Mr. Tshombé was issued threatening the fullest possible resistance to the United Nations. The United Nations thereupon launched an action to restore the security of ONUC by expelling the gendarmerie and to assert their freedom of movement by clearing all road-blocks and, after this had succeeded around Elisabethville, troops operating from the Kamina base occupied Kaminaville and Kipushi and a rapid advance to Jadotville occurred which appeared to have been decided upon by the ONUC military officers on the spot without specific instructions from the Secretary-General. Kolwezi was entered, unopposed, on 21 January.[13] This operation was subsequently described by the Secretary-General as "highly successful"[14] and, indeed, on 14 January Mr. Tshombé indicated that he was ready to proclaim the end of the secession of Katanga, to grant freedom of

---

[10] S/5053/Add. 12 and Corr. 1.
[11] S/5053/Add. 14. In particular, Portugal, the U.K. and the Union of S. Africa were asked to stop shipments of copper through their territories until such time as the question of payments by the Union Minière to Katanga had been settled. On 15 January 1963 representatives of the Union Minière signed an agreement with representatives of the Central Government in Leopoldville whereby all export proceeds would be remitted to the Monetary Council of the Central Government.
[12] *Ibid.*
[13] See the Report to the Secretary-General by the Officer-in-Charge, covering events from 26 November–4 January (S/5053/Add. 14) and from 5–23 January (S/5053/Add. 15).
[14] Report by the Secretary-General of 4 February 1963: S/5240 and Add. 1.

movement to the United Nations and to co-operate with them.[15]   On 23 January Mr. Ileo arrived in Elisabethville as the Minister Resident of the Central Government.

With this operation the *de facto* secession of Katanga was virtually ended.[16]   Certainly problems of reconstruction, of maintaining order, and of integrating the Katangese gendarmerie into the ANC, remained.[17]   Moreover, the political problems, of a constitutional nature, which lay before the Congolese authorities were considerable; but, clearly, the stage had been reached at which the military side of ONUC could be gradually liquidated.[18]   It is appropriate, therefore, to turn from this *historique* to consideration of the separate problems which arose and which directly concern the establishment and operation of ONUC.

II. THE CONSTITUTIONAL BASIS OF THE RESOLUTIONS ADOPTED

The complexity of this question results from the facts that the Resolutions stemmed from two different organs, the Security Council and the General Assembly, that neither organ specifically stated the Charter provisions upon which particular Resolutions were based and that individual Resolutions were, in their various operative paragraphs, addressed to the Secretary-General, to States and even to non-State entities.   Clearly a separation of Resolutions adopted by the Assembly from those adopted by the Council is essential to any understanding of their constitutional basis.   Moreover, it is equally essential to distinguish those Resolutions, or parts of Resolutions, which were concerned with the creation of ONUC and its operation from those addressed to States or non-State entities.   Whether the actual conduct of ONUC, or of States, was consistent with the Resolutions is, again, a quite separate question which will be dealt with under heads IV, VII and VIII below.

[15] *Ibid.*   Mr. Tshombé had left Elisabethville on 28 December, visiting Salisbury in N. Rhodesia; he returned to Elisabethville on 8 January, left again on 12 January for the Rhodesian border, returning again on 17 January.

[16] Although it was not until 25 June 1963 that the Congolese Parliament by bill "abolished" Katanga as a separate province and integrated it into a new province called East Katanga : *New York Times*, 26 June 1963.

[17] The Secretary-General on 20 March informed the Advisory Committee that, in response to a request from Prime Minister Adoula, the UN would establish a co-ordinating group to help in this process of integration and in the training and modernisation of the ANC.   By April 1963 it had become apparent that disagreement between Adoula and the Secretary-General had arisen over the extent to which the Congo could arrange, on a bilateral basis, for assistance from States without UN concurrence; see *News Summaries* for April/May, releases 17–21/63.   The UN eventually refused to take part in a training programme for the ANC which involved the provision of experts on a bilateral basis, by agreement between the Congolese Government and certain Member States, *outside* the organisation and control of ONUC.   See Report by the Secretary-General on Military Disengagement in the Congo, *U.N. Review*, Vol. 10, No. 9, October 1963, p. 44.

[18] See *post*, p. 235.

1. *The creation of ONUC by the Security Council*

The creation, or establishment, of ONUC was accomplished by the Secretary-General under the express authorisation of the Security Council. The Resolution of 14 July 1960,[19] para. 2:

"Decides to authorise the Secretary-General to take the necessary steps in consultation with the Government of the Republic of the Congo, to provide the Government with such military assistance as may be necessary, until, through the efforts of the Congolese Government with the technical assistance of the United Nations, the national security forces may be able, in the opinion of the Government, to meet fully their tasks."

On one view, advanced with great authority by Schachter,[20] this decision was taken under Chapter VII of the Charter, and, more specifically, under Article 40 of that Chapter. Certainly the absence of a specific finding under Article 39 of the Charter that there existed a "threat to the peace, breach of the peace or act of aggression" is not, according to the practice of the Council,[21] contrary to this view of the applicability of Chapter VII. Moreover the initial cables from the Congolese Government, which referred to "external aggression which is a threat to international peace," [22] the Secretary-General's own recourse to Article 99 in requesting an immediate meeting of the Council [23] and the statements of representatives within the Council,[24] all indicated a general acceptance of the view that the Council was faced with a "Chapter VII situation," that is to say a threat to or breach of international peace and security. The Secretary-General, in his First Report of 18 July, referred to "a threat to peace and security justifying United Nations intervention on the basis of the explicit request of the Government of the Republic of the Congo." [25] Moreover the references to Articles 25 and 49 of the Charter found in statements by the Secretary-General [26] and in the Security Council's Resolution of 9 August 1960 [27] equally indicate that binding decisions were being taken and, therefore, that Chapter VII was applicable to the situation. However, it was not until its Resolution of 21 February [28] that the Council itself used the actual phrase "threat to international peace and security." The

[19] S/4387.
[20] "Legal aspects of the United Nations action in the Congo," (1961) 55 A.J. 1. Also R. Y. Jennings, "The United Nations Force and the Congo," *The Listener*, 19 October 1961.
[21] *Repertory of practice of UN Organs*, Vol. 2, pp. 338–341.
[22] S/4382.
[23] *Ante*, p. 153.
[24] See *Off. Rec. S.C.*, 15th yr., 873rd Mtg., *passim*: the U.S.S.R., Poland and Tunisia referred to Belgian "aggression" (though no condemnation was made—see *ante*, p. 161) and Ecuador, Italy and France regarded the situation as one of potential international conflict. The Assembly took a similar view in Resol. 1600 (XV): *Off. Rec. G.A.*, 15th Sess., Suppl. No. 16A, p. 17.
[25] S/4389, p. 2.
[26] *Off. Rec. S.C.*, 15th yr., 884th Mtg., p. 4; and see the letter to the Katangese authorities, S/4417, p. 5.
[27] S/4426.
[28] S/4741.

International Court of Justice, in its Opinion of 20 July 1962, never-theless had little hesitation in stating that:

" The Resolution (of 14 July 1960), in the light of the appeal from the Govern-ment of the Congo, the report of the Secretary-General and the debate in the Security Council, was clearly adopted with a view to maintaining international peace and security." [29]

Accepting that ONUC was created under Chapter VII, the problem of finding the precise article within that Chapter upon which its creation rested remains. Certainly ONUC was not a force created under Article 42; the purposes of the Force were essentially different from those for which, at San Francisco, forces used under Article 42 were contemplated,[30] and the Secretary-General himself stressed that the ONUC action was not taken under Articles 41 or 42.[31] The International Court of Justice, in its Opinion of 20 July 1962,[32] found that " it is not necessary for the Court to express an opinion as to which article or articles of the Charter were the basis for the Resolutions of the Security Council" but added that " the operation did not involve ' preventive or enforcement measures' against any State under Chapter VII . . ." [33] Whilst this is not conclusive on the non-applicability of Articles 41 and 42,[34] it suggests that the Court did not feel these to be the appropriate articles. It is really in relation to the eventual authorisation to use force, contained in the Resolution of 21 February, that one is tempted to regard the constitutional basis of ONUC as having shifted to Article 42.[35] However, as we shall see in examining the function of ONUC, force was to be limited to the specific purposes of preventing civil war, and later, by the Resolution of 24 November, of expelling mercenaries. Whilst these Resolutions clearly entitled ONUC to go beyond mere self-defence, they cannot properly be regarded as authorising " enforcement action," or shifting the constitutional basis to Article 42; both the Opinion of the Court and the fact that no re-negotiation with contributing States took place support this view,[36] and, indeed, the Secretary-General throughout denied that enforcement measures under Article 42 were authorised.

---

[29] *I.C.J. Reports*, 1962, p. 175.   [30] UNCIO, vol. 12, 334, 580–581.
[31] Statement by the Secretary-General, 13 December 1960: *Off. Rec. S.C.*, 15th yr., 920th Mtg., pp. 18–19.
[32] *I.C.J. Reports*, 1962, p. 151.   [33] *Ibid.*, at p. 177.
[34] This because the words used in Arts. 41 and 42 do not necessarily pre-suppose that the action has to be enforcement action *against a State*: see Schachter, *loc. cit.*, pp. 7–8.
[35] Seyersted, "United Nations Forces," (1961) 37 *B.Y.I.L.* at p. 446, however, considers that it is possible " that since 21 February 1961 (or since August/September 1961) the Force has been acting under Article 42 [although] . . . it is also possible to treat the United Nations action as one under Article 40." But he admits that it is difficult to use these articles as relevant to the inception of the Force. Jennings, "The United Nations Force and the Congo," *The Listener*, 19 October 1961, also regards this Resolution of 21 February as authorising " enforcement measures."
[36] See Riad, "The United Nations Action in the Congo and its Legal Basis," (1961) 17 *Revue Egyptienne de droit International*, at p. 29. The Secretary-

Article 41, in referring to "measures involving the use of armed force" might conceivably be used as a basis for some kinds of peace-keeping operations, and indeed it was an article cited by the Secretary-General on at least one occasion.[37] However, it is scarcely appropriate to ONUC whose mandate was extended to include the right to use armed force. Moreover it had originally been envisaged as applicable to a form of enforcement action comparable to Article 42, but different in degree in that "economic" rather than "military" sanctions would be used.[38]

One is therefore tempted to turn, almost inevitably, to Article 40 as the possible constitutional basis of the decision to create the Force. Indeed, the Secretary-General himself cited this article when addressing the Security Council on 8 August 1960,[39] and again on 13 December 1960 said explicitly that:

"My own view, which I have expressed to the Council, is that the Resolutions may be considered as implicitly taken under Article 40 and, in that sense, as based on an implicit finding under Article 39."[40]

Moreover he was later to make repeated reference to this article when dealing with the question of control over the bases at Kitona, Ndjili and Kimona.[41] For these reasons, coupled with the constant insistence on the principle of non-intervention and the relevance of Article 2 (7) of the Charter[42]—which would not have applied to enforcement measures under Articles 41 or 42—the "official" United Nations view, at least of the Secretary-General, and that adopted by Schachter, is that it is in Article 40 that the constitutional basis of the Force is to be found. This is certainly a tenable view. Article 40 was certainly the basis of certain parts of the Resolutions addressed to Belgium, the Republic of the Congo and Member States. And, whilst it may be argued that a "call upon the parties concerned to comply with such provisional measures as it deems necessary or desirable" is essentially different from a decision to authorise the Secretary-General to provide military assistance, it may be reasoned that whenever the Council makes a call for provisional measures under Article 40 it may establish, either directly or by delegation to the Secretary-General, a subsidiary organ whose function shall be to

General had, in a statement to the Council on 20 February 1961, stated that a change in mandate would require a new consent from contributing States (*Off. Rec. S.C.*, 942nd Mtg., para. 218). His own view of the Resolution of 21 February was that "without any change of the United Nations mandate [it] widens its scope and application": S/4752, Annex I and Annex VII (a letter to African States). See also the Secretary-General's statement in *Off. Rec. G.A.*, 4th Emergency Sess., 859th Mtg., p. 34. As late as 17 April 1961 the Secretary-General was adamant that ONUC was not using force under Art. 42: A/C.5/864, statement at the 839th Mtg. of the Fifth Committee.

[37] *Off. Rec. S.C.*, 15th yr., 884th Mtg., para. 26.
[38] *Post*, p. 279.
[39] *Off. Rec. S.C.*, 15th yr., 884th Mtg., p. 4.
[40] *Ibid.*, 920th Mtg., p. 19.
[41] *Post*, p. 234.
[42] *Post*, pp. 196–200.

supervise or assist in the compliance by the parties with these provisional measures. Hence Article 40, coupled with the power to establish subsidiary organs in Article 29, affords a satisfactory basis for the Force, rather in the way in which these two provisions of the Charter provided a basis for certain of the observer groups which the Council has established.[43] The present writer's difficulty in accepting this as a complete answer to the question of the constitutional basis of ONUC is that, whilst the supervision of compliance with the call for provisional measures was a major part of ONUC's function, it was not the entire function: it is for this reason that a somewhat broader basis in Article 39 is preferred. Before turning to a consideration of Article 39, however, some reference must be made to alternatives suggested by various writers.

Draper[44] finds Article 29 in itself a satisfactory basis, a view which is unacceptable to the present writer since, whilst the Force may certainly be regarded as a subsidiary organ of the Security Council, it is unthinkable that it could have been created by a simple, procedural vote which is all that the application of that article requires.[45] The establishment of a subsidiary organ simply cannot be divorced from the *functions* entrusted to the organ; otherwise the Council could create a standing army, by a simple, procedural vote, even for enforcement action under Chapter VII.[46] In other words a Resolution which contemplates a subsidiary organ with a given function has to find its constitutional basis first and foremost in the articles justifying the function—and not in an article giving a general power to establish subsidiary organs.

The view of Halderman[47] is that ONUC has its substantive legal basis in Article 1 (1) of the Charter whereby a stated purpose of the Charter is:

"To maintain international peace and security, and to that end: to take effective collective measures for the prevention and removal of threats to the peace, and for the suppression of acts of aggression or other breaches of the peace . . ."

Certainly once it is conceded that the Security Council had acted on the assumption that there existed in the Congo a threat to international peace this article would make " collective measures " *intra vires* the Organisation. The term " collective measures " is nowhere defined, but it is believed the threefold criterion of Halderman is correct, namely:

[43] *Ante*, pp. 61–68.
[44] "The legal limitation upon the employment of weapons by the United Nations Force in the Congo," (1963) 12 I.C.L.Q. at p. 392.
[45] See *Repertory*, Vol. 2, pp. 72–73 for a discussion of the decision of 24 May 1948 on the Czechoslovak question.
[46] This reasoning is supported by the fact that, whilst Draper similarly indicates Art. 22 as the constitutional basis of UNEF (*ibid.*, p. 391), the I.C.J. in the *Expenses Case* did not rely on this article but turned to the more substantive articles dealing with the powers of the General Assembly, in particular Art. 14: see *post*, p. 289.
[47] "Legal Basis for United Nations Armed Forces," (1962) 56 A.J. 971.

" (1) They are measures taken by the United Nations;
   (2) They entail the application of tangible, as distinct from moral, pressures
       to international situations;
   (3) They are to be applied only in situations amounting to threats to the
       peace, breaches of the peace or acts of aggression." [48]

It is also believed that ONUC meets this criterion. The only real difficulty is whether one can rely on the general terms of Article 1 (1) without reference to the specific powers of the particular organ which decides upon, or possibly recommends,[49] such measures. It is believed that a simple reliance on Article 1 (1) is not enough, for it divorces the question entirely from the equally important question whether a particular organ has power to undertake a given course of action : otherwise it could be argued that ECOSOC could establish a Force like ONUC. Hence, in the Congo, the Security Council had to find a constitutional basis for its action not only in Article 1 (1) but also in Chapter VII of the Charter. As has been shown, whilst the Congo situation was clearly a " Chapter VII situation," a situation involving a threat to international peace and security (and therefore appropriate for " collective measures"), no specific article of Chapter VII quite fits the Resolutions adopted—at least so far as the establishment of the Force is concerned. It is perhaps a trite observation to say that at San Francisco, and therefore in the specific wording of Chapter VII, action like the Congo action simply was not contemplated. Yet, given that the Congo action was *intra vires* the Organisation, by virtue of Article 1 (1), it is not permissible to assume that in the absence of a specific power the Security Council had no power to create ONUC for the purposes entrusted to it. To do so would be to deny the essentially dynamic character of the Charter and the doctrine of *implied* powers which has become a prominent feature of the jurisprudence of the International Court of Justice in dealing with constitutional questions.[50] Moreover, as the Court has said in the *Expenses Case* :

" But when the Organisation takes action which warrants the assertion that it was appropriate for the fulfilment of one of the stated purposes of the United Nations, the presumption is that such action is not *ultra vires* the Organisation." [51]

There is little doubt that the Security Council could have created ONUC by means of recommendations to Member States under Article 39, rather in the way it had made recommendations to States with regard to assisting the Republic of Korea in June 1950. It chose, instead, to achieve the same result by way of authorising the Secretary-General to provide military assistance, knowing that the

[48] *Ibid.*, p. 974.
[49] As in the case of the Korean Force and of UNEF; see *post*, p. 307 for further development of this argument.
[50] See Seyersted, *loc. cit.*, pp. 447–471; Bowett, *The Law of International Institutions* (1963) pp. 274–280; and, generally, *post*, pp. 307–311.
[51] *I.C.J. Reports*, 1962, p. 168.

Secretary-General, who under Article 98 " Shall perform such other functions as are entrusted to him," would do this by way of negotiating with Member States for such assistance, following the UNEF precedent. Our conclusion is, therefore, that the establishment of ONUC was by Resolution of the Security Council to achieve the general purpose of the Organisation set out in Article 1 (1), in fulfilment of the Council's "primary responsibility for the maintenance of international peace and security," conferred by Article 24; and that, having made an implicit finding under Article 39, the Council acted under Chapter VII of the Charter so as to establish a United Nations Force for the purpose of supervising and enforcing compliance with the provisional measures ordered under Article 40 and for other purposes which were consistent with the general powers of the Council under Article 39.[52] In so acting the Council utilised its further powers under Article 98 to use the Secretary-General as its agent.

It may finally be added that whereas the Secretary-General found it necessary to refer to the explicit request or consent of the Republic of the Congo as a legal basis for the United Nations intervention in the Congo—regarding this as an element of the same order as the implicit finding of a threat to international peace and security[53]— it is believed that the question of consent to the presence of the Force is extraneous to the question of the constitutionality of its creation, which is all we are concerned with at this juncture. The existence of consent may certainly be regarded as evidence that ONUC was not in the nature of an "enforcement action" under Article 42 of the Charter, and, indeed, the International Court of Justice in the *Expenses Case* appears to have stressed the fact of consent as evidence of this. But the Charter provisions, on which ONUC's constitutional basis must be found, nowhere make any reference to consent by the host State. The question of consent to the presence of the Force on the territory of the Congo, and of whether such consent was strictly necessary, is postponed until section VIII (1) below, dealing with relations with the host State.

2. *The instructions to States given by the Security Council*

All the Resolutions adopted by the Security Council embody operative paragraphs addressed to States. There are, first, those paragraphs by which the Council called upon Belgium to withdraw its troops[54]

---

[52] This is not dissimilar from Seyersted's conclusion, *loc. cit.*, p. 446, although he is less sure about Chapter VII being applicable at all. Similarly Riad, *loc. cit.*, p. 19, accepts that Chapter VII was applicable but, like Schachter, regards Art. 40 as the applicable provision within that chapter. Certain of the statements made during the pleadings in the *Expenses Case* support the views advanced in the text above. See *I.C.J. Pleadings, Certain Expenses of the United Nations*, p. 162 (written statement of Denmark), pp. 302–305 (oral statement of Canada), p. 370 (statement of Norway).
[53] First Report, 18 July 1960, S/4389, p. 2.
[54] 14 July 1960, S/4387, para. 1; 22 July 1960, S/4405, para. 1; 9 August 1960, S/4426, para. 2.

and there is little doubt that, for them, an adequate constitutional basis can be found in Article 40.

Then there are various paragraphs addressed either to *all* States [55] or to all *Member* States,[56] and these are framed in terms of a " request " or a " call upon." The only clear difference between the two categories is that it is only in the case of those paragraphs addressed to *Member* States that Articles 25 and 49 are specifically invoked; there would, of course, be some difficulty about assuming that the obligations of those articles extend to non-Members. But with regard to non-Member States the Organisation has the general power of Article 2 (6) of the Charter and, moreover, when acting under Articles 39 or 40 the Security Council is not limited to acting in relation to Member States. Certainly the reference to Articles 25 and 49 [57] was clear indication that the instructions to Members were mandatory. The precise constitutional basis for these various requests and commands is never stated in the Resolutions and there is some difficulty in assuming Article 40 to provide this basis since that article speaks of a call to the " parties," and not all the Member States could be considered as " parties." However, even if Article 40 was not applicable, there is little difficulty in finding sufficient authorisation for the Security Council's action. The various requests and commands could be considered either as the " recommendations " envisaged under Article 39 or even the " measures . . . to be employed to give effect to its decisions . . ." under Article 41; even the general obligation contained in the first part of Article 2 (5) would provide a sufficient basis for the instructions to Member States.

3. *The instructions to non-State entities given by the Security Council*

Apart from the various directives given to the Secretary-General and the Force under Article 98 of the Charter, there are certain paragraphs which, directly or indirectly, convey instructions to the secessionist and other factions within the Congo. The Resolution of 9 August 1960, declaring that entry of ONUC into Katanga was necessary, the Resolution of 21 February 1961, urging that measures be taken for the withdrawal and evacuation of mercenaries and urging the convening of Parliament and reorganisation of Congolese armed units were, in a very real sense, directed at non-State entities. Even more directly the Resolution of 24 November 1961 strongly deprecated "the secessionist activities illegally carried out by the provincial administration of Katanga . . . [and] the armed action against United Nations forces . . ." It *insisted* that such activities should cease and called upon " all concerned " to desist. There is, as we have seen,[58] nothing

[55] S/4405, para. 2; S/4741, para. 3 (Resol. A) and para. 3 (Resol. B); S/5002, para. 6.
[56] S/4426, para. 5; S/5002, para. 7.
[57] S/4426, para. 5; see also General Assembly Resol. 1474 (ES–IV), para. 5 and S/4741, para. 5.
[58] *Ante*, p. 30.

novel in the proposition that the Security Council can address itself to entities other than States, and the legal basis for such action in the present case can be regarded as under Articles 39 or 40.

It may be noted that, as early as 4 August 1960, the Secretary-General had expressed the view (which no member of the Security Council disputed) that the Security Council Resolutions were mandatory on all factions within the Congo. In a reply to Tshombé he stated:

"The Secretary-General wishes to draw attention to Article 25 of the United Nations Charter, as also to Article 49, which Articles confer on the Security Council an authority applicable directly to governments, and *a fortiori* to subordinate territorial non-governmental authorities of Member nations." [59]

4. *The Resolutions of the General Assembly*

These were largely in the nature of an endorsement of the actions of the Security Council and the Secretary-General and were not concerned with the creation of the Force; they were all in the nature of "requests," "appeals" (as in the "appeal" to "all Congolese" to solve their internal conflicts [60]) and "urges," with the exception of the "calls" to the Congolese authorities to desist from attempting a military solution,[61] and "calls" to Belgium to comply with the will of the Security Council and General Assembly [62] and the "calls" to all States to refrain from unilateral assistance.[63] These would not, however, be of themselves mandatory. There is, however, the somewhat unusual *decision* that all Belgian and other foreign military, para-military personnel, political advisers and mercenaries shall be completely withdrawn and evacuated: this formed part of the Resolution of 15 April 1961.[64] Prima facie, the Assembly cannot take decisions binding on States; however, this particular "decision" may be regarded as one addressed not to States but to ONUC, or even as a simple endorsement of the Security Council's earlier Resolution of 21 February 1961. The general constitutional authority of the Assembly to make these Resolutions may be found in Article 14 [65] which, it may be recalled, unlike Articles 10 or 11, does not limit the addressees of recommendations of the Assembly to Member States and the Security Council.

---

[59] Second Report, S/4417, p. 5.
[60] Resol. 1474 /Rev. 1 (ES–IV), 20 September 1960.
[61] Resol. 1600 (XV) of 17 April 1961.
[62] Resol. 1599 (XV) of 15 April 1961.
[63] Resol. 1474/Rev. 1 (ES–IV).
[64] Resol. 1599 (XV). For a detailed survey of the Assembly's Resolutions, and their constitutional basis, see Riad, *loc. cit.*, pp. 22–27, 31–32.
[65] It may be recalled that it was in this article that the I.C.J. found the constitutional basis for UNEF in its opinion of 20 July 1962: see *ante*, p. 98.

III. THE ROLE OF THE SECRETARY-GENERAL

It is convenient after dealing with the Resolutions of the Security Council and General Assembly, and before turning to a detailed discussion of the functions of ONUC, to discuss the role of the Secretary-General. The Congo operation was, by the initial Resolution of 14 July, to be entrusted to the Secretary-General by a mandate which, in employing the phrase " to take the necessary steps," could scarcely have been wider. The technique, which had proved successful in the past, particularly with UNEF, has been accurately summarised in the phrase " leave it to Dag! " [66] However, whilst the means to be used were largely left to his discretion, the purposes of the " military assistance " were broadly set out in the Resolution of 14 July, and subsequent Resolutions further defined them, as we shall see in the next section in dealing with the functions of the Force. Initially, however, it was left very much to the Secretary-General to give substance to the vague terms of the Resolution of 14 July, and this he did by formulating the principles he conceived to be applicable to the Force, having indicated even prior to the adoption of that Resolution, in his statement to the Council, that he would follow the pattern and principles which had served for UNEF.[67] The Secretary-General took the position, in his First Report, that since the Resolution had been adopted in response to his initial statement to the Council—in which he had set out these principles—that statement became a " basic document in the interpretation of the mandate."

These principles which emerged for ONUC, and based on the UNEF experience, were:

1. The exclusive nature of the United Nations' control over the Force.[68]
2. The composition of the Force on the basis of assistance from African nations, but qualified by an element of universality essential to any United Nations' operation.[69]
3. The prohibition against interference in the internal, domestic affairs of the host State—the principle of non-intervention.[70]
4. The limitation of the Force to action in self-defence.[71]
5. The freedom of movement of the Force.[72]

Whilst not one of these principles went unchallenged as events

---

[66] Statement by the representative of the U.A.R., 9 December 1960: *Off. Rec. S.C.*, 15th yr., 960th Mtg., para. 90. He went on " this escapism on the part of United Nations bodies was hardly fair either to the Secretariat or to the United Nations as a whole."

[67] *Off. Rec. S.C.*, 15th yr., 873rd Mtg., para. 28 and, later, 885th Mtg., para. 65. These principles had been set out in the *Summary Study of Experience*, dated 9 October 1958: *Off. Rec. G.A.*, 13th Sess., Agenda item 65 (c), A/3943.

[68] First Report by the Secretary-General, S/4389, p. 3; and see *post*, pp. 233–236.

[69] *Ibid.*, p. 6; and see *post*, pp. 205–208.

[70] *Ibid.*, p. 5; and see *post*, pp. 196–200.

[71] *Ibid.*, p. 5; and see *post*, pp. 200–203.

[72] *Ibid.*, p. 3; and see *post*, pp. 203–205.

developed, it was the principle of non-intervention which, in its application, brought upon the Secretary-General the strongest criticism —and eventually the call by the Soviets for his resignation. The application of this principle, and the other principles, will be considered in detail after the functions of the Force have been outlined, for the very reason that the validity of these principles can only be tested in relation to the functions of the Force. For the moment our immediate interest is to see by what means, given these challenges to his interpretation of the mandate and his application of these principles, the Secretary-General sought to avoid the accusation that he was failing to carry out his mandate.

First, and naturally enough, he sought clarification of the mandate from the organ which had issued it. When Prime Minister Lumumba challenged the Secretary-General's view that ONUC could not be used to conquer Katanga, and end secession, by force [73] the Secretary-General on 21 August sought clarification of the mandate, and confirmation of his interpretation, from the Security Council.[74] This, tragically, was not forthcoming in any formal Resolution, although nine of the eleven members voiced their approval of his interpretation. This left the Secretary-General no choice, as he was to remind the General Assembly on 26 September, after Mr. Kruschev had called for his resignation, in words which are worth quoting:

"Sometimes one gets the impression that the Congo operation is looked at as being in the hands of the Secretary-General, as somehow distinct from the United Nations. No: this is your operation, gentlemen. . . . It is for you to indicate what you want to be done. As the agent of the Organisation, I am grateful for any positive advice, but if no such positive advice is forthcoming— as happened in the Security Council on August 21, when my line of implementation had been challenged from outside—then I have no choice but to follow my own conviction, guided by the principles to which I have just referred." [75]

This was not entirely a new position for the Secretary-General to be in, and he had on earlier occasions outlined the way in which his own office should be fulfilled in the absence of clear instructions from the political organs,[76] but it is true that on no previous occasion had this course of action been fraught with greater dangers. That the Secretary-General was reluctant to assume this burden of responsibility is apparent from his gentle admonition to the political organs. Speaking on 13 December 1960, the Secretary-General said:

---

[73] *Ante*, p. 157.   [74] *Off. Rec. S.C.*, 15th yr., 887th Mtg., p. 2.
[75] *Off. Rec. G.A.*, 15th Sess., 871st Plen. Mtg., p. 96.
[76] For example, his decision in July 1958 to enlarge UNOGIL, his role in Laos in 1959 and his discussions with the Union of South Africa in 1960 on the apartheid issue.

For three excellent discussions of the concept of the office of Secretary-General, as conceived by Hammarskjoeld, see Hammarskjoeld's own address to Oxford University on 30 May 1961, *The International Civil Servant in Law and in Fact* (Clarendon Press); Schachter, " Dag Hammarskjoeld and the relation of law to politics," (1962) 56 A.J. 1 and Stein, " Mr. Hammarskjoeld, the Charter Law and the future role of the UN Secretary-General," *ibid.*, p. 33.

" . . . there are daily decisions, involving interpretations in detail of the extent of our power, which I and my collaborators now have had to take alone for five months. Representatives of the Council or the Assembly might well shoulder on behalf of the General Assembly or the Council the fair share of the responsibility of those organs for current interpretations of the mandate." [77]

The second means used by the Secretary-General to ensure a fulfilment of his mandate in a way which was politically acceptable to United Nations' Members (or the majority of them, at least) was to seek advice and guidance from an Advisory Group. It may be recalled that a similar Advisory Committee had been established to assist the Secretary-General with UNEF.[78] When, therefore, the rift between the Secretary-General and Mr. Lumumba developed in August 1960, and Mr. Gizenga had called on the Secretary-General to "share his responsibilities" with a group of neutral Afro-Asian States,[79] the Secretary-General replied that he would welcome a "more formal and regular arrangement for the . . . consultation which I have with contributing States" [80] and proposed establishing an *advisory* committee, following the UNEF pattern. He was, and remained, unwilling to surrender or even share the actual control of ONUC with such a group.[81] However, his reliance on this Committee of contributing States became a normal feature of his policy, and was particularly evident in relation to implementing the Resolution of 21 February 1961 [82] and in the procedure for investigating Mr. Lumumba's death.[83]

A third means was for the Secretary-General to rely on draft Resolutions which failed of adoption but which, in the discussion in the Security Council, attained sufficient support for them to be regarded as an expression of the opinion of the Members, even though not formally adopted by them. This happened when, in a letter of 21 December 1960 to President Kasavubu,[84] he relied on the Four Power draft Resolution which had been vetoed in the Security Council on 14 December.[85] Again, after the Three Power draft Resolution [86] had failed of adoption on 21 February, the Secretary-General said:

"I note that there has been no difference of opinion, if I understand the situation correctly, as regards the operative paragraphs. Under such circumstances I feel entitled to use these operative paragraphs with the full moral value which they have in our efforts in the Congo." [87]

This recourse to unadopted draft Resolutions, whilst understandable in view of the disagreements within the Security Council and the

---

[77] *Off. Rec. S.C.*, 15th yr., 920th Mtg.
[78] Resol. 1001 (ES–1); and see *Summary Study of Experience*, etc. (A/3943), p. 15.
[79] *Off. Rec. S.C.*, 15th yr., 887th Mtg., paras. 78–79.
[80] *Off. Rec. S.C.*, 15th yr., 887th Mtg., paras. 36 and 108.
[81] See *post*, p. 212.
[82] S/4752, 27 February 1961.
[83] S/4771; and see *post*, p. 213.
[84] S/4606, p. 2.
[85] *Ante*, p. 163.
[86] S/4733; see *ante*, p. 165.
[87] *Off. Rec. S.C.*, 16th yr., 942nd Mtg., pp. 40–41.

necessity, nonetheless, to continue with the ONUC operation, is an unfortunate development. The Secretary-General admittedly claimed for such Resolutions a moral rather than a legal value, but there is considerable danger in any course which treats such Resolutions otherwise than as completely inoperative.

IV. THE FUNCTIONS OF THE FORCE

These functions were conveniently re-stated, in the form of the "policies and purposes of the United Nations with respect to the Congo," in the preamble to the Resolution of the Security Council of 24 November 1961.[88] It will be convenient to adopt, as "heads" of function, the tabulation adopted in that Resolution.

1. "To maintain the territorial integrity and the political independence of the Republic of the Congo"

Initially the threat to international peace and security was seen as resulting from the Belgian intervention in the Congo and, more indirectly, from the possibility that other States might intervene also. Hence the initial Resolution of the Council of 14 July called on Belgium to withdraw and the Secretary-General regarded ONUC's presence as a factor contributing to an early withdrawal as well as a barrier to other possible interventions by States. In explaining the mandate of ONUC, and having referred to the necessity of re-establishing "the instruments of government for the maintenance of order," he said:

"... it was the breakdown of those instruments which had created a situation which through its consequences represented a threat to peace and security justifying United Nations intervention on the basis of the explicit request of the Government of the Republic of the Congo ... I pointed out that, on the basis of the interpretation I had given, it would be understood that, were the United Nations to act as I proposed, the Belgian Government 'would see its way to a withdrawal' and the Council itself called upon the Belgian Government to withdraw their troops." [89]

The analogy of this line of thought to that which had prevailed over UNEF is obvious.

Hence, whilst it was never contemplated that ONUC would use force to compel a Belgian withdrawal,[90] a primary function of ONUC was undoubtedly to enable such withdrawal to take place, and more urgent requests for this withdrawal followed in the Resolution of 9 August [91] and in the letters from the Secretary-General to the Belgian Foreign Minister in September 1960.[92]

[88] S/5002.
[89] First Report, S/4389, p. 2. That this position seemed to be accepted by Belgium appears clear from the statement by the Belgian Minister of Foreign Affairs on 2 August: S/4417, p. 4.
[90] The draft Soviet Resolution, S/4425, which came nearest to this since it contemplated calling on the Secretary-General to use "any means" to remove Belgian troops, was never pressed to a vote.
[91] S/4426, para. 2.
[92] *Ante*, p. 158.

It was also clear that by " the Congo," the Security Council meant the entire Congo, including Katanga, and this was made explicit in the Resolution of 9 August 1960. The notion of maintaining the " territorial integrity and the political independence " of the Congo also implied an insistence on the Congo as a territorial and political unity—and opposition to any secessionist movement—and this will become even more relevant to the function of preventing civil war, examined below.

Since, however, the Belgian intervention had been due to the breakdown of internal law and order, consequent upon the mutiny of the Force Publique, it followed that the maintenance of *internal* law and order was a necessary precondition to Belgian withdrawal and to the successful accomplishment of the maintenance of *international* peace and security.[93] We therefore turn to the second and closely related function.

2. " To assist the Central Government of the Congo in the restoration and maintenance of law and order "

This second function, whilst implicit in the first Resolution of 14 July [94] (since the maintenance of *internal* law and order may be assumed to be the normal task of the " national security forces " which the Secretary-General was asked to assist in), became explicit in the Resolution of 22 July which considered " that the complete restoration of law and order in the Republic of the Congo would effectively contribute to the maintenance of international peace and security." The General Assembly, in its Resolution of 20 September 1960 [95] addressed an even more explicit request to the Secretary-General to assist in the maintenance of law and order.

In practice the measures taken by ONUC to perform this function were the protection of life and property from unlawful violence, the disarming of elements whose activities threatened internal law and order, and assistance in the reorganisation of ANC.

Protection of life and property, as an essential function of ONUC, was stressed in the Secretary-General's First Report [96] and remained a primary task throughout the operation. The need for such protection sprang not only from the mutinous Force Publique, but from the frequent inter-tribal warfare in Kasai, where the Baluba were attacked by the Lulua, and in Equateur and Katanga. Moreover, the tribes were subsequently, and often according to their political sympathies, threatened either by the Katangese gendarmerie,[97] or by

---

[93] See Schachter, *loc. cit.*, p. 14.
[94] *Off. Rec. S.C.*, 15th yr., 873rd Mtg., pp. 8–10.
[95] Resol. 1474 (ES–IV).
[96] S/4389, p. 3 and Add. 1 (Report of Bunche), p. 1 where it was said that " the complete protection of all sectors of the population is the primary and most immediate purpose of the United Nations operation here." See also the First Progress Report from Dayal (S/4531, pp. 4–6) and the later Report of 25 February 1961 (S/4750).
[97] See the protest of the Secretary-General to Tshombé, 18 September 1960 (S/4529); also S/4557, paras. 75–78.

the ANC under Colonel Mobutu,[98] or by troops owing allegiance to Mr. Kalonji in Kasai.[99] The efficacy of measures taken by ONUC depended very much on ONUC's strength in the area. In Leopoldville, for example, patrolling, route-marches, concentrated shows of strength at critical points and even the transport of ANC troops by United Nations planes (to obviate pillage along the route of march) were all measures tried by ONUC to protect life and property. Negotiations with troop commanders were sometimes successful in persuading them to withdraw or, as in Leopoldville on 26 October 1960, to confine troops to barracks. When the numbers of ONUC were so few as to make any general protection impossible recourse was had to the practice of setting up " protected areas," [1] a practice which increased after the Security Council's Resolution of 21 February 1961 had authorised the " use of force . . . in the last resort." [2]

Protection was offered to all in danger of unlawful violence, without any discrimination; hence political leaders, including Mr. Lumumba,[3] from time to time enjoyed United Nations protection, often in the form of " asylum " in guarded premises. The principles applied by the United Nations in affording asylum in protected areas were set out in a special report dated 2 March 1961.[4]

The disarming of those elements which threatened life and property was a measure necessarily linked to the function of protecting life and property and, more generally, to the function of maintaining law and order. So far as Katangese and other secessionist forces were concerned, any disarming could also be linked with the functions of preventing civil war and expelling mercenaries. However, these functions were not specifically entrusted to ONUC until the Resolution of 21 February 1961, and on 16 January 1961 the Secretary-General had refused President Kasavubu's request that ONUC disarm " the rebellious bands of Gizenga and Lundula," on the ground that " this cannot be done by me or the United Nations Force short of new instructions from the Security Council." [5] How far the Resolution of 21 February authorised such a course is questionable, for a positive policy of disarming rebel forces would, in the face of opposition, really have amounted to " enforcement action " which, as we have seen, even this Resolution did not authorise. When, early in February, discussion of the policy of disarming

---

[98] Second Progress Report of Mr. Dayal, S/4557, 2 November 1960, paras. 60–66.
[99] *Ibid.*, paras. 72–73.
[1] S/4557, para. 79; S/4757, 2 March 1961, lists the protected areas.
[2] In fact the Secretary-General had previously said in the Security Council on 15 February 1961 that " instructions have already been given to the Force to protect the civilian population against attacks from armed units, whoever the authority under which they are acting . . . this is on the outer margin of the mandate of the United Nations . . .": *Off. Rec. S.C.*, 16th yr., 935th Mtg., para. 27. [3] S/4571.
[4] S/4757. These principles were, briefly, that asylum was granted to persons in real danger of violence or persecution, but not to enable a lawful prosecution to be avoided, and on condition that the person abstained from conducting political activities and was free to leave at any time.
[5] S/4629, p. 4.

the various military factions arose in the Security Council, Mr. Tshombé protested by letter dated 9 February 1961 against this policy. Indeed, no general attempt was made to disarm the rebel forces as such; excluding the foreign mercenaries, who were disarmed as part of the "expulsion" process, disarming of rebel forces appears to have occurred only as an incident to their capture in an action which, from ONUC's point of view, was an action in self-defence or to arrest mercenaries.[6] The emphasis, even to the end, was placed on the integration of these forces into the ANC, rather than disarming them and destroying their military character.

It was, somewhat paradoxically, in relation to the ANC that the question of disarming troops became acute. Even during August/September 1960 the Secretary-General had envisaged a "temporary disarming" of mutinous ANC forces,[7] in particular those engaged in action against the Baluba in Kasai, whose conduct was described as "having the characteristics of the crime of genocide."[8] Yet the Secretary-General based such action by ONUC on the decision of the Congolese Government, not on any specific power in the mandate of ONUC,[9] and action taken was limited to mutinous troops.[10] Hence, during the controversy between Major-General Alexander, the Ghanaian Chief of Staff, and Bunche,[11] the latter made it quite clear that, since no Security Council Resolution ordered such action, ONUC was limited to acting with the concurrence of the Congolese Government; there could be no question of disarming the ANC contrary to that Government's wishes. Moreover, the Soviet draft Resolution[12] introduced on 15 February, which had specifically envisaged the disarming of the ANC under the control of Colonel Mobutu, was rejected. When the Resolution of 21 February gave additional powers to ONUC, and was followed by clashes between ONUC and ANC,[13] the ANC Headquarters announced its intention to resist by force any attempt to disarm the ANC forces.[14] The Secretary-General hastened to assure President Kasavubu that para. A–1 of the Resolution, authorising the "use of force," referred to measures for the prevention of civil war and did not apply to B–2, urging the reorganisation of the ANC.[15]

---

[6] An exception would seem to have been the disarming of drunken Katangese gendarmerie in December 1961: *Off. Rec. G.A.*, 17th Sess., Suppl. No. 1 (A/5201), p. 14.

[7] S/4482, para. 12. [8] *Off. Rec. S.C.*, 15th yr., 896th Mtg., p. 18.

[9] Statement to the Security Council, 8 August 1960: *Off. Rec. S.C.*, 15th yr., 990th Mtg., p. 38.

[10] As in the disarming of the ANC at Luluabourg, the capital of Kasai province, in November 1961. See the statement by the Secretary-General in his cable of 8 March 1961, S/4775, p. 5, referring to "such units as might have broken loose from their own command and threatened the population." See also O'Brien, *op. cit.*, p. 312 who tells of giving instructions to disarm an ANC unit in November 1961 when they began looting.

[11] S/4445, Annex II, dated 19 August 1960, contains the report by Alexander: the reply by Bunche is given in S/4451.

[12] S/4706. [13] See *ante*, p. 166.

[14] S/4758, 3 March 1961.

[15] S/4775, p. 5, cable of 8 March 1961.

Thus, deprived of the function of taking "enforcement action," ONUC had throughout little real authority to disarm either rebel or ANC troops; the disarming which occurred was incidental to its other functions and, in the case of the ANC, apparently dependent upon the concurrence of the Central Government. The dilemma is apparent. The original mandate to provide that Government with military assistance could not be reconciled with the disarming of its own forces; such a course would have been clear "intervention." [16] The basis upon which President Nkrumah had called for the disarming of Colonel Mobutu's forces in his speech to the General Assembly on 23 September 1960 was one of distinguishing between "the legal authorities and the law breakers." [17] However, in so far as this rested on a construction of Congolese constitutional law, it was a distinction which would, in the making, involve a certain intervention and, even more important, it was a distinction which neither the Assembly nor the Security Council was itself prepared to make. Yet, this being admitted, it cannot be doubted that the need to isolate the ANC from politics was apparent from September 1960, and, had the whole basis of ONUC's mandate not prevented it, General Alexander's policy of disarming and neutralising the ANC would have vastly eased the entire situation.[18]

The "constitutional" difficulties in the way of disarming *rebel* forces were not nearly so great. There is something to be said for the view that, whenever ONUC became engaged with rebel forces which denied by force the "freedom of movement" to which ONUC was entitled, it would have been legitimate, in self-defence, to have disarmed such forces. Certainly by the Resolution of 21 February the express mandate to prevent the occurrence of civil war could, when coupled with the later stand in the Resolution of 24 November that secession was illegal, have justified actual disarming of rebel forces. However, this being said, it is clear that had the Secretary-General pursued such a policy it would have met with tremendous criticism, both from certain contributing States [19] and from States which, like the United Kingdom, Belgium and Greece, were quick to oppose the assumption of military initiative by ONUC in December 1961 and again in December/January 1962.[20]

[16] See statement by the Secretary-General, 10 December 1960, pointing out that the ANC under Colonel Mobutu "is sanctioned by and under the authority of President Kasavubu": *Off. Rec. S.C.*, 15th yr., 917th Mtg., para. 63.

[17] *Off. Rec. G.A.*, 15th Sess., 869th Mtg., paras. 17–18.

[18] See also Okumu, *op. cit.*, pp. 167, 180; O'Brien, *op. cit.*, p. 312.

[19] See *post*, p. 214.

[20] *Ante*, pp. 171, 173. See also the differences of opinion on how far ONUC could, or should, disarm rebel forces and the ANC in the debate in the Assembly in September 1960: *Off. Rec. G.A.*, 15th Sess., 859th and 860th Mtgs. Tunisia (859th Mtg., para. 27) called for disarming of all irregular forces and those acting against the Central Government. Ghana (860th Mtg., para. 145) called for disarming of all militarist forces. Similarly, in the Security Council in December 1960, Ceylon wanted the disarming of all private armies (917th Mtg., paras. 52–53); India disliked disarming and suggested the ANC should go on leave (*ibid.*, para. 194); and France opposed disarming (918th Mtg., para. 63).

The juxtaposition of the two authorities, one international and the other national, in the field of maintenance of *internal* law and order was something which, even in the most stable conditions, called for complete liaison and mutual confidence. In the Congo the conditions were far from stable, and liaison and mutual confidence all too rarely existed. It was in the light of the experience of conflict with the local authorities, rather than co-operation with them, that the Agreement of 27 November 1961 included detailed provisions on liaison and guidance on the delimitation of the respective functions of ONUC and the local authorities.[21]

It may be noted, finally, that it is in general no part of the United Nations' function to provide internal security forces for a State. The assumption of such a function by the United Nations in the case of the Congo is explicable by the fact that maintenance of internal order became a necessary ancillary function in order that the United Nations might operate in conditions which permitted the elimination of the threat to *international* peace and so as to eliminate any justification for intervention by outside Powers. As the Secretary-General was later to state in his Report on Military Disengagement in the Congo:

"It seems to me to be reasonable not to expect the United Nations to underwrite for any country permanent insurance against internal disorders and disturbances, by indefinitely providing an important part of the internal police power for exclusively internal use, when external threats have ended."[22]

3. "To prevent the occurrence of civil war in the Congo"

It is important to realise that when ONUC was first established, pursuant to the Resolution of 14 July 1960, there was no civil war in being in the Congo. The maintenance of internal law and order, and the elimination of lawlessness brought about by mutinous ANC forces, are functions vastly different in degree from the prevention of civil war.

Prima facie the United Nations have no power to intervene in a civil war within a State, and it is believed that this remains the position even when a request for assistance has been made to the United Nations by the authorities generally recognised as the lawful government. However, ONUC was never specifically authorised to assist the Central Government in this sense, hence the Secretary-General's position in refusing to accede to Lumumba's demand that ONUC should be so used in August 1960.[23] The Secretary-General had, in his initial statement to the Council, declared that the Force would not be entitled to "take any action which would make them a party to internal conflicts in the country."[24] The Resolution of 9 August, in paragraph 4, gave the reassurance to Tshombé that:

[21] See *post*, pp. 239–240.
[22] *U.N. Review*, Vol. 10, No. 9, October 1963, p. 44.
[23] *Ante*, p. 157.
[24] *Off. Rec. S.C.*, 15th yr., 873rd Mtg., para. 28.

" . . . the United Nations Force in the Congo will not be a party to or in any way intervene in or be used to influence the outcome of any internal conflict, constitutional or otherwise : . . ."

In his memorandum on the implementation of this paragraph,[25] the Secretary-General, having surveyed the precedents of UNOGIL and Hungary, came to the following conclusions :

1. ONUC could not be used on behalf of the Central Government to subdue or to force the provincial government to a specific line of action.

2. ONUC's facilities could not be used, for example, to transport civilian or military representatives, under the authority of the Central Government, to Katanga against the decision of the Katanga provincial government.[26]

3. ONUC had no duty, or right, to protect civilian or military personnel, representing the Central Government, arriving in Katanga, beyond what followed from its general duty to maintain law and order.

4. The United Nations had no right to refuse the Central Government to take any action which, by their own means, in accordance with the purposes and principles of the Charter, they could carry through in relation to Katanga.

5. These conclusions apply, *mutatis mutandis*, as regards the provincial government in its relations with the Central Government.

This interpretation, which represents an " absolute neutrality," was challenged in the Security Council in August only by the U.S.S.R. and Poland.[27] Their challenge was not so much to the principle of non-intervention in domestic affairs, but rather to the Secretary-General's assumption that this was a domestic, internal conflict. They regarded the Katangese secession, and resistance, as supported by Belgian intervention, so that it thereby ceased to be a " domestic " matter. This view also found support in the Assembly,[28] and, indeed, the Assembly's Resolution of 20 September,[29] in calling upon States to refrain from direct and indirect provision of arms, or military personnel and other assistance for military purposes, suggested strongly that the civil conflict was not entirely " domestic." However, the Security Council, in its Resolution of 21 February, did not authorise intervention against the secessionists; it authorised only the use of force for the *prevention* of civil war via the media of

---

[25] S/4417/Add. 6, 12 August 1960.

[26] For examples of this principle in practice, see *ante*, p. 155.

[27] *Off. Rec. S.C.*, 15th yr., 888th and 889th Mtgs.

[28] *Off. Rec. G.A.*, 4th Emergency Special Sess., Plen. Mtgs., 859th Mtg., paras. 60–61, 98, 139, 186.

[29] Resol. 1474 (ES–IV). This view became even more evident in the Assembly's Resolution 1599 (XV) of 17 April 1961, in which the Assembly was " convinced that the central factor in the present grave situation in the Congo is the continued presence of Belgian and other foreign military and paramilitary personnel and political advisers, and mercenaries . . ."

cease-fires, halting of military operations and prevention of clashes.[30] Even the Resolution of 24 November, despite its rejection of the Katangese claim to independent statehood and its declaration that secessionist activities were illegal, did not authorise the assumption of military initiative against the rebel forces as such: the use of force was to be confined to removing from those forces the " foreign " element.

Whether or not the ONUC actions of August and September 1961,[31] December 1961 [32] and December/January 1963 [33] became in fact military actions directed against the Katangese forces as such, with a view to terminating the rebellion by force, is a matter of some dispute. Certainly the United Nations' view of these actions, as contained in the reports from the Officer-in-Charge, indicates that the objectives of ONUC were far more limited and were restricted to the apprehension of mercenaries, the securing of freedom of movement, and measures in self-defence.

The action in August 1961 was most certainly designed simply to apprehend and expel mercenaries and to bring about compliance with the Security Council's Resolution of 21 February which Mr. Tshombé had delayed by every conceivable means. It was, moreover, an action taken at the request of the Central Government which had passed Ordinance No. 70 for the expulsion of " all the non-Congolese officers and mercenaries." [34] The action the following month was, according to O'Brien, designed to carry out the arrests of the Katangese leaders, ordered by the warrants issued from the Central Government.[35] The extent to which the Secretary-General knew of this design *in advance* is unclear,[36] but O'Brien, then the United Nations Representative in Elisabethville, has indicated that, in his view, the purpose behind the arrests was to end the secession by force. If that was the intention behind the action it was not justified by the Resolutions of the Security Council. His view that para. 1 of Resolution A of 21 February justified such action

---

[30] See, for example, the statement by the U.K. representative, Sir Patrick Dean: " I must explain that the interpretation which my delegation puts upon the words at the end of that paragraph, namely, ' and the use of force, if necessary, in the last resort ' is that force will only be used to prevent a clash between hostile Congolese troops. There can be no question of empowering the United Nations to use its forces to impose a political settlement ": 942nd Mtg., para. 21. Note that the U.K. abstained in the vote adopting the Resolution of 24 November.

[31] *Ante*, p. 169. For a description of this operation, see O'Brien, *op. cit.*, Chap. 13.

[32] *Ante*, p. 171.

[33] *Ante*, p. 173.

[34] S/4940, 14 September. It was this unhappy experience of an attempt by ONUC to apply and enforce local law that perhaps led to the provision in para. 43 (a) of the Agreement of 27 November 1961 that ONUC " shall not apply domestic regulations and procedures, but shall act in accordance with its interpretation of the mission assigned to it by the Security Council." See *post*, p. 239.

[35] See O'Brien, Chap. 15. At p. 249 he recounts the instruction to " avoid a clash with the gendarmerie."

[36] *Ibid.*, p. 262.

(despite being contrary to para. 4 of the Resolution of 9 August) is untenable. Particularly disturbing is O'Brien's rejection of the truth of the official version of the action given in the Report of the Officer-in-Charge on 14 September,[37] for he regards this official version as largely a fabrication to make the action more palatable to States which, like the United Kingdom, were opposed to force.

The action by ONUC beginning on 5 December 1961 was also described as "defensive action to restore law and order in Elisabeth-ville and to regain freedom of movement"; this was in the face of "manifest preparations for a concerted attack on United Nations positions [which] made it imperative . . . to take the essential measures necessary in self-defence for the maintenance of public order and restoration of freedom of movement."[38] The United Nations was clearly, in this action, basing its military initiative on the anticipatory right of self-defence, coupled with its right to assert freedom of movement. There was no attempt to assert a general right to end secession by force.

After the action in late December 1962 and early January 1963, the Officer-in-Charge reported that "the Katangese gendarmerie as an organised fighting force had ceased to exist."[39] However, whilst the end result was the same as if an operation aimed at the destruction of the Katangese forces had been launched, the reports to the Secretary-General, having recounted the harassment of United Nations personnel, attacks on United Nations troops and property and the establishment of road blocks placing ONUC "in a position akin to siege,"[40] based ONUC's action on self-defence and the right to restore freedom of movement. The latter right was invoked specifically to justify the advance on Jadotville from 1–4 January. The view that this action was a desperate attempt by the United Nations to end civil war and the Katangese secession, and to impose on Tshombé the Secretary-General's Plan of National Reconciliation, is, therefore, not one which can be deduced from any United Nations source.

---

[37] S/4940, para. 15 described the action as "security precautions . . . to prevent inflammatory broadcasts or other threats to the maintenance of law and order"; it contained no mention of the attempt to execute the warrants of arrest. For O'Brien's version, see pp. 247–267; his own announcement after the action that "the secession of Katanga is at an end" was premature and inconsistent with the official version of the affair. He says at p. 276: "We had taken action to end the secession, under the authority, as we thought, of the 'civil war' proviso, but it soon became clear that that was not what we were supposed to be doing. We were supposed to be defending ourselves; so we defended ourselves." Gordon, *op. cit.*, pp. 124–127 is probably right in stating that, whilst the Secretary-General and his advisers in New York had been ignorant of the intentions of O'Brien and Khiary to execute the warrants for arrest and regarded the action as a continuance of the 28 August action, O'Brien and Khiary assumed that the plan had been approved. It would seem that, if the official report (S/4940) is to be criticised, it is in its failure to note that a serious misunderstanding had occurred.
[38] S/4940/Add.17 and 18; and see Annual Report of the Secretary-General, *Off. Rec. G.A.*, 17th Sess., Suppl. No. 1 (A/5201), pp. 13–15.
[39] S/5053/Add.15, para. 37.
[40] S/5053/Add.14, para. 2.

4. *" To secure the immediate withdrawal and evacuation from the Congo of all foreign military, para-military and advisory personnel, not under the United Nations Command, and all mercenaries."*

Initially the Security Council had placed the main emphasis on the withdrawal of Belgian troops, and the Resolutions of 14 July, 22 July and 9 August dealt almost entirely with the "official" Belgian presence. By the beginning of September it had become apparent that, whilst this particular aim was likely to be achieved reasonably soon, an "unofficial" presence had become apparent in the form of Belgian and other foreign officers attached to the Katangese gendarmerie. By October a similar presence had been observed in the political and administrative departments of government, both central and secessionist, to the detriment of the little co-operation which had existed with the United Nations.[41] The reinforcement of the secessionist military forces by mercenaries, other than Belgians, also became both evident and ominous.

It was to meet this new situation that the General Assembly Resolution of 20 September [42] and, more particularly, the Security Council Resolution of 21 February,[43] para. 2A were adopted. The express authorisation to use force, if necessary, for the apprehension and deportation of such foreign elements came only with the Council's Resolution of 24 November 1961.[44]

It is clear that the express authorisation to use force came only after all other means had failed. A detailed description of the various means proposed by the United Nations is perhaps unnecessary in a study of United Nations Forces. Suffice it to say that, whilst it was never the United Nations' intention to exclude the "technicians" who were, indeed, vital to the continued operation of many sectors of the economy of the Congo, the problem of identifying, apprehending and deporting the foreign element which had become politically and militarily involved was one which the United Nations had attempted to solve on the basis of agreement with the Congolese authorities, central and provincial.[45] It was only when it became

[41] *Ante,* pp. 162–193.
[42] Resol. 1474/Rev.1 (ES–IV), para. 6.
[43] S/4741. This dealt only very indirectly with this problem. It may be recalled that Kasavubu's reaction to this Resolution was almost as strong as that of Tshombé (S/3743, cable dated 22 February, and see *ante*, p. 166).
[44] S/5002. By this Resolution the Council finally accepted the view which the Secretary-General had urged since the previous October.
[45] After the Resolution of 21 February the Secretary-General sent notes to Belgium and other States calling for their co-operation (S/4752, Annexes I and II) and wrote to both President Kasavubu and Mr. Tshombé (S/4752/ Add. 1, B. C), calling for accurate information on the personnel covered by the Resolution. The visit of Gardiner and Nwokedi was for the purpose of arranging an appropriate means of executing the Resolution. Some arrests were made in April (S/4790), but by June 510 remained in Katanga (208 Belgian and 302 foreign mercenaries). The joint commissions established by ONUC and Tshombé in June were largely used to delay matters, and Tshombé's announcement of the termination of all their services, on 28 August 1961, and his promise to evacuate was accepted by ONUC so

abundantly clear that no co-operation from the Katangese authorities could be expected that resort to force was used.

O'Brien has regarded the Resolution of 24 November as retro-actively validating operation " Rumpunch," the operation to arrest the mercenaries begun in Elisabethville in August.[46] The assumption behind this is that, prior to 24 November, ONUC possessed no authority to use force for this purpose. Perhaps the difference between the Resolution of 21 February and that of 24 November is really only one of degree. The Security Council could scarcely have believed, in February, that ONUC could carry out the instruction without force: every arrest or measure of detention is, in one sense, a use of force and the degree of force used will vary with the degree of resistance offered. It may be suggested that whereas it was implicit in the earlier Resolution that force might have to be used against the mercenaries, the November Resolution was passed on the basis that force might also have to be used against Katangese forces as well, in order to carry out the Resolution. It must also be remembered that the Central Government, by Ordinance No. 70, had ordered the arrest and deportation and called on ONUC to execute it; so that, quite apart from the Security Council's mandate, there existed an authority for ONUC to act under municipal law—which ONUC had, from the outset, been called on to assist in maintaining as part of the " maintenance of law and order " mandate.[47]

V. THE RESTRICTIONS ON ONUC INHERENT IN THE PRINCIPLE OF NON-INTERVENTION AND IN THE PRINCIPLE THAT ONUC SHOULD ACT ONLY IN SELF-DEFENCE

1. *The principle of non-intervention*

The applicability of this principle to UNEF, where no civil strife existed on the territory of Egypt, or even to UNOGIL where, although

that they suspended their own searches. By September substantial rein-filtration was apparent and on 11 September ONUC gave the Katangese authorities 24 hours within which to evacuate all personnel covered by the Resolution. The ONUC operations beginning on 13 September were, accord-ing to the " official " UN view (see *ante*, p. 194) merely a resumption of the August measures to apprehend and expel the personnel covered by the Resolution. Following this Tshombé and ONUC exchanged lists of per-sonnel and, in February 1962, two Commissions of civilian and military representatives were established to finalise the list of personnel (A/5201, pp. 19–20). That even these measures were not entirely successful is proved by the participation by mercenaries in the fighting at Elisabethville, Jadot-ville and Kolwezi in late December/early January 1963. For an outline of the measures taken to eliminate the personnel covered by the Resolution of 21 February, see *U.N. Yearbook 1960*, p. 61 and 1961, p. 76; also Gordon, *op. cit.*, pp. 123–127, 162–164.

[46] *Op. cit.*, p. 318.

[47] The Report of the Officer-in-Charge, 14 September 1961 (S/4940, para. 2) described the Congolese Ordinance and request for assistance in executing it as giving the UN " legal rights within the Congo corresponding to the terms of the . . . Resolution." But see *post*, p. 239 for the text of para. 43 (a) of the Agreement of 27 November, forbidding ONUC to apply " domestic regulations and procedures."

civil strife existed in the Lebanon, the Group's function was restricted to observation, was undoubtedly right. It was also understandable that the Secretary-General should initially assume this principle to be applicable to ONUC.[48] The wisdom of a continued adherence to this principle when faced with secessionist movements backed by outside interference is by no means as understandable. The Secretary-General's view was that, since no "enforcement action" had been authorised, the proviso to Article 2 (7) of the Charter did not apply and therefore the "domestic jurisdiction" limitation on the power of the United Nations *did* apply, obliging the United Nations to maintain a policy of non-intervention. As we have seen,[49] many Member States did not regard the secessionist movements as a purely domestic matter, since the evidence of external support for them was overwhelming. Even apart from this, there is considerable doubt whether, in a situation where there exists a threat to international peace, there is any justification for so general a reliance on the "domestic jurisdiction" limitation on the powers of the United Nations.[50] A threat to *international* peace can never, by definition, be a purely domestic matter. There are, however, two different contexts in which the appropriateness of the non-intervention principle must be judged. The first is that of the secessionist movements, notably the Katangese secession; the second is that of the competition for political power *within* the Central Government.

The implications of this principle in relation to Katangese secession were stated by the Secretary-General in his memorandum on implementing paragraph 4 of the Resolution of 9 August,[51] and these have already been set out in detail.[52] It was this interpretation which was so strongly challenged by Lumumba[53] and led to the Secretary-General's request to the Security Council for clarification, without result.[54]

As we have already indicated,[55] the basic principle that the United Nations has no right to interfere in a purely civil war, which does not of itself constitute a threat to international peace and security, is certainly right. Quite apart from the general limitations on the Security Council's (and, indeed, the United Nations') powers which confine it to situations with an "international" aspect, there is the principle of "self-determination" which, despite its difficulty of definition and uncertain legal status, would suggest that it is not for the United Nations to dictate to a people which government it should have, or even whether a part of the people should remain within a

[48] See his initial statement to the Council: *Off. Rec. S.C.*, 15th yr., 873rd Mtg., para. 28; also First Report, S/4389, p. 5, Second Report, S/4417, pp. 6, 11.
[49] *Ante*, p. 192.
[50] See, for similar doubts, Jennings, *loc. cit.*, p. 590.
[51] S/4417/Add.6, 12 August 1960.
[52] *Ante*, p. 192.
[53] *Ante*, p. 157.
[54] *Ante*, p. 158.
[55] *Ante*, p. 191.

particular State. But for the fact that secession of Katanga was not simply an expression of the political will of its people, but prompted by outside interference, the Security Council's rejection of Katangese independence and its declaration that secessionist activities were illegal under the *Loi Fondamentale* (and should therefore cease) embodied in the Resolution of 24 November would have been intervention and *ultra vires* the United Nations Organisation. However, given that there were serious doubts over how far the secessionist movements could be regarded as a genuine expression of the will of the people in the territory,[56] given that there was abundant evidence of the support for secession coming from foreign interests and elements,[57] and given that the situation contained a threat to international peace and security, a principle which involved absolute neutrality by the United Nations could scarcely be applicable to that situation. Whilst it is, admittedly, an easy task to criticise when equipped with hindsight, it may be said that the efforts of the United Nations should have been more forcibly directed to the prevention of civil war *and the creation of conditions in which the genuinely-expressed desires of the people for their political future could operate.* In other words, whilst ONUC should not have been committed to a war with the Katangese forces, the assertion of its right to freedom of movement and the execution of the mandate to expel the foreign element should have been far more forceful (and military action taken as necessary to achieve these ends rather than as a result of a more general policy of destroying Katangese forces). However, the eventual aim should have been to bring about the complete elimination of foreign elements, thus leaving the Congolese people free to effect a political settlement of the problem through the ordinary democratic processes.

The responsibility for the failure to re-appraise the suitability of a policy of absolute neutrality to the radically changed conditions of the Congo from late August onwards (as compared with late July)

---

[56] The secessionist policy of Tshombé's Conakat had not been an issue put to the electorate in the elections of May 1960, which gave the Conakat 25 of the 60 seats in the Provincial Assembly. The Conakat Government was elected without a quorum according to the *Loi Fondamentale*, but under an amended procedure voted by the Belgian Parliament. It was this Government which, without any referendum, declared independence on 11 July 1960. See Davister, *Katanga Enjeu du Monde*, p. 53; O'Brien, *op. cit.*, pp. 84–85. And note the denial by the representative of Chile that Katangese secession was based on self-determination (S/PV.977, p. 3).

[57] *Ante*, p. 192. And see Riad, *loc. cit.*, pp. 37–38. It has been said that the Belgian forces in July 1960 disarmed and returned to their tribes the sections of the Force Publique in Katanga who were loyal to the Central Government and opposed to Tshombé's plans for secession, thus ensuring that there would be no effective opposition to the secession. Certainly the Belgian military commanders indicated that their forces were at the disposal of the Government of Tshombé (and not, therefore, limited to protecting Belgian lives): see *L'Essor du Congo*, 18 July 1960. The general directions given to Belgian troops are reproduced in *Congo 1960*, Vol. II, p. 557; as to Katanga they say simply "occupation de tous les centres importants, notamment Kolwezi et gares frontières et Sakania et Dilolo."

can only in small part be laid at the feet of Mr. Hammarskjoeld. His own tenacity in adhering to that principle certainly affected the position but the essential need was for a re-direction of ONUC by the Security Council, and it is the Member States which must really share the responsibility for failing to direct ONUC's operations in the way which the changed conditions demanded. The reluctance of the Member States so to do may be ascribed in part to the hope that, through conciliation and negotiation, a political solution could be reached between the Congolese leaders, in part to the fact that the economic interests of some States would have benefited from Katangese secession,[58] in part to the fear that too forceful a policy by the United Nations might create a precedent which would, in the future, enable the United Nations to intervene in the domestic affairs of a State,[59] and in large part to the fact that the problem of the Congo became entangled in the East-West conflict, with both sides attempting to ensure that the Congolese authorities finally established in power would be " Eastern " or " Western " in their political sympathies.

Within the context of the struggle for power *within* the Central Government the adherence to a principle of non-intervention was undoubtedly right. Whilst, certainly, the failure of the Lumumba Government was regarded differently by different States, it could not be said that this particular struggle was one which, by reason of outside interference,[60] had assumed the character of a threat to

[58] The future security of the Union Minière (in the sense of freedom from expropriation) would probably be higher in an independent Katanga than in a unified Congo, and, being Belgian-owned, this would certainly be one factor in Belgium's policy. The Union Minière, the world's chief producer of cobalt and third producer of copper, formed the largest unit in the Congolese economy, contributing, prior to independence, between 50 and 60 per cent. to the total resources of the Congo, and three-sevenths of the total exchequer income. See Chomé, *La Crise Congolaise*, p. 36, citing the Belgian *Agence Economique et Financière*. The shareholdings in Union Minière in 1960 were Tanganyika Concessions (Tanks—a British company) 179,760 shares; Société Générale (Belgian) 59,685; Comité special du Katanga (Belgian) 315,675; Compagnie du Katanga (Belgian) 18,800; others (mainly French and Belgian small holdings) 860,380. Tanganyika Concessions, apart from its holdings in the Union Minière, owned the Benguela Railway, carrying 20 per cent. of the mineral output from Katanga. The shares in Tanks were held as to 30 per cent. in England, 40 per cent. in Belgium and 20 per cent. in France. Quite apart from the Union Minière, there were 35 government-owned but autonomously administered public corporations providing rail and river transport, electric power and various financial and welfare services. See *Katanga and Congolese Independence* (1962) Document Division of Ministry of Foreign Affairs, Republic of the Congo.

[59] This, far more than any " economic " involvement or pressure from the so-called " Katanga lobby," may perhaps have been the basic element in the United Kingdom's policy. It is believed that, apart from its apprehension about creating an undesirable precedent, the basis of Her Majesty's Government's policy was the belief that a solution could be found by conciliation and without resorting to force. This may have been an over-optimistic belief, but it was no part of the policy of H.M.G. to support the secession of any part of the Congo.

[60] That there was some outside assistance to the parties seems clear, see *post*, p. 227, but it is not believed that it was of such an order as to change the nature of the struggle from a " domestic " to an " international " matter.

international peace and security: it was, essentially, a struggle of a "domestic" character. The very existence of the struggle created, as we have seen, enormous difficulties for ONUC, but strict impartiality between the contestants, principally Kasavubu and Lumumba, was essential for ONUC.

Indeed, the criticism of ONUC has in general been that it was *not* neutral in this struggle. Although ONUC refused, on 15 September 1960, to permit the arrest of Lumumba, and again on 11 October, on a warrant issued under President Kasavubu's authority,[61] it has been said that ONUC's action in closing the Leopoldville radio station and airport on 11 September [62] effectively denied to Lumumba the possibility of appealing for popular support and ensured Kasavubu's triumph in the struggle for power.[63] It is believed, however, that, whether or not this was the eventual result of this action, it was not the result intended by ONUC. The intention of these actions, as subsequently explained by the Secretary-General,[64] was to prevent the outbreak of civil war which seemed likely had Lumumba been able to appeal to the people to take up arms against President Kasavubu's Government and to fly in from Kasai the troops loyal to Lumumba on the aircraft which the Soviet Union had provided. As such the action was the only reasonable action ONUC could have taken. It could scarcely be consistent with a "partisan" policy, favouring Kasavubu, that ONUC should itself have been accused by Kasavubu of interference in protecting Lumumba [65] and that it should have declined to deal with the College of Commissioners-General—established by decree of the President on 11 October—as the legal government, since it was a régime founded on military power.[66]

2. The restriction of ONUC to action in self-defence

The restriction of ONUC to action in self-defence was, again on the basis of the UNEF precedent, assumed by Mr. Hammarskjoeld to be an essential principle applicable to the operations of the Force. In his First Report the Secretary-General stated:

"In my initial statement I recalled the rule applied in previous United Nations operations to the effect that the military units would be entitled to act only in self-defence. In amplification of this statement I would like to quote the following passage from the report to which I referred:

[61] S/4505/Add. 2 and S/4531, para. 27.
[62] S/4505 and S/4531, para. 24.
[63] See Okumu, *op. cit.*, p. 138; Chomé, *Le gouvernement congolaise et l'ONU —Un paradoxe tragique*, Etudes Congolaise, No. 6, p. 83; Dinant, *L'ONU face à la crise congolaise—la politique d'Hammarskjoeld*, pp. 67–72.
[64] *Off. Rec. S.C.*, 890th Mtg., p. 17. For a justification of the ONUC action, see Gordon, *op. cit.*, pp. 55–58. It should be pointed out that, although the temporary closure of the Leopoldville radio station was effective against Kasavubu also, it favoured Kasavubu in the sense that he had access to, and used, the powerful Radio Brazzaville.
[65] S/4571/Add. 1, dated 8 December 1960.
[66] See *post*, p. 231.

'. . . men engaged in the operation may never take the initiative in the use of armed force, but are entitled to respond with force to an attack with arms, including attempts to use force to make them withdraw from positions which they occupy under orders from the Commander, . . .'

acting under the authority of the Security Council and within the scope of its Resolution. 'The basic element involved is clearly the prohibition against any initiative in the use of armed force '." [67]

This principle was embodied in the instructions issued to every member of ONUC upon arrival in the Congo,[68] it was assumed to prevent entry into Katanga by force,[69] and was stated in the Secretary-General's cable to Mr. Tshombé of 10 August,[70] almost by way of reassurance and as a corollary to the principle of non-intervention.[71] It was also assumed that, since ONUC had no power to take "enforcement action," it was necessarily limited to self-defence and could not, therefore, take the military initiative necessary to disarm ANC.[72]

However, it became apparent reasonably soon that ONUC's role with regard to the maintenance of law and order was one which, for its fulfilment, placed considerable strain on the concept of self-defence. The use of force to protect the civilian population was scarcely self-defence and the Secretary-General was obliged to describe it as "on the outer margin of the mandate of the United Nations." [73] A similar embarrassment, due to the restrictions involved in the concept of self-defence, was evident in the Secretary-General's inquiry of the Security Council on 15 February 1961 whether it was prepared to enlarge ONUC's mandate by conferring a right of search so as to check the imports of arms into the country; limited to self-defence, ONUC could not take such measures.

What did emerge from the Security Council, in the Resolution of 21 February, was a mandate to use force for the prevention of civil war "including arrangements for cease-fires, the halting of all military operations, the prevention of clashes . . ." Since this involved, for example,[74] the use of force against units which had, *in attacking non-United Nations units,* broken cease-fire arrangements, it is difficult to avoid the conclusion that the Security Council by this Resolution abandoned a strict reliance on the principle of

---

[67] S/4389, p. 5. See also the Second Report, S/4417, p. 10.
[68] Press Release Co/15, 19 July 1960.
[69] S/4417, p. 10.
[70] S/4417, Add. 4.
[71] For a linking of these two principles, see Dayal's First Progress Report, S/4531, para. 36.
[72] *Ante,* pp. 189–190.
[73] Statement to Security Council, 15 February 1961: *Off. Rec. S.C.,* 16th yr., 935th Mtg., para. 27. Note that this authorisation, in the rather vague form of power to take "necessary and effective measures," came not from the Security Council but from the General Assembly in Resol. 1600 (XV) of 17 April 1961.
[74] See the warning by ONUC given on 31 October 1961 that it would take counteraction against any breach of the cease-fire agreements which would result from a clash between the Katangese forces and the ANC in Kasai province.

self-defence. However, in a letter to African States, appealing for reinforcements for ONUC,[75] the Secretary-General, having stated that the Resolution of 21 February, "without any change of the United Nations mandate, widens its scope and application," continued:

"If . . . United Nations troops engage in defensive action, when attacked while holding positions occupied in prevention of a civil war risk, this would not, in my opinion, mean that they may become a party to a conflict, while the possibility of becoming such a party would be open were troops to take the initiative in an armed attack on an organised army group in the Congo."

This statement reveals a clinging to the "self-defence" concept which was unfortunate in the context of measures to prevent a civil war, just as it reveals a clinging to the UNEF precedent of an "interposition" force. Yet, in the Congo, true "interposition," in the strategic sense, was not always possible, so that an attack by one Congolese unit on another would not necessarily be an attack through positions held by ONUC. What was really required was the assertion of a right (which is not the right of self-defence but a more general right to maintain peace between the rival factions) to act against any unit which began military action in defiance of the Security Council Resolutions. There was perhaps no need to describe an initiative of this kind, which has its parallel in the initiative of the policeman who stops a street brawl, as carrying the risk of intervention in the political affairs of the Congo.

The Resolution of 24 November contemplated, and authorised, the use of force for the expulsion of mercenaries and other personnel included in paragraph A-2 of the Resolution of 21 February; this, too, marked an abandonment of the self-defence limitation. Significantly, the Status Agreement of 27 November 1961 provided that "the United Nations shall not have recourse to the use of force except as a last resort and subject to the restrictions imposed by its mandate and by the Resolutions of the Security Council and the General Assembly"[76]; there was, here, no attempt to limit ONUC to self-defence.

It also became apparent that, quite apart from the wider powers afforded by these two Resolutions, even when ONUC relied upon the right of self-defence it had in due course to abandon the rather strict definition which had originally been offered by the Secretary-General, prohibiting the taking of the initiative in any military action. The operations in September and December 1961 were in the nature of "anticipatory" measures of self-defence[77] rather than reactions to an actual armed attack.

It may be concluded, therefore, that the emphasis on self-defence was too rigid in view of the functions which ONUC had to assume;

[75] S/4752, Annex VII.
[76] S/5004, para. 43 (b).
[77] *Ante*, p. 171.

and in practice it could not be adhered to.[78] Even more important, perhaps, is the fact that in August 1960, the Secretary-General assumed that the limitation of ONUC to self-defence prevented an entry into Katanga by force. This, it is believed, was due to a failure to appreciate the essential link between the right of self-defence and the right of freedom of movement. It is to this latter right that we now turn.

3. *The right to freedom of movement*

The Secretary-General, in addressing the Security Council on 20 July 1960, and with specific reference to the agreement with the host State which would in due course have to be negotiated, stated:

"... I would like to stress that ... there cannot from my viewpoint exist any hesitation as regards what is the area of operation. The Resolution of the Security Council, in response to the appeal of the Government of the Congo, clearly applies to the whole of the territory of the Republic as it existed when the Security Council only a few days earlier recommended the Congo for admission as a Member of the United Nations. Thus, in my view, the United Nations Force, under the Resolution and on the basis of the request of the Government of the Congo, is entitled to access to all parts of the territory in fulfilment of its duties." [79]

On this point, therefore, the Secretary-General had, from the outset, perceived that there would have to be one important distinction between UNEF and ONUC, namely, that the latter Force would have to have freedom of movement throughout the entire territory of the Congo. Without adopting a position that this freedom of movement was unlimited, it could be said that it was to be limited only by the mandate of the Force; that is to say, ONUC was to have the freedom of movement necessary to fulfil the functions assigned to it. The Central Government appears to have accepted this position in the Basic Agreement of 29 July,[80] paragraph 1 of which stated:

"The Government of the Republic of the Congo ... states that it will ensure the freedom of movement of the Force in the interior of the country ..."

The Security Council's Resolution of 9 August, declaring that "the entry of the United Nations Force into the Province of Katanga is necessary for the full implementation of this Resolution," was a sufficient confirmation of the Secretary-General's view that the freedom of movement applied throughout the Congo.

In these circumstances it is difficult to understand why, when opposition to the entry into Katanga was threatened by Tshombé in early August, the Secretary-General took the view that "the aims of the Resolutions cannot be achieved by the use of the United

---

[78] Draper, "The Legal limitation upon the employment of weapons by the United Nations Force in the Congo" (1963) 12 I.C.L.Q. p. 400, describes the policy of adhering to the self-defence principle, bearing in mind the possibility of combat action, as "lacking in realism."

[79] *Off. Rec. S.C.*, 15th yr., 877th Mtg., para. 15. See also First Report, S/4389, p. 3, and Second Report, S/4417, p. 7.

[80] S/4389/Add. 5.

Nations Force, as its mandate has been defined." [81] A decision that, in terms of military strength and preparedness, to enter Katanga and risk combat action was not opportune at that time would have been understandable, but not a decision that ONUC lacked legal authority to do so. It is believed that this error arose from a failure to appreciate the essential link between the freedom of movement and the right of self-defence.[82] In simple terms, it may be said that ONUC was entitled to assert its freedom of movement and to resort to self-defence against any action constituting a denial of freedom of movement: this would not have meant abandoning the principle, then operative, that ONUC could not take the initiative in military action.[83] The principle, which it is believed was the right principle, was expressed by the representative of the Soviet Union on 8 August in the Security Council; he said that he did not propose that ONUC "should ever be the first to have recourse to arms," but, in accordance with the Resolutions of 14 and 22 July,

". . . if the troops introduced into the territory of the Republic of the Congo by decision of the Security Council met with armed resistance they may overcome it by any means available to them. This means, then, that the United Nations troops can and should resort to arms for the purpose of overcoming armed resistance as a matter of protection or self-defence." [84]

In political terms there may have been misgivings amongst certain of the contributing States, but it is clear that others would have fully supported such a stand.[85]

The occasions on which freedom of movement was denied were, unhappily, all too frequent, and one or two examples will suffice to show the different ways, and the different degrees, in which interference occurred. One of the most serious incidents arose from the attack on the ONUC position at the port of Matadi by ANC forces, compelling the Sudanese contingent of ONUC to withdraw on 5 March 1961. In the exchange of correspondence which followed between the Secretary-General and President Kasavubu [86] the Secretary-General invoked the freedom of movement undertaking in the Basic Agreement as well as the Council's Resolution of 9 August, which referred to the obligations on all Member States under Articles 25 and 49 of the Charter. The Secretary-General regarded

---

[81] S/4417, para. 10; and see *ante*, pp. 155–156.

[82] See also Draper, *loc. cit.*, pp. 400–401.

[83] Support for this view, in terms of general international law, can be found in the judgment of the I.C.J. in the *Corfu Channel Case (Merits)*, I.C.J. *Reports*, 1949, p. 5, to the effect that the United Kingdom was not bound to abstain from asserting its right of passage through the Channel merely because of the possibility that Albania might use force to deny the right of passage.

[84] *Off. Rec. S.C.*, 15th yr., 886th Mtg., pp. 42–44.

[85] See, for example, the cable dated 7 August from Guinea (S/4417/Add.1/ Rev.1); Note Verbale from Ghana dated 6 August (S/4420); telegram from the Congolese Prime Minister dated 7 August (S/4421). See also letter from the Representative of the U.S.S.R., 6 August (S/4418).

[86] S/4775. And see the Report of the Secretary-General from his Special Representative, S/4761.

Matadi as essential to a "vital line of communication," so that, without it, ONUC's freedom of movement would be restricted. The demand from the Minister of Foreign Affairs of the Central Government, on 1 March 1961, that ONUC should evacuate the air base at Ndjili, and not enter Congolese military camps, was another example.[87] Another form of interference came with the instructions given by officials of the Central Government to OTRACO (Office d'Exploitation des Transports Coloniaux) which resulted in depriving ONUC of essential supplies, which were held up in transit. Again the Secretary-General invoked the freedom of movement clause and Articles 25 and 29 of the Charter.[88]

In Katanga the interference ranged from the molesting of ONUC personnel at the Elisabethville airport to the more serious attempts to place a siege on ONUC positions in Elisabethville in December 1961 and, again, in December 1962. These events have already been described,[89] but the point must be re-emphasised now that the substantial military actions which ONUC became engaged in were in part designed to restore, and justified legally on, the freedom of movement to which ONUC was entitled. These two instances demonstrate very forcibly the point made above that a combination of the right to freedom of movement and the right of self-defence was sufficient to enable ONUC to deal with any armed opposition to its complete freedom of movement: the Acting Secretary-General therefore adopted, on these occasions, a view which his predecessor, Hammarskjoeld, had been reluctant to adopt in August 1960.

It may be noted that the Agreement of 27 November 1961,[90] which was given retroactive application, provided in paragraph 30 for "full freedom of movement throughout Congolese territory and to and from points of access to Congolese territory." It also confined Congolese personnel controlling air traffic at airports used by the United Nations to *civilian* personnel, and limited even their jurisdiction to air traffic other than United Nations traffic (para. 42). These provisions clearly reflect the experience of ONUC, and the difficulties of this experience, in relation to its freedom of movement.

VI. RELATIONS BETWEEN THE UNITED NATIONS AND CONTRIBUTING STATES

1. *Composition of the Force*

Arrangements for the contribution of contingents to ONUC by Member States were made between the Secretary-General and the States concerned by correspondence rather than by formal agreement. However, it was left to the Secretary-General to select the States

[87] *Post*, p. 234.
[88] *Off. Rec. S.C.*, 16th yr., 960th Mtg., para. 7. See on this incident generally, *U.N. Yearbook*, 1961, p. 73.
[89] *Ante*, pp. 171, 173.
[90] *Post*, pp. 237–240.

whose contributions would be desirable as part of ONUC and he had, on the 13 July 1960, made it clear that, in following the UNEF precedent, contingents from Permanent Members of the Security Council would be excluded but that, in so far as contingents from African States would *not* be excluded, there was less implication that States in geographical proximity to the Congo would have the " special interest in the conflict " which was a ground for exclusion from UNEF. Indeed, in his First Report, he went on to say that ONUC would be " built around a hard core of military units from African States," [91] whilst at the same time " maintaining the universal character of a United Nations operation." [92] Hence contingents from Asia (India, Pakistan, Malaya, Indonesia), Europe (Austria, Ireland, Italy, Netherlands, Sweden), South America (Brazil) and even North America (Canada) were in fact used at various stages. An indication of the extent of contributions of personnel can be gathered from the table reproduced below,[93] which gives the strength of ONUC as at 5 May 1962.

The Secretary-General made it clear that, whilst the views of the host State were one factor to be considered in composing the Force, and normally a serious objection to a specific contributing country would be accepted by the United Nations, ultimately it was for the United Nations to decide on the question of composition.[94] The need for this exclusive control over composition quickly became apparent when, on 15 August, Mr. Lumumba asked that only African

[91] S/4389, p. 6.
[92] *Ibid.*, p. 9.
[93] Strength of ONUC troop contingents and other units as at 5 May 1962 :

Countries	Total	Staff	Troops	Air	Adm.
Austria	47	1			46
Brazil	49	3		46	
Canada	308	23		15	270
Denmark	90	8		5	77
Ethiopia	3,018	14	2,952	52	
Ghana	674	2	672		
India	6,194	42	5,151	135	866
Ireland	715	27	683		5
Italy	135	2		86	47
Liberia	235	3	232		
Malaya	1,518	9	1,509		
Netherlands	6	1			5
Nigeria	1,642	5	1,637		
Norway	145	17		67	61
Pakistan	680	29			651
Sierra Leone	110		110		
Sweden	1,017	15	781	149	72
Tunisia	1,049	2	1,047		
Total :	17,632	203	14,774	555	2,100

In September 1960 (see S/4531, Annex 1) there had also been contingents from Argentina (10), Burma (9), Ceylon (9), Guinea (1,349), Indonesia (1,152), Mali (577), Morocco (3,257), New Zealand (1), Sudan (398), Switzerland (22), United Arab Republic (519) and Yugoslavia (20). The Ghana contingent had then stood at 2,291.

[94] *Ibid.*, p. 4.

troops be sent into Katanga[95] and, on 20 August, demanded the withdrawal of the "white" troops who had been involved in an incident at Ndjili Airport.[96] The Status Agreement of 27 November 1961 not surprisingly provided, therefore, that:

"The United Nations shall possess sole competence with respect to decisions concerning the composition of the military units sent to the Congo, it being understood at the same time that the United Nations shall, in determining their composition, give every consideration to the opinion of the Government as one of the most important factors to be borne in mind in connection with recruitment."[97]

The pressure to turn ONUC into an exclusively African force did not only come from the Congolese Prime Minister. The Soviet Union had, at the 873rd Meeting of the Security Council, made the same suggestion, and later the Soviet Union was to protest at the inclusion of contingents from NATO powers and allies of Belgium.[98] The contingent affected was the Canadian contingent, whose inclusion in ONUC was justified by the Secretary-General on the grounds that the Canadian contingent was a bilingual signals unit, essential for such an operation, which could not be found in any other country; moreover, he did not regard participation in NATO or the Warsaw Treaty Organisation as, of itself, a ground for exclusion.[99]

Increases in the strength of the Force occurred from time to time. On 20 February 1961 the Secretary-General mentioned that the broadening of the functions of the Force, envisaged in the draft Resolution before the Security Council, would require an increase in strength.[1] This was effected either through an appeal to other Member States for contingents or for an increase in the size of a contingent already with ONUC. However, the Secretary-General did not regard an increase in the size of a contingent as requiring any re-negotiation of the agreement between the United Nations and the State concerned: whereas he did take the view that to have altered the legal basis upon which the Force was operating, *i.e.*, to have changed it from a "peace-keeping" operation into an "enforcement action," would have required a re-negotiation and, indeed, a new consent by the contributing State to the use of its contingent.[2]

An idea of both the fluctuations in the size of the Force (due to withdrawals and/or the changing military situation) and the different types of personnel supplied by States can be gained by looking at the

---

[95] Press Release Co/20/Add. 4 and S/4417/Add. 7.
[96] Co/20/Add. 5. p. 2. The "white" troops were Canadian troops, who on 18 August had been disarmed and manhandled by ANC units at the airport (see S/4417/Add. 8).
[97] S/4986, para. 2.
[98] S/4418, p. 3. Note that the Secretary-General refused to allow Belgian troops to be used for the restoration of order at Stanleyville on 18 July 1960: this is referred to in the Belgian Note Verbale of 7 December 1960, S/4585, p. 6.
[99] Statement on 21 August 1960: *Off. Rec. S.C.*, 15th yr., 888th Mtg., para. 96.
[1] *Off. Rec. S.C.*, 16th yr., 942nd Mtg., para. 218, and see S/4752, paras. 7 and 8.
[2] *Ibid.*, 942nd Mtg., para. 218.

table reproduced above.[3] It must also be remembered that certain States, like the United Kingdom and the United States, whilst not contributing States in the strict sense, provided air transport for contingents from contributing States.[4]

2. *Withdrawal of contingents*

Since all the contingents were provided voluntarily by Member States (there being no stand-by agreements with the Security Council), it seems to have been assumed both by contributing States and by the Secretary-General that any contributing State had the legal right to withdraw its contingent when it wished. Whether this assumption was necessarily correct is not altogether clear, for the principle of good faith and the obligations of Articles 2 (5), 25 and 49 may suggest certain limitations on any absolute right of withdrawal, and this is a problem to which reference must be made at a later stage.[5] However, the very serious implications which such withdrawals could have on the security, and future, of the Force are obvious and, indeed, the Secretary-General's concern was such that he addressed a special report [6] on this problem to the Security Council on 26 January 1961. At that time Guinea (749 officers and men) and Yugoslavia (21) had both withdrawn and Indonesia (1,150), Morocco (3,240) and the United Arab Republic (510) had notified their intention to withdraw. To the extent that these threats of withdrawal were designed to influence, or to express dissatisfaction over, the actual conduct of ONUC's operations, this is a question which will be dealt with below.[7]

One very important point, consequent upon withdrawal, was the status of a contingent which was withdrawn from ONUC but which chose to remain in the Congo to assist the Congolese Government independently of ONUC. The Permanent Representative of Ghana, on 18 August, notified the Secretary-General that, if the United Nations was unable to carry out the instructions of the Security Council, Ghana " in agreement with the Government of the Congo and, if necessary, in concert with other African Bodies, [would] be justified in taking independent action." [8] The Secretary-General's view on this problem was stated to the Security Council on 9 September 1960 :

" Were a national contingent to leave the United Nations Force, they would have to be regarded as foreign troops introduced into the Congo, and the Security Council would have to consider their continued presence in the Congo, as well as its consequences for the United Nations operation, in this light." [9]

---

[3] *Ante*, p. 206, n. 93.
[4] S/4389, p. 10. Soviet planes flew in food and other supplies : *ibid.*, p. 11, and see *post*, pp. 218–219, under " logistic support."   [5] *Post*, pp. 379–385.
[6] S/4640.   [7] *Post*, p. 214.
[8] S/4427.
[9] *Off. Rec. S.C.*, 15th yr., 896th Mtg., para. 109. See also the Secretary-General's reaction to the order from the Moroccan Government to its brigade to " cease to perform its functions " in January 1961. The Secretary-General reiterated that the contingent could only remain as part of ONUC, and that any other position was untenable (S/4668).

This view was undoubtedly right. The assumption of an independent power of action by the contingent of a Member State within the Congo could not be consistent with the demand for the cessation of all unilateral action which became so prominent in the General Assembly's Resolution of 20 September 1960.[10] A situation in which a Member State was employing its own forces in the territory of another State, at variance with the purposes for which a United Nations Force was being employed in the same territory, would be potentially anarchical; it would also amount to a clear defiance of the Member's obligations under Articles 25 and 49 of the Charter. However, the Casablanca Declaration of 7 January 1961, issued by the Conference of Independent African States, embodied a decision that, " if the United Nations Command failed to realise the objectives which were stated in the Declaration (a statement not fully in accord with Security Council Resolutions) the parties would reserve the right to take appropriate action." [11] If illustration of the inadvisability of the Secretary-General's acting on this kind of unilateral interpretation of the Security Council's mandate be sought, then it can surely be found in the fact that the Brazzaville Conference of twelve African States condemned the resolutions of the Casablanca Conference as calling for interference in the affairs of the Congo.[12]

3. Command structure

The command structure can best be illustrated in diagrammatic form. This illustrates, strikingly, the extent to which the political arm controlled the military; it stands in marked contrast to the paucity of political control over the military in Korea. Hence the command was headed by the Secretary-General who, in turn, carried out the mandate given to him by the political organs.[13]

Regulation 11 of the ONUC Regulations stated:

"The Secretary-General, under the authority of the Security Council and the General Assembly, has full command authority over the Force. The Commander is operationally responsible to the Secretary-General through the officer-in-charge for the performance of all functions assigned to the Force by the United Nations, and for the deployment and assignment of troops placed at the disposal of the Force."

Under Regulation 16 the Secretary-General was stated to have authority over " all administrative, executive and financial matters affecting the Force and shall be responsible for the negotiation and conclusion of agreements, with governments concerning the Force."

[10] Resol. 1474 (ES–IV), and see *ante*, p. 160.
[11] S/4626. Brackets mine.
[12] See statement by the representative of the Congo (Brazzaville) on 15 February: *Off. Rec. S.C.*, 16th yr., 937th Mtg., paras. 54–60.
[13] See *ante*, pp. 183–186. The fact that the Secretary-General turned for advice to the General Assembly, as well as the Security Council, did not in practice lead to difficulties, since he was never subjected to contradictory directions from the two organs. Had that situation ever arisen then, in principle, since the Security Council has " primary responsibility " (Art. 24) and had in fact established ONUC as a subsidiary organ, the directions of the Security Council should prevail.

The United Nations Force in the Congo (ONUC)

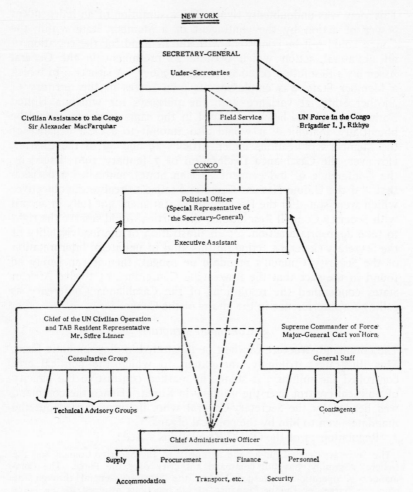

Reproduced from Official Records of the Security Council,
15th yr., Suppl. for July, August and September 1960, p. 66.

At headquarters, in New York, the Secretary-General was *controlled* only by the political organs of the United Nations and *advised* by the Advisory Committee of contributing States. He was *assisted* by his own staff, including a military adviser (Brigadier Rikhye) and an adviser on civilian assistance. The independent and equal status of these two advisers brings out the two-fold character of ONUC which was at the same time both a military operation and an operation of technical assistance to the Congo.

In the field the same structure is evident in the supremacy of the Special Representative of the Secretary-General (later called "Officer-in-Charge"), a political officer responsible solely to the Secretary-General, who directed both the United Nations Civilian operation (with its own Chief, Dr. Linner) and the Military operations, under the command of a Commander appointed by the Secretary-General. The Commander of the Force, assisted by a multi-national General Staff,[14] would translate into military commands to the national commanders of each contingent the political directives emanating from the Secretary-General or his Special Representative.[15] Regulation 12 made explicit the "full and exclusive authority" of the Commander over all members of his Headquarters Staff and of all members of the Force, "including the deployment and movement of all contingents in the Force and units thereof." Regulation 13 stated his "general responsibility for the good order and discipline of the Force," although disciplinary action was to be taken by national contingent commanders, subject to reports to the Commander. Regulation 15 provided for Military Police, with power of arrest over any member of the Force. Regulation 17 gave the Commander responsibility for the operation of the Force, but, as we shall see in examining the ONUC regulations, his subjection to political control was very much more marked than in the case of UNEF.

National contingents were normally kept under their own commands, but, as the Secretary-General pointed out when India attempted to impose this as a condition of the employment of Indian troops:

". . . certain operational situations occasionally necessitate the detachment of a company or more to other areas, functions or contingents for limited periods. On such occasions, however, detachments are kept in recognised military size under command of their own officers." [16]

Certainly the United Nations Command abandoned the principle used in Korea that there must be a *minimum* size of contingent, at about battalion strength (1,200 men),[17] so that, with smaller contingents, some integration of national contingents could on occasions be expected.

One feature of the initial stages of establishing ONUC was the reliance on UNEF and UNTSO, just as in establishing UNEF reliance had been placed on UNTSO.[18] Hence a nucleus of a command was created initially by the appointment of General Von Horn, Chief of

---

[14] Twenty-nine nations contributed staff officers and other ranks to man the headquarters: see Bloomfield, "Headquarters—Field Relations," in "International Force—A Symposium," *International Organisation*, Vol. 17, No. 2 (1963) p. 381.

[15] See ONUC Regulation 4: "The Commander may issue Orders not inconsistent with the Resolutions of the Security Council and the General Assembly relating to the Force, with these Regulations and amendments thereto, or with the supplemental instructions of the Secretary-General and of the Officer-in-Charge:
(a) in the discharge of his duties as Commander of the Force; or
(b) in implementation or explanation of these Regulations. Command Orders shall be subject to review by the Secretary-General and by the Officer-in-Charge."

[16] Press Release SG/1016, 4 March 1961, in reply to letter given in Press Release SG/1015.

[17] *Ante*, p. 37.

[18] *Ante*, p. 109.

Staff of UNTSO, and several UNTSO officers, and a Swedish battalion was detached from UNEF on a temporary basis.[19]

The degree of integration of the Command could not be expected to approach that which can be expected within a national force. Even apart from the difficulties of differences of language, training, equipment and disciplinary standards, the Force faced a problem which does not normally face a fighting force, namely, the severe restrictions on their ability to use force and to pursue objectives which, from the military point of view, might appear desirable. The disagreement between General Alexander and Bunche over the disarming of the Force Publique is the obvious example of this. In a sense, the differences of political opinion as to the objectives of the Force could not help but permeate through to the military level, so that the degree of co-operation by different contingents in the United Nations' objectives was rather variable. In an extreme form it was manifested in a threat of disobedience to United Nations Command orders [20]; in a less extreme form it was manifested in the conditions which a contributing State might impose on the use of its forces.[21]

Thus the larger problem, which is inevitably linked with that of the command structure, was one of strategic and political control.

4. *Strategic and political control*

The exercise of political control over ONUC should have been, and to some extent was, a matter for the Security Council. The lack of continuity, and at times even the absence, of this obvious form of control has been emphasised in the earlier parts of this chapter; but certainly the orthodox line of control was Security Council, through to the Secretary-General, and then through to the United Nations Command.[22]

In principle, this control lay exclusively in the United Nations, and not in the hands of either the host State or any single Member of the United Nations, whether a contributing State or not. As the Secretary-General said in his first report:

" Although the United Nations Force under the Resolution is dispatched to the Congo at the request of the Government and will be present in the Congo with its consent . . . the Force is necessarily under the exclusive command of the United Nations, vested in the Secretary-General under the control of the Security Council. This is in accordance with the principles generally applied by the Organisation. The Force is thus not under the orders of the Government nor can it . . . be permitted to become a party to any internal conflict. A departure from this principle would seriously endanger the impartiality of the United Nations and of the operation . . .

[19] S/4389, pp. 7–8.
[20] See the letter dated 1 February 1961 from the Moroccan Permanent Representative to the Secretary-General and the reply of the Secretary-General (S/4668).
[21] *Post*, pp. 214–215.
[22] See statement of the Secretary-General on 8 August 1960: *Off. Rec. S.C.*, 15th yr., 885th Mtg., para. 127.

" It also follows from the above-mentioned statement that the United Nations, in this case as in any mission of the Organisation, acts solely under the authority of the main organs of the Organisation, representing only the Organisation, and supporting only the principles and purposes of the Organisation." [23]

The lack of continual and efficacious political direction from the Council thrust on the Secretary-General a burden of political control which he was, as we have seen, not entirely happy to assume. Hence he established the Advisory Committee of contributing States on 23 August 1960 when his policy of non-intervention in relation to Katanga came under criticism.[24] However, this Committee remained essentially advisory, and whilst there were many occasions on which the Secretary-General made clear that he was acting on the advice of this Committee,[25] the effective decisions were those of the Secretary-General. The full extent of the Secretary-General's reliance on the Advisory Committee is difficult to estimate, since no records of the meetings were published.

Within the Secretariat the Secretary-General relied on his own body of advisers and, almost of necessity, the day-to-day surveillance and direction of the activities of ONUC lay with this group—the so-called " Congo Club." [26] The fact that this Secretariat group was composed of persons of a predominantly " Western " background has led to a certain amount of criticism,[27] and it may be noted that U Thant, on succeeding Mr. Hammarskjoeld, broadened the basis upon which this direction rested.[28] It may equally be noted that this made little difference to United Nations policy as directed by the Secretary-General and his staff; indeed, from the point of view of certain States, the actions of ONUC in December 1961 and 1962 were even less acceptable than the actions of ONUC under Mr. Hammarskjoeld in August and September 1961.

Criticism of the source and content of this political control assumed various forms. There was first the demand by the Soviet Union for the replacing of a single Secretary-General by a " troika,"

[23] S/4389, p. 3.
[24] *Off.Rec.S.C.*, 15th yr., 887th Mtg., para. 36.
[25] For example, see S/4752 for the reference to the " guidance " of the Committee on the implementation of the Resolution of 21 February; also S/4771, in which the Secretary-General made it clear that the terms of reference of the Committee of Investigation into Lumumba's death were set by the Advisory Committee. The Conciliation Commission was also created by the Advisory Committee pursuant to General Assembly Resol. 1474 (ES–IV) of 20 September 1960. It is also clear that the ONUC Regulations (ST/SGB/ONUC/1) were issued following consultation with the Advisory Committee.
[26] See O'Brien, *op. cit.*, Chap. 2, where he accepts that this group " put the interests of the United Nations first " but argues that " their conceptions of what constituted the interests of the United Nations were profoundly and involuntarily affected by (among other things) their own national formation " (p. 59).
[27] See, for example, O'Brien, *op. cit.*, pp. 53–59; Okumu, *op. cit.*, p. 443; Woddis, " Lessons of the Congo," *Marxism Today*, May 1963, p. 138.
[28] See U Thant's statement on election to office on 3 November 1961 (*U.N. Review*, December 1961, p. 20).

a triumvirate of one Western, one Socialist ("Eastern" or "Communist") and one "non-aligned" or "neutral" member.[29] The essential difficulty in this proposal was that it would have injected into the office of Secretary-General the same power of veto—and possibly the same fundamental political divergencies—which had paralysed the Security Council. So that, instead of having an ineffective Council but an effective Secretary-General, there would have been both an ineffective Council and an ineffective Secretary-General. In other words, it was likely to substitute for a policy which aroused antagonism no policy at all. The proposal failed to secure support from either the West or the Afro-Asian powers and, based on a personal attack on the integrity of Mr. Hammarskjoeld, it can only be described as a serious tactical error by the Soviet Union.

The other form which criticism assumed was that of an attempt by individual contributing States to force a change of policy. In so far as this might be made as part of the debate and discussion within either the Security Council or the General Assembly there is, of course, no possible objection to this. The attempt to influence policy becomes suspect only when it is made outside those bodies, as a form of pressure on the Secretary-General, in order to force him to accept a policy which the State knew would not be acceptable to the political organs representing the United Nations as a whole. It is from this point of view that the withdrawal of national contingents,[30] or the ordering of national contingents to cease to execute the commands of the United Nations Command,[31] or even the imposition unilaterally of conditions on which their contingents might be used,[32] may be suspect. Admitting that all contingents were provided on a voluntary basis, it may yet be said that if a contributing State wished to challenge the interpretation of the Secretary-General of the mandate of the Security Council the place for that challenge to be made was the Security Council or the General Assembly. Otherwise the contributing States were both morally and legally bound to accept

---

[29] See statement by Mr. Krushchev, *Off. Rec. G.A.*, 15th Sess., 882nd Mtg., para. 40; on the implications of this proposal see Bailey, "The troika and the future of the UN," (1962) *International Conciliation*, No. 538.

[30] *Ante*, p. 208.

[31] *Ante*, p. 212, for the Moroccan position (S/4668; and *ante*, p. 208, for the position assumed by Ghana on 18 August 1960, that it was content to leave its contingent under the UN Command only so long as the UN carried out the Resolutions of the Security Council (S/4427).

[32] See in particular the letter from the Indian Permanent Representative dated 3 March 1961, offering additions to its contingent but stating the conditions on which the Indian forces were to be used (Press Release S.G./1015) and the Secretary-General's reply (S.G./1016). Similar conditions were imposed by Ethiopia, Sudan and Tunisia earlier on 27 February 1961 (S/4752). The particular conditions, so far as they simply reiterated the Security Council's own conditions, were unobjectionable; the danger lies more in the general position assumed by these States that a legitimate way of asserting their own interpretation of the Resolutions of the Security Council is by communication with the Secretary-General in this way, rather than by argument before the political organs of the UN.

the decisions of the Security Council and not to substitute a unilateral interpretation of those decisions for that made by the Secretary-General as agent of the Security Council.

A third form of criticism of the political control was the proposal made to transfer such control from the hands of the Secretary-General, as agent for the Security Council, to a "unified African command" responsible directly to the Security Council.[33] This, in itself, was a perfectly permissible proposal, but on grounds of political and practical desirability its wisdom may be questioned. It would have suffered from the same drawbacks which the Korean action suffered in being entrusted to the United States Government, namely, that the policy might in fact have become (and would certainly have been so regarded by many States) a policy of one or more Member States and not the policy of the United Nations as such. However difficult it may be for the political organs of the United Nations to agree upon and formulate a continuing policy, it is considered that there is extraordinary danger in the proposal to entrust any United Nations operation involving the use of force in the name of the United Nations to a limited group of States. This would be tantamount, virtually, to an abdication by the United Nations of its responsibility in favour of a grouping of States, generally regional in character, which could then, in the name of the United Nations (and with all the moral and even financial backing which that implies) pursue a policy unacceptable to the collectivity of States.

Yet a fourth form of criticism was to be seen in the refusal by some States to contribute towards the cost of the ONUC operations. This is a matter dealt with in detail later,[34] but it may be stated now that the International Court rejected the criticism in this context. It stated, after reviewing the Resolutions of both Security Council and General Assembly:

"In the light of such a record of reiterated consideration, confirmation, approval and ratification by the Security Council and by the General Assembly of the actions of the Secretary-General in implementing the Resolution of 14 July 1960, it is impossible to reach the conclusion that the operations in question usurped or impinged upon the prerogatives conferred by the Charter on the Security Council."[35]

The translation of the guiding political directives into strategic terms seems to have been a task assumed by the Secretary-General and his military advisers as much as by the Supreme Commander in the field. The absence of any attempt to use the Military Staff Committee, which, under the terms of the Charter, could possibly have been used to advise on strategic direction of the Force, is only partially explicable by reference to the fact that the operations were

---

[33] See statement by Nkrumah in the General Assembly on 23 September 1960: *Off.Rec.G.A.*, 15th Sess., 869th Mtg., para. 30.
[34] *Post*, pp. 249–254.
[35] *I.C.J. Reports*, 1962, p. 177.

entrusted to the Secretary-General rather than assumed by the Security Council itself and were not in the nature of enforcement action under Article 42.[36] The larger part of the explanation is certainly to be found in the Secretary-General's adherence to the principle that ONUC should not include (and, *semble*, be directed by) any of the Permanent Members of the Council and also in the history of the Military Staff Committee[37] which suggested that coherent advice would not be forthcoming from such a body but, rather, that the Committee would simply have reflected the basic political differences of the Members of the Security Council and thus led to a frustration of the enterprise rather than its successful prosecution. Thus the strategic direction of the Force became a matter essentially for the Secretariat to provide, from its own resources, and subject to the immediate responsibility of the Secretary-General, which would tend to place the main stress on political rather than strategic control and direction. This was, no doubt, to some extent inevitable since, unlike a normal military campaign, no general political directive to destroy all opposing forces could be given, and every military step was fraught with serious political repercussions.

However, the instances when, in the field, action was taken which went beyond what had been envisaged by the Secretary-General and his staff in New York indicate that effective liaison was lacking not only between the political side and the military side, but also between the political side in New York and the political side in the Congo. The events of September 1961 have already been described,[38] and, if O'Brien is to be believed, it is apparent that as the political representative in Elisabethville his ideas of what was authorised did not coincide with those held in New York. In December/January 1963, the action began in Elisabethville and led to the move to Jadotville on 4 January, a move which appears to have been dictated by strategic and military considerations, and determined by the military commanders on the spot upon finding that little resistance was offered to the advance, rather than by the Secretary-General. The newspaper talk of a "general's revolt" at that time[39] was dramatic, but scarcely accurate; what had occurred, under combat conditions, was a serious breakdown in communications. As the Report of the Officer-in-Charge confessed:

"The Jadotville operation was the first experience of a strictly United Nations armed force under United Nations command with combat conditions in the field. The stress and strain of battle revealed serious deficiencies in communication and co-ordination as among United Nations Headquarters in New York,

[36] See *I.C.J. Pleadings, Certain expenses of the United Nations*, pp. 161, 302.
[37] *Ante*, p. 12. [38] *Ante*, p. 169.
[39] See *The Sunday Times*, 6 January 1963; also *The Times*, 5 January 1963 and the *New York Times*, 4 January 1963. It would seem that the Secretary-General had assured the Belgian ambassador that no advance on Jadotville would be made, in the hope that this would avoid sabotage to the refining installations at Jadotville, but that this "standstill" order had not been communicated to the Force Commander in Katanga.

the Leopoldville Headquarters in the Congo operation, and the military detachments in action in the field. It should also be pointed out that the telecommunications facilities between Leopoldville and Elisabethville are badly hampered by weather conditions during this time of the year, which is the rainy season. Urgent measures are being taken to correct these defects and it may be accepted with confidence that there will be no recurrence of the Jadotville lapses." [40]

The subsequent report by Bunche emphasised that the problem was essentially one of deficient communications and that he " found nothing to suggest that the authority of the Secretary-General and his full control over the Force and the operation as a whole has ever been questioned by anyone in the Organisation . . . there was and is no question of the military branch of the operation exceeding authority . . ." [41] However, perhaps the most illuminating observation is the "home-truth" which has to be accepted if combat operations are contemplated : Bunche phrased it in these terms :

" It has to be soberly reckoned with at United Nations Headquarters, that once a fighting situation develops—and particularly when a plan is being executed in an area of combat activity—efforts to regulate the details of military moves and tactics by political levers at Headquarters may put many men's lives in jeopardy. Once a military action is afoot there can be no push-button action at Headquarters to control that action in response to political or other considerations, without doing violence to sound military judgment and tactics, at serious cost to the security of the troops involved and of the local population." [42]

Bunche's own proposed solution was the attachment of a " mature reporting officer " from the ONUC Headquarters to every unit likely to see fighting action, whose sole responsibility would be to report to the Force Commander on the progress of the action. Also, on the staff of the Force Commander, there should be senior officers assigned the duty of reporting to United Nations Headquarters in New York. Finally, he suggested a high level liaison officer, between the Officer-in-Charge (the Secretary-General's political representative) and the Force Commander.

Quite apart from the inadequacy of the communications and liaison systems, the strategic control of the Force suffered from a lack of any military intelligence unit. Mr. Hammarskjoeld is reported as having admitted to the Advisory Committee that this was a serious handicap,[43] and O'Brien has stated that, in Katanga, the United Nations was forced to rely on one Greek ex-policeman, with an imperfect knowledge of French, and some Baluba houseboys.[44] The principle will probably have to be accepted, in future, that, however distasteful the notion of a United Nations " espionage " or intelligence system may be, in a situation involving combat possibilities it may be necessary to save the lives of United Nations soldiers.

[40] S/5053/Add. 14, para. 74.
[41] S/5053/Add. 14, Annex.
[42] *Ibid.* See, on this problem, Bloomfield, *loc. cit.*, pp. 386–388.
[43] O'Brien, *op. cit.*, p. 76.
[44] *Ibid.*

5. *Logistical support*

The hastily improvised character of ONUC was nowhere more apparent than in the arrangements for logistical support of the Force. The initial task of transporting contingents to the Congo was accomplished only by the supply of air transportation by the United States [45] and, to a lesser extent, the United Kingdom, Ethiopia, Canada and, in respect of supplies, the Soviet Union. Aircraft were chartered also from commercial air lines such as Swissair, and, indeed, the system of air transport was in due course based very largely on commercial aircraft. Staging depots were established at Pisa in Italy and Kano in Nigeria.

Once within the Congo the problems of transport within the Congo, supply and maintenance of the troops and communications remained to be solved. Given the nature and size of the country, air transport proved the most expeditious and ONUC built up its own Air Transport Force [46] but this remained inadequate as the situation deteriorated and rapid deployment of troops was required,[47] the more so as maintenance of aircraft, due to lack of both technicians and spares, proved difficult. The lack of any meteorological services initially was yet a further handicap to air operations. Road transport equally presented problems, of a similar nature, and these were not eased by the variety of different types of vehicles used, about forty in number.

Supplies for continuing support of the troops were either airlifted into the Congo or else imported by sea via the port of Matadi, hence the concern of the Secretary-General to ensure United Nations control over the port.[48] Troops arriving were normally expected to be self-sustaining for the first few days, but thereafter supplies were the concern of the United Nations and, because of the variety of the troops, no single rationing scheme could be devised for all troops.

Communications by wireless were provided for the main command by a Canadian signals squadron, and a Canadian detachment was also established at each of the four territorial commands. Within each command national contingents provided communications, but additional equipment had to be provided to cope with the great distances.[49] An Indian signals company subsequently took over communications for Katanga province.[50]

Hospital services were provided by an Indian base hospital at

---

[45] See *U.S. Participation in the UN*, Report by the President to Congress for 1961, Dept. State Pub. 7413, Int. Org. Conference Series 33, August 1962, p. 87, which reveals that the U.S.A. had, by the end of 1961, airlifted 46,000 troops and 7,800 tons of supplies to and from the Congo. The U.S.A. also "sealifted" 13,000 troops, 4,860 tons of supplies and 612 vehicles.

[46] See Dayal's First Report, S/4531, Annex 3.

[47] Dayal's Second Report, S/4557, p. 27.

[48] *Ante*, p. 204.

[49] S/4531, Annex 2.

[50] S/4557, p. 31.

Leopoldville, with other units in Luluabourg and Coquilhatville, and an Italian hospital at Albertville.[51] It is perhaps fortunate that no serious epidemic or severe casualties occurred to test these health services.

The procurement system for supplies rested on the logistic staffs attached to each of the four territorial commands, the logistic staff at Headquarters in Leopoldville, and, from there, in general, to the Chief Administration Officer who, with regard to procurement, was under direct instructions from the Field Operations Service in New York, where, in fact, most of the purchasing was done.[52] Both military and civilian (*i.e.*, for the Civilian Operations side of ONUC) supplies were purchased via the New York Field Operations Service. It may be noted that, under ONUC Regulations No. 21, it was the Officer-in-Charge, not the Commander, who had responsibility for billeting, food supplies, transportation, procurement of supplies and equipment, maintenance and other services.[53] Even the Commander's authority to enter into contracts was, under Regulation 22, by delegation from the Officer-in-Charge and all recruitment of local personnel or Secretariat staff was done by the Officer-in-Charge. The efficiency of this system has been severely criticised on the ground of lack of advance planning, of readily available supplies, of trained logistic personnel and of co-ordination.[54] Proposals for a solution to these defects are examined in detail at a later stage.[55]

6. *The Regulations for the United Nations Force in the Congo*

The Regulations for ONUC,[56] like those for UNEF, are directed mainly to problems arising from the relationship between the United Nations and participating States so that they may be considered appropriately at this juncture. They are based very much on the UNEF regulations and, although published officially only on 15 July 1963, they are stated to be deemed to have taken effect on the date of the arrival of the first elements of ONUC in the Congo and to " continue in effect the policies and practices which have been followed in respect of the Force since it came into existence."

The " international character " of the Force was laid down in Regulation 6, as in the case of UNEF; it never became a matter of dispute as in the case of the Korean force, except to the extent that

---

[51] *Ibid.*, p. 30.
[52] The CAO had a discretion to make his own purchases locally up to $5,000. See the very informative article by Bowman and Fanning " Logistics Problems of a UN Military Force," (1963) *International Organisation*, Vol. 17, No. 2, p. 364.
[53] But note that, under Reg. 17 the Commander's responsibility also related to " the provision of facilities, supplies and auxiliary services "; in the exercise of this authority he was to " act in consultation with the Secretary-General through the Officer-in-Charge."
[54] Bowman and Fanning, *loc. cit.*, pp. 368–376.
[55] *Post*, pp. 403–406.
[56] ST/SGB/ONUC/1, 15 July 1963, issued by the Secretary-General.

objections were lodged as to its composition,[57] or to the manner in which it was being employed.[58]   However, the pressures which were applied both by contributing States and by the host State were in part a reflection of an unwillingness to accept the principle stated in Regulation 6, namely, that:

" . . . The members of the Force, although remaining in their national service, are, during the period of their assignment to the Force, international personnel under the authority of the United Nations and subject to the instructions of the Commander, through the chain of command.   The functions of the Force are exclusively international and members of the Force shall discharge these functions and regulate their conduct with the interest of the United Nations only in view."

The authorisation to use the United Nations flag,[59] the provision requiring a "distinctive United Nations mark and licence" on all transportation of the Force,[60] and the provisions on privileges and immunities of the Force,[61] are all indicative of the international character of ONUC.

The detailed provisions are best not summarised here, but rather dealt with under the appropriate sub-heads of this chapter. However, it may be useful here to summarise the principal changes which can be discerned in the ONUC regulations as compared to the UNEF regulations.

Firstly, there is the reference to the establishment of ONUC by the Resolution of the Security Council [62]; in the case of UNEF it was the Assembly which created the subsidiary organ.

Secondly, there is the very much more specific statement of the authority of the Secretary-General, an authority in many cases assumed by him rather than by the Commander, as was the case with UNEF.   Whereas in UNEF the power of the Secretary-General to issue supplemental regulations lay "with respect to matters not delegated to the Commander," [63] in the case of ONUC there is no such sphere of matters which are excluded from the Secretary-General's regulatory powers.[64]   Moreover, the Commander is, in ONUC, appointed by the Secretary-General [65] and not by the Assembly, as was the case with UNEF.[66]   Command authority is vested in the Secretary-General and not directly in the Commander.[67] Changes in commanders of national contingents are to be made not as a matter for consultation between the Commander and the participating State but in consultation with the Secretary-General.[68]

[57] *Ante*, p. 207.
[58] *Ante*, p. 214.
[59] Reg. 7.
[60] Reg. 9.
[61] Reg. 10 and Chapter V; and see *post*, pp. 237–239.
[62] Regs. 4, 5 (b).
[63] UNEF, Reg. 3.
[64] Reg. 3.
[65] Reg. 5 (c).
[66] UNEF, Reg. 5 (a).
[67] Reg. 11.
[68] Reg. 12.

The Commander is, in the exercise of his duties and responsibilities, to receive from the Secretary-General " appropriate guidance through the Officer-in-Charge . . . ," [69] whereas in UNEF the comparable regulation omitted that clause.[70] Even in the relatively minor matter of the accompaniment of members of the Force by their dependants it is the Secretary-General and not the Commander who prescribes the conditions on which this is to be permitted.[71]

Thirdly, there is the frequent recognition in the Regulations of the role of the " Officer-in-Charge "—an officer non-existent in UNEF. He may issue supplemental instructions binding on the Commander [72] and may review Command Orders [73]; it is he who is given " over-all command and direction for all United Nations activities in the Republic of the Congo (Leopoldville), civil and military." [74] It is the Officer-in-Charge who acts as intermediary between the Commander and the Secretary-General,[75] and who takes over recruitment of Secretariat and local personnel, general administration, power to make contracts and all public information activities [76]—all these being powers vested in the Commander in UNEF. All this is symptomatic of the fact that in ONUC, as compared with UNEF, the predominance of the political control over the military is very marked indeed, as we have seen in examining the command structure.[77]

Fourthly, the Commander, apart from having this very much more specific statement of his subordination to the political control of the Secretary-General and the Officer-in-Charge, has an increased power of investigating into matters relating to the good order and discipline of the Force,[78] and into incidents, accidents or losses affecting the Force or its members or property used by the Force.[79]

Fifthly, there are two minor changes affecting the Force itself, relating to the overseas service allowance [80] and compensation to members for loss of personal effects [81]; and there are the more significant changes in the regulations on privileges and immunities,[82] which are described in detail below.[83]

Lastly, there is a new Chapter VI to the Regulations, dealing with relations between the participating governments and the United

---

[69] Reg. 16.
[70] UNEF, Reg. 15.
[71] Reg. 36.
[72] Regs. 3, 4.
[73] Reg. 4 (b).
[74] Reg. 5 (a).
[75] Regs. 16, 17.
[76] Regs. 20, 21, 22, 23 and 27.
[77] *Ante*, pp. 209–212.
[78] Reg. 13.
[79] Reg. 14. There is no comparable regulation in UNEF.
[80] Reg. 34 does not contain the rigid $1 per day maximum which Reg. 39 of UNEF did.
[81] Reg. 35. There is no comparable regulation in UNEF.
[82] Regs. 10, 29 (b).
[83] *Post*, pp. 237–239.

Nations. Regulation 39 prescribes the United Nations Headquarters in New York as the proper channel for communications concerning their units, through the Permanent Missions of the participating governments, and Regulation 40 provides for visits to the Force by officials of the participating governments to be arranged with the Commander via the United Nations Headquarters in New York. Then there are new provisions on the financial relations between the United Nations and the participating States, and these will be dealt with later.[84]

7. *The application of the laws of war*

The application of the laws of war to ONUC operations merits separate mention because, although it was referred to specifically in the ONUC Regulations, it raises wider questions of principle. Regulation 43, which finds its counterpart in Regulation 44 of UNEF, provided that:

" The Force shall observe the principles and spirit of the general international Conventions applicable to the conduct of military personnel."

Whilst, clearly, there was never any question of ONUC (or rather the United Nations) assuming a belligerent status in the Congo, it became obvious that the fulfilment of the tasks assigned to it involved a high risk of combat activity, and the regulation cited indicates the intention of ONUC to abide by the general international conventions applicable to military personnel engaged in armed combat. In taking this position the United Nations made a number of questionable assumptions which are discussed in detail later [85]; at this juncture, however, it may be useful to indicate the factual context within which this question arose in the Congo and the attitude of various Member States and the United Nations itself.

The weapons used by the United Nations in the course of activities based on the Security Council Resolutions—and not on the rights and duties inherent in lawful belligerency—included fighter and bomber aircraft,[86] mortars, anti-tank and anti-aircraft weapons, machine guns and small-arms. These weapons caused casualties to both military and civilian life and property, mainly in the course of actions between the Katangese gendarmerie and ONUC.

However, whilst Belgium had on 8 December 1961 called on the United Nations to observe the Geneva Conventions of 1949,[87] the International Committee of the Red Cross had been less clear about the total applicability of even these Conventions: its communiqué of 17 November 1961 stated that:

[84] *Post*, p. 249.
[85] *Post*, pp. 506–516.
[86] For the abortive negotiations with the U.K. in December 1961, for the supply of bombs, see O'Brien, *op. cit.*, p. 329. The U.K. finally decided not to supply bombs and expressed concern at UN attacks on non-military targets. In fact no bombs were actually used by the UN.
[87] S/5025.

" Le Comité internationale a constamment rappelé aux autorités congo-
laises de droit et de fait les exigences *minima*, decoulent de l'application des
Conventions de Genève." [88]

This tended to suggest that the view was being taken that what was
involved was the minimum of limited humanitarian rules applicable
under Article 3 of the 1949 Conventions to " internal conflicts," [89]
and not the laws of war as such, or even the " general international
conventions applicable to the conduct of military personnel," to use
the phrase of the ONUC Regulations.[90]

Prisoners were certainly taken, on both sides, but were not
regarded as prisoners of war in the sense of personnel to whom the
1949 Convention applied, and the normal procedure was for prisoners
to be disarmed and returned as soon as practicable [91]; the only
exception to this was in the case of the mercenaries who were
deported.

There were numerous occasions on which the Congolese and the
United Nations Forces were accused of acts which could have been
characterised as violations of the laws of war by reference to specific
provisions of the Hague Regulations or the Geneva Conventions, had
those been regarded as strictly applicable.[92]   In practice, however,
the United Nations ordered an investigation into " violations " or
" offences," without further specification; the notion of " war
crimes " was not used by United Nations spokesmen.[93]

It is believed that a good deal of the publicity given to the " war
crimes " committed, or alleged to have been committed, by ONUC
was based upon a desire to discredit the United Nations operations
by any available means.[94]   Hostilities of the kind which began in

[88] *Revue Int. de la Croix Rouge*, 1961, p. 603 (italics added): copies and
information about the Conventions were distributed in Swahili amongst
the various forces in the Congo.
[89] See also the Report of the Commission of Experts, *ibid.*, February 1963,
pp. 79–80, although this does not refer specifically to the Congo.
[90] And see Draper, *loc. cit.*, p. 410, who regards it as doubtful whether even
Art. 3 had any application.
[91] The cease-fire agreements contained this provision: see S/4940/Add. 11.
[92] The destruction on 13 December 1961, of an ambulance of the Red Cross
by bazooka fire, and the killing of 3 Red Cross personnel, was investigated
by the Acting Secretary-General, although no evidence could be obtained
to attribute this to UN Forces (see Draper, *loc. cit.*, p. 410).   The killing
of a Frenchwoman on 29 December 1962, was similarly investigated by
the UN with the help of Interpol (see *Summary Chronology of UN Action
Relating to the Congo*, Part XXI, 1 February).   Accusations against Irish and
Ethiopian troops were made, but never substantiated, by Monseigneur
Kileshie, Vicar-General at Elisabethville and were in fact denied by the
Officer-in-Charge, Mr. Gardiner (*ibid.*, 15 February).   On the part of the
non-UN forces there were numerous incidents, of which the most shocking
was perhaps the murder of 13 Italian airmen by Stanleyville troops in
September 1961 (S/4940/Add. 13).
[93] The Minister of Justice of S. Kasai did, on one occasion, justify executions
as being for " war crimes " and invoked the parallel of the Allied punishment of the Axis war leaders (S/4727/Add. 2, 20 February 1961): this
scarcely merits comment.
[94] Extreme examples of this are the booklet entitled " 46 Angry Men," an
indictment of ONUC action by specific reference to the Geneva Conventions and purporting to emanate from 46 civilian doctors in Elisabethville

December 1961 and 1962 cannot, especially when taking place in a town like Elisabethville, avoid damage to life and property[95]; there is, however, a vast difference between death or injury to innocent bystanders which may occur without design, but as an inevitable consequence of warlike operations, and the deliberate infliction of such harm. The only clear evidence of violations of the rules to which the United Nations had pledged itself was in relation to occasional cases of looting and rape, and such isolated cases occur in the best-regulated armies. The most that can be expected is due diligence in investigating allegations of such acts, and punishment of the offenders. On 25 January 1962 a United Nations information officer gave the assurance that " those found guilty of these violations of the strict orders of the United Nations Command either already have been punished or will be after due process." [96]

It follows, however, from the immunity of ONUC personnel from the criminal jurisdiction of the host State and from the lack of any United Nations disciplinary procedures (military codes, courts-martial, etc.) that the jurisdiction of the participating States was the only feasible jurisdiction, and the ONUC regulations so provided.[97]

VII. RELATIONS BETWEEN THE UNITED NATIONS AND MEMBER STATES GENERALLY

The United Nations, as a system for collective security, rests on the assumption that when action is decided upon, via the constitutional processes provided for in the Charter, it will be action supported by the entirety of the membership; the quality and kind of support may vary from State to State, but support there must be. Hence Article 2 (5) provides:

" All Members shall give the United Nations every assistance in any action it takes in accordance with the present Charter, and shall refrain from giving assistance to any State against which the United Nations is taking preventive or enforcement action."

Since ONUC was not in the nature of " preventive or enforcement action " against a State, the latter (and negative) part of the obligation was inapplicable; yet the first was certainly applicable and it is

---

or the pamphlet " What truly happened on the 17 July of 1962 ": both were printed in Belgium, and, whilst they contain horrifying pictures, they contain little in the way of proof that the victims had suffered at the hands of ONUC personnel in a way contrary to the Geneva Conventions.

[95] See Report by Officer-in-Charge on Events in Katanga from 26 November to 4 January 1963 for the estimate of civilian casualties due to the fighting from 24 December to 4 January 1963, as being between 40 and 50. ONUC casualties were 9 dead and 72 wounded.

[96] UN Information Release of 25 January 1962, p. 5, statement by Mr. Ivan Smith. See also *The Times*, 8 February 1962, for the statement in the House of Commons by a Government spokesman to the effect that the UN had assured the British Government that ONUC personnel guilty of offences were punished (also in H.C.Parl.Deb., Vol. 671, col. 741, 7 February).

[97] ONUC Reg. 29 (a).

surprising to find a complete absence in the official records of any reference to this general undertaking to give assistance. Instead, as we have seen,[98] the Secretary-General, and in due course the Security Council, chose to invoke Articles 25 and 49 as a reminder to Members generally that the Resolutions of the Council involved obligations on States other than the participating States, or even the State of Belgium to which specific demands had been addressed. However, the obligation to " accept and carry out " the decisions of the Council and to " join in affording mutual assistance in carrying out the measures decided upon by the Security Council," came as close to the obligation in Article 2 (5) to give " every assistance " as would make little difference—it being assumed that the contribution of forces was on a purely voluntary basis. Certainly Articles 25 and 49 were adequate criteria by which one can assess the extent to which Member States generally conformed to the obligations assumed under the Charter, and to the Resolutions of the Security Council and the General Assembly addressed to them.

The contexts within which it becomes necessary to examine the conduct of Member States, so as to ascertain the extent to which co-operation and assistance were accorded to the United Nations, are perhaps four.

1. Expulsion of foreign military, para-military personnel, political advisers and mercenaries

The degrees by which expulsion of these foreign elements became an express aim of United Nations action has already been described.[99] In the prosecution of this particular aim the assistance afforded to the United Nations was scarcely impressive. The efforts by the Secretary-General to secure full compliance by Belgium were a constant testimony to the failure of Belgium to co-operate. To his protest on 4 September 1960 over the attachment of Belgian officers, formerly serving with the Force Publique, to the newly created Katangese forces the Belgian reply was, essentially, that this was " technical assistance." [1] Following the Council's Resolution of 21 February 1961, a series of exchanges between the Secretary-General and Belgium occurred,[2] with Belgium making withdrawal conditional on United Nations guarantees of protection for Belgian life, justifying the attachment of Belgian officers under Article 250 of the *Loi Fondamentale*, and stating that recruitment of Belgians would be stopped,[3] but that Belgium could only compel under Belgian law the return to Belgium of such Belgian nationals serving in the Congo as had not fulfilled their obligations of military service.

---

[98] *Ante*, pp. 175, 181.
[99] *Ante*, pp. 165–172, 195–196.
[1] S/4482/Add. 3.
[2] S/4752/and Add. 1.
[3] Directions to the Belgian police appear to have been given only in February 1961 (S/4752/Annex II, B).

The Secretary-General rejected the view that Belgium could make its compliance with the Council's Resolutions conditional, or that reliance on Article 250 of the *Loi Fondamentale* could override those Resolutions: he also invoked Article 103 of the Charter.[4] The Secretary-General subsequently described the Belgian attitude as showing " a reluctance which, on some occasions, came close to putting in doubt its very acceptance of the Resolution in principle." [5] It was certainly inadequate for Belgium to rely upon the limitations of her own national law as a reason for not enforcing the return of those mercenaries already in Katanga: no principle of international law is clearer than the principle that a State may not invoke its own municipal law as a reason for evading its international obligations.[6]

The need for co-operation by Member States in this matter was not confined to Belgium. It had become clear that nationals of many States were being recruited as mercenaries,[7] and the Resolution of 21 February was clear in its reference to Belgian " and other " foreign personnel. Moreover, from evidence given by captured mercenaries, it became clear that recruiting centres were established in Brussels, Johannesburg (South Africa) and Bulawayo (Southern Rhodesia).[8] Hence, whilst the action of a Member in allowing this to occur in its territory could scarcely have been regarded as consistent with the general obligation to assist the United Nations, or the Security Council Resolutions of 22 July, para. 2, or 9 August, para. 5, or the General Assembly Resolution of 20 September, paras. 5 and 6, it became necessary for the Resolution of 21 February to spell out the call to all States "to take immediate and energetic measures to prevent the departure of such personnel from their territories, and for the denial of transit and other facilities for them." The United Nations representative in Elisabethville had, on 9 September 1961, called for the assistance of the various Consuls in Elisabethville in securing the withdrawal of mercenaries; according to O'Brien this assistance was not forthcoming,[9] but the evidence on this point is inconclusive.

4 S/4752/Add. 1. The Belgian reply of 4 March (S/4752/Add. 2) showed little change of opinion. The negotiations between the Secretary-General and Belgium are reviewed in the Secretary-General's Progress Report of 17 May 1961 (S/4807).
5 S/4807, para. 4.
6 *Advisory Opinion on the Treatment of Polish Nationals in the Danzig Territory*, P.C.I.J. Ser. A/B, No. 44.
7 See the Report to the Secretary-General from the Special Representative, dated 14 April 1961, S/4790, giving a list of the names and nationalities of the 30 mercenaries captured at Kabalo airfield on 7 April 1961 : they included British, South African, Italian, and Greek nationals.
8 *Ibid.*, paras. 8–10; see also S/5053/Add. 12 for further evidence of recruitment.
9 O'Brien, *op. cit.*, p. 220 says that operation Rumpunch, the rounding-up of mercenaries in August 1961, was stopped partly at the request of the Consuls and in return for an undertaking that they would undertake the repatriation of the mercenaries.

2. *Other forms of assistance to the factions within the Congo*

The principle which the Secretary-General had regarded as fundamental,[10] and which the General Assembly endorsed on 20 September
1960, was that all assistance to the Congo should be channelled
through the United Nations and not afforded by States unilaterally.
This Assembly Resolution called on Members:

". . . to refrain from the direct and indirect provision of arms or other
materials of war and military personnel and other assistance for military
purposes in the Congo during the temporary period of military assistance
through the United Nations, except upon the request of the United Nations
through the Secretary General . . ."

Despite this there was, as we have seen,[11] the threat by certain
African States to afford military assistance to the Congolese Government independently of the United Nations. There was also the
assistance provided prior to the Resolution of 20 September by the
Soviet Union, on a purely bilateral basis, consisting of Ilyushin
transport aircraft and trucks.[12] The position taken by the Soviet
Union was that it was within the sovereign right of the Government
of the Congo to negotiate bilateral agreements for such assistance,
and, indeed, President Kasavubu later adopted the same position.[13]
The difficulty about this position, even if one assumes that it was
prompted by the feeling that the Secretary-General was failing to
give the required assistance, was that it could only serve to increase
the possibilities of civil war, not to diminish them. For example,
the Soviet aid, and the African offer of assistance, were destined to
assist Mr. Lumumba in his struggle for power with President Kasavubu and the ANC forces under the control of Colonel Mobutu. In
that context it was assistance which was scarcely likely to be conducive to a unity of policy by the United Nations as a whole and to
the suppression of civil war.

The assistance provided to the secessionist forces lacked even the
moral justification which lay behind the Soviet standpoint, for this
was clearly designed to be used against the Central Government with
a view to destroying the unity of the Congo which, for the United
Nations, was the basis of its policy. The Secretary-General's protest
to Belgium about the transmission by air to Elisabethville of cargoes
of weapons [14] was met by an admission of "the incompetence of an
ill-informed official" of the Belgian Government.[15] A similar protest
to the Federal Republic of Germany on 12 April 1961 [16] concerning
the transport of arms to Kolwezi revealed that, whilst the arms had
been neither manufactured nor loaded in German territory, they had

---

[10] Fourth Report of the Secretary-General (S/4482/Add. 1).
[11] *Ante,* p. 208.
[12] See note verbale from Secretary-General to the Delegation of the U.S.S.R.,
dated 5 September (S/4503).
[13] S/4630, para. 6, 16 January 1961.
[14] S/4482/Add. 1, 8 September 1960.
[15] S/4482/Add. 2.
[16] S/4789.

been shipped by a German aircraft under charter to Sabena, the Belgian airline. The Report of the Officer-in-Charge, dated 8 October 1962,[17] showed that Katangese air strength was being built up by the addition of a jet Fouga Magister fighter, 5 Dornier aircraft, 5 Piper aircraft, 3 German-built Klemm aircraft, 7 Harvard aircraft and 4 Vampire aircraft. These purchases were apparently made in countries like South Africa, Germany and France, and there was evidence of shipment through Portuguese Angola. Certainly it was a reinforcement to Katangese military strength which betokened a degree of laxity in the efforts of certain Member States to see the Resolutions of the Assembly enforced.

3. *The use of Member States' territories*

The situation which developed when units of the ANC landed at Usumbura airfield in the Belgian trust-territory of Ruanda-Urundi on 30 December 1960 and proceeded some ninety miles by trucks to initiate action in Kivu province [18] provides the most glaring example of the provision of a form of assistance to one of the factions in the Congo, in direct contravention of paragraph 6 of Resolution 1474 (ES–IV) of 20 September. The explanation of Belgium was that the authorities in Brussels knew of this only at the same time that the contingent landed, and thereafter instructed the local Belgian authorities to see that the ANC contingent left for the frontier [19]; this can only be regarded as unsatisfactory since it amounts to a denial of responsibility for the conduct of the Belgian officials in Ruanda-Urundi; certainly there were many Member States who regarded this as unsatisfactory, for a demand was even made for the termination of Belgium's trusteeship.[20]

A further example of indifferent co-operation can be seen in the refusal of the Portuguese and British Governments to accept the suggestion of the Secretary-General on 29 and 30 December 1960 [21] that observers be stationed on their territory to check the infiltration into Katanga from Angola and Northern Rhodesia of mercenaries and military supplies. Again, in relation to Northern Rhodesia, there was the incident in December 1961 when Ndola airport, in Northern Rhodesia, was being used as a base for aircraft of the Katangese air force, operating against ONUC.[22] The British Government was,

---

[17] S/5053/Add. 12.
[18] S/4606 and Add. 1.
[19] *Ibid.*, note verbale from the Belgian Representative to the Secretary-General, 31 December 1960, and S/4621, note verbale dated 11 January 1961.
[20] See the draft Resolution S/4625, introduced in the Security Council by Ceylon, Liberia and the U.A.R., but not adopted; also the letter dated 11 January 1961, from the Representative of the U.S.S.R., S/4622.
[21] *Off.Rec.G.A.*, 17th Sess., Suppl. No. 1 (A/5201), p. 19. The counter-offer by the Rhodesian Government that the Secretary-General should visit the Federation to discuss all aspects of traffic across the border was not accepted by the Secretary-General.
[22] UN Note to Correspondents, 2467, 26 December 1961, referred to in Gordon, *op. cit.*, p. 137.

admittedly, in a particularly difficult position in that its control over a fully self-governing territory like Northern Rhodesia was minimal. However, the general principle that all States should prevent transit of supplies or materials of war across their territories, "except in accordance with decisions, policies and purposes of the United Nations," was clearly laid down in the request to States in paragraph 6 of the Resolution of 24 November 1961.

The above examples relate to the use of Member States' territory by non-United Nations forces in a way which ran counter to, rather than assisted, the operations of United Nations forces. In one case, however, the lack of co-operation took the form of a refusal by a State, the Congo (Brazzaville), to allow to ONUC planes a right of overflight over its territory.[23]

4. *The call for economic measures to prevent secession*

On 31 July 1962 U Thant, the Secretary-General, had appealed to Member States generally to consider "economic pressure upon the Katangese authorities" and, in the last resort, "barring all trade and financial relations." [24] This was followed, on 2 August, by a special appeal to Belgium to bring pressure to bear on the Union Minière, with whose financial support the Katangese authorities were able to maintain the armed forces backing the secession. An appeal was even made to the Universal Postal Union to treat as invalid the postage issued by the provincial authorities of Katanga. In December 1962 Prime Minister Adoula appealed to seventeen States to join in an economic boycott of Katanga.[25] There is perhaps little doubt that economic sanctions, sincerely applied, could have ended Katangese secession and yet there is little evidence of economic sanctions being applied by Member States. The difficulty was that, even after the Security Council had on 24 November 1961 gone to the extent of declaring Katangese secession to be illegal, there was room for doubt whether the termination of secession was, *per se*, the proper objective for the United Nations to pursue [26]; moreover the plan for an economic boycott was never endorsed by the Security Council. Indeed, had the simple aim of termination of secession ever been accepted by the Security Council, it is probable that this could have been achieved by economic sanctions and with very little recourse to force by United Nations Forces.

The very clear impression which remains after this brief survey of the relations between the United Nations and Member States

---

[23] A/5201, p. 16. Gordon, *op. cit.*, p. 137, also states that the U.K. refused to allow Ethiopian planes, provided for the UN, to have refuelling rights at Kampala (in the former protectorate of Uganda) until after Hammarskjoeld's death.

[24] S/5053/Add. 11/Annex XXV.

[25] *Le Monde*, 14 December 1962.

[26] *Ante*, pp. 197–198: and see the British view against such sanctions to enforce a political settlement, in the statement by the Foreign Secretary, Lord Home, reported in *The Times*, 5 December 1962.

generally is that there was never a complete, general support of United Nations policy; indeed, in the case of Belgium, the attitude was one of obstruction rather than co-operation. One of the conclusions reached by the Conciliation Commission in its report to the Assembly of 20 March 1961 [27] was that "the deliberate violations of this injunction [the Security Council and General Assembly Resolutions calling upon States to refrain from sending military assistance which could be used for military purposes to any side, except through the United Nations itself], open or secret, are largely responsible for the continuing deterioration of the situation and the drift of the country towards civil war and disintegration." Without going into the merits of the Soviet view that assistance should have been given to Lumumba, or the Belgian view that withdrawal must be conditional on ONUC's fulfilling certain duties, or the British view that a political solution must not be brought about by force, it is believed that the Congo operations demonstrated all too frequently a refusal by Member States to accept and carry out the decisions of the United Nations organs, arrived at by the majority vote requisite under the Charter. It can scarcely be expected that every Member will agree with the majority; but it can be expected (and this is surely the essence of majority rule) that, once adopted, a Member will sublimate its particular doubts and accept the majority decision. This Members were clearly unwilling to do, and they perpetuated this opposition to the majority view in the different forms of non-co-operation which have just been described. To argue, as Ghana and the Soviet Union argued, that opposition was to the interpretation by the Secretary-General of the Security Council Resolutions, and not to the Resolutions as such, is scarcely to refute this principle for, again, the place in which to challenge that interpretation was within the Security Council, by a majority vote: if support for the challenge was not forthcoming then the Soviet Union, or Ghana, or the United Kingdom, or Belgium—or any other State—had no business to continue its challenge by unilateral action or failure to co-operate.

VIII. RELATIONS BETWEEN THE UNITED NATIONS AND THE "HOST" STATE

Not least of the problems facing the United Nations in its operations in the Congo was the absence of a stable government with which the United Nations could deal as representative of the host State. The problem was not so much one of the secessionist provincial authorities, for the United Nations in fact declined to give any recognition to these,[28] but rather of the persons who could be regarded as representative of the Central Government. The internal rift between Lumumba as Prime Minister and Kasavubu as President [29] and the

---

[27] A/4711 and Add. 1 and 2 (*Off.Rec.G.A.*, 15th Sess., Agenda item 85), at p. 49.
[28] *Post*, pp. 240–241. [29] *Ante*, pp. 159–162.

rise to power of Colonel Mobutu who, on 14 September, established the " Collège des universitaires " placed the Secretary-General in a position to which he found the solution in recognising the President as Head of State and dealing with him direct. The United Nations, acting through the Secretary-General, declined to deal with any other representative of a régime founded on military force as a representative of the Government : such relations as were continued with the Collège and the succeeding Council of Commissioners-General were on a purely technical plane and limited to what was necessary for the actual functioning of ONUC.[30] The recognition of the credentials of the Kasavubu delegation by the General Assembly on 22 November to some extent vindicated the Secretary-General's stand but this did not solve the problem of relationship within the Congo itself. This solution necessarily awaited the restoration of internal stability which came in February 1961 with the establishment of the Ileo Government. Thus, for a period of four months, the United Nations operated on the basis of an extremely unsatisfactory relationship with the host State, and this accounted for the delay in negotiating a Status Agreement.

Apart from this particular period of difficulty there were several major issues which the relationship between the host State and the United Nations raised, and these must now be considered.

1. *The relevance of " consent " by the host State to the presence of ONUC and the manner of performance of its functions*

The Secretary-General had, in outlining the basis upon which ONUC operated, placed the consent of the host State on a footing equivalent to the Security Council's implied determination of a threat to international peace and security.[31] A primary issue became that of the extent to which the operations of ONUC should be conditional on the consent, or agreement, of the host State. This issue does not permit of a simple, uniform answer.

As already indicated,[32] the consent of the host State had no relation to the constitutional basis of the Force in terms of the United Nations Charter : that could only be a question of the construction of the Charter. There is, however, the further question of whether this consent was necessary for ONUC to enter the territory of the Congo, and to regard the fact of consent to the presence of the Force as evidence that the Force was not taking enforcement action under Article 42 (as the International Court of Justice did in the *Expenses Case*) is by no means the same thing as saying that the consent of the Republic of the Congo was legally

[30] Second Report of Mr. Dayal, S/4557, paras. 28–31. The UN Commander dealt directly with Colonel Mobutu (para. 31).
[31] *Ante*, p. 180.
[32] *Ante*, p. 180.

necessary or the Force to operate on Congolese territory. This raises a general problem which is dealt with in Chapter 12,[33] but it may be stated here that nothing in Chapter VII of the Charter indicates that the consent of a State is necessary, as a matter of law as opposed to political expediency, when the Security Council establishes a Force to deal with a situation which constitutes a threat to international peace and security. Indeed, it may be argued that a decision to establish a Force to deal with a threat to international peace and security within a State's territory is a decision which, under Articles 2 (5), 25 and 49, is binding on the State in the sense that it must admit the Force to its territory—even though there be no question of the Force taking preventive or enforcement action against that State as an " aggressor " State. However, in the Congo there was no need for the Security Council to make any kind of ruling on this question since military assistance had in fact been requested, and the initial Resolution of 14 July proceeded on that basis, regarding the operation as one in which the Secretary-General could proceed on the basis of this invitation. To this extent the Congo operations do not provide any precedent for a ruling on the question we are now posing.[34]

Consent once given to the presence of a United Nations Force does not, however, extend to the control of the operations of the Force or even to the control over the duration of the stay of the Force. These limitations on the relevance of the consent of the host State can clearly be seen to have been operative in the Congo. The initial consent, expressed in the invitation by cable on July 12, was supplemented by the Basic Agreement of 27 July 1960.[35] This had but four operative paragraphs containing, essentially, an agreement by the Congo to be guided, in " good faith," by the fact that it had requested United Nations assistance and by its acceptance of the Resolutions of 14 and 22 July; an agreement to ensure freedom of movement in the interior of the country; and an agreement to accord the requisite privileges and immunities. On the part of the United Nations there was an equal undertaking to be guided, in good faith, by the task assigned to the Force by the Resolutions and to maintain the Force in the Congo " until such time as it deems the latter's task to have been fully accomplished." These bare provisions were, in practice, to be supplemented by an insistence by the United Nations on its exclusive control over ONUC which emphasised the limits within which the consent of the host State was applicable to ONUC's operations.

---

[33] *Post*, pp. 413–417.
[34] Halderman, " Legal Basis for United Nations Armed Forces " (1962) 56 A.J. at p. 972 appears to suggest that action justified as " collective measures " under Art. 1 (1) does not require such consent: if this is his suggestion, it is believed to be too broad a statement, for it would apply equally to collective measures recommended by the Assembly.
[35] S/4389/Add. 5.

2. The exclusiveness of United Nations authority and control over the Force

In his First Report the Secretary-General made it abundantly clear that, even though the Force might be regarded as " serving as an arm of the Government for the maintenance of order and protection of life," it " is necessarily under the exclusive command of the United Nations . . . [and] not under the orders of the Government." [36] It was fundamental to the policy of the United Nations that the Force should preserve its " international character," despite the juxtaposition of its roles in the maintenance of international and internal order. This was a principle which Mr. Lumumba failed to grasp, and this led to his accusations against the Secretary-General of failure to co-operate with the Government.[37] It also led to his demand for ONUC's withdrawal from airports and the broadcasting station in Leopoldville which had been closed temporarily by the United Nations as a measure to avoid civil war.[38]

In due course President Kasavubu made the same error when, as part of his initial opposition to the Security Council Resolution of 21 February 1961, he called for complete consultation with his Government on both the military and civilian aspects of ONUC operations.[39] Even earlier, in January 1961, he had regarded his request for the removal of Mr. Dayal as something which the Secretary-General must necessarily comply with.[40] The latter was obliged, in reply,[41] to point out that Mr. Dayal was not an ambassador to whom the principle *persona non grata* applied, but someone exclusively under the Secretary-General's authority. The principle involved was, fundamentally, the same as that which dictated that the composition of ONUC was a matter for the United Nations, with the views of the host State being but one of the factors to be taken into account.[42]

The other context in which the exclusiveness of United Nations authority had to be asserted was that of the bases and airfields occupied by the United Nations. The Secretary-General had, on 21 August,[43] indicated that the assumption of control by the United

[36] S/4389, p. 3.
[37] See Telegram dated 7 August 1960 (S/4421) and Telegram dated 20 August 1960 (S/4448).
[38] See S/4531 and *ante*, p. 200.
[39] Cable dated 22 February 1961 (S/4743). See also the Congolese memorandum of 7 January 1961, S/4630, criticising the UN's unilateral action and " exclusive assumption of responsibilities."
[40] Letter dated 14 January 1961 (S/4629) and Cable dated 24 January (S/4629/Add. 1).
[41] Letter dated 15 January (S/4629). It may be noted that whilst, in principle, the Secretary-General was right, in practice it became impossible to continue with a Special Representative unacceptable to the host Government, and Dayal was finally recalled by the Secretary-General on 10 March.
[42] *Ante*, p. 206.
[43] *Off.Rec.S.C.* 15th yr., 887th Mtg., para. 31. And see Third Report, S/4475, para. 3 and letter to Belgium of 21 January 1961, S/4651.

Nations over the bases formerly held by Belgian forces was in the nature of a provisional measure under Article 40 and did not prejudice the questions of title to, or payment for, any property in these bases. It soon became apparent that the problem of bases was one which concerned not only Belgium, but also the host State which evidenced a desire to control these bases. When, on 13 December 1960, ANC forces entered Kitona base, despite protest by the United Nations Commander, the Secretary-General protested at the "flagrant violation" of the rights of the United Nations and reaffirmed the exclusive nature of United Nations authority as administrator of the base.[44] On 1 March 1961 the host Government called for the evacuation from the air force installations at Ndjili, from Parc Hembise, and forbade entry into ANC military camps; it also protested at the establishment of "neutral zones" without consultation with the host Government.[45] This the Secretary-General regarded as a violation of the guarantee of freedom of movement contained in the basic agreement of 27 July 1960 and of the general undertaking to carry out in good faith the obligations incumbent on the host State under Security Council Resolutions: accordingly he declined this request.[46] The clashes between ONUC and the ANC at Moanda, Banana and Matadi between 3 and 5 March 1961 involved the same principle.[47] In a telegram dated 5 March 1961 the Secretary-General informed the President of the Republic of the Congo that:

" . . . United Nations under Security Council mandate must keep complete freedom of decision as regards the deployment of national contingents in performance of United Nations operation. In the exercise of its responsibility the placement of specific contingents will, of course, always be made with due regard to all the relevant circumstances. I am bound to consider unacceptable any attempt by force or otherwise to influence ONUC in this respect, including the setting conditions as to the selection of units for Matadi." [48]

On 8 March the Secretary-General re-stated fully the legal implications of the United Nations presence.[49] He emphasised that the relationship was not simply a contractual one, with the consent of the host State being the determining element, but rather that "the status, rights and functions of the United Nations are basically determined by the fact that the action was taken in order to counteract an international threat to peace." Therefore, relying on the "good faith" clause in the basic agreement, on the right to freedom of

---

[44] S/4599, Letter dated 14 December 1960, from the Secretary-General to President Kasavubu.
[45] S/4758.
[46] S/4758/Add. 1.
[47] S/4578/Add. 2, Add. 3, Add. 4 and S/4761.
[48] S/4578/Add. 4. A similar issue arose when the Central Government demanded, and the Secretary-General refused, exclusion of all but African troops from the entry into Katanga (Press Release Co/2o/Add. 4 and 5) and, later, of the entire Indian contingent from Katanga.
[49] S/4775, Message of 8 March 1961. And see the further message of 12 March (*ibid.*, p. 11).

movement and on the fact that all Member States, including the Congo, were bound under Articles 25 and 49 to abide by the Resolutions of the Council, he concluded that:

" . . . the relationship between the United Nations and the Government of the Republic of the Congo is not merely a contractual relationship in which the Republic can impose its conditions as host State and thereby determine the circumstances under which the United Nations operates. It is rather a relationship governed by mandatory decisions of the Secco (Security Council). The consequence of this is that no Government, including the host Government, can by unilateral action determine how measures taken by the Secco in this context should be carried out. Such a determination can be made only by the Secco itself or on the basis of its explicit delegation of authority. It is of special importance that only the Secco can decide on the discontinuance of the operation."

The last point is of special importance, for it raises the vital question of the termination of ONUC's mission. The disagreement in March 1961 was not the first occasion on which the host State had threatened to terminate the mission: Lumumba had formally called on the United Nations to withdraw on 16 September 1960,[50] although this was after he had been dismissed by the President. The Resolution of 14 July had, in using the phrase " until . . . the national security forces may be able, in the opinion of the Government to meet fully their tasks," tended to raise the implication that it was for the Government to decide when the mission had been completed. However, the Basic Agreement contained quite the reverse implication, for that stated that the United Nations would maintain the Force in the Congo " until such time as it deems the latter's task to have been fully accomplished"; the " it " referred unmistakably to the Organisation, not the Government.

The eventual Agreement of 27 November 1961 reiterated the " sole competence " of the United Nations with regard to the composition of ONUC. It did not specifically deal with the withdrawal of the Force, except to the extent of providing in para. 48 that the Agreement should remain in force until the departure from the Congo of the last elements of the Force and its equipment. The question of who determines the time for withdrawal therefrom remained governed by the basic agreement of 29 July and the general principles governing United Nations action.

In the event the Secretary-General clearly interpreted the situation as one in which it was for the United Nations to decide on withdrawal. His Report on Military Disengagement in the Congo [51] disclosed a rejection of the request of Prime Minister Adoula [52] for the retention of 3,000 troops, and an intention to " phase out " ONUC so as to withdraw completely by the end of 1963. In fact that has

[50] See Report of the UN Conciliation Commission, A/4711/Add. 1, p. 25. The Chamber of Representatives had on 9 September called for ONUC's withdrawal from aerodromes, broadcasting stations and the withdrawal from the Congo of all troops belonging to NATO powers: *ibid.*, p. 2.

[51] *U.N. Review*, Vol. 10, No. 9, October 1963, p. 44.

[52] Letter dated 22 August 1963, Annex 1 to the Report.

not occurred, and at the time of writing [53] ONUC still remains in the Congo.

The Congo experience therefore suggests that, at least in a situation in which there is a threat to international peace and security and a United Nations Force is operating under Resolutions which impose binding obligations on States, whether or not the consent of the host State is essential to the initial right of entry into its territory, it is thereafter not essential either to a determination of the composition of the Force, of the functions of the Force, or even of the area of operations of the Force (although this might be different if the freedom of movement had been carefully circumscribed by agreement with the host State).[54] Moreover the termination of the mission of the Force is, similarly, a matter for the United Nations and not for the host State. Perhaps one explanation for the assumption that it was for the Government to decide when ONUC should withdraw was the reasoning that, since the Government had given its consent to the entry of the Force, that consent was *legally* necessary to the presence of ONUC on Congolese territory. It has already been suggested that this reasoning is highly suspect.[55] But even were this reasoning correct, it may still be maintained that consent, once given, cannot be revoked at will: the principle of good faith and the obligations on a Member State under Articles 2 (5), 25 and 49 would suggest severe restrictions on arbitrary action by a host State of this kind. In all these questions the notion of co-operation between the United Nations and the host State involves an obligation to consider in good faith the views of the host State: it does not involve an obligation to act in conformity with those views.

Whilst this question did not arise in the Congo, nor, indeed, in any United Nations military operation to date, it may be suggested that the only clear situation in which a host State can unilaterally terminate the mission of a United Nations Force is where the United Nations has determined that there no longer exists a threat to international peace and security.

3. *Status of Forces Agreements*

The original Basic Agreement of 27 July 1960 contained guarantees by the Republic of the Congo of freedom of movement and of the requisite privileges and immunities, but these general provisions obviously needed supplementation on the lines of the comprehensive agreement between the United Nations and Egypt of 8 February 1957.[56]

So far as privileges and immunities of the Force were concerned,

[53] 30 January 1964. Complete military withdrawal occurred 30 June 1964.
[54] On the various disagreements which arose over the right to freedom of movement, see *ante*, pp. 204–205.
[55] *Ante*, p. 232.
[56] U.N.T.S. Vol. 260, p. 61.

since ONUC was a subsidiary organ of the Security Council, Article 105 of the Charter applied (and this was specifically stated in Regulation 10 of the Regulations of the Force), but this, too, was scarcely detailed enough to provide for the various, specific problems apt to arise from a United Nations-host State relationship. Hence, on 27 November 1961 a comprehensive " Agreement relating to the legal status, facilities, privileges and immunities of the United Nations Organisation in the Congo " was signed in New York.[57] It may be added that attempts to negotiate such an agreement had begun in August 1960, but had been postponed due to the internal political instability which then developed and which left the United Nations with no established government with which to negotiate an agreement.[58] The first, and striking, feature of the Agreement was that it was given retroactive effect, as from the date of arrival of the first elements of ONUC in the Congo (para. 48).

The second striking feature was the exclusion of the jurisdictional competence of the host State. Paragraph 9, like the UNEF Agreement, gave complete immunity from the criminal jurisdiction of the Congo to all Members of the Force.[59] Moreover, in contrast to the UNEF Agreement,[60] which contemplated a certain amount of civil jurisdiction in the local Egyptian courts, paragraph 10 of the Congo Agreement virtually substituted for the jurisdictional competence of the Congolese courts in cases of any " official act " a process of negotiation between the United Nations and the Congo and, failing agreement, recourse to arbitration.[61] In the case of civil law obligations *not* arising out of an official act (or, more properly, " any act performed by a Member of the Force . . . in the course of his official duties "), the United Nations was to use its good offices to assist the parties in arriving at a settlement. In the absence of a settlement, it was to go to arbitration at the request of either party. The Representative of the Secretary-General was given authority, under paragraph 11, to arrange for any necessary arbitral proceedings, and was also given power to establish a Claims Commission to deal with non-penal matters. The United Nations and the Congo also

---

[57] U.N.T.S. Vol. 414, p. 229; also A/4986—S/5004.

[58] S/4531, para. 19; S/4557, para. 29.

[59] See also ONUC Regulation 29 (a) which provided :

" Members of the Force shall be subject to the criminal jurisdiction of their respective national States in accordance with the laws and regulations of those States. They shall not be subject to the criminal jurisdiction of the host State. Responsibility for the exercise of criminal jurisdiction shall rest with the authorities of the State concerned, including, as appropriate, the commanders of the national contingents."
The immunity from the criminal jurisdiction of the Congo of UN officials, as compared to Members of the Force, was not so absolute but, under paragraph 10, was dependent on an agreement between the UN and the Congo on whether the UN should discipline the official or the Congolese authorities should institute proceedings.

[60] See *ante*, p. 125.

[61] And see ONUC Reg. 29 (b). Note that the Officer-in-Charge and the Commander were given full diplomatic immunity : ONUC Reg. 20 (a).

agreed, under paragraph 13, that they would each exercise a power of arrest over the military personnel of the other only when the competent authorities to whom such personnel were responsible were unable to act with the necessary speed to apprehend them at the time when they committed, or attemped to commit, an offence which may result in serious harm to persons or property. In such cases the personnel were to be " delivered immediately to the nearest authority to whom the person in question is responsible."

The provisions on privileges and immunities are spelt out in detail [62] and not by reference to the 1946 Convention on the Privileges and Immunities of the United Nations, as was the case with the UNEF Agreement. This difference in technique was no doubt due to the fact that, whilst Egypt was a party to the 1946 Convention, the Congo was not. Hence the United Nations, its property and assets, and also the property and assets of States participating in ONUC, were specifically stated to be immune from any form of legal process, search and requisition and from any other form of governmental interference.[63] There was, similarly, exemption from taxes, from customs duties and prohibitions or restrictions on imports and exports. The funds, currencies and accounts of the United Nations were to be free from financial controls,[64] and Congolese currency was to be made available at the most favourable official rate of exchange.[65] The Congolese Government was to provide any necessary accommodation, buildings or camps—all of which were to be inviolable.[66] The United Nations also had rights to use its flag on its premises, vehicles and vessels,[67] to recruit local personnel,[68] and to " full freedom of movement throughout Congolese territory and to and from points of access to Congolese territory." [69] Authorisation for the establishment and use of communications installations, free from any form of interference and censorship, was granted,[70] as was also the right to the use of public services such as water, electricity and other public utilities at normal rates.[71]

Members of the Force enjoyed exemption from direct taxes and personal contributions and inviolability of their papers and documents.[72] They also had the right of free importation of personal effects, subject to restrictions on sale within the Congo, and exemption from inspection of their personal baggage.[73] Members of the Force

---

[62] They are briefly referred to also in Regs. 10 and 29 of the ONUC Regulations.
[63] Para. 15. See *ante*, p. 204, on the affair at Matadi where the Congo appears to have been in breach of this obligation.
[64] Para. 20.
[65] Para. 21.
[66] Para. 24.
[67] Para. 26.
[68] Para. 27. These enjoyed immunity only in respect of official acts.
[69] Para. 30. And see *ante*, pp. 203–205.
[70] Paras. 33–38.
[71] Para. 38.
[72] Para. 16.
[73] Para. 18.

would normally wear uniform but could wear civilian dress on conditions prescribed by the Force Commander and, whilst on duty, were
entitled to carry arms.[74]

A further, interesting, contrast with the UNEF Agreement is the
emphasis on liaison. The UNEF Agreement had only a brief article
on this (Art. 41), but this topic occupies four reasonably lengthy paragraphs (paras. 41–44) of the Congo Agreement. The system of liaison
comprised liaison officers, on a reciprocal basis, at staff headquarters
and, when useful, at the regional commands of the ANC and ONUC.
Liaison was to be effected at airports, at which the United Nations
was to have exclusive control over aircraft operating on its behalf,
and such government officials as controlled other traffic were to be
civilian and not military. The essential differences of the mandates
of ONUC and the Congolese authorities were stressed, by way of
guidance to the parties in carrying out their liaison duties, in the
following terms :

Para. 43. " . . .
    (a) Full responsibility for the implementation of domestic legislation and
        regulations shall remain with the Congolese authorities. The United
        Nations shall be as an international Force and as such its respon-
        sibilities shall be exercised for the purposes of maintaining public
        order, peace and security; in so doing it shall not apply domestic
        regulations and procedures, but shall act in accordance with its
        interpretation of the mission assigned to it by the Security Council.
    (b) In the performance of their duties, the Congolese authorities respon-
        sible for enforcing the law shall have the right to resort to force in
        conformity with the law. The United Nations shall not have recourse
        to the use of force except as a last resort and subject to the restric-
        tions imposed by its mandate and by the Resolutions of the Security
        Council and the General Assembly."

Paragraph 44 recognised " the impossibility of having two security
systems acting in competition " and thus enjoined on both parties the
duty of consultation to " co-ordinate their actions in the maintenance
of public order."

The Agreement also contained a paragraph 45, enabling supplementary provisions to be entered into between the Congolese authorities on the one hand and either the Special Representative of the
Secretary-General or the Supreme Commander on the other. Finally,
it contained a review procedure and a compromissory clause providing for arbitration on any dispute between the United Nations and
the Government concerning the interpretation and application of the
Agreement.

The Agreement, particularly in its jurisdictional provisions (paras.
9–14), the liaison provisions (paras. 41–43), and the very much wider
freedom of movement clause (para. 30) afford a contrast with the
UNEF Agreement which reflects the essentially different character
of the operation. Not only was the mandate of ONUC to maintain
internal law and order one which carried a high risk of competition

[74] Para. 39.

with the local authorities—hence the need for "liaison"—it also demanded full freedom of movement: these particular provisions were no doubt drafted in the light of the experience already gained by November 1961, showing that clashes with the local authorities, in particular the ANC, had to be anticipated and prevented by as careful a delimitation of the respective roles of ONUC and the local authorities as possible. The insistence on only Congolese *civilian* personnel at airports servicing the United Nations also betokens the wisdom of experience. The jurisdictional provisions, which well-nigh exclude the jurisdiction of the local courts, are perhaps explicable in the light of the complete breakdown of the judiciary which had occurred: the attribution of jurisdictional competence to a very imperfectly functioning judiciary would certainly have been unwise.

4. *Relations between the United Nations and provincial authorities*

As has already been shown,[75] the United Nations never accepted the secession of any of the provinces, and maintained the view that the Congo remained a single, unitary State. Hence the general position of the United Nations was that its relations with the host State, the Congo, were to be conducted with the Central Government, and this was explicitly recognised in the Agreement of 27 November 1961 which provided in paragraph 47 that:

"The Central Government of the Republic of the Congo shall have the ultimate responsibility for the fulfilment of such obligations by the competent Congolese authorities, whether central, provincial or local."

In practice, however, large areas of the Congo remained, for different periods of time, in control of the secessionist factions in Katanga, in South Kasai and in Equateur-Orientale Province under the leadership of Tshombé, Kalonji and Gizenga respectively. To this extent, and assuming ONUC was not to be committed to military action against any forces opposing it but rather to seek co-operation, the fulfilment of its mandate was not simply a matter of United Nations–Central Government relationships, but also of a relationship with the authorities in *de facto* control of those parts of Congolese territory to which ONUC deemed its mandate to apply.

Therefore, in August 1960, Mr. Hammarskjoeld felt obliged to "negotiate" his way into Katanga rather than to enter by force,[76] and, having taken this decision,[77] he had virtually no alternative but to negotiate with Mr. Tshombé. The extent to which he allowed Tshombé to impose conditions on United Nations entry into Katanga is not altogether clear.[78] What is clear is that this policy of negotiating

[75] *Ante*, pp. 171, 198.
[76] *Ante*, p. 157.
[77] *Ante*, p. 203, for a discussion of the *legal* necessity for this decision.
[78] See *Congo 1960*, Vol. II, pp. 751–752 for the 10 conditions put by Tshombé on 4 August of which, on 12 August, Tshombé declared 9 had been accepted: however the joint communiqué said nothing of any acceptance of these conditions and Hammarskjoeld's cable of 10 August 1960 (S/4417/ Add. 4) had contained a refusal to allow conditions to be imposed.

with the " rebels " drew forth strong criticism from the Central Government [79] and from Member States like the Soviet Union who regarded Hammarskjoeld as having accorded " *de facto* " recognition to the Tshombé régime.[80] Hammarskjoeld, who had previously explained to the Security Council that he had not acted without consulting the Congolese Central Government,[81] justified the necessity for this negotiation with Tshombé, and denied that there were any implications of recognition, to the Assembly's Emergency Session on 18 September by the remark: " In such negotiations you do not recognise any constitutional position or any rights, but a situation *de facto.*" [82]

Later, and very necessary, political contacts between the United Nations and the Katangese authorities can be seen, for example, in the Secretary-General's letter to Tshombé regarding the implementation of the Security Council's Resolution of 21 February [83] and in the agreement on 17 January 1963 for ONUC's entry into Kolwezi.

In respect of the need to protect human life it was even more essential for the United Nations to deal with the authorities whose activities threatened human life: there was simply no point in addressing to the Central Government protests about the treatment of Balubas by the Katangese authorities. Thus the Secretary-General reproached Mr. Tshombé directly on this score [84] and, on 17 October 1960, an agreement between the United Nations and the Katangese authorities was reached on the establishment of " neutral zones " within which the United Nations was to assume responsibility for the civilian personnel.[85] Protests about the restrictions placed on the movement of foreign nationals,[86] or about the activities of the ANC under Gizenga's control, or about the summary executions taking place in South Kasai,[87] or about the maltreatment of Europeans after the news of Mr. Lumumba's death,[88] were sent to the responsible authorities in the person of Gizenga or Kalonji. Of a similar nature were the direct protests to Tshombé about the treatment of Mr. Lumumba himself.[89]

In the field of military operations the United Nations necessarily concluded cease-fire agreements with the authorities in control of the forces with whom hostilities had begun. Cease-fire agreements

---

[79] S/4417/Add. 7 (II).
[80] *Off.Rec.S.C*, 15th yr., 918th Mtg., p. 5, 12 December 1960.
[81] *Ibid.*, 15th yr., 887th Mtg., 21 August 1960.
[82] *Off.Rec.G.A*, 4th Emergency Special Sess., 18 September 1960.
[83] S/4752/Add. 1.
[84] Message dated 18 September 1960 (S/4529).
[85] *Congo 1960*, Vol. II, p. 794.
[86] S/4637.
[87] S/4727/Add. 3.
[88] S/4745.
[89] S/4637, S/4688/Add. 2.

were accordingly concluded with Tshombé[90] and with the officers commanding Kalonji's forces in Kasai.[91]

IX. CLAIMS AND RESPONSIBILITY

The nature of the operations undertaken by ONUC gave rise to several different categories of potential claims. The first was a category of claims between the United Nations and the Republic of the Congo and, after the *Reparations Case*,[92] there could be little doubt that the United Nations was a capable plaintiff against a State like the Congo. Moreover, in justice, the United Nations could scarcely refuse to meet claims as a defendant, and had already done so in Korea and in UNEF.[93] The frequent allegations by the United Nations of breaches of obligations assumed towards the United Nations by the Congo, either by reference to defiance of the Security Council Resolutions or of the Status Agreement, have already been referred to.[94] Moreover, since ONUC personnel could be regarded as "agents" of the United Nations, and since ONUC Regulation 25 provided that: "Members of the Force are entitled to the legal protection of the United Nations and shall be regarded as agents of the United Nations for the purpose of such protection," there could be little doubt that in respect of the all too frequent attacks by Congolese forces on ONUC personnel the United Nations right of "functional" protection could be validly exercised.

However, the Status Agreement of 27 November 1961[95] contained a compromissory clause, Article 46, which was confined to disputes "between the United Nations and the Government concerning the interpretation and application of this Agreement." For such disputes, failing settlement by other agreed means, arbitration was envisaged. There were conceivably other disputes which could arise, in particular those involving responsibility for attacks on ONUC personnel, which might not find their basis in the Agreement, so that in respect of these other disputes any settlement by arbitration would

---

[90] See the agreement of 20 September 1961 (S/4940/Add. 7) and the further agreement of 13 October (S/4940/Add. 11) concluded after Hammarskjoeld's death and signed by senior ONUC personnel (Mahmoud Khiary). S/4940/Add. 11, para. 9 stressed that these agreements were "of a strictly military character and by nature therefore limited in their application solely to the relations between the parties." See also the text of approval by UN Headquarters (*ibid.*, Annex II, para. 2). The U.S.S.R. protested at this agreement and described it as "not operative" (S/4962, S/5003): the basis of this protest was that the Security Council alone could authorise the conclusion of a cease-fire agreement.

[91] S/4557, paras. 70–72. This does not make it clear whether there were simply negotiations with Colonels Gillet and Crèvecoeur, with a view to implementing the cease-fire order made by President Kasavubu, or whether an actual agreement was eventually reached.

[92] *I.C.J. Reports*, 1949, p. 175.

[93] *Ante*, pp. 57, 149–151. Judge Krylov in the *Reparations Case* (at p. 219) had expressly referred to the position of the UN as a defendant.

[94] *Ante*, p. 234.

[95] U.N.T.S. Vol. 414, p. 231.

have had to be on a voluntary basis and not by virtue of the pre-existing obligation to arbitrate under Article 46. Moreover, unlike the UNEF Agreement[96] (which had a counterpart to Article 46 in its own Article 40) there was no provision for settlement of claims of a private law character between the United Nations and the host State. The reason for this paucity of settlement procedures, as compared with UNEF, may well have been that, since the United Nations was heavily committed to the financial support of the Congo, there was little point in providing for lengthy procedures for settlement which would in the result mean little more than a book-keeping exercise with the figures showing what financial assistance had been provided to the Congo.

In practice it is believed that no claims were made against the Congo, nor has the arbitration procedure of Article 46 been used. United Nations action has been confined to protest, and in the many protests about the maltreatment or killing of ONUC personnel,[97] the protests did not cite specific articles of the Basic Agreement or the Status Agreement and rested content with a demand for the prosecution of the offenders rather than for damages in addition.

On occasions the State whose nationals the ONUC personnel were also lodged a protest.[98] However, these were in the nature of an association of the State with the formal United Nations protest and did not attempt to press a separate claim on the basis of a breach of the Congo's duties towards aliens[99]: there was, therefore, no question of concurrent protection, functional and diplomatic, on two different bases, for both protests were based on the fact that the personnel were United Nations personnel and neither protest involved an actual claim.

A second category of claims was that of claims between the United Nations and Congolese civilians in which, as a normal rule (if the UNEF experience was any guide) the United Nations would be in the position of defendant. Article 10 (*b*) of the Status Agreement provided that:

"If as a result of any act performed by a member of the Force or an official in the course of his official duties, it is alleged that loss or damage that may give rise to civil proceedings has been caused to a citizen or resident of the Congo, the United Nations shall settle the dispute by negotiation or by any other method agreed between the Parties; if it is not found possible to arrive

---

[96] Art. 38 (*b*) (iii).
[97] S/4417/Add. 8; S/4753; S/4940/Add. 13, 15, Annex II, and 16, Annex I.
[98] See Swedish protest over the incident at Port Franqui in April 1961, cited in Seyersted, *loc. cit.* (1961) *B.Y.B.I.L.*, p. 425.
[99] Whilst, in general, it is believed that the UN and not the participating State is the primary claimant in respect of injuries to ONUC personnel (even though the I.C.J. has declared that there is "no rule of law which assigns priority to the one or to the other": *I.C.J. Reports,* 1949, p. 185) this would only be true where the agent was injured in the course of his official duties as agent. If he were, for example, on leave it may well be that the right of functional protection has no basis and only the national State could claim: see *I.C.J. Reports,* 1949, at p. 182; also Seyersted, *loc. cit.,* p. 424.

at an agreement in this manner, the matter shall be submitted to arbitration at the request of either Party."

Evidently, since the acts were the official acts of agents of the United Nations, the United Nations would be the defendant, assuming a form of vicarious responsibility for all such acts. In the absence of settlement, arbitration was compulsory at the request of either party. Article 11 and ONUC Regulation 29 (d) authorised the Special Representative of the Secretary-General to arrange for any necessary arbitral procedure, or even to establish a Claims Commission. The jurisdiction of the Congolese courts was not to be exercised until after all these procedures had been exhausted.

A third category of claims would be those for "non-official" acts, where the parties were the Congolese civilian and the member of the Force. Then Article 10 (c) applied, providing that the United Nations should "use its good offices to assist the parties in arriving at a settlement." In the absence of a settlement, again, arbitration was the remedy as in the previous category, although, presumably, the United Nations would not be a party.

A fourth category of claims would be those between United Nations and non-Congolese civilians, such as the foreign corporations providing goods and services. These were not, of course, dealt with in the Status Agreement and would, in accordance with the United Nations' established practice [1] be dealt with, presumably, by arbitration.

It is apparent that at least the last three categories are categories of *civil* claims; indeed Article 10 (b) and (c) are specifically limited to civil law obligations. Not least of the problems faced by a Claims Commission attempting to deal with civil claims against the United Nations is the absence of an agreed "proper law," for it is by no means clear that the *lex loci* will be applied or will even be suitable. The Claims Commission of UNEF dealt with the matter on a purely pragmatic basis, and it may be that such Commissions are forced to rely on general principles of law rather than on any defined legal system,[2] although they should doubtless operate *sur place*, if only for reasons of availability of witnesses.

It was also conceivable that members of the Force would commit criminal acts, either by reference to the Congolese law which, under Article 1 of the Status Agreement, all members of the Force and the United Nations officials were bound to respect, or by reference to a more general notion of acts being criminal as contrary to the accepted

---

[1] See generally Jenks, *The Proper Law of International Organisations* (1962), Part. III.

[2] A Report by the League Belge pour la défense des droits de l'homme of 28 August 1963, circulated to the Institut de Droit International, suggested that ". . . pour les réclamations, addressées par des personnes privées directement à l'ONU, les conditions de la responsabilité devraient être établies par une création d'un droit de la responsabilité civile interne à l'organisation fondé sur 'les principes généraux du droit reconnus par les nations civilisées'." This Report deals in detail with the problems of claims by and against both UNEF and ONUC.

laws and usages regulating the conduct of hostilities. It was clear that Articles 9 and 10 (c) of the Status Agreement and ONUC Regulation 29 (a) excluded Congolese criminal jurisdiction, vesting this exclusively in the authorities of the participating State from whose contingent the member came. Yet this exclusion of jurisdictional competence did not solve the ultimate question of liability, and here the Republic of the Congo and the States whose nationals or property might have been affected appear as potential claimants against the United Nations. It is believed that no claims could be made against the participating State, at least to the extent that the criminal acts were committed in the course of the individual agent's official duties and subject to what is said below about the possibility of a claim against a participating State which refused to exercise its own criminal jurisdiction against the individual. The character of the Force as an international, United Nations Force, a subsidiary organ of the Security Council, the exclusiveness of the United Nations control over the Force, and the determination in ONUC Regulation 25 that members of the Force are " agents " of the United Nations, support the view that the United Nations would be the proper recipient of any claims arising from the official duties of the Force member.[3] Where the acts are not part of the official duties of the member of the Force, but are criminal under Congolese law or breaches of the laws of war, the primary claim must be, in essence, a claim that the participating State to whose contingent the member belongs should exercise criminal jurisdiction over him. So far as the host State is concerned, this claim could be presented on the basis that its own surrender of criminal jurisdiction was conditional on the assumption that Article 9 of the Agreement between it and the United Nations, vesting criminal jurisdiction in the participating States exclusively, would be exercised in good faith.[4] A very real difficulty arises in the case where the claimant State is a third State whose nationals have been injured due to the criminal acts of Force members, for the Agreement with the host State and also the Agreement between the United Nations and the participating State are *res inter alios acta*. It might, of course, be argued that such third States could insist, as a matter of general international law, that the participating State was bound to bring to justice an offender whose crimes had injured their own nationals since, due to the surrender of jurisdiction by the territorial host State, it was the only State with effective jurisdiction.[5] However, there would be an advantage in

---

[3] But see the views of Judge Koretsky in the *Expenses Case, I.C.J. Reports,* 1962, p. 257.

[4] For this reason the present writer disagrees with Seyersted, *op. cit.*, pp. 414–415 who regards the Status Agreement as *not* being a *pactum in favorem tertii* and therefore concludes that the host State has no rights as against participating States.

[5] Although, normally, the State against which a complaint of this kind is made is the territorial State, there seems no reason why a complaint should not be made against a State simply on the basis that, without having sovereignty over the territory on which the acts were committed, it has

the future in drafting the Agreements with host States and participating States so as to ensure that host States and third States have this right to insist on the exercise by the participating State of its exclusive jurisdiction : refusal to do so would then constitute a clear breach of obligation and ground a distinct international claim. There is no basis in general international law for regarding the participating States as being under any duty other than the duty to prosecute; in particular, there would be no basis for a claim for compensation from the participating State in respect of a *private*, " non-official " criminal act by a member of its contingent.

So far as the responsibility of the United Nations is concerned, a distinction must be drawn between acts criminal by reference to Congolese law and not arising from the official duties of the members of the Force (such as rape, or theft) and acts which do arise from the performance of official duties. In the first case, though none is known to the writer, in principle the only obligation of the United Nations is to do all within its power to investigate the alleged offence [6] and to insist that the participating State fulfil its obligation to punish the offender.[7] ONUC Regulations 13 and 29 are clear in that the ultimate responsibility for both disciplinary action and criminal jurisdiction rests with the authorities of the participating State.

In the second case, where the criminal acts are also " official " acts, it is clear that the United Nations must assume responsibility. If the act is simply criminal under the law of the host State, the United Nations responsibility is satisfied by its fulfilling its duties to investigate, to insist upon the participating State exercising jurisdiction *and* to make whatever monetary compensation is appropriate. However, acts which occur as part of the actual conduct of hostilities by ONUC call for quite separate consideration and, again, two different sets of circumstances must be presupposed. The first is that the acts causing the damage are *illegal* acts in the sense either of acts *ultra vires* the mandate of the Force (this being contained in the Resolutions of the Security Council and of the General Assembly) or of acts violative of the " principles and spirit of the general international Conventions applicable to the conduct of military personnel." [8] In principle such acts would form the basis of a proper claim for compensation against the United Nations provided that they were attributable to the United Nations by reason of their being within the performance of official duties or because of specific authorisation or subsequent ratification by the United Nations, acting through the Secretary-General or possibly also

effective jurisdiction over the offender. See the Panamanian protest to the U.S.A. over acts of U.S. Forces in the Panama Canal Zone in *The Times,* 18 April 1963.

[6] See the powers of the Commander under ONUC Reg. 14.

[7] Conceivably the difficulty could arise that the act, criminal by Congolese law, was not criminal by the law of the participating State, although this would be unlikely when the crime was a serious one.

[8] ONUC Reg. 43.

the Officer-in-Charge or Commander. However, it would also be obligatory on the participating State to punish the individual offender where the acts were in violation of the laws of war, whereas, in the case of acts *ultra vires* the mandate, there would be no such claim against the participating State but only the claim against the United Nations.

When the claim failed to establish the illegality of the acts, in the sense described above, it is believed that the United Nations would be under no responsibility.[9] By analogy with the rules of international law which acquit a State from responsibility for damage to aliens and their property caused in the otherwise lawful exercise of hostilities against rebel forces or even against the forces of another State,[10] the United Nations should be under no liability in similar situations.[11]

It is not known whether any States have in fact submitted such claims to the United Nations, but the Joint Under-Secretary of State for Foreign Affairs stated in the British Parliament on 7 March 1962 :

" . . . Dependent upon the facts of each case there appear to be three parties against whom claims might lie for damage which has taken place in Katanga. . . . These three parties are the Central Government, the Provincial Government and the United Nations.

With this in mind, Her Majesty's Government have been looking into the various reports by British subjects who have suffered damage or injury during the fighting. In cases where United Nations responsibility appears to be established, I certainly see no reason why the claims should not be taken up with them by the persons concerned." [12]

Presumably the British Government would base responsibility on the illegality of the conduct of United Nations personnel (and not, after its own argument in the *Expenses Case*, on the ground that the actions were *ultra vires*), the illegality being in the " wanton and unnecessary " nature of the acts or in their being contrary to the Hague Regulations. It is also of interest to note that, in the last sentence quoted, the British Government appears to be thinking of a claim, in the first instance, by the persons concerned. In other words, and rightly,[13] when the injuries are to persons and their property, a rule

---

9 See S/4940/Add. 10, para. 2 for the rejection by UN Headquarters of Tshombé's claim for " war damages."

10 See Eagleton, *The Responsibility of States in International Law* (1928), pp. 141–156, who, however, points out that " due diligence " is required to avoid responsibility; Oppenheim, *International Law*, 8th ed., Vol. I, pp. 364, 366–367; McNair, *International Law Opinions*, Vol. 11, pp. 277–287, especially p. 277 where he states that liability exists only where the damage is " wanton and unnecessary." It is believed that such " wanton and unnecessary " damage would be contrary to the Hague Regulations.

11 The Report of the League Belge (*ante*, n. 2) makes the suggestion that the UN should establish a fund for compensation of victims in such cases, based on voluntary contributions by States.

12 H.C.Deb., Vol. 655, cols. 551–552. The Belgian Government certainly seem to have contemplated such claims. A report of the Committee on Foreign Affairs of the Belgian State, Document 87, p. 16, is cited to this effect in the Report by the League Belge, etc., referred to above in footnote 2.

13 See Ritter, " La protection diplomatique à l'égard d'une organisation internationale," *Ann.Fr.de D.I.* (1962), at p. 454.

akin to the rule of exhaustion of local remedies would apply so that the Government would take up the claim against the United Nations only when there had been, via the United Nations own procedures for setlement of claims, a " denial of justice."

X. CIVILIAN RELIEF OPERATIONS

A detailed description of the civilian relief operations in the Congo would be out of place in this present study of United Nations Forces. However, the point has been made earlier [14] that Allied experience during the Second World War, and the Korean experience of the United Nations itself, suggest strongly that military operations by a United Nations Force may have to find a counterpart in a comprehensive operation for civilian relief, and this became very much the case in the Congo.

The importance of the civilian aspects of the Congo operations was evident in the fact that, although the civilian operations were distinct from the military operations, and had separate chiefs,[15] they were both under the direction of the Representative of the Secretary-General in the Congo (later the " Officer-in-Charge ") and, in practice, the two sides of assistance were conceived as being interrelated and mutually supporting. The Security Council Resolution of 22 July 1960 invited the co-operation of the specialised agencies and the Chief of Civilian Operations became, on 26 July 1960, simultaneously the Resident Representative of the Technical Assistance Board and, on 11 August, the Chairman of a Consultative Group composed of the senior experts in each of the major fields of civilian assistance sent by the specialised agencies. Members of the Group assumed the dual role of consultants to the Chief of Civilian Operations and advisers to the Ministries of the Congolese Government.

The shortage of trained, local personnel, coupled with the flight of Belgian and other foreign technical personnel, meant that the civilian operations scheme had to provide expert personnel in the fields of general administration, public health, civil aviation, telecommunications, the judicature, agriculture, finance and education.[16] This was in addition to the provision of actual supplies of food to cope with the famine in South Kasai in 1960–1961 and, of course, financial assistance.[17] Refugees, alone, constituted a problem of some magnitude: in September 1961 there were 35,000 refugees (mainly Balubas) in Elisabethville itself. The actual financing of the Civilian Operations Scheme was separate from the financing of the military side of ONUC and was based on voluntary contributions to the United

[14] *Ante*, p. 58.
[15] *Ante*, p. 211.
[16] For details of the civilian operations see S/4417/Add. 5, S/4447, Dayal's First Report, S/4531, Section IV, and Second Report, S/4557, Section VIII. Also the appropriate sections of the *U.N. Yearbook*, 1960, pp. 108–118, 1961, pp. 82–86; also Gordon, *op. cit.*, pp. 63–74.
[17] An agreement for financial assistance was signed between the Secretary-General and the President of the Congo on 12 June 1961.

Nations Fund for the Congo, a fund which rose from $10 million in 1960 to $33 million by the end of 1961.

XI. FINANCING OF ONUC

It was clear that with ONUC, as with UNEF, the United Nations would not be faced with the problem of meeting the *total* cost of the operations—for, even in the absence of specific agreements, the rough division of costs between participating States and the United Nations which had been arrived at with UNEF [18] was being applied to ONUC [19]—yet there remained a net cost which was heavier than had ever been the case with UNEF.

In one sense, the occurrence of the Congo crisis at a time when the Organisation was financially heavily committed over UNEF was singularly unfortunate, yet in another it was fortunate in that, in relation to UNEF, the principle had already been established that the financing of peace-keeping operations was a collective responsibility upon all Member States.[20]

In July 1960 the Advisory Committee on Administrative and Budgetary Questions authorised the Secretary-General to expend up to $15 million, a limit soon raised to $40 million in September, and by December the Secretary-General was warning the Committee of a cost of nearer $66 million: the Committee advised that the total cost for 1960 should be held to $60 million.[21]

The General Assembly, by Resolution 1583 (XV) of 20 December 1960,[22] adopted by forty-six votes to seventeen, with twenty-four

---

[18] See *ante*, pp. 139–142.
[19] Secretary-General's Note of 21 January 1963 on the Budgetary and Financial Practices of the UN, A/AC. 113/1, paras. 258–263. There were some slight differences. In relation to compensation for deterioration of equipment, since difficulties arose in assessing worn out equipment only at the end of the total period during which a government provided troops, particularly in the case of ONUC, this was amended to permit reimbursement on a current basis, at agreed standard rates, at the expiry of the period of service of particular units: Resol. 1575 (XV), para. 5, approving paras. 67–70 of the Secretary-General's Report on UNEF, A/4486, *Off.Rec.G.A.*, Agenda item 27, 15th Sess. 1956–57, Annexes. Another difference was the *per diem* allowed to members of contingents, designed to meet their personal and recreational needs and to equalise their disadvantages by comparison with troops stationed at regular military establishments. In the case of UNEF the amount was originally fixed by the Military Advisory Group at $1 a day for all ranks; this was reduced to 86 cents from 17 December 1956, at which it has since remained. Paid in local currency, it is referred to amongst the UNEF soldiers as "piastre pay." A similar allowance, presently amounting to $1.30 a day is paid in the case of ONUC: see 22nd Report of the Advisory Committee on Administrative and Budgetary Questions, A/3402, *Off.Rec.G.A.* Agenda item 66, 11th Sess. 1956–57, Annexes; Report of the Secretary-General, A/3694; *Off.Rec.G.A.* Agenda item 65, 12th Sess. 1957, Annexes; Reg. 39 of the UNEF Regulations; and see the Report of the Secretary-General, A/C.5/836, *Off.Rec.G.A.*, Agenda items 49/50, 15th Sess. 1960–61, Annexes.
[20] *Ante*, p. 145.   [21] A/4580.
[22] *Off.Rec.G.A.* 15th Sess. Annexes, Agenda items 49/50 (A/4676, paras. 7, 10). The U.S.A. and U.S.S.R. had previously announced the waiver of their claims to $10 million and $1.5 million respectively for the initial transport of troops to the Congo.

abstentions the first basic Resolution on the financing of ONUC which:

" *Recognising* that the expenses involved in the United Nations operations in the Congo for 1960 constitute 'expenses of the Organisation' within the meaning of Article 17, paragraph 2, of the Charter of the United Nations, and that the assessment thereof against Member States creates binding legal obligations on such States to pay their assessed shares. . .

1. *Decides* to establish an *ad hoc* account for the expenses of the United Nations in the Congo, . . .
3. Notes that the waiver of airlift costs announced by certain Governments will reduce the level of expenses from the amount of $60 million recommended by the Advisory Committee on Administration and Budgetary Questions to the amount of $48·5 million;
4. *Decides* that the amount of $48·5 million shall be apportioned among the Member States on the basis of the regular scale of assessment . . . ;
6. *Calls upon* the former administering power of the Republic of the Congo (Leopoldville) to make a substantial contribution . . ."

On the same day the Assembly adopted a further Resolution [23] authorising expenditure of a further $24 million during January-March pending the resumption of the fifteenth session of the Assembly. On 3 April 1961 the Assembly authorised expenditure up to $8 million per month,[24] and on 21 April the Assembly commuted this to a total authorisation of $100 million to cover the period from 1 January to 31 October 1961. Further appropriations followed of $10 million per month from 31 October 1961 onwards,[25] and of a further $80 million to cover the period 1 November 1961 to 30 June 1962.[26]

By this time, however, the refusal of many States to pay their assessments had led to a financial crisis which had resulted in the request to the International Court of Justice for an Advisory Opinion. The request was formulated in Resolution 1731 (XVI) of the Assembly of 20 December 1961: in so far as it affected the financing of UNEF, this has been dealt with in Chapter 4.[27] In so far as it affected ONUC it was phrased in the following terms:

" Do the expenditures authorised in General Assembly Resolutions 1583 (XV) and 1590 (XV) of 20 December 1960, 1595 (XV) of 3 April 1961, 1619 (XV) of 21 April 1961 and 1633 (XVI) of 30 October 1961 relating to the United Nations operations in the Congo undertaken in pursuance of the Security Council Resolutions of 14 July, 22 July and 9 August 1960, and 21 February and 24 November 1961 . . . constitute 'expenses of the Organisation' within the meaning of Article 17, paragraph 2, of the Charter of the United Nations."

The Opinion of the Court [28] rightly distinguished between three separate questions, and it will be convenient to continue this treatment of the problem of financing ONUC by way of a discussion of these three separate questions.

[23] Resol. 1590 (XV).   [24] Resol. 1595 (XV).
[25] Resol. 1633 (XVI).
[26] Resol. 1732 (XVI), adopted 20 December 1961.
[27] *Ante*, pp. 142–148.
[28] *Advisory Opinion on Certain Expenses of the United Nations* (Article 17, paragraph 2, of the Charter), 20 July 1962, *I.C.J. Reports*, 1962, p. 152, adopted by 9 votes to 5.

1. *The question of identifying what are " the expenses of the Organisation "*

The majority opinion of the Court rejected the argument that there existed a distinction between the " administrative " and " operational " budgets of the United Nations so as to bring only the former within the scope of Article 17 (2).[29] It similarly rejected the argument that the budgetary authority of the Assembly, or the power to apportion expenses, did not extend to the expenses resulting from operations for the maintenance of international peace and security.[30] For the Court the question was essentially one of determining whether the expenses were incurred in connection with the purposes of the United Nations:

" . . . such expenditures must be tested by their relationship to the purposes of the United Nations in the sense that if an expenditure were made for a purpose which is not one of the purposes of the United Nations, it could not be considered an ' expense of the Organisation '." [31]

Applying this test to ONUC expenses, the Court noted that the Resolution of 14 July 1960 " was clearly adopted with a view to maintaining international peace and security." [32] It rejected the argument that the Secretary-General had utilised ONUC in a way contrary to his mandate: having reviewed the succession of Resolutions approving the Secretary-General's conduct of the operations it concluded that:

" In the light of such a record of reiterated consideration, confirmation, approval and ratification by the Security Council and by the General Assembly of the actions of the Secretary-General in implementing the Resolution of 14 July 1960, it is impossible to reach the conclusion that the operations in question usurped or impinged upon the prerogatives conferred by the Charter on the Security Council." [33]

---

[29] *Ibid.*, pp. 158–162. The handling of the finances by way of an *ad hoc* Account has been criticised as giving support to the argument that Member States were not, in respect of such *ad hoc* Account, under the same obligations as applied to the regular budget (see Rosner, *The United Nations Emergency Force* (1963) pp. 182–183). However, the Court stated that: " In this context, it is of no legal significance whether, as a matter of book-keeping or accounting, the General Assembly chooses to have the item in question included under one of the standard established sections of the ' regular ' budget or whether it is separately listed in some special account or fund." (*ibid.*, p. 169.) Similarly, the reference, in the preamble to the Assembly Resolution 1619 (XV) of 21 April 1961, to " extraordinary expenses . . . essentially different in nature from the expenses of the Organisation under the regular budget " was treated by the Court as referring to the desirability of a different method of apportionment (*ibid.*, pp. 178–179).

[30] *Ibid.*, pp. 162–165. This, the Soviet argument, had been based on the view that such expenses lay within the province of the Security Council and that agreements between the Council and States under Art. 43 would deal with apportionment.

[31] *Ibid.*, p. 167. Note that it was only in relation to UNEF, not ONUC, that the Court had to deal with the question whether the expenses were incurred by the wrong organ (in terms of the distribution of powers between the Assembly and Security Council): since ONUC was established by the Security Council there was no problem of this kind.

[32] *Ibid.*, p. 175.   [33] *Ibid.*, p. 177.

The Court therefore concluded that the ONUC expenses were properly regarded as "expenses of the Organisation" within the meaning of Article 17 (2): this opinion was "accepted" by Resolution of the General Assembly on 19 December 1962, by seventy-six votes to seventeen, with eight abstentions.[34]

However, it must not be assumed that this settled the problems arising over finance. Firstly, the opinion of the Court was still an "opinion," and not a "judgment," so that, as the result of the voting on the Resolution of 19 December 1962 shows, there were many States which did not regard themselves as legally bound to accept this opinion. Secondly, as the Court itself emphasised, its opinion concerned only the first of three questions, so that it is to the second and third questions that we must now turn.

2. *The question of apportionment by the Assembly*

The apportionment of ONUC expenses according to the regular scale of assessment was determined by the Resolution of 20 December 1960,[35] but it was clearly not the only method of apportionment open to the Assembly and, indeed, this method had already been under attack in relation to UNEF expenses.[36] The Resolution of 21 April 1961 gave further support to the view that this was an essentially provisional method of apportionment: according to its terms the General Assembly:

"...

Bearing in mind that the extraordinary expenses for the United Nations operations in the Congo are essentially different in nature from the expenses of the Organisation under the regular budget and that therefore a procedure different from that applied in the case of the regular budget is required for meeting these extraordinary expenses,

. . .

3. *Decides* to appropriate an amount of $100 million for the operations of the United Nations in the Congo from 1 January to 31 October 1961;
4. *Decides further* to apportion as expenses of the Organisation the amount of $100 million among the Member States . . . ;
5. *Urges* the permanent members of the Security Council to make sizeable additional contributions;
6. *Appeals* to all other Member States who are in a position to assist to make voluntary contributions;
7. *Calls upon* the Government of Belgium, a State directly concerned with the situation in the Republic of the Congo (Leopoldville) to make a substantial contribution . . ."

This Resolution already reflected the criteria which some Members were arguing should be applied in determining a different scale of assessments, but it did so by way of an appeal for voluntary contributions and not by way of a decision upon a different method of

[34] Resol. 1854 (XVII).
[35] Resol. 1583 (XV).
[36] *Ante*, p. 145.

assessment. The first real step away from the regular scale of assessments came on 20 December 1961 when the General Assembly,[37] in appropriating $80 million, for the period 1 November 1961 to 30 June 1962, introduced a sliding scale whereby it reduced by 80 per cent. the contributions of Members whose regular budget contributions ranged from 0·04 to 0·25 per cent. or who were receiving assistance under the Expanded Technical Assistance Programme and who contributed in the range of 0·26 to 1·25 per cent.; and by 50 per cent. the contributions of Members receiving technical assistance but contributing 1·26 per cent. and above. The deficit was to be made good by the additional voluntary contributions called for under paras. 6, 7 and 8 of the same Resolution.

The difficulty of that system was that the reductions for the less prosperous States came as a matter of course, whereas the voluntary contributions did not. Hence it was found advisable to devise a scheme whereby the voluntary contributions would be paid into the Congo *ad hoc* Account in proportion to the amounts paid in by the less prosperous States so as to minimise the extent to which these less prosperous States would tend to rely on voluntary contributions from their wealthier colleagues. The Assembly's Resolution of 27 June 1963 [38] sought to achieve this, and also to supply the scale of reduction for the less prosperous States, in a Resolution which merits citation *in extenso* : by its terms the Assembly :

" . . .

1. *Decides* to continue the *ad hoc* Account for the expenses of the United Nations operation in the Congo;

. . .

3. *Decides* to appropriate an amount of $33 million for the United Nations operation in the Congo for the period 1 July to 31 December 1963;

4. *Decides* to apportion :

(a) The amount of $3 million among all Member States in accordance with the regular scale of assessments for 1963;

(b) The $30 million balance of the amount appropriated in paragraph 3 above among the Member States in accordance with the regular scale of assessments for 1963, except that each ' economically less developed country ' shall be assessed an amount calculated at 45 per cent. of its rate under the regular scale of assessments for 1963;

provided that this apportionment shall constitute an *ad hoc* arrangement for the present phase of this peace-keeping operation, and shall not constitute a precedent for the future;

5. *Decides* that, for the purpose of the present Resolution, the term ' economically less developed countries ' shall mean all Member States except Australia, Austria, Belgium, Byelorussian S.S.R., Canada, Czechoslovakia, Denmark, Finland, France, Hungary, Iceland, Ireland, Italy, Japan, Luxembourg, Netherlands, New Zealand, Norway, Poland, Roumania, South Africa, Sweden, Ukrainian S.S.R., U.S.S.R., U.K. and the U.S.A.;

[37] Resol. 1732 (XVI), adopted by 67–13–15. A similar step away from the regular scale of assessments had been made in relation to UNEF by Resol. 1441 (XIV) on 5 December 1959 : see *ante*, pp. 147–148.

[38] Resol. 1876 (S–IV); the " companion " Resolution of the same date, dealing with the general principles to govern the costs of *future* peace-keeping operations, adopted on the same date (Resol. 1874 (S–IV)) is discussed *post*, pp. 474–477.

6. *Recommends* that the Member States named in paragraph 5 above make voluntary contributions in addition to their assessments under the present Resolution in order to finance authorised expenditures in excess of the total amount assessed under the present Resolution, such voluntary contributions to be credited to a special account by the Secretary-General and transferred to the Congo *ad hoc* Account as and when an economically less developed country has once paid to the credit of the latter account its assessment under paragraph 4 (b) of above or an equal amount, the transfer to be of an amount which bears the same proportion to the total of such voluntary contributions as the amount of such payment bears to the total of the assessments on economically less developed countries under paragraph 4 (b); any amount left in such special account on 31 December 1965, shall revert to the Member States that made such voluntary contributions in proportion to their respective voluntary contributions;

7. *Appeals* to all other Member States which are in a position to assist to make similar voluntary contributions or alternatively to forgo having their assessments calculated at the rate mentioned in the exception contained in paragraph 4 (b) above;

8. *Decides* that the voluntary contributions referred to in paragraphs 6 and 7 above may be made by a Member State, at its option, in the form of services and supplies, acceptable to the Secretary-General, furnished for use in connection with the United Nations operation in the Congo during the period 1 July to 31 December 1963, for which the Member State does not require reimbursement, the Member State to be credited with the fair value thereof as agreed upon by the Member State and by the Secretary-General."

It may be noted that this particular method of assessment is treated as *ad hoc*, and not a precedent for the future.

The search for agreed general principles upon which to base assessment of financial obligations arising out of future peace-keeping operations has continued in a wider context than the ONUC context. It now represents a general problem not confined to ONUC, so that an examination of the criteria suggested for apportionment, and of the progress so far made, had best be postponed until the section on financing in Part Two of the present study.[39] The purpose of the present section has been to state the actual basis upon which ONUC expenses have been assessed and apportioned to date.

3. *The question of the interpretation of the phrase "shall be borne by the Members"*

This third question was, likewise, not dealt with by the majority opinion of the Court except in so far as the Court stated that:

". . . the exercise of the power of apportionment creates the *obligation*, specifically stated in Article 17, paragraph 2, of each Member to bear that part of the expenses which is apportioned to it by the General Assembly." [40]

This question has never been settled in relation to ONUC finances and, clearly, the question of how far there exists a legal obligation to pay the assessments made by the Assembly is one of general application, not confined to ONUC. It had therefore best be postponed until Part Two of the present study.[41]

---

[39] *Post*, pp. 474–483.
[41] *Post*, pp. 477–480.

[40] *Ibid.*, p. 164 (italics added).

7

The United Nations
Temporary Executive Authority (UNTEA)

IT may be recalled that when, in the Charter of the Transfer of Sovereignty drawn up at the Hague in August 1949, the Netherlands had transferred complete sovereignty over Indonesia to the Republic of Indonesia this transfer was expressly stated to exclude West New Guinea. This particular territory remained the subject of a dispute between the two States which for twelve years evaded solution. The question was considered by the Assembly at successive sessions, in 1954, 1955, 1956, 1957 and 1961, and in December 1961 hostilities broke out in the area between Netherlands and Indonesian forces. At this stage the Secretary-General, U Thant, invited both parties to discuss with him the possibilities of a peaceful settlement and he appointed Ambassador Bunker, of the United States, to act as mediator, representing the Secretary-General. This mediation was successful in that it culminated in the Agreement between the Netherlands and Indonesia of 15 August 1962.[1] The Agreement envisaged the temporary transfer of administration of the territory to a United Nations Temporary Executive Authority, to be established by and to be under the jurisdiction of the Secretary-General[2] and to be assisted by a security force (UNSF).[3] However, since the assumption of these responsibilities was deemed to be a matter requiring the authorisation of the General Assembly, the Agreement contained an undertaking by both parties that they would jointly introduce in the General Assembly a Resolution granting this authority to the Secretary-General,[4] and the Agreement was to enter into force only upon the date of this Resolution of the General Assembly.[5]

I. THE ACTION OF THE GENERAL ASSEMBLY

On 21 September 1962 the General Assembly passed the following Resolution:

". . . *Considering* that the Governments of Indonesia and the Netherlands have resolved their dispute concerning West New Guinea (West Irian),

---

[1] Text in *U.N. Review*, Vol. 9, No. 9 (September 1962), p. 39 and in A/5170 and Corr. 1 and Add. 1.　　　　　　　　　　　　　　　　　　　[2] Art. II.
[3] Art. VII.
[4] Art. I.
[5] Art. XXVIII.

255

> *Noting with appreciation* the successful efforts of the Acting Secretary-General to bring about this peaceful settlement,
> *Having taken cognizance* of the Agreement between the Republic of Indonesia and the Kingdom of the Netherlands concerning West New Guinea (West Irian),
> 1. *Takes note* of the Agreement;
> 2. *Acknowledges* the role conferred upon the Secretary-General in the Agreement;
> 3. *Authorises* the Secretary-General to carry out the tasks entrusted to him in the Agreement." [6]

Thus, despite the misgivings which during the Congo operations had been expressed over the policy of entrusting to the Secretary-General the primary responsibility for control of a United Nations operation, the Assembly gave a general authorisation to the Secretary-General to discharge all the tasks which the parties in their Agreement—and not the Assembly—had formulated. One of these tasks, with which we are primarily concerned, was the creation and control of the United Nations Security Force envisaged under Article VII of the Agreement.

The constitutional basis of the Assembly's action is not, of course, specified in the Resolution, but it is thought to lie in Article 14 of the Charter although, rather than acting by way of a recommendation of " measures for the peaceful adjustment of any situation, regardless of origin," it acted by way of an authorisation to the Secretary-General. It must be emphasised that the Assembly's authorisation was in the context of a situation which had occupied the Assembly's attention over many sessions and which, in December 1961, had erupted into open hostilities between two Member States.[7] This can therefore be seen as yet another " peace-keeping " operation, dealing with a situation which had presented a threat to international peace and security but which, by reason of the cease-fire and the Agreement between the parties, offered an opportunity for a peaceful solution provided the United Nations could assume certain functions. As Ambassador Bunker is reported to have said:

"The United Nations, instead of being called upon to extinguish the fire after it had started, as was often the case, sought to prevent the conflagration from starting." [8]

It may be regarded, therefore, as broadly similar to UNEF so far as its constitutional basis in the Charter is concerned. There is certainly no justification for regarding UNTEA as a precedent for the United Nations supplying any State with internal security forces

---

[6] Resol. 1752 (XVII), adopted 21 September 1962 by 89-0-14 in A/5217 (*Off.Rec.G.A.*, 17th Sess., Suppl. No. 17). For the debate on this draft Resolution see A/PV. 1127.

[7] The letter by both parties to the Secretary-General, dated 13 August 1962 (and reproduced in an Annex to the Agreement) mentioned specifically that " the functions conferred upon the Secretary-General [are] in order to give the earliest possible effect to the cessation of hostilities " and spoke also of " the urgent necessity for your assistance and that of the United Nations personnel in implementing the agreement on cessation of hostilities."

[8] *U.N. Review*, Vol. 9, No. 9, September 1962, p. 5.

simply because its own security forces were inadequate for their tasks. As in the Congo, the situation was one in which there was, or had been, a threat to *international* peace and security. Moreover, in the case of UNTEA, since it was assuming governmental powers by the consent of both parties, it was obviously desirable that it should have the backing of an international United Nations Force, rather than rely entirely on local forces, even for internal " police " functions.

II. THE FUNCTIONS OF UNTEA GENERALLY, AND OF THE UNSF IN PARTICULAR

UNTEA itself became, in effect, the government of the territory for the period of its administration. This was perhaps the most unique feature of the Agreement. The extent of its governmental powers can be seen in the conferment upon the United Nations Administrator [9] of " full authority under the direction of the Secretary-General to administer the territory . . .",[10] of power to appoint governmental officials and members of the representative councils,[11] of power to legislate for the territory,[12] of power to issue travel documents to Papuans for travel abroad [13] and in the commitments and guarantees undertaken by UNTEA with regard to civil liberties and property rights.[14] Above all it can be seen in the duty of the Secretary-General to provide UNTEA with " such security forces as the United Nations Administrator deems necessary . . ." [15]

In the light of the governmental power assumed by UNTEA it was not surprising that the function, at least the primary function, of the Security Force was " to maintain internal law and order." As Article VII stated :

" . . . such forces will primarily supplement existing Papuan police in the task of maintaining law and order. The Papuan Volunteer Corps, which on the arrival of the United Nations Administrator will cease being part of the Netherlands armed forces, and the Indonesian armed forces in the territory will be under the authority of, and at the disposal of, the Secretary-General for the same purpose. The United Nations Administrator will, to the extent feasible, use the Papuan police as a United Nations security force to maintain law and order and, at his discretion, use Indonesian armed forces. The Netherlands armed forces will be repatriated as rapidly as possible and while still in the territory will be under the authority of the UNTEA."

Thus, in one sense, the United Nations Force was to assume a " police " function, a task similar to that assumed by ONUC.

---

[9] An Iranian, Dr. Abdoh, was appointed on 22 October.　　[10] Art. V.
[11] Arts. IX and XXIII.
[12] Art. XI. This power was subject to the terms of the Agreement and the obligation to consult the representative councils.
[13] See the annexed " Agreement Relating to Travel Documents and Consular Assistance and Protection Abroad to Papuans (West Irianese)." The two parties to the agreement undertook to provide consular assistance and protection abroad at the request of the Secretary-General.
[14] Art. XXII.
[15] Art. VII.

257

However, there were important differences, for in the case of UNTEA the United Nations Force was not to assist the government of a State but to assist a United Nations subsidiary organ which had assumed exclusively the powers of government. Moreover, the United Nations Force was to have integrated within it—at least in the sense that they should be used under the direction and control of the United Nations Administrator—the local Papuan police and, where necessary, the Indonesian armed forces remaining in the territory. In retrospect one cannot help but reflect on how much easier the ONUC operation would have been had a similar authority been conferred on the United Nations. None of the problems of a relationship with a " host " State, or of existing side-by-side with the armed forces and militia of that State, were to exist in the case of UNTEA.

This was not, however, the only function conferred on UNTEA. In the " Memorandum of Understanding on Cessation of Hostilities constituting an Agreement between the Republic of Indonesia and the Kingdom of the Netherlands " [16] UNTEA was to assume an observer function comparable more to the observer functions of UNTSO than to ONUC. Paragraph 1 (c) of the Memorandum provided:

"The Secretary-General of the United Nations will assign United Nations personnel (i) to observe the implementation of this agreement and (ii) in particular to take necessary steps for the prevention of any acts endangering the security of forces of both parties to this agreement."

This " observer " function was coupled with the Secretary-General's role in assisting in repatriation of Indonesian prisoners,[17] as has often been the case in practice with an observer group,[18] and it was evidently assumed that the Security Force would be distinct from the Observer Group. However, since the function of the Security Force was described as being *primarily* to maintain law and order, and not *exclusively*, it may be suggested that nothing in the Agreements would have prevented the Secretary-General from utilising members of the Security Force for this other function of observing the cease-fire. Indeed, bearing in mind the smallness of the Observer Group,[19] it might have been imperative for him to do so in order to take the " necessary steps for the prevention of any acts endangering the security of forces of both parties," had any attempt at renewal of hostilities been made. Fortunately, no such attempt was made.

It may be noted, further, that the Agreements envisaged yet another function for the United Nations, that of supervising the plebiscite which is to take place in the territory in 1969. Articles XVI–XVIII envisage that a Representative of the Secretary-General,

[16] Annex A to the letter to the Acting Secretary-General of 13 August 1962.
[17] *Ibid.*, para. 8.
[18] *Ante*, p. 78.
[19] *Post*, p. 260.

together with a staff, will " advise, assist and participate in arrangements which are the responsibility of Indonesia for the act of free
choice " by the inhabitants. However, since this will occur long
after the withdrawal of UNTEA and the Security Force, it is not a
function to be assumed by them. Whether a United Nations Force
will be necessary to supervise the plebiscite is highly doubtful, and
it is certainly not provided for in the Agreement.

Finally, there was never any problem over the termination of the
functions of UNTEA. Article XIII provided expressly for the withdrawal of all United Nations security forces upon the transfer of
administration to Indonesia, and in an *Aide-mémoire* this transfer was
stated to take effect as soon as possible after 1 May 1963. In fact,
the United Nations flag [20] was lowered on that precise date and all
United Nations troops were evacuated.

III. COMPOSITION OF THE FORCE

Article VII of the Agreement did not itself specify the size or
composition of the United Nations Force, but paragraph 7 of the
Cease-Fire Agreement specified " a United Nations security force
including an infantry battalion with ancillary arms and services " to
be included in the Force. However, this imposed a minimum rather
than a maximum limit. In fact, the Secretary-General arranged for
a Force largely made up of a contingent from Pakistan. On 10
November the size of the Force totalled 1,596, of which 1,485 were
Pakistanis and 12 were Canadian and 99 were United States air force
personnel.[21] The Force was commanded by a Pakistani Brigadier-
General.

The Force thus contained little in the way of an admixture of
national contingents to give it that " international " character which
had been stressed particularly in UNEF and ONUC. No doubt this
almost exclusive reliance on the contingent from one State was due
to the fact that it was estimated that about one battalion was all
that was needed, and it would have led to unnecessary complications
to accept small contingents from several States in order to make up
the one battalion required. The more striking feature was something
which had never been attempted before, namely, the admixture—at
least in terms of control by UNTEA—of the Papuan police, the
Volunteer Corps, and even the Indonesian troops.[22]

---

[20] Art. VI provided for the flying of the UN flag during the UN administration
and, in para. 2, left the question of which other flags (Indonesian and
Netherlands) should be flown together with it for subsequent agreement.
In fact the Indonesian flag was hoisted side by side with the UN flag on
31 December 1962, the date on which the Netherlands flag was lowered.

[21] *U.N. Review*, Vol. 9, No. 12, December 1962, p. 36. Note that the Pakistanis
took over 9 vessels transferred from the Netherlands Navy, thus
constituting the first UN " Navy."

[22] The provision on liaison between the UN and Indonesia in para. 6 of the
cease-fire agreement related only to the observer functions; there were
no provisions directed specifically to the problems of liaison with UNSF.

The Observer Group was distinct from the Force. This was headed by Brigadier Rikhye, who also acted as Military Adviser to the Secretary-General. This Group consisted of some twenty-one members, deployed at six observation points, and drawn from the existing personnel of UNTSO.

IV. PRIVILEGES AND IMMUNITIES

Since the United Nations did not become sovereign over the territory,[23] but simply the temporary administrator, it followed that the actual sovereign should grant to the United Nations the privileges and immunities necessary for the fulfilment of its tasks. The fact that sovereignty was in dispute suggested that both Indonesia and the Netherlands should join in the grant, and, accordingly, Article XXVI provided that:

"For the purposes of the present agreement, Indonesia and the Netherlands will apply to United Nations property, funds, assets and officials the provisions of the Convention on the Privileges and Immunities of the United Nations. In particular, the United Nations Administrator, appointed pursuant to Article IV, and the United Nations Representative, appointed pursuant to Article XVII, will enjoy the privileges and immunities specified in section 19 of the Convention on the Privileges and Immunities of the United Nations."

This Article does not refer specifically to UNSF, nor could its members be comprised within the definition of "officials," and no separate Status Agreement relating to the Force seems to have been concluded. In terms of drafting, therefore, the Article scarcely seems comprehensive enough. The fact that UNTEA was to assume the functions of government for the duration of the stay of the Force rendered unlikely any difficulties in this respect and it is believed that none occurred.

V. FINANCE

A second unique feature of the establishment of UNTEA (and one which, without undue scepticism, may be regarded as being in part responsible for the Assembly's alacrity in accepting the idea) was that the entire financial burden of UNTEA, including the UNSF, was to be borne equally by the two parties, Netherlands and Indonesia. There was to be no charge on the funds of the Organisation. Under Article XXIV the parties agreed that, whilst the Secretary-General was to have the final decision on financial questions relating to UNTEA,[24] they would reimburse "all costs incurred by the United

---

[23] Art. XII of the Agreement spoke of the transfer of the "administration" (not of "sovereignty") to Indonesia by the UNTEA at the end of the first phase; the *Aide-mémoire* used the term "transfer of authority."

[24] A special "Memorandum of Understanding constituting an Agreement between the Republic of Indonesia and the Kingdom of the Netherlands on Certain Financial Matters" established a committee of representatives of both parties and of the Secretary-General to advise the Secretary-General on UNTEA's budget: it also fixed the rate of exchange of the New Guinea guilder in terms of U.S. dollars.

Nations under the present agreement." Deficits in the budget of the territory during the administration of UNTEA, and all costs of UNTEA itself, were to be shared equally by the parties.

By way of conclusion of this brief chapter on UNTEA, it may be said that the administration appears to have been a complete success. The experiment had many novel features and it now affords a precedent for a United Nations role which places the United Nations, supported by an international force, in charge of the actual government of a territory. This role could only have been assumed on the basis of the consent of the States concerned, yet it is to be hoped that, in the future, States involved in this kind of transfer of territory will seek to utilise the United Nations in a similar way. The plebiscite phase of the transfer of territory in the case of UNTEA is postponed until Indonesia has assumed authority and UNTEA has withdrawn. In principle, however, there is no reason why a United Nations subsidiary organ, supported by its own forces, should not assume administration of a territory during an actual plebiscite.[25]

[25] See *ante*, Chap. I.

Part Two

Introduction

There are many who regard the future of mankind as dependent upon an agreement between States on general disarmament. Whether this is too sanguine, or too simple, a belief is open to question, but what is clear is that, for the purposes of the present study, a radical distinction has to be made in projecting our minds into the future according to whether we are thinking in terms of the immediate, short-term future—in which no agreement on general and complete disarmament exists—and the distant, long-term future in which there may be such an agreement. Lord McNair, speaking in the House of Lords on 20 February 1963, put the distinction in the following terms:

" As I see it, there are two objectives. There is a major and ultimate one, and a minor and immediate one. This major and ultimate objective is an international armed force operating under the direction of a world authority, particularly linked with the process of disarmament, and designed also to preserve peace in a world of States or other units which are restricted to the use of force for internal purposes. The minor and more immediate objective is an international police force equipped for such purposes as dealing with the liquidation of the Suez crisis or with the Congo affair." [1]

Part Two is therefore limited to the immediate future, a future which is already with us, and the entirety of this Part is based upon the following assumptions:

(1) There is no agreement on general and complete disarmament;
(2) The nation-States remain heavily armed;
(3) The United Nations continues in being and unreformed.

It will be seen that, on these assumptions, the particular problems dealt with in the various sections offer certain solutions, in which very great reliance can be placed on the experience of the past which has been reviewed in Part One. Other solutions are theoretically possible, but scarcely practical on these assumptions, and these are therefore postponed to Part Three dealing with Disarmament and an International Force. To give but one example, to talk of a permanent Force capable of assuming enforcement functions is simply impracticable in the immediate future. If directed against a major Power such a Force would produce world war, not world peace, and even to be directed against any sizeable Power the Force would have to be of a size which, in terms of finance alone, would make the suggestion impractical. A permanent Force designed to take enforcement action becomes a practical proposition only in a disarmed world and is therefore relevant to Part Three, but not Part Two.

The discussion of problems which follows is therefore limited by the assumptions made above.

[1] Parl. Debates (Hansard) H.L., Vol. 246, No. 43, col. 1395.

8

The Functions and Constitutional Bases of United Nations Forces

ALTHOUGH the Charter of the United Nations specifically envisages only one sort of United Nations Force—a Force for the purpose of carrying out enforcement measures decided upon by the Security Council—United Nations Forces have in fact been established for other purposes. Indeed, the striking feature of all the United Nations military Forces established so far is that not one of them has been of the type specifically envisaged—the " Article 42 " Force. The first part of this study has revealed a wide variety of Forces, established for a variety of functions; moreover, it is also possible to envisage the establishment of new Forces, or the adaptation of existing ones, for yet different functions. There exists an essential relationship between the functions or tasks of a Force and the constitutional provisions under which it is set up; certain procedures of establishment may be proper for one type of Force, but improper for another. Once it has been decided that a United Nations military Force is necessary to secure certain objectives, it must then be decided which organ may appropriately establish such a Force and under what authority. On occasion it occurs that the choice of organ is clear, and that it is then required to mount a Force whose functions and scope are limited by that choice.[1] In either event, constitutional provisions and the functions of United Nations Forces must be discussed together. In classifying the different kinds of functions which may be entrusted to a United Nations military Force it is proposed to accept the broad distinction made in the opinion of the International Court of Justice between " enforcement " action, or functions, which presuppose the taking of military action *against* a State (or possibly other authority) and " peace-keeping operations," or functions, which do not.[2] The further categories of function will be listed for completeness although it will be seen that they represent categories of *possible* functions rather than functions already assumed by the United Nations.

---

[1] " Clearly an organ constituted in a particular way will tend to carry out a given function in a different way from an organ differently constituted, and will have been entrusted with that function for that reason, *inter alia*." Judge Sir Gerald Fitzmaurice, Separate Opinion, *Certain Expenses of the United Nations, I.C.J. Reports*, 1962, p. 200, n. 3.
[2] *Ibid.*, pp. 163–5, 166–7, 177.

I. ENFORCEMENT FUNCTIONS

It is anticipated in Chapter VII of the Charter that the United Nations may, in the last resort, have to take armed action against a State which has been deemed an aggressor and has refused to heed the directives of the Security Council. It is also possible under Chapter VII that United Nations Forces may have to enforce the decisions of the Security Council for ending a breach of the peace, or even a serious threat to the peace in circumstances in which, though no State has been determined to be an " aggressor," one or both parties refuse to comply with an order for provisional measures under Article 40. In such circumstances, a United Nations Force is likely to be acting *against* certain elements or governments, will be engaged in hostilities, and will need to be a fully fighting, military Force. Loosely speaking, it may be said to be engaged in " belligerent functions " though the term " enforcement measures " is to be preferred.[3] It is also possible that a United Nations Force could be used to enforce a judicial decision, although this has never yet been done. This could be done by the Security Council characterising a State's refusal to comply with the decision as a " threat to the peace, breach of the peace, or act of aggression " under Article 39, and hence using its power under Chapter VII to secure this end: or it may be that, in relation to judgments of the International Court of Justice, Article 94 of the Charter gives an entirely separate legal foundation for such action.[4] In any event, the action would be directed against the recalcitrant State and would partake of the character of enforcement action whether technically taken under Chapter VII or not.

So far, the only unequivocal United Nations enforcement action has been in the case of the Korean conflict, though doubts have been expressed as to the correctness of designating the military effort a " United Nations Force." On 27 June 1950 the Security Council recommended that members " furnish such assistance to the Republic of Korea as may be necessary to repel the armed attack and to restore international peace and security in the area." [5] The view has been expressed in Chapter 3 [6] that, whilst the Korean action was not that which the Charter specifically envisaged in Article 42, it was nevertheless enforcement action under Chapter VII of the Charter.

II. " PEACE-KEEPING OPERATIONS " FOR THE MAINTENANCE OF INTERNATIONAL PEACE AND SECURITY

A United Nations Force may also be established for the purpose of maintaining international peace and security rather than enforcing

---

[3] See *post*, pp. 485, 496–499.
[4] For an examination of the right of the United Nations to use force for this purpose and a thorough review of the authorities on this question, see Schachter, " The Enforcement of International Judicial and Arbitral Decisions " (1960) 54 A.J.I.L. 14–24.
[5] UN Doc. S/1511.
[6] *Ante*, p. 32.

its restoration. Such a Force is different in nature from the one described above, for although it may be armed and become involved in fighting, its main purpose and intention is not military. There are many different situations in which such a Force might be used, and indeed has been used, for the circumstances in which international peace might be jeopardised vary considerably. To some extent, therefore, it is possible to indicate various sub-categories within this rather broad category, though these are not mutually exclusive. The first five are in fact functions already assumed by United Nations Forces: the remaining categories, 6–9, are functions which may be anticipated in the future.

1. *Ceasefire, truce and armistice functions entrusted to "observer" groups*

After a cessation of hostilities has been agreed upon in principle, there frequently remains the problem of sufficiently guaranteeing the good faith of all the parties concerned in order that a ceasefire may be implemented. Further, there may be genuine technical difficulties in securing a ceasefire. The practice which has been summarised in Chapter 4[7] has shown that a United Nations Force can fulfil these functions most effectively. This role is to be sharply distinguished from enforcement action by United Nations Forces, even where it is assumed under Chapter VII of the Charter rather than Chapter VI. Even where the observer group is unarmed, there may be situations in which there is a need for a United Nations Force of some kind to afford to the observers a minimum of protection in the execution of their duties. The proposals of Trygve Lie, as Secretary-General, for a "United Nations Guard Force" had precisely this kind of function in mind.[8]

There is little doubt that, once a ceasefire has been agreed upon, comparatively small United Nations Forces are singularly well suited to aiding in its implementation, and they could perform this role in many possible future situations. The recent examples of UNTEA[9] and the Group in the Yemen[10] show an adaptation of this role to the task of supervising the implementation by States of a "disengagement" agreement where, as also in the cases of the Group in Indonesia and of UNTSO in Palestine, military forces are to be withdrawn by agreement. The role may even include the supervision of the exchange of prisoners of war.

---

[7] *Ante*, pp. 73–78.
[8] *Ante*, pp. 18–20.
[9] *Ante*, pp. 255–258. The 21-member team—which was "para-military" in nature though not a fighting force—covered West Irian by aircraft, dropping pamphlets to inform troops in the bush of the end of hostilities. It also looked after the repatriation of prisoners, re-supplied Indonesian forces with non-military materials, and formed a military liaison team comprising Indonesian, Netherlands and United Nations members: see UN Press Release WNG/8, 28 August 1962.
[10] *Ante*, pp. 66, 74.

2. *Frontier control*

A United Nations Force can also usefully perform the function of frontier control,[11] thus helping to reduce the tension between two hostile States. Such a Force could be established by request of both parties—or of one party if it were to patrol solely that side of the border—where there existed a dispute as to illegal infiltration of the frontier. The Force could also be used for patrol of a frontier agreed upon in an armistice or ceasefire and to this extent this particular function would become a part of the broader functions referred to in the previous category; it was for this task that the Truce Supervision Commission was set up in 1948. Its task was to assist in supervising the implementation of Security Council Resolutions on a ceasefire in Palestine, and border patrol was inherent in this task. After the armistice agreements were signed between Israel and the Arab States, UNTSO became established as a subsidiary organ of the United Nations and assumed this task.

There are very many situations of international tension or hostility which do not involve an armistice, truce or ceasefire but yet in which one can envisage a useful border-patrolling role being played by the United Nations: UNOGIL is a case in point.[12] Such frontier control might involve the manning of entry points at the border and the checking of documents for legal movement across the border; it is, of course, conceivable that the United Nations could play such a role in Berlin at a future date.

3. *Interpositionary functions*

A United Nations Force could be used for interpositionary functions between two belligerents. Such a Force could be effective only if the vital interests of the two parties did not, in their own eyes, necessitate the continuation of hostilities irrespective of public opinion and diplomatic pressures. It would not be essential for the United Nations Force to be large enough to engage in a full-scale armed combat itself, against one or both of the parties. Rather its function would be one of insulation, or the provision of a " trip-wire." In these circumstances a Force of limited size and equipment would suffice. It is thought that in certain circumstances the mere presence of United Nations personnel and insignia would suffice as a barrier.[13]

An interposition Force could be used not only when the belligerents were still engaged in hostilities, provided it was clear that neither belligerent would attack the United Nations Force, so as to bring about a *de facto* separation and ceasefire, but also immediately after a truce or ceasefire has been agreed upon by the parties, in order to maintain the agreed separation between the former

[11] *Ante*, pp. 71–72.
[12] *Ante*, p. 65.
[13] For some views on the usefulness of interpositionary activities, see James, " UN Action for Peace," *World Today*, November and December 1962.

combatants. Interpositionary functions are thus sometimes carried out by Forces whose primary task is to secure a cessation of hostilities but whose task thereafter becomes one of maintaining the cessation. Thus border patrolling may also be considered part of the interposition function, so, to this extent, there would be an overlapping with the previous function. The United Nations Emergency Force, UNEF, was an interposition Force, and took over the responsibility previously held by UNTSO for the maintenance of order and for patrolling the Gaza Strip demarcation line.[14]

A Force with interposition functions could also be set up in an area of high tension, but where there had yet occurred no military hostilities. Its duties there would be preventive rather than restorative.

4. Defence and security of United Nations zones or areas placed under United Nations control

When the United Nations assumes control of a territory or a zone it may need an armed Force to provide defence and security and to maintain internal law and order. A United Nations Force established for these purposes will thus perform both the role of army and of police. There are several situations in which such a need can arise. In 1948 the General Assembly, in one of the many attempts to solve the Palestine problem, drew up a Plan of Partition for Palestine under which Jerusalem would become an international city. The Plan envisaged the formation of responsible Jewish and Arab militias, but it was noted that these would not have been formed by the time that the British withdrew upon the termination of the mandate. The Secretariat reported that there would be a need for an International Police Force, to keep public order and security. Moreover, in view of the particular situation, it was "obvious . . . that order and security are necessary not only for the implementation of the Plan but also generally for avoiding anarchy and chaos and for minimising bloodshed and to prevent breach of international peace." [15] This is true of almost any situation that can be envisaged in which the United Nations assumes territorial responsibilities, including, though perhaps to a lesser degree, the designation of the United Nations as an Administering Authority for its own trusteeship territory. In the case of Jerusalem it would have been—had not the Plan proved abortive—essential to maintain free communications and

---

[14] See generally *ante*, Chap. 5.
[15] See Working Paper by the Secretariat, UN Doc.A/AC.21/13, pp. 7 and 10. The Secretary-General referred also to the situation in which the Security Council did not find that there existed a threat to international peace and security but nevertheless wished to establish a Force, saying that "an international armed Force set up on this basis . . . would not be one in the sense of Chapter VII of the Charter. It would have the character of an international police force for the maintenance of law and order in a territory for which the international society is still responsible" (*ibid.*, pp. 8-11).

to protect Holy Places and religious buildings. The International Police Force was to perform these functions.

Further, and this time practical, proof of the need for a Force to perform these functions in a zone controlled by the United Nations has been given in the settlement of the West Irian dispute. West Irian (West New Guinea), having for some years been a territory disputed between the Netherlands and Indonesia, was finally placed under the temporary administration of the United Nations under the Agreement of August 1962, and a United Nations Security Force was established as part of the United Nations Administration (UNTEA).[16]

It is possible to envisage many situations in which the administration of disputed territory is transferred temporarily to the United Nations, and UNTEA has clearly indicated the useful functions which a United Nations Force can play in these circumstances. The possibility of the United Nations assuming control over Berlin, with its own United Nations Security Force, is one which is frequently referred to.

5. The maintenance of law and order in a State

The precedent of the Congo has shown that the United Nations may be willing to establish a Force not only to assist in bringing about the withdrawal of foreign forces, but also to aid in the maintenance or restoration of public order in a State, at that State's request, and where the breakdown in law and order has been caused by or resulted in the intervention of foreign forces, and where the situation constitutes a threat to international peace. Even then, ONUC was not regarded as in any way a substitute for the police or militia forces of the Republic of the Congo and never assumed the function of enforcing municipal law as such. On the contrary, paragraph 43 (a) of the Agreement of 27 November 1961 between the United Nations and the Congo provided expressly that ONUC " shall not apply domestic regulations and procedures, but shall act in accordance with its interpretation of the mission assigned to it by the Security Council." [17] There was, therefore, a distinction (albeit a difficult one) between the mandate to assist in the restoration and maintenance of law and order and a mandate to enforce Congolese law : the first refers to " law and order " in the quite general sense of stability—hence concentrating on the protection of life and property from arbitrary violence from any source—and was ultimately linked with the function of preventing civil war, whereas the latter would have required ONUC to act as the executive arm of the Government to enforce Congolese law in toto.

Perhaps the only situations in which a United Nations Force can properly assume the function of maintaining internal law and order in the strict sense in which local police or militia forces do so is

[16] Ante, Chap. 7.
[17] See ante, pp. 193, 239.

where, as with UNTEA,[18] the United Nations itself becomes the effective administration for the territory or, possibly, where a United Nations Force is sent into a territory devastated by a natural disaster.[19]

The other, and distinct, problem which the Congo operations suggest is whether or not the United Nations may assume the function of maintaining law and order in a State where the breakdown of law and order is neither caused by, nor likely to occasion, foreign intervention. In such a situation it would be difficult for a United Nations organ to make any finding that there existed a threat to *international* peace: the situation would, unlike the Congo, be one affecting *internal* peace. Apart from situations like the UNTEA situation, referred to in the preceding paragraph, it is believed that the United Nations may not assume this function, at least by means of a United Nations Force. If the breakdown in law and order was caused merely through anarchist rioting and ill-discipline, the response of the United Nations could possibly be in the nature of technical assistance, albeit of a military and police nature.[20] But this would be confined to military advisers and the like, such as experts on police organisation: it is inconceivable that a United Nations military Force could be despatched in the guise of "technical assistance." If, however, the breakdown was caused by the actions of rebel groups aiming at the overthrow of the government, then the United Nations would be certainly ill-advised and perhaps acting illegally in sending a Force for their suppression.[21] It is not a proper function of the United Nations to offer Forces to maintain one particular government in power and, indeed, such action runs directly counter to the right of self-determination. It is far from certain that a government is at liberty to aid another government in the suppression of a rebellion, certainly if no external intervention is involved.[22] This may be true even where the rebellion has not yet assumed the proportions which entitle the rebels to the rights of belligerency and brings into operation the rule of non-intervention by third parties; the reason being that if any government feels compelled to resort to foreign aid in these circumstances, then almost by definition the rebellion *has*

---

[18] *Ante*, p. 257.

[19] *Post*, p. 273.

[20] The technical assistance aspect was mentioned in the case of ONUC, in the first Resolution (S/4387), but in practice was regarded as being relevant to the civilian operations or to the assistance in reorganising the ANC. There was, of course, the possibility that the UN could have given technical assistance in the form of assistance in the training of the ANC, but this was, in the event, refused due to the Congolese Government's desire to arrange for this on a bilateral basis with Member States and thus exclude the UN from exclusive control of the assistance: see *ante*, p. 174.

[21] For discussion of the principle of non-intervention in the Congo see *ante*, p. 196, and, more generally, *post*, Chap. 12.

[22] For a recent, and thorough, examination of the views of writers and of State practice on this question see Brownlie, *International Law and the Use of Force by States* (1963) pp. 321–327.

assumed belligerent proportions.[23]   It therefore behoves the United Nations even more *not* to establish a Force with these functions.

6. *Plebiscite supervision*

The United Nations may recommend a plebiscite to determine the status of a territory disputed between two sovereign States, or for the purpose of deciding the future of a dependent territory prior to its independence.   In such a case the assistance of the United Nations may well be required to organise and administer the plebiscite[24]; and although this requires expert civilian personnel, a small United Nations Force could also play a useful role by the maintenance of order and the distribution of information and instructions to the inhabitants of the territory.   The desirability of an international United Nations Force to assist the civil side of plebiscite administration will, of course, depend upon the extent to which serious internal disorders—or even the threat of intervention by foreign elements—can be anticipated.   However, sufficient has been said on plebiscite functions in the first Chapter of this study[25] to warrant the assertion that, whilst no United Nations Force has yet assumed such functions, they must be regarded as functions eminently suitable for a United Nations Force.

7. *Assistance and relief for national disasters*

The United Nations and its specialised agencies have a special and vital concern with social and humanitarian problems, and are frequently called upon to provide relief and aid of various sorts to countries and peoples suffering from the effects of floods, famine, epidemics and war itself.   While it is usually civilian experts of the United Nations and specialised agencies who respond to these disasters, it may in some circumstances be appropriate for a United Nations Force to fulfil these functions.   The existence of panic and disorder as a result of these calamities might prove a case in point.

[23] However, where there has been foreign intervention, it may be that a government can legally call for the aid of an ally in suppressing the rebellion, even if that rebellion has reached the dimensions of a civil war. For a fuller discussion of these questions see E. Lauterpacht, " Intervention by Invitation," (1958) 7 I.C.L.Q., 99; and Higgins "Legal Limits to the Use of Force by Sovereign States—United Nations Practice," (1961) 37 B.Y.I.L. 308–311.

[24] See, for example, the plebiscite in Togoland under British administration in 1955: UN Doc.A/3173 and Add. 1, and T/1269 and Add. 1; the United Nations has also helped in the organisation of two plebiscites in the Northern Cameroons and two plebiscites in the Southern Cameroons: see General Assembly Resolutions 1350 (XIII), 1352 (XIV) and 1473 (XIV). It played a similar role in Western Samoa: General Assembly Resolution 1569 (XV). In each case the plebiscite was organised by the administering authority, " in consultation with and under the supervision of" the UN Plebiscite Commissioner. For a very interesting memorandum on plebiscites held under the supervision of international organisations, see A/C.4/351, 26 February 1957.

[25] *Ante,* pp. 7–11.

The United Nations Force would in such a situation be performing functions similar to those of a national armed force responding to a national disaster—distribution of medical aid, food and water, reopening of communications, the maintenance of order and enforcement of quarantine precautions, and so forth.

8. *Prevention of international crimes*

Certain crimes are so universally recognised—either by custom,[26] or by treaty,[27] or by common affirmation [28]—that it has been thought possible to establish an international Force for their prevention and control. Traffic in slavery and narcotics, piracy and genocide are all examples which come readily to mind. In the immediate post-war era attempts were made to build on the Nuremberg precedent by establishing a court with international criminal jurisdiction.[29] It was thought that a United Nations Force could in effect act as a police force in relation to those generally acknowledged international crimes. In the event the hopes of an international criminal court have proved abortive; and it is difficult to see how a Force could usefully be employed for these functions except as an arm of such a judicial body. This particular function is one which may only be realised by a United Nations Force when States are prepared to envisage the United Nations as a body capable of assuming "supra-national" authority, yet it merits both mention and attention. In the United Kingdom the Parliamentary Group for World Government has made detailed proposals for the establishment of a Force with precisely this function.

9. *Disarmament functions*

These functions are to be envisaged in the distant, long-term future when a treaty on complete and general disarmament is agreed upon. They are therefore more appropriately dealt with in Part Three of the present study, and not this Part which is concerned with the immediate, short-term future prior to general disarmament.

III. CONSTITUTIONAL BASES

1. *The functions of the Security Council*

The functions of the Security Council are described in Articles 24–26 of the Charter, while the specific powers at its disposal for the

---

[26] For example, piracy.
[27] Such as the Genocide Convention, and the many conventions on the control of illicit trade in narcotics.
[28] See the affirmation in General Assembly Resolution 95 (1) of the Nuremberg principles, and the Draft Code of Offences Against Peace and Security of Mankind which includes the crime of "terrorism" in addition to genocide, (1955) 49 A.J.I.L., Spec. Suppl. 19.
[29] Kuhn, "International Criminal Jurisdiction" (1947) 41 A.J.I.L. 430; and note by Liang (1949) 43 A.J.I.L. 479; and Roling, "On Aggression, on International Criminal Law, on International Criminal Jurisdiction" (1955) 2 Ned. Tijd. Int. Recht. 167.

discharge of these functions are laid down in Chapters VI, VII, VIII and XII. The Security Council is given primary responsibility for the maintenance of international peace and security (Article 24 (1)) and, towards that end, bears responsibility for formulating, with the assistance of a Military Staff Committee, plans to be submitted to United Nations Members for the regulation of armaments (Article 26).

Chapter VI of the Charter provides for functions of the Security Council relating to the pacific settlement of disputes the continuation of which is likely to endanger international peace and security. It has been seen in Chapter 4 on United Nations observer groups that certain of these groups, notably UNOGIL, and possibly the Group in the Yemen, may be regarded as having been established under Chapter VI rather than Chapter VII of the Charter.[30] Moreover, the view has been expressed earlier [31] that whether the group is regarded as an organ for purposes of investigation under Article 34 or for wider purposes of assisting in Security Council action under Chapter VI is of little relevance to the authority of the Council to establish such a group: Article 34 is a specific illustration of the very wide powers of the Council under Chapter VI which the Council can fulfil by means of a subsidiary organ established under Article 29. In both cases the vote to assume the *functions* should be non-procedural, even though the vote to establish the subsidiary organ under Article 29 may perhaps be regarded as procedural. The essential distinction between the Council acting under Chapter VI and Chapter VII is, it is believed, that in the former case the action of the Council will be recommendatory rather than mandatory.

Chapter VII of the Charter—entitled " Action with Respect to Threats to the Peace, Breaches of the Peace, and Acts of Aggression " —provides the means for the fulfilment of the Security Council's functions other than those under Chapter VI relating to the pacific settlement of disputes. Under Article 39, that organ " shall determine the existence of any threat to the peace, breach of the peace, or act of aggression and shall make recommendations, or decide what measures shall be taken in accordance with Articles 41 and 42, to maintain or restore international peace and security." Article 41 authorises the Security Council to decide upon the use of measures short of armed force, including " complete or partial interruption of economic relations and of rail, sea, air, postal, telegraphic, radio, and

---

[30] *Ante,* pp. 65–68. In relation to UNOGIL the precise Charter authority for its establishment was never clearly stated, even by Sweden, the sponsoring State (UN Doc. S/4023), or by the Secretary-General in his First Report (UN Doc. S/4029). Only the Panamanian delegate referred to UNOGIL as a subsidiary organ of the Security Council under Article 29. He denied that it could be set up under Article 34 of the Charter, for that refers to the investigation of a dispute, which in turn implies an examination of the causes of a situation; UNOGIL, however, was limited to observation of the current situation. It was therefore to be regarded, thought the Panamanian representative, as " similar in character to the Peace Observation Commission, established by the ' Uniting for Peace Resolution.' " *Off.Rec.S.C.,* 13th yr., 825th Mtg.

[31] *Ante,* p. 66.

other means of communication, and the severance of diplomatic relations." Article 42 goes further, and permits such military action "by air, sea, or land forces as may be necessary to maintain or restore international peace and security."

From the wording of Article 39 it is possible that the Security Council could make recommendations for the establishment of a United Nations Force, without further deciding upon measures under Articles 41 and 42. While the Resolutions by which the Korea Force was established referred to no specific Charter authority, they all determined the existence of a breach of the peace and made recommendations for the use of force.[32] It is therefore reasonable to suppose that there was an implied finding under Article 39, and a recommendation thereunder that Member States furnish assistance voluntarily.[33] The United Kingdom delegate was among those who believed that Article 39, standing on its own, was sufficient basis for the establishment of a Force to restore international peace and security.[34]

This interpretation of the powers inherent in Article 39 is of especial significance in the light of a body of opinion which regards action under Article 42 as having been made impossible by the failure to implement Article 43. Article 43 had envisaged the conclusion of agreements between the Security Council and other United Nations Members for the provision of national armed forces to be made available to the Security Council; it is well known that these hopes have proved abortive.[35] The position is taken by the Soviet Union and other Communist States that the result of the non-implementation of Article 43 is an inability on the part of the Security Council to establish a United Nations Force, on the grounds that Articles 42 and 43 are essentially related[36]; moreover, the ability

[32] UN Docs. S/1501, Resolution of 25 June 1950; S/1511, Resolution of 27 June 1950; and S/1588, Resolution of 7 July 1950. These Resolutions also referred to an "armed attack," thus pointing to Article 51: on this aspect, see *post*, pp. 302–303.

[33] See *ante*, Chap. 3, pp. 32–36. It is argued by some that this caused the Korean action to be undertaken by States, and not by the United Nations itself, and that the delegation of the Unified Command to the United States confirms this view. On this controversy see Frankenstein, *L'Organisation des Nations Unies devant le Conflit Coréen* (1952), and Goodrich, "Korea: Collective Measures against Aggression," *International Conciliation*, 1953, No. 494. After the establishment of the Force in Korea by the Security Council, the day-to-day consideration of the Korean question switched to the General Assembly, due to the return of the previously absent Soviet delegate to the former organ and a resultant loss of unanimity among the Permanent Members. The Unified Command continued to act on behalf of the Security Council, however.

[34] *Off.Rec.S.C.*, 5th yr., 476th Mtg., pp. 3–4.

[35] See *ante*, Chap. 2, pp. 12–18: and see Goodrich and Simons, *The United Nations and the Maintenance of International Peace and Security* (1955), pp. 398–405; and Blaisdell, "Arms for the United Nations," 1 *Dept. of State Documents and State Papers* (1948), pp. 141–158.

[36] For the latest reaffirmation of this view by the Soviet representative see the Conference of the Eighteen-Nation Committee on Disarmament in 1962. ENDC/P.V. 55, at pp. 55–56. Occasional lapses in consistency may be seen, however: thus in 1956 the Soviet Union urged that "in accordance

of the Council to establish a United Nations Force by recommendation under Article 39 is denied. Several other States, while rejecting
the restrictive Soviet interpretation of Article 39, share its views
about the mutual dependency of Articles 42 and 43.[37]

While the wording of Article 39 does not seem to necessitate that
recommendations thereunder refer to Articles 41 or 42 it equally
seems untenable to argue that Article 42 can only be applied on the
basis of agreements concluded under Article 43. The wording of
Article 42 is broad, leaving open both the method of recruiting the
Forces and the precise nature of their command.[38] The absence of
agreements under Article 43 merely ensures that States cannot be
compelled to contribute to United Nations action under Article 42;
but action under Article 42 may be recommended by the Security
Council, pursuant to a finding under Article 39.[39] Some evidence to
the contrary is perhaps presented by Article 106 of the Charter,
which stipulates that " pending the coming into force " of the special
arrangements in Article 43, the parties to the Four-Power Declaration
of 1943 and France shall consult together " with a view to such joint
action on behalf of the Organisation as may be necessary for the
purpose of maintaining international peace and security." It is,
however, generally accepted that Article 106 was intended to be of a
temporary nature, and that the failure to implement Article 43
cannot be said to have extended indefinitely its application.[40]

It can, therefore, be seen that a United Nations Force may be
established by a recommendation under Article 39 *simpliciter*, or by
a recommendation under Article 39 referring to Article 42.[41] It is

with Article 42 . . . all States Members of the United Nations . . .
should give military aid and other assistance to the Republic of Egypt."
See *Repertory of Practice of the Security Council*, Suppl. 1956-8, p. 172,
and Seyersted, " United Nations Forces, some legal problems" (1961), 37
B.Y.I.L. at p. 439. Nor did the Soviet Union object to the Security Council
Resolution under which ONUC was established; while it was true that
ONUC was not set up under Article 42, it nonetheless was set up outside
the framework of Article 43. UN Docs. S/4387 and *Certain Expenses of the
United Nations, I.C.J. Pleadings*, 1962, p. 270; and see *ante*, pp. 175-180.

[37] *Off.Rec.S.C.*, 5th yr., 476th Mtg., p. 4.

[38] Sohn has correctly observed that only the use of national contingents
depends on the prior conclusion of special agreements under Article 43.
"The Authority of the United Nations to Establish and Maintain a
Permanent Force" (1958), 52 A.J.I.L. 230. All that can be inferred from
Article 43 is that national contingents cannot be compelled to fight on
behalf of the United Nations without Special Agreements being concluded;
but their services under Article 42 could be offered by Member States in
response to a recommendation under Article 39. To this effect also, see
Seyersted, *op. cit.*, at p. 439.

[39] Article 42 nowhere stipulates that the forces there used are only to be
those provided by arrangements made under Article 43. See *I.C.J. Pleadings, Certain Expenses of the UN*, Statement of Mr. Chayes (U.S.A.),
p. 423.

[40] See Halderman, " Legal basis for United Nations Armed Forces" (1962), 56
A.J.I.L. at p. 985.

[41] Halderman has pointed out that the power of "recommendation" has
both a substantive and a procedural aspect; the Security Council may
"recommend" under Article 39 that certain measures be carried out (as
was the probable basis for action in Korea), or, once collective measures

further arguable that a *decision* could be made under Article 39 to set up a Force under Article 42 by means of direct individual recruitment, and that this would not violate Article 43. The political practicality of this last constitutional method is, of course, a separate matter. The establishment of a Force under Article 42, subsequent to a finding under Article 39, would point to a Force of a decidedly military nature. However, contrary to common belief, nothing in the text of Article 42 necessitates that the action which it authorises should constitute "sanctions" against a State; all that is required is that military measures be adopted to maintain or restore international peace and security. In other words, the establishment of a United Nations military unit under Article 42 does not necessarily depend upon an intention to combat a named "aggressor." Because of this broad wording, it has been argued by some writers that the United Nations Force in the Congo, certainly once it became actively engaged in military action, was operating under Article 42.[42] However, the use of force permitted to ONUC in the Congo was for the purpose of maintaining internal law and order, thus enabling Belgian troops to be withdrawn and removing the threat to international peace.[43] Moreover, while Article 42 does not strictly require that military action be directed against a specifically designated government or authority, the *travaux préparatoires* certainly indicate that this was what was intended and expected.[44] The undoubtedly deliberate refusal of the Security Council to classify ONUC as a measure under Article 42 [45] supports the view that on this occasion the constitutional basis was to be looked for elsewhere. The initial limitation of the use of force permitted to ONUC to that of self-defence, and the continuous regard paid by the United Nations to the principle of non-intervention in Congolese sovereignty or domestic affairs confirm that there was no intention of taking measures under Article 42.[46] This view is upheld both by the Resolutions of the Security Council and by the agreement between the Government of the Congo Republic and the United Nations covering the presence and functions of ONUC in that country.[47]

Whereas the use of force permitted to ONUC was originally strictly limited to cases of self-defence, it must be admitted both that "self-defence" has been widely interpreted to include freedom of

have been decided upon, the procedure may be adopted of using recommendations to carry them out. *Ibid.*, p. 987. The ability of the Security Council to decide upon "collective measures" when Article 43 has not been implemented is another question, and one to which we shall return later; *post*, p. 311.

[42] See *ante*, p. 176.

[43] On this question, in some detail, see Schachter, "Legal Aspects of the United Nations Action in the Congo" (1961), 55 A.J.I.L. 7–8; and see the detailed description of the mandate of ONUC in Chap. 6, *ante*, pp. 186–196.

[44] 12 UNCIO Docs. 334, and 580–581.

[45] *Ante*, p. 176.

[46] *Ante*, pp. 196–203.

[47] UN Doc. S/4389/Add. 5; *ante*, pp. 236–240.

movement and that the Resolutions of 21 February 1961 and 24 November 1961 go beyond even liberal interpretations of self-defence. The former Resolution provided for "all appropriate measures to prevent the occurrence of civil war in the Congo, including . . . the use of force, if necessary, in the last resort," and the latter clarified the scope of this provision by stipulating that a "requisite measure of force" may be employed, if necessary, to apprehend, detain and deport certain groups of foreign personnel and mercenaries. It nonetheless remains true that this particular employment of force as a last resort still falls short of, and is of a nature different from, military measures within the scope of Articles 42–46 of the Charter. The military action taken under these Resolutions did not:

"serve the purpose of enforcing decisions of the United Nations against national authorities which are internationally responsible for their conduct, but (served) the much more limited purposes of preserving law and order in the Republic of the Congo, of preventing civil war, and of apprehending certain groups of individuals whose activities were particularly prejudicial to the maintenance of law and order." [48]

A further possible constitutional basis for a United Nations Force is to be found in Article 41 of the Charter, which provides for the use of "measures not involving the use of armed force" in order that the Security Council may "give effect to its decisions." It may be argued that the Security Council is able to make a finding under Article 39 of a threat to the peace, breach of the peace, or act of aggression, and decide that an interposition Force should be established as a measure "not involving the use of armed force" in order to stabilise the situation. The right of such an interposition or "barrier" Force to use arms in self-defence would not change its essential non-military nature.[49] While Article 41, like Article 42, has generally been assumed to authorise enforcement measures, its wording also allows the view that other decisions to restore international peace, involving neither the use of armed force nor the employment of sanctions, may be taken under its authority.[50] It

[48] *Certain Expenses of the United Nations, I.C.J. Pleadings,* 1962, written statement of the Kingdom of Denmark, p. 161. The Court itself offered the opinion that the ONUC operation was not an enforcement action within Chapter VII of the Charter, and that therefore Article 43 had no applicability. *I.C.J. Reports,* 1962, p. 166.

[49] "The fact that the Force may use its weapons in self-defence affects its status as little as does a civilian's exercise of his right of self-defence under municipal law," Schwarzenberger, *Report on Problems of a UN Force, Int. Law Association, Hamburg Conference,* 1960, p. 7. He refers to seven different ways of establishing an "interposition" Force by the Security Council, but treats Arts. 41 and 48 with some reserve, relying more on Arts. 39, 40, 42 and 53.

[50] The technical assistance given to the Congo by the United Nations was thought of "as a means to strengthen the government of the country and to improve internal conditions and . . . these, in turn, would directly reduce the risk of external intervention. One might conceivably regard such measures as within the broad language of Article 41 . . ."; Schachter, (1961), 55 A.J.I.L. at p. 8. However, the civilian operations, though part of ONUC, were in a sense different from the UN Force.

may be observed that the Secretary-General has mentioned this Article in connection with the Congo operations,[51] though he did not consider it to be his sole, or even primary, constitutional authority in this case. Article 41 is, therefore, a possible basis for a United Nations Force with functions which do not comprise the use of armed force, such as an observer group or perhaps even an interposition Force.[52] However, this is clearly not the kind of measure which was contemplated as being appropriate to this Article at San Francisco, and it is unlikely that situations will arise in which Article 41 becomes the sole constitutional basis for a decision by the Security Council: Articles 39, 40 or 42 will generally be adequate enough without recourse to Article 41.

Article 40 of the Charter would seem to provide possible constitutional authority for a United Nations Force. It states:

" In order to prevent an aggravation of the situation, the Security Council may, before making the recommendations or deciding upon the measures provided for in Article 39, call upon the parties concerned to comply with such provisional measures as it deems necessary or desirable. . ."

The wording of this Article seems to envisage the employment of " provisional " measures which could require supervision or enforcement by military means; ceasefire orders, truces,[53] interim injunctions on the movement of persons and weapons, all afford examples. Once there has been a finding, express or implied, of a threat to the peace, breach of the peace, or act of aggression under Article 39, and a provisional measure of the sort indicated has been called for, there is no reason why a Force should not be set up by the Security Council to supervise the truce or ceasefire.[54] Indeed, as Chapter 4 has shown, most of the United Nations observer groups to date may be regarded as based on Article 40. This same Article also affords a partial, but not complete, basis for the establishment of ONUC since ONUC may be regarded as a subsidiary organ established in part to supervise and assist in the implementation of provisional measures ordered under Article 40.[55]

Further, it is arguable that the establishment and employment of an interposition Force could of itself constitute a provisional measure under Article 40; in other words, although a finding under Article 39 is required, it is not necessary that a ceasefire or a truce or any similar measure should have been called for before Article 40 can sustain a Force. Indeed, if there is merely a threat to the peace, such measures might well be inappropriate. However, this involves a certain distortion of the language of the Article, which speaks of

[51] *Off.Rec.S.C.*, 15th yr., 884th Mtg., para. 26.
[52] Supporting this view see Sohn, " The authority of the United Nations to Establish and Maintain a permanent Force " (1958), 52 A.J.I.L. 230.
[53] For the distinction between these various forms of provisional measures, see Stone, *Legal Controls of International Conflict* (1954), pp. 643–647, and *ante*, p. 73.
[54] Sohn, *loc. cit.*, p. 230.
[55] *Ante*, pp. 175–180.

a " call upon the parties," and it is difficult to see how a decision by the Council to establish a Force is a " call upon the parties." In general, one would expect to find a separate call for provisional measures, addressed to the parties by the Council, and the establishment of a Force would be linked with this .in the form of a decision under Article 29 to establish a subsidiary organ to assume functions directly related to the action of the Council under Article 40 : but it could not in itself be strictly a " measure " under Article 40.

It will be noted that Article 40 authorises the Security Council to " call upon " Members to comply with provisional measures and the question therefore arises of how far the " call " imposes legal obligations on Members to comply with that call. Generally speaking, it is to be expected that Article 40 would be brought into operation in cases of threats to the peace or breaches of the peace; it is difficult to envisage it being an appropriate measure where there has been a clear finding of aggression—though a State may be called upon to cease fire, and its refusal to obey such a call may well provide further, and final, evidence of its aggressive intent. In such a case the call of the Security Council for provisional action would seem properly to constitute " preventive action " within the terms of Article 2 (5), and Members would be required to " refrain from giving assistance to any State against which the United Nations is taking preventive . . . action." This pattern was followed in the cease fire Resolution of 25 June 1950,[56] in the Korean conflict.

If Article 40 is used to indicate provisional measures and to establish a Force to supervise or assist in the implementation of these measures, is the term " call upon " to be characterised as mandatory? Kelsen has contended that the Security Council always has the option of making the " call " under Article 40 a simple recommendation or a legally binding decision, for in language it falls between " recommendations " of Chapter VI and " deciding on measures " in Chapter VII.[57] However, Article 40 is part of Chapter VII, and there seems no reason why action taken under it should not be binding if the Council so intends.[58] The stipulation in the last sentence of the Article that : " The Security Council shall duly take account of failure to comply with such provisional measures " seems to confirm this view.[59] In the Congo operations the Secretary-General and the Security Council adopted the position that the calls under Article 40

---

[56] UN Doc.S/1501. See *ante*, pp. 30–31, and also Stone, *op. cit.*, at p. 233.
[57] Kelsen, *The Law of the United Nations* (1950), at p. 740.
[58] To same effect, Stone, *Legal Controls of International Conflict*, at p. 220. He correctly observes that the term " call " as used in Articles 43 and 44, however, commands less than mandatory force " since by the very terms of those Articles the ' call ' there imposes no obligation except on a particular Member who has entered into a special agreement to make forces available." *Ibid.*
[59] On this point, and for a most useful discussion of Article 40 generally, see Schachter, " Legal Aspects of United Nations Action in the Congo ' (1961), 55 A.J.I.L. 1, at p. 6.

were mandatory and directly invoked the application of Articles 25 and 49 of the Charter.[60]

The opinion that the United Nations action in the Congo finds its basis in Article 40 is supported by the emphasis placed upon non-interference in the internal affairs of that country. This non-interference comprised the refusal to adjudicate between contending factions claiming to represent the Congo, and between varying interpretations of the *Loi Fondémentale*.[61] It did not mean, however, that no action was to be taken against the foreign support for Katangese secession.[62] Significantly, the first Resolution on the Congo to be passed after the death of Hammarskjoeld went so far as to declare the secession to be illegal *per se*, being contrary to the *Loi Fondémentale*. This departure from the previous position taken by the United Nations—that the ONUC's mandate in Katanga rested essentially on the foreign, mercenary support for Mr. Tshombé, and not a contravention of a domestic constitution—is to be regretted.[63] Be that as it may, the repeated statements by both the late Secretary-General and Members of the Security Council concerning the necessity of respect for the sovereignty of the Congo [64] tend to indicate that action was based on Article 40.

Whilst the adherence to a principle of non-intervention may certainly be regarded as evidence that the constitutional basis of the Force is Article 40 rather than Article 42, it is believed that there is a very real danger of conclusions being drawn from the wording of Article 2 (7) which are unwarranted. This is a matter more fully dealt with in section III of Chapter 12, but certain observations may be made at this juncture. In the first place, even where the action taken is undoubtedly "enforcement action" against an aggressor State, the non-applicability of the domestic jurisdiction clause to United Nations action can never be absolute, for United Nations action is always limited by the purposes and principles of the Charter. To give an example, United Nations action against an aggressor State could certainly comprise, without any possibility of objection on the basis of a plea of "domestic" jurisdiction, the invasion of its territory or the sequestration of its national banks and funds. But it is doubtful whether the United Nations could

---

[60] *Ante*, pp. 156–157, 225.
[61] See Security Council Resolution S/4426, and First Report of the Secretary-General on ONUC, UN Doc.S/4389; also S/4791, para. 25. For a fuller discussion of the principle of non-intervention, see *ante*, pp. 196–200.
[62] Security Council Resolutions S/4741 and S/5002.
[63] Seyersted seeks to explain this by suggesting that after the establishment of a new constitutional Government in the Congo in August 1961, the United Nations felt entitled to guarantee that it would direct no military action against any "offensive police operation" undertaken by that Government, 1961, 37 B.Y.I.L. at pp. 401–402. This falls considerably short, however, of volunteering the view that secession is contrary to the *Loi Fondémentale*.
[64] *e.g., Off.Rec.S.C.*, 15th yr., 886th Mtg., paras. 42–44, 70–71, 80; 887th Mtg., para. 44; 889th Mtg., para. 114; 913rd Mtg., paras. 17, 31; and 915th Mtg., para. 22.

nationalise its railways, once in occupation of its territory, or even dictate to the inhabitants which political party they shall return to power on the withdrawal of United Nations control over the territory. Such matters are, in a sense, still "domestic jurisdiction" or, perhaps more properly, matters outside the scope of the purposes for which United Nations action was taken.

In the second place, even where action is undoubtedly under Article 40,[65] since the whole of Chapter VII is predicated upon the assumption that there exists a threat to or breach of *international* peace, the situation cannot be realistically described as one of "domestic jurisdiction." Hence, as has already been suggested,[66] the Security Council's adherence to the principle of non-intervention during the Congo operations, on the assumption that because ONUC was not "enforcement action" it was therefore bound by Article 2 (7), was unnecessarily rigid and absolute—and indeed had to be departed from in practice. The difference between action under Articles 40 and 42 is, in this respect, a difference of degree, for the difference in the aims and purposes of the action will alone give an indication of which matters are necessarily connected with the successful fulfilment of the purposes of the United Nations action and which are not: the former will not be protected by the "domestic jurisdiction" limitation, the latter will.

We may conclude, therefore, that the establishment of a United Nations Force might well be based on Article 40 in the sense that it is established as a subsidiary organ of the Security Council for purposes which either include, or are even confined to, the super-vision of (and assistance in the compliance by parties with) provi-sional measures addressed to them by the Council under Article 40. Moreover, when the Council indicates that its measures are manda-tory, these "calls" will be tantamount to decisions of the Council to which Articles 2 (5), 25 and 49 will apply; thus all Member States, and even non-Members, will be under duties of action to promote (and not impede) the operations of the Force.[67]

This being said, it must be observed that the occasions on which *specific* reliance on Article 40 is to be found are few.[68] In the most

---

[65] It may perhaps be argued that as action under Article 40 may be taken pursuant to a finding of aggression, as well as a finding of a threat to the peace or breach of the peace, such action would in these circumstances constitute a "sanction," and in consequence would not be subject to Article 2 (7). (This seems to be the position taken by Kelsen, *The Law of the United Nations*, at p. 757; cf. Schachter (1961), 55 A.J.I.L. at p. 5.) However, the clause of Article 40 which clearly states that "such pro-visional measures shall be without prejudice to the rights, claims or position of the parties concerned" must be taken to apply to *all* pro-visional measures, even if they are aimed at checking aggression. The legislative history of this Article at San Francisco supports this view. (UNCIO Docs. 505, 6, 7, 8, 580).

[66] *Ante*, p. 198.

[67] *Ante*, pp. 224–230, for a survey of the obligations imposed on States relative to the operations of ONUC.

[68] *Ante*, Chap. 4, p. 61.

controversial case so far, that of the Congo, no specific finding to this effect was ever made by the Council, and we have previously indicated [69] that it affords only a partial basis for the ONUC operations. Moreover, the International Court of Justice, in its advisory opinion on *Certain Expenses of the United Nations*, failed to give support to the view that ONUC's constitutional basis is to be found in Article 40. The Court decided that the constitutional basis of either UNEF or ONUC was, strictly speaking, not a matter essential to the opinion required in the case; however, it did offer the general view, *obiter*, that the Resolutions on ONUC fell within Chapter VII of the Charter, though they certainly did not constitute enforcement measures.[70] The Court did *not* continue by deducing that ONUC thus fell within the scope of Article 40, but left the point open, preferring to emphasise the consent which had been given to the operation by the Congo Government and the right of the Security Council, under Chapter VII, " to police a situation even though it does not resort to enforcement action against a State." [71] No specific basis for this right was cited. Judge Koretsky, in his dissenting opinion, denied the possible applicability of Article 40, insisting that it is "closely connected with Articles 41 and 42 of the Charter through Article 39," and thus subject to agreement under Article 43.[72]

Article 48, paragraph 1, of the Charter states that "The action required to carry out the decisions of the Security Council for the maintenance of international peace and security shall be taken by all the Members of the United Nations or by some of them, as the Security Council may determine." Does this provide a separate constitutional basis for the establishment of a United Nations Force? It seems very doubtful that it does, for the Security Council decisions for the maintenance of peace, to which this Article refers, must be taken under some other authority in the Charter; and Article 48 (1) merely regulates the nature and extent of the participation in the decision already taken. In other words, Article 48 (1) could regulate the implementation of a decision for a United Nations Force, but not provide the actual basis for its establishment.

This view has been taken by the Soviet Government in connection with its refusal to contribute its assessed proportion towards the

---

[69] *Ante*, pp. 178–180.
[70] *I.C.J. Reports*, 1962, p. 166. Cf. the position taken by dissenting Judge Quintana, that "any use of armed force intended for whatever purpose implies by definition enforcement action" and that "when there have been dead and wounded, bombardments on both sides, when civilian populations have paid the price, when a ceasefire and other military agreements have been negotiated between two belligerent groups, it is not easy (to evade the conclusion that this constitutes) enforcement action . . . ." *ibid.*, p. 246. Parentheses added.
[71] *Ibid.*, p. 167.
[72] *Ibid.*, p. 275. Judge Koretsky offered the caustic comment that the only reason the Secretary-General could have had for relying on Article 40 was that "This provision had apparently been suggested to their chief by his legal advisers, who had in mind what had been said in literature or what they themselves had published."

expenses of ONUC. It has taken the position that the Resolution of 13 July 1960 establishing ONUC was valid; but that it was implemented illegally because, *inter alia*, Article 48 (1) stipulates that the Security Council, and not the Secretary-General, should determine the list of States to participate in ONUC.[73] It is possible to reject this particular interpretation of Article 48 (1) (and this is a point to which we shall return later [74]) while accepting the premise upon which it is based—namely, that this particular provision can provide no separate title giving authority to establish a Force. The Soviet Union further offered the view that the "decisions" referred to in Article 48 may only be implemented on the basis of special agreements concluded under Article 43. It is therefore easy to see why it regarded Article 48 as illegally applied in the case of ONUC; what is less easy to see is on what basis that Government ever regarded the establishment of ONUC by Resolution S/4387 as legal. It is the Soviet position that Articles 39, 42, 43 and 48 are essentially related, and that only the Security Council may recommend or decide upon the use of force by the United Nations; this being so, it seems spurious to assert that the establishment of the Force—even at the request of the Congolese Government—was legal, and that the operation then became illegal by reason of the failure to carry it out by means of agreements under Article 43. Neither in the Security Council nor before the International Court of Justice has the Soviet Union explained the legal basis for its vote in favour of the Resolution establishing ONUC.

Some authority for the establishment of a United Nations Force may also be found in Article 29 of the Charter, which provides that "The Security Council may establish such subsidiary organs as it deems necessary for the performance of its functions." While this Article cannot *per se* support an armed Force, provided the requisite authority is to be found within Chapters VI or VII of the Charter, the Force may be set up and operated as a subsidiary organ of the Security Council.[75]

2. *Functions of the General Assembly : The Charter provisions*

There are several provisions in the Charter which would seem to authorise the General Assembly to establish a United Nations Force in certain circumstances. Under the terms of Article 10 the General Assembly "may discuss any questions or any matters within the scope of the present Charter . . . and, except as provided in Article 12, may make recommendations to the Members of the United Nations or to the Security Council or to both . . ." The exception referred to in Article 12 provides that the Assembly shall not make recommendations on a dispute or situation "while the

---

[73] *Certain Expenses of the United Nations, I.C.J. Pleadings*, 1962, pp. 272 and 400.
[74] *Post*, p. 301.
[75] See *ante*, p. 178.

Security Council is exercising in respect of (that) dispute or situation the functions assigned to it in the present Charter." It will be noted that, even with this stipulation, the powers of the Assembly under Article 10 are very wide.

Article 11 (2) is also relevant [76]; this authorises the General Assembly to discuss any question relating to the maintenance of peace and security, and—again with the exception contained in Article 12—it may "make recommendations with regard to such question to the State or States concerned, to the Security Council, or to both." The final sentence of this paragraph stipulates that " Any such question on which action is necessary shall be referred to the Security Council by the General Assembly either before or after discussion."

A further basis for an interposition Force may be found in the broad wording of Article 14, which, subject to the provisions of Article 12, permits the Assembly to "recommend measures for the peaceful adjustment of any situation, regardless of origin, which it deems likely to impair the general welfare or friendly relations among nations, including situations resulting from a violation of the provisions of the present Charter setting forth the purposes and principles of the United Nations." The Purposes and Principles of the Charter are, of course, laid down in Articles 1 and 2, and include such basic and fundamental prohibitions as that of the threat or use of force in Article 2 (4).[77]

Moreover, Article 22 states that the General Assembly may " establish such organs as it deems necessary for the performance of its functions." It is perhaps arguable that Article 22 was intended to cover bodies such as committees or commissions, which would assist " the Assembly in its deliberative, quasi-legislative and investigatory functions." [78] However, a permissible view is that a dynamic interpretation of the Charter would permit Article 22 to sustain an interposition Force, for :

" once . . . it has been accepted that mediators or commissions, appointed by the Assembly to supervise a truce agreement or the observance of the Resolutions of the Assembly, might need additional personnel for the exercise of their functions, there seems to be no logical limit to the number of persons

---

[76] Article 11 (1) is relevant only in so far as it authorises the General Assembly to formulate *a priori* principles which might then be applied to a United Nations Force subsequently formed; it cannot provide the basis for a recommendation that Members make available to the United Nations a specified armed Force. Sohn, *op. cit.* (1958), 52 *A.J.I.L.* at p. 231. Article 11 (1) provides " The General Assembly may consider the general principles of co-operation in the maintenance of international peace and security, including the principles governing disarmament and the regulation of armaments, and may make recommendations with regard to such principles to the Members or to the Security Council or to both."

[77] Article 2 (4) says : " All Members shall refrain in their international relations from the threat or use of force against the territorial integrity or political independence of any State, or in any other manner inconsistent with the purposes of the United Nations."

[78] Sohn, *op. cit.* (1958) 52 A.J.I.L. at p. 234.

needed. Similarly, if military personnel are added to United Nations missions and guards are sent to defend the personnel and the property of such missions, it is difficult to draw the line between permitted and prohibited types of personnel. . ." [79]

There are grounds, however, for asserting that Article 22 cannot *per se* sustain the establishment of a United Nations Force: it is necessary in addition to show that the functions of the Force fall within the proper powers of the Assembly as indicated in Articles 10, 11 or 14. [80]

The United Nations Emergency Force was classified by the Secretary-General as a "subsidiary organ of the General Assembly," [81] and this position has found fairly general support. Bearing in mind that Article 22 is limited by the scope of the Assembly's functions as they are defined elsewhere in the Charter, a detailed examination of the Articles in question is called for. This in turn depends upon an analysis of the division of authority between the General Assembly and the Security Council.

Article 10 of the Charter, authorising the Assembly to make recommendations to Members on any matter within the scope of the Charter, is subject only to the limitation contained in Article 12. Provided that the Security Council is not exercising its functions in respect of the same dispute or matter, the General Assembly may recommend under Article 10 that Members support the formation of a Force. The power of the Assembly here being only recommendatory, Members would be under no compulsion to contribute contingents towards such a Force. It is possible to regard UNEF as a Force complying with these conditions, though perhaps its constitutional basis is more accurately to be found in other Articles.

Article 11 (2) raises questions of more complexity. The last sentence in this Article requires reference to the Security Council of

---

[79] *Ibid.*

[80] Stone, *Aggression and World Order*, p. 197, draws attention to a parallel situation caused by the establishment of the Administrative Tribunal of the United Nations under Article 22: the International Court found that the Assembly had authority to create this organ for the effective implementation of the provisions in Article 107 concerning regulations for United Nations staff. *Effect of Awards of Compensation made by the United Nations Administrative Tribunal, I.C.J. Reports*, 1954, p. 71. For confirmation that Article 22 cannot of itself give title to the establishment of a Force, see Kelsen, *The Law of the United Nations* (1950), pp. 391–392; and Andrassy, in *Report on Problems of a UN Force, Int. Law Association (Hamburg Conference* 1960), p. 8, n. 206.

[81] Introduction to the Regulations for the United Nations Emergency Force, UN Doc. A/3552; and Agreement between the United Nations and Egypt, 8 February 1957, UN Doc. A/3527, pp. 2 and 7. However, in the actual Regulations UNEF is referred to as "a subsidiary organ of the United Nations." Article 7 of the Charter refers to the establishment of subsidiary organs "in accordance with the present Charter." For support of the Secretary-General's view see Chapman, "UNEF—legal status" (1958–9) 57 Michigan L.R. 56; Chaumont, "La Situation Juridique des Etats Membres à l'Egard de la Force d'Urgence des Nations-Unies," (1958) 4 *Ann.Français de Droit International* 403; Poirier, *La Force Internationale d'Urgence* (1962) p. 147.

any question relating to the maintenance of peace on which "action" is required. If the "recommendations" permitted in Article 11 (2) suggest the formation of a United Nations Force, is this to be deemed "action," and hence impermissible without reference to the Security Council? The Soviet Union has answered this question affirmatively.[82] On the other hand, it is to be noted that paragraph 4 of Article 11 stipulates that that Article is complementary to, rather than a limitation upon, Article 10. Accordingly:

"Article 11, para. 2, *in fine*, does no more than state the obvious fact that if the General Assembly is of the opinion that the dispute or situation calls for the "action" of the Security Council, expressly provided for in the Charter, it should refer this matter to the Security Council. Actually this is nothing else but an application of Article 10, which empowers the General Assembly to make recommendations to the Security Council." [83]

In its advisory opinion on the case of *Certain Expenses of the United Nations, Article 17 (2) of the Charter*, the International Court had some interesting observations to make on this point. It rejected the Soviet contention on the grounds that if the word "action" in Article 11 (2) were interpreted to mean that the General Assembly could make recommendations only of a general character affecting peace and security in the abstract, then the paragraph would not have provided that the General Assembly may make recommendations on questions brought before it by States or the Security Council. The position was that "the kind of action referred to in Article 11 (2), is coercive or enforcement action" [84]; and the word "action" must mean such action as is solely within the province of the Security Council.[85]

It is not clear from these statements whether the Court would view provisional measures under Article 40—especially those establishing a Force, as was perhaps the case with ONUC—as "action . . . solely within the province of the Security Council." It seems to be open to the Assembly to call for "provisional" measures under Articles 10 or 11 (2). Moreover, by implication the Court seems to be rejecting the popular and long-held view that the essential distinction between the powers of the Assembly and Security Council is that the former—with certain exceptions—may only recommend,[86]

---

[82] *Certain Expenses of the United Nations, I.C.J. Pleadings*, 1962, at p. 174, *per* the Netherlands.

[83] *Per* the United States representative, *ibid.*, p. 206.

[84] *I.C.J. Reports*, 1962, p. 164.

[85] *Ibid.*, p. 165.

[86] For sensible reaffirmations by the Secretary-General, which, at this stage, are salutary, that, in law, a recommendation is a recommendation and no more, cf. Section 9 of the Second and Final Report by the Secretary-General on the Plan for UNEF, 6 November 1956 (UN Doc. A/3302) and Section 19 of the further Report by the Secretary-General of 11 February 1957 (A/3527): "The Charter has given to the Security Council means of enforcement and the right to take decisions with mandatory effect. No such authority is given to the General Assembly, which can only recommend action to Member governments which, in turn, may follow the recommendations or disregard them . . . In this case also [recommendations under the Uniting for Peace Resolution], the recommendation has not

while the latter may order; in other words, that the Assembly may do by recommendation all that the Security Council can do under Chapter VII. The Court's definition of "action" is "coercive or enforcement action" not because that is the only *mandatory* form of action, but rather because this is the action that is "solely within the province of the Security Council." There is a strong suggestion in the language employed by the Court that coercive action is the sole prerogative of the Security Council, even if mobilised by means of recommendations.[87]

What the Court does make clear, however, is that the Assembly is entitled to implement its recommendations by the setting up of commissions and other bodies, for "such implementation is a normal feature of the functioning of the United Nations" and is not to be considered "action" within the terms of Article 11 (2), requiring reference to the Security Council. It is, therefore, clear that a United Nations Force may be set up under Article 11 (2) provided that it is not for the purpose of coercive and enforcement action; and such a Force may also constitute a subsidiary organ under Article 22. It has been unequivocally shown that the employment of UNEF was never intended as an enforcement action, and never became one [88]; although it was a military Force and was not limited to mere observation, its role fell short of initiating military action.[89]

The Court, however, has preferred the view that UNEF is based upon Article 14 of the Charter; its attention to Article 11 (2) was largely for the purpose of rebutting the view that the Security Council has a monopoly in matters of action concerning the peace, rather than for the purpose of providing authority for UNEF. The preference for Article 14, which is stated only obliquely, is perhaps surprising, for that Article refers to the "peaceful adjustment of any situation . . . which it deems likely to impair the general welfare or friendly relations among nations," which seems to err on the side

compulsory force." The General Assembly may take certain *decisions*—see Articles 5, 6 and 18,—and in some cases it has mandatory powers—see Article 17. Moreover, a State is bound to consider in good faith the application of a recommendation by the Assembly, and to offer reasons for its non-compliance: see further, *ibid.*, s. 20; the Separate Opinions by Judges Klaestad and Lauterpacht in the Advisory Opinion of the I.C.J. on *Voting Procedure on Questions relating to Reports and Petitions concerning the Territory of South-West Africa, I.C.J. Reports,* 1955, pp. 87–88 and 115–121; and the balanced evaluations by Sloan ((1948) 25 B.Y.I.L., p. 1 *et seq.*); Johnson ((1957) 33 B.Y.I.L., p. 97 *et seq.*), and Brugière, *Les Pouvoirs de l'Assemblée Générale des Nations Unies* (1955) p. 15.

[87] This point is very relevant to the constitutional authority to be found in the Uniting for Peace Resolution, which is largely based on the assumption that the Assembly may by means of recommendation do all that the Council can do under Chapter VII. It is perhaps significant that the Court omits completely in its opinion all reference to this Resolution. This aspect of the question is dealt with in more detail *post*, pp. 291–293.

[88] The Court, going well beyond what was juridically necessary for it to arrive at its opinion, confirmed that neither UNEF nor ONUC were enforcement actions. *I.C.J. Reports,* 1962, p. 166.

[89] For a discussion of the functions of UNEF, see *ante*, pp. 105–109.

of understatement as a description of the situation following the intervention in Egypt in 1956. The terminology of Article 11 (2) would have seemed more appropriate.[90] The reasoning of the Court on the relevance of Article 14 to UNEF is not very clearly presented. It notes that the first Assembly Resolution on the Middle East operations provides in paragraph 5:

"*Requests* the Secretary-General to observe and report promptly on the compliance with the present Resolution to the Security Council *and* to the General Assembly, for such further *action as they may deem appropriate in accordance with the Charter.*"[91]

The italicised words reveal an understanding, states the Court, that either of the two organs may take " action "; and

"The Court notes that these ' actions ' may be considered ' measures ' recommended under Article 14, rather than ' action ' recommended under Article 11."

The Court had also insisted that " action " under Article 11 (2) must be taken to mean " enforcement action."[92] It now suggests that " the word ' measures ' implies some kind of action " and:

" . . . since the Resolutions of the General Assembly in question do not mention upon which Article they are based, and since the language used in most of them might imply reference to either Article 14 or Article 11, it cannot be excluded that they were based upon the former rather than the latter Article."[93]

3. The Resolution on Uniting for Peace

By Resolution 377A(V) the General Assembly recommended the adoption of certain measures aimed at improving the machinery of the United Nations for preserving peace. This Resolution was passed after the outbreak of hostilities in Korea and refers to the failure of the Security Council to discharge its responsibilities on behalf of the Member States, especially with respect to lack of restraint in the use of the veto and its non-implementation of Article 43. Section A of the Resolution [94] resolves that if the Security Council, because of lack of unanimity among the Permanent Members, fails to exercise its primary responsibility for the maintenance of international peace and security in any case where there " appears to be a threat to the

---

[90] Though the Court expressly denies this point of view. *I.C.J. Reports*, 1962, p. 172.
[91] *Ibid.* Italics as in text.
[92] This view has always been upheld by Kelsen, *op.cit.*, p. 204. The Soviet delegates have upheld this interpretation, though to them " action " was to be equated with the use of armed forces. Thus armed forces engaged in policing measures are still " action " in the Soviet view, but enforcement measures short of the use of armed force are not " action "; and the latter falls within the domain of the Assembly while the former does not. See *Off.Rec.G.A.* 5th Sess., A/C.1/362, p. 122.
[93] p. 172.
[94] Hereinafter referred to as the " Uniting for Peace Resolution "; though in fact this is Resolution A of three " Uniting for Peace Resolutions " adopted on 3 November 1950. Resolutions B and C are beyond the scope of the present discussion.

peace, breach of the peace or act of aggression, the General Assembly shall consider the matter immediately with a view to making appropriate recommendations to Members for collective measures, including in the case of a breach of the peace or act of aggression the use of armed force when necessary, to maintain or restore international peace and security." Section A also provides for the calling of an emergency meeting of the Assembly, should it not be in session at that time.[95]

The underlying assumption of this section of the Uniting for Peace Resolution is that the General Assembly may do by recommendation anything that the Security Council can do by decision under Chapter VII. The Communist States have always denied this, insisting that all matters concerning the use of force are reserved exclusively to the Security Council. They base this viewpoint on Articles 11 (2), 43 and 47, and Article 24. The relationship between the Security Council and the General Assembly as revealed by Articles 11 (2) and 43 has already been discussed above.[96] It must be repeated that the International Court, during its advisory opinion on the *Expenses Case* interpreted the term " action " in Article 11 (2) to mean " enforcement action." Whereas this view indicates that the Assembly is free to take many other types of action without referring to the Security Council, it also implies that it may never, even by recommendation, undertake enforcement action. It is possible that the Court did not intend to convey this impression, and the point is not directly germane to its conclusions on the matter of expenses. It does, nevertheless, only mention the authority of the Assembly to take " action " under Article 11 (2) when this involves the organisation of " peace-keeping " operations, at the request, or with the consent, of the States concerned.[97] At no time does the Court uphold the right of the Assembly to *recommend* enforcement measures (though it emphasises repeatedly that only the Council may order coercive action), either under the Charter generally or under the Uniting for Peace Resolution. Moreover, the opinion of the Court studiously avoids all mention of that Resolution, even though it was much discussed in the Pleadings.

Article 24 of the Charter provides that the members of the United Nations " confer upon the Security Council primary responsibility for the maintenance of international peace and security." In support of the Uniting for Peace Resolution attention has been drawn to the fact that Article 24 gives the Security Council only " primary " responsibility, and not exclusive responsibility in matters affecting international peace. The secondary or residual responsibility of the General Assembly is apparent, as Articles 10, 11 and 14 testify. The

---

[95] For a detailed discussion on the compatibility of this provision with the procedure of the Assembly, see Andrassy, " Uniting for Peace " (1956) 50 A.J.I.L. 574–578.
[96] *Supra*, pp. 286–290.
[97] *I.C.J. Reports*, 1962, p. 164.

International Court has also upheld this view of the secondary responsibility of the Assembly under Article 24 (1), though without seeking to relate its comments on this point to the Uniting for Peace Resolution.[98]

Some mention must also be made at this stage of Article 12, for its guidance on the spheres of competence of the Assembly and Council is also instructive so far as the Uniting for Peace Resolution is concerned. Under the terms of this Article the General Assembly may make no recommendation on a question while the Security Council is exercising its functions in respect of that question, unless the Security Council so requests. Article 12 does not seem to prevent the General Assembly from *discussing* a situation which is being dealt with by the Security Council, nor does it specify that the Permanent Members of the Security Council all have to favour a request from that organ that the Assembly make a recommendation. The provision in Section A of the Uniting for Peace Resolution for the convening of an emergency session of the Assembly on the vote of any seven members when the Council " fails to exercise its primary responsibility for the maintenance of international peace and security is thus compatible with the terms of the Charter. Section A also provides for the calling of an emergency session " by a majority of the Members of the United Nations "; as this would not occur until the Council had failed to act, and the residual responsibility of the Assembly implied by Article 24 (1) came into play, it cannot be accepted that this is contrary to the Charter.

Article 12 (2) stipulates that the Secretary-General shall inform the Assembly at each session of matters relating to the maintenance of peace which are being dealt with by the Security Council, and shall also inform them when the Council ceases to deal with such matters. The argument has therefore been heard that until such " clearance " is received from the Secretary-General, the Assembly may make no recommendations on a situation, even if the Security Council is in deadlock. The better view, however, is that paragraph 2 of Article 12 is concerned with procedure, and not substance. It provides the appropriate procedure for keeping the Assembly informed of the work of the Council; but the test for whether the Council has actually ceased to deal with a matter is by interpretation of Article 12 (1), and not by notification by the Secretary-General.[99]

---

[98] *I.C.J. Reports*, 1962, p. 163. It may further be argued that as Article 24 (2) states that the Security Council shall act in accordance with the Purposes and Principles of the Charter, it has failed to do so if it does not maintain international peace and security " by effective collective measures," which are mentioned in the Purposes in Article 1.

[99] See Andrassy, " Uniting for Peace," *op. cit.*, pp. 568–569. He observes that the mere fact that a matter is not actually being considered by the Security Council is not conclusive for the Assembly where the matter has been deemed deliberately to require a certain delay. *e.g.*, in order to achieve a direct agreement between the parties. That such a delay would be appropriate in cases covered by Article 39 is unlikely. *Ibid.*, p. 569, n. 23.

Whether the Council is "exercising its functions" cannot depend upon mere formality.

It may therefore be concluded that the authority of the Assembly to recommend military operations under Part A of the Uniting for Peace Resolution does not go beyond the proper limits of its authority as defined in the Charter, certainly if the operations are "peace-keeping" operations and not "enforcement action" in the sense of action directed *against* a State or other authority. Interestingly, the Resolution reserves the use of armed force for breaches of the peace or for acts of aggression, although under Article 39 of the Charter the Security Council may determine a threat to the peace, breach of peace, or act of aggression, and under Article 42 may recommend military measures subsequent to a finding of any of these three situations. Only the Security Council is given express authority to make such a finding and it has been argued by some scholars that, by inference, the Assembly possesses no such authority.[1] The present writer rejects this view (believing the right of the Council under Article 39 was only specifically enunciated in order to make clear the conditions for the operation of Article 42, and there was no need for such enunciation in the case of the Assembly, as it possesses no binding authority equivalent to that of Article 42). The opinion that in any event the Assembly has no need to make such a finding before recommending the use of force is also to be doubted[2]—it can hardly be allowed more freedom in the field of military measures than the Security Council. Under Part A of the Uniting for Peace Resolution it is to be assumed therefore that the General Assembly will determine the existence of a breach of the peace or act of aggression before recommending collective measures.

Parts C and D of the Uniting for Peace Resolution were intended to provide the teeth for the collective enforcement measures envisaged under Part A. In Part C Members of the United Nations are invited to survey their resources in order to determine the nature and scope of the assistance they would offer in response to a recommendation by the Assembly. It suggests the earmarking and training of troops who could be made available to the United Nations "upon recommendation by the Security Council or the General Assembly without prejudice to the use of such elements in exercise of the right of individual or collective self-defence recognised in Article 51 of the Charter." Further, the Secretary-General is requested to appoint a panel of military experts. Thus, it is clear that a constitutional basis for United Nations Forces could in certain circumstances be found in Section A of the Uniting for Peace Resolution, and

[1] See Kelsen, *Recent Trends in the Law of the United Nations*, pp. 978–979; and Goodrich, "Development of the General Assembly," *International Conciliation* (1951) No. 471, pp. 267, 274.
[2] The contrary view is expressed by Andrassy, *op. cit.*, p. 578.

implemented by reference to Section C. Section C itself falls easily within the scope of Article 11 (1) of the Charter and finds further strength in the provisions of the Preamble and Article 2 (5).

Section D of the Uniting for Peace Resolution establishes a Collective Measures Committee of fourteen members whose task was to consult with the Secretary-General and Member States, and to report by September 1951 on methods, including those in Section C, "which might be used to maintain and strengthen international peace and security in accordance with the Purposes and Principles of the Charter, taking account of collective self-defence and regional arrangements (Articles 51 and 52 of the Charter)." [3] The Communist countries have opposed both Sections C and D on the grounds that they derogate from the rightful authority of the Security Council in matters affecting the maintenance of peace and security. More specifically, they argue that under the Charter it is the Security Council to which States shall make armed forces available, and Article 47 provides that such forces should be regulated by the Military Staff Committee. It was contended that both the panel of experts and the Collective Measures Committee by-passed the Military Staff Committee and were illegal. Moreover, it was alleged that these bodies could not properly be considered as subsidiary organs of the Assembly within the terms of Article 22, as they were intended to fulfil functions that were both inappropriate and properly within the province of the Military Staff Committee. Part D of the Resolution, especially, was deemed to entail in reality the liquidation of that Committee and the emasculation of Security Council powers under Chapter VII.

However, the fact must not be ignored that this machinery is only to be used in case of the failure of the Security Council to function. Indeed, the Resolution itself expressly reiterates the primary responsibility of the Council in these matters. The option is always open to the Permanent Members to implement Article 43. Section C of the Uniting for Peace Resolution thus at least confirms a basis in Charter Law for the establishment of a permanent fighting Force. It is not a new or unique basis, for there is nothing in the Charter which would prevent members from surveying their defence resources and holding troops ready for United Nations service; nor can it be said that anything significant is added to the provisions of Article 11 (1). Section D could equally be useful, should the reports of the Collective Measures Committee ever be adopted by the General Assembly.[4] More broadly both the General Assembly and the Security Council can recommend the establishment of Forces under

---

[3] See Report of the Collective Measures Committee (1951), UN Doc. A/1891. For a fuller discussion of the reports of the Collective Measures Committee see *ante*, pp. 21–28.

[4] For the three reports of the Collective Measures Committee see *ante*, pp. 21–28.

paragraph 8 of the Resolution, employing any particular non-obligatory method which they care to use.[5]

It is not easy to assess how much these provisions have actually been used in practice, partly because of sometimes deliberate ambiguity in stating the basis of a United Nations action, and partly because the Resolution covers not only the establishment of a Force, but the calling of an Emergency Special Session. It is thus possible for an Emergency Special Session to be called under Resolution 377 (v), without any recommendations being made thereunder for the use of force. In the case of the Anglo-French intervention in Suez in 1956, failure to pass any Resolution in the Security Council resulted in a suggestion by Yugoslavia that an Emergency Session be called under the terms of the Uniting for Peace Resolution. The Soviet Union, despite its previously avowed opposition to that Resolution, supported this move.[6] The Yugoslavian suggestion was adopted, but not before the United Kingdom had unsuccessfully contended that the Resolutions which it and France had voted against were not "substantive decisions within Chapter VII" and hence the conditions for Uniting for Peace did not exist.[7] Thus the Assembly in 1956 certainly met by virtue of this Resolution; whether UNEF was set up under it is another matter which requires further examination.

It is impossible to decide the constitutional authority for UNEF without reference to the functions and purposes for which it was set up. These functions and purposes have already been described above, but it may now be repeated that at no time was it considered that UNEF be employed to carry out enforcement measures. It was not to engage in armed combat, though it could use force in self-defence. On the other hand, it was considered to be more than a

---

[5] See Andrassy, "Uniting for Peace" (1956), 50 A.J.I.L. 563–582; McDougal and Gardner, "The Veto and the Charter: an interpretation for Survival" (1951) 60 *Yale Law Journal*, 258; Goodrich and Rosner: "The United Nations Emergency Force" (1957) 11 *International Organisation*, 413. "United Nations Armed Forces, Military Staff Committee and Collective Measures Committee," *Commonwealth Survey*, 27 November 1956, p. 1019; Schwarzenberger, "Problems of a United Nations Force" (1959) 12 *Current Legal Problems*, 247.

[6] The Soviet Union rejected the contention of the Danish Government (*I.C.J. Pleadings*, 1962, p. 154) that it was estopped from denying the legality of UNEF by virtue of its acquiescence in a Security Council Resolution which relied on Assembly Resolution 377 (V). Professor Tunkin stated that the Soviet Union had been in favour of the Assembly making "appropriate recommendations" but that they could not include a recommendation to use force, which was exclusively within the province of the Security Council. As the Soviet Government was aware that the whole basis of Resolution 377 (V) was the provision of enforcement measures by the Assembly, it may perhaps be thought that this explanation lacks conviction. *Ibid.*, at p. 399.

[7] *Off.Rec.S.C.*, 11th yr., 751st Mtg., at pp. 13–14. Presumably the United Kingdom representative was contending that both a finding under Article 39 and a decision to use enforcement measures under Articles 41 and 42 had to be rejected before an Emergency Special Session of the Assembly could be called. This interpretation was rejected by 6 votes to 4, with one abstention.

mere observer corps. The Secretary-General suggested that UNEF would function " on the basis of a decision reached under the terms of Resolution 377 (V), Uniting for Peace." [8] The General Assembly Resolutions contain no clear reference to a specific authority, but Resolution 1000 (ES–1) did " note with satisfaction " the first Report of the Secretary-General on his plan for UNEF. Professor Sohn has written that " the United Nations seems to have proceeded on the assumption, not entirely justified, that no forces were available to it . . . (and) that the decision (to establish the Force) was based on Section A rather than on Section C of that Resolution." [9] He concedes, however, that there is no clear support for this view.

The purposes for which UNEF was set up were different in kind from those envisaged under Section A of the Uniting for Peace Resolution, and from the measures proposed by the Collective Measures Committee. It is true that Section A envisages the recommendation of the use of force in cases where there has been a breach of the peace or act of aggression, and that the situation in the Middle East could reasonably be classified as the former, and possibly also as the latter. However, like Article 42, this section anticipates—even though it is not expressly provided—that the action would take place against the aggressor or the State designated to have breached the peace. In other words, the Uniting for Peace Resolution was to be used to recommend enforcement measures. The great emphasis on the limited purposes and objectives of UNEF made it clear that it was a Force of a different nature. It seems insufficient to base UNEF on the Uniting for Peace Resolution on the grounds that " the right to establish such a smaller Force is implicit in the right to establish a large fighting Force." [10] Rather, it is preferable to seek the basis in the general provisions of the Charter; and UNEF, given the views on the division of powers between the Assembly and Council, and the meaning of " action " in Article 11 (2), discussed above, seems properly to fall within the scope of Articles 10, 11, and —in the view of the International Court—Article 14.[11]

---

[8] UN Doc. A/3302 and A/3289.

[9] Sohn, *op. cit.*, (1958), 52 A.J.I.L. at pp. 233–234.

[10] Sohn, *op. cit.*, at p. 234. The present writer's viewpoint is shared by Seyersted, *op. cit.*, at pp. 440–41. It is also shared by Stone, but for rather different reasons. He rejects the legality of the Uniting for Peace Resolution as a possible basis for a United Nations Force, taking the position that in so far as peace enforcement is concerned, " the view must be adopted that the General Assembly cannot as such exercise functions attributed by the Charter only to the Security Council," and to attempt to replace Article 43 by the provisions of the Uniting for Peace Resolution, cannot " overcome the constitutional difficulties involved." *Aggression and World Order*, p. 193. The International Court, in the advisory opinion on *Certain Expenses*, had no occasion to pronounce upon the legality of the Uniting for Peace Resolution, or UNEF's relationship to it; but it did deny, *obiter*, that Article 43 constitutes a *lex specialis*, for " It cannot be said that the Charter has left the Security Council impotent in the face of an emergency situation when agreements under Article 43 have not been concluded." *I.C.J. Reports*, 1962, p. 167.

[11] See *ante*, p. 98. For discussions on UNEF, see Goodrich and Rosner,

Although it is unlikely that the Uniting for Peace Resolution has to date provided the authority for any United Nations Force, several emergency sessions have been called under its terms. In the question of Hungary, failure to agree upon action in the Security Council led to the adoption of a Resolution, by ten votes to one, to call an emergency special session of the Assembly " as provided for in General Assembly Resolution 377 (V)." [12] The Lebanon question in 1958 is rather curious in that although no agreement could be reached in the Security Council on appropriate measures, all the Permanent Members were in favour of calling upon the General Assembly to deal with the matter. Ostensibly, this is a clear case of the application of Article 20; and, indeed, the Resolution in question [13] made no reference to the Uniting for Peace provisions. It did, however, refer to the calling of " an emergency special session " rather than a " special session " of the Assembly. The United Nations Observation Group in the Lebanon had already been instituted before the case was put in the hands of the Assembly. The Congo operation is another example of using the Uniting for Peace Resolution [14] to refer a matter to the Assembly, though with no intention that the Assembly should " recommend . . . the use of force," for ONUC had already been set up by the Council.

This line of precedent, briefly explained, leads to some interesting questions about the relationship between Article 20 and the Uniting for Peace Resolution—questions which seem to have received virtually no attention in either United Nations practice or in the writings of jurists. Article 20 of the Charter provides that " Special sessions (of the Assembly) shall be convoked by the Secretary-General at the request of the Security Council, or of a majority of the Members of the United Nations." This may be compared with Section A of Resolution 377 (V): " Such emergency special sessions shall be called if requested by the Security Council on the vote of any seven members, or by a majority of the Members of the United Nations." Other than the term " emergency " Special Session, the latter provision only differs from the former in that it expressly stipulates

op. cit. (1957) 11 Int.Org., 413; Wilcox, " View of the Department of State on Creating a Permanent United Nations Emergency Force," 39 *Dept. of State Bull.,* p. 324 (25 August 1958); Chaumont, " La situation juridique des états membres à l'égard de la Force d'Urgence des Nations Unies " (1958) 4 Ann.Fr. de Droit Int., 399; Kay, " The United Nations Forces in Korea and Sinai " (1961) 2 *International Relations,* 168; Hudson, " The United Nations Emergency Force—a notable precedent " (1960) 38 *Current History,* 326; M. Cohen, " UNEF " (1957) *International Journal,* 109; Pearson, " Force for the United Nations (1957) *Foreign Affairs,* 395; Munro, " Can the United Nations Enforce Peace? " (1960) *Foreign Affairs,* 209; Chapman, " UNEF—legal status " (1958) 57 *Michigan Law Review,* 56; James, " United Nations Action for Peace," *World Today,* November and December 1962; Stone, *Aggression and World Order* (1958), pp. 184–200.

[12] Security Council Resolution S/3733.
[13] UN Doc. S/4083.
[14] UN Doc. S/4526.

that the calling of such a session is a procedural matter, not subject to the veto voting rule of Article 27. It is doubtful, however, that Article 20 should be treated as a substantive matter.[15] The alternative contained therein of allowing a special Assembly to be called by the will of a majority of the Members of the United Nations hardly seems compatible with the retention of a right of veto in the clause dealing with the calling of a special session by Security Council request. Moreover, the removal of an item from the Security Council's agenda—which is the easiest way of allowing the Assembly to make recommendations on it—is certainly treated as a procedural matter. The only occasion on which a special Assembly Session under Article 20 was convened at the request of the Security Council[16] was in April 1948, when that body was deadlocked over the Palestine question. The Resolution calling for the Special Assembly Session—" in accordance with Article 20 of the Charter " was passed by nine votes to none, with two abstentions, including the Soviet Union.[17] Whereas it has subsequently become established in United Nations practice that an abstention is not to be considered equivalent to a negative vote in the context of Article 27 (3), this was by no means established in 1948. It would therefore have been expected, had the matter been thought substantive, that there would at least have been some debate on this point or some protest registered. There was none.

This reasoning leads to the conclusion that, generally speaking, it is unnecessary to rely on the Uniting for Peace Resolution to refer a matter on which the Security Council is unable to act to the General Assembly. If the Security Council wishes to relieve itself altogether of responsibility for the matter concerned, it can remove it from its agenda; if there is some pressing reason for retaining the matter on its agenda,—as there was in the case of the Congo, where ONUC was set up by and under the command of the Security Council—then Article 20 may be used. Certainly to rely on the Uniting for Peace Resolution where the Permanent Members of the Council are in agreement in their wish to send the matter to the Assembly, is completely unnecessary. Yet there are indications that those provisions of the Uniting For Peace Resolution which allow for the mounting of a United Nations Force have been avoided (the principle of " consent " or reliance on Articles 11, 14 and 40 being preferred), and instead the Resolution is being used merely as a device to call the General Assembly into special session.

[15] For the contrary opinion, see Bentwich and Martin, *A Commentary on the Charter of the United Nations* (1951), p. 54, n. 2.
[16] A special session was convened in 1947, also on the Palestine question, at the request of a majority of Members of the United Nations. See UN Docs. A/286, A/295 and Corr. 1. An attempt to use the same procedure over the Tunisian question in 1952 failed, a majority of members failing to support the request of a group of States. See UN Docs. A/2137 and A/2143.
[17] Security Council Resolution S/714.

4. *The functions of the Secretariat and the Secretary-General*

A United Nations Force could also be established under the authority of the Secretariat, though the relevant Charter Articles indicate certain limitations which would have to be borne in mind. Article 97 states that "The Secretariat shall comprise a Secretary-General and such staff as the Organisation may require." It is for the Secretary-General, as the Chief Administrative Officer of the United Nations, to decide upon the size of the Secretariat needed for the effective functioning of the Organisation. There is within Article 97 no limitation upon the number of staff members he may recruit. Furthermore, it is possible to read this article as permitting the establishment of a United Nations Force *within the Secretariat*. However, a reading of other parts of the Charter supports the view that if such a Force were intended to perform more than very limited functions, additional authorisation from the General Assembly or Security Council would be required.

Within the terms of Article 97, *simpliciter*, the Secretary-General would certainly be entitled to recruit Secretariat staff, versed in the use of and equipped with weapons, for the protection of other Secretariat members, field missions, subsidiary commissions of inquiry, conciliation or mediation, and for the guarding of United Nations archives and property. Indeed, the functions of the guards at United Nations headquarters are along these lines, though of course they do not constitute a "United Nations Force." The first Secretary-General proposed the establishment of a "Guard Force" for these purposes,[18] and had no doubt as to his constitutional authority under Articles 97 and 98. The Secretary-General emphasised that the Guard would not (and presumably could not) be used for enforcement functions under Article 42. In the event, as we have seen,[19] the Assembly approved the modified plan for a normally unarmed Field Service for guard, transport and communication services and a Panel of Observers. Whereas a possible exception may have been made to the monopoly of the Council over enforcement measures by General Assembly recommendations under the Uniting for Peace Resolution, the Secretariat remains incapable of mounting such a Force within the terms of Article 97 alone. The freedom of the Secretary-General to decide what staff is required by the Organisation does not amount to a freedom to decide that members of the Secretariat should carry out enforcement measures.[20] However, should the General Assembly recommend that the Secretariat should establish military units, then Article 97, taken together with General Assembly Resolution 13 (1), would seem broad enough to sustain such action. By Resolution 13 (1) of 13 February 1946 the General Assembly asked the Secretary-General to establish an:

[18] See *ante*, pp. 18–20.
[19] *Ante*, p. 20.
[20] See Report of Secretary-General on a United Nations Guard, UN Doc. A/656, p. 7, para. 7.

" administrative organisation which will permit of the effective discharge of his administrative and general responsibilities under the Charter, and the efficient performance of those functions and services required to meet the needs of the several organs of the United Nations."

The authority of the Secretary-General to establish an interposition or fighting Force is thus seen to be exclusively a delegated authority.[21]

It will be noted that, regardless of whether the Secretariat Force is for the purpose of protection of United Nations personnel and property, or for the maintenance of international peace and security, budgetary approval from the General Assembly is necessary.[22] In other words, " If the General Assembly were willing to make the necessary financial appropriations, the Secretary-General could recruit as many individuals as the Assembly should authorise, provide for their training as military units of the Secretariat, and send them on such missions as the Assembly might direct." [23]

A Force established by the Secretariat should ideally be individually and directly recruited, and not composed of national contingents. However, it is probably incorrect to assume that the terms of Article 100 of the Charter, under which the staff of the Secretariat undertake not to " seek or receive instructions from any government or from any other authority external to the Organisation," necessarily precludes the use of national contingents in a Force established by the Secretary-General under Articles 97 and 98. The Regulations for both UNEF and ONUC, both of which were based on national contingents, adopted principles almost identical to Article 100 so as to ensure that members of the Force should be " international personnel under the authority of the United Nations." [24]

Article 98 of the Charter is relevant in relation to the authority of the Secretariat in the planning and operation of United Nations Forces established by either the Assembly or the Security Council. It provides that the Secretary-General " shall perform such . . . functions as are entrusted to him by (the main) organs." Thus the General Assembly delegated authority to the Secretary-General for certain responsibilities in connection with UNEF [25]; and the day-to-day decisions concerning ONUC have also fallen upon the Secretary-General for discharge.[26] During the case of *Certain Expenses of the United Nations*, the Soviet memorandum placed before the Court the interesting contention that the Secretary-General had acted illegally in determining the composition of ONUC. The Soviet Union pointed

---

[21] The present writer here agrees with Professor Andrassy, *Report on Problems of a UN Force*, Int. Law Association, Hamburg Conference, 1960, p. 14, n. 41. Cf. the view of the International Committee, *ibid.*

[22] *Ibid.*, paras. 10–11 and 28.

[23] Sohn, *op. cit.*, p. 235.

[24] See UNEF and ONUC Regulations 6 (*ante*, pp. 122–123, 220). The assumption referred to has been made by Schwarzenberger, *loc. cit.*, p. 12.

[25] In which he is assisted by an Advisory Committee (of which he is Chairman) composed of the representatives of seven Member States: UN Doc. A/3943, Sects. 26 *et seq.*, 84 *et seq.*, 172 and 174.

[26] *Ante*, pp. 183, 213.

to Article 48 (1), and found in this a usurpation of the Security Council's authority by the Secretary-General, inasmuch as he himself had determined which States were to participate in the Congo operation.[27] The Court, however, rejected this argument, observing that the Charter does not forbid the Security Council to act through instruments of its own choice, and that Articles 29 and 98 are significant for this purpose.[28] Further, that the Secretary-General was authorised by the Security Council to make arrangements which in other circumstances might have been made by the Security Council under Article 48 (1) was to be deduced from the many Resolutions of that organ approving the work of the Secretary-General.[29]

While the limited authority of the Secretariat to establish a United Nations Force is thus clear, no United Nations Force has yet been established by this organ. The first Secretary-General's proposals for a Guard Force proved abortive [30] and the United Nations Field Service cannot properly be described as a military force.[31] The Field Service was established by the Secretary-General under his own authority, and the General Assembly passed a Resolution noting his intentions. No mention was made of specific Charter provisions, but they observed that the Field Service would enable United Nations missions to operate more efficiently, and that the Secretary-General possessed the necessary authority.[32] A reference to both Articles 97 and 98 was thus implied.

In 1952 Trygve Lie suggested that those States whose resources were too limited to contribute the military units contemplated in paragraph 8 of the Uniting for Peace Resolution, might support a United Nations Volunteer Reserve, whereby individuals could be recruited into special United Nations reserve groups. However, this proposal failed to receive widespread support and came to nothing; nor was it clear that it would have involved the establishment of a Force by the Secretariat, as it anticipated the recruiting and training being carried out within national volunteer reserve establishments, pending " mobilisation by the United Nations." [33]

---

[27] *I.C.J. Pleadings*, 1962, pp. 272 and 400.   [28] *I.C.J. Pleadings*, 1962, p. 177.

[29] See para. 3 of Security Council Resol. S/4387; para. 3 of Security Council Resol. S/4405; para. 1 of Resol. S/4426; General Assembly Resol. 1474 (ES–IV); Security Council Resol. S/4741; and paras. 4 and 5 of Resol. S/5002. None of these Resolutions was subject to a dissenting vote.

[30] For a resumé see *ante*, pp. 18–20, and see also Schwebel, "A United Nations 'Guard' and a United Nations 'Legion,'" in Frye, *A United Nations Peace Force* (1957) pp. 206–208.

[31] See Report of Special Committee on a Field Service, *Off.Rec.G.A.*, 3rd Sess., Pt. 2, Plenary Mtgs., Annexes p. 10. The Field Service comprises 300 men recruited as Secretariat Staff, wearing United Nations uniforms and only rarely carrying arms. See *Off.Rec.G.A.*, 4th Sess., Suppl. No. 13, and Seyersted, *op. cit.*, pp. 353–4.

[32] General Assembly Resol. 297 (IV). For a detailed discussion, see Schwebel, *op. cit.*, pp. 202–203.

[33] Report of the Collective Measures Committee, *Off.Rec.G.A.*, 7th Sess. Suppl. No. 17 (A/2215), p. 12. See *ante*, pp. 25–26, and see also Schwebel, *op. cit.*, pp. 210–216.

5. Collective defence arrangements under Article 51
of the Charter

Article 51 of the Charter stipulates that:

" Nothing in the present Charter shall impair the inherent right of individual or collective self-defence if an armed attack occurs against a Member of the United Nations, until the Security Council has taken the measures necessary to maintain international peace and security. Measures taken by Members in the exercise of this right of self-defence shall be immediately reported to the Security Council and shall not in any way affect the authority and responsibility of the Security Council under the present Charter to take at any time such action as it deems necessary in order to maintain or restore international peace and security."

It will be seen that Article 51 is concerned with the right of States to act in self-defence on their own behalf until the Security Council has taken action to maintain or restore peace. If, after being apprised of events, the Security Council fails to take such action, then the right of States to act in self-defence continues. It has been suggested that if the overwhelming majority of United Nations Members act in co-ordinated self-defence, then such arrangements could take on the nature of " United Nations action." The establishment of a United Nations command at the head of an action for co-ordinated self-defence, subsequent to a finding by the Security Council [34] of an armed attack against a Member, would come very close to basing the authority for a United Nations Force on the right to collective self-defence under Article 51. In other words, it is contended that the licence to use force under Article 51,[35] though aimed at securing the traditional liberties of individual States, can also serve as a title to United Nations action even when the Security Council is unable to make a decision under Article 42.

Some evidence in support of this theoretical proposition is found in the status of the United Nations Forces in Korea. The Security Council recommended that Member States aid South Korea in

---

[34] Or possibly by the General Assembly; though Professor Kelsen has insisted that the Security Council has exclusive power to determine when an " armed attack " has taken place justifying self-defence under Article 51: *Recent Trends in the Law of the United Nations*, at p. 979.

[35] Stone, *Legal Controls of International Conflict* (1959), p. 234, suggests that the licence to States to use force, finding expression in recommendations that they do so by the Assembly, rests on two bases. The first of these is the inherent right of individual or collective self-defence, and the second " the liberty of each State to resort to war under customary International Law, which still exists even for United Nations members, except where prohibited by the Charter." The present writer disagrees that this second basis exists, believing that the Charter has limited the use of force to licensed self-defence, legal enforcement measures and illegal coercion. To rely, as does Stone, upon the wording of Article 2 (4) (". . . against the territorial integrity and political independence of any state ") to uphold a licence to resort to war for the purpose of " maintaining international peace and security " when the Security Council is unable to take a decision under Chapter VII is to ignore the very intention of the Charter. This view also involves a curious interpretation of Articles 1 and 2. Moreover, the existence under international law of a duty to maintain international peace and to redress violations thereof is very doubtful: see Stowell, *Intervention in International Law* (1921), p. 48.

repelling the armed attack mounted against her, and the national contingents made available in response to this recommendation were placed under the United Nations flag, even though the Command was given to the United States. If one takes the broad view of the right of collective self-defence—namely, that any State may aid another State defending itself against armed attack,[36]—then it is certainly arguable that the United Nations action did nothing more than co-ordinate such defensive measures. It must be noticed, however, that Article 51 refers only to armed attack against a Member, and South Korea was not a Member of the United Nations. It is true that Article 2 (6) resolves that the Organisation shall ensure that non-Members act in accordance with Charter principles so far as may be necessary for the maintenance of peace and security, but this seems to refer to enforcement measures rather than a right of collective self-defence under Article 51; to interpret Article 2 (6) otherwise is to strain its natural meaning.[37] Any right of collective self-defence with a non-Member—and against a non-Member—exists not under Articles 51 and 2 (6), but under customary international law.

Professor Julius Stone, while believing that the Korean action is to be explained as Collective Self-Defence, denies the possibility that it can also be designated a " United Nations action." [38] It has been thought in some quarters that if there is a finding of an armed attack, followed by recommendations that States jointly resist such aggression, then Article 2 (5), by which Members are to give every assistance to the United Nations in any action it takes, comes into operation and classifies the response as " United Nations action." [39] Professor Stone rejects this argument on the grounds that it confuses a Council or Assembly recommendation with a collective decision imposing Charter obligations on Members. This reasoning, however, presupposes that the " action " referred to in Article 2 (5) is only enforcement action undertaken by means of a binding decision of the Security Council; yet the International Court has pointed out that many forms of " action " are undertaken by the General Assembly.[40] More broadly, though Article 2 (5) cannot make Members bound by

---

[36] Cf. Bowett, "Collective Self-Defence under the Charter of the United Nations" (1955–56), 32 B.Y.I.L. 137, where it is argued that this is too broad a view and that, for States to be acting in collective self-defence, the aggressor State must have been in breach of duty to each of them. Thus if State A violates the legally protected interests of State B, and State C joins State B in collective action, State C is *not* acting in collective self-defence. An exception may occur where, for reasons of geographic proximity, political or economic dependence, State C's interests are indirectly so greatly affected by the attack on State B that is may be deemed to act in collective self-defence.

[37] Cf. Stone, *Legal Controls of International Conflict*, p. 234, n. 33, who believes that Article 2 (6) resolves the difficulty of relying upon Article 51 where a non-Member is concerned.

[38] *Op. cit.*, p. 234, and see *ante*, pp. 33–34.

[39] Gross, " Voting in the Security Council " (1951) 60 Yale L.J. at pp. 254–5.

[40] *Certain Expenses of the United Nations, I.C.J. Reports*, 1962, at p. 163.

mere recommendations in the field of military measures, it points to a general obligation to act in good faith in assisting the United Nations in securing its legitimate objectives.

It has been suggested by certain writers that the Uniting for Peace Resolution, if it is to stand at all, must base its legality, and the legality to establish forces thereunder, on the right of collective self-defence. If one holds the view that Resolution 377 (V) is *ultra vires* in so far as it purports to recommend enforcement action,[41] then it is still possible to seek its justification in Article 51. The difficulty in so doing is that the intention of its drafters was certainly very far from a mere enunciation of their rights under Article 51; more-over, paragraphs 8 and 11 of the Uniting for Peace Resolution tend to imply another legal basis, for the former recommends the main-taining of national units for United Nations service "without prejudice" to the use of such units under Article 51, while the latter mentions that in planning collective measures account shall be taken of collective self-defence and regional arrangements. Moreover, a recommendation under Section A to use force may or may not involve what is correctly self-defence, according to the circumstances. Not every breach of the peace or act of aggression anywhere in the world gives rise to a right of self-defence by all United Nations Members. Nor, in the opinion of the present writer, does the fact that "each Member remains legally free to act or not act on such recommendation" lead logically to the immediately ensuing con-clusion of Professor Stone that "If it acts it does so in accordance with its right of self-defence under Article 51."[42] It only acts under such right if its legal "self" has been subjected to armed attack.[43] The essential nature of self-defence does not lie in the fact that it is in response to a recommendation rather than a binding obligation.

While the right of collective self-defence is not based upon the existence of a treaty arrangement between participating States, it would presumably be possible nevertheless for the United Nations to recommend that action be taken within the scope of a multilateral defence treaty. Doubts that the United Nations would wish to associate itself in action by a limited inter-State defence arrangement are to some extent assuaged by Article 53, which shows that the Organisation may employ regional arrangements for enforcement purposes.[44] A fortiori, it may be argued, non-universal defence

---

[41] For this position, see Stone, *Legal Controls of International Conflict*, pp. 268–272. [42] *Ibid.*, p. 275.
[43] What constitutes the legal "self" in respect of a right of self-defence is another question, beyond the scope of this Chapter. But see Bowett, *Self-Defence in International Law*, pp. 3–18, 201–248; and Higgins, "The Legal Limits to the use of Force by Sovereign States" (1961) 37 B.Y.I.L. at pp. 306–7. For a different view see Browlie, *International Law and the Use of Force by States* (1963), Chap. XVII.
[44] However, it is probable that a regional arrangement within the terms of Article 53 is one aimed at the maintenance of peace *between its members* and *within its own region*; if so, this argument is largely illusory. See *post*, pp. 306–307.

arrangements could be used by the United Nations for action under its authority.

Indeed, since Member States may agree *ad hoc* to place forces at the disposal of the United Nations for use as part of a United Nations Force, it is difficult to see why a group of States, already organised via a treaty for collective self-defence, cannot offer their forces collectively and the United Nations accept that offer. However, the constitutional basis of the United Nations Force would, in that event, not be Article 51 but rather Article 1 (1) coupled with either Articles 11 (2) or 14 or Chapter VII according to whether the Assembly or the Security Council became the organ initiating the action. The action would cease to be collective self-defence and would be a collective United Nations action : the former requires no prior authorisation, whereas the latter is essentially based on authorisation by a competent United Nations organ. An authorisation by the Security Council or a recommendation by the Assembly under the Uniting for Peace Resolution that collective measures be taken for the international security changes both the nature of the action and its consequences. It thus avoids the need that there should exist among the participating States the community of interests that is needed legally to support an action in collective self-defence. It has already been suggested that the proper application of collective self-defence usually entails a certain geographical proximity or political or economic interdependence; in other words, each of the participating States should have the right of individual self-defence in the circumstances before it can act collectively in self-defence.[45] It will readily be seen that this leads to difficulty in practice in distinguishing collective self-defence arrangements under Article 51 from regional arrangements under Article 53. Unless treaties for collective self-defence are, however, kept within these limits, one will find that :

" as a whole Article 51 is being used more and more as a substitute, as Ersatz for the non-existing general collective security and sanctions. But self-defence under Article 51 gains, under such conditions, a very different meaning and becomes a technique pretty near to the old fashioned right to resort to war."[46]

6. *Regional arrangements under Article 53 of the Charter*

Article 52 (1), appearing at the beginning of Chapter VIII of the Charter, provides that "Nothing in the present Charter precludes the existence of regional arrangements or agencies for dealing with such matters relating to the maintenance of international peace and security as are appropriate for regional action, provided that such arrangements or agencies and their activities are consistent with the

---

[45] Bowett, *op. cit.* (1955–6) 32 B.Y.I.L. 152–154; and *Self-Defence in International Law* (1958), p. 238. *Cf.* the detailed reply to this view by McDougal and Feliciano, *Law and Minimum World Public Order* (1961) pp. 247–253.
[46] Kunz, "The Inter-American Treaty of Reciprocal Assistance" (1948) 42 A.J.I.L. 120. For an examination of the *casus foederis* of collective self-defence arrangements, see Bowett, *op. cit.* (1955–6) 32 B.Y.I.L., 142–149.

Purposes and Principles of the United Nations." Article 53 permits the Security Council to "utilise such regional arrangements or agencies for enforcement action under its authority." However, the regional agencies shall undertake no enforcement action without the authorisation of the Security Council,[47] and under the terms of Article 54 regional arrangements and agencies are to keep the Security Council fully informed of activities undertaken or in contemplation for the maintenance of international peace and security.

Quite clearly, Article 53 provides constitutional authority for the use of certain Forces by the United Nations; however, the scope of this authority merits further examination. Freedom of military action under Article 53 being limited, the reason for the establishment of many collective arrangements of regional character under Article 51 is apparent. Given that collective self-defence arrangements are frequently concerned with the protection of a particular area, what is the essential difference between such groupings and these under Article 53? On one view the hall-mark of a regional arrangement is that it is directed against aggression between its members *inter se*.[48] In other words, the "underlying concept is that of common action for peace and security within (and not merely ' of ') the region." [49] Moreover, under Article 52 (3) the Security Council is to encourage the pacific settlement of "local" disputes: it is therefore assumed that peace enforcement by regional agencies refers to the same area. Further, this interpretation of the meaning of a regional arrangement is the only one which avoids absurdity, for, as Professor Stone has pointed out: " If an alliance for defence against a Permanent Member from *outside* the region were a ' regional arrangement,' even military staff plans would have to be disclosed in advance to the potential aggressor; and the potential aggressor's own consent obtained before he could be resisted." [50] Such an alliance is more correctly regarded as a preparatory measure for collective self-defence, reportable only after such measures have been taken. On this view neither the North Atlantic Treaty nor the Brussels Treaty are to be regarded as

---

[47] With the exception of measures against any State which was an enemy during the Second World War, or falling within Article 107.

[48] Beckett, *The North Atlantic Treaty, the Brussels Treaty and the Charter* (1950) p. 20. For a discussion of Beckett's and Kelsen's views see Bowett, *Self-Defence in International Law* (1958) pp. 220–223.

[49] Stone, *Legal Controls of International Conflict*, p. 247.

[50] See Beckett, *op. cit.*; Kelsen, " Is the North Atlantic Treaty a Regional Arrangement? " (1951) 45 A.J.I.L. 162; Van Kleffens, "Regionalism and Political Pacts " (1949) 44 A.J.I.L. 666; and also the Soviet view that the Pact failed as a regional arrangement within Article 52 because "it has not as its aim the settlement of any regional issues": *Note of Protest*, March 31, 1949. *Cf.* Tucker, "The Interpretation of War " (1951) 4 *Int. Law Quarterly*, 11. Stone seems to fall into the error of arguing that because no reports of preparatory measures have been made under the North Atlantic Treaty, and because it would be contrary to its interests to disclose such information, that therefore the Treaty is not to be considered a "regional arrangement": *Legal Controls*, etc., pp. 249–50. It is because the North Atlantic Treaty does not fall within Articles 52–54 that it is exempt from such actions, and not vice versa.

regional arrangements, and they cannot be used as United Nations Forces under Article 53. This is so in spite of the employment of certain terminology in these treaties which might indicate otherwise.[51]

However, whilst it is perhaps true that the intent of the Charter was to allow regional arrangements to be used by the United Nations for enforcement action *within* the region, this simply means that Chapter VIII of the Charter only affords a constitutional basis for such United Nations action in that case. It does not mean that States Members of a regional arrangement may not offer their forces for use by the United Nations under some alternative constitutional basis: an offer, *ad hoc*, either individually or collectively could be made under Article 42, for example, in a similar way to that in which States Members of a collective self-defence organisation could offer their forces. The difference would be that the constitutional basis of the Force would lie in Chapter VII, and not in Chapter VIII or Article 51, as the case may be. So far, the United Nations has never attempted to establish a Force under Article 53, though the possibility remains. There has, indeed, been comparatively little practice generally under Chapter VIII of the Charter.[52]

7. The United Nations Charter generally and the " effectiveness " principle of construction

Having now looked at the various articles of the Charter and Resolutions of the Assembly which may be said to provide a constitutional basis for United Nations Forces, it behoves us to ask one further question: is it necessary at all to locate specifically in the Charter provisions the constitutional authority for United Nations Forces? In other words, cannot a more general argument for their legality be relied upon?

To answer this question it is necessary to examine, even if briefly, the legal nature of the powers of international organisations. It was a fairly common view during the early, tentative days of the United Nations, that it could only exercise powers specifically granted to it under its constitution. The constitution was a finite instrument which contained the full total of powers delegated by the founding sovereign States to the international organisation. While this static view has been persisted in by a minority of jurists,[53] it has generally

---

[51] And see *Dept. State Bull.*, 20 March 1949, which treats the pact as concerned with the security of a region.

[52] In the Palestine hostilities the Syrian representative claimed, *inter alia*, that the Arab League was pacifying a local dispute in Palestine under the authorisation of Article 52, *Off.Rec.S.C.*, 2nd yr., 299th Mtg. In 1960 and in 1962 the question has arisen as to whether non-military sanctions by the Organisation of American States (rupture of diplomatic relations in the former case, and expulsion from membership in the latter) constituted an enforcement measure under Article 53 requiring the approval of the Security Council: see UN Docs. S/4491 and S/5095.

[53] Kelsen's *Law of the United Nations* is perhaps the prime example of rigid interpretation and a refusal to go beyond the strict letter of the law. Lauterpacht has referred to the outcome as " an example of the pessimistic

come to be acknowledged that international constitutional instruments are to be interpreted dynamically, and that the powers of an international organisation may go beyond those specifically allocated to it.

This is not the place for a detailed discussion of general, but not specifically named, powers that are inherent in intergovernmental organisations. It may merely be said that the treaty-making power of such organisations is often only implied, and that even where it is specific the nature and scope of the agreements to which it applies may still have not been explicitly stated.[54] The authority which the United Nations exercises in internal administrative matters is only very broadly based on provisions in the Charter. Again, that organisation has taken certain actions which were not foreseen in the terms of the Charter: its willingness to assume certain "governmental" and "territorial" functions in Jerusalem,[55] Trieste[56] and West Irian[57] were cases in point.

All these examples of non-specifically delegated powers have one element in common—they were all performed for the furtherance of the Principles and Purposes of the United Nations. The International Court of Justice in 1949 advised that specific authority was not essential, though it confined its viewpoint to the explanation that:

"Under international law, the Organisation must be deemed to have those powers which, though not expressly provided in the Charter, are conferred upon it *by necessary implication as being essential to the performance of its duties.*"[58]

What is or is not essential to the performance of the United Nations duties "arises by necessary intendment out of the Charter."[59] This

tendency to exact the largest possible element of absurdity from an admittedly imperfect document." (1947) 70 *Recueil des Cours,* I, at p. 24.
[54] See Kasmé, *La Capacité de l'Organisation des Nations Unies de Conclure des Traités* (1960), p. 40; Seyersted, *op. cit.,* p. 449; and Parry, "The Treaty-making power of the United Nations" (1949) 26 B.Y.I.L. 108.
[55] The Assembly's plan for the partition of Palestine included the establishment of an international city of Jerusalem, which would have been administered through a Governor, appointed by the Trusteeship Council, and with authority extending to the conduct of international affairs. However, Jerusalem was not to be a trust territory within the terms of Chapters XII–XIII: G.A.Res. 181, Annex, pt. III. For detailed comments, see Seyersted, *op. cit.,* p. 452.
[56] The Peace Treaty with Italy provided for the assumption of certain responsibilities of the Security Council in respect of the Free Territory of Trieste. These included ensuring the independence and integrity of the Territory; determining when its Permanent Statute should enter into force; amending it, if desired; and appointing a Governor. The Security Council was required to approve the instruments of Trieste and to accept the responsibilities thereunder. In spite of some protests that it had no authority under the Charter to undertake these sorts of duties, the Security Council agreed to do so, being guided by the view of the Secretary-General that sufficient inherent powers flowed from Article 24 of the Charter: 49 U.N.T.S. 186; and *Off.Rec.S.C.,* 2nd. yr., No. 3, pp. 44–45. For a detailed discussion see Schachter, in (1948) 25 B.Y.I.L., 96–101.
[57] *Ante,* pp. 255–261.   [58] *I.C.J. Reports,* 1949, p. 182. Italics added.
[59] *Ibid.,* p. 184.

was confirmed in 1954, when the Court deemed valid the establishment of an Administrative Tribunal to regulate disputes between the United Nations and its employees, for although the Charter contained "no express provision for the establishment of judicial bodies or organs" such provision could be inferred "by necessary intendment out of the Charter." [60]

It has been observed elsewhere that in practice the powers of the United Nations have not even been restricted to those which, even if not explicitly provided for, were "essential to the performance of its duties." It was hardly "essential" that United Nations medals be awarded to personnel in Korea and the Congo, for example.[61] The position is therefore more accurately stated by saying that the United Nations may perform any action which is not specifically forbidden under the Charter, provided that it is within the Principles and Purposes of the Charter. This indeed was the attitude taken by the United Kingdom Government over UNEF; it declined to seek specific Charter authority for its establishment, but noted that no Article prevented its being set up.[62] It is at least arguable that this general basis is also more realistic for the ONUC action in the Congo, rather than the somewhat tortuous reliance on either Article 40 or Article 42.[63] In this particular case, however, the prevention of civil war and, ultimately, the suppression of secession, are sufficiently doubtful general objectives for the United Nations for a specific mandate also to be required.[64]

There remains, of course, the question of interpretation as to whether or not certain actions *are* forbidden by existing Articles of the Charter. So far as the establishment of United Nations Forces is concerned, Articles 39, 43, 46 and 47 are relevant in this context. Does the existence in these Articles of specific provisions for the use of force (Article 39 listing situations appropriate for the use of force by the United Nations, and referring to Articles 41 and 42, and Articles 43, 46 and 47 stating the modalities to be used for such measures) render invalid the formation of a United Nations Force

---

[60] *Effects of Awards of Compensation made by the United Nations Administrative Tribunal, I.C.J. Reports,* 1954, pp. 56–57.

[61] For a very helpful statement and illustration of this point, see Seyersted, *op. cit.,* pp. 455–460. And see General Assembly Resolution 483 (V).

[62] *Ante,* p. 94, and see E. Lauterpacht, "Survey of British Practice," in (1957) 6 I.C.L.Q. at p. 322.

[63] *Ante,* pp. 179–180.

[64] The International Court, in the *Expenses Case,* lent some weight to the view that the doctrine of implied powers is to be liberally construed so as to permit all actions within the purposes of the UN; indeed, it said that "when the Organisation takes action which warrants the assertion that it was appropriate for the fulfilment of one of the stated purposes of the United Nations, *the presumption is that such action is not ultra vires the Organisation.*" I.C.J. Reports, 1962, p. 168. Moreover, if the action is within the scope of the functions of the United Nations, but taken by the wrong organ, or in an irregular manner, any expense incurred *vis à vis* a third party was still an expense of the Organisation within Article 17 (2): *ibid.* In view of this last pronouncement by the Court exception must be taken to Seyersted's comments on constitutionality, inherent powers and binding obligations: *op. cit.* (1961), 37 B.Y.I.L. at pp. 459–60.

under general, inherent powers? In other words, are these particular Charter provisions to be interpreted *a contrario*? The argument for insisting that they must be is that otherwise the specific Charter provisions become meaningless. However, the basic purposes and objectives of the Organisation are paramount, and " this interpretation has not been adopted in practice any more than *a contrario* interpretation has been adopted in most other cases where an international constitution specifies certain inherent powers." [65] Further, the International Court itself, in the *Expenses Case*, has refused to interpret Article 43 in this manner. The Court stated that the failure to implement Article 43 did not exclude the possibility " that the Security Council might act under some other Article of the Charter . . . It cannot be said that the Charter has left the Security Council impotent in the face of an emergency situation when agreements under Article 43 have not been concluded." [66]

It will readily be seen that this broad view of " necessary intendment " in the United Nations Charter is in keeping with the principle of effectiveness in treaty interpretation. The general rule of interpretation by which the parties are supposed to favour the effectiveness of a treaty they have agreed upon,[67] also guides the interpretation of international constitutions. The relationship of this principle to the doctrine of implied powers is apparent. The emphasis of the International Court on the principle of effectiveness in reference to the *Reparation for Injuries Case* has already been commented upon. Not only the advisory opinion on the *United Nations Administrative Tribunal Case*, but also that on the *Reservations to the Genocide Convention*, relied strongly on the effectiveness of treaties.[68] This principle has its limits—as can be seen from the case on the *Interpretation of Peace Treaties* [69]—but so far as the establishment of

---

[65] Seyersted, *op. cit.*, p. 461.

[66] *I.C.J. Reports*, 1962, at p. 167. See also the statement of the Danish Government before that Court, to the same effect. The Danish Government considered Articles 42–46 inapplicable to the Congo, but thought this irrelevant because the Congo operations " are firmly based on the implied powers of the United Nations, if not any specific article of the Charter." *I.C.J. Pleadings*, 1962, p. 162.

[67] On the principle of effectiveness in treaty interpretation see Lauterpacht, *The development of International Law by the International Court* (1958), Part IV. In the *Expenses Case* the Danish Government also made haste to avail itself of this principle, declaring that to maintain that " the responsibility of the Security Council for the preservation of international peace and security can only be discharged under the conditions and modalities laid down in Chapter VII would be tantamount to reducing the United Nations to an extremely inefficient instrument for the realisation of the purposes and principles to which member states are committed under Article 1." *I.C.J. Pleadings*, 1962, p. 162.

[68] See the *Effect of Awards of Compensation made by the United Nations Administrative Tribunal, I.C.J. Reports*, 1954, p. 57; and *Reservations to the Genocide Convention, I.C.J. Reports*, 1951, p. 24. This principle of interpretation was also known to the League: *Competence of the International Labour Organisation*, Series B, No. 13, p. 18.

[69] *I.C.J. Reports*, 1950, p. 221. For an invaluable discussion of the limits of the doctrine of effectiveness, see Lauterpacht, *op. cit.*, pp. 282–293.

United Nations Forces is concerned, these limits lie more in the principle that the doctrine of implied powers cannot be divorced from the question of which organ chooses to exercise powers which may be legitimately implied for the Organisation. Thus the power to establish a Force for particular purposes cannot be implied for a particular organ except upon the basis of construction of the general and express powers of *that* organ.

If one seeks a basis for ONUC and UNEF in the doctrine of implied powers and the principle of effectiveness, it is necessary to ask what uses of force, other than for enforcement measures under Articles 41 and 42, are inherent in the Charter and within the purposes and principles of the Charter. Article 1 (1) is of considerable guidance here, for it states that:

" the Purposes of the United Nations are:
1. To maintain international peace and security, and to that end: to take effective collective measures for the prevention and removal of threats to the peace, and for the suppression of acts of aggression or other breaches of the peace. . ."

It is arguable therefore, that the United Nations has the inherent power to establish Forces for these named purposes; and this inherent power exists even if the Forces designated for these tasks are of a more limited nature than those anticipated for enforcement measures under Chapter VII.[70]

8. *The principle of " consent "*

The view has already been expressed[71] that the constitutional basis of a United Nations Force is not to be found in the consent of any State upon whose territory the Force may be required to operate: such constitutional basis is to be found in the Charter and not in matters extraneous to the Charter (for the Charter nowhere refers to the necessity for such consent). Hence the existence of such a consent may be relied upon to indicate that the operations are in the nature of " peace-keeping " operations rather than " preventive or enforcement action," but this is to treat consent as evidence of a particular Charter basis, not to accept consent as in itself a constitutional basis. Even here, the consent of a particular State is not

---

[70] Further than this it does not seem possible to go. The present writer is unable to agree with the contention put forward by Halderman, " Legal Basis for United Nations Armed Forces" (1962) 56 A.J.I.L. 971, that Article 1 (1) of itself provides *substantive authority* for the establishment of a United Nations Force. The initiation of such measures must still be by a particular organ of the UN, and the question whether that organ has such an express or implied power must still be answered: otherwise one might be tempted to conclude that *any* organ, ECOSOC for example, could do so. It is this fault of attempting to disassociate Article 1 (1) from the powers of the particular organ which, it is believed, has led Halderman into the error of asserting that the Assembly, acting under Article 1 (1), is not limited to a mere power of making recommendations to States but can decide to apply " tangible pressures." See further, *ante*, pp. 178–179.
[71] *Ante*, pp. 180, 231–232.

conclusive: it is not difficult to imagine a United Nations enforcement action being taken in the territory of a State, which is the
victim of aggression, with its consent in order to oust the forces of
an aggressor.

Thus it is believed that the question of the right of the United
Nations to place a United Nations Force in the territory of a State
is best dealt with as a question separate from the constitutional basis
of the Force, and this question is therefore postponed until Chapter
12 below.[72]

---

[72] *Post*, pp. 412–427.

9

Structure and Control of United Nations Forces

I. TYPES OF FORCE

THERE is no scarcity of plans for "international police Forces" or "United Nations Peace Forces" or however a Force for the United Nations may be called. In 1930 Lord Davies identified three main schemes for the organisation of an "international police Force":

(1) A Force might be made up of quotas drawn from members of the League of Nations under the supervision of a general staff at the headquarters of the international authority, remaining under national control in peacetime, and falling automatically under command of the international authority on being mobilised;

(2) A Force comprising, after abolition of all national forces, a complete self-contained international army, navy and air force under the sole direction and control of the international authority;

(3) A composite Force made up of national quotas formed around a specialised contingent enlisted, equipped and controlled by the international authority.[1]

He said with great penetration that, "It may be possible to produce a host of proposals, but these will probably be variations of one of the three schemes . . . ," and in weighing the advantages and disadvantages of each of his three schemes, displayed an uncanny acumen.[2]

Hence, Clark and Sohn's 1958 "Gestalt" scheme[3] is an elaboration of Lord Davies' second scheme. Annex II of "World Peace through World Law" sets out a plan for the organisation, command and maintenance of a world peace Force whose growth would accompany a stage-by-stage disarmament of the world.

In a monograph entitled "International Policing," published by the New Commonwealth Institute in March 1935, Professor Hans Wehberg concluded that League members should try "to create at least the nucleus of an international police." This, he thought, would be "a new and great experiment" which mankind must have the

---

[1] Davies, *The Problem of the Twentieth Century* (1930), at p. 368.
[2] After each of his three schemes, Lord Davies set out its advantages and disadvantages, anticipating the American International Law Society's *Report of Committee on Study of Legal Problems of the United Nations*, Proceedings, American Society of International Law (1957) at pp. 227–228.
[3] *World Peace through World Law* (1960) 2nd ed. (revised), Annex II.

courage to try. Wehberg's is a modest variation of Lord Davies' third scheme.

In a work under the title "International Sanctions," [4] published under the auspices of the Royal Institute of International Affairs in 1938 the group of members responsible for the report identified the following types of "international police Forces":

(1) An overwhelmingly powerful Force, consisting of all arms, under the complete control of an international body;

(2) A Force made up of ear-marked national contingents; or

(3) A combination of (1) and (2), *i.e.*, a centrally controlled Force around which ear-marked national contingents would form.

The resemblance between these and those proposed by Lord Davies is obvious.

In 1962 a monograph entitled "Keeping the Peace" [5] was published by the Wyndham Place Trust. The group responsible for the work saw the ultimate International Peace Force developing in stages:

(1) The present stage of *ad hoc* Forces, constituted for particular emergencies;

(2) Forces made up of ear-marked national units;

(3) Light standing Forces operating in a fully armed world;

(4) A stronger standing force in a fully armed world;

(5) A Force becoming supra-national, in a disarming world; and

(6) A world peace Force in a disarmed world.

If we eliminate, at this stage, those proposals which deal with a type of Force appropriate to some stage of disarmament and concentrate on types appropriate to the immediate future it becomes clear that there are three basic types of Force:

(1) A Force made up of national contingents provided by United Nations Member States but under the control of the United Nations;

(2) A permanent Force, established as a permanent organ of the United Nations and under its control;

(3) A composite Force combining a permanent nucleus with supporting national contingents, *i.e.*, a combination of (1) and (2).

Which type is appropriate, or even feasible, depends upon what functions one envisages for the Force, and the functions will determine not only the type appropriate but also questions of command structure, operational role, desirable methods of raising, of financing, the application of the laws of war, the necessity for bases, logistic support and permanent legal arrangements. Hence it will be necessary to consider each basic type, and any variations within that

[4] Royal Institute of International Affairs, *International Sanctions* (1938) at pp. 122, 123.
[5] Wyndham Place Trust, *Keeping the Peace* (1962).

basic type, in terms of the different functions which may be envisaged for the Force.

1. *A Force made up of national contingents provided by United Nations Member States but under the control of the United Nations*

This type of Force is, essentially, the type provided for in Chapter VII of the Charter, and also the type of Force which, although not the same as the Force contemplated in Articles 42 and 43 of the Charter, has been used by the United Nations in Korea, UNEF, ONUC, UNTEA and various observer groups.

The kind of national contingents required will, of course, depend upon the functions envisaged for the Force, hence the following broad generalisations are possible.

(a) *Enforcement functions*—military units equipped for armed hostilities on a scale (and of a size) dependent on the degree of resistance likely to be encountered;

(b) *Peace-keeping operations*—either military units lightly armed, *or* military observers recruited from governments as individuals rather than as units; *or* a combination of both when the observers may need armed protection.

The provision of these units, or individual personnel, can be either by way of a prior undertaking by States to contribute—the Article 43 Agreements with the Security Council or other " stand-by agreements " with either the Council or the General Assembly—or else on a voluntary, *ad hoc* basis as has so far been the case. There is the important variant of these which lies in between these two methods of providing forces in that it envisages that contributions will be voluntary but nevertheless planned for in advance, as when a State complies with the Assembly's invitation in the Resolution on Uniting for Peace to maintain within its armed forces units capable of being used at short notice upon call by the Assembly or the Council. This was essentially the " Pearson Plan " for peace-keeping operations: Mr. Pearson, the Canadian Secretary of State for External Affairs, suggested that:

" Even if governments are unable to give the United Nations a ' fighting ' force ready and organised to serve it on the decision of the Security Council, they should be willing to earmark smaller forces for the more limited duty of securing a cease fire already agreed upon by the belligerents. We might in this way be able to construct a halfway house at the crossroads of war, and utilise an intermediate technique between merely passing Resolutions and actually fighting." [6]

As a first step he proposed the establishment of a " permanent mechanism by which units of the armed forces of member countries could be endowed with the authority of the United Nations and made available at short notice for supervisory police duties."

[6] Pearson, "Force for the UN" (1957) 35 *Foreign Affairs* at p. 401. For a similar proposal see the U.K. Foreign Secretary, Mr. Selwyn Lloyd at the 14th Session: *Off.Rec.G.A.*, 14th Sess., 798th Plen. Mtg., 17 September 1959.

Admitting that he was not proposing "anything very new," Mr. Pearson:

(1) Urged that non-permanent Members of the Security Council " should be invited to signify a willingness in principle to contribute contingents to the United Nations for purposes that are essentially noncombatant, such as, for example, the supervision of agreed cease fires and comparable peace supervisory functions";

(2) Suggested as a concomitant of effective organisation " some type of central United Nations machinery " made up of the Secretary-General, a permanent Military Adviser and a small staff;

(3) Recommended the use of an advisory committee similar to that constituted when UNEF was established;

(4) Recommended the revitalisation of the Peace Observation Commission of which the Peace Supervision Force would be an " extension in space "; and

(5) Suggested that model agreements be prepared in advance governing financial, administrative and legal procedures under which national contingents would be made available to the United Nations.

The " Pearson Plan " was really a proposal for certain steps to improve the UNEF prototype. It remains, therefore, a plan for this first type of Force, and not a plan for a permanent Force. The second of the suggestions enumerated above is the only one that comes anything near to a proposal for a permanent nucleus, but even this is really directed to increasing the strength of the personnel within the Secretariat on whom the Secretary-General may rely for advice: it is not the kind of permanent United Nations Military Staff which is referred to below in connection with the composite type of Force.

2. *A permanent Force, established as a permanent organ of the United Nations and under its control*

The initial attractions of this idea are apt to be lessened when one distinguishes between the different functions to be envisaged for a United Nations Force.

(a) ENFORCEMENT FUNCTIONS

These will require military units as outlined in 1 (a) above.

However, once the Force is envisaged as a permanent Force rather than composed of national contingents, there arise a number of problems of which perhaps the greatest is finance.[7] To be within the

---

[7] See Frye, *A United Nations Peace Force* (1957), pp. 72–73 : he estimates that a Force of 500,000 would cost a minimum of $1,500 million per year, approximately 30 times the normal UN budget. One possibility of reducing the size of a UN permanent Force, capable of undertaking major enforcement actions, would be to give to the UN Force an overwhelming weapons

scope of the sort of finance which States may be expected to provide for a United Nations Force (and prior to any real reduction of the costs of maintaining national forces consequent upon disarmament) the Force would have to be of so minimal a size as to be useless against any but the smallest States. The inherent injustice in financing a Force capable of use against only the small, under-developed States is likely to make any proposal for such a force totally unaccept- able. Clark and Sohn, neither of whom can be said to be lacking in optimism, reach this same conclusion that at the present time. or in the immediate future and pending complete disarmament, a permanent Force for enforcement functions is impractical.[8]

However, the fact is that such proposals are being made, and at the eleventh session of the Assembly the Foreign Minister of Pakistan expressed the hope that:

". . . without undue delay the international Force envisaged in Chapter VII of the Charter will be established on a permanent basis for enforcing the rule of law in all international disputes. Even though this permanent international Force may not be stronger than the national armed forces, its moral force, with the backing of the whole civilised world, would be an effective deterrent to any potential aggressor. This international Force, comprising for the present the units made available to the United Nations by the armed forces of Member States under General Assembly Resolution 337 (V), should eventually be recruited and paid for by this Organisation and located, under its own commanders, in various strategic areas of the world." [9]

The Pakistani proposal thus looks beyond the stage of what may be called the " Pearson Plan " to a stage at which a truly international and permanent Force should be created. No details were given of the size and cost of the Force envisaged.

(b) PEACE-KEEPING OPERATIONS

For this function the proposal for a permanent Force begins to be feasible, for it could generally be expected to be on a smaller scale than the Force required under (a) above. However, ONUC developed to a size of 20,000, so that the financial implications must not be under-estimated. A more realistic size might be in the region of 5-10,000.

The scheme put forth by Cannon and Jordan [10] in 1957 envisaged a lightly armed infantry brigade of 7,000 men, formed of national contingents from nations other than the Permanent Members of the Security Council and controlled by the General Assembly, not the Security Council. The financing of the Force was to be borne (by

superiority. But this is only feasible as a long-term plan in conjunction with general disarmament, and was so conceived by Lord Davies, *op. cit.,* p. 377. For suggestions that, under disarmament, the UN Force might retain a monopoly of the atomic weapon, see *post,* pp. 544–545.

[8] *World Peace through World Law,* p. 315.
[9] *Off.Rec.G.A.,* 11th Sess., Plen. Mtgs., Vol. 1, 601st Mtg.
[10] " Military aspects of a Permanent UN Force," in Frye, *A United Nations Peace Force* (1957) pp. 161–171.

apportionment by the Assembly) by all United Nations Members with the exception of those contributing troops: States would be entitled to an allowance for the facilities, services or equipment donated by them.

There would not seem to be any real need to confine the power to control the Force to the Assembly: indeed, it may be surmised that any proposal to do so would meet with the bitterest opposition by the Soviet Union.[11] The most that could be expected, and even this is highly problematical, is an acceptance of the principle which the International Court of Justice accepted in the *Expenses Case*, and which in a sense [12] lies behind the Resolution on Uniting for Peace, that, if the Security Council by reason of the veto fails to discharge its responsibilities and instruct the use of the Force in situations clearly calling for its use, the Assembly has the power to do so.

The International Law Association has recently devoted a good deal of attention to the problem of establishing a permanent United Nations Force for peace-keeping operations only (and to this extent its inquiry was more limited than the very wide terms of the Pakistani proposal). Professor Schwarzenberger, the Rapporteur of the Committee on the Charter of the United Nations, argued strongly for a study of a proposal to establish a permanent Peace Force of between 2,000 and 10,000 men,[13] and a definite proposal was submitted by which the Conference would have resolved:

" 1. To recommend that the General Assembly of the United Nations consider at its next session, as a matter of urgency, the establishment of a permanent United Nations Peace Force and Observer Corps to assist the Organisation in the fulfilment of its obligations regarding the maintenance of world peace and international security;

2. To request the Committee on the Charter of the United Nations to examine . . . any of the problems raised in the Rapporteur's Report, as well as those involved in the establishment of a permanent United Nations Peace Force and Observer Corps, with a view to submitting a Report to the next Conference." [14]

This resolution was not, however, adopted: instead the Conference requested the Committee:

" To examine, if necessary with the assistance of outside experts, any of the problems raised in the Rapporteur's Report, as well as those involved in the establishment of a permanent United Nations Peace Force and Observer Corps, with a view to submitting a Report to the next Conference." [15]

[11] See Schwarzenberger's *Report on Legal Problems of a UN Force, Report of the 49th Conference of the I.L.A.*, p. 151: " . . . proposals for a permanent United Nations Force might appear less extravagant than while it had to be taken for granted that such a Force would have to operate under the direction of the General Assembly." He lists five situations in which the Security Council might find it possible to operate an " interposition " Force.
[12] " In a sense " because the literal wording of the Resolution on Uniting for Peace is apt to include enforcement action as well as " peace-keeping operations," and it is only the latter which concern us here.
[13] *Report of the 48th Conference of the I.L.A.* (New York, 1958) at p. 510.
[14] *Ibid.*, p. 519.
[15] *Ibid.*, p. xiv.

Notwithstanding his excellent Report to the 49th Conference at Hamburg in 1960,[16] which he supported by the most persuasive arguments, Dr. Schwarzenberger failed to gain even the Committee's approval of that part of a draft resolution which *considered*:

" in the light of the experiences gained in the practice of the United Nations, *that* the establishment and maintenance of United Nations Forces on the pattern of the United Nations Emergency Force is entirely in accordance with the letter and spirit of the Charter of the United Nations, and that further developments on these lines, especially in the direction of creating some more permanent framework and cadres of military and technical personnel, are in the best interest of the United Nations." [17]

Rather the Conference requested the Committee to carry out a further study with a view to reporting at an early date on the following specific questions:

(1) Whether it would be useful to prepare draft standing orders for the guidance of United Nations Commands in case of need;

(2) What are the respective legal implications, advantages and disadvantages, on the one hand, of *ad hoc* United Nations Forces and, on the other, permanent United Nations Forces;

(3) What are the respective legal implications, advantages and disadvantages, on the one hand, of United Nations Forces, consisting of contingents contributed by Member States and, on the other hand, a United Nations Force, based on the method of individual enlistment; and

(4) What are the rules governing civil and criminal liability resulting from the activities of a United Nations Force and the proper jurisdiction to which such matters should be referred.[18]

The reactions of the International Law Association to these proposals are instructive in that they indicate very clearly that reserve (or even hostility) to the idea of a permanent Force is not confined to politicians.

3. *A composite Force combining a permanent nucleus with supporting national contingents*

It was this kind of compromise, composite type of Force which, in 1930, Lord Davies felt to offer the best solution.[19] Again, however, one has to distinguish the two different types of function to be envisaged for the Force before the type of composite Force becomes clear.

---

[16] *Report of the 49th Conference of the I.L.A.* (Hamburg, 1960), at pp. 96, 130; and see for reference to this report, *ante*, pp. 279, 287.

[17] *Ibid.* (49th) at p. 112.

[18] *Ibid.* (49th) at p. 124.

[19] *Op. cit.*, p. 380. But note that the functions of the " international police force " were, for him, essentially those of repelling aggression and enforcing decisions of judicial and arbitral tribunals: these are the functions in practice least exercised so far by UN Forces. The permanent element would, in his plan, have had a marked weapons superiority over the national contingents.

(a) ENFORCEMENT FUNCTIONS

In all likelihood the permanent nucleus would have to be on a reasonably substantial scale. The permanent Force of 7,000 planned by Cannon and Jordan was, in the event of a situation developing which called for enforcement action or even serious military combat falling short of that (as in the Congo) to be either withdrawn or reinforced by national contingents.[20] Thus, in the event of reinforcement, the United Nations Force of one brigade would be no more than a permanent nucleus for a larger Force of this composite type.

There is, however, no axiomatic size for such a nucleus; the reasons for a smaller, or larger, nucleus of a permanent character would be reasons of finance, political acceptability, military convenience and the like. It is possible that the permanent nucleus could be no more than a standing Headquarters Military Staff from which could be drawn a United Nations Command, and this is a proposal which we shall develop under the next head.

(b) PEACE-KEEPING OPERATIONS

Prima facie, a permanent nucleus for this kind of function would be smaller than that required for enforcement functions. The proposals of Trygve Lie, as Secretary-General, in 1948,[21] for a United Nations Guard of 800 (500 of which would be reservists) was one kind of nucleus, although envisaged for somewhat more limited functions than the entire " peace-keeping " bracket includes. His later proposals for a United Nations " Legion " in 1951 [22] envisaged a quasi-permanent nucleus in the form of a United Nations Volunteer Reserve, although these would have been designed for enforcement action.

It may well be that a modest beginning could be made by establishing as a permanent nucleus only a United Nations Headquarters Military Staff which could be entrusted with advance planning of different kinds of operations, both enforcement and peace-keeping, and with the training of officers from States which were in principle, or even by commitment in a stand-by agreement, prepared to contribute national contingents to serve under this nucleus. In the event of an actual operation the United Nations Military Staff would then use the national contingents, and assume command over them, in a somewhat less *ad hoc*, or improvised, way than has been the United Nations' practice hitherto. Such a beginning, combined with the co-operation of Member States in the form of a definite ear-marking of units of their national forces or, even better, the conclusion of stand-by agreements whereby States undertook an obligation to make such units available to the United Nations, would signify a real advance in methods of maintaining international peace.

[20] *Loc. cit.*, p. 162.
[21] *Ante*, pp. 18–20.
[22] *Ante*, pp. 25–26.

Lord Robertson (formerly General Robertson), in the House of Lords debate on 20 February 1963, advocated "the immediate creation . . . of a headquarters, containing a strong political and military planning staff and a logistic nucleus. . . . This staff should owe allegiance to the Secretary-General through its own Chief of Staff . . . they should be the servants of the United Nations." He continued:

"Such a headquarters would, in my view, have functions roughly as follows. In the first place, it would make a study of the various kinds of intervention that the United Nations might be called upon to make, whether by force or by showing a presence, and a study of those ancillary activities which might be associated with intervention, such as the temporary assumption of responsibility for civil affairs, to which the Motion most properly draws attention. Second, as part of this study, the staff should devise and recommend a sensible system of control to ensure proper, prompt and constant direction and a reasonable chain of military command. Thirdly, it should collect information and collate it on the various parts of the world where information might be needed. Fourth, and most important, it should be authorised to consult with the governments of those States who agree, and who should be pressed to agree, to earmark forces . . . to consult them about their composition, their state of readiness, their training and so forth, and to make inspections. Fifth, this staff should plan the logistics of intervention, and the infrastructures needed for it—by which I mean the telecommunications, the chain of airfields and so on." [23]

There is increasing evidence of a recognition that the creation of a permanent Headquarters Military Staff is a logical and necessary next step in the improvement of the United Nations peace-keeping machinery. A study by the World Veterans Federation concluded that "all members of the Study Group agreed that a permanent planning organisation within the United Nations should be set up as soon as possible." [24] Significantly, this study was based upon the comments of senior military officers who had had actual experience with United Nations military operations.[25] Similar conclusions have recently been made in specialist papers prepared for the International Conference on United Nations Security Forces as a Means to Promoting Peace, to convene in Oslo in February 1964.[26]

---

[23] Parl.Debates (Hansard) H.L., Vol. 246, No. 43, cols. 1392–1393. See also Lord McNair (*ibid.*, col. 1402), speaking in like vein, Lord Tweedsmuir (col. 1405) and the Earl of Lucan (col. 1409).

[24] *The Functioning of Ad hoc United Nations Forces* (1963), p. 13. The functions to be assumed by the planning organisation included 1. A periodic review of national availabilities of Member States in supplying units for an *ad hoc* emergency Force; 2. The operational, logistical and administrative problems to be encountered, including the question of standardisation of equipment, particularly vehicles and light arms, and the establishment of standard operational procedures; 3. Preliminary arrangements for the establishment of a UN Force headquarters, once authorised.

[25] *Ibid.*, Annex A. The officers were General Burns, Air Marshal Miller, Lieut.-General Sean MacEvin and Maj.-General von Horn.

[26] "Earmarking of Forces for the Use of the UN," p. 8; "Establishment of a Permanent Planning Staff within the UN Secretariat"—Introduction to Second Lecture; Bowitz, "The Central and Military Administration of UN Forces," p. 13.

321

It will be one of the major aims of the present study to argue for the creation of such a United Nations Headquarters Military Staff, and the functions which such a Staff could perform will be outlined in the succeeding sections of this study.

4. *The pros and cons of permanent and ad hoc Forces*

It would be inappropriate to reach the above conclusions without a brief examination of the kind of points which are made for and against a permanent Force, an examination all the more interesting since it shows that the objections to a permanent Force relate either to a Force of a kind totally different to that which we now propose, or else are largely misconceived.

(a) THE ARGUMENTS FOR A PERMANENT FORCE

These have been put by various people, in various forms, at different times.[27]   Essentially they are the following:

(1) The improvisation inherent in an *ad hoc* Force leads to inefficient use of resources, uncertainty as to whether a suitable Force can be collected together, and delay in the use of the Force, which could have serious consequences for international peace.[28]

(2) With the dissipation of an *ad hoc* Force, and with no permanent Force remaining in being, much of the experience gained is lost.   It is not enough to commit experience to paper for future reference: experience means also the experience of people in handling a given set of problems, so that permanent personnel become more important than permanent records.[29]

(3) The decision to use the Force must always remain a political decision, but the additional decision of how to constitute a Force—which is necessary when reliance is placed on *ad hoc* Forces—adds further complicating factors which could be avoided if a permanent Force were established.[30]

(4) Personnel of a permanent Force recruited as individuals would not remain members of national forces and would therefore be able to assume the international loyalty and *esprit de corps* which

---

[27] See Lord Davies, *op. cit.*, pp. 377–9; Schwarzenberger's *Report on Legal Problems of a United Nations Force, loc. cit.*, pp. 96–98 and the discussion following this Report at pp. 99–123; *Report of Committee on Study of Legal Problems of the United Nations, Proceedings of A.S.I.L.* (1957) pp. 227–8; Frye, *op. cit.*, Chap. VII.

[28] For a frank confession of these weaknesses see the address by U Thant to the Harvard Alumni Association at Cambridge, Massachusetts, on 13 June 1963 (Press Release SG/1520).

[29] The post-UNEF assurance of the Secretary-General that the experience of the UN was satisfactorily embodied in such records as his *Summary Study of Experience, etc.* (A/3943) and in the experience of the UN Secretariat (para. 186) must be regarded as having been shaken by the Congo operations.

[30] See Green in *Report of the 49th Conference of the I.L.A.*, pp. 114–116; and see *ante*, pp. 109–111, 206–207, on problems of composition of UN Forces.

Secretariat members assume, and would become subject to rights and obligations under Article 100 of the Charter.[31]

(5) The possibility of recruitment of individuals in a permanent Force secures, in addition to the advantages in (4) above, a Force which cannot be dissipated by the withdrawal of national contingents.[32]

(6) In operations of an indefinite nature States are unwilling to see contingents of their national forces committed indefinitely.[33]

(7) Member States might be more prepared to finance a permanent international Force, than a Force comprised of relatively few national contingents.

(8) Service with a United Nations Force requires special skills [34] which cannot be readily imparted to an *ad hoc* Force, and which should be retained.

(9) Consent to the presence of the Force would be more readily forthcoming.[35]

(10) Unity of command and better control over the Force could be achieved.[36]

(11) The permanent Force could become a nucleus around which a larger Force could be constituted, by the contribution of national contingents, for the larger peace-keeping operations (like the Congo) or even enforcement action.

(12) The permanent Force would constitute a " pilot scheme " so as to build up the experience and confidence necessary for the progression to general disarmament, in which a larger United Nations Force would be necessary.

(b) THE ARGUMENTS AGAINST A PERMANENT FORCE

(1) The type of Force required for a particular operation will vary according to the situation, and *ad hoc* Forces give the necessary flexibility to meet different situations.

This was very much the argument used by Hammarskjoeld in his *Summary Study of the Experience derived from the establishment and operation of the Force* (UNEF).[37] Interestingly enough,

---

[31] On the status of members of UNEF see A/3943, para. 128.
[32] See *ante*, pp. 113, 208–209, on withdrawal of national contingents.
[33] For the reservations of States in contributing national contingents see *post*, p. 381.
[34] For example, skills in dealing with communications problems on a bilingual basis or in " policing " a situation with all the limitations on the use of arms inherent in that function as opposed to normal combat operations.
[35] *Proceedings of the A.S.I.L.* (1957) p. 228. This " advantage " was stated to exist on the assumption that *ad hoc* Forces required the consent of the territorial State for their operation: on the reasons for not entirely sharing this assumption see *post*, pp. 413–417.
[36] For the impact of this on matters of discipline and the application of the laws of war see *post*, pp. 511–513.
[37] A/3943, paras. 153–154. For his acceptance of the idea of an expanded military staff within the Secretariat see para. 185. He visualised a " standing group of military experts " to keep under review any stand-by arrangements which States might be prepared to conclude with the UN.

U Thant, speaking on 13 June 1963,[38] continued the Secretary-General's traditional opposition. He stated that:

"In my opinion, a permanent United Nations Force is not a practical proposition at the present time . . . Many difficulties still stand in the way of its evolution. Personally, I have no doubt that the world should eventually have an international police Force which will be accepted as an integral and essential part of life in the same way as national police forces are accepted."

However, the reasons against a permanent Force given by U Thant are not the variety of situations to be encountered, and the flexibility of the *ad hoc* system, but rather doubts " whether many governments in the world would yet be prepared to accept the political implications of such an institution and, in the light of our current experience with financial problems, I am sure that they would have very serious difficulties in accepting the financial implications." Hence, the Secretary-General advanced no more reasons of an intrinsically persuasive character against a permanent Force, but rather the simple political fact that governments are not prepared to accept the idea.

(2) The selection of personnel for a permanent Force would be difficult.[39]

This argument has never seemed particularly persuasive to the present writer. Whether secondment from national forces or individual recruitment is chosen, the problems are much the same as in recruiting the United Nations Secretariat—and this has never seemed insurmountable! Clearly some kind of quota system could be devised to prevent over-reliance on a few nationalities,[40] and, even though exclusion of nationals from the Permanent Members might be desirable, there would still be plenty of available and sufficiently expert personnel of the right calibre and qualifications.

(3) The financial implications.

This is, in a relative sense, an extremely strong objection and it is, as we have seen, still the objection which U Thant is raising. No one with any knowledge of the financial difficulties which the United Nations has experienced over UNEF and ONUC would deny the seriousness of this objection. However, it has to be placed in perspective, and it must first be said that, as one conceives of a peace-keeping Force or even a permanent Military Staff, and not a Force capable of enforcement action, so does one's conception of the cost involved alter, and the validity of the objection diminish. It may be recalled that the Secretary-General's estimate for his 800-man Guard Force in 1949 was $4m. per annum.[41] Frye's estimate for a force of

---

[38] SG/1520.
[39] See Saario in *Report of the 49th Conference of the I.L.A.*, p. 103. A similar argument was used by the U.K. in opposing the Secretary-General's proposals for a UN Guard in 1949: see *ante*, p. 20.
[40] The formula suggested by Clark and Sohn for a disarmament Force (*op. cit.*, p. 324) limiting the number of any one nationality to 3 per cent. of the total strength is one kind of solution: in relation to the UN Secretariat there has long been a fixing of the desirable number of posts for any one nationality.   [41] *Ante*, p. 19.

7,000 men was $25m. per annum when not in action.[42]   UNEF, of 6,000 strong in 1958, was costing approximately $20m., and ONUC, of 16,000, approximately $120m.; in both cases, however, large parts of the upkeep was the burden of the participating States and not the United Nations.[43]   Astronomic though these sums might be, viewed relatively they are reduced to their proper perspective, and they make a rather favourable comparison to the sums States are prepared to spend on their defence budgets or even single items in those budgets.[44]   Moreover, as the recent examples of UNTEA and the Yemen Group show,[45] on some occasions the States directly concerned may be prepared to assume the entire cost of the operations.

Basically, the objection of finance is an objection to the assessment of a permanent Force as an institution of high priority in the maintenance of peace and security.   The moment that one accepts that such a Force could make a contribution to the maintenance of international peace and security of the same order as the vast standing armies of the Member States, the objection of finance loses a great deal of its force.

Finally, it may be said that what is proposed above is not even, as a first step, a standing, permanent Force but rather a permanent Headquarters Military Staff.   If one visualises a Staff of, say, fifty experienced officers,[46] the cost may well be in the order of $500,000 per annum : by any standards a not oppressive sum for more than a hundred Member States.

(4) Political unacceptance of the idea.

There is little doubt that the majority of Member States, as represented by their governments, show relatively little enthusiasm for the idea.[47]   Quite apart from the question of cost, there are

---

[42] *Op. cit.*, pp. 78, 167.   This cost is likely to be doubled when the Force is deployed in a State's territory on a peace-keeping operation.   The cost of ONUC at a strength of 6,000 for six months only has recently been estimated by the Secretary-General to be $25m : *UN Review*, Vol. 10, No. 9, October 1963, p. 45.

[43] *Post*, pp. 468–471.

[44] Frye, *op. cit.*, p. 78 cites the cost of a Forrestal aircraft-carrier as $200m. In *NATO, Facts about the North Atlantic Treaty Organisation* (1962) at p. 105 the total defence expenditures for the NATO countries are given, and the following figures are taken from the table there produced :

Currency Unit	1958	1959	1960	1961 (Forecast)
Canada Million Can. $	1,740	1,642	1,654	1,703
France Million New Frs.	16,569	17,926	18,940	19,800
U.K. Million £s Strlg.	1,591	1,589	1,652	1,701
U.S.A. Million U.S. $	45,503	46,614	46,545	51,093

It is believed that the Soviet Union's defence expenditure in 1961 was £4,960 million.

[45] *Ante*, pp. 85, 260.

[46] For details see *post*, p. 350.

[47] For observations on the sectional interests of States, real or imaginary, which militate against a permanent Force, see Frye, *op. cit.*, p. 34.

many [48] who distrust the idea because of a fear that the Force may be used to interfere with State sovereignty, or may be used to augment the Secretary-General's power in an improper way,[49] or used by a group or *bloc* of States in a way designed to further their regional interests rather than the purposes and principles of the Charter and the interests of the Members as a whole.[50] There is a certain validity in these objections, but they go to the desirability of establishing a proper system of political control [51] rather than to the establishment of a permanent Force as such. Moreover, since we are for the present talking in terms of a permanent United Nations Military Staff, and in the more remote future perhaps a permanent Force of 5–10,000 men, the very limited size of the Force is such that it can scarcely be regarded as a potential aggressor against States.

It may be that governments also instinctively dislike proposals which imply some restraint on their freedom of action—and certainly a permanent United Nations Force will be utilised to curb certain forms of action—but this is scarcely an objection which ought to carry much weight once the Force is conceived as an instrument designed to ensure that governments abide by the obligations they have already assumed under the Charter with regard to the limitation of the use of force. The other comment which must be made on the objection of " political unacceptance " is that governments may be becoming divorced from the opinions of their people. Ill-informed as the general public may be, gallup polls in the United States have revealed a majority view in favour of a permanent Force for the United Nations,[52] and one suspects that a good many States would find a similar view amongst their people.[53]

---

[48] See *Report of the 49th Conference of the I.L.A.* for observations by Tunkin (U.S.S.R.), p. 104, Perera (Ceylon), p. 109.

[49] *Ibid.*, statement by Sztucki (Poland), p. 121.

[50] See *ante*, p. 215, for comments on the role of the African States in the Congo operations.

[51] As to this see *post*, p. 353 *et seq.*

[52] For details see Frye, *op. cit.*, pp. 66–67. See also the celebrated Resolution 109 of the U.S. Congress in July 1958 that :
" (a) A Force of a similar character (to UNEF) should be made a permanent arm of the United Nations;
(b) Such a Force should be composed of units made available by members of the United Nations : provided, that no such units should be accepted from the Permanent Members of the Security Council;
(c) Consideration should be given to arrangements whereby individuals would be allowed to volunteer for service with such a Force : provided, that individuals who are nationals of permanent Members of the Security Council such not be acceptable;
(d) Equipment and expenses of such a force should be provided by the United Nations out of its regular budget."
Hearings before the Sub-committee on International Organisation and Movements of the Committee on Foreign Affairs, House of Representatives, 85th Congress, 2d Session (July 24, 1958).

[53] For a very instructive debate on a United Nations Force in the House of Lords on 20 February 1963 see Parl.Debates (Hansard) H.L., Vol. 246, No. 43, cols. 1371-1436. Lord Ogmore called for a small permanent Force, recruited

A final, and perhaps the most important, comment is that unless a beginning is made in this modest way it is difficult to see how the long-term plans for general disarmament which (at least from the standpoint of the proposals of the United States) envisage a United Nations Force of a permanent kind can ever be found acceptable. An experiment to build up confidence must be begun soon.

(5) The unconstitutionality of the proposal in terms of the United Nations Charter.

The objection has been made [54] that, since the Charter envisages a Force constituted by means of national contingents provided by States pursuant to agreements under Article 43, to establish a permanent Force would be to act *ultra vires*. This is an objection which has, in one sense, already been rejected by Member States generally and by the International Court of Justice in the *Expenses Case*, for it rests on the premise that the only type of Force permissible for the United Nations is the Article 43 type of Force: not one of the Forces so far established has been of this type and the different constitutional bases for United Nations Forces have already been examined to demonstrate the invalidity of this premise.[55]

However, to show the invalidity of this premise is not to answer the whole objection, for no permanent Force has yet been established. The full answer to the objection lies in the doctrine of implied powers [56] : as Seyersted has said:

"Indeed, it appears that while intergovernmental organisations, unlike States, are restricted by specific provisions in their constitutions as to the aims for which they shall work, such organisations are, like States, in principle free to perform any sovereign act, or any act under international law, which they are in a factual position to perform to attain these aims, provided that their constitutions do not preclude such acts." [57]

Nothing in the Charter specifically precludes the establishment of a permanent Force, and, as we have seen,[58] both the Assembly and the Security Council have powers wide enough to enable them to establish a permanent Force as a subsidiary organ for purposes necessary to the maintenance of international peace and security.[59]

as individuals on a long-term basis, with a UN Command and having combined "military, naval and air units and a military-civil affairs component" (col. 1375). He also argued for a permanent Command structure immediately, and a gradual build-up of the individually-recruited element of the Force, gradually displacing the national contingents. He was supported by Earl Attlee, the Lord Bishop of Chichester, Lord Robertson, Lord McNair, Lord Tweedsmuir, and the Earl of Lucan.

[54] *Report of the 49th Conference of the I.L.A.*, observations by Tunkin (U.S.S.R.), p. 104; Litwin (Poland), p. 106; Krishna Rao (India), p. 116.
[55] *Ante*, pp. 274–312.
[56] See generally Seyersted, "United Nations Forces" (1961), B.Y.I.L. pp. 447–470.
[57] *Ibid.*, p. 456.
[58] *Ante*, pp. 274–312.
[59] But see *ante*, pp. 288, 291–293, on the question whether the functions of a Force established by the Assembly can include "enforcement action."

5. *Military, paramilitary or police Force?*

In the Second and final (UNEF) Report [60] to the General Assembly the Secretary-General described UNEF as a "paramilitary" body. This troubled General Burns, who made the following comment in his book:

"I objected to the use of the term 'paramilitary' to describe UNEF or its functions. The Oxford English Dictionary defines 'paramilitary' as 'having a status or function ancillary to that of military forces.' Examples are constabularies or gendarmeries organised more or less on military lines and having functions of maintaining order in turbulent areas, with a regular military force behind them. But UNEF was and is unquestionably formed of military units, from the regular forces of the nations contributing. It is not ancillary to any 'other' military force.

This inappropriate (in my view) use of the term 'paramilitary' perhaps arises from a misapprehension that a military force in all situations invariably and necessarily uses all the arms and means at its disposal to achieve its object. This, of course, is not so, as an army can give 'aid to the civil power' under great restrictions as to its use of arms. In my view, *UNEF is certainly a military force*, but with a strictly limited and defined task and mode of action prescribed for it.

"Possibly 'paramilitary' in the text was used to allay the doubts of some supporters of the Resolution." [61]

When Trygve Lie made his proposal for a United Nations Guard he took pains to emphasise that it would be "entirely non-military." Soviet spokesmen objected even to the light arming of the Guard suggested by the Secretary-General, arguing that so armed the Guard would be a "real armed force" and, for that reason alone, unacceptable.

During the interval between the World Wars it became fashionable to speak of an "International Police Force." The abbreviation "IPF" was used as if it were as generally known as "UN" is today. Others referred to an "international army" or simply an "international force." Frye entitled his book *The United Nations Peace Force*. Mr. L. B. Pearson, Canadian Minister for External Affairs in 1957, now the Prime Minister of Canada, coined the expression "Peace Supervision Force" in his article in the April 1957 quarterly issue of *Foreign Affairs*. For West New Guinea (West Irian) the Secretary-General created a "United Nations Security Force." The United Nations Force in the Congo has not yet been given a distinctive name but is referred to indifferently as the "United Nations Force in the Congo," or the "ONUC (UNOC) Force" or, simply, but inaccurately, "ONUC" or "UNOC." The expressions a "United Nations Military Force" or a "United Nations Armed Force" are consciously, almost self-consciously, avoided.

This preference for euphemisms can be explained, in part, by the feeling that the United Nations ought to be engaged in keeping the peace and not in fighting wars: it overlooks the fact that the United Nations may have to engage in hostilities indistinguishable from

[60] A/3302, para. 10.   [61] *Op. cit.*, p. 313.

warfare in their practical effect in order to keep the peace. The larger explanation is due to a desire to distinguish between the different functions which have in the past been, and may in the future be, entrusted to a United Nations Force.[62]

According to function, UNEF, ONUC and the UNSF are more "police" than "military." The fact remains that a United Nations Force made up of national military contingents will, and is expected to, behave like a military force. The distinguishing mark of a military force is its disciplined response to command, not the fact that its members bear arms and are uniformed.

Many purely civilian organisations wear uniforms and lawfully bear arms. In his article in the *British Year Book* (1961), Dr. Seyersted treats the United Nations Guard and the United Nations Field Service as examples of United Nations "semi-military" bodies. Dr. Seyersted also treats as "semi-military" United Nations military observer groups, UNTSO, UNOGIL and UNMOGIP. The observers are "military" but are not organised as a military body under formal military command. In dealing with his role as "Chief of Staff" of UNTSO General Burns said:

"The title 'Chief of Staff' in military usage denotes a senior officer controlling a more or less extensive staff, and responsible either to a military commander or to a Minister of Defence, or to a Government.

"The Chief of Staff UNTSO is not at the head of a staff, but is the administrator of the corps of United Nations Military Observers and the director of their operations. He is responsible to and receives instructions from the Security Council, usually in the form of its Resolutions. He communicates with the Security Council through the Secretary-General, to whom in the first instance he addresses his routine and day-by-day reports.

"The title, though not terminologically accurate, has established itself through usage." [63]

Kelsen had this to say about the accuracy of designating an armed Force as a police Force:

"Another terminology, the correctness of which is doubtful is to designate as an international 'police' Force only a permanent and separate armed Force at the direct disposal of the central organ of an international security community. A police force is an armed force used in the performance of a police action. A police action is any enforcement action performed by an organ of a community for the welfare of its members, their health, morals, prosperity and, especially, their security. However, it is not a sanitary police force or a police force for the purpose of morals or economics, but a *security police force* with which an international security organisation is concerned . . .The difference between a 'police force' for the maintenance of internal order and an 'armed force' for defence against external aggression is irrelevant within an international security organisation." [64]

---

[62] Thus Poirier, *La Force Internationale d'Urgence* (1962) Part Two, Chaps. I and II, devotes two chapters to the role and nature of UNEF to arrive at the conclusion that UNEF is an international police force and not a military force in the sense of the Charter. Burns was convinced that UNEF was a military force.

[63] *Op. cit.*, p. 295.

[64] U.S. Naval War College, *International Law Studies—Collective Security under International Law, 1954* (1956) at pp. 114-5.

Kelsen's views of the functions of a " security police force " are essentially pre-UNEF; that is to say, they are stated far too narrowly and do not include the variety of functions which have been listed above.[65] This whole controversy over nomenclature seems a somewhat sterile one. The analysis of functions attempted above discloses that United Nations Forces may be entrusted with tasks which involve a greater or lesser risk of combat activity, or even no risk at all: they will accordingly be armed to a greater or lesser extent, or not at all (as with many of the observer groups). The present study has adopted the all-embracing title of " United Nations Forces " to allow for the discussion of United Nations bodies *composed of military personnel*, as opposed to the civilian Secretariat, for whatever purpose or function.

The problem of nomenclature does, of course, assume importance when one discusses proposals for a permanent Force since it will raise the problem of the size, type and equipment of the Force and, indeed, one of the arguments against a permanent Force has been that it would commit the United Nations to a particular type of Force when other types may well be needed. It is believed that this argument has little merit. The permanent nucleus which should be aimed at in the immediate future, namely, a Headquarters Military Staff and soon afterwards a small unit of 5–10,000 men, would be a *military* Force: but it would have to be a versatile Force so that it would be trained, and in the event either armed or not armed, to tackle any of the various functions we have listed. The outstanding merit of the Ghanaian and Nigerian riot police (220 and 120 strong respectively) in the Congo stemmed from their training, not the fact that they were called " police " rather than " military," and there is no reason why a military unit should not be trained to deal with riots as well as armed hostilities. Equally there is no reason why its officers should not be trained in the duties of observers, although a reserve panel of observers might be necessary for situations in which greater numbers of observers would be required,[66] and part of the Force, if necessary, detailed to act as guards for the observers.

II. METHODS OF RAISING UNITED NATIONS FORCES

The methods available to the United Nations for raising forces are closely related to the type of Force envisaged. It will be convenient, therefore, to consider these methods under the same broad heads of types of Force as have been used under Section I.

1. *Ad hoc Forces made up of national contingents provided by United Nations Member States*

The pattern so far has been to rely on agreements *ad hoc*, made between the United Nations (represented in Korea by the United

---

[65] *Ante*, pp. 267–274.
[66] *Post*, p. 548.

States and in UNEF by the Secretary-General) and particular contributing States. The content of these agreements is outlined in
Chapter 10 below. This particular method of raising forces is, of
course, dependent entirely on the voluntary co-operation of Member
States, and it raises, on each occasion, a host of problems of composition, transport, logistics, finance and permanence—for a right
to withdraw contingents voluntarily provided has generally been
assumed. It has, in brief, the questionable advantage of flexibility
and all the disadvantages of hasty improvisation.

An alternative system is that envisaged under Article 43 of the
Charter, namely, that Member States would enter into pre-existing
legal commitments to provide contingents and "ancillary support"
in the form of transport facilities, transit facilities, rights of passage,
etc. The pattern of such agreements emerged clearly from the
discussion in the Military Staff Committee and the Security Council
in 1946–1948, as did the obstacles in the way of such agreements.[67]
However, these negotiations were conducted on the basis of a large-
scale Force designed for enforcement action, and it may well be that
if either the Security Council or the General Assembly were to
attempt a new negotiation of "stand-by" agreements for a "peace-
keeping" Force many of the obstacles would disappear, for the
assumptions basic to these negotiations will have changed radically.
It may be recalled that the major obstacles, or areas of disagreement,
were:

(1) Relative sizes of the contributions of the Permanent Members:
it is likely that, not only would this problem diminish as the total
size of the Force diminished, but the problem would disappear
entirely due to the general acceptance of the principle that peace-
keeping Forces shall not include contingents from the Permanent
Members.

(2) Location of the contingents pending use by the United
Nations: here again practice has been to withdraw contingents made
available for peace-keeping operations back to their national territories, so that to continue existing practice would be to solve the
dispute over this particular question.

(3) Provision of assistance and facilities, including rights of
passage: again practice has been to negotiate any agreements *ad hoc*
and not to secure a general guarantee of such facilities in advance.
To this extent practice has been of the kind which the U.S.S.R.
envisaged, even under Article 43 agreements. However, this is by
no means an ideal situation, as the section on transit and operational
bases will show,[68] and either a general guarantee of facilities or an
agreement in advance of any particular operation would be far
preferable. It may well be that the Soviet opposition to such
guarantees—general or limited—in advance would diminish once a

[67] *Ante*, pp. 12–18.   [68] *Post*, pp. 455–458.

peace-keeping Force of 5–10,000 were envisaged rather than an enforcement Force of 125–300,000 men.

(4) Logistical support: it may be recalled that the Military Staff Committee adopted the basic principle that each national contingent would provide full logistical support, and disagreement arose mainly over the question of how far a Member was entitled to seek assistance from another Member State when it found itself incapable of fulfilling its obligation in this respect. In practice, however, the United Nations peace-keeping Forces so far used have not been regarded as logistically self-sufficient within each national contingent, and logistical support has become more and more a central, United Nations problem, so that here, too, the obstacle to agreement may simply not exist in relation to peace-keeping Forces.

It thus appears that the major obstacles to the conclusion of stand-by agreements which frustrated the Military Staff Committee and the Security Council in their attempts to implement Article 43 may disappear once one thinks in terms of a " peace-keeping " Force. The possibility that the Security Council could renew its efforts to conclude stand-by agreements with States, but for " peace-keeping " Forces and not, at this stage, enforcement Forces, cannot be excluded. It is perhaps more likely, however, especially now that the exclusion of contingents from Permanent Members seems to be the general rule, that the General Assembly will be the more suitable organ to negotiate stand-by agreements between the United Nations and Member States.

This possibility has existed ever since the Resolution on Uniting for Peace, although the Collective Measures Committee did not think in these terms but rather in terms of Member States making arrangements unilaterally to maintain components of their national forces available, on a voluntary basis, to the United Nations and of agreements being made *ad hoc*, when the occasion arose. There seems to be no reason, however, why the General Assembly should not proceed to negotiate stand-by agreements with States for the provision of peace-keeping Forces. It is clear that, in content, such agreements would have to take account of any parallel developments in the nature of permanent regulations for a United Nations Force, standard agreements with host States (Status of Forces Agreements), the establishment of a permanent Headquarters Military Staff and standing Resolutions on financial arrangements: but the basic political difficulties which plagued the Military Staff Committee and Security Council may no longer be relevant.

The Assembly would also have to look to its own organisational structure in order to be in a position to effectively use such Forces when the occasion arose. As will be suggested in Section IV of this Chapter, it will probably need a committee of limited membership to act as a political control organ.

This being said, it must be admitted that so far there is little evidence of the Assembly moving in this direction. Such progress as is being made is in the direction of Mr. Pearson's "half-way" concept of States making, unilaterally, such internal legal and administrative arrangements as may be necessary to enable their national armed forces, or special units of these, to be made available to the United Nations. This seems to be the basis of the recent Scandinavian and Canadian initiatives and it appears to have been as the result of the Secretary-General's request in 1960 rather than by way of an implementation of the recommendation addressed to Member States in the Resolution on Uniting for Peace. What seems to be involved is not a binding commitment to make such forces available, but rather a declaration of willingness, in principle, to do so.[69] It is certainly an advance on the *ad hoc* system used so far,

---

[69] So far six States appear to have offered forces. Netherlands a self-contained Marine Corps unit and a number of Staff Officers; Finland an infantry battalion; Canada a regular army battalion with its own air-lift; and the Scandinavian countries a combined Nordic force of approximately 3,000 men consisting of the following: Denmark one infantry battalion, one signals unit, one medical unit, one military police unit, staff personnel, observers, EME-personnel and movement control personnel totalling about 930 men; Norway both naval and air force units, one movement control team, one military police unit, one surgical unit for emergency purposes, one hygiene unit and Staff personnel, totalling about 500 men; Sweden about 1,200 men already in service in the Congo.

The Secretary-General's Press Release of 1 October 1963 (SG/1588) stated that:

"Communications concerning offers of 'stand-by' military units which could be made available to the United Nations on request have been addressed recently to the Secretary-General by the Governments of Denmark, Finland, Netherlands, Norway and Sweden. Informal approaches on the same subject have been made by some other Governments. The units in question would be for use in United Nations peace-keeping operations and would be kept in readiness for assignment to United Nations duties.

The Secretary-General, in welcoming and accepting these offers, has emphasised the conditions implicit in them, namely that the troops thus designated would be available to the United Nations whenever they might be called for by the Organisation to meet a peace-keeping need, and that unless and until the troops should be called for, the offer to make them available would have no financial consequences for the United Nations.

The Secretary-General has also pointed out that generally the peace-keeping operations of the United Nations in which military personnel are employed are undertaken on the basis of specific authorisation by one of the component United Nations organs. The exact composition of the military body required by the specific operation, as regards particularly such factors as nationality and language, is necessarily and largely influenced by the *locus* and the nature of the situation giving rise to the need for the peace-keeping operation. There is, of course, no authorisation for the creation of a standing or stand-by United Nations Force as such."

No comprehensive "stand-by" agreement seems to have been concluded, and whilst the Secretary-General puts his statement in terms of an offer and an acceptance, thus suggesting a legal commitment on the part of the offering States, it is more likely that the commitment is of a political nature, a commitment "in principle," which could scarcely, in any event, be backed up by any legal process or sanction if it was broken. At this rather rudimentary stage of commitment the distinction between a political and a legal commitment is probably without much meaning; the matter will, of course, be otherwise when a comprehensive stand-by agreement is concluded.

and represents another method of raising Forces, but it is a limited advance and should not be regarded as the best available method for this type of Force: it is bound to remain less satisfactory than a binding agreement between Members and the United Nations.

2. *A permanent Force*

Whereas the Forces contemplated in the preceding type would be constituted *ad hoc*, as and when the occasion arose (and whether by virtue of a voluntary contribution or a pre-existing stand-by agreement), the kind of Force we must now consider is one which is permanently in being as a United Nations Force under United Nations command. It has already been suggested that such a Force can, in practical terms, only be envisaged in the immediate future for peace-keeping operations: a Force of this type could be raised either by calling on national contingents or by resorting to individual recruitment.

(a) COMPOSED OF NATIONAL CONTINGENTS

A scheme could well be devised, perhaps in conjunction with stand-by agreements, for Member States to provide, on a rotation basis, limited contingents for a fixed period of years—say, three years at a time—which would for the duration of that period be completely detached from their national armed forces and placed under exclusive United Nations command. Such a scheme could ensure that, at any one time, there would be national contingents of the right size and kind and drawn from different regions of the world so as to maintain an equitable geographical distribution; moreover, replacement of contingents could be staggered so that there existed a permanent Force with an experienced and trained core. It would be highly desirable, however, for such a system to revolve around a permanent Headquarters Military Staff of which a nucleus at least were individually recruited on a longer contract than three years.

Such a Force could be utilised for peace-keeping operations by either the Security Council or the General Assembly, on the assumption that the latter organ develops its own institutional structure to provide effective political control.

Even with a permanent Force of this kind it would be necessary to make permanent legal arrangements so as to provide for a base or bases for the Force, for its own internal disciplinary system, for a standing set of Regulations for the Force, for a standard Status of Forces Agreement to become operative whenever the Force moved into a State's territory, and for the financing and logistical support of the Force. These permanent legal arrangements are considered in further detail later in Chapters 10, 11 and 13.

(b) COMPOSED OF INDIVIDUALS RECRUITED AS SUCH

The advantages of individual recruitment are, of course, tied up with the more general question of the advantages of a permanent

Force dealt with above. In particular they are that it would be easier to inculcate the international loyalty desirable and to apply rigorously Article 100 of the Charter; that the individuals could serve for longer periods than a national contingent can be released for, say five to seven years rather than three, with a consequent increase in efficiency of the Force; that they could not be withdrawn like a national contingent [70]; that a fully integrated system of training, command, equipment, logistics and discipline could be achieved; and that the financing would be simplified (even though not necessarily reduced in overall cost) in that the United Nations would assume complete responsibility and there would be no problems of accounting as between the United Nations, contributing States and other United Nations Members. It might also be easier to raise finance from non-governmental sources if the Force was individually recruited.

Recruitment could be entrusted either to States or, preferably, undertaken by the United Nations itself as is now the case with the Secretariat.[71] Recruiting centres could be established in all capitals, provided any obstacles in municipal law were removed, and it is believed that there would be no shortage of recruits, particularly if this were regarded as in substitution for any compulsory national service. However, recruitment for the United Nations would remain entirely voluntary. It might also be possible, on the basis of individual recruitment, to get away from the principle now used in *ad hoc* Forces—and which is in some respects regrettable—that nationals of the Permanent Members of the Security Council cannot be employed.

Safeguards could be applied so as to prevent any undue prominence by individuals of any one nationality: for example, it could be provided that no nationality should comprise more than 3 per cent. of the Force or of any one unit of the Force more than fifty strong.[72] The highest echelon of command, immediately under the

[70] This remains a possibility even under (a) above, for it would be difficult to prevent a State breaking its obligations under such a scheme for a permanent Force and withdrawing its national contingent.

[71] The individual recruitment we are here concerned with is direct recruitment into a permanent UN Force. The system advocated by the paper "Earmarking of Forces for the Use of the United Nations," prepared for the International Conference on UN Security Forces, Oslo, February 1964 is the same, and is described as the "ideal" system: but it is different from that which the Scandinavian countries are now envisaging for recruitment of volunteers into the UN stand-by units. The Swedish Parliament in 1961 is reported as having provided for recruitment of volunteers from the existing Swedish forces, these volunteers being given special training and then assigned to the stand-by units: see *The Functioning of Ad hoc. UN Emergency Forces* (1963) p. 20. One of the best discussions of individual recruitment is by Singer. "The Internal Operations and Organisation of an International Police Force" in *Quis Custodiet?* (1963) Vol. 11, Appendices D–18 to D–22.

[72] See the provisions outlined by Clark and Sohn for a Disarmament Force in *Draft of a Proposed Treaty Establishing a World Disarmament and World Development Organisation within the framework of the UN* (May, 1962) Art. 69 (13) and (14). For other possible criteria of quotas see Singer,

Commander, could also reflect the "troika" principle, once it had been agreed to permit recruitment of nationals of Permanent Members of the Security Council.

The terms of service could be made attractive by normal standards of military service, with a salary free from national taxation and pension rights for long service.[73] The standard of personnel would necessarily have to be high, not only because of the nature of the missions to be undertaken but also because the Force would presumably be bilingual—perhaps English and French—and recruits would have to pass proficiency tests in these languages either before, or soon after, recruitment.

The complex of permanent legal arrangements required for a permanent Force on the basis of national contingents would be equally necessary in the case of individual recruitment, with certain modifications. For example, the Regulations of the Force would reflect, and perhaps embody, a service agreement. Since the Force would be entirely independent logistically, an arms purchasing agency would be necessary, perhaps as part of a general procurement agency. The details of these are best postponed until Section II (6) of Chapter 11.

3. *A composite Force combining a permanent Staff and Command Structure with supporting national contingents*

This, it will be recalled, was the type of Force we have suggested as offering the best chance of an immediate, progressive development. So far as the supporting national contingents are concerned, the problems of raising them, and the methods by which they can be raised, are the same as in 1. above. So far as the Headquarters Military Staff and the nucleus of a Command Structure is concerned this would be substantially the same problem as in 2. above, but on a smaller scale. For example, it would no longer be essential to think in terms of permanent bases—but only of training facilities (which States might be readier to concede). It would no longer be essential to have the United Nations establish its own system of military law and discipline, although still desirable. It would no longer be necessary to think in terms of a heavy burden of finance or a completely self-sufficient logistics system. The whole emphasis would be on the recruitment by the United Nations of experienced military officers on an equitable geographical basis, and by arrangements through governments, as *international officials*. The one

---

loc. cit., D–23. Singer also deals with the difficult question of whether units should be confined to recruits from one nationality and, if so, what size of unit; his own argument is for a completely mixed, heterogeneous unit. Clearly this is one of the questions which it would be for the UN Headquarters Military Staff to consider and even experiment with during the initial planning stages.

[73] Eligibility for renewal of contracts after, say, 8 years would probably have to be the exceptional case so long as the Force remained small and it was felt desirable to give maximum opportunities for participation.

condition would be that the personnel should cease to be members of national armed forces and should, for periods of between five to eight years, assume an undivided loyalty to the United Nations.[74] Theirs would be the task of advanced planning for the various kinds of peace-keeping operations which the United Nations might assume on the basis of national contingents provided *ad hoc*, or under stand-by agreements. Included in this task could be the holding of training courses at which officers from States prepared to provide national contingents could be instructed in the problems peculiar to United Nations operations and perhaps also of planning exercises jointly with those national contingents in their own territory.

III. COMMAND STRUCTURE

1. *Ad hoc Forces*

Reviewing the patterns so far established in the strictly military Forces like those in Korea, UNEF and ONUC, it is clear that no standard structure of command has yet been established.

(a) APPOINTMENT OF COMMANDER AND STAFF

It may be recalled that the Military Staff Committee in 1947 had no hesitation in ascribing the responsibility for appointment of a Commander of the Forces envisaged under Chapter VII of the Charter to the Security Council: the difference of opinion was as to whether the appointment of the commanders-in-chief of naval, land and air forces was similarly to be a matter for the Council or for the " Supreme " or " overall " commander.[75]

In Korea the problem was circumvented by entrusting the appointment to the United States, so that the " Unified Command " became in practice fully integrated with the United States Far East Command[76]: that there were decided disadvantages to this has already been shown.[77] An awareness of these was evident in the Report of the Collective Measures Committee which envisaged that the appointment of a Commander-in-Chief should be by the " executive military authority " the State or group of States nominated as such by the Assembly. It would, presumably, be open to the Assembly to entrust command to a group of States already organised as a

---

[74] The Study Group of Strategic Studies of the Norwegian Institute of International Affairs suggests the alternative of attachment of officers from national forces for short periods in order that a balanced rotation may be obtained. It concludes that permanent appointment of officers and NCO's would probably not be right. The present writer disagrees with this view, at least to the extent that it involves the notion that the *entire* Headquarters Staff should consist of short-term secondments. The need is for permanent personnel, as well as permanent machinery, and the position is comparable to that within the international Secretariat where the core consists of permanent officials.

[75] *Ante*, p. 17.

[76] *Ante*, p. 40.

[77] *Ante*, p. 43.

regional arrangement or an organisation for collective self-defence and having an existing command structure. This idea has initial attractions, and indeed is partly anticipated by Chapter VIII of the Charter which envisages that the Security Council may utilise regional arrangements under its authority. However, the fact that many of these organisations are, in terms of the East-West rift, "partisan" or "aligned," would suggest that to entrust to them a United Nations Command would be to invite extreme opposition from other Members of the United Nations, certainly if they were to command Forces in the name of the United Nations operating outside the territories of their own members, and probably also even if designed to meet a situation internal to the regional organisation itself. The plan which President Makarios appears to suggest for the Cyprus problem in February 1964 is along these lines, in that the Security Council would authorise a United Nations Peace-keeping Force to be composed of contingents from the Commonwealth countries, and even a Commonwealth command. At the time of writing the plan has not been put to the Security Council, but its acceptance there is deemed to be unlikely. In any event, great care would have to be taken to ensure that any regional organisation entrusted with a United Nations Command remained subject to close United Nations political control so as to ensure that the political objectives of the operations remained those of the United Nations and not of that particular group of States. Otherwise one might find that a group of, say, Arab or African States would be left free, in the name of the United Nations, to solve the Israeli or South African problems in a way which would be totally unacceptable to the United Nations as a whole. On balance it is believed that to entrust command to a group of States is not a suitable solution to the problems of a United Nations Command structure.

However, in UNEF the Commander was appointed directly by the General Assembly,[78] and in ONUC by the Secretary-General.[79] The Commander of UNEF was, moreover, left free to recruit his staff officers, in consultation with the Secretary-General, and initially relied heavily on the UNTSO personnel, replacing these gradually by the officers of the national contingents from the participating States. The Commanders of both UNEF and ONUC had no control over the appointment of the commanders of the various national contingents, although the Regulations of the Force [80] provided for consultation with him by the authorities of the participating governments before making any changes in their commanders

(b) CHAIN OF COMMAND

The Chain of Command for the Force in Korea was highly unusual [81] and is unlikely to provide a pattern for the future. In UNEF, Regulations 11 and 12 provided:

---

[78] *Ante,* p. 115; UNEF Reg. 5 (a).   [79] ONUC Reg. 5 (c).
[80] UNEF Reg. 12 and ONUC Reg. 12 (the latter provided for consultation with the Secretary-General also).   [81] *Ante,* p. 41.

" 11. *Command Authority*. The Commander has full command authority over the Force. He is operationally responsible for the performance of all functions assigned to the Force by the United Nations, and for the deployment and assignment of troops placed at the disposal of the Force.

" 12. *Chain of Command and Delegation of Authority*. The Commander shall designate the chain of command for the Force, making use of the officers of the United Nations Command and the commanders of the national contingents made available by participating governments. He may delegate his authority through the chain of command. Changes in commanders of national contingents made available by participating governments shall be made in consultation between the Commander of the UNEF and the appropriate authorities of the participating government. The Commander of the UNEF may make such provisional emergency assignments as may be required. The Commander of the UNEF has full authority with respect to all assignments of members of the United Nations Command and, through the chain of command, of all members of the Force. Instructions from principal organs of the United Nations shall be channelled by the Secretary-General through the Commander and the chain of command designated by him."

The military staff organisation was headed by a Chief-of-Staff, who acted for the Commander in his absence,[82] and the Headquarters Staff comprised three sections: (1) personnel, (2) operations, and (3) logistics. There was also a Special Staff "composed of a number of specialised officers who advise and assist the Commander in particular fields and, in some cases, co-ordinate, supervise or carry out functional activities." [83] Liaison officers were established at Cairo and at Tel Aviv.

The national contingents received orders from the Commander, to whom the commanders of these contingents were responsible, and contingents furnishing units for more than one functional task would designate commanders of each functional activity to clarify responsibility in such matters when they affected personnel of national contingents.

In contrast with the above arrangement for UNEF, the ONUC Command Structure was headed by the Secretary-General. ONUC Regulation 11 provided:

"*Command authority*. The Secretary-General, under the authority of the Security Council and the General Assembly, has full command authority over the Force. The Commander is operationally responsible to the Secretary-General through the Officer-in-Charge for the performance of all functions assigned to the Force by the United Nations, and for the deployment and assignment of troops placed at the disposal of the Force."

Regulation 12 was identical to that of UNEF with the exception that changes in the commanders of national contingents required consultation with the Secretary-General, and instructions from the principal organs were to be channelled by the Secretary-General through the Officer-in-Charge, a post unknown in UNEF.

---

[82] The post of Deputy Commander was tried for a time but found to be unnecessary.

[83] A/3943, para. 78.

(c) DELINEATION OF AUTHORITY OF SECRETARY-GENERAL AND COMMANDER

In contrast to Korea, where the Commander's connection with the Secretary-General was minimal,[84] the UNEF Regulations carefully delineated the respective authorities of Commander and Secretary-General. Regulations 15 and 16 provided:

"15. *Authority of the Secretary-General.* The Secretary-General of the United Nations shall have authority for all administrative, executive and financial matters affecting the Force and shall be responsible for the negotiation and conclusion of agreements with governments concerning the Force. He shall make provisions for the settlement of claims arising with respect to the Force.

"16. *Authority of the Commander.* The Commander shall have direct authority for the operation of the Force and for arrangements for the provision of facilities, supplies and auxiliary services. In the exercise of this authority he shall act in consultation with the Secretary-General and in accordance with the administrative and financial principles contained in Regulations 17–28 following."

The Commander was responsible for designating the chain of command; negotiating changes in national commanders; assignments of members of the Command and, through the chain of command, all members of the Force [85]; good order and discipline of the Force [86]; provision of military police [87]; establishing the Headquarters of the Force and other operational centres and liaison offices [88]; recruitment of officers for the Command; arranging detailment of Secretariat Staff with the Secretary-General; recruitment of local personnel [89]; billeting and provision of food and amenities [90]; transportation [91]; procurement of supplies and equipment [92]; the inclusion in the Force of units for telecommunications and postal services [93]; maintenance and repairs [94]; provision of medical, dental and sanitary services [95]; contracts [96] and public information.[97]

The Congo Regulations revealed a very marked change of emphasis. Not only did the Secretary-General assume command authority, but Regulation 16 included the additional phrase that "He shall provide appropriate guidance through the Officer-in-Charge to the Commander in the exercise of the latter's duties and responsibilities . . ." Regulation 21 placed responsibility for administration in the hands of the Officer-in-Charge—including billeting, procurement

---

[84] *Ante*, p. 42.
[85] Reg. 12.
[86] Reg. 13.
[87] Reg. 14.
[88] Reg. 17.
[89] Reg. 19.
[90] Reg. 20.
[91] Reg. 21.
[92] Regs. 22 and 23.
[93] Reg. 24.
[94] Reg. 25.
[95] Reg. 26.
[96] Reg. 27.
[97] Reg. 28.

of food, supplies and equipment, transportation, maintenance and other services, telecommunications and postal services, provision of medical, dental and sanitary services, contracts, public information and recruitment of local personnel.

Thus, whereas in UNEF the Commander had the dual role of military commander and political representative of the United Nations,[98] in the Congo he lost the latter role to the Officer-in-Charge, a civilian representative of the Secretary-General, and he also lost responsibility for most of the administrative side of the functioning of the Force. These changes are perhaps explicable and justifiable by reference to the size of the civilian operations, which existed side by side with the military, and by the very much more delicate nature of the political problems involved.

However, the fact that the Secretary-General—and through him the Officer-in-Charge—assumed command authority over the Commander and the Force is less explicable, for it implies an infusion of the political or civilian element into the domain of command which is strange to Western conceptions of the unity of military command,[99] and, indeed, somewhat difficult to reconcile with Regulation 31 of UNEF and 26 of ONUC which provided that:

" In the performance of their duties the members of the Force shall receive their instructions only from the Commander and the chain of command designated by him."

In all of the Western armed forces, unity of command is axiomatic. The introduction of political commissars in the Soviet military structure after the Revolution created an illogical (in Western eyes) joint command of the Red Army that has waxed and waned according to the fortunes of the Army in war and in peace. Illogical and traditionally inconsistent though the Soviet innovation may appear to be, the notion may be quite the reverse in the context of a United Nations Force that is assigned a politico-military mission. The extent to which the Special Representatives of the Secretary-General in the Congo or West Irian have intruded themselves directly into the formulation of orders issued to the troops is not known. It is fair to assume that the appointed United Nations Commanders have not avoided the influence of the presence of the Special Representatives

[98] A/3943, paras. 76 and 77.
[99] " Military command " is simply a *means* by which a military commander exercises his command in carrying out policy laid down for him. The U.S. Army's Staff Officers' Field Manual defines " staff " as " the staff of a unit consists of the officers who assist the commander in the exercise of his command." Brigadier General James D. Hittle, U.S. Marine Corps, Retired, describes the basic and common staff functions as " procuring information for the commander, preparing details of his plans, *translating his decisions and plans into orders*, and then *causing the orders to be transmitted to the troops*." (Hittle, *The Military Staff—Its History and Development* (3rd ed. 1961) at p. 3). General Hittle takes for granted that orders issued to troops under command will be executed because it is axiomatic that a military force must be subjected to some form of code of service discipline or special régime of law to which soldiers are subject over and above the ordinary law.

in the theatres of their operations.[1] Indeed, one suspects that, had the signing of the cease-fire agreements in Katanga been left to the military commanders—as a matter of military judgment—and had not been done by Mr. Khiary, much of the criticism of them could have been avoided.[2]

It may be difficult for the United Nations staff members to grasp the full significance of the military principle of unity of command, but as long as the United Nations wishes to use a military Force as a peace-keeping mechanism, the principle must be maintained. This is not to say that the United Nations Secretariat staff accompanying the Force should have no powers—of course their powers must be commensurate with their responsibilities. It is clear that political direction and control must not be assumed by the Commander, but must emanate from the political organs and through the Secretary-General and representatives chosen by him; but there is an important distinction to be made between political direction and control[3] on the one hand and military command on the other. What the Secretariat should not assume is the power of military command. Military command is a heady wine for those unused to it and may give rise to illusions of power. Decisions and directions of the United Nations Secretariat, made within the scope of their powers and responsibilities, should be reflected in orders issued by the Commander or on his behalf. In the Canadian National Defence Act it is provided that all orders and instructions to the three Canadian Services "that are required to give effect to the decisions and to carry out the directions of the Government of Canada, or the Minister, shall be issued by or through"[4] the Service Chief of Staff concerned. Without derogating from the paramountcy of civil authority, this statutory provision recognises and maintains the principle of unity of military command.

One would not wish to give the impression of having failed to take into account the differences between the primary aim of a United Nations Force and that of national trained forces. The United Nations Force is not intended to engage in war—the latter exists for that purpose. A national armed force is, therefore, influenced by "principles of war," a United Nations Force by "principles of peace." To function successfully under either set of principles, however, the Force must be subject to a Commander, not to several co-Commanders, some of whom are not military. Within national forces there is room for combined command, that is, where two national services are acting in a combined operation, but in this case the command is still military and not civilian-military.

In his 1958 UNEF Experience Report Mr. Hammarskjoeld devoted one paragraph under the heading "Joint civilian-military organisation" of UNEF. It is worth quoting *in extenso*:

---

[1] See O'Brien, *To Katanga and Back* (1962) pp. 245, 249–287 for an account of his part in the hostitilies in Katanga in August and September 1961.
[2] *Ante*, p. 169.
[3] *Post*, pp. 353–360.
[4] Revised Statutes of Canada, 1952, Chap. 184, s. 19 (5).

"The fusion of military and civilian activities requires considerable understanding as well as knowledge on the part of the Commander, who is the
only officer of the Force operating in both a military and a civilian capacity,
as also on the part of the senior military and civilian officers. In practice,
in the day-to-day activities, it falls mainly to the Chief of Staff to set the
tone for civil-military relationships. The possibility of friction, stemming
from differences in background, training and discipline, is always present and
deserves special attention. There are some areas so clearly defined as to
allow little occasion for military-civil misunderstanding. Among them are
military operations, air operations, health services, military police, legal
affairs, public information, and relations with other United Nations agencies.
Only slight difficulty has been experienced in some other areas where
civilian-military responsibilities are mixed, such as personnel, maintenance
and construction, welfare programmes, supervision of mess facilities and
canteens, rotation of contingents and, finally though they have always been
solved, problems of this kind have arisen in connection with logistics, finance
and travel, and the issuance of directives and instructions covering the general
administration of the Force. With regard to senior officers on the civilian
side and staff officers on the military side, it may be said that too frequent
rotation has been a hindrance to the development and consolidation of
maximum efficiency in administration." [5]

The principle of unity of command is applicable not only to the
possibility of Secretariat intrusion into the command sphere but also
to the attitude of the national contingents, for it follows that they,
too, must respect the complete authority of the Commander
appointed by the United Nations. On the whole, the record seems
to have been excellent, but the Congo operations did reveal a
tendency of certain States to challenge the Secretary-General's interpretation of the role of ONUC by means of instructing their national
contingents to refuse to comply with orders of the Commander or by
proposals to divest the United Nations of command and vest it in an
African Command, composed of nominees of the African participating
States.[6] Such conduct is to be deplored on both political and military
grounds: there are other, and more suitable, means whereby participating States can raise this kind of challenge.[7] This is not to deny
the right of commanders of national contingents to communicate
with their governments on matters affecting their contingent: this
was recognised by the Military Staff Committee,[8] the Collective
Measures Committee [9] and not prohibited by the UNEF and ONUC
Regulations.[10]

(d) DISCIPLINE

The inter-dependence of command authority and disciplinary
powers is normally an axiom of military organisation: without the

[5] A/3943, para. 87.
[6] *Ante*, pp. 214–215.
[7] *Ante*, p. 214.
[8] *Ante*, p. 15.
[9] *Ante*, p. 24.
[10] The use of "liaison officers," not part of UNEF but representing the
interests of the participating State at Headquarters, was evidently tried
during the early days of UNEF, but the Secretary-General's "*Summary
Study, etc. . . .*" (A/3943, para. 82) described their position as "anomalous"
and is critical in tone.

latter the former is in constant jeopardy. However, in *ad hoc* United Nations Forces the system of discipline has so far contradicted this axiom. Regulation 13 of UNEF provided:

" 13. *Good Order and Discipline.* The Commander of the UNEF shall have general responsibility for the good order of the Force. Responsibility for disciplinary action in national contingents provided for the Force rests with the commanders of the national contingents. Reports concerning disciplinary action shall be communicated to the Commander of the UNEF who may consult with the commander of the national contingent and if necessary the authorities of the participating State concerned."

The comparable regulation of ONUC differed only in the specific grant to the Commander of a power to make investigations and require reports. Commenting on this position, the Secretary-General concluded that:

"The disciplinary system in UNEF, from the strictly military point of view, is rather anomalous. Normally, the commander of a force has power both of command and punishment, whereas the Commander of UNEF has power only of command. Disciplinary power resides in the commanding officer of each national contingent. To confer such powers upon the Commander would probably require specific legislation in most participating States." [11]

One can, in fact, find a precedent capable of adaptation to United Nations Forces in the arrangements made by legislation for contingents of different members of the British Commonwealth which might be engaged in joint operations.

To provide for the case of Commonwealth forces "serving together" or "acting in combination," it was considered necessary in 1933 to enact reciprocal legislation by each of the old Commonwealth members. Subsection (5) of section 6 of the Canadian version of the Visiting Forces (British Commonwealth) Act [12] provides:

"(5) When a home (Canadian) force and another force to which this section applies (British, Australian, New Zealand) are serving together, whether alone or not.

    (a) any member of the other force shall be treated and shall have over members of the home force the like powers of command as if he were a member of the home force of relative rank, and

    (b) if the forces are acting in combination, any officer of the other force appointed by Her Majesty, or in accordance with regulations made by or by authority of Her Majesty, to command the combined force, or any part thereof, shall be treated and shall have over members of the home force the like powers of command *and punishment,* and may be invested with the like authority to convene and confirm the findings and sentences of, courts martial as if he were an officer of the home force of relative rank and holding the same command."

It will be observed that when Commonwealth forces are only "serving together," mutual powers of command subsist as between individual members of the several forces. Where the forces are acting

---

[11] A/3943, para. 139.
[12] Revised Statutes of Canada, 1952, Chap. 283, s. 6 (5), italics added. The comparable English statutory provision is the Visiting Forces (British Commonwealth) Act, 1933, s. 4.

in combination, however, the officer appointed to command the combined force has not only powers of command but also powers of punishment, that is to say, disciplinary powers. The present United States proposals for integration of NATO forces on NATO vessels equipped with nuclear weapons are not yet implemented : if, and when, they are they will certainly represent an even greater degree of integration.[13]

Canadian Army elements in the Commonwealth Division of the United Nations Forces in Korea " acted in combination " with British, Australian and New Zealand military elements under an Australian Commander. British Army contingents training in Canada with Canadian Army elements are " serving together." British and Canadian Forces in NATO's NORTHAG " serve together." Even the state of " serving together " makes for easier co-operation and understanding between Commonwealth forces. Adoption by national Commonwealth force commanders of common orders while the forces are " serving together " approaches the effective integration possible under conditions of " acting in combination." The principles underlying the Visiting Forces (British Commonwealth) Act, are, of course, practical where the forces involved apply common basic training, operational and administrative practices. Where fundamental differences exist between national forces the system may be quite impracticable. Moreover the system, to be adapted to United Nations needs, would require the United Nations to promulgate its own code of military discipline, either by " adopting " that of an existing Member State or by legislating anew.[14]

Norway, Sweden and Denmark have agreed to man a joint force of 3,000 for United Nations service, Sweden contributing 1,600, Norway 500, and Denmark 900. It will be interesting to see what legislation, if any, the three countries will enact to integrate the

---

[13] The proposed MLF will not be the first example of integration; the dual key system of tactical atomic weapons or the mobile reserve force of 5 battalions are also examples of integration.

[14] Under Article 5 of Annex II of Clark and Sohn's Revised Charter (p. 331 of *World Peace etc.*) military and civilian members of the UN Peace Force and their dependants are subject to the exclusive criminal and disciplinary jurisdiction of the United Nations, presumably conferred by the basic and other laws and regulations enacted by the General Assembly under sub-paragraph (b) of paragraph 3 of Article 2 and paragraph 1 of Article 3. A State's signature of the Revised Charter would not of itself necessarily confer jurisdiction of any kind on the United Nations. Implementing legislation would certainly be required in the United Kingdom, and in any Member State where international agreements do not become the domestic law of the land upon their being accepted in accordance with domestic constitutional law.

It is observed in the Clark and Sohn scheme that UN jurisdiction is exercisable only in the leased area of bases and in relation to offences committed therein. With respect, this would be impractical. Take the likely case of insubordination occurring outside the leased area. It is unlikely that this common military offence would be triable by the host national authorities, and, being committed outside the leased area it would not be subject to UN jurisdiction. Absenteeism without leave is another common military offence—is this offence committed in or out of the leased area?

"Scandinavian United Nations Standby Force," which is a logical development of the "Danor" battalion serving with UNEF.

If all Member States were prepared to enact legislation similar to the Visiting Forces (British Commonwealth) Acts respecting their national forces acting in combination with the national contingents of other Member States, all under the command of a commander appointed by a United Nations authority, complete integration would be achieved in a UNEF-type of force. Such action has not yet been taken among the NATO States and it is perhaps unlikely that it would be universally accepted in a United Nations context.

In practice, however, it is not essential that the officer commanding the combined Force be vested with disciplinary powers if commanders of national contingents are directed by their governments to respect the views of the Commander respecting the military order and discipline of their troops under his command. Given a clearly defined common interest among participating states, the UNEF Regulations quoted above are workable. From experience it appears they work, and, judging from the Secretary-General's Annual UNEF Reports, discipline among the troops is being maintained. It is true that should a national commander fail to take into account the Commander's views respecting the maintenance of good order in the national contingent concerned, there is nothing the Commander can do directly to enforce his will. From a practical point of view, though, the Commander's right of consultation under UNEF Regulation 13 would have the desired result but not, of course, in the case of a participating State that interprets "consultation" as undesirable "interference." If a participating State has accepted the obligation to contribute troops to the United Nations Force on the terms set out in Regulations approved by the General Assembly, it is as reasonable to assume that it will discharge its obligations as it is to assume that it will not.

The actual supervision of discipline is largely a matter for military police and Regulations 14 and 15 of UNEF and ONUC were almost identical.

"The Commander shall provide for military police for any camps, establishments, or other premises which are occupied by the Force in a host State and for such areas where the Force is deployed in the performance of its functions. Elsewhere military police of the Force may be employed, in so far as such employment is necessary to maintain discipline and order among members of the Force, [or to conduct investigations relating to the Force or its members] (subject to arrangements with the authorities of the host State concerned, and in liaison with those authorities). For the purpose of this Regulation the military police of the Force shall have the power of arrest over members of the Force. Nothing in this Regulation is in derogation of the authority of arrest conferred upon members of a national contingent vis-à-vis one another." [15]

[15] UNEF Reg 14: the insertions in square brackets are the additions for ONUC, and the phrase in round brackets was deleted for ONUC. Presumably the relative efficacy of the Egyptian and Congolese local police accounts for these changes.

(e) JOINT CIVILIAN-MILITARY OPERATIONS

The juxtaposition of a military operation and a civilian operation in the sense of a technical assistance programme poses similar, but separate, problems to those examined above in considering the extent to which the fusion of military and civilian (Secretariat) personnel occurs in the command of United Nations military operations. This juxtaposition in fact occurred in the Congo, and the civilian operations side was given equal standing with the military in that the Chief of Civilian Operations was given a rank equal to the United Nations Commander: neither was subject to the authority of the other, but both were subject to the authority of the Officer-in-Charge and, through him, the Secretary-General.

The extent to which this solution proved successful is not easy to estimate, for no report by the Secretary-General comparable to the "Summary of experience, etc." published after UNEF has been published for the Congo operations. The impression one has from reading the documents on the Congo operation is that the separation worked well. Such problems as there were related more to the common use, by both military and civilian sides, of Secretariat services for procurement, communications, etc.

However, the coexistence of the two sides clearly points to a need for liaison and co-ordination, for it is not difficult to imagine competing claims to priority in matters of supply, finance and transport. This was, no doubt, one justification for placing a civilian Officer-in-Charge at the head of both sides of the operation.

2. Permanent Forces

(a) APPOINTMENT OF COMMANDER AND STAFF

The principle of appointment of the Commander [16] by the political organs, which was assumed to be applicable during the early discussions on the implementation of Chapter VII, was undoubtedly right: the departures from that principle, notably in Korea and in the Congo, were explicable, as to Korea, by the fact that command was delegated to one State, and, as to the Congo, by the fact that the Secretary-General himself assumed command authority, so that for him to appoint the Commander seemed a natural and logical step.

However, it is submitted that it may be unwise to vest the direct power of appointment in the Secretary-General for this tends to heighten the degree of subordination of the Commander to him. This is not to question the obligation of the Commander to carry out the political directives of the political organs, as transmitted and even interpreted to him by the Secretary-General, but it is believed

---

[16] The term "Commander" is used here to denote the military officer in supreme military command. It may be, as we shall suggest later, that in a permanent Headquarters Military Staff, this officer could be a Chief-of-Staff with a "Commander" operating under him and appointed by the Chief-of-Staff: see *post*, pp. 351–352.

that a more marked separation of the Commander and his staff from the Secretariat would be preferable in any permanent Force, and this is the more likely to be achieved if the Secretary-General does not have direct power of appointment. It is believed to be even more imperative that the Secretary-General does not himself assume command authority.

Appointment by a comparatively small body, like the Security Council, is prima facie an easier task than appointment by the whole membership of the General Assembly. The problem in the Security Council is clearly that of the veto, but it is really a similar problem to appointment of a Secretary-General, so that, on the assumption that a national of one of the Permanent Members would not be eligible, it is likely that agreement can be reached: moreover, it is highly desirable for the Commander of a permanent Force, like the Secretary-General, to enjoy the confidence and support of all the Permanent Members.

The ideal would be a relinquishment of the power of veto in the matter of appointment of the Commander. Failing that, provision would have to be made for a transfer of competence to the Assembly. This shift of the power of appointment from the Council to the Assembly could be provided for by an agreement between the Members of the Council in advance (or, preferably, even, by a provision in the Statute of the Force) that when a majority resolved that no decision on appointment could be reached or positive recommendation to the Assembly be made,[17] the matter would pass to the Assembly. Appointment by the Assembly would presumably require a sifting of possible appointees by a smaller committee of the Assembly, and thereafter a two-thirds majority vote.

The Soviet notion of a " troika "—a body of three persons of whom one would represent the West, one the East, and one the " non-aligned " States—has been suggested as an appropriate device for fairly representing the different political interests, both in the appointment of a Secretary-General and in the appointment of a Commander of a United Nations Force under a disarmament plan.[18] It may be presumed that, if the Soviets were ever to agree to a *permanent* Force prior to disarmament, the same proposal would be made. It is a proposal which must be rejected, for it destroys the unity of command essential to the operation of any military force and will tend to introduce the veto not only in the Security Council, in so far as it falls to that organ to issue the political directives, but also in the Command itself when these come to be carried into operation.

The principle of appointment by the political organ should, it is believed, apply to the Commanders-in-Chief of the land, sea and air

[17] Assuming that the appointment required the concurrence of the Council and Assembly as in Art. 97 of the Charter for appointment of a Secretary-General.

[18] *Post,* p. 534.

branches of the Force and to any Regional Commanders if a United Nations Force ever achieves a sufficient size to be sub-divided into regional commands. Below that level appointment could be by the Commander, in consultation with the Secretary-General and any political Committee of States established in connection with the Force.

The tenure of an appointment should be limited in time, say for a period of five years, in all cases where the appointment is a political appointment. The relatively short period of office of the highest officers in the Force would not be so necessary when the Force is of very limited size, or no more than a Military Staff from which the Command would be drawn : but the principle of limited tenure would become of importance in a large Force at the completion of disarmament,[19] for it would be one of the devices to ensure that a military clique did not develop to which the Force might develop an allegiance replacing its allegiance to the United Nations. For this reason it may be desirable to establish this principle from the beginning. Staggering of appointments would be desirable so as to ensure continuity of experience in the Command.

So long as the permanent Force consisted of national contingents, placed under the authority of the Command by virtue of a pre-existing obligation on Member States, and presumably in rotation, it would probably remain for the State to designate the Commander of its own particular contingent. Should the Force ever be recruited on an individual basis this particular feature would doubtless disappear.

The whole appointments procedure would have to be scaled down to deal with the initial stages of establishing a United Nations Force. Thinking in terms of a permanent Headquarters Military Staff, and no more, it is probable that only the Chief-of-Staff and Commander need be politically appointed : recruitment of the remaining staff officers could be by the Secretary-General, in consultation with the Chief-of-Staff and a Committee of Member States, set up by the organ establishing the Force. Even if, at a later stage, a Force of 5,000–10,000 were established, the same procedure would probably suffice. It would only be at the more ambitious stages of developing a full military Force with land, sea and air branches, that the range of political appointments would have to be extended.

The exclusion of nationals of Permanent Members of the Security Council from this Headquarters Military Staff would, from several points of view, be regrettable. However, whether or not they were to be recruited would clearly rest on a political decision by the organ establishing the Staff, and the most that might be said at this stage is that an alternative way of including such experts would be to recruit them as *ad hoc* experts for short periods, to assist in the early planning stages, without making them part of the permanent Staff.

---

[19] See *post*, p. 531.

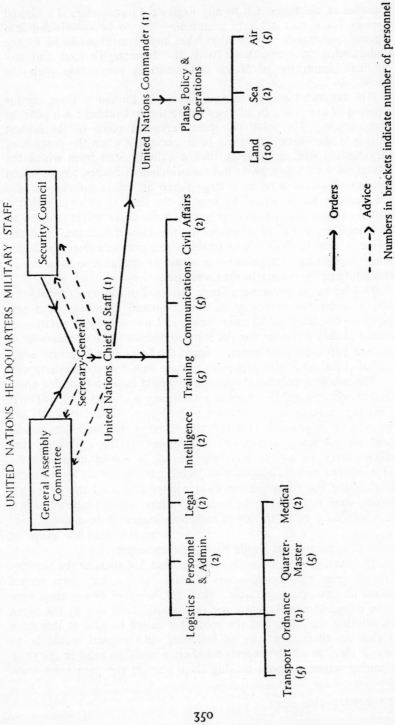

UNITED NATIONS HEADQUARTERS MILITARY STAFF

General Assembly Committee

Security Council

Secretary-General

United Nations Chief of Staff (1)

United Nations Commander (1)

Plans, Policy & Operations

Land (10)   Sea (2)   Air (5)

Logistics   Personnel & Admin. (2)   Legal (2)   Intelligence (2)   Training (5)   Communications (5)   Civil Affairs (2)

Transport (5)   Ordnance (2)   Quarter-Master (5)   Medical (2)

Orders ——→
Advice – – →
Numbers in brackets indicate number of personnel

(b) CHAIN OF COMMAND

The Command Structure would vary, in the degree of complexity, with the size of the Force contemplated. For a Force of 20,000, without a naval arm, the ONUC structure could be adapted, subject to what has been said above about the desirability of a greater separation between the Secretariat civilian side and the military command, and the exclusion of the Secretary-General or his representatives from direct military command.

A very realistic structure has been proposed by Cannon and Jordan [20] for a single United Nations infantry brigade of 7,000. It is probable, however, that the command structure has to be adapted both to the size of the Force actually being employed on a particular operation and to the kind of operation, or function, involved. Hence it should be possible for a permanent Headquarters Military Staff to draw up different plans for command structures required for different operations, relying on past United Nations experience with forces as varied as UNEF, ONUC, UNTEA and even the observer groups like UNTSO, UNOGIL and the Group in the Yemen: these plans could then be put into operation as occasion required and the Military Staff could, in the initial stages, before a permanent Force is created, itself provide the key officers to form the skeleton of the appropriate command structure.

The diagram produced opposite illustrates, therefore, not a " chain of command " in the sense in which the Cannon and Jordan diagram envisages chain of command, but more the structure of the permanent Headquarters Military Staff, which we envisage as the essential, first step, before any permanent Force can be brought into being. The Chief of Staff would be the highest military officer and serving under him as part of his staff would be a Commander who would normally be entrusted with command of a United Nations Force in the field. The Chief-of-Staff would remain at United Nations Headquarters, together with the Headquarters Staff; however, the Staff would be large enough to enable officers to be detached from it to serve with the Commander in the field as his own Staff, forming the essential skeleton staff into which officers from national contingents could be integrated. This system would not only ensure that an adequate military staff remained at United Nations Headquarters during military operations, with day-to-day liaison with the political bodies from whom political directives would come, but also that the staff in the field with the Commander and the Headquarters Staff in New York would be people who had worked and planned together for the kind of operations in which they found themselves. Moreover, if one can assume that the United Nations Military Staff would have trained in advance with the contingents provided by States, whether in the course of exercises in their home countries

[20] " Military Aspects of a Permanent UN Force " in Frye, *A United Nations Peace Force* (1957) p. 161.

or during training courses at a United Nations Staff College, there would be a reasonable chance of providing a co-ordinated military Force.

If, and when, a United Nations Force is composed of units permanently attached to the United Nations—whether by way of secondment as national contingents by Member States for a fixed period of two to three years or by way of the individual recruitment of a Force—the occasion will arise for separating what is essentially a Headquarters Military Staff from the command structure proper. The latter will then assume its own form, on the basis of experience, and will be headed by the Commander assisted by his own staff distinct from the Headquarters Military Staff, which could then perhaps be reduced in size. Until that stage, however, there is an advantage in combining what is really a military planning staff with a body of officers who will form the nucleus of a command structure when a Force is created for a particular occasion.

Unity of command should be preserved and, since the Headquarters Military Staff and the key officers of the Command in the field would be international servants,[21] this unity of command would not be disrupted by their subordination to the military authorities of their national States: for the period of their service they, and their States, would be subject to Article 100 of the Charter.

(c) DELINEATION OF AUTHORITIES OF SECRETARY-GENERAL AND THE MILITARY STAFF

The respective spheres of competence, or authority, of the military commanders—the Chief-of-Staff at United Nations Headquarters and the Commander in the field—on the one hand and the Secretary-General on the other should, it is submitted, follow the general UNEF pattern and not that followed in ONUC. The reasons for divorcing the Secretary-General from command authority are dealt with below under the section on political control. In general, the intrusion of a political directorate, whether this be the Secretary-General or a political committee of the political organs of the United Nations, into the sphere of command authority is to be regretted. Indeed, with a permanent Military Staff one would expect a higher degree of confidence to be placed in the Staff and correspondingly less intrusion into the normal sphere of command authority. Moreover, whereas, necessarily, with an *ad hoc* Force much of the administrative side has to be dealt with by the permanent Secretariat officials, in a permanent Force or even with a permanent Military Staff a separate administrative staff could be established and trained to deal with those needs of the Force which were exclusive and did not require reliance on the United Nations Secretariat.

This insistence on the separateness of the command authority is not intended to suggest that the military are in every respect free

[21] On their status see *post*, p. 445.

from political control. Command authority would not include a right to initiate armed action, except in self-defence,[22] and complete obedience to the political directorate would be essential. However, in the operational control of the Force the Commander should be given full and exclusive authority.

(d) DISCIPLINE

So long as the Force remained largely constituted of national contingents the problems of discipline outlined above[23] would remain, and the only real solution to this would be for Member States to legislate so as to confer disciplinary powers on the United Nations Command for the period of service with the United Nations of any contingent from their armed forces. The United Nations would, on its part, have to prescribe a system of military law and establish courts-martial.

A Force individually recruited would not require the same degree of legislation by Member States, although some States may have to amend any legislation imposing restrictions on their nationals with regard to enlistment in " foreign " forces. It would require the same kind of legislation by the United Nations.

Such legislation would have to cover not merely matters of discipline, but matters of pay, allowances, leave, pensions for injury or death, legal protection by the United Nations, the establishment of military police, and terms of service generally.

IV. POLITICAL CONTROL OF UNITED NATIONS FORCES

1. *The organs of control*

The notion of an uncontrolled military force is abhorrent to all civilised communities, and one of the major problems involved in the creation of a United Nations Force is that of devising a satisfactory system of political control. This is not to assume that such control

---

[22] The right of Commanders in the field to take all necessary measures for the protection of units under their command is believed to be essential: authority to conclude a ceasefire, operative within the area of the command, or to surrender, would also be implicit in command authority. When the termination of the Occupation Régime in the Federal Republic of Germany was being negotiated, Adenauer officially stated in his letter dated 23 October 1954, to the U.S., British and French Secretaries of State (*Documents relating to the Termination of the Occupation Régime in the Federal Republic of Germany*, Cmd. 9368, January 1955, at p. 162):

" I refer to paragraph 7 of Article 5 of the Convention on Relations between the Three Powers and the Federal Republic of Germany signed at Bonn on 26 May 1952, which provides that, independently of a state of emergency, any military commander may, if his Forces are imminently menaced, take such immediate action appropriate for their protection (including the use of armed force) as is requisite to remove the danger. The Federal Government is of the opinion that this is the inherent right of any military commander according to international law and therefore German law."

[23] *Ante*, p. 343.

is the only form of control, for, as we shall see,[24] techniques of judicial control can also be developed, but the *primary* control must be political.

The absence of such control leads either to confusion as to what the proper task of the Force is to be—and such confusion has existed to some extent in Korea,[25] in UNEF [26] and in ONUC [27]—or, possibly, at a stage of disarmament when a United Nations Force assumes dominant military power, to the Force itself becoming a threat to society.

In the immediate future it is the first of these dangers against which one must guard, and the potential sources of political control are really three: the Security Council, the General Assembly and the Secretary-General.

(a) THE SECURITY COUNCIL

The Security Council should clearly be looked to as the primary organ of control, for Article 24 of the Charter is clear in entrusting this organ with "primary responsibility for the maintenance of international peace and security." However, the record of the United Nations in using Forces, summarised in Part One of this study, shows that the Council may either fail to establish the Force—so that control immediately passes to the General Assembly (as in UNEF)— or, having established the Force, may fail to maintain a consensus of agreement as to the political directives to be issued to the Force: this was in a very real sense the tragedy of the Congo. In both cases the root of the failure has been the serious political differences which are characterised by the phrases " the East-West rift " or " the cold war." The veto simply becomes the means whereby the

---

[24] *Post*, pp. 463–467, 550–551, 565–566.   [25] *Ante*, p. 43.

[26] The difficulties over UNEF were perhaps due more to the hasty improvisation of the Force, but, even allowing for this, the General Assembly Resolutions could scarcely be described as adequate political directives. See the statement by General Burns, the UNEF Commander, in his book *Between Arab and Israeli* (1962), p. 218:

"... there was no chance for the unhurried talk I should have liked in order to clear my mind as to my task and general responsibilities. It is the practice, when a commander is sent out with a military expeditionary force, to provide him with a general instruction as to what he is expected to achieve, what his relations should be with allies or the authorities of the country in which he is to operate, and other guiding principles for his action. Of course, in the circumstances, it was impossible for such a document to be drawn up by the UN Secretariat, since so many matters relating to UNEF were improvised, and so much was dependent on political conditions, which were fluid and in the course of development. I understand this, but my difficulties were increased by the absence of a definite instruction as to how it was intended that the Force would be constituted and would function, and its relations to the Egyptian authorities."

In other words, all General Burns felt he needed was a clear statement of UN policy upon which he could formulate decisions and plans. His was a politico-military mission which he was obliged to accomplish with a military staff and national contingent commanders who likewise had been inadequately instructed.

[27] *Ante*, pp. 186–196.

Permanent Member or Members [28] check the majority view from being adopted.

The solutions, apart from the obvious solution of those Permanent Members improving their political relations, are either for the veto to be abandoned in matters relating to the creation or direction of a United Nations Force, or for means to be devised for passing responsibility to some other organ when the Security Council becomes ineffective as an organ of political control. The relinquishment of the veto is probably not practical politics. The second solution is the one already in being, so that we must turn to the Assembly as the next appropriate organ of political control.

(b) THE GENERAL ASSEMBLY

The General Assembly's constitutional authority to establish a Force has already been dealt with.[29] If a permanent Force were established it would be desirable to establish this as a United Nations organ, and not a subsidiary organ of the Security Council, in order to obviate difficulties about the Assembly assuming power to issue directives to a Security Council subsidiary organ: similarly, if the Force were to be constituted by national contingents, these should preferably be made available to " the United Nations " and not " the Security Council." How far the Assembly has authority to control a Force equivalent to that of the Security Council is not altogether clear: there may be some doubt about the Assembly's power to direct (even by way of recommendation) enforcement action against States.[30] However, as we have already indicated, in the initial stages a permanent Force would probably have to be confined to " peacekeeping " operations, so that this particular problem arises only in relation to *ad hoc* Forces, or to a permanent Force utilised as a nucleus around which national contingents contributed *ad hoc* could be formed, authorised to take enforcement action.

The decision to authorise the use of a United Nations Force could well be a decision of the whole Assembly. It is probably impractical, however, to envisage the Assembly as a whole as a suitable organ for the continuing political supervision which a Force would require: delegation to a smaller committee of the Assembly would be imperative. The Resolution on Uniting for Peace [31] established the Peace Observation Commission of fourteen Member States, with functions wide enough to enable it to use and control a part of a

---

[28] It is perhaps wrong to characterise the negative votes of more than one Permanent Member as a " veto ": but the point has to be made that it may not be a single Permanent Member which opposes the majority. Britain and France were united in their opposition to Security Council action in Suez (see *ante*, p. 90), and in the Congo it is by no means clear that, quite apart from the Soviet Union, these two Members would have subscribed to the same views as the U.S.A. over the political directives to be given to the Force.

[29] *Ante*, pp. 285–298.

[30] *Ante*, p. 291.

[31] *Ante*, p. 290.

United Nations Force for strictly observer functions; it also established the Collective Measures Committee [32] : but neither are, under that Resolution, appropriately endowed with the functions of political control which we now envisage. However, it should be possible to extend the functions of one or other of these committees so as to provide the Assembly with an appropriate committee—or a new committee could be appointed. It is highly doubtful whether any such committee could, in the foreseeable future, become a committee of individuals (as opposed to a Committee of States): nor is it likely that any kind of weighted or balanced voting system could be agreed upon to replace the existing rule in the Assembly of equality of voting. But criteria could be specified so as to produce a generally acceptable committee in terms of its composition. For example, the exclusion of the Permanent Members of the Security Council would be one possible criterion: this would be justifiable not only because the assertion of responsibility by the Assembly could be predicated upon the assumption that the Permanent Members had failed to agree in the Security Council but also because the Force would not include contingents from the Permanent Members. The other criterion would be one designed to secure equitable geographical representation so that the different regions of the world would be adequately represented: within this criterion some reflection of the Soviet demand for a "troika" could be embodied, in that States from the East, the West, and the "non-aligned" areas of the world could be included (but not the Permanent Members). Voting would be by majority, either simple or two-thirds. Hence the committee would replace the advisory committees of contributing States used by the Secretary-General in UNEF and ONUC and would become not merely an advisory body but the effective political directorate responsible only to the General Assembly.[33]

It would also be desirable for the Secretary-General to be the permanent Chairman of this Committee,[34] though without a right to vote; thus he could provide guidance and a point of view which was not conditioned by any national policy but simply by his own concept of the interests and aims of the Organisation.

This whole scheme for using the General Assembly in cases where the Security Council is unable to function effectively runs the risk of being boycotted by the Soviet Union and its allies, just as the scheme envisaged in the Resolution on Uniting for Peace has been boycotted. However, the scheme could be operated without Soviet

[32] *Ante,* p. 294.
[33] It is assumed that the machinery for summoning an emergency session of the whole Assembly under the Resolution on Uniting for Peace would be utilised in cases where the committee required guidance or approval of the Assembly. Indeed, a minority of, say, 6 out of 14 members could be given the right to convene an emergency session: perhaps a similar right could also be given to the Secretary-General.
[34] The Secretary-General of NATO is the permanent Chairman of the NATO Council: there is also a President who changes annually.

participation, however undesirable in principle that may be: indeed, it may have to be so operated unless Member States are prepared to revert to a situation in which the Security Council has a monopoly over both enforcement action and peace-keeping operations and action by the United Nations becomes highly unlikely.

(c) THE SECRETARY-GENERAL

The Secretary-General is the third possible instrument of political control over a United Nations Force: the basis, and limits, of his constitutional authority to establish a Force have already been examined.[35]   His authority to assume political control over such a Force would, in those cases where it was established by him, tend to follow from that fact: in all other cases he would assume political control only by delegation from either the Council or the Assembly.

If one assumes that *both* the Security Council and the General Assembly have powers to establish and control United Nations Forces there is little reason to fall back upon the Secretary-General's own (but more limited) powers.   It is noticeable that, even in the case of UNTEA, General Assembly authorisation was sought and, in the case of the Yemen Observer Group, the Soviets opposed the Secretary-General acting on his own authority.

The likelihood will be, therefore, that any political control assumed by the Secretary-General will in the future be by delegation from the Council or the Assembly, and not upon his own authority. The reasons for such delegation have largely been in the past that this process of delegation avoided the continued entanglement of the operations with the East-West rift and that, in the case of the Assembly, no existing machinery was available to undertake the task.   Practice has tended to show, in the case of UNEF, that a committee of contributing States, in an advisory capacity, was desirable, if not essential, and the same became true in ONUC, although for different reasons.   There the reasons were not the unwieldy size of the Assembly, but the certainty, from August 1960 onwards, that no clear policy could be agreed upon in the Council: the size of the Council was never the disadvantage.

The question for the future is whether it is wise to rest the enormous responsibility for political direction on the Secretary-General.   Our present feeling is that it is unwise and may tend to weaken, rather than strengthen, the position of the Secretary-General whose role of "quiet diplomacy" is probably more important than his role as political directorate of a United Nations Force: this will certainly be true if, as is now suggested, the General Assembly establishes a committee to perform this function in cases where the Security Council cannot.[36]   An advisory committee is not enough,

[35] *Ante*, pp. 299–301.
[36] See the statement by Earl Attlee in the debate in the House of Lords on 20 February 1963: "The structure of UNO at the present time puts an almost unbearable burden on the Secretary-General.   I look forward to a

for such a committee cannot assume final responsibility, and it is final responsibility which really counts. The Secretary-General might be the permanent Chairman of such a committee, although without a right to vote; he would be there to advise and caution, to represent the United Nations' point of view rather than a national point of view, and perhaps with a right to summon an emergency session of the Assembly if he believed the committee to be embarking upon a policy opposed to the purposes and principles of the Charter. Thus these suggestions, which aim at divesting the Secretary-General of effective responsibility for political control—and the suggestion made above for separating the Secretary-General and the civilian Secretariat from operational command of United Nations Forces—are made not to weaken the Secretariat but to preserve it. It is believed that the Secretary-General and the Secretariat have for years shouldered responsibilities which should have been assumed by the Member States, and, in so doing, have acquitted themselves well. Yet this has not prevented a series of attacks on the Secretariat and it is perhaps necessary now, in order to preserve the Secretariat for its essential functions, to divest them of these responsibilities and powers which, if continued to be assumed, might destroy the office of the Secretary-General and the Secretariat as we now know them.

The whole problem of political control is essentially a problem of devising an appropriate control mechanism within the United Nations. Therefore what has been said applies in general equally to a United Nations Force composed *ad hoc* of national contingents as to a permanent United Nations Force, whether composed of national contingents seconded to the United Nations for a fixed period or of individuals directly recruited. However, experience in the Congo suggests that so long as national contingents play a part in a United Nations Force the States contributing them will demand some say in the control of the Force. Hence, whether the Security Council or the Assembly assumes control, there will probably be a need to allow for co-opting such States onto the committee or other body assuming political control where these are not already represented.

Subject to this it is believed to be imperative that States do not interfere indirectly—*i.e.*, except through the normal procedures of the political directorate in which they may rightly express their views—with the control of the Force. Important as unity of command is,[37] unity of political direction is even more important

development of the United Nations in which there will be an executive body responsible to the United Nations, to whom the world police force will look for its orders." *Parl. Debates* (Hansard) H.L., Vol. 246, No. 43, col. 1379. Lord McNair raised the interesting though limited analogy of the I.C.J. as an organ—the principal judicial organ—of the UN but entirely independent of the UN in the performance of its functions, and suggested that this technique might be used so as to provide for a permanent Force which, once its mandate is prescribed, may be left free to carry it out without a continual reference to an organ of the UN (*ibid.*, col. 1396).

[37] *Ante*, p. 341.

and no instructions or orders to national contingents should be given by States which may conflict with their command orders or the orders of the political directorate. Perhaps the main advantage of the system of individual recruitment is, as we shall see,[38] that the Force will cease to be subject to this form of indirect political control either by threats to withdraw contingents, or by orders to them inconsistent with those emanating from the United Nations Command.

2. *The techniques of political control*

Whatever the organ entrusted with political control over a permanent Force, it would be possible to exercise control by the following means:

(1) Power of appointment and dismissal of the Chief-of-Staff, Commander, Commanders-in-Chief of air, sea and land forces and even any regional commanders who might be appointed;

(2) The authority of the Chief-of-Staff and Commander would be circumscribed and defined in the Statute and Regulations for the Force;

(3) The size and composition of the Force would be determined by the control organ;

(4) No movement of the Force from any permanent base could be made without prior authorisation;

(5) The Chief-of-Staff would be under a duty to submit to the control organs periodic reports on the Force and its activities.

3. *Strategic direction*

By this term we mean the translation of the political directives into military terms. As such it is a task for the military experts, not the politicians, and it was for this reason that the Security Council was to be advised and assisted by a Military Staff Committee comprising the Chiefs-of-Staff of the Permanent Members of the Council.[39] The task is also different from that of actual command which we have considered above: no committee is suitable for actual command, which must rest on the principle of unity of command.

So far as the Security Council is concerned there is no reason why the Military Staff Committee should not assume the task of giving strategic direction to the political directives of the Council in situations in which the Council can effectively operate. In that event the Military Staff Committee would be interposed between the Security Council and the Chief-of-Staff of the United Nations Military Headquarters in the diagram reproduced above.[40] However, the Charter, in establishing the Military Staff Committee, had envisaged the Security Council assuming responsibility for very sizeable military

---

[38] *Post*, p. 386.
[39] Arts. 46 and 47 of the Charter.
[40] *Ante*, p. 350.

operations, without any assistance from a permanent United Nations military staff of the kind we have envisaged above, so that the existence of the Military Staff Committee in addition to the United Nations Headquarters Military Staff would be of doubtful advantage.

If we assume that the General Assembly, operating through its Committee, becomes the political directorate, then there is not this complication for it possesses no established organ for giving military advice. Hence it could be expected that the Assembly's Committee would be prepared to utilise the Chief-of-Staff at Headquarters both for the purpose of obtaining reports and advice on military problems and as a channel through which to communicate its political instructions—these being translated by the Chief-of-Staff into military terms for action either by his Headquarters Staff or by the United Nations Commander in the field.

10

Agreements between the United Nations and Participating States for the Provision of Forces

---

I. " AD HOC " AGREEMENTS

UNDER the system of security created by the Charter it was intended that Member States should place units of their armed forces at the disposal of the Security Council, in order that prompt and effective action might be taken, as determined by that body, to maintain or restore international peace and security. It is clear from the report of the Military Staff Committee to the Security Council in 1947, setting out proposed " General Principles " relating to the organisation of such forces,[1] that it was assumed that the agreements to be entered into under Article 43 of the Charter would be on a permanent basis, designed to enable troops to be made available at any time for use by the Security Council. However, owing to failure to agree on the principles to be embodied in the texts of the agreements between the Security Council and Member States, no such agreements have been concluded and the requisite troops have not in fact been placed at the disposal of the United Nations; nor has any United Nations Force come into existence as a standing body. Instead, successive United Nations peace-keeping operations have been dependent on the consent of Member States given as each occasion arose. Thus, not only have Member States been called upon to pass the necessary Resolution setting up an *ad hoc* United Nations Force to deal with a particular emergency, but they have also had to decide, as individual States, whether or not they wished to provide contingents from their national armies to enable the Force to be constituted. The range of circumstances in which the relevant Resolutions may be adopted, whether by the Security Council or by the General Assembly, and the varying disputes with which different United Nations Forces may have to deal, make it difficult to forecast with

---

[1] The text of the articles in the report, as amended by the Security Council, is contained in the *Repertory of Practice of United Nations Organs*, Vol. II, p. 396 *et seq.* For the basic differences which the discussions in the Military Staff Committee and the Security Council revealed, see *ante*, pp. 15–18.

accuracy when Member States may agree to give such consent, and what conditions they may impose in particular instances as regards the availability of their troops.

The contents of any *ad hoc* agreement may be influenced to a considerable extent by the choice of the party with whom the agreement is made on the United Nations' behalf. There would appear to be at least four different bodies with which such agreements may be concluded by a participating State. Firstly, as in the case of the United Nations operations in Korea, one Member State may be given major responsibilities for carrying out an Assembly or Security Council recommendation and other governments may be requested to make their assistance available to that State. Accordingly, agreements may be entered into between the State acting as agent for the United Nations and other States in order to determine the conditions under which armed forces are to be provided for the collective action. In the agreements of this kind concluded between the United States and other States during the Korean struggle, the United States expressly declared that it was acting as " the executive agent of the United Nations Forces in Korea," although the agreements were registered with the United Nations only as bilateral treaties between the two Governments concerned. The Organisation *qua* Secretariat was given responsibility merely in respect of the civilian relief operations in Korea and, as requested by the Unified Command, for acting as a transmission channel between Member States and the Unified Command regarding proposed contributions. This system (if, indeed, it can be called a system and not itself an *ad hoc* arrangement), of concluding agreements regarding contributions with a body outside the immediate framework of the United Nations, could obviously be extended to a group of States, as the Collective Measures Committee contemplated, and an existing group, such as those belonging to NATO or to the Warsaw Pact, or to a standing regional organisation, like the Organisation of American States or the Arab League, could be utilised if the Assembly or Security Council so chose.[2] In this case the various *ad hoc* agreements would no doubt largely reflect the security arrangements already made amongst the States concerned under the pre-existing

[2] It may be noted that Article 53, paragraph 1, of the Charter provides as follows:
"The Security Council shall, where appropriate, utilise such regional arrangements or agencies for enforcement action under its authority. But no enforcement action shall be taken under regional arrangements or by regional agencies without the authorisation of the Security Council, with the exception of measures against any enemy State, as defined in paragraph 2 of this Article, provided for pursuant to Article 107 or in regional arrangements directed against renewal of aggressive policy on the part of any such State, until such time as the Organisation may, on request of the Governments concerned, be charged with the responsibility for preventing further aggression by such a State."
For a discussion of the constitutional basis for utilising regional organisations see *ante*, pp. 305–307.

treaty. The disadvantages of this kind of delegation by a United Nations organ to either one State, or even a regional grouping of States, have already been discussed in relation to Korea [3] and in relation to the proposals to entrust the command of ONUC to a unified African command.[4]

The other three entities with which *ad hoc* agreements might be made are the Security Council, the General Assembly, and the Secretary-General, all forming part of the permanent structure of the United Nations. In the case of UNEF and ONUC it has in fact been the Secretary-General who has negotiated the necessary agreements on behalf of the United Nations. Whilst it might have been argued that authority for him to do so was to be implied from his general position as the chief executive of the Organisation, in practice the Secretary-General ensured each time that clear authorisation had been given in the pertinent Resolutions.

It has also been clear from the practice so far that the United Nations has decided (albeit indirectly, through, in the case of Korea, the United States Government as its agent, and in other cases through the Secretary-General) which particular Member States should contribute forces. There has been no recognition of a *right* of a United Nations Member State to contribute forces to any particular United Nations operation.

Turning to the contents of the various agreements, those entered into during the Korean conflict between the United States and nations providing forces or other assistance to the Unified Command, followed a uniform pattern.[5] The United States undertook to provide the unit with "available materials, supplies, services and facilities," [6] which the national government was unable to furnish, against reimbursement under appropriate technical and administrative arrangements. It was agreed that the two Governments would not bring claims against one another in respect of injury or death incurred by members of their respective forces, or for the loss, damage or destruction of property, caused by the other. Claims brought by the national government of a contingent against other States, or vice versa, including those in respect of supplies furnished by third governments, were to be settled by direct negotiation. It was also provided that contingents should be supplied with Korean currency under arrangements determined by the Commander, in

---

[3] *Ante,* p. 43.

[4] *Ante,* p. 215.

[5] The agreements contained in the *United Nations Treaty Series* are as follows: United States—Norway, Vol. 140, No. 1895, p. 313; United States—Sweden, Vol. 148, No. 1937, p. 77; United States—Netherlands, Vol. 177, No. 2321, p. 233; United States—South Africa, *ibid.*, No. 2322, p. 241; United States—Belgium, Vol. 223, No. 3040, p. 3; and United States—Germany, *ibid.*, No. 3064, p. 153.

[6] See, *e.g.*, Article 1 of the Agreement between the United States and the Netherlands, U.N.T.S., Vol. 177, No. 2321, p. 233, at p. 234. But note that the British Commonwealth division maintained a separate logistical supply line: *ante,* p. 37.

accordance with the Agreement between the United States and the Republic of Korea regarding expenditures by United Nations troops.[7] As regards control over the Force, the agreements specified that the orders given by the Commander were to be obeyed by the unit commander, subject to the right of the State concerned to make a formal protest at a later stage in the event of disagreement.

The arrangements made with States providing contingents for UNEF have also followed a uniform pattern. Nothing has been published, however, relating to the agreements concluded in the case of ONUC, apart from isolated references, although it was stated at the outset that the procedures adopted for the establishment of UNEF were being followed as closely as possible. It may, therefore, be presumed that, at least in outline, the same general arrangements have been made in both instances. Nevertheless, the exchange of letters between the Secretary-General and States furnishing troops for UNEF differed considerably from the agreements concluded by the United States during the Korean struggle. In his letter to participating States of 21 June 1957 the Secretary-General first referred to the Resolutions 1000(ES–1) and 1001(ES–1), of 5 and 7 November 1956, which had provided the basis for the establishment of the Force. He recalled that in the latter Resolution the Assembly had approved the guiding principles for the organisation and functioning of the Force set out in his Second and Final Report of 6 November 1956,[8] and had authorised him to take all necessary administrative and executive action. Pursuant to this Resolution he had therefore concluded an agreement on the status of UNEF in Egypt with the Egyptian Government, which had been approved by the General Assembly,[9] and had issued Regulations for the Force following consultation with the Advisory Committee, the participating States and the Commander of the Force. Copies of the exchange of letters with the Egyptian Government and of the Regulations were annexed to the Secretary-General's letter. The international character of the Force as a subsidiary organ of the General Assembly had been affirmed in the Regulations, which also defined the conditions under which members of the Force served. The independent exercise of the functions of the Force was secured through the privileges and immunities granted to its members, as specified in the Regulations and as agreed to by the Egyptian Government. The Secretary-General drew the attention of participating States particularly to the provisions relating to their exclusive jurisdiction over criminal offences committed by their soldiers, pointing out that this immunity had been granted on the understanding that such jurisdiction would in fact be exercised by their respective national States. The Regulations

[7] U.N.T.S., Vol. 140, No. 1883, p. 57.
[8] *Second and final report of the Secretary-General on the plan for an emergency international United Nations Force, A/3302, Off.Rec.G.A., 1st Emergency Special Sess.*, 1956, Annexes, Agenda item 5. See *ante*, pp. 99–100.
[9] In Resolution 1126 (XI), of 22 February 1957.

also provided that, whilst the Commander of the Force would have general responsibility for the good order of the Force, responsibility for disciplinary action within national contingents rested with the unit commander. The Secretary-General therefore sought appropriate assurances from participating States that unit commanders would be in a position to exercise the necessary disciplinary authority and that criminal offences would be tried by the Force State.

National contingents might be withdrawn, at the initiative of either the government concerned, subject to appropriate notice being given, or of the United Nations. Command authority rested with the Commander of the Force, who was empowered to designate the chain of command and to delegate authority; changes in unit commanders were to be made in consultation with the Commander and the appropriate national authorities. The question of the alloca-tion of expenses between the participating State and the United Nations was left to be dealt with in a supplemental agreement, in the light of the relevant Resolutions of the Assembly. Provision was also made for the settlement of disputes between the United Nations and the government concerned by means of arbitration, if they were not settled by negotiation or other agreed mode of settlement.

The participating States submitted short replies, accepting the contents of the Secretary-General's letter and undertaking to exercise jurisdiction. The agreement between the United Nations and the State concerned then came into effect from the date the national contingent left its home country, and was registered accordingly by the United Nations.[10]

The distinct lack of similarity between the agreements concluded by the United States in respect of the Korean operation, and by the Secretary-General on behalf of the United Nations as regards UNEF and ONUC, makes it difficult to determine what are the essential, or even the likely, features of any future agreements. The matter is made more complex by the issue of the Regulations for the Force, in which much of the general organisation of the Force was laid down by the United Nations. In addition, the fact that neither UNEF nor ONUC was an instrument of enforcement action as such had a clear bearing on the range of matters for which specific provision was made. However, the following would appear to be the principal issues which participating States and the United Nations may be expected to include, either expressly or by reference, in the majority of future *ad hoc* agreements.

The first, and most general, issue concerns the scope of the functions of the Force. A distinction may be noted here between agreements relating to enforcement action and those concerned with peace-keeping and " police " operations, such as UNEF and ONUC.

[10] U.N.T.S. Vol. 271, No. 3913, p. 135 (Finland); *ibid.*, No. 3914, p. 187 (Sweden): *ibid.*, No. 3914, p. 223 (Norway); Vol. 274, No. 3957, p. 47 (Canada); *ibid.*, No. 3959, p. 81 (Denmark); *ibid.*, No. 3966, p. 199 (Brazil); *ibid.*, No. 3968. p. 233 (India); and Vol. 277, No. 4006, p. 191 (Yugoslavia).

The 1947 report of the Military Staff Committee [11] referred to the general purposes for which the prospective armed Forces might be used by the Security Council, in accordance with the relevant provisions of the Charter, and attempted to limit, so far as possible, the length of time for which the Forces would actually be engaged. However, no further description was given, or indeed could be given in the circumstances, of the extent of the functions to be undertaken in relation to any particular situation. Similarly in the Korean agreements, reference was made only to the Resolutions under which the Unified Command was created; the functions of the United Nations Forces were left unstated, presumably because it was known and recognised by all concerned that troops were to be used for a particular armed conflict in a given country. Even here, however, the matter proved to be not without difficulty. Did the task entrusted to the United Nations Forces necessitate the crossing of the 38th parallel? Did the Unified Command have sufficient authority to conclude an armistice? Both these questions were answered at the time by reference to the implied powers of the military commander in the field.[12] It seems to have been agreed, however, that the functions of the Commander of the Unified Command did not extend to the negotiation of a political settlement on behalf of the United Nations.[13]

Where measures less than full armed conflict have been involved in the course of dealing with a particular situation, as in the case of UNEF and ONUC, the functions of the Force have been more closely defined. In the opening paragraph of his letter to participating States in UNEF, the Secretary-General was at pains to refer to the pertinent Assembly Resolutions in which the purpose of the Force had been described. It may be noted, moreover, that several States furnishing troops to UNEF stated expressly that they were doing so on condition that the troops were used only for the tasks indicated in the Assembly's Resolutions. This issue has also arisen, on occasions critically, in the course of the ONUC operation. The matter has been resolved satisfactorily in each instance, although the functions of UNEF and more particularly ONUC have broadened appreciably since their inception.[14] In the case of UNEF, the Force has become a peace observation unit, patrolling the Armistice Demarcation Line, after being initially established in order to secure the cessation of the hostilities of the 1956 Suez campaign and to ensure an orderly withdrawal of the invading troops. The functions of ONUC have been extended considerably since July 1960. This has, however, raised the question of the extent to which the functions could be changed, once Member States had provided troops upon the assumption that the functions of the Force would be those stated in

[11] See Chapters I and V of the report.
[12] *Ante*, p. 43.
[13] *Ante*, p. 52.
[14] *Ante*, pp. 106–108, 186–196.

the initial Resolutions. As has been seen,[15] the Secretary-General took the view that none of the successive Resolutions of the Security Council, in particular those of 21 February 1961 and 24 November 1961, changed the *constitutional basis* of the Force—although they clearly extended its functions—hence no renegotiation of the agreements with participating States was necessary. Whilst it is difficult to pursue consideration of all the issues involved in this question without reference to a particular situation, it is clear that in future *ad hoc* agreements the functions of the Force will need to be defined as fully as possible, if only by incorporation of the pertinent Resolutions, and that participating States will continue to attach central importance to this matter.

Perhaps the second most important item for inclusion in the majority of *ad hoc* agreements concerns the question of whether the consent of the host State or States has been given to the presence of the Force. The extent to which the consent of a State is legally necessary to the presence of a United Nations Force on its territory is a controversial question which has been dealt with elsewhere.[16] However, in both the UNEF and ONUC operations this issue has been of crucial significance since a number of States predicated their willingness to contribute contingents on the consent of the host State to receive the Force.[17] The need for the participating State to consider its relations with the host government will no doubt continue to operate as a factor determining the availability or otherwise of national contingents. This consideration has not operated too severely in the case of UNEF or ONUC since it was a basic principle of the operations that such consent had been given. Complications may arise, however, if such consent should be withdrawn, perhaps with respect to certain contingents only, or if there should be a change of governments in unsettled circumstances, as occurred in the Congo.

Independent of the two questions considered above is that of the internal organisation and chain of command of the Force. Whereas in a national army these matters will normally be accepted and established, in an international Force, composed *ad hoc* of units from different States, the structure and system of command has so far been laid down *de novo*. To some extent the problem involved is one of scale; the Allied forces which fought in Europe during the Second World War did so on a basis of staff co-ordination rather than through a merger of combat units. In the Korean conflict, on the other hand, although non-American contingents retained their identity, the preponderant role borne by United States troops made it inevitable that other units should be " fitted in " to the American strategy and fighting pattern.[18] Nevertheless, although these units

[15] *Ante,* p. 176.　　　　　　　　　　　　　　　　[16] See *post.* Chap. 12.
[17] The problem relating to the consent of the Katanga authorities raises separate considerations, discussed *ante,* pp. 203–204, 240–241.
[18] *Ante,* p. 40.

were obliged to accept the instructions given by the Commander, opportunity was given to the government concerned to bring a formal protest at a later stage. The political influence of the *ad hoc* " Committee of Sixteen," which met in Washington, should, moreover, not be ignored.[19]

In the case of UNEF and ONUC, the situation has been different again in that no large units have been involved, on the scale of national armies, but only a number of contingents, of limited size, each capable of performing one or more of the military functions required of the Force. Since the internal organisation of contingents has been maintained,[20] it was imperative that a chain of command should be laid down which would enable the Commander to exercise effective authority in respect of the Force as a whole, without impinging too far on the responsibilities retained by the unit commanders. Broadly speaking, the matter has been resolved in terms of "Force" requirements and "unit" requirements; whilst orders flow from the Commander to the unit commanders, and are obeyed accordingly, within the unit the national commander has authority, including that in respect of disciplinary action. However, the significant difference between UNEF and ONUC, in terms of command structure, lay in the assumption of command authority over ONUC by the Secretary-General and, through him, his civilian representatives. It has been suggested earlier [21] that the UNEF pattern is preferable and should be followed in future *ad hoc* agreements.

As regards logistics support and transportation for the Force, it is probable that in future operations on the scale of UNEF and ONUC these will form part of the direct responsibility of the United Nations, subject to the direction of the Force Commander. If the number of United Nations troops involved were to be increased considerably, however, as in the Korean struggle, arrangements would probably tend to reflect an increasing necessity for reliance upon national governments. Similarly as regards equipment; the arrangements made during the Korean operations have little in common with those made for UNEF and ONUC. Until the scale of the operation is known one cannot therefore forecast with any great accuracy what arrangements are likely to be made, except perhaps to note that the United Nations has in general found it more economical and practical to purchase equipment for UNEF and ONUC, rather than to use contingent-owned equipment and to be liable for its accelerated deterioration. In any event it is clear that proper arrangements should be made regarding the custodianship of

[19] Nor, on the other hand, should it be exaggerated according to Goodrich, "Korea: Collective Measures Against Aggression," *International Conciliation*, 1953, No. 494, p. 131, and see *ante*, p. 42.
[20] An exception may be noted in the case of the joint Danish-Norwegian battalion serving with UNEF. See *United Nations Emergency Force*, Background Information Paper, 3 February 1962, at p. 13.
[21] *Ante*, p. 340.

all equipment and supplies and that the accounting and control methods should be specified in some detail.

The financial arrangements to be made will also need to be covered in the various *ad hoc* agreements. In the Korean treaties reference was made only to the fact that other governments would need to repay the United States in respect of American materials, supplies and equipment, furnished to their contingents. In the case of UNEF, the Secretary-General's letter suggested that financial arrangements should be the subject of a supplementary agreement, in the light of the pertinent Assembly Resolutions. In practice, financial arrangements between the United Nations and States contributing troops to UNEF and ONUC have been handled at an administrative level, without any formal agreements being entered into. Broadly, as stated in the UNEF Regulations, national States have remained liable for the pay and other normal costs of their troops, whilst the operating expenses of the Force have been met by the United Nations.[22] It may also be noted that, judging from the Korean and UNEF operations, arrangements may be required to enable local currency to be provided for participating States, in conjunction with the authorities of the host State. In view of the importance which may be attached to the financial arrangements by participating States, a quick solution will need to be found at the very outset of the operation.

The international character of the Force, implicit in its functions, also raises the question of its privileges and immunities in so far as these affect the participating States. The national units and the individual members of the Force will, of course, owe full loyalty to the United Nations and will be required to carry out the orders given to them without reference to their respective home authorities. More specifically, it may be noted that it was provided in the exchange of letters on the Status of UNEF in Egypt that members of the Force should not be subject to Egyptian taxation in respect of their emoluments, whether received from the United Nations or from participating States. It was also agreed that the property, funds and assets of the latter should benefit from the provisions of Article II of the Convention on the Privileges and Immunities of the United Nations.[23] The general question of privileges and immunities is linked to that of criminal and civil jurisdiction over members of the Force. The classic problem of jurisdiction over armed forces acting outside national frontiers is plainly increased in difficulty where a multi-national Force is involved. The facts of international life suggest that the great majority of States are reluctant to yield jurisdiction over offences committed by their troops, and that this may prove a significant factor, as was noted in the

[22] See *ante*, pp. 139–142, for a more detailed account of the financial arrangements.

[23] Agreement on the Status of UNEF in Egypt, paragraph 23, U.N.T.S., Vol. 260, No. 3704, p. 61 : see generally, *ante*, pp. 125–136.

Summary Study,[24] in determining the availability of contingents. Subject to obtaining the consent of the host State where this is required, arrangements will therefore need to be made to ensure that participating States are able to exercise jurisdiction and, so far as possible, assurances sought from them that they will in fact exercise this jurisdiction. In his letter to States contributing troops to UNEF the Secretary-General dwelt at length on this point and has subsequently referred to the matter on several occasions. There would also be a decided advantage in dealing specifically with the question of who has authority to waive any immunities—the Secretary-General (or Commander, perhaps) or the authorities of the participating State, and it looks to be certain that, for members of their national contingents, this right of waiver will be retained by the authorities of the participating States. A distinct advance would be the insertion of clause obliging the participating State to exercise its own jurisdiction *in situ*: the problems of securing a fair trial of an issue, whether civil or criminal, in the home State are enormous, and not least because the witnesses from the host State will seldom ever be available.

A more general issue concerns that of responsibility for the acts of the Force. In the Korean campaign the United States insisted that Russian and Chinese complaints regarding flights over their territory by planes forming part of the United Nations Forces should be considered by the United Nations, although the United States itself offered to pay compensation, as assessed by a United Nations Commission, for any damage done.[25] Unless the arrangements made in respect of the Korean conflict are to be repeated, however, it may be expected that the United Nations will be more directly responsible for the acts of its troops in future operations. In the case of UNEF and ONUC the United Nations has met claims presented following accidents caused during the performance of official duties, and this primary responsibility *vis-à-vis* third parties will no doubt continue where the United Nations itself is exercising immediate authority over the troops concerned. Both in respect to the concession of civil jurisdiction to the host State and in the provision of a machinery for dealing with claims, the more sophisticated system of UNEF is to be preferred to the rudimentary system of ONUC: the latter should be regarded as being confined to the exceptional case where, by reason of the breakdown of internal law and order, it would be folly to envisage jurisdiction in the local courts or a detailed system of claims procedures—at least in so far as they would result in compensating the government of the host State or the United Nations. The need to compensate private individuals will always remain and should be provided for. Where the situation is one in which the

---

[24] *Summary Study,* A/3943, paragraph 163.
[25] See S/1856 and *Off.Rec.S.C.,* 5th yr., 493rd Mtg., 31 August 1950, p. 26; and see *ante,* p. 57.

United Nations would wish to exercise its right of functional protection, and present claims on its own behalf or on behalf of the
personnel of the Force, it would be advisable for the agreements to
embody a clause whereby the participating States conceded that, in
respect of injury or damage to personnel of the contingent suffered
in the course of their official duties, the primary right to protection
against the authorities of the host State lay with the United Nations.
This would be far preferable to a situation in which the host State
would have to face a series of claims by different participating States
and would emphasise the international character of the Force.

A suitable claims machinery will also need to be established
between the United Nations and participating States, in order to
settle disputes which may arise regarding, for example, the allocation
of expenses or the payment of compensation to third parties. In the
Korean agreements, arrangements were made for direct negotiations
and settlement of claims between governments. In cases similar to
UNEF and ONUC, however, where the United Nations has exercised
more direct control, the claims machinery will normally operate
only between participating States and the United Nations. In this
respect the provisions of the UNEF agreements, providing for international arbitration in the event of failure to reach an amicable
settlement, would appear to be a suitable precedent.

II. " STAND-BY " AGREEMENTS

The argument has already been made [26] that " stand-by " agreements
between the United Nations and Member States would be very much
preferable to the present system which relies on *" ad hoc "* agreements which have to be negotiated for each operation and then made
to operate retrospectively. At the present time the United Nations
has been forced to authorise operations without knowing with any
real certainty that the necessary forces can be found to carry out
the operations: a comprehensive series of stand-by agreements
whereby States would agree *in advance* to provide certain forces
must be a more effective means of ensuring that the United Nations
can fulfil its responsibility to maintain international peace and
security.

A preliminary difficulty is that of deciding whether the Permanent
Members of the Security Council should be asked to participate in
this system of stand-by agreements. As we have seen, both in UNEF
and ONUC the forces of such Member States were excluded from
participation as a matter of principle: this principle is clearly based
on political rather than military considerations, for it cannot be
doubted that the Permanent Members are in many ways the very

---

[26] *Ante,* p. 334. For a discussion of the arrangements which have already
been made with States like the Netherlands, Finland, Canada and the
Scandinavian countries, and which appear to fall half-way between the
" *Ad hoc* " and the true " Stand-by " arrangement, see *ante,* p. 333.

States best equipped to provide effective contingents for a United Nations Force, and to this extent the principle is a regrettable one. However, it is likely that, for the immediate future at least, this principle will have to be adhered to.[27]   An abandonment of the principle can occur either at a stage when the relations between East and West improve to such an extent as to remove the basic political justification for the principle or at a stage when a United Nations Force is recruited individually rather than constituted via the national contingents provided pursuant to stand-by agreements.

Turning to the actual content of the agreements, it must first be emphasised that these agreements will not stand in isolation but will operate in conjunction with (and will be interpreted together with) the Regulations for the Force[28] and, in most cases,[29] the United Nations Status of Forces Agreement.   Certain matters which are perfectly capable of insertion into the stand-by agreements may, therefore, be felt to be more appropriately dealt with in one or other of these two instruments.

It would seem that the basic agreement between the United Nations and participating States which operated in UNEF, and which was followed in ONUC, must provide the model upon which stand-by agreements will be based.   Yet, in the light of experience and of the fact that stand-by agreements anticipate operations in the future, certain modifications seem desirable.

Whereas in the *ad hoc* agreements it has been possible to define the functions of the Force by reference to the Resolutions of either the Security Council or General Assembly authorising the operations, this will clearly not be possible with stand-by agreements.   What is suggested, therefore, is that the agreements should specify in the broadest possible terms that the State is making its contingent available for (i) " peace-keeping " operations authorised by the Security Council and/or the General Assembly and/or (ii) enforcement action authorised by the Security Council and/or the General Assembly.[30]   A State will, therefore, opt for a larger or smaller category of functions.   It may also be necessary to allow States to specify that their contingents can be used only on the territory of a

---

[27] The principle operates so as to exclude *contingents* from the Permanent Members: it does not involve the exclusion of individuals, recruited as such, of the nationality of the Permanent Members who might be recruited to the UN Military Headquarters Planning Staff at an earlier stage: see *ante*, pp. 349–352.

[28] *Post*, p. 376.

[29] Not in all cases, for in the event of the Force taking action against a State—enforcement action—or possibly even engaging in a peace-keeping operation without the consent of the State on whose territory it operates (*post*, pp. 413–417) the Standing Agreement on the Status of UN Forces will not regulate relations between the Force and the "host" State, for there will be no "host" State in that sense.

[30] Whether the Assembly can, under its present constitutional powers, authorise enforcement action is not entirely clear: on this problem see *ante*, pp. 291–293.

State which has consented to the presence of the Force,[31] or even to specify that it shall not be used in particular geographical areas. There are, of course, certain disadvantages in allowing for this variety of legal commitments, but it is believed that at the present time these disadvantages are offset by the paramount need to secure as wide as possible a participation in a system of stand-by agreements by Member States.

The principle that, for any particular operation, it would be for the United Nations exclusively to determine the composition of a United Nations Force should be clearly spelt out: no agreement would give a State the *right* to participate in any given operation.

The agreements will also have to provide for the exact type, size, degree of readiness and location of the contingent which the State agrees to provide; obviously this particular clause will vary considerably from agreement to agreement. Similarly, there is no need to anticipate uniformity in the clauses dealing with the transport of the contingent or its logistical supply, for whereas some States may be able to provide their own transport and considerable portions of the supplies necessary to maintain it, others may be able to provide little more than the personnel. Rotation of contingents should be limited to rotation after service of not less than twelve months' duration, and changes in the command of national contingents should be made subject to prior consultation with the United Nations Commander.

It would also be desirable to have a clause dealing with the financial arrangements between the participating State and the United Nations, rather than leave this to a supplemental agreement as was done with UNEF and ONUC.[32] It may well be that it will be necessary in this clause only to refer to standing financial arrangements in so far as the United Nations is able to establish such arrangements on a permanent basis,[33] but deviations from the standard arrangements could be provided for in particular cases. For example, certain States might be prepared to contribute a contingent only on the basis that the United Nations assumed full responsibility for pay, whereas the standard arrangements make this the responsibility of the participating State, with the United Nations providing only a *per diem*. The agreements could, in effect, make such modifications to the standard financial arrangements as would be necessary to secure the participation of the relatively less well-endowed Members.

The United Nations should undertake to provide all necessary local currency for the needs of a contingent and adequate accounting procedures would have to be provided for, either in the agreement

---

[31] We have rejected the view that the distinction between " peace-keeping " and " enforcement " operations necessarily turns on this question of consent: *ante*, pp. 311–312.

[32] These arrangements would not, of course, cover the *whole* cost of the Force: see *post*, pp. 468–480.

[33] *Post*, p. 481.

or by a reference in the agreement to standing accounting procedures set up in the permanent financial arrangements. This procedure would ideally provide that all supplies furnished by the United Nations should remain the property of the United Nations and, in the event of withdrawal of a contingent or disbandment of the Force consequent upon completion of the mission, should be returned to the United Nations.

The character of the Force as an international, United Nations Force should be emphasised and, as a corollary, it should be made clear that, for the duration of the assignment of a contingent to United Nations service, the contingent would come under the exclusive command of the United Nations, and it would be for the United Nations alone to determine the manner in which a particular mandate of the Force should be carried out and the question of when a particular mandate had been fulfilled. The actual obligations of members of contingents, details of command structure and of discipline could be more appropriately left to the permanent Regulations for the Force. However, the stand-by agreements should, consistently with the more detailed provisions of the United Nations Status of Forces Agreement, provide for the problems of civil and criminal jurisdiction over members of the Force and property of contingents other than United Nations-owned property. The arrangements for UNEF [34] seem in general an adequate pattern, more so than the arrangements for ONUC,[35] but it would seem desirable to modify even these to the extent that participating States would agree to legislate so as to ensure that they possessed full jurisdiction over any acts criminal under their own law and committed by members of their contingents whilst in United Nations service. Moreover, they should be obliged to legislate so as to permit the exercise of this jurisdiction *in situ* whenever, in the opinion of the United Nations Commander of the Force, this was desirable either from the standpoint of availability of witnesses or for any other reason based on the necessity for maintaining discipline or the good reputation of the Force. One further modification would seem desirable, and that is to provide that in any civil action against a member of the Force it should be for the United Nations Commander, after consultation with the contingent commander, to waive any immunity from the jurisdiction of the local courts when to do so would not interfere with the proper functioning of the Force and would be consistent with the promotion of justice.

Linked with problems of privileges and immunities, there should be provisions dealing with claims and responsibility.[36] The United Nations should not only agree to afford international legal protection to all members of the Force but the participating States should agree that, in matters arising out of the performance of their official duties,

[34] *Ante*, pp. 131–136.
[35] *Ante*, pp. 236–238.
[36] See generally *post*, pp. 445–448.

the United Nations should have the primary right to exercise this protection over members of the Force. Moreover, in order to ensure legal responsibility for breaches of the conventional rules of warfare, participating States should agree that, at least for purposes of service with the United Nations, their contingents would be fully subject to the Hague Regulations of 1907 and the Geneva Conventions of 1949 and should undertake so to instruct these contingents.[37]

A withdrawal clause (permitting withdrawal of the contingent) should be made an optional clause: this problem requires particular attention and is dealt with in more detail later.[38] A revision clause would also be desirable, permitting negotiations for revision of the agreement to be opened at the request of either the United Nations or the participating State at any time after three years from the entry into force of the agreement or of a revised agreement: changes in military strength or even economic strength suggest this to be highly desirable.

Disputes clauses would certainly be necessary. For disputes arising from the interpretation or application of the agreement between the United Nations and the participating State arbitration, following the UNEF precedent, would be most suitable. For disputes between a host State or its nationals and the Force or its members the United Nations Status of Forces Agreement will obviously make provision, and perhaps no more is necessary in the stand-by agreement than to provide that the United Nations shall make provision for the settlement of such disputes as disputes to which the United Nations is a party, and not the participating State. Similarly, disputes arising between different participating States arising from the employment of their contingents in the same operation should be considered as disputes between a claimant State and the United Nations and dealt with by a Claims Commission. The United Nations should, of course, in the stand-by agreement, have a right to indemnity against a participating State in respect of any liability arising from the acts of a contingent which were unauthorised by the United Nations Command or from the use of equipment and *matériel* not provided by the United Nations. The purpose of such provisions would be to prevent a multiplicity of claims—and possibly acrimony between participating States—so that the United Nations would in all cases appear as the nominal defendant. This would emphasise the character of the Force as a United Nations Force and would facilitate general settlements of liability, leaving the matter as an accounting problem except in the cases where a participating State disagreed that a particular liability ought to be attributed to its own account; the matter would then go to arbitration (if turning on the interpretation of the stand-by agreement) or to the Claims Commission.

[37] On this problem see *post*, pp. 507–516.
[38] *Post*, pp. 379–386.

The negotiation of these agreements will certainly be no easy matter and it is likely that it will have to proceed in stages. The first stage could be one in which the basic provisions are drafted by a United Nations Committee, preferably under the chairmanship of the Secretary-General. It is, of course, true that the Article 43 agreements were to be negotiated with States by the Security Council. However, the Security Council has, for a period of twenty years, failed to negotiate such agreements; moreover, the "stand-by" agreements we now envisage are broader than the Article 43 agreements since they envisage the provision of forces for functions wider than the enforcement functions of Chapter VII (*i.e.*, they include "peace-keeping" functions) and further, that the General Assembly may in addition to the Security Council assume control over a United Nations Force constituted via these stand-by agreements. Hence, there is every reason for not regarding the drafting and negotiation of these stand-by agreements as exclusively within the province of the Security Council. There would be good sense in having this United Nations Committee a joint Committee of both the Security Council and the General Assembly, or a Committee of the Assembly upon which the five Permanent Members of the Security Council are represented: but it must be clear from the outset that no veto will be applicable at any stage of its work.

The Committee will be "political," but with the representatives of States elected to the Committee having the right to be accompanied by military advisers. Ideally, if the United Nations Military Headquarters Staff has been established by that time, the Staff could propose a draft to form the basis of discussion and could be represented on the Committee, without a right of vote. These basic provisions would not be subject to negotiation once adopted by the General Assembly, and, after adoption, the Assembly could call on all Member States, with the exception of the Permanent Members, to communicate to the Secretary-General their willingness to enter into negotiations with the United Nations, via this same United Nations Committee, so as to complete the agreement in the sense of negotiating the outstanding clauses dealing with size, location and degree of readiness of the contingent, obligations of logistical support, etc. The agreements could then enter into force upon signature by the representatives of the Member State and the Secretary-General.

It should also be planned that, at the time of "adopting" the basic provisions of stand-by agreements, the General Assembly will also have before it for adoption the permanent Regulations for a United Nations Force and the United Nations Status of Forces Agreement, for these will form a coherent whole together with the stand-by agreements. These could, similarly, be prepared by the same United Nations Committee, and, particularly with regard to the Regulations for the Force, it would be highly desirable for the United

Nations Headquarters Military Staff to be already in existence and to have prepared initial drafts upon which the United Nations Committee could work. Yet another useful function which the Headquarters Staff could perform at this stage would be that of entering into exploratory discussions with the military representatives of Member States so as to work out the details of the outstanding clauses of the stand-by agreements which are primarily of a " military " character. The advantage would be that the Member State could then present to the United Nations Committee a series of proposals which were in principle acceptable to the Headquarters Staff.

One further possible function relating to the " stand-by " agreements can be envisaged for the Headquarters Staff. Assuming that these agreements come into force, it will be necessary for the United Nations to satisfy itself that the Member States are in a position to implement these agreements. Thus the Headquarters Staff, perhaps in the person of the Commander and a few aides, could act as an Inspectorate, making visits to the national contingents held ready under the stand-by agreements so as to ensure that their state of readiness conformed to that prescribed in the agreement. They could, at the same time, exercise a useful liaison function, reporting back to Headquarters on any difficulties experienced by the participating State. It might also be no small advantage for troops to have seen the Commander who will, in the event of any United Nations operation, assume command over them.

III. AGREEMENTS FOR A PERMANENT FORCE

In so far as a stage is reached at which the entire United Nations Force is individually recruited, then there will be no participating States in the strict sense : such agreements as may have to be concluded with States will cover incidental matters such as the obligation to remove any restrictions on the enlistment of a State's nationals in United Nations service, perhaps the right of a recruit to treat service with the United Nations Force as counting for exemption from any compulsory, national, military service, the right of the United Nations to establish recruiting centres in a State's territory, and so forth.

However, we have suggested earlier [39] that a gradual transition from a non-permanent Force based on stand-by agreements to a truly permanent Force could be made either by gradually strengthening the components of the Force individually recruited, and thus building up the permanent element, *or* (and this method is additional rather than alternative) by persuading States to substitute for stand-by agreements an agreement whereby they would place their contingents at the disposal of the United Nations for a period of, say, three years. During this period the contingent would, for all practical purposes, be divorced from the national army and become

[39] *Ante*, p. 334.

fully integrated into the United Nations Force: it would move to one of the United Nations bases or training areas.

In this event the agreements would already differ from the stand-by agreements: there would be no question of withdrawal, the United Nations would presumably assume full responsibility for all pay, allowances and pensions for death or injury, a more complete logistics responsibility, complete responsibility for all acts of the contingent without any right of indemnity against the participating State, and so forth. It would be desirable for the United Nations by this stage to have its own system of courts-martial and military law and to assume criminal and disciplinary jurisdiction over the contingents so provided. Moreover, by this time the necessity for a permanent base or bases would have become compelling, and thus the agreements would have to be read together with both the United Nations Status of Forces Agreement *and* the special bases agreements [40] covering the bases where these contingents would be trained and deployed pending a particular operation.

The agreements would, therefore, increase in complexity, but since these would come at a stage subsequent to the stand-by agreements there would be time for the operation of the stand-by agreements themselves to be examined in the light of experience, and full examination of the complexities of permanent agreements of the kind now envisaged could be undertaken by the United Nations Committee together with the United Nations Headquarters Military Staff.

Not least of the problems would be to provide a rota system to determine which particular States were, at any one time, to furnish the contingents to be permanently attached to the United Nations Force. On the assumption that a good many States were agreeable to such a system, and yet the permanent Force was to be kept to a " peace-keeping " size of perhaps 10,000–25,000 men, not all the States would be required to implement their agreements at one and the same time. Hence a rota system, designed to ensure sufficient contingents of the right size and kind, and drawn from different parts of the world in order to maintain an equitable geographical distribution, would have to be devised. Whether such a scheme would present greater difficulties than a scheme which depended entirely on individual recruitment remains to be seen. Certainly, in the view of the present writer, the scheme for individually recruiting a permanent Force seems the simpler and better scheme, but it may be that the kind of agreements we now envisage could be utilised to establish a permanent Force if, in the event and for political reasons, Member States felt reluctant to envisage a Force recruited as individuals in its entirety.[41]

[40] See *post*, pp. 458–467.
[41] We are assuming that there would already be a certain part of the Force so recruited, *i.e.*, the UN Military Headquarters Staff and certain of the specialist units, such as the bilingual signals units, maintenance and transport personnel, etc.

IV. WITHDRAWAL OF NATIONAL CONTINGENTS

1. *Under ad hoc agreements*

A characteristic weakness of the United Nations Forces raised on the basis of an *ad hoc* agreement has been the possibility of participating States withdrawing their national contingents. The report of the Military Staff Committee in 1947, dealing with the agreements contemplated under Article 43, had certainly not contemplated that Members would retain a complete freedom to withdraw their contingents, for the essence of these agreements was to have been a continuing obligation to provide forces upon the call of the Security Council. Unilateral withdrawal would therefore have constituted a breach of the obligation. The only reference in the Military Staff Committee's report relating to withdrawal was that proposed by China and France. This provided as follows:

" In the case of self-defence (Article 51 of the Charter) and of national emergencies, Member Nations will have the right to make use of armed forces, which they have made available to the Security Council in conformity with the terms of special agreements. They undertake, however, to assume anew all of their obligations within the shortest possible space of time." [42]

This suggestion, which would have enabled participating States to reserve the right of withdrawal in the two cases mentioned, proved unacceptable to the other three Permanent Members. Even if it had been adopted, moreover, it would have been necessary for individual Member States to make a clear reservation in their respective special agreements; it appears to have been assumed that without such a reservation the right to withdraw a contingent would have been lost.

In the Korean agreements, no provision was included for withdrawal; indeed, having regard to the intensity with which the campaign was waged on both sides, such a reference was hardly to be expected. However, in the absence of agreements concluded under Article 43, the *ad hoc* consent of Member States has been required before troops could be made available to help meet a particular emergency; the principle has thus emerged that, unless Member States agree to provide troops for a fixed period and then seek to withdraw them before that period has expired, or restrict their discretion in some other way, they will retain the right to withdraw their contingents at any time. This appears to have been the position accepted by the United Nations in respect of States providing troops for UNEF and ONUC, except that Member States were, in the case of UNEF, expressly required to give adequate notice. In his letter of 21 June 1957 to States contributing troops to UNEF, the Secretary-General therefore provided expressly that units might be withdrawn by the national State concerned, subject only to adequate notice being given in order that appropriate

[42] Article 17, Report of the Military Staff Committee, *Repertory of Practice of United Nations Organs*, Vol. II, p. 396, at p. 400.

arrangements might be made relating to the recruitment of fresh troops.[43] Arrangements made in the case of contingents forming part of ONUC appear to have been based on similar considerations, although no written agreements have been entered into between the United Nations and participating States. The Secretary-General sought to persuade the Casablanca Powers not to withdraw their troops, after they had informed him of their intention to do so owing to their disagreement with the interpretation given to the mandate of the Force.[44] Following the failure of his efforts, the actual withdrawal operation itself appears to have proceeded smoothly. There was a complication in the withdrawal of the Moroccan contingent, however, in that it appeared likely that there would be a gap between its withdrawal from the Force and the date of its repatriation. The Secretary-General therefore instructed that the contingent should remain subject to the orders of the ONUC Commander until it actually left the Congo, and this instruction was accepted.[45] There was, of course, in the Congo the additional complication that troops withdrawing from ONUC might remain within the Congo and act independently of the United Nations, taking instructions from their own governments and intervening in the civil war. The Secretary-General's position on this was, as we have seen,[46] that this would bring about an impossible situation and that all troops remaining on Congolese territory, but not under ONUC's command, would become foreign military personnel and therefore liable to expulsion by ONUC under the Resolutions of the Security Council. This position was undoubtedly right.

There is, however, little doubt that the success of a United Nations military operation is likely to be imperilled so long as the right of unilateral withdrawal exists: even the requirement of reasonable notice may not prevent a dangerous situation from arising, for it does no more than give the United Nations time to make other arrangements. There is no certainty that troop replacements will be found.

In his communications to the Casablanca Powers, the Secretary-General pointed out the dangers which would arise if there was a general withdrawal of troops from the Congo.[47] Indeed, the withdrawal of those units left the United Nations Forces seriously under-manned and contributed to several incidents, most notably that at Matadi, where a small Sudanese detachment, covering up for the Moroccan troops who had been withdrawn, was overwhelmed by Congolese troops.[48]

---

[43] A/3943, Annex I, paragraph 8, *Off.Rec.G.A.*, Agenda item 65, Annexes, 13th Sess., 1958. Chaumont, in (1958) *Ann.Fr.D.I.*, pp. 432–433 takes the view that withdrawal could only occur by agreement with the UN.
[44] S/4640, *Off.Rec.S.C.*, 16th yr., Suppl. January–March 1961; and see *ante*, pp. 208–209, 214.
[45] S/4668 and Add. 1, *ibid.*
[46] *Ante*, pp. 208–209.
[47] S/4640, Annexes I and II, *ibid.*   [48] S/4761, paragraphs 5 and 17, *ibid.*

Past experience, particularly in the Congo, would suggest that whenever United Nations Forces are established via *ad hoc* agreements in the future, a more specific regulation of the right of withdrawal ought to be made in the agreements. Naturally, this will have to be based upon a realistic appraisal of the reasons why States wish to withdraw their contingents, and past experience indicates the following possible reasons:

(1) A State's need to recall contingents for its own self-defence or other national emergency.[49]

(2) A State's inability or unwillingness to have its contingent (or even replacements for a particular contingent) committed to an operation which had originally been anticipated as one of short duration but which transpires to be one of indefinite duration.[50]

(3) A State's disagreement with the manner in which the original mandate of the Force is being interpreted or executed.[51]

(4) A State's disagreement with an extension or alteration of the original mandate.

The first two reasons are certainly understandable and must be reckoned with in any future *ad hoc* agreements. Assuming that the reasons are bona fide—and there may be some doubt about the first of these reasons when the contingent in question is small in size as compared with the overall size of the national armed forces of the State demanding recall—there would seem to be a need for providing that *a State may recall its contingent, following consultation with the appropriate organ of the United Nations, for reasons of self-defence or a national emergency or upon the expiration of the time for which the State has specified that the contingent is to be available, provided that (where the reason is one of self-defence or national emergency) reasonable notice is given to the United Nations and provided that in all cases the withdrawal does not, in the opinion of the appropriate organ of the United Nations, jeopardise the security or mission of the Force.*

The third reason is not believed to be an acceptable reason for withdrawal of the contingent. Any State participating in a measure of collective security, or collective action for the maintenance of international peace and security, must be prepared to accept the collective decision as to the manner in which the action is to be conducted: the provisions of Articles 25 and 49 clearly indicate this in relation to action authorised by decision of the Security Council

---

[49] Such was the case with the withdrawal of the Tunisian contingent from ONUC during the Bizerta crisis (S/4940/Add. 12, para. 16); or that of the Mali contingent during a constitutional crisis (Dayal's Second Report, S/4557, para. 82).

[50] As with the Finnish and Indonesian contingents with UNEF (A/3943, para. 50) and the Indonesian, Nigerian and Liberian contingents with ONUC (S/4940/Add. 12, para. 16).

[51] As with the Moroccan withdrawal from ONUC (S/4668, para. B.2); and see *ante*, p. 208.

and, even in relation to action authorised by the Assembly, Article 2 (5) and the general principle of good faith would suggest that any other construction is inconsistent with the essential principle upon which a system of collective security is based. This will be even more fundamental when, as we have suggested above,[52] the interpretation or execution of the original mandate is discharged by the political organs of the United Nations—or their sub-committees— and not by the Secretary-General on the basis of his individual decision. To allow individual States to exert a minority view by means of the threat of withdrawal of their national contingents is fundamentally wrong. The view of a participating State that the mission of the Force had been accomplished and that, therefore, its contingent should withdraw, would fall into this category.

The fourth reason cannot be quite so categorically rejected as unacceptable, even though it may in some cases be difficult to distinguish from the third reason. It may well be that some States are prepared to provide contingents for " peace-keeping " operations, but not for " enforcement action " and, should an alteration of so radical a nature occur in the mandate laid down by the competent United Nations organ as to change the nature of the action from one to the other, then in principle it is difficult to see why a State consenting to the former use of its contingent only should be prevented from withdrawing its contingent.[53] With anything less than this kind of radical alteration of the mandate it should not, in principle, be permissible for a State to withdraw its contingent, for otherwise the way is opened up for States to rely on what we have already rejected as the third reason, namely, a difference of view as to the execution of a general mandate.

One further point, already made in the case of ONUC, should be inserted in any future agreements and that is that, pending withdrawal, the contingent must remain fully subject to United Nations command.

Ad hoc agreements might, finally, contain provisions relating to the provision and cost of transport necessary for contingents being repatriated, and their equipment; moreover, a procedure should be established for verifying that all equipment, arms, ammunition and stores supplied by the United Nations and not essential to the contingent as part of the repatriation procedure (*e.g.*, certain foodstuffs and clothing) had been surrendered and checked.

Following the withdrawal of national contingents it will be necessary for the United Nations and the participating State to settle their accounts. Arguably, if a participating State has withdrawn its troops in such a way as to cause extra expense to the United Nations, the latter would be entitled to debit the State accordingly,

---

[52] *Ante*, p. 357.
[53] For the same view see Virally, " Les Nations Unies et l'Affaire du Congo," (1960) *Ann.Fr.D.I.* pp. 518–519; also Chaumont, *loc. cit.*, p. 433. In the same sense see the *Summary Study, etc.*, A/3943, para. 178.

although such a ruling appears an unlikely course for the United Nations to adopt. No suggestion to this effect was made when troops were withdrawn from ONUC at the request of national States, although considerable inconvenience was caused to the United Nations effort as a result. The financial arrangements which were made therefore, other than those relating to the logistics of the actual transfer home, have consisted of payment by the United Nations of all the " extra and extraordinary costs " incurred by the Member State up to the time of withdrawal, according to the principles governing the allocation of expenses which have been evolved by the United Nations.[54] Apart from pay and allowances falling under this heading—which would merely need to be calculated up to the due date—the evaluation of the cost of deterioration of equipment, *matériel* and supplies furnished by the government has been the major item. Such deterioration was originally estimated solely at the moment of withdrawal, but it is now calculated at the time each unit is rotated. In future, therefore, as regards equipment, it will merely be necessary to treat the withdrawal of a contingent to which the United Nations has agreed in the same way as the return of a rotating unit to the home State.

Arrangements will also need to be made in respect of cases of service-incurred illness, accident or death. The United Nations will, no doubt, wish to commute periodic payments due under national law into a lump sum settlement, possibly covering the entire contingent. In the event of cases only arising after withdrawal—a small class—the United Nations will continue to be responsible for reimbursing the national State, at its demand.

It is cases such as these which will render it difficult to arrange for a prompt and final settlement of all issues. Budgetary adjustments may also result in some delay, both as regards the presentation of claims by participating States and in meeting them. This will be particularly so as regards reimbursement to the United Nations of any local currency which it may have supplied in order to help the participating State pay wages and allowances to its troops in the area of operations.

Lastly, the claims machinery left extant between the United Nations and the participating State, even after withdrawal, may produce further sums to be met by one or other side. Possibly, for example, the United Nations may incur expense as a result of paying compensation for the private, *ultra vires* acts of individual soldiers and may seek appropriate reimbursement from the national State. More complex issues may also arise in the case of dissolution of common facilities, to which the particular State contributed along with others, or where a number of participating States are involved. Consideration of these items will need to await the particular facts; the possibility of such claims should not, however, be ignored.

[54] See *ante*, pp. 139–142.

So far we have assumed that withdrawal takes place at the request of the participating State. However, another possible situation is that the United Nations might call for the withdrawal of a particular national contingent. It would seem axiomatic that the United Nations should have the right to order the withdrawal of a particular national contingent if it so decides. However, as so often with axiomatic truths, no clear authority exists to support this right and the matter is left to be inferred from general principles relating to the means by and purpose for which the Force was established. If a United Nations Force has been established as a result of a decision by the General Assembly or Security Council, the United Nations would normally have sufficient authority over it to determine its composition, both initially and subsequently. In the case of the Korean conflict, where the United Nations itself played little or no part in the organisation of the troops which fought in its name, it is unlikely that either the Security Council or the Assembly would have decided that a particular contingent should be withdrawn, or that such a decision, if adopted, would necessarily have been accepted. As. contrasted with this decentralised action, however, one may look to the arrangements envisaged under the framework of Article 43. The Security Council would clearly have retained sufficient authority to decide and ensure that a particular contingent should be withdrawn, if agreements had been concluded with Member States. Such a decision, however, would have been one made largely on political grounds, involving the concurrent votes of the five Permanent Members. It is hard to imagine any one of the latter agreeing to the withdrawal of its own troops at other than its own request, although conceivably some intricate " horse-trading" between East and West might have resulted in such a negotiated withdrawal. This, however, is to move into the realm of conjecture rather than of well-established fact.

The more likely circumstances concern the withdrawal, at the request of the United Nations, of a contingent from a force similar to UNEF or ONUC. Unless the withdrawal were to be on strictly technical grounds—the troops supplied being specialists for which there was no longer any need, for example—the Secretary-General would, no doubt, seek the opinion and authorisation of the Security Council, or of the Assembly, before proceeding to the issue of an actual order for withdrawal. Particularly where the Force operated in territory on the basis of the consent of the host State, a demand by the host State for the withdrawal of a particular contingent might be accepted as a matter of policy (though not legal obligation) by the United Nations.[55] Failure of a contingent to observe the laws of war, or to comply with orders of the United Nations Command, would be other examples of reasons for compelling the withdrawal

[55] It may be recalled that the Congolese authorities called for the withdrawal of the U.A.R. contingent; see *ante*, p. 164.

of a national contingent. The normal pattern would be for negotiations to take place between the Secretary-General and the participating State, and only if these failed, the State concerned for some reason refusing to withdraw, would the Secretary-General need to go further. The Agreement concluded between the Secretary-General and States participating in UNEF provided expressly that ". . . should circumstances render the service of some national contingent with the Force no longer necessary, the Secretary-General undertakes to consult with your Government and to give adequate prior notification concerning its withdrawal." [56] It may be noted that no objection appears to have been raised at any stage to the assumption that the United Nations possesses the right to order withdrawal subject to adequate, prior notice. The efficiency of any similar United Nations Force, as a functional body designed to achieve a particular object, could hardly be maintained if this were not to be the case.

2. *Under permanent arrangements*

If we envisage future permanent arrangements as being in the form of " stand-by " agreements in which States undertake legal obligations to provide contingents *in advance* of any particular operation—and the desirability of these arrangements has been strongly emphasised above [57]—then slightly different considerations will apply to the question of withdrawal of contingents.

Under either the Article 43 agreements or more general " stand-by " agreements whereby States agree to place contingents at the disposal of *any* competent United Nations organ (the latter being preferable) it is probable that a certain latitude ought to be allowed to Member States so as to permit them to opt for an agreement of the kind envisaged by the Military Staff Committee or a less comprehensive agreement. For example, it may be useful to give States the option of committing their contingents to any action authorised by a competent United Nations organ and consistent with the purposes and principles of the Charter *or* to " peace-keeping" operations only. Some States might be prepared to agree only to the latter so that, in the event, their contingents could not be called for enforcement action or, should an operation change from a peace-keeping operation to an enforcement action, they would exercise a right to call for the withdrawal of their contingent.

Similarly, it may be useful to allow States to choose whether a " self-defence or national emergency " clause permitting recall should be inserted: this may be important to small States but of less importance to larger States to whom a small United Nations " earmarked " contingent would make little difference.

Again, some States might be prepared to enter into a legal commitment for a limited period of years, or even a commitment that

---

[56] A/3943, Annex I, exchange of letters dated 21 June 1957.   [57] *Ante,* p. 371.

its contingent should only be used for a limited period at any one time, rather than a commitment without any limitation in time.

By and large, it is believed preferable to maximise the number of such agreements by providing for such options rather than to insist upon extensive commitments which few States, at least pending disarmament, are prepared to accept. Thus a withdrawal clause somewhat like the clause suggested for the *ad hoc* agreements above [58] could be inserted in " stand-by " agreements in which States availed themselves of these options. Subject to this, the same kind of clauses regarding the subjection of the contingent to United Nations command pending recall, the costs of recall, surrender and verification of equipment, etc., and legal arrangements for the settlement of outstanding financial questions and claims would be required.

The disadvantage of permitting withdrawal or recall of national contingents under these closely specified conditions is, of course, that it would tend to diminish the forces available to the United Nations. However, the object must be to persuade as many States as possible to enter into these permanent arrangements, if only because it is not really feasible that a few States will indefinitely remain committed in a stringent manner whilst the vast majority of Member States stand idly by, allowing the few to shoulder the burden of maintaining international peace and security. If this object is attained there should be a sufficient number of States legally committed to provide forces that the occasional withdrawal of a particular national contingent, subject to the agreed conditions and in consultation with the competent United Nations organ, will not seriously affect the efficiency of any United Nations Force.

Another possibility is that a rota system might be worked out whereby only a certain number of these States under legal commitments to provide forces should be called upon at any one time, although the difficulties of working out an equitable rota system would be such as to suggest that this possibility ought to be explored *after*, and not before, the initial stand-by agreements are completed. On balance, the rota system is thought to be more suitable for the later stage in the development of United Nations Forces in which national contingents become permanently attached to a United Nations Force for a period of years and, for that period, separated from their national forces.[59] Only at that stage would it be desirable to exclude altogether the right to withdrawal of a national contingent.

It may be added, finally, that once the Force became a Force recruited on the basis of individual recruitment the concept of the " national contingent " would disappear, and with it this problem of withdrawal. This is perhaps one of the strongest arguments in favour of moving towards a truly permanent Force based on individual recruitment.[60]

[58] *Ante*, p. 381.   [59] See *ante*, pp. 320, 334.
[60] *Ante*, p. 323.

11

Logistical Support and Movement of United Nations Forces

I. ARRANGEMENTS BETWEEN THE UNITED NATIONS AND MEMBER STATES
FOR LOGISTICAL SUPPORT

MEMBER nations may be called upon to provide logistical support for United Nations Forces under two distinct sets of legal conditions. Under the first, the Member State concerned may be required to furnish logistical support as part of the preventive or enforcement measures which the Security Council has decided to take under the mandatory powers given to it in respect of threats to peace, breaches of the peace and acts of aggression, under Chapter VII of the Charter. Under the second, the Security Council or the General Assembly may decide to recommend that Member States should give assistance, including logistical support, to United Nations Forces, and individual Member States may agree to comply with the request.

Dealing with the first class, Chapter VII provides that, if the Security Council considers that measures short of armed force are, or may prove, inadequate to maintain or restore international peace and security, " it may take such action by air, sea or land forces as may be necessary."[1] Apart from the general obligation of Member States under Article 25 to accept and carry out Security Council decisions, Article 49 provides specifically that Member nations " shall join in affording mutual assistance in carrying out the measures decided upon by the Security Council." Members of the United Nations might thus be called upon under this Article to provide logistical support for Forces acting in accordance with decisions of the Security Council taken under Article 42.[2]

This general authority possessed by the Security Council is supplemented by the provisions of Article 43, under which Member States " undertake to make available to the Security Council, on its call and in accordance with a special agreement or agreements, armed forces, assistance and facilities, including rights of passage,

---

[1] Art. 42 of the Charter.
[2] That a " call " can be regarded as mandatory was clearly illustrated in the Congo operations: see *ante*, pp. 181, 225. Arguably the reference in Article 49 to " measures " is intended to relate solely to measures taken by the Security Council under Article 41, *i.e.*, to those not involving the use of armed force under Article 42. However, the word is used more generally in both Articles 39 and 50 to include enforcement action

necessary for the purpose of maintaining international peace and security." Under paragraph 2 of the Article, the agreements are to determine, inter alia, " the nature of the facilities and assistance to be provided." Owing to the failure of the Permanent Members of the Security Council to find an acceptable formula regarding the conditions under which national units should be made available, no agreements have in fact been concluded under Article 43. However, in their report to the Security Council in 1947,[3] the Military Staff Committee included three articles dealing with logistical support to be furnished for any forces which might be available. Articles 29 and 30, both of which were adopted by the Security Council, provided as follows:

Article 29
Member Nations of the United Nations which, in accordance with special agreements, have placed armed forces at the disposal of the Security Council on its call for the carrying out of measures envisaged in Article 42 of the Charter, will provide their respective forces with all necessary replacements in personnel and equipment and with all necessary supplies and transport.

Article 30
Each Member Nation will at all times maintain a specified level of reserves to replace initial personnel, transport, equipment, spare parts, ammunition and all other forms of supply for the forces which it has agreed to place at the disposal of the Security Council on its call. This reserve level will be prescribed in the special agreements under Article 43 of the Charter.

The text of the remaining Article in the Chapter was not adopted. Two drafts were put forward, however, by the delegations of China, the United Kingdom and the United States, and by the delegations of France and the Union of Soviet Socialist Republics respectively.

Article 31
(Text accepted by the delegations of China, the United Kingdom and the United States of America):

Member Nations, in the event of inability to discharge to the full extent their responsibilities under Article 29 above, may invoke the aid of the Security Council, which, on the advice of the Military Staff Committee, will negotiate with other appropriate Member Nations for the provision of such assistance as it deems necessary. The agreement of Member Nations concerned must be obtained by the Security Council before the deficiencies in the contribution of one Member Nation can be made up by transfers from the contribution of another Member State.

(Text accepted by the delegations of France and the Union of Soviet Socialist Republics):

Deviations from the principle stated in Article 29 above shall be permitted in individual instances at the request of a Member Nation, by special decision of the Security Council on the advice of the Military Staff Committee, if this Member Nation desires to have supplies and transport made available

---

[3] The report is contained in *Repertory of Practice of United Nations Organs*, Vol. II, p. 396.

to it for the proper provision of the armed forces placed by this Member Nation at the disposal of the Security Council.

In the absence of agreement regarding the report as a whole, no further steps have been taken by the Security Council. It is difficult therefore to offer extensive comments on the Articles relating to logistical support. It may be noted, however, that it seems to have been generally agreed that self-contained units should be made available and that participating states should themselves be responsible for keeping their troops properly supplied when in the field and for maintaining adequate reserves of men and materials. The assumption that the national contingents in a United Nations Force would be logistically self-contained was perhaps understandable in view of the size of the Force which the Military Staff Committee contemplated, but whether the assumption was soundly based is very questionable. Certainly the NATO experience suggests [4] that the efficient utilisation of a multinational force may demand a very much more centralised, and standardised, system of logistical support, and it is by no means certain that any future " stand-by " agreements will necessarily adopt the principle of " logistical self-sufficiency." [5]

In the event the only agreements which have been made between the United Nations and Member nations regarding the provision of logistical support have been based on non-obligatory Resolutions of the General Assembly and Security Council. An initial distinction may perhaps be noted, however, between bodies such as UNTSO and UNOGIL, and larger organs, such as UNEF and ONUC. In the former case there has been relatively little need for full-scale logistical support and the United Nations has met the needs of the Force largely out of its own immediate resources, acting through United Nations procurement channels. Arrangements have been made, however, for seeking the assistance of the host authorities in several instances. Thus in the Agreement between the United Nations and Jordan regarding the Spinelli mission it was provided that the Special Representative of the Secretary-General might call upon the Jordanian Government for the procurement of locally available supplies and equipment, subject to repayment at reasonable rates.[6] These instances concern, however, small units consisting of less than 600 men at most. In the case of larger bodies, such as the forces serving under the Unified Command in Korea, or as part of UNEF and ONUC, the problem of ensuring logistical support has been one of appreciably larger dimensions, necessitating recourse to Member States for the

---

[4] See *NATO, Facts about the North Atlantic Treaty Organisation*, published by the NATO Information Service, January 1962, Chap. 10. Apart from the NATO Common Infrastructure Programme, NATO undertook a programme of codification of equipment, after studies by the Military Agency for Standardisation, and a NATO Supply Centre exists for maintaining a common fund of supplies for aircraft, spare parts of aircraft and other modern weapons.

[5] *Ante*, p. 373.

[6] U.N.T.S. Vol. 315, No. 4564, p. 125.

supply of food, equipment, war material, and means of transport, in the course of an extensive international operation.

No agreements for the provision of logistical support were made by the United Nations itself, however, during the Korean conflict. Forces and other means of assistance were made available by Member nations, under Security Council and General Assembly Resolutions, to the Unified Command appointed by the United States. The only functions given to the Secretary-General were those of providing assistance to the civilian population of Korea and of acting as a transmission channel in respect of offers of assistance. Offers were communicated to the Secretary-General in broad terms and relayed to the United States Government, which then entered into direct consultations with the other governments concerned.

In the agreements made between the United States and other governments which offered assistance, it was stated that, where the participating State was unable to furnish its unit with necessary supplies, these should be provided by the United States against subsequent reimbursement. Thus Article 1 of the Agreement between the United States and the Netherlands "concerning participation of the Netherlands forces in United Nations Operations in Korea"[7] provided as follows:

"The Government of the United States of America agrees to furnish the Netherlands forces with available materials, supplies, services, and facilities which the Netherlands forces will require for these operations, and which the Government of the Netherlands is unable to furnish. The Government of the United States of America and the Government of the Netherlands will maintain accounts of materials, supplies, services, and facilities furnished by the Government of the United States of America to the Government of the Netherlands, its forces or agencies. Reimbursement for such materials, supplies, services, and facilities will be accomplished by the Government of the Netherlands upon presentation of statements of account by the Government of the United States of America. Such payment will be affected by the Government of the Netherlands in United States dollars. Issues of materials and supplies to the Netherlands forces will not operate to transfer title to the Government of the Netherlands in advance of reimbursement."

In addition, the Government of the Netherlands was required to maintain accounts of materials, supplies, services, and facilities furnished by governments other than the United States and to settle any claims directly with the governments concerned.[8] The large preponderance of American troops participating in the conflict on behalf of the United Nations made it essential for operational purposes that there should be only one logistical supply line. An exception was made, however, as regards units from the British Commonwealth and others using British-type equipment. Although various problems arose regarding the training of men in the use of

---

[7] U.N.T.S. Vol. 177, No. 2321, p. 233, at p. 234. The other agreements contain substantially the same provisions.
[8] *Ibid.*, Article 5.

the new weapons and the cost of new equipment, the overall advantage in having one principal source of supply was undoubtedly considerable.[9]

Mention should also be made of the Agreement concluded between the United States and the Republic of Korea relating to economic co-ordination between the Unified Command and Korea, in furtherance of the pertinent United Nations Resolutions.[10] Although the Agreement was concerned largely with the provision of civilian relief and the maintenance of the Korean economy, the arrangements made also covered the furnishing of logistical support to the Korean forces serving under the Unified Command and for the procurement of "equipment, supplies and services" by the Unified Command, in conjunction with the Korean Government.

The validity of the various agreements concluded by the United States during the Korean conflict as specifically United Nations agreements is doubtful; it has been argued that they were not agreements entered into between the United Nations and a particular State, but agreements between two States, in furtherance of the Security Council Resolutions calling upon Member nations to assist the Unified Command.[11] Whilst this view does somewhat less than justice to the particular responsibilities given to the Unified Command by the Security Council, in strict point of law it would appear to be correct.

For actual examples of agreements concluded between the United Nations and Member States regarding logistical support it is necessary to turn to the operations of UNEF and ONUC. In each of these instances the Secretary-General, having been called upon to establish the Force, was given authority to take the necessary administrative steps and it was under this heading that he arranged for the logistical support and movement of the United Nations Force concerned. The non-mandatory nature of the pertinent United Nations Resolutions has meant that not only were Member States not obliged to make any positive contribution at all, but also that, if they did agree to send troops, then almost of necessity they were not accepting the obligation to send troops fully trained and equipped. However, there was initially an implication that States providing contingents should, whenever possible, be in a position to maintain them logistically. This implication was clearly brought out in Resolution 337 (A) (V), "Uniting for Peace," in which the General Assembly recommended that each Member of the United Nations "maintain within its national armed forces elements so trained, organised and equipped that they could promptly be made available, in accordance with its constitutional processes, for service as a United Nations unit or units,

---

[9] See Goodrich, "Korea: Collective Measures against Aggression," *International Conciliation*, 1953, No. 494, p. 131, at p. 159.
[10] U.N.T.S., Vol. 179, No. 2353, p. 23.
[11] See Baxter, "Constitutional Forms and Some Legal Problems of International Military Command" (1952), B.Y.I.L., 325.

upon recommendation by the Security Council or the General Assembly. . . ." Although the details of negotiations between the United Nations and Member States who offered forces for UNEF and ONUC have necessarily remained confidential, there can be little doubt that the need for units to be adequately equipped and ready for service has remained important. However, at least for the peace-keeping operations such as UNEF and ONUC, whilst the expectation was retained that the contingent would be initially self-supporting for a limited time, the tendency has been for the United Nations to assume more and more of a logistics responsibility, and it may be presumed that any similar Force established in the future is a United Nations responsibility, subject to Assembly or Security Council Resolutions calling upon Member States to provide appropriate assistance to the Force.[12] The following is a brief description of the arrangements in operation between the United Nations and States contributing troops to UNEF and ONUC.

First, each participating State is responsible for ensuring that the troop units which it sends to the theatre of operations have their full complement of men and equipment, together with a basic supply of ammunition, in accordance with the standards laid down by the government in its so-called "Tables of Organisation and Equipment," or equivalent regulations.[13] Besides personal weapons and equipment, each soldier is required to have sufficient clothing, other than that to be supplied by the United Nations, to last him during his tour of duty according to the percentage of wastage accepted by the participating government concerned. If necessary, reserve stocks must be brought to the theatre of operations. The participating government is also required to send copies of its Tables of Organisation and Equipment, or their equivalent, and of its regulations for basic loads of ammunition, to the United Nations Headquarters, and to the Chief Logistics Officer of the particular United Nations Force. At the same time the participating government is asked to submit lists of any critical materials which it is unable to supply, in order that the United Nations may itself take steps to obtain them.

Once a particular unit has entered the area of operations, all supplies which it requires, and which the United Nations may be

---

[12] For example, paragraph 10 of Resolution 1001 (ES–1), requesting all Member States to afford assistance as necessary to the United Nations Command in the performance of its functions.

[13] The participating States in ONUC were expected to provide the following items:
    (i) Personal clothing of contingent members;
    (ii) Personal equipment such as rucksacks, kitbags, sleeping-bags, canteens, cooking and eating utensils, etc.;
    (iii) Small arms and ammunition.
These items apart, equipment was procured and paid for by the UN through its own procurement channels even if, in special cases, it had been requisitioned from the participating States: see Report of the Secretary-General of 13 September 1960, A/4486, paras. 67–70: *Off.Rec.G.A.*, 15th Sess., Annexes, A.i.27, p. 20, approved by General-Assembly Resol. 1575 (XV) of 20 December 1960.

called upon to pay for, must be requisitioned through the logistics channels of the United Nations Force. In the case of ordinary items, such as food, tentage, fuel and spare parts for vehicles, for example, this arrangement ensures that the goods concerned are purchased at the cheapest price the United Nations can obtain, via its procurement network, compatible with the needs of the Force as a military unit. It also enables the United Nations to take steps in appropriate instances to try to obtain items from governments as contributions in kind, either in lieu of, or in addition to, their normal United Nations budgetary contribution. When essential items are peculiar to a contingent, however, as in the case of ordnance stores and ammunition, and the participating government is the logical source of supply, requisitions are placed by the United Nations Headquarters under the " Assist Letter Scheme " with the government concerned. Under this scheme, agreement having been given beforehand to the arrangement, a numbered " Assist Letter " is sent to the government by the United Nations in respect of a particular service or quantity of supplies required. Having supplied the item requested, the government, which may have furnished similar supplies at its own cost to its contingent when it was dispatched, then submits a bill to the United Nations referring to the relevant " Assist Letter." This reference acts as proof of authorised expenditure on the item in question, thereby facilitating early settlement of the claim.

The United Nations assumes responsibility for the continuing operation of units of the Force once they are within the area of operations. As part of this responsibility the United Nations provides billeting and rations for the troops, including the rental and purchase of premises. Units are expected, however, to bring standard field messing equipment with them. The United Nations is also responsible for communication facilities, for the costs of transporting and issuing supplies, and for furnishing expendable items, such as ammunition and cleaning materials; spare parts for motor-vehicles, together with maintenance, and petrol, oil and lubricants; and for providing United Nations uniforms, according to the scales of issue prescribed by the United Nations. The United Nations also supplies items of special equipment which a unit may require whilst with the Force and which do not form part of the unit's standard establishment. Examples under this heading have included the provision of vehicles suitable for use in the sandy country in which UNEF operates and tropical equipment in the case of ONUC. Lastly, the United Nations also assumes responsibility for the miscellaneous " extra services," such as cobblering, tailoring, laundrying and haircutting, which the Force may require.

One feature of the United Nations logistics system which makes it particularly unique, as well as extremely difficult to describe in simple terms, lies in the amalgam of military and civilian techniques which has been evolved. In military logistics work, supply requirements are usually met by preparing requisitions based on standard supply tables; the procurement action is then carried out without further review. In the case of United Nations Forces, however, no such standard supply tables have existed, at least initially; UNEF now possesses such tables, and they are known to have been in the course of preparation for ONUC. The requisitioning officer, forming part of the Logistics Section of the Force, has therefore tended to rely on the standard tables of his national army, or, failing that, has selected what seemed to him to be the necessary alternative. The Chief Procurement Officer—who in the case of both UNEF and ONUC is a member of the Secretariat—has been accustomed to a different method of operation, however, and has had to assure himself that each requisition was in respect of essential supplies only and that no suitable alternatives existed.

Moreover, in the early stages of a military operation it is imperative to have an assured source of supply; it is only after the supply " pipeline " has been established and the Force settled into its positions that consideration can be given to other, more economic, sources. Thus during the initial emergency period when UNEF and ONUC were being established, heavy reliance was placed on the resources of participating States and on such other sources, notably those provided by the United States, which could meet the immediate demands of the Force. It was only after this period that more flexible arrangements could be devised, in which relative cost evaluation has played a larger part. The principal sources of supply for UNEF and ONUC at the present time are the following: the participating governments (chiefly under the " Assist Letter " scheme described above), notably in respect of items which are peculiar to their respective contingents and of which they are virtually the sole source of supply; different countries throughout the world, via United Nations Headquarters, in respect of those goods, chiefly durable supplies, which can be most economically secured through United Nations procurement offices; and, lastly, local purchase, particularly, of course, in respect of fresh food, when price comparisons show that this is the most practical course.[14]

II. MOVEMENT AND SUPPLIES

1. *Transportation*

(a) THE " AIR-LIFT "

The initial problem is one of getting the Force to the area where it is needed, and, in the past, since speed has tended to be an essential ingredient of success, the problem has been solved by recourse to an air-lift of sizeable proportions.

At the time when the Charter was drafted it was envisaged that air units would be amongst the forces which Member States would place at the disposal of the Security Council, under agreements concluded in accordance with the provisions of Article 43. Although

---

[14] *Summary Study*, paragraphs 91–93.

no mention is made of an air-lift as such, the wide terms of Article 43, and the references in Articles 42 and 45 to air operations and to the availability of air force contingents, would have provided sufficient authority to permit arrangements regarding an air-lift to be included in such agreements. In any case, however, if a series of agreements under Article 43 were concluded, the five Permanent Members could no doubt arrange for an air-lift to be furnished without much practical difficulty. It may be assumed that each of these would have adequate air power to transport its own land forces; the issue would only arise in a crucial form therefore in respect of the transport to be provided, presumably by one of the Permanent Members, for troops offered by smaller nations. This arrangement appears to have been envisaged by the Military Staff Committee in their 1947 report to the Security Council.[15] The Security Council agreed that the forces to be made available should include air units normally forming part of the Member's armed forces,[16] and that they should be sufficient "to enable the Security Council to take prompt action."[17] More directly still, it was suggested that Member nations should be required to provide logistical support, including necessary transport for their armed forces[18]; if a Member nation was unable to discharge this responsibility, then arrangements were proposed to enable the requisite supplies and transport to be provided by another State.[19]

In the event, no agreements have been concluded under the provisions of Article 43, and the United Nations has lacked air transport, no less than armed forces, upon which it could rely when any threat to the maintenance of international peace and security occurred. In the Korean conflict, the only instance in which the Security Council has recommended that direct enforcement action should be taken against aggression, overall responsibility was given to one Member nation, the United States. Although other Member States responded to the request that every assistance should be given to the efforts of the Unified Command in Korea, the predominant position of the United States, both in respect of the number of troops engaged and the availability of aircraft, meant that air transport was very largely provided from American sources. Thus in the Agreement entered into between the United States and the Federal Republic of Germany, providing for the operation of a German Red Cross Hospital in Korea, it was agreed that the United States should supply all facilities, including transportation to and from Korea.[20] The American troops

---

[15] The articles in the report, as amended by the Security Council, are contained in *Repertory of the United Nations Organs*, Vol. II, p. 396.

[16] *Ibid.*, Article 3.

[17] *Ibid.*, Article 6. See also Chapter VI of the report, "Degree of Readiness of Armed Forces."

[18] *Ibid.*, Article 29.

[19] *Ibid.*, Article 31. The Permanent Members were unable to agree on the text of this Article, but both versions put forward provided for arrangements to be made along the lines indicated.

[20] U.N.T.S. Vol. 223, No. 3064. Article III.

who formed the overwhelming majority of troops serving under the Unified Command, other than those from the Republic of Korea itself, were brought to Korea by means of facilities, including air transport, provided by the United States.

It was not until the establishment of UNEF that a full United Nations air-lift was provided as such. A number of States who offered troops when proposals were first made regarding UNEF indicated that they did so on the understanding that transport was to be provided by the United Nations.[21] Since communication of these offers followed negotiations with the Secretary-General, it may be presumed that the United Nations had itself taken the initiative in offering air transport from the home country, if suitable troops were ready there, following the declaration of the United States representative at the 564th meeting of the General Assembly on 5 November 1956, that the United States Government was prepared to make air-lift facilities available. Following the adoption of Resolution 1001 (ES–1), and further consultations, the United States Government informed the Secretary-General that it would undertake to provide "necessary air and surface transport of troop units currently estimated to be of the order of 3,500 to 5,000 men and their equipment to staging areas and areas of operation as requested by the Chief of Command of the Emergency Force." [22] The policy of excluding military units of the Permanent Members of the Security Council from participation in the United Nations Force did not therefore extend to the provision of planes, air and ground crews, and related facilities. The question of the nationality of the planes to be used did threaten to provide some difficulty, however, *vis-à-vis* the Egyptian Government.[23] Arrangements were therefore made to have troops carried by U.S.A.F. planes only as far as the staging area established at Capodichino Airport, near Naples, and to provide planes of more acceptable nationality for the journey between Italy and Egypt. The United Nations, in the person of the Secretary-General, entered into a commercial contract with the Swissair Company, for the transport of troops and equipment from Naples to Abu Suweir, near Ismailia, from 13 to 26 November.[24] These flights by Swissair were subsequently taken over by the Royal Canadian Air Force (R.C.A.F.) and, to a lesser extent in respect of supplies, by the Italian Air Force.[25] The U.S.A.F., however, brought the majority of troops to the staging area at Naples, and later to Beirut.

[21] See, *e.g.*, Communication of the Government of India, A/3302, Add. 4/Rev. 1, *Off.Rec.G.A.*, Agenda item 5, Annexes, 1st Emergency Special Sess., 1956; and of the Government of Ceylon, A/3302, Add. 15, *idem.*

[22] A/3302, Add. 20, *Off.Rec.G.A.*, Agenda item 66, Annexes, 11th Sess., 1956–1957. The estimated cost to the U.S.A. was $2½ million.

[23] See *Summary Study, etc.* (A/3943), paragraph 38.

[24] See communication from the Government of Switzerland of 11 December 1956, A/3302, Add. 29, *Off.Rec.G.A.*, Agenda item 66, Annexes, 11th Sess.; 1956–1957.

[25] *Idem*, A/3302, Add. 30 and 22nd Report of the Advisory Committee on Administrative and Budgetary Questions, A/3402, paragraph 6. See also *Summary Study, etc.*, para. 38.

The initial movement of troops was arranged through United Nations Headquarters in New York. The representatives of participating States first informed the Secretariat of the numbers and the amount of equipment involved, and of the state of readiness of the unit; the Secretariat then relayed this information to the State providing the aircraft, chiefly the United States. The latter in turn notified the United Nations of the detailed arrangements for transporting the particular unit, and this information was conveyed to the authorities in the participating State by its military representative in New York.

More routine arrangements regarding flights were developed after the Force had taken up its duties along the Armistice Demarcation Line. A U.S.A.F. DC-3 type aircraft, which had been chartered for the use of the Commander in December 1956, was dispensed with and returned to the United States Government in April 1957.[26] By the end of 1957 air support for UNEF consisted of two flights of the Royal Canadian Air Force.[27] 114 Communications Flight, consisting of four (originally twelve) C-119 aircraft based on Naples, was responsible for the heavy lift of mails and priority cargo and passengers between Italy and Egypt. 115 Communications Flight, which moved from Abu Suweir to El Arish, just south of the Gaza Strip, in September 1957, consisted of four Otter and two DC-3 planes; its function was to provide internal transport for the Force, as well as to perform reconnaissance and similar duties. In January 1958 the 114 Communications Flight was withdrawn and the UNEF base at Capodichino Airport closed.[28] The 115 Flight was supplemented by a DC-3 and its name changed to that of 115 Air Transport Unit; it has continued to provide flights within the area of operations of the Force, as well as a shuttle service to Beirut. During 1961 the strength of the Flight was reduced slightly with the introduction of Caribou-type aircraft and it now consists of three Caribou and two Otter planes.[29]

In addition to these local flights, the R.C.A.F. has maintained a series of regular logistical flights between Canada and El Arish, via Pisa. During 1960 the number of these flights was reduced from fifty-two to forty a year. At the present time the flights between Canada and Pisa, which also serve ONUC, are performed by Comet aircraft. A North Star Detachment, based on Pisa, carries troops and supplies to El Arish. Arrangements have been made, by the Commander,[30] to co-ordinate these R.C.A.F. flights with the regular

[26] A/3694 and Add. 1. Report of Secretary-General of 9 October 1957, Section IX. *Off.Rec.G.A.*, Agenda item 65, Annexes, 12th Sess., 1957.
[27] *Ibid.*, para. 12.
[28] Report of the Secretary-General, 27 August 1958, para. 8, A/3899, *Off.Rec.G.A.*, Agenda item 65, Annexes, 13th Sess., 1958.
[29] Report of the Secretary-General, 30 August 1961, paragraph 5, A/4857 and UNEF, Cost Estimates for the Maintenance of the Force, A/5187, 12 September 1962, *Off.Rec.G.A.*, 17th Sess., 1962.
[30] Under UNEF Regulation 21 the Commander is given authority to arrange for the transportation of persons and equipment to and from the area of

weekly SCANAP[31] service between Pisa and the Scandinavian countries. When the available R.C.A.F. planes are unable to carry all the essential air cargo received on SCANAP flights, authorisation is given for extended flights to be made between Pisa and El Arish by C-119s of the Norwegian Air Force.

The routine nature of the operations presently performed by UNEF has made it comparatively easy to evolve regular flight schedules in which maximum use is made of available facilities. In the case of the Congo, however, the larger scale of the operations, the greater distances to be covered, and the more difficult problems encountered, hindered the emergence of a clear pattern of flights in support of the United Nations Force there. Considerable use was made, however, of the experience gained in establishing and maintaining UNEF. As regards the initial air lift, offers made by non-African countries were accepted, including those made by Permanent Members of the Security Council,[32] although the bulk of the ONUC Force was itself drawn from African States. In his first Report the Secretary-General declared that, in view of the urgency of the situation, he was appealing to the States which could provide the required facilities in the shortest possible time.[33] The Ethiopian contingent came in Ethiopian Air Force planes; the Ghanaian troops were carried in R.A.F. transport planes and later in planes provided by the U.S.S.R.[34] The remainder were brought largely by U.S.A.F. aircraft, in response to the Secretary-General's appeal, during a round-the-clock air lift operated through the world.[35] Other countries which participated in the United Nations air lift were: Canada, Italy, Switzerland, and the United Arab Republic.

States were also asked to provide aircraft and pilots for service with the actual ONUC Force. Although a number of air and ground crew personnel were recruited in this way, from a wide number of

operations and to co-ordinate the use of all transportation facilities furnished by governments. The Secretary-General, however, is responsible for concluding agreements with governments regarding required services. Report of the Secretary-General on Administrative and Financial Arrangements for UNEF, A/3383 and Rev. 1, 21 November 1956. *Off.Rec.G.A.*, Agenda item 66, Annexes, 11th Sess., 1956–1957.

[31] So called because flights were originally between Scandinavia and Naples. See generally, Cost Estimates for Maintenance of Force, Report of Secretary-General, 13 July 1961, A/4784, *Off.Rec.G.A.*, Agenda item 26, Annexes, 15th Sess., 1960.

[32] It may be noted that planes supplied by the Permanent Members did not operate between points within the Congo, either directly for the Force itself or indirectly for national contingents. See the exchange of communications between the Secretary-General and the U.S.S.R. S/4503, *Off.Rec.S.C.*, 15th yr., Suppl., July-September 1960.

[33] First Report of the Secretary-General on Implementation of Security Council Resolution S/4387, 18 July 1960: S/4389, *Off.Rec.S.C.*, 15th yr., Suppl. July-September 1960, pp. 21–22.

[34] *Ibid.*, p. 23.

[35] Communication of the United States, S/4400, 20 July 1960, *ibid.* For details of the U.S. air lift see *ante*, p. 218.

countries,[36] governments proved unable or reluctant to offer suitable planes, unless the United Nations was prepared to buy the aircraft outright.[37] The United Nations therefore chose to charter a number of aircraft, mainly for use on logistical flights. It was on a plane chartered from the Swedish Transair Company that Mr. Hammarskjoeld, the late Secretary-General, lost his life in September 1961. As in the case of UNEF, the major logistical air service has been provided by the Royal Canadian Air Force. A twice weekly shuttle service is maintained by North Star planes between the Congo and Pisa, while a Comet carries troops, equipment and supplies between Canada and Italy.

It may be noted that participating States have also operated flights direct to their own troops, in order to provide them with supplies over and above those made available through the normal logistical channels maintained by the United Nations. One such flight, by a United Arab Republic Ilyushin, operating without a flying or landing clearance, resulted in an incident in which United Arab Republic troops refused to allow the Congolese authorities to approach the plane. The reply given by the United Nations to the complaint of the Congolese Government made it clear that the flight had not been in accordance with ONUC instructions regarding direct air support from participating States.[38] This incident appears, however, to have been an isolated one.

(b) CONTINUING SUPPORT

With UNEF, once within Egyptian territory, land transportation provided a reasonable means of moving the troops to their positions. However, since in the early stages the Swissair transports from Capodichino had been unable to transport vehicles, the troops arrived without surface transport and jeeps had to be purchased from the United Kingdom forces, from Gaza and from the Egyptian authorities.[39] The rather motley collection of land vehicles was gradually replaced with standard pieces—the trucks British Bedfords, the cars French Citröens, and the jeeps the standard American variety. Continuing support in the form of transportation of supplies, troops replacements, etc., was mainly by sea, with 80 to 90 per cent. of UNEF's supplies coming in by sea to Port Said and being transported from there by trucks: the main exception was that of foodstuffs

---

[36] Pilots were provided by Argentina, Brazil, Ethiopia, India, Norway, Sweden and Yugoslavia, S/4389, Add. 6, *ibid.*

[37] See the statement of the United Nations Controller, Fifth Committee, Congo Finances 1961, 24 March 1961, p. 3. *Off.Rec.G.A.*, 15th Sess.

[38] In particular in that no opportunity had been given for the ONUC authorities to attempt to obtain permission from the Congolese Government for the flight to be made, in accordance with the usual procedure in the case of direct flights by participating States. See S/4630 and S/4724, *Off.Rec.S.C.*, 16th yr., Suppl. January–March 1961.

[39] Bowman and Fanning, "The Logistics Problems of a UN Military Force," (1963) 17 *International Organisation*, 359–360.

which were collected at Pisa and flown in by a Canadian weekly charter flight.

In the Congo, because of the nature and size of the country and the initial paralysis of surface transportation, air deliveries of men and materials to Ndjili, the Leopoldville airport, had to be distributed by an internal air-lift. This intra-Congo air-lift posed a number of problems, and the facts that some aircraft were on loan from Member States, some were chartered, and neither the loans nor the charters were indefinite, meant that gradually the United Nations phased in a system of transport based almost solely on commercial aircraft.[40] But the lack of serviced airstrips, of aircrews and technical services —including meteorologists—posed very serious problems. However, it was this internal air-lift which was largely responsible for transporting supplies from the port of Matadi, where the bulk of sea-borne supplies were unloaded, to the supply points in the three territorial commands. The supplies to the fourth command in Leopoldville were able to be transported by rail. Once at the supply points, further distribution was by road transport. The United Nations attempted to keep on hand sufficient supplies to provide for three months of operations.

The rotation of national contingents is a problem which can normally be handled by sea transport, since it is normally provided for well in advance after consultation with the United Nations Commander and the Secretary-General and does not arise as a matter of urgency. However, the relatively frequent rotation of contingents does increase the cost of operating the Force, as well as having possible repercussions on its efficiency.

2. *Communications*

Apart from communications by transport, dealt with above, the United Nations in the Congo found great difficulty in establishing a satisfactory communications system. The Congo situation especially presented, both in terms of the size of the territories and the breakdown of the existing communications system, a challenge which the United Nations had never previously encountered. In September 1960, two months after the arrival of the first troops, Mr. Dayal reported that:

"Communications of all kinds have hitherto been at a minimum. When a brigade of three battalions is responsible for an area the size of France which is beset by problems ranging from famine to tribal war, the lack of communications aggravates the already exhausting task of the troops. At present radio communications have been established by the Force signals between ONUC headquarters and the majority of the territorial commands. There are, however, still some territorial commands which depend for their link with headquarters on borrowed or public facilities. The situation within the territorial commands is also not completely satisfactory, many of the units being without radio communications between their headquarters and subunits . . . With the voluntary departure of European personnel incident

[40] *Ibid.*, p. 363.

to independence, there was virtually no trained staff to supervise the operation of telephone, telex and radio transmission installations and these facilities are in operation to-day only because of the presence of a large United Nations—International Telecommunications Union Team." [41]

The need for bilingual operators, filled in part by the Canadian unit, was an obvious one. Moreover, there were serious deficiencies in the communications system between the Congo and New York and, as we have seen,[42] the United Nations was forced to concede that the advances made by United Nations troops in January 1962 were not intended and resulted from a breakdown in communications.

Coupled with problems of wireless and telex communications were the even more rudimentary problems stemming from the absence of maps, of meteorologists to forecast flight conditions, and of movement control teams.

3. *Military equipment and matériel*

Given that the United Nations has tended increasingly to provide the bulk of the military equipment needed by a United Nations Force, it is clear that the United Nations has to rely a good deal on the goodwill of Member States to sell such equipment as it needs, and this has been largely forthcoming. Procurements are made via the "assists" agreements,[43] or via isolated requests for the supply of equipment. To this extent there is always a risk of a refusal of equipment, and it is known that the United States refused tanks to ONUC (offering armoured-cars instead)[44] and the United Kingdom refused bombs.[45] Whether these refusals were right, as a matter of policy, is arguable, but these instances point to a difficulty which the United Nations is bound to face in making *ad hoc* purchases from Members. The further difficulty which this *ad hoc* purchasing system raises is that, whilst the assumption by the United Nations of the major responsibility for logistical supply has the clear advantage of offering some chance of standardising the equipment in use by the Force,[46] this advantage could be reduced if, on a particular occasion, the United Nations were forced to rely on the goodwill of Members to provide specific items of equipment in an emergency: the result might be to force the United Nations to acquire different kinds of similar equipment simply because no source of supply was available of the quantity required of the same kind of equipment. The immediate availability of large stocks of munitions, military equipment or even food is not to be relied upon or assumed, and one

---

[41] *Off.Rec.S.C.*, 15th yr., Suppl. for July, August and September 1960, pp. 185–8.
[42] *Ante*, pp. 216–217.
[43] *Ante*, p. 393.
[44] Bowman and Fanning, *loc. cit.*, pp. 367–8.
[45] *Ante*, p. 222.
[46] Standardisation is not always possible. Food supplies for ONUC had to take account of a variety of dietary habits existing amongst the different contingents.

suspects that the United Nations has had its share of good fortune in this respect. For example, with UNEF the United States was able to supply large stocks of food rations from its own stores at Leghorn in Italy and at Metz and Dreux in France.

In practice the equipment most needed has been trucks and road transport, radio communications equipment and aircraft: helicopters have proved essential to many of the observer groups,[47] and transport and later fighter aircraft were desperately needed by ONUC.[48]

4. *Medical services*

Provision of medical services for UNEF did not constitute a major problem since the Force never became involved in combat duty and never, therefore, had large numbers of personnel requiring treatment. Most contingents carried some medical staffs and a central hospital at Rafah base was operated under joint Canadian-Norwegian administration.[49] Arrangements were also made for evacuation of personnel to a number of countries where advanced or specialised medical treatment could be afforded to UNEF personnel.

The Congo clearly posed greater problems, both in terms of casualties and inaccessibility of the areas in which ONUC was forced to operate. However, hospital services were provided additional to the medical services within individual contingents by the Indian base hospital at Leopoldville, an Italian hospital at Albertville and other units at Luluabourg and Coquilhatville.[50] Evacuation problems gave rise to an unusually high dependence on aircraft.

5. *The procurement system and logistics staff*

It has been said, with considerable justification, that " the United Nations is simply not designed to initiate and sustain large military missions." [51] The problems created by the lack of trained, logistic personnel and of advance planning were not confined to logistics in the field; they were equally evident in the procurement system used by the United Nations.

The Office of General Services stands as the main logistical component of the Secretariat, and part of this Office, the Field Operations Service,[52] has assumed the main responsibility for field missions; however, Purchasing and Transportation has dealt with purchase of supplies and transport arrangements, and Communications and Records has maintained the United Nations radio network.

---

[47] *Ante*, pp. 70–71.
[48] *Ante*, p. 222.
[49] There were, prior to 1957, separate facilities at Rafah (Canadian) and Gaza (Norwegian) but these were consolidated in late 1957: A/3943, para. 38.
[50] S/4557, p. 30.
[51] Bowman and Fanning, *loc. cit.*, p. 356.
[52] The UN Field Service, established in 1949 to provide technical services to field missions, is a part of this: see *ante*, p. 19.

The Field Operations Service in New York controls the Chief Administrative Officer (CAO) attached to the Force and, in UNEF, it was the CAO who handled all matters of finance and who received the requisitions—or statements of requirements—from the military staff which were then transmitted to the Field Operations Service in New York. Thus, whilst the military staff had a limited logistical function, and whilst the CAO could himself purchase supplies on a requisition for an amount less than $5,000, the bulk of the purchases were made from New York. It has been estimated that from the date on which the requisition is transmitted from the CAO in Gaza to New York, it takes between four to six months for the supplies, arriving by sea, to reach Gaza.

The system for ONUC was similar, but in the Congo there was the additional procurement burden of supplying not only the military operations but also the civilian operations and, again, financial power and procurement rested with the CAO. Moreover, in view of the area of the operations, there had to be four territorial commands, with logistics staff attached to each command as integral parts of troop contingents: the headquarters logistics staff comprised the special, large detachments such as the Pakistani ordnance unit, the Canadian signals unit and the Indian supply unit.

6. Proposals for rationalisation

The recent survey by Bowman and Fanning [53] concluded by listing the problems of logistics in this way:

(a) READINESS PROBLEMS

(1) Insufficient provision for administrative co-ordination. Here the main criticism was that, assuming the situation was, like that in the Congo, constantly changing and could not operate on a set plan at a lower level of administration, the highest level of administration (the team of Secretary-General, Under-Secretary for Special Political Affairs, the Military Adviser and the Adviser on Civilian Activities) was overburdened and inadequately staffed for effective co-ordination.

(2) Insufficient capability for large-scale planning. Here the criticism was twofold: first, that there was no advance planning for the kind of operations the United Nations became involved in and, second, that there was no staff of sufficient size to carry through even the *ad hoc* plan which emerged, let alone the necessary advance planning. This criticism is more applicable to the ONUC operation than to UNEF, for in his report on UNEF [54] the Secretary-General revealed a decided complacency about the Secretariat's planning abilities. He stated:

" It may be reiterated in passing that the United Nations Secretariat has by now had extensive experience in establishing and maintaining United Nations operations involving military personnel and, without improvising or augmenting unduly, can quickly provide operations of that nature with efficient

[53] *Loc. cit.*, p. 368. [54] *Summary Study*, etc. (A/3943), p. 73.

communications service in the field, with headquarters, with transportation and vehicles for local transport, with well-tested administrative and accounting systems and expert personnel to man them, and with effective procurement and security arrangements."

There is certainly considerable justification for this faith in the Secretariat's capabilities if one looks to UNEF, although even there it is impossible to ignore the initial inadequacies of the operations,[55] but the Congo experience shattered any such complacency. Without decrying in any way the extraordinary accomplishments of the Secretariat, it is clear that the Secretariat did not have within it the structure or personnel capable of carrying through the ONUC operations with real efficiency.

(3) Lack of immediately available supplies, equipment and transportation. The reliance on United States air lift, on United States stockpiles of equipment in Europe, and on the lesser degrees of contributions by other Member States and private sources of transport and supply was, at best, a risky and piecemeal operation.[56] There is a strong argument for United Nations stockpiles or, at least, advance planning which would involve arrangements with States or private corporations and guarantee the immediate availability of supplies, equipment and transportation.

(4) Lack of immediately available logistics personnel. Here the criticism is that, whilst contingents provided their own personnel for logistics *within* the contingent, the United Nations had to make special requests for units—such as the Canadian signals unit—to handle logistical tasks external to the national contingents. Moreover, the United Nations had no real advance knowledge of which States could provide the kind of units required.

(b) OPERATING PROBLEMS

(1) Inadequate administrative co-ordination and procedures. This is really a criticism based on the absence of standard operating procedures which national forces develop to a high standard; in other words, no " organisation manual."

(2) Insufficiently standardised equipment and supplies. Essentially this criticism is that, relying on national contingents, the United Nations is forced to support different national systems of equipment and supply rather than establish a United Nations system although, after some considerable time, it has proved possible to move over to a more standardised system : it is a problem of the initial stage rather than of a semi-permanent Force like UNEF.

(3) Political staffing considerations. This criticism relates to the problem which, in one sense, affects all international organisations, and that is that efficiency may have to give way to policy in the selection of personnel. The exclusion of the Permanent Members

---

[55] See Burns, *Between Arab and Israeli*, pp. 209–218.
[56] See Frye, *A United Nations Peace Force* (1957), p. 85, for specific illustrations of the UNEF problems of locating supplies.

from peace-keeping operations is, from this point of view, a policy consideration which is secured at the cost of eliminating the personnel most likely to bring real experience to bear.

(4) Frequent turnover of personnel. This affects not only the cost of the Force, since frequent transportation of contingents is necessarily costly, but also the efficiency of the Force. Obviously, contingents retained for very long periods may reveal a decline in efficiency, but a six-monthly rotation is likely to prove both costly and detrimental to efficiency.

(5) Air transport reliability. Here there are two separate problems; one is that of having a reliable supply of aircraft, and the other is that of maintaining the aircraft in a condition of reliability. The reports from the Congo (and, indeed, Mr. Hammarskjoeld's death) suggest that standards of reliability, whether due to lack of spares or servicing, left much to be desired.[57]

One does not necessarily have to agree with all these criticisms to agree with the proposition that, with an adequate, permanent United Nations Headquarters Military Staff, many of these defects in the system of logistical supply and movement of the United Nations Forces used to date could be remedied. Advance planning and training of key personnel; prior knowledge of the availability of supplies, transportation, specialist, logistical, medical[58] and communications units; the conclusion of agreements in advance with Member States for the supply of troops, equipment and transport, or with private firms for the chartering of aircraft—all this could be done and the efficiency of the operations correspondingly increased. At a later stage, when the permanent Military Headquarters Staff begins to be supported by a small, permanent Force, the experience in the logistics field suggests that the emphasis should be placed on individual recruitment of logistics personnel. A large part of the permanent Force could include the more specialised personnel and units upon which the supply and communications lifelines of a force depend, leaving the provision of the bulk of the infantry to the stand-by agreements which, it would be hoped, States would enter into so as to ensure that the small, permanent nucleus would be strengthened to whatever size the occasion demanded.

The establishment of a special procurement agency might well be contemplated so as to purchase and stockpile in preparation for operations those items of transport, supplies and equipment, deemed vital for United Nations military operations: the stockpiles could be maintained in the territory of Member States or, ideally, in base areas as and when the United Nations acquires permanent bases for a

---

[57] Bowman and Fanning, *loc. cit.*, p. 376.
[58] Conceivably the World Health Organisation could assist in the provision of medical personnel and supplies and arrangements to this effect could be concluded in advance by the UN Headquarters Military Staff which we have envisaged (*ante*, p. 350) should include medical officers.

permanent Force. Options to purchase other supplies could be taken up as and when needed. The existence of such an agency would thus relieve the Secretariat of this additional burden which it faces whenever a military operation is begun. The exact form of the agency is, of course, a problem to which alternative solutions are possible. It could be a part of the United Nations Headquarters Military Staff, but, of course, subject to financial and policy control by a Committee of the General Assembly,[59] or it could be a special sub-committee of the Assembly itself operating in close co-operation with the Headquarters Staff.

III. FINANCIAL ARRANGEMENTS BETWEEN THE UNITED NATIONS AND MEMBER STATES

1. *Logistical support*

The financial arrangements to be entered into between the United Nations and Member States in respect of the logistical support required for a United Nations Force form only one part of the overall pattern of financial arrangements. In so far as the United Nations itself assumes liability for providing logistical support, the expenses of doing so will be the responsibility of the United Nations, to be met out of Members' contributions. If Members provide necessary supplies direct to their own troops, however, or furnish the United Nations with services or items at its request, to be used for the support of the Force, questions of reimbursement and of the correct allocation of expenses may arise.

In their 1947 report[60] to the Security Council the Military Staff Committee made no suggestion regarding the financial arrangements to be entered into after Member States had made armed units available to the Security Council, as envisaged in Article 43 of the Charter. The Military Staff Committee proposed, however, that, at least as a general rule, Member States should supply fully equipped units, up to combat standard if necessary, and should thereafter be responsible for providing logistical support. Whether this pre-supposed that Member States would do so at their own cost, or that they would be entitled to claim that the cost should be offset against their budgetary contributions to the " expenses of the Organisation," has remained an open question in the absence of any agreements under Article 43. In principle, however, there would seem to be no reason why expenses incurred through providing logistical support in the course of operations decided upon by the Security Council

[59] See *ante*, p. 356. It may be that the Committee we have envisaged as responsible for political control of the Force would prefer to entrust financial control to the Fifth Committee: in any event the financial implications of its policy would become the concern both of the Fifth Committee and, at an earlier stage, of the Committee on Administrative and Budgetary Questions.

[60] The report is contained in *Repertory of Practice of United Nations Organs*, Vol. II, p. 396: and see *ante*, pp. 12–18.

should not constitute such expenses, subject to any ruling which might be made regarding the special responsibilities of the Permanent Members.

In the case of the Korean conflict, however, where the Security Council, and subsequently the General Assembly, merely recommended that Member States should take collective action against an act of aggression, the Member States who responded to this request thereby became responsible for providing logistical support for their own contingents. In practice, however, arrangements were made to utilise United States facilities as far as possible, in order to ease the logistical burden. With the exception of the Commonwealth division which maintained an independent line of logistical supply, States which offered assistance agreed that their units should be furnished with necessary supplies by the United States, against reimbursement in United States currency. In the case where assistance was provided from other sources, provision was made for claims to be settled direct. In the agreement between the United States and Belgium, regulating the financial settlement for the logistical support which the Belgian contingent received, it was agreed that payment should be based on :

" (a) a sum representing the cost price covering initial supplies of equipment and services furnished to the Belgian forces;
(b) a fixed sum per man and per day for maintenance of personnel and equipment from date of arrival in Korea;
(c) a fixed sum for ammunition;
(d) a sum representing the cost price covering pieces of heavy equipment having a minimum unit value of 1,000 dollars and supplies subsequent to initial delivery, as well as hospitalisation services;
(e) a sum representing the cost, real or estimated, of transportation costs." [61]

Whilst there is no indication that the same breakdown of costs was used in relation to the costs incurred by other States, since the basic agreements with the United States were very largely the same there is at least some ground for thinking that similar arrangements were made in other cases.

In UNEF and ONUC the logistical support initially received by contingents from their respective States has largely consisted of the equipment, *matériel* and expendable supplies which units have brought with them to the area of operations. In the case of UNEF,[62] steady efforts have been made to reduce the proportion of contingent-owned equipment, so that virtually only the personal equipment of individual members, together with small-arms and ammunition, are now contingent-owned. In ONUC this policy has been adopted, so far as was practical, from the beginning. As regards items which have been used, however, the United Nations has agreed to reimburse participating States in respect of deterioration

[61] Article 1, U.N.T.S. Vol. 223, No. 3041, p. 11, at p. 13.
[62] *Ante*, pp. 139–141.

or consumption at a rate faster than that laid down in the relevant national schedules.[63]   Under present United Nations procedures such supplies, particularly equipment, are surveyed on the arrival of a unit in the theatre of operations, and at its departure, by the appropriate United Nations authorities; reimbursement is then made on a current basis.

2. *Costs of movement*

In general it may be said that the allocation of expenses between the United Nations and Member States in respect of the movement of the Force follows the same pattern as the allocation of expenses incurred in providing logistical support.   No specific mention is made in Article 43 of how the costs of making armed forces available are to be met.   From the central position of that Article within the framework of Chapter VII, which sets out the principal means by which international security is to be maintained under the Charter, it may be presumed that it was intended that the costs of any steps taken were to form " expenses of the Organisation " under Article 17.   The report of the Military Staff Committee, although referring to the provision by Member nations of necessary transport, as well as of supplies, for their own forces,[64] makes no mention, however, of how the costs of such transport were to be allocated.   Such matters were presumably amongst those to be dealt with in the detailed agreements between the Security Council and Member States.

It appears to have been assumed during the Korean struggle that the responsibility given to the United States carried with it the burden of paying for the movement of its own forces at least, as well as of arranging for the movement of other troops serving under the Unified Command.   In the various agreements made between the United States and other Members of the United Nations who responded to the request of the Security Council that they should support the United Nations action in Korea, reference is made to the provision by the United States of " services and facilities," [65] against subsequent reimbursement by the State concerned, a phrase which is wide enough to cover the use of, and later payment for, American transport.   In two cases express reference was made to the question of transportation.   In the Agreement between the United States and the Federal Republic of Germany regarding the operation of a German Red Cross Hospital in Korea, it was stated that the United States should supply transportation to and from Korea, as well as all services and facilities supplied to similar units in the field, against

[63] See *ante*, p. 249, for the slight differences made in ONUC, as compared with UNEF, with regard to compensation for deterioration of equipment.
[64] *Loc. cit.*, Article 29.
[65] See, *e.g.*, Article 1 of the Agreement between the United States and Belgium, U.N.T.S. Vol. 223, No. 3040, p. 3, at p. 5.

reimbursement by Germany.[66] In the Agreement between Belgium and the United States, regarding financial arrangements between the two countries in respect of the Belgian contingent, mention was made of the payment by Belgium of the cost of transport supplied by the United States.[67]

Apart from these instances, which appear to reflect an *ad hoc* response to a particular situation rather than a precedent for use by the United Nations in making arrangements with a participating State, the United Nations first dealt with the problem when considering the allocation of the expenses incurred in establishing UNEF. The "basic rule" governing expenses, which stated that all direct costs which participating States would not otherwise have incurred should be borne by the United Nations,[68] carried with it the natural implication that the United Nations would pay for all transport costs outside the home country, unless Member States chose to provide facilities for transportation free of charge. At an early stage the United States declared that, for its part, it would provide all "necessary air and surface transport" for United Nations contingents, without cost to the United Nations.[69] The Advisory Committee on Administrative and Budgetary Questions thought it worthwhile to note that the transport furnished would also be at no charge to the participating State.[70] The Swiss Federal Council undertook to meet the costs of the commercial contract with the Swissair Company which the United Nations had entered into in order to provide the initial air lift between Naples and Abu Suweir.[71] The sum paid included both the cost of the air lift proper and that of insuring the Company's staff from all risks, other than those arising from acts of war. The Canadian and Scandinavian Governments also paid for air lifts for their troops to Egypt or Naples. The Italian Government for its part provided facilities, including planes, without charge, during the initial air operations.[72]

In the *Summary Study* the Secretary-General set out the various items which formed part of the expenses met by the United Nations in connection with the setting up and operation of UNEF.[73] On the basis of Resolutions 1001(ES–1), 1089(XI), and 1151(XII), these expenses included the costs of rotation of national contingents; travel within the area of operations; motor transport and heavy mobile equipment; spare parts, maintenance and fuels and lubricants for vehicles; the flying costs of the R.C.A.F. planes; and also the costs of

---

[66] *Ibid.*, Vol. 223, No. 3064, p. 153.   [67] *Ibid.*, Vol. 223, No. 3041, p. 11.
[68] *Ante*, p. 139.
[69] A/3302/Add. 20, *Off.Rec.G.A.*, Agenda item 66, 11th Sess., 1956–1957, Annexes.
[70] 22nd Report of the Advisory Committee on Administrative and Budgetary Questions, A/3402, *Off.Rec.G.A.*, Agenda item 66, 11th Sess., 1956–1957, Annexes.   [71] A/3302/Add. 29, *ibid.*
[72] Report of the Secretary-General, A/3694 and Add. 1, *Off.Rec.G.A.*, Agenda item 65, 12th Sess., 1957, Annexes.
[73] *Summary Study* etc., A/3943, paragraph 120.

transporting and issuing supplies. As regards troop rotation, the United Nations has, from the outset, made all necessary arrangements for the transport of units, although it has attempted to persuade States to reduce the frequency of such rotations so far as possible. In the absence of scheduled services between the area of operations, or if no government offered to provide transport facilities, the United Nations has sought to obtain transport at the lowest commercial rates. The Canadian and Scandinavian contingents have mostly been rotated in Government planes, on a partly reimbursable basis. Most of the other contingents, however, have travelled by ship. The Brazilian unit has been transported by vessels of the Brazilian Navy, on a reduced cost basis. Whilst no ruling appears to have been given, it seems that the United Nations responsibility for rotation ceases once the troops concerned reach the home country; travel within the country concerned is the responsibility of the participating State and of the individual soldier.

Besides the cost of rotation, the United Nations has also provided for the cost of the operational transport of the Force, a heavy item in view of the long distances involved and the constant patrolling of the Armistice Demarcation Line performed by UNEF, and for the cost of transporting supplies. At the same time the vehicle requirements of UNEF have been systematically standardised and reduced to minimum requirements compatible with efficiency, in order to cut down overheads and to simplify the problem of maintenance. Excess contingent-owned vehicles have been returned to the home country or, where they were worn out, or their value was less than the cost of transport, disposed of in the best interests of the United Nations.[74] It may be noted that the United Nations has also met the cost of all traffic accidents in which members of the Force have been involved in the course of their duties.

In the case of air transport, the United Nations has paid the Canadian Government a standard rate per flying hour which includes elements for fuel and oil, maintenance of the air frame, engines and propellors, and attrition, but no element of the initial capital cost, depreciation, obsolescence or overheads, or for the pay and allowance of the air and ground crews. Unlike the position adopted in the case of equipment it appears to have been agreed that no claims would be presented in respect of aircraft which may be worn out or destroyed.[75] The introduction of Caribou aircraft for internal transport has enabled the Canadian Government to reduce its rates appreciably. It may also be noted that, prior to the ONUC operation, the costs of RCAF flights between Canada and Italy were shared

---

[74] Chapter III, Cost estimates for the maintenance of the Force: report of the Secretary-General, A/4784. *Off.Rec.G.A.*, Agenda item 26, 16th Sess., 1961–1962, Annexes.

[75] 2nd Report of the Advisory Committee on Administrative and Budgetary Questions: budget estimates for the period 1 January to 31 December 1958, paragraph 14, A/3839, *Off.Rec.G.A.*, Agenda item 65, 13th Sess., 1958, Annexes.

between UNEF and the Canadian Government, since they were not used solely for UNEF. Since the ONUC operation they have been split between UNEF, ONUC and the Canadian Government, according to the approximate proportion of space occupied and weight carried. The flights made by the Norwegian Air Force between Pisa and the Scandinavian countries as part of the SCANAP service have been provided without cost to UNEF.

Regarding two smaller operations, it may be noted that although the Spinelli Mission to Jordan in 1958 was provided with United Nations transport, at the cost of the Organisation, in the case of the United Nations Observation Group in Lebanon the Lebanese Government undertook to furnish transportation and other facilities to assist the functioning of the Group.[76] Special considerations applied in each case, not least in the relatively small number of personnel involved and the nature of the mission to be performed.

As regards operations in the Congo, the Secretary-General, in announcing the cost estimates for the initial period, pointed out that they would be reduced appreciably in the event that governments who had furnished supplies, special services, and facilities, particularly the air lift, chose to make these available without charge.[77] The cost of the initial air lift formed, indeed, the largest single cost element of the establishment of the Force. The major part of this cost—$14 million—was borne by the United States; the remainder, incurred by a number of States including Canada, Ethiopia, Ghana, Italy, Sweden, the United Arab Republic, the United Kingdom and the U.S.S.R., amounted to $1 million. The United Nations, however, has paid for the air crews provided under arrangements similar to those covering provision of contingents, and for the maintenance and operation of aircraft, as well as of vehicles, whether owned by contingents or by the United Nations. The United Nations has also paid the assumed costs of fuel and lubricants, depreciation, inspection and handling charges. Arrangements have thus varied appreciably from those made in the case of UNEF. As regards chartered aircraft, contracts have been made so far as possible on an all-inclusive basis.[78] It may be noted that several Members who provided transportation facilities for the Congo operation agreed to make the cost a voluntary contribution, dependent on a decision that the expenses of ONUC would be considered as expenses of the Organisation; if this should not be the case, they agreed to forgo their claim. As with UNEF, the costs of operational movement of the Force, together with the cost of troop rotation and of transporting supplies, have been borne by the United Nations except to the extent to which facilities have been provided without charge by Member States.

[76] U.N.T.S. Vol. 315, No. 4564, p. 125 and *ibid.*, Vol. 303, No. 4386, p. 271.
[77] Report of the Secretary-General, A/C.5/836, *Off.Rec.G.A.*, Agenda item 49/50, 15th Sess., 1960, Annexes.
[78] Report of the Advisory Committee on Administrative and Budgetary Questions, A/4580.

12

The Relevance of Consent to the Presence of a United Nations Force

I. THE QUESTION WHETHER THE CONSENT OF A STATE IS REQUIRED
FOR THE PRESENCE OF A UNITED NATIONS FORCE UPON ITS
TERRITORY

1. The " aggressor " State

No principle seems clearer but that a State determined by a competent United Nations organ to be an " aggressor," and against which sanctions—or " preventive or enforcement action "—are either recommended or decided upon cannot stultify United Nations action by withholding its consent to the presence of a United Nations Force upon its territory. By its own conduct it has forfeited the right to inviolability of its territory. In the only case in which a situation similar to this has occurred, that of Korea, the forces operating under the United Nations Command did in fact cross the 38th parallel and such reservations as have been expressed about that step related more to the political wisdom of such a step rather than to doubts as to the legality of such a step in the absence of the consent of the North Korean authorities.[1] It was, moreover, implicit in the Secretary-General's statements on the entry of ONUC into Katanga that, had ONUC been taking enforcement action under Chapter VII of the Charter, such entry could have been effected by force.[2]

There has been a tendency however—though again it is here suggested that political wisdom and not legal necessity has been the motive—to obtain the consent even of parties whose actions might have been deemed illegal, though not unequivocally an aggression. The Secretary-General thus felt that UNEF could not be stationed on Israeli territory without the consent of the Israeli Government, which was not, in the event, forthcoming.[3] Moreover, there was some talk at the time of obtaining the consent of Israel, France and the United Kingdom for the placing of UNEF on Egyptian territory[4]; the

---

[1] *Ante*, p. 43.
[2] *Ante*, pp. 156, 204. For a discussion of the legal basis upon which the UN would conduct its relations with the authorities and population of the territorial State see *post*, pp. 490–491.
[3] UN Doc. A/3512 para. 5.
[4] Canada tabled a proposal to this effect: *Off.Rec.G.A.*, 1st emergency Special Sess., p. 69. Certain States raised objections of principle: *ibid.*, pp. 70, 83, 87; and A/3302, para. 9; and see also the terms of General Assembly Resol. 998 (ES–1) of 4 November 1956.

Secretary-General's position on this point was ambiguous,[5] and in the event clarification was not needed as consent was forthcoming from all quarters, and many participating States required that all parties should approve the plan. Moreover, the UNEF operations were initiated by the Assembly and not the Security Council, and this may well be the vital consideration.[6]

2. The " victim " State or other " host " State

Where the territorial State has not itself been designated as an "aggressor," but is either the victim State or, where the action is simply a "peace-keeping" operation, a State on whose territory operations by United Nations Forces become necessary in the interests of maintaining international peace and security, the legal basis for the presence of these Forces obviously has to be sought in some principle other than the "forfeiture" principle applied to the aggressor State.

Where the United Nations action is initiated by the Security Council and is in the nature of enforcement action under Chapter VII it is believed that, certainly in so far as the Council *decides* upon such action, the victim State is bound to admit and assist the United Nations Force into its territory. A refusal of consent is perhaps unlikely, but Articles 2 (5), 25 and 49 would provide sufficient basis for an obligation of this kind. The obligation of other States to provide transit or other operational facilities is another matter (though difficult to distinguish in principle) and is dealt with elsewhere.[7] A mere recommendation that such action be taken, at least if addressed to the States upon whose territory the Force would be required to operate,[8] would not impose such an obligation and, if the operations were considered essential in the interests of international peace and security, the Council would presumably act by way of a decision rather than a recommendation. A fortiori, peace-keeping operations under Charter VI, possibly in the nature of an observer group or Force, would, being based on that Chapter, be recommendatory rather than obligatory, thus requiring the consent of the territorial State, and practice to date supports that view.[9]

The same view has prevailed where a United Nations Force has operated under the authority of the Security Council, carrying out

---

[5] The Secretary-General referred merely to the necessity of consent of " the parties concerned." *Ibid.*, Annexes, p. 20.

[6] *Post*, p. 416.

[7] *Post*, pp. 417–419.

[8] It is conceivable that the Council could proceed by way of recommending Member States to provide the necessary forces and, upon being assured of a sufficient Force, *decide* that the Force shall proceed to the territory of the victim State.

[9] It has on occasion been suggested that a decision of the Council under Article 34 of Chapter VI, to send an investigating committee to a territory to determine whether a dispute is likely to endanger peace, does not require the consent of the State concerned. See statements in the Greek Case, *Off.Rec.S.C.*, 2nd yr., Nos. 61, 63 and 64, pp. 1423, 1523 and 1540–1541 : see further *ante*, pp. 67–68.

measures which were more limited than enforcement action under Article 42, namely " peace-keeping " operations under Chapter VII. Thus with regard to ONUC repeated emphasis has been placed on the invitation by the Congo Government to the United Nations.[10] In this case the point proved of vital importance, for it was used as proof that the United Nations—even during the later phases of the Congo operation—was not acting under Article 42, and consequently remained bound by the domestic jurisdiction provisions of Article 2 (7) of the Charter. Moreover, the position of ONUC, should the Congolese Central Government insist upon its withdrawal, has been regarded as very doubtful.[11] Equal emphasis on the principle of consent was laid by the International Court, which found the fact that UNEF and ONUC had been set up with the approval of the host State a significant factor in the assessment of their status as legal.[12]

It may be suggested that this particular view of the requirement of consent is ill-conceived and unnecessary, and that it does not automatically follow that every military action short of enforcement measures decided upon by the Security Council requires the consent of the State on whose territory such action occurs. Undoubtedly it is politically most desirable that such consent *should* be obtained. Where there is an effective government and a limited United Nations Force, the latter cannot possibly act effectively in fulfilment of its mandate if its presence is opposed by the former: this was appreciated in Egypt.[13] Even where the " host " government is not strong, failure to obtain its consent may well meet with the violent opposition of States in sympathy with its policies, or fearful of a United Nations " tutelage ": such was the case in the Congo. However, there may still occur cases where the political disadvantages in waiting for consent for United Nations action in a territory may outweigh such considerations as these; and in all these cases, it is submitted, the Security Council is legally entitled to act without consent should it avail itself of the political option to do so.

Once there has been a finding, express or implied under Article 39 of the Charter, of a threat to the peace, breach of the peace, or act

---

[10] First Report by the Secretary-General on the implementation of Security Council Resolution S/4387: UN Doc. S/4389, p. 2; and see generally *ante*, pp. 231–232.

[11] See *post*, p. 421.

[12] *Certain Expenses of the United Nations, I.C.J. Reports*, 1962, pp. 170–1 and 175.

[13] " From the practical as well as the legal point of view the continuing consent of the host State seems essential to the functioning of UNEF. How could the UN maintain a particular activity or position in the face of insistent demands by the host State that it cease or withdraw? The Force is small, poorly armed, and its line of communications is difficult to protect. Its contingents probably are subject to withdrawal under pressure from Egypt. Any intimation by the Secretary-General that the Force might be ordered to stand its ground against Egyptian armed forces would raise the most difficult practical questions for the nations whose contingents were included in the Force." Noyes, "The Problem of 'Consent' in Relation to a UN Force" in Frye, *A United Nations Peace Force*, at p. 152.

of aggression, then the Security Council has a responsibility to take decisions or to make recommendations to maintain or restore international peace and security. This responsibility is in no way tempered by a need to obtain the consent of the State on whose territory such threat or breach of the peace is occurring. Article 39 does not limit the right of the Security Council to take action— whether by recommendation or decision—to cases involving overt aggression. Psychologically, of course, States are cautious about taking military action of a police or interpositary nature where there is only a threat to the peace or breach of the peace; yet the Charter authority exists. It is sometimes hard to allocate specifically the responsibility for a threat to the peace or a breach of the peace; yet Article 39 does not stipulate that recommendations or decisions for the restoration or maintenance of peace in these circumstances must include an allocation of responsibility. Nor even, it may be noted, does Article 42. It may therefore be deduced that legally the Security Council may recommend or decide upon action to safeguard international peace, even on the territory of a State which is not responsible for the breach or threat thereto, much less for an aggression, and that where the Council *decides* that such action is necessary the State must accept the presence of a United Nations Force.

However, in advancing this view it has to be conceded that an alternative view is possible, namely that the requirement of consent can only be eliminated when the action taken is in the nature of an enforcement action and that *all* peace-keeping operations, whether under Chapter VI or Chapter VII of the Charter, and whether based on a decision or recommendation of the Security Council, require the consent of the territorial State. It has further to be conceded that practice to date under Chapter VII has always been in situations in which such consent existed. Moreover, the International Court of Justice placed great stress on the existence of consent to the presence of ONUC when dealing with the *Expenses Case*, and this has been the approach consistently adopted by the Secretary-General. This, then, is weighty evidence which cannot be ignored. However, the fact remains that the Charter does not specifically require consent from the territorial State to any operations undertaken pursuant to a *decision* under Chapter VII, and Article 25 may on one construction be regarded as a giving of consent in advance by all Members. Further, not one single operation under Chapter VII has clearly raised this issue in the sense of a territorial State refusing consent to an operation decided upon by the Council under Chapter VII: the occasional refusals, noted earlier in Chapter 4, have all been to Chapter VI observer groups. Thus, both views remain possible and it really remains for the Security Council to determine this issue. What is fairly clear is that, if the unanimous votes of all the Permanent Members could be placed on the side of the view first advanced—the view the present writer prefers—there would be a considerable strengthening of the powers of the Security Council in the interest of maintaining international peace and security.

The position of a United Nations Force operating under the authority of the General Assembly cannot be regarded as necessarily analogous to that of a Force operating under the Security Council. There is considerable doubt whether, despite the rather broad terms of the Resolution on Uniting for Peace, the Assembly can initiate, even by way of a recommendation, action directed against a State,[14] so that the whole position of anything analogous to " enforcement action " taken by the Assembly is unclear. If the Assembly may lawfully initiate coercive action against an " aggressor " State, then the same principle of forfeiture as applies in the case of enforcement action by the Security Council would seem to operate, and no consent by that State would be required. The position of the victim State is far less clear, for no reliance on the " forfeiture " principle can apply, nor can the obligations of Articles 25 and 49 be said to apply: the only basis upon which an obligation to admit a United Nations Force into its territory can rest is the rather general obligation in Article 2 (5).

However, so far as the Assembly authorises a " peace-keeping " operation, as it did in the case of UNEF, it has been commonly assumed that such an operation could only proceed on the basis of the consent of the State upon whose territory the operation is to take place. The Secretary-General explicitly supported this view-point in respect of UNEF, commenting that UNEF cannot " be stationed or operate on the territory of a given country without the consent of that country." He then continued to say that he did not exclude, on the other hand, " the possibility that the Security Council could use such a Force within the wider margins provided under Chapter VII." [15] This remark must be taken to mean that consent would not be necessary were the Security Council taking enforcement measures; it cannot be understood to reflect the opinion that UNEF was a suitable Force for sanctions under Chapter VII, when it was established for an entirely different purpose. This opinion has been confirmed by the Secretary-General at a later date,[16] and supported by the United Kingdom Government.[17] Moreover, this view has been generally held by writers and jurists.[18]

This limitation upon Forces operating on the basis of an authorisation from the General Assembly does not arise from the

---

[14] *Ante*, pp. 291–293.
[15] Second Report of Secretary-General on the plan for UNEF, UN Doc. A/3302, para. 9. See also UN Doc. A/3512, paras. 5 (b) and 20.
[16] See *Summary Study of the Experience etc.*, A/3943, para. 15.
[17] (1957) 6 I.C.L.Q. 322. See also General Assembly Resolution 503 (VI), which, in reference to the Uniting for Peace Resolution, " recognises that nothing in the present Resolution shall be construed to permit any measures to be taken in any State without the free and express consent of that State."
[18] See, for example, Sohn (1958), 52 A.J.I.L. p. 238; Seyersted (1961), 37 B.Y.I.L. p. 466, and Rosner, " UNEF," (1957) 11 *Int. Organisation* 419.

fact that the operations are only of a " peace-keeping " character : it has been suggested above that peace-keeping operations decided upon by the Security Council do not require the consent of the territorial State. Rather does the limitation arise from the fact that the Assembly has no power to take decisions binding upon States outside the field of its own internal structure and functioning and the limited Charter provisions—such as those on the admission of new Members and the budgetary decisions under Article 17—which envisage a power to make binding decisions.[19]

It may be added that non-Member States are not likely to be in a position much different from Member States.[20] Consent will, in general, not be required of Members in those cases where the Security Council is operating under Chapter VII, and this is very much the kind of situation to which Article 2 (6) of the Charter applies. It can, of course, be argued that Article 2 (6) will not cover " peace-keeping " operations decided upon by the Security Council or the General Assembly, so that no power of compulsion over non-Members can be exercised in respect of such operations, but it is equally likely that the Council at least will assimilate all its actions under Chapter VII in this respect and decide what to do in relation to non-Members on the basis of political expediency rather than by recognising a legal limitation on its powers. The more likely situation is that which in fact occurred in the Congo, where the non-Member requested United Nations assistance and in which, therefore, an obligation to consent to the presence of the Force is really self-imposed. Moreover, this may involve the further obligation to accept decisions of the Security Council relating to the operations of the Force.[21] This further obligation would seem to be better viewed as a corollary to the initial request rather than a kind of obligation arising from an inchoate membership, for a non-Member State might not be in the course of applying for membership, as was the Congo.

3. *Other States in whose territory transit facilities or bases are required*

The position of States in whose territory the main operations are not being carried out, but in which transit rights are required, will be considered in more detail later.[22] However, for the sake of completeness it may be appropriate to anticipate our later conclusions at this stage by stating that, whilst in practice such transit

[19] See Sloan, "The binding force of a recommendation of the General Assembly," (1948) 25 B.Y.B.I.L. 1; Johnson, "The effect of resolutions of the General Assembly of the UN" (1955-56), 32 *ibid.* 97; also the views of Judge Lauterpacht in the *A.O. on S.W. Africa—Voting Procedure*, I.C.J. *Reports*, 1955, 118–119 and Judge Sir Gerald Fitzmaurice in the *Expenses Case*, I.C.J. *Reports*, 1962, pp. 208–211.
[20] See, on this question, Seyersted, "United Nations Forces" (1961) 37 B.Y.I.L. 472.
[21] See *ante*, pp. 224–230.
[22] *Post*, pp. 455–458.

rights have always been acquired under specific agreements, the State whose co-operation is needed in the form of transit facilities is legally in no different position from any other host State, so that what has been said in relation to host States in the preceding section applies equally to the " transit " State : the Security Council has power, under Chapter VII, to compel the grant of transit facilities when these are necessary to an enforcement action under Chapter VII. The duty of a Member State to " accept and carry out " the *decisions* of the Security Council, a duty expressly recognised in Article 25 and supplemented by Articles 2 (5) and 49 is wide enough to embrace an obligation to accord transit rights. This is not, of course, to deny the obvious advantages of securing transit rights by agreement, and, indeed, it will later be argued [23] that the conclusion of transit agreements in advance of any particular operation would be highly desirable. The argument is simply that a Member State cannot, by withholding transit facilities, frustrate the Security Council in an attempt to fulfil its own obligation to take enforcement action under Chapter VII to maintain or restore international peace and security. The weakness of this argument lies, of course, in the fact that Article 43 makes the undertaking to provide " assistance, and facilities, including rights of passage " subject to " a special agreement or agreements " : the undertaking might appear, therefore, as no more than a *pactum de contrahendo*, and as an undertaking of the same imperfect character as the obligation to provide armed forces. Yet it is by no means clear from the *travaux préparatoires* that this result was intended. The Dumbarton Oaks Proposals spoke of " a special agreement or agreements " for the provision of " armed forces, facilities and assistance necessary for the purpose of maintaining international peace and security." [24] It was only at the San Francisco Conference that the phrase " including rights of passage " was inserted at the request of France, and of this the Report of Committee III said the following :

> "Taking into consideration the desire expressed by France, the right of passage is specifically mentioned in the text as one of the 'facilities' to be furnished by Member States, although this mention is not intended to exclude the granting of other facilities. The Committee agreed to this inclusion *in the light of the precedent contained in the Covenant of the League of Nations, but with the conviction that this important international obligation should not be violated or disregarded as has occurred so often in the past."* [25]

Now it may be recalled that Article 16 (3) of the Covenant of the League contained an undertaking, without more, that Member States

---

[23] *Post*, pp. 455–458.
[24] Ch. VIII, Section B, 5.
[25] Doc. 881, III/3/46, UNCIO, Vol. 12, p. 510 : the emphasis is added. The reference to " the past " must be taken as referring to the refusal by Scandinavian countries to allow the transit of British and French troops across their territories in order to go to the assistance of Finland when attacked by the U.S.S.R. in 1939.

"will take the necessary steps to afford passage through their territory to the forces of any of the Members of the League which are co-operating to protect the covenant of the League." Thus, the Covenant contained a pre-existing obligation to accord rights of transit, not dependent on subsequent agreements, and the avowed purpose of the French amendments was to ensure "greater effectiveness in the provisions relating to the composition, the stationing and the use of forces placed at the disposal of the Security Council," and to "fill in the gaps and to correct the errors which may have been noted in the Articles of the Covenant . . ." [26] It would thus be a curious interpretation of the French amendment if it in fact reduced the obligations of Member States as compared with the obligations of members of the League under the Covenant! Hence there is good reason for suggesting that Committee III conceived agreements regarding transit to be desirable to supplement and particularise a pre-existing obligation to accord transit rights to Forces operating under the authority of the Security Council contained in Chapter VII of the Charter. However, it must again be admitted that practice to date has been based entirely on the *voluntary* provision of transit rights, and practice tends to assume in the interpretation of the Charter more importance than the *travaux préparatoires* of half its membership, twenty years ago. Moreover, the Military Staff Committee and the Collective Measures Committee dealt with this question on the assumption that an agreement would be necessary. Thus, as with the view advanced above in section 2, the view we now advance is a possible view but one which the Security Council would have to adopt as a matter of policy and against the run of practice so far: yet there is a strong argument for saying that such a view would be permissible under the Charter.

The position of a State providing a permanent base is, however, different; not only would it be ludicrous to suggest that a permanent base for a United Nations Force could be secured and maintained against the opposition of the host State but, moreover, such a base would be required for the Force pending operations. Thus it would be required for long periods when no breach of international peace or act of aggression was in existence, so for these long periods the Security Council could not rely on its compulsive powers under Chapter VII. From every point of view it is desirable to regard permanent bases as being dependent upon a specific consent and agreement of the host State.

[26] Commentary of the French Government on the Dumbarton Oaks Proposals, UNCIO, Vol. 3, pp. 379–80. Included in the "General Principles" drafted by the Military Staff Committee in 1947 was a text proposed by France for Article 26 dealing with the provision of assistance and facilities, including rights of passage, for armed forces. However, this text clearly contemplated that special agreements would be concluded and it was even less "generous" than the China/U.K./U.S.A. draft which contemplated a general guarantee of rights of passage: see *ante*, p. 16.

II. THE EFFECT OF WITHDRAWAL OF CONSENT TO THE PRESENCE OF THE FORCE BY THE HOST STATE

A good deal of uncertainly surrounds this question due to the facts that, in cases like the Congo, a great deal of emphasis was placed on the existence of consent to the presence of the Force (and the question of whether such consent was legally necessary carefully avoided) and that, with both UNEF and ONUC, the matter became regulated by agreement with the host State. Before attempting a statement of the legal principles applicable to this problem, it may be useful, briefly, to examine the main precedents.

Excluding cases like UNTEA, or even the Observer Group in the Yemen, where the presence was based on a " disengagement " agreement and was envisaged for a fixed period of time,[27] the principal precedent from the observer groups is that of UNOGIL. It may be recalled that, whilst the Group had itself indicated that its task was completed, and whilst the decision to withdraw the Group was effectively that of the Secretary-General, this withdrawal was on the basis of a plan acceptable to the Lebanese Government and followed the request from that Government to the Security Council to delete its complaint from the agenda of the Council.[28] Thus, the precedent is somewhat inconclusive: the issue we are now concerned with never arose as such.

With UNEF, it must be remembered that not only was the Force established under the authority of the Assembly, and not the Security Council, but that the basic agreement (*Aide-mémoire*) with Egypt [29] specifically regulated the question of withdrawal of the Force. However, the terms in which this issue was regulated leave a good deal to be desired in the way of clarity, and writers have expressed divergent views on how far the withdrawal of Egypt's consent could terminate the mission.[30]

---

[27] *Ante*, pp. 85, 259.   [28] *Ante*, pp. 69, 81.

[29] A/3375, Annex (emphasis and brackets added):

" . . .

1. The Government of Egypt declares that, when exercising its sovereign rights on any matter concerning the presence and functioning of UNEF, it will be guided, *in good faith*, by its acceptance of General Assembly Resolution 1000 (ES–I) . . .

2. *The United Nations takes note of this declaration* . . . and declares *that the activities of UNEF will be guided, in good faith, by the task* established for the Force in . . . Resolutions [1000 (ES–I) and 1001 (ES–I)]; in particular, the *United Nations, understanding this to correspond to the wishes of the Government of Egypt, reaffirms its willingness to maintain UNEF until its task is completed.*

3. The Government of Egypt and the Secretary-General declare that it is their intention to proceed forthwith, in the light of points 1 and 2 above, to explore jointly concrete aspects of the functioning of UNEF. . .; the Government of Egypt, *confirming its intention to facilitate the functioning of UNEF, and the United Nations are agreed to expedite in co-operation the implementation of guiding principles [so] arrived at . . .*"

[30] Compare Franck, " United Nations Law in Africa: The Congo Operations as a Case Study " (1962) 27 *Law and Contemporary Problems*, 632, 639, 643 where he regards UNEF as being in Egypt on sufferance; and Weiss-

The Secretary-General in his summary of experience, although clearly taking the point that in ensuring the independence of the Force it was necessary to curb the Egyptian Government's unilateral right to require withdrawal, did not assert that Egypt's right was entirely abrogated and that the United Nations could exclusively decide on the question of withdrawal:

"The consequence of such a bilateral declaration is that, were either side to act unilaterally in refusing continued presence or deciding on withdrawal, and were the other side to find that such action was contrary to a good-faith interpretation of the purposes of the operation, an exchange of views would be called for towards harmonising the positions. This does not imply any infringement of the sovereign right of the host government, nor any restriction of the right of the United Nations to decide on the termination of its own operation whenever it might see fit to do so. But it does mean a mutual recognition of the fact that the operation, being based on collaboration between the host government and the United Nations, should be carried on in forms natural to such collaboration, and especially so with regard to the questions of presence and maintenance." [31]

It will also be recalled that he forecast that it would be unlikely that any government or the United Nations would go further than in the *Aide-mémoire*.[32]

ONUC was, in contrast, a Force established by the Security Council under Chapter VII of the Charter,[33] and, moreover, in response to a specific request from the Congolese Government for military assistance.[34] The original Security Council Resolution of 14 July 1960,[35] which in effect accepted the request of the Congolese Government, authorised the Secretary-General to provide military assistance "until . . . the national security forces might be able, *in the opinion of the Government*, to meet fully their tasks" (emphasis added). Later the Secretary-General made it clear that it was his view that the Secretary-General could make binding decisions and indeed in the basic agreement, as has already been seen,[36] the United Nations reaffirmed, "considering it to be in accordance with the wishes of the Government of the Republic of the Congo, that it is prepared to maintain the United Nations Force in the Congo until such time as it [clearly the United Nations] deems the latter's task to have been fully accomplished." [37] The fact that, apparently contrary to the Secretary-General's expectation, the Congolese Government was prepared to go further than the Egyptian Government and to relinquish any unilateral right to require withdrawal is

berg, *The International Status of the UN* (1961) pp. 131–40 for the view that "Egypt would violate her duties if she were to evict UNEF on the basis of her own unilateral decision."
[31] *Summary Study* etc., A/3943, para. 158.
[32] *Ibid.*, para. 159.
[33] *Ante*, pp. 124–125.
[34] *Ante*, p. 153.
[35] S/4387.
[36] *Ante*, p. 232.
[37] S/4389/Add. 5: brackets added.

probably explained by the fact that it was not in a position to surrender such a right: it did not possess it.

It is on the basis of these somewhat inconclusive precedents that we venture to state the following propositions:

(1) That the fact that a State has consented to the presence of the Force does not of itself imply that the State retains the right to withdraw such consent and unilaterally terminate the mission of the Force.

(2) That in all cases where consent to the presence of the Force is not initially required as a matter of law,[38] the unilateral withdrawal of consent cannot terminate the mission of the Force.

(3) That where consent is a legal prerequisite to the presence of the Force then, prima facie, the Force must withdraw in reasonable time upon the termination of such consent.

(4) However, where, prima facie, this right to terminate the mission of the Force is retained by the host State this may be waived *either* by a specific agreement with the United Nations, *or* by a unilateral undertaking—which operates as an estoppel [39]—or even by an undertaking, express or implied, to act in good faith with regard to the continued presence of the Force. This last, whilst it may fall short of a specific agreement waiving entirely the right to call for a withdrawal of the Force, would demand that such a call must follow adequate negotiations with the United Nations, adequate notice to the United Nations, and be accompanied by adequate and bona fide reasons.

(5) That, subject to any agreement with the host State and to the same considerations of an estoppel and good faith, the United Nations has the exclusive right to terminate the mission of the Force in all cases where the presence of the Force is not dependent in law entirely on the consent of the host State.

III. CONSENT AND THE RULE OF NON-INTERVENTION

We have already indicated that, in our view, consent is not part of the constitutional basis of a United Nations Force: the constitutional basis must be found in the Charter, not in consent *per se*, so that consent becomes no more than evidence that a particular Force is engaged in a peace-keeping operation rather than enforcement action.[40]

It remains for us to ask whether "consent" by a government can render legal certain actions or functions of a United Nations Force which would otherwise be illegal. In other words, if there

---

[38] See the preceding section.
[39] For example, such an undertaking might be given in the course of the debates in the UN organ establishing the Force, or even in the form of an affirmative vote for a Resolution which envisages that it shall be for the UN to terminate the mission of the Force.
[40] *Ante*, p. 311.

exists no Charter authority for certain actions by the United Nations, can the "consent" of a host government to such action on its territory provide a legal basis therefor? To some extent this is an illusory question, for an implied constitutional basis for many actions may be found in the inherent powers of the organisation, and a request from a State may merely underline that the occasion is appropriate for their use.

One aspect of this problem can be raised by the question whether the consent of the territorial State could authorise action by an organ, such as the General Assembly, which would otherwise be *ultra vires* that organ—and this might well be the position with enforcement action. The International Court of Justice has at least touched on this question in its Advisory Opinion on *Certain Expenses of the United Nations*. In the context of legally binding expenses of the Organisation it drew a distinction between actions which were contrary to the Purposes of the Charter and actions which were *ultra vires* through being executed by the wrong organ, in the wrong form, etc.[41] The Court was in fact drawing a traditional distinction of treaty law between internal unconstitutionality and external unconstitutionality. Where the act was merely illegal internally a valid expense of the Organisation is incurred, binding upon all States. It is therefore implied that if consent—on which the Court relied strongly as evidence of legality—is given to the performance of an action by the United Nations which is within the scope of its Principles and Purposes, then even if other articles of the Charter are contravened, a valid expense is still incurred. Can this pronouncement, which is broad enough as it stands, be extended to questions other than expenses? If a decision is made, with the consent of the parties concerned, to perform an action within the purposes and principles of the Charter, but by an inappropriate organ, is that action to be deemed legal for *all* purposes? If the action were the establishment of a United Nations Force, could doubtful States not only refuse to participate (which loophole they already have because of the non-implementation of Article 43) but also to co-operate in matters of rights of passage, etc.? For purposes other than the assessment of legal expenses, the distinction between acts internally legal and externally legal seems artificial, for in the Charter the two aspects are vitally interwoven. Two levels of legality in United Nations operations would introduce an undesirable element of uncertainty. An action performed by an incompetent organ, even if consented to by the affected State, is not to be considered legal.

The other, and more likely, aspect of this problem is the general question of the limits imposed upon action by United Nations Forces by general international law and the Charter and of whether the consent of the territorial State affects the definition of those limits:

[41] *I.C.J. Reports*, 1962, p. 168.

in short, how far does the rule of non-intervention apply and how far does the giving of consent to a particular function make permissible a function otherwise contravening this rule?

It may first be noted that, in relation to the general international law applicable between States, there is no clear consensus of opinion on the question of whether consent permits in all cases action by a foreign State which would otherwise constitute intervention. However, it is believed that the problem in relation to the United Nations is not necessarily analogous to the problem between States, if only for the reason that the powers of the United Nations are circumscribed by the Charter, so that it may be possible to give an answer on the position of the United Nations with a greater degree of confidence. Yet to do so it is necessary to distinguish between the following situations.

1. *Enforcement action*

Here the proviso to Article 2 (7) makes it clear that the rule of non-intervention is of limited application. It would be wrong to assume it had no application, for there are clearly limits to United Nations action even against the aggressor State. Unlike the belligerent of traditional international law, the United Nations may not impose such conditions as it sees fit, for its conduct is to be directed to the maintenance or restoration of international peace and security. Thus it may be doubted whether, after the defeat of the aggressor, the United Nations could impose a particular form of government on the State, or confiscate State assets wholesale,[42] or partition the territory of the State: there would be limits to the intervention possible, namely, those limits imposed by the necessity to restore and maintain international peace and security and no more.

2. *Peace-keeping operations*

(a) IN SITUATIONS HAVING AN "INTERNATIONAL" ELEMENT

Here the "international" element may vary in the degree of its intensity. Given that there is a threat to, or breach of, *international* peace and security—and this, it will be argued, is the precondition of even a peace-keeping operation—the situation can scarcely be regarded as one of purely domestic concern, so that the principle of Article 2 (7) is immediately limited in its application to such situations. What is and what is not of purely domestic concern can only be determined in the light of the particular threat to international peace, the particular international element in the situation. In situations such as that faced by UNEF, when an interposition Force is required between two States, this element is clear and a United Nations Force may resort to actions such as the closing of borders,

---

[42] This would not exclude a certain degree of penal confiscation so as to oblige the aggressor to make reparation for the damage it had caused.

the prevention of illegal incursions across borders and so on. The territorial State cannot argue that such measures constitute "intervention" and are therefore impermissible. The test of what is permissible is, in our view, to be determined by the necessity to preserve international peace and security and to protect the security of the Force itself. The consent of the territorial State cannot, in general, either curtail or extend the functions of the Force which stem from the mandate of the Force laid down by the parent organ. The only exception to this would be where the presence of the Force was dependent upon consent and, *in the giving of that consent*,[43] the territorial State had imposed clear restrictions. We have suggested above that this situation need only arise as a matter of law when the General Assembly establishes the Force, or when the Security Council chooses to act under Chapter VI or by a mere recommendation under Chapter VII: but not when it acts by a decision under Chapter VII. It would be for the United Nations to decide whether it chose to operate a Force under such restrictions.

In so far as the territorial State requested the Force to assume functions *not* necessary for the maintenance of international peace and security (a "supplemental" as opposed to a "restrictive" consent) these functions should not be accepted by a United Nations Force. They might be assumed as a form of technical assistance, but not by a United Nations Force as such.

A more limited international element can be seen in cases like the Congo where the situation is, or becomes, basically a situation of civil strife but one which is given an international character either by support to the internal factions from outside or by the existence or threat of intervention from outside Powers. This was true of the Congo [44] and is probably true of the present situation in Cyprus.[45] In this situation it is believed that a United Nations Force should be confined to excluding the "foreign" elements and taking such other measures as are necessary for its own security and freedom of movement. The application of this principle to the Congo has already been examined in some detail,[46] but it may be repeated that measures such as the sealing off of frontiers, the expulsion of foreign troops or mercenaries, the disarming even of local forces whose actions impeded these tasks—these would all be permissible functions.

Further than this the United Nations should not go, and no consent by the territorial State (or the recognised government of that

---

[43] Restrictions imposed subsequently and designed to impede the exercise of the functions of the Force could well be treated as a breach of faith and rejected by the UN. For a similar view see Eide and Midgaard, "UN Security Forces: Some General Problems," p. 4 (a paper prepared for the International Conference on UN Security Forces as a Means to Promoting Peace, to be convened by the Norwegian Group of Strategic Studies in Oslo, 20–21 February 1964).

[44] *Ante*, pp. 154, 186–187.

[45] In the sense that a deterioration of the situation might lead to the intervention of Greek and Turkish forces.

[46] *Ante*, pp. 186–200.

State) can authorise functions which do not stem from the necessity to maintain or restore *international* peace and security.[47] Hence the problems of *internal* peace are not, as such, problems for which a United Nations Force should assume any functional responsibility. The prevention of secession, the support of a particular government against even a violent opposition which is of a genuine indigenous character, or the enforcement of a particular political solution upon the internal parties to a civil strife are thus not permissible functions, whether with or without the consent of the established government.

To embark upon such functions, even with the consent of the host government, would involve the United Nations Force in what is plainly a domestic matter and not one affecting *international* peace. It would involve a suppression of the right to self-determination which must still, at the present stage of evolution of international society, be deemed to include a right to revolt whether for the purpose of secession or for the purpose of overthrowing an unpopular government.[48] The United Nations might conceivably assume a role of political mediator or conciliator—and, indeed, commissions for this purpose were established in the Congo—but this role would not be one for a United Nations Force to assume. Moreover, since it is inconceivable that the United Nations could support a rebellious faction *against* the government, any support must be *for* the government and this would necessarily involve a political choice which could fail to carry general support of the Member States. This would be even more likely where the internal struggle for power is waged between rival groups both claiming to represent the government: the rift between Lumumba and Kasavubu in the Congo was thus reflected in a rift between Member States. There is, finally, the purely financial consideration which would suggest that the United Nations cannot afford to assume functions related solely to the *internal* stability of a State, in the absence of a threat to international peace and security.

On this view, therefore, an *internal* policing role is not one which a United Nations Force might assume. To the extent that a United Nations Force could take action to suppress measures of genocide, gross violation of human rights by arbitrary violence and attacks on aliens within the territory,[49] this would be justified by reference to a concept that such measures are likely to endanger *international* peace

---

[47] Burns and Heathcote, *Peace-keeping by UN Forces from Suez to the Congo* (1963) p. 167 go much further in advocating a "policing" role for UN Forces. Eide and Midgaard, *loc. cit.*, pp. 10–18 are more restrictive and come nearer to the present writer's views, as also does Millis, "The Political Control of an International Force" in *Quis Custodiet?: Controlling the Police in a Disarmed World* (1963) Appendices, Vol. III, at p. 39, although he is referring to a police force operating after disarmament.

[48] See Eide and Midgaard, *loc. cit.*, p. 14: "There are good reasons to believe that the Charter protects what might be called the right of revolution, which means that the people of a country has a right to decide for themselves the form and structure of their government and constitution."

[49] For the functions of ONUC in this regard see *ante*, pp. 187–191.

by producing exactly the conditions which would encourage intervention by outside Powers. Yet any United Nations action of this
kind would be directed at the groups responsible for these measures,
which might conceivably be groups representing the established
government rather than those opposing it, so that the action would
be devoid of political bias and based upon the desire to protect those
elementary human rights which are recognised in the Charter. Such
action would also be designed to create the conditions in which a
political reconciliation or a democratic solution to the problems
might prove possible, but it would not in any way prejudice that
solution.

(b) IN SITUATIONS HAVING NO " INTERNATIONAL " ELEMENT

In these purely " civil " strifes, when the problem is simply one
of the internal order and stability of a State, it follows from what
has been said above that no United Nations Force should be used.
The United Nations might conceivably afford technical assistance in
the form of military or police experts, capable of assisting in the
organisation and disciplining of internal security forces, but even
this assistance would have to be tempered by caution. It would,
for example, be highly questionable policy for the United Nations to
afford even this kind of technical assistance to a State which intended
to use its internal security forces for the suppression of the democratic processes by which the people of a State are able freely to
choose their own form of government. So long as the United
Nations remains an organisation based upon the co-operation of
sovereign States for the preservation of international peace and
security—and not a federal or " supra-national " organisation—it
should in principle refrain from any form of coercion in respect of
internal, civil disorders.

13

Agreements with "Host" States

THE circumstances in which the consent of the territorial State is legally necessary for the entry and operations of a United Nations Force on that territory have already been examined.[1] It may be reiterated, however, that in certain cases, even when consent is not legally required, there will be marked advantages in the United Nations operating on the basis of consent as a matter of practical convenience, so that it would be wrong to assume that agreements with "host" States will only arise in cases where such agreement is legally necessary.

Four types of agreements must be distinguished, and this not so much because they must be distinguished as a matter of law but rather because, in practice, they are better so distinguished: these are (1) the "basic" agreement determining the nature and purpose of the operations of the United Nations Force; (2) the detailed Status of Forces Agreement (SOFA); (3) agreements for transit rights; and (4) agreements for permanent bases.

I. THE BASIC AGREEMENT

In the past, and very likely in the future, time has been at a premium in the early stages of planning a Force. This has been, in part, the explanation for the fact that either a brief "basic" agreement has been concluded between the United Nations and the host State—as in the cases of UNEF and ONUC—or that no such agreement has been concluded at all.[2] There is, however, little doubt that for the larger United Nations military operations a basic agreement is highly desirable, and covering more than a simple acceptance of the Resolutions of the United Nations organ setting out

---

[1] *Ante*, pp. 412–420.
[2] In Korea, no basic agreement (not even an SOFA) was concluded with the Republic of Korea by the UN: *ante*, pp. 57–58. With UNTEA there was, similarly, no basic agreement in the usual sense, although the General Assembly "adopted" the Netherlands/Indonesian Agreement of 15 August 1962: *ante*, pp. 255–260. With the observer groups, similarly, no basic agreement comparable to the UNEF and ONUC Agreements was concluded. Either the UN adopted a statement of the functions of the group contained in an agreement between the parties (as with UNTSO and the Group in the Yemen) or itself specified the mandate of the group in Resolutions which the States concerned accepted as the purposes for which they agreed to entry of the group (as with UNOGIL, UNMOGIP and UNCOK). On the observer groups see generally *ante*, Chap. 4, pp. 83–84.

the mandate of the Force. Following Suez, from the Resolution of the Assembly of 4 November 1956 requesting the Secretary-General to submit plans for the setting up of a Force [3] to the conclusion of the basic agreement between Egypt and the United Nations on 18 November,[4] only fourteen days elapsed. In the Congo, from the initial cables of 12 and 13 July 1960 [5] requesting assistance until the conclusion of a basic agreement on 27 July,[6] again only fourteen days elapsed. Whilst in neither case did the entry of the United Nations troops have to await the conclusion of these basic agreements, since consent had been given in general terms previously, it is clear that the early conclusion of a short agreement defining the scope of the operations of the Force was regarded as a matter of urgency.[7]

The terms of the basic agreements relating to both UNEF and ONUC were brief. The agreement over UNEF contained three paragraphs:

" 1. The Government of Egypt declares that, when exercising its sovereign rights on any matter concerning the presence and functioning of UNEF, it will be guided, in good faith, by its acceptance of General Assembly Resolution 1000 (ES-1) of 5 November 1956.

2. The United Nations takes note of this declaration of the Government of Egypt and declares that the activities of UNEF will be guided, in good faith, by the task established for the Force in the aforementioned Resolution; in particular, the United Nations, understanding this to correspond to the wishes of the Government of Egypt, reaffirms its willingness to maintain UNEF until its task is completed.

3. The Government of Egypt and the Secretary-General declare that it is their intention to proceed forthwith, in the light of the points 1 and 2 above, to explore jointly concrete aspects of the functioning of UNEF, including its stationing and the question of its lines of communication and supply; the Government of Egypt, confirming its intention to facilitate the functioning of UNEF, and the United Nations are agreed to expedite in co-operation the implementation of guiding principles arrived at as a result of that joint exploration on the basis of the Resolutions of the General Assembly."

The agreement over ONUC was slightly more detailed, and provided as follows:

"The Government of the Republic of the Congo states that, in the exercise of its sovereign rights with respect to any question concerning the presence and functioning of the United Nations Force in the Congo, it will be guided, in good faith, by the fact that it has requested military assistance from the United Nations and by its acceptance of the Resolutions of the Security Council of 14 and 22 July 1960; it likewise states that it will ensure the freedom of movement of the Force in the interior of the country and will accord the requisite privileges and immunities to all personnel associated with the activities of the Force.

The United Nations takes note of the statement of the Government of the Republic of the Congo and states that, with regard to the activities of the United Nations Force in the Congo, it will be guided, in good faith, by the task

---

[3] Resol. 998 (ES-1): see *ante*, p. 92.
[4] A/3375, Annex and A/3943, paras. 132–133: *ante*, p. 125.
[5] S/4382: see *ante*, p. 153.
[6] S/4389/Add. 5: *ante*, p. 236.
[7] A/3943, para. 133.

assigned to the Force in the aforementioned Resolutions; in particular the United Nations reaffirms, considering it to be in accordance with the wishes of the Government of the Republic of the Congo, that it is prepared to maintain the United Nations Force in the Congo until such time as it deems the latter's task to have been fully accomplished."

The agreements thus have in common the acceptance by the host State of the Resolutions of the United Nations organ establishing the Force and the undertaking to be guided " in good faith " by those Resolutions; the undertaking by the United Nations to be guided " in good faith " by those same Resolutions; and the undertaking by the United Nations to maintain the Force until its task is completed.

Their dissimilarities lie in the fact that the ONUC Agreement contained rather more detail: it affirmed the freedom of movement of the Force and also obliged the Congo to accord the requisite privileges and immunities to the Force. These matters were, in UNEF, left to the subsequent Status of Forces Agreement which was possibly anticipated in the third paragraph.[8]

The experience with UNEF and ONUC suggest that, for future basic agreements with host States, the matters to be appropriately included are the following:

(1) An acceptance by both the host State and the United Nations of the Resolutions of the United Nations organ establishing the Force —or initiating a particular operation of any permanent Force—as definitive of the mandate of the Force and an agreement to be guided, in " good faith," by those Resolutions. It is believed that, in principle, this mandate, as a statement of the purposes and functions of the Force, should stem from a Resolution of the Security Council or the General Assembly. In so far as the mission of the Force is stated in a request by the host State, this should become definitive of the mandate of the Force only to the extent that it is incorporated in the appropriate Resolutions.[9]

(2) A guarantee of such freedom of movement for the Force as may be necessary to enable the Force to discharge its mandate, both within the territory and to and from points of access to the territory.[10]

(3) An agreement that the United Nations shall have exclusive control over the Force: in particular, that, whilst under an obligation to consider any views expressed by the host State on these matters,

---

[8] The explanation of the need to insert a provision on privileges and immunities in the ONUC Agreement is in part that the Congo was not a Member of the UN nor a party to the 1946 Convention on Privileges and Immunities (as Egypt was): however, this cannot be the entire explanation for, as we shall see, supplemental provisions dealing with privileges and immunities had to be negotiated with Egypt. Neither the Charter nor the 1946 Convention are really adequate for a detailed SOFA.

[9] Thus General Assembly Resol. 1752 (XVII) of 21 September 1962 " adopted " the mandate for UNTEA and the UN Security Force prescribed in the Netherlands/Indonesian Agreement of 15 August 1962: see *ante*, pp. 255–260.

[10] Nowhere is the importance of freedom of movement more amply demonstrated than in the Congo operations: see *ante*, pp. 203–205.

the United Nations shall determine the composition of the Force and have exclusive control over the operations of the Force and over installations and property belonging to it or placed under its control.[11]

(4) An agreement that the United Nations Status of Forces Agreement [12] shall be applicable, assuming this to be in existence, or, if not, that such an agreement will be negotiated.

(5) An agreement that the United Nations will maintain the Force until the completion of its mandate but that the question whether the mandate for the Force, as specified in the Resolutions of either the Security Council or the General Assembly, has been fulfilled is for the United Nations to decide: and that the termination of the mission of the Force for any other reason shall occur only as the result of an agreement between the host State and the United Nations.[13]

It must be noted, finally, that the basic agreements hitherto concluded have included no provisions for the settlement of any disputes which may arise under them. There may be several reasons why a customary compromissory clause would not be appropriate.

In the first place the terms of the agreement are very broad and the normal procedures for arbitral or judicial settlement of disputes would not reasonably apply. The extent to which their terms have been complied with will raise questions calling for an appreciation of the conduct of the parties which is essentially political rather than judicial. The scope for the settlement of major disputes could not be delimited in legal terms. This leads to a second point; even if the dispute arising under the basic agreement could be contained within a legal framework it would often be most unlikely that a judicial or arbitral settlement would be acceptable to either the United Nations or to interested States. Broad political issues are involved, and there must be both flexibility and reasonable expedition in their resolution: the whole operation could be hamstrung by lengthy technical and legal argument. The political organs of the United Nations or liaison committees on the spot are therefore the appropriate *fori* for such questions. The more precise legal obligations relating to the operation of the Force have in practice been defined in the later SOFA, which have accordingly provided for the settlement of the disputes which arise under them.

Thus the remedies available to either party, if it took the view that a serious breach of the basic agreement had occurred, would be of a political nature. The United Nations could, on its part, ultimately resort to the withdrawal of the Force or, if a breach of international peace was still in existence, to mandatory measures under Chapter VII which would not depend on the agreement of the host State.[14] The host State could effectively deny further

[11] *Ante*, pp. 110, 120–123, 127, 233–236.
[12] *Post*, pp. 432–455.
[13] *Ante*, pp. 420–422.
[14] *Ante*, pp. 267, 412.

co-operation to the United Nations and force the United Nations to take one or other of these two alternatives.

II. UNITED NATIONS STATUS OF FORCES AGREEMENTS

1. *General considerations*

Exterritoriality, the traditional justification for diplomatic privileges and immunities, has now been generally discredited. Superseded first by the representative theory (that the Head of State's privileges and immunities should be granted to his diplomatic representatives), it has been supplemented by a third which seems now to be generally accepted—the functional theory. The functional test therefore provides a justification for privileges and immunities generally and a particular test to measure the extent of specific immunities. The functional basis for immunities is even more emphatically recognised in the case of privileges and immunities of international organisations.[15]

The general question to be asked therefore is whether the privilege or immunity in issue is necessary for the efficient functioning of the organisation. Dr. Jenks has said: " . . . the current régime of international immunities has been evolved as the result of a thorough appraisal by governments of the functional needs of effective international organisations. It is these functional needs which constitute both the justification for and the measure of international immunities." [16]

It follows from this, of course, that, as in the case of diplomatic and consular privileges and immunities, the privileges and immunities are granted not in the interests of the individuals concerned but for the benefit of the organisation. This is expressly acknowledged in many of the relevant instruments. The General Convention, for instance, provides as follows:

" Privileges and immunities are granted to officials in the interests of the United Nations and not for the personal benefit of the individuals themselves . . . " [17]

Similarly, the UNEF Agreement [18] records that the arrangements respecting criminal and civil jurisdiction are made having regard to the special functions of the Force and to the interests of the United Nations, and not for the personal benefit of the members of the Force (para. 10).

The corollaries of the functional basis of the immunities are (1) that the persons entitled to the immunities are nevertheless obliged to comply with local law; (2) that there should be some procedure for meeting just claims in respect of which immunity may be claimed including, possibly, some provision for waiving the immunity concerned. The necessity for waiver is greater in the case

---

[15] See for example Art. 105 of the Charter of the United Nations.
[16] *International Immunities* (1961) pp. xxxvii–xxxviii and see his Chap. 2.
[17] Art. V, Section 20, see also Art. IV, Section 14, and Art. VI, Section 23.
[18] Agreement of 8 February 1957 : U.N.T.S. Vol. 260, p. 61.

of an international official who is entitled to full immunities than in the case of a diplomat for the reason that there is no "sending" State, the courts of which would have jurisdiction over the individual.

Two broad and important aspects of the functional effectiveness of a United Nations Force may be noted at this stage (they will be developed further later): the independence of the Force from control by interested States; and freedom of movement (this latter being a specific aspect of the former).

A further factor relevant to the determination of the status of the Force is the existence of the relevant provisions of the Charter and the General Convention. Those provisions laid down certain rules which clearly apply to all organs of the United Nations, but they were not intended to regulate, and do not adequately regulate, the whole complex of privileges and immunities required for a United Nations Force. There is, for instance, considerable doubt whether members of a Force who are members of national contingents may properly be called "officials" of the United Nations.[19] Equally the status of the property of the contributing States may be in doubt.[20]

Jenks refers to three major differences between international immunities on the one hand and diplomatic immunities on the other: (1) nationals who are diplomats can be appointed only with the consent of the receiving State; (2) as we have already noted, there is no "sending" State whose courts have jurisdiction. This, however, is subject to modification in the case of the members of national contingents of United Nations Forces. Both the UNEF and ONUC Agreements have contemplated the exercise by the authorities of national contingents of criminal jurisdiction over members of the contingents, and the Secretary-General has secured undertakings to that effect from the governments of participating States[21]; (3) the principle of reciprocity does not operate as in the case of diplomatic privileges and immunities.

Whilst the first and third of these differences might suggest that international privileges and immunities need to be more restricted than diplomatic privileges and immunities, it must be remembered that in dealing with a United Nations Force we are dealing with operations undertaken by military forces—not simply Secretariat officials—and often in conditions which place these forces on an operational footing. Hence it may be surmised that the general law relating to the status of friendly visiting forces (and even forces in "belligerent" occupation of friendly territory) may offer a more adequate guide to the proper status of a United Nations Military Force.

[19] *Ante*, p. 132.
[20] *Ante*, p. 131.
[21] *Ante*, pp. 132, 245.

Indeed, the United Nations SOFA concluded to date represent compromises and shifts between the law of visiting forces on the one hand and the law of international privileges and immunities on the other, against the background of functional necessity. The impact of the general law of visiting forces will be further examined below, but certain differences between the typical contemporary visiting force situation and the United Nations Force situation may be noted here: (1) the United Nations Force is not that of an ally: indeed it will generally be completely independent of the local authorities; (2) the Force generally may be actually operating, in the military sense, within the territory of the State and not merely stationed there.

To date there have been a number of agreements regulating the status of United Nations Forces. These have been briefly mentioned, separately, in Part One of the present study [22] in relation to particular Forces. It is appropriate in this section to attempt some synthesis and to project the experience gained from these agreements into future proposals both for a standing United Nations Status of Forces Agreement—which could become operative immediately a United Nations Force entered a State's territory by consent for a particular operation—and for a permanent United Nations Force. Two agreements—those relating to UNEF and ONUC—have been much more detailed than the remainder and it is to them that attention will chiefly be paid. In spite of the fact that the two operations and the functions of the two Forces differ greatly, there was quite remarkable uniformity on several important issues. As we have already seen, the Secretary-General in his Report in 1958 stressed the importance of several basic principles, which should, he said, be recognised in any United Nations operation. Two of those principles have now been established in all the SOFA; freedom of movement and full immunity from the exercise of local criminal jurisdiction. These are, however, merely two aspects, admittedly of the greatest importance, of the independent status of the Force and flow, the Secretary-General would argue, from the necessity for the independent functioning of the Force.

2. *Freedom of movement*

It is essential that freedom of movement, which is fundamental to successful operations by a United Nations Force,[23] should be acknowledged by the host State as early as possible. That right should be recognised in the basic agreement, but the details of the right should be worked out in the SOFA. In the first place, the host government should guarantee entry facilities. Members of the Force must have unrestricted access to the host State. This means that passport, visa, and immigration regulations and the laws relating to the alien

[22] *Ante,* pp. 84, 125, 236, 260.
[23] See *ante,* pp. 128, 203.

registration must be waived.[24]   Force identity cards, and, in the case of Secretariat officials, United Nations *laissez-passer*, should be accepted as sufficient entry documents.   Any other regulation of entry would give the host State unilateral control over the composition and indeed over the functioning of the Force.[25]   Freedom of movement was more specifically defined in paragraph 33 of the UNEF Agreement as follows:

" The Force shall have the right to the use of roads, bridges, canals and other waters, port facilities and airfields without the payment of dues, tolls or charges either by way of registration or otherwise, in the area of operations and the normal points of access, except for charges that are related directly to services rendered.   The Egyptian authorities, subject to special arrangements, will give the most favourable consideration to requests for the grant to members of the Force of travelling facilities on its railways and of concessions with regard to fares." [26]

Since the Gaza harbour is not equipped for handling freight, the greater proportion of UNEF supplies arriving by sea has been landed at Beirut and Port Said; in the latter case they have then been transported, either by rail or road, to Rafah, at the Southern end of the Gaza Strip, so that this degree of freedom of movement was essential.[27]

The position within the host country in respect of freedom of movement and the provision of transport facilities has not always been an easy one and the Congo operations demonstrated how crucial freedom of movement can be[28]; to an appreciable extent the struggle between the Congolese authorities and the United Nations was waged over the question of control of the means of communication.   Whilst the matter has already been described by reference to its specific context in Chapter 6, it may be noted that in the Agreement between the United Nations and the Congolese Government of 27 November 1961, provision was made to enable members of the Force to enter the country freely, without formalities.[29]   It was also agreed that:

" The United Nations shall have the right to the use of roads, bridges, waterways, port facilities and airfields without payment of dues, tolls or charges by way of registration or otherwise, except for charges collected directly or remuneration for specified services." [30]

As regards air transport, the United Nations was given sole control at airports necessary for the effective functioning of the Force

---

[24] See para. 7 of the UNEF Agreement and paras. 4 and 5 of the ONUC Agreement.

[25] The undesirability of such control by the host State has already been stressed: *ante*, pp. 120–123, 233–236.

[26] A/3526, para. 33: and see the similar provision in the Congo Agreement, A/4986, para. 31.

[27] Report of the Secretary-General, A/3694, *Off.Rec.G.A.*, Agenda item 65, Annexes, 12th Sess., 1957; Report of the Secretary-General, A/3899, *Off.Rec.G.A.*, Agenda item 65, Annexes, 13th Sess., 1958.

[28] *Ante*, pp. 203–205.

[29] A/4986, S/5004, 27 November 1961, para. 4 *et seq.*

[30] *Ibid.*, para. 31.

over arrivals and departures of all aircraft operating on its behalf, whether these were transporting civilian or military personnel or supplies.[31]   Serious disputes have, however, occurred in the past regarding the use of airfields.[32]   It may also be noted that armed conflict broke out between Congolese and ONUC troops at the port of Matadi, the only port capable of receiving ocean-going vessels and which the United Nations had succeeded in opening to traffic.   The ONUC Forces were obliged to withdraw, although eventually they reoccupied the town and ensured that this essential supply line remained open.[33]

Clearly such freedom of movement requires certain safeguards for the host State : the nature of the operations will determine whether, as in the Congo, freedom of movement is necessary throughout the entire territory or, as in Suez, merely between the Force and its supply points, access points, etc.   Moreover, in the UNEF Agreement the Commander was, perfectly reasonably, required to consult with the Egyptian authorities " with respect to large movements of persons, stores or vehicles on railways or roads used for general traffic." [34]   The right to move or use vessels, vehicles, aircraft and equipment [35] presupposes their proper identification as United Nations property,[36] even though United Nations registration of any vehicles and United Nations driving licences must be accepted without any additional requirement of local registration.[37]

In the case of the less extensive operations in the Lebanon and Jordan it was found sufficient merely to ensure with little additional detail " full freedom of movement," except that, for the operation of the Spinelli Mission, the Agreement between the United Nations and the Jordanian Government provided specifically for " the use of airfields by aircraft in the service of the United Nations without the payment of fees or charges except those directly related to services rendered." [38]   The Agreement with Lebanon regarding the status of the United Nations Observation Group in Lebanon went somewhat further in providing that the Lebanese Government would itself furnish the necessary means of transportation, as well as all other facilities for the Group.[39]

3. *Immunity from criminal jurisdiction*

It is necessary to distinguish between Secretariat officials who are not military members of the Force and military members of a United

---

[31] *Ibid.*, para. 42.
[32] For details of an incident at Ndjili airport see S/4417/Add. 8.   *Off.Rec.S.C.*, 15th yr., Suppl. July–September 1960 : and see *ante*, p. 205.
[33] See First Progress Report to the Secretary-General from Mr. Dayal, para. 44, S/4521, *ibid.*; S/4758/Add. 6, *Off.Rec.S.C.*, 16th yr., Suppl. January–March 1961; S/4761, *ibid.*, S/4775, *ibid.*   [34] A/3526, para. 32.
[35] A/4986, para. 30.
[36] A/3526, paras. 20, 21.
[37] A/3526, para. 21; A/4986, para. 32.
[38] U.N.T.S. Vol. 315, No. 4564, para. 2.
[39] *Ibid.*, Vol. 303, No. 4386, p. 271 at p. 274 : and see *ante*, p. 84.

Nations Force. That distinction is necessary for two reasons: in the first place the ordinary rules as to visiting forces hardly apply to officials; and, secondly, as we have already seen, there has in the past been in the case of members of the Force a "sending" State which not only is competent but is obliged to exercise jurisdiction over them. So long as that practice continues there is a case for saying that the members of such a Force are entitled to greater immunities than Secretariat officials, who are, of course, subject to no such jurisdiction.

It now seems to be accepted, despite occasional statements to the contrary, that visiting forces generally are subject to the exercise of concurrent criminal jurisdiction not only of the authorities of the forces to which they belong but also of the host State. This appears most clearly, it is suggested, from an almost consistent practice since 1945: the Agreement of the Brussels Powers, the NATO SOFA, the Agreement for the United Nations Force in Japan, the Agreements concluded between U.S.S.R. and other Eastern States, and the United Kingdom/Malayan Defence Agreement, are all examples of agreements which recognise the right both of the host State and of the sending State to exercise jurisdiction over offences committed against their laws.[40] On the other hand, however, agreements concluded by the United Nations with Egypt, Lebanon, Jordan, and the Congo provided that the members of the Force are subject to the exclusive criminal jurisdiction of the participating State; and the Secretary-General in his report has stated "the position established for UNEF should be maintained in future arrangements" (para. 163). Can this "divergence" [41] be justified?

It has already been noted that there are certain distinctions between a United Nations Force and the ordinary present-day visiting force. In the first place the United Nations Force may actually be operating in the field and may, indeed, be in control of certain areas of State territory. What is the status of the Force and of its members in those areas where it is actually in occupation, albeit with the territorial State's consent? Indeed, it seems to be well established that a force in occupation by consent not only has exclusive jurisdiction over its own members but in addition may have certain jurisdiction over other persons in the territory. Whether the United Nations could have this latter jurisdiction would depend on the terms of the consent: it would seem that in none of the operations to date has it possessed such jurisdiction.[42] Whether a United Nations Force constitutes a force in occupation by consent will depend on the nature of its function and on all the circumstances

---

[40] For a comprehensive survey of the agreements concluded by the United States, and reflecting a general acceptance of the principle of concurrent jurisdiction, see Stambuck, *American Military Forces Abroad* (1963) esp. Chap. III.
[41] "The United Nations Emergency Force" (1957) II *International Organisation*, p. 413, at p. 426.
[42] *Ante*, pp. 108, 201–202, 239.

of the case, but it is clear that a United Nations Force will invariably be completely independent of and rarely, if ever, allied to the local forces. For this very reason the considerations which apply to forces stationed indefinitely in the territory of an ally, training and generally co-operating with the local forces, and becoming to a not inconsiderable degree assimilated in the society in which they are stationed, without being immediately involved in actual operations, lose much of their cogency in the case of a United Nations Force as arguments in favour of denying total immunity.

Accordingly there seems to be some case for according to the members of the United Nations Forces which are involved in operations (as they almost invariably will be) absolute immunity from the jurisdiction of the local courts.[43]   There may, therefore, be justification for the Secretary-General's comment that the provision in the UNEF Agreement giving the participating States *exclusive* criminal jurisdiction is essential to the successful recruitment by the United Nations of national contingents, that it has set a most valuable precedent and that such a rule should be maintained in the future.[44]

It is important to ensure that such an exception to the general rule is not abused. Three matters are relevant : first, it should be clearly understood that the privileges and immunities are not granted for the benefit of the individual concerned; secondly, there should be machinery for prosecuting offenders against local law and an obligation to use that machinery (the question of suitable procedures to settle *civil* claims when there is immunity will be considered below); and thirdly, the immunity should not be unjustifiably extended.

That the privileges and immunities are granted to ensure the effective functioning of the Force and not for the benefit of the individuals concerned has been made quite clear in the case of the UNEF and ONUC Agreements. Articles 10 and 11 (first sentence) of those agreements respectively provide that :

" The following arrangements respecting criminal and civil jurisdiction are made having regard to the special functions of the Force and to the interests of the United Nations, and not for the personal benefit of the members of the Force."

Equally it should be made clear that the immunity is from *the exercise of jurisdiction* and not from compliance with the law : the members of the Force, although not subject to the jurisdiction of the courts, are bound by the substantive law. The UNEF and ONUC Agreements (Articles 6 and 1) require the members of the Forces and United Nations officials to respect the local laws and regulations : that obligation is reiterated in the Regulations for UNEF.[45]

As to the second, the UNEF precedent should be followed. The

---

[43] The situation of a UN Force occupying a base pending operations is dealt with *post*, pp. 458–467.
[44] A/3943, para. 163.
[45] ST/SGB/UNEF/1, Chapter V, para. 29.

UNEF Agreement (para. 11) providing for the exclusive jurisdiction of the service authorities of the participating State was "based on the undertaking that the authorities of the participating States would exercise such jurisdiction as might be necessary with respect to crimes or offences committed in Egypt by any members of the Force." [46] The Secretary-General accordingly asked for and obtained assurances from those States that they would be prepared to exercise jurisdiction with respect to any crime or offence committed by a member of a national contingent.[47] Further, in the agreement with Egypt the Force authorities agreed to undertake "measures within their power with respect to crimes or offences committed against Egyptian citizens by members of the Force." [48] It would seem most desirable to include such provisions in future agreements. Further, as has already been suggested in discussing "stand-by" agreements, those agreements with participating States should contain an obligation to legislate so as to ensure that this jurisdiction over the members of their national contingents is in fact possessed by them and, moreover, that their courts-martial should have power to conduct trials *in situ*, and not after transfer of the accused to the home State.[49] Naturally this obligation is reciprocal, and the host State must similarly undertake obligations: hence paragraph 18 of the UNEF Agreement included the undertaking by Egypt to "ensure the prosecution of persons subject to its criminal jurisdiction who are accused of acts in relation to the Force or its members which, if committed in relation to the Egyptian forces or its members, would have rendered them liable to prosecution." The absence of a similar clause from the Congo Agreement was only justifiable by reference to the judicial chaos in the Congo and should not normally be a feature of any United Nations Status of Forces Agreement.

Agreements relating to the status of United Nations Forces on leave have been concluded with Japan in 1954,[50] and, second, with the Lebanon in 1956 in relation to UNEF. The former (which replaced an earlier protocol dealing solely with criminal jurisdiction),[51] is clearly patterned on the NATO SOFA Agreement, being almost identical with it. In other words, members of the United Nations Force when on leave in Japan were subject to the *concurrent* jurisdiction of the service courts and local courts when they transgressed against both legal systems. Priorities of jurisdiction were established as in the NATO SOFA. It is significant that the agreement conceding the jurisdiction of the local courts was concluded by the United States—as the State providing the Unified Command of the Korean operation—a State which had previously been thought

---

[46] A/3943, Annex 1, para. 5.
[47] *Ibid.*, para. 7.
[48] Para. 18.
[49] *Ante*, p. 374; and see A/3943, para. 137.
[50] 214 U.N.T.S. 51.
[51] 207 U.N.T.S. 237.

to hold most firmly to the view that its forces were totally immune from local jurisdiction.[52]

It is accordingly surprising to find that the agreement with the Lebanon contains the following provision:

" A member of the Force shall be subject to the exclusive criminal jurisdiction of the competent authorities of the participating State to which he belongs. . . ." [53]

It is suggested that there is no justification, apart from the purely political justification that it is only upon this basis that States will provide contingents, for this grant of immunity except perhaps in the case of the Force Commander and other senior officials. They may perhaps be treated as equivalent to the Secretary-General and Assistant Secretaries-General who in terms of the General Convention are entitled to an immunity equivalent to diplomatic immunity, in respect of *all* acts.[54] These immunities apparently have been accorded not only for functional reasons but also on a representational basis. More recently, for instance, the Netherlands and Indonesian Governments in their agreements concerning what is now Irian Barat agreed to accord to the United Nations Administrator and Representative the full (*i.e.*, diplomatic) immunities which the Secretary-General enjoys under the General Convention.[55]

It is also important that the immunity from criminal jurisdiction should not be unjustifiably extended to non-military personnel unless this is considered to be functionally necessary, or in the case of senior officials (who might be said to be in the position of senior diplomats) to be required by virtue of their dignity and status. In fact, the two agreements with Egypt and the Congo recognise that immunity from criminal prosecution should not be indiscriminately extended. Article 24 of the 1957 agreement with Egypt recognised that members of the United Nations Secretariat remain entitled to the privileges and immunities accorded by Articles V and VII of the General Convention. In other words, they are immune from legal process in respect of all acts performed by them in their official capacity [56] but not, as this phrase has always been construed, from criminal liability.[57] After providing for immunity for members of the Force, Article 9 of the ONUC Agreement similarly accords to ONUC officials immunity from legal process in respect of official acts. In addition, they are immune from *any* form of arrest or detention

---

[52] See the statement by the Senate on ratifying the NATO SOFA that the criminal jurisdiction provisions in Article 7 do not constitute a precedent for future agreements: 199 U.N.T.S. 67, 68, n. 1.
[53] Exchange of letters constituting a Provisional Agreement between the United Nations and Lebanon concerning the UNEF Leave Centre in Lebanon, Beirut 20/29 April and 1 May 1957, 226 U.N.T.S. 125, para. 13.
[54] See, *e.g.*, the UNOGIL and Jordanian Agreements: 303 U.N.T.S. 271, 315 U.N.T.S. 125.
[55] S/5169, Article XXVI.
[56] Section 18 (a).
[57] Jenks, *op. cit.*, pp. 114–120.

and this, so far as it extends to protect an official from arrest for a crime, goes beyond the immunity accorded under the General Convention and, therefore, the UNEF Agreement. The question arises whether such exemptions are justified. Presumably in the Congo situation it was considered that the effective functioning of the civil part of the operation required such ample immunities. The grant of such an exception should always be carefully considered in the light of the necessities of the Force.

In summary the following suggestions are advanced:

(1) Members of a United Nations Force in the areas in which they are operating and their environs (which might properly, as in the case of the Congo, extend to the whole of the territory of the host State) may properly be accorded immunity from the criminal jurisdiction of the local courts.

(2) Such an immunity is only justified as a means of assuring the functional effectiveness of the Force and if it can be established that immunity is not so required it should not be accorded. In this connection there arises a matter which has not already been discussed. Privileges and immunities agreements relating to the United Nations or international organisations generally give the Secretary-General or other administrative head the right and the duty to waive the immunity when, in his opinion, the immunity would impede the course of justice and could be waived without prejudice to the interests of the organisation.[58] The question arises whether the Commander-in-Chief or national contingent Commander should not be entitled to waive the immunity of a member of a United Nations Force. Political pressures apart, he may even prefer to allow prosecution in the local courts in special cases. It might be felt that the alleged offender can be more properly dealt with by the local authorities; or there might be difficulties in securing witnesses or prosecuting a charge before a national court-martial; and it is understood that in the case of UNEF some participating States have wanted to request the local authorities to exercise jurisdiction. This has not been permitted: indeed it may be doubted whether under the agreements as drafted the immunity can be waived. Moreover, in the event that a United Nations Force becomes individually recruited (as it is hoped it will), there will be no participating State to exercise jurisdiction, so that a complete jurisdictional vacuum will arise. The member of the Force will, in most cases, have a nationality and a national State, but it is highly doubtful if such a State will or even can exercise a general criminal jurisdiction over one of its nationals who has enlisted in a United Nations Force. It will, therefore, at that stage in the development of a United Nations Force be absolutely crucial both to establish a United Nations Code of

---

[58] See, *e.g.*, the General Convention, Article V, section 20, also Article IV, section 14 and Article VI, section 23; see generally Jenks, *op. cit.*, pp. 118–119.

Military Law, a United Nations Courts-Martial and, *preferably*, a power in the Commander of the Force to waive his immunity (subject to guarantees of fair trial, etc.).

(3) It should be stressed that the members of the Force are to respect the local law and that the immunities from jurisdiction are in the interests of the United Nations and not of the individual members.

(4) Non-military members of the Force should be immune from criminal process only in respect of official acts. Some senior officials only may be equated to an Assistant Secretary-General and granted full diplomatic privileges and immunities. The local courts should accept as conclusive the certificate of the Commander of the Force that the acts are " official," [59] leaving disputes which raise a question of principle to be raised by the host State before the Arbitration Tribunal provided for the settlement of disputes relating to the interpretation or application of the agreement.

4. *Status, privileges and immunities of the Force*

At some point in any SOFA the status and privileges and immunities of the Force itself—as opposed to its individual members—should be established. In this regard the position will be governed (for those States which are bound by the two instruments) by Article 104 of the Charter and Articles I and II of the General Convention: the Force, as a subsidiary organ, will be entitled to the privileges and immunities of the United Nations.[60] Even where the host State is a party to the General Convention, however, it may be appropriate to spell out the obligations in the SOFA. In the first place it is obviously desirable to establish that the property of the participating States used in connection with the Force should receive the same treatment as the property of the Force itself.[61] This is, therefore, in paragraph 15 of the ONUC Agreement, made immune from every form of legal process, from search and requisition and from any other kind of governmental interference: such a provision is crucial. Secondly, to take one example, the UNEF and ONUC Agreements (paras. 23 and 16) show that the immunities from the payment of customs duties may well need to be specified in more detail if the Force is large and not temporary: imports for the Force's canteen for instance. This is particularly important in so far as provisions and supplies may belong to the participating States and not to the United Nations.

---

[59] The UNEF Agreement, para. 13 did not make it clear whether this was in fact so, and the ONUC Agreement omitted any reference to such certification; however, it is believed that in practice the Egyptian courts accepted the certificate as conclusive. This is a very considerable problem under the general body of treaty-law on SOFA: for a detailed discussion see Stambuk, *op. cit.*, pp. 85–92.

[60] *Ante*, p. 130.

[61] *Ante*, p. 131.

Where the State concerned is not a party to the General Convention it is even more desirable that the relevant provisions of that Convention should be imported into the SOFA (unless, of course, a bilateral agreement has already been concluded with the United Nations *generally* regulating the United Nations' status) [62] : the general provisions of Articles 104 and 105 of the Charter clearly require filling out. The details will always depend on all the circumstances, but the ideal would be to have a standard United Nations SOFA capable of immediate operation, but capable of being adapted or modified in the light of these circumstances.

(a) ZONE AREAS

If the Force is to operate effectively it will require areas and buildings for accommodation: the parallel with diplomatic missions is clearly apparent.[63] In the Agreement between the United Nations and Egypt, it was specified that the Egyptian Government should provide " such areas for headquarters, camps or other premises as may be necessary for the accommodation and the fulfilment of the functions of the Force." [64] Such of these properties as were Government owned have been provided free. More complex arrangements have been made in the case of privately owned land, according to whether or not the land was required for operational or other purposes connected with the comfort and convenience of the Force; where the land is required for operational purposes it is surveyed in conjunction with the local authorities and payment made by UNEF. The United Nations has, however, reserved its position *vis-à-vis* the Egyptian Government regarding a possible claim for reimbursement on the basis of its rights under the Agreement.[65]

Broadly similar arrangements have been made in the case of ONUC. Paragraph 24 of the Agreement between the United Nations and the Congo of 27 November 1961 states that the Government shall provide " such buildings or areas for headquarters, camps or other premises as may be necessary for the accommodation of the personnel and services of the United Nations and enable them to carry out their functions. Without prejudice to the fact that all such premises remain Congolese territory, they shall be inviolable and subject to the exclusive control and authority of the United Nations." [66]

Whilst not a great deal has been mentioned regarding the operation of this provision in the pertinent United Nations reports, the question of the former Belgian bases in the Congo has figured

[62] See 135 U.N.T.S. 305, 104 U.N.T.S. 323 for Japan and Korea.
[63] Compare Article 21 of the Vienna Convention on Diplomatic Relations, Cmnd. 1368.
[64] Paragraph 19 of the Secretary-General's letter, A/3526. *Off.Rec.G.A.*, Agenda item 66, 11th Sess., 1956–1957, Annexes.
[65] *Summary Study* etc., A/3943, para. 142.
[66] A/4986, S/5004, 27 November 1961.

prominently. The United Nations took over these bases when Belgian troops withdrew " as a provisional measure in the sense of Article 40 of the Charter, necessary under the mandate given to the Secretary-General for the achievement of the withdrawal of Belgian troops ' under speedy modalities determined by the Secretary-General '." [67] The bases were not, therefore, occupied for use as operational facilities in the usual sense of the term, although an air maintenance unit was later established at Kamina. A number of difficulties arose, however, regarding the future status of the bases and of the war *matériel* and stores they contained. The Congolese Government brought pressure on the United Nations authorities in an effort to obtain possession of the bases and the Belgian Government also sought to interfere with the stand taken by the United Nations. The position maintained by the United Nations was that its custodianship of the bases, and of the supplies there, was without prejudice to their future ownership or possession, but that it should itself continue to occupy the bases so long as this appeared necessary for the fulfilment of its mandate.[68] One further point relating to zone areas and bases should be noted. In the conditions prevalent in the Congo, and having regard to the mandate of ONUC, the United Nations occasionally granted asylum within those areas to persons likely to be physically harmed by unlawful violence [69] : that experience suggests that the United Nations should not forgo entirely the right to afford asylum in these areas.

(b) ARREST, INVESTIGATION, ETC.

Whatever international law may provide in relation to the immunity from criminal jurisdiction of members of visiting forces such members are, and are universally admitted to be, subject to arrest and detention by the authorities of the host State. This appears quite clearly, for instance, from the United States of America (Visiting Forces) Act, 1942, section 1 (2), which, while granting *exclusive* criminal jurisdiction to the United States authorities, expressly provided that nothing in the Act affected any powers of arrest, search, entry, or custody exercisable under English law. The same rule has also been recognised by the UNEF and ONUC Agreements (paras. 16 and 13) which provide that the Egyptian and Congolese authorities may take members of the Force into custody in order *immediately* to deliver them to the Force authorities (1) where requested and (2) where the members are apprehended

[67] Third Report of the Secretary-General on the implementation of various Security Council Resolutions, S/4475, para. 3; *Off.Rec.S.C.*, 15th yr., Suppl. July–September 1960.

[68] See Second Progress Report, A/4557, pp. 16–17; *Off.Rec.G.A.*, Agenda item 85, 15th Sess., 1960–1961, Annexes; A/4652, *ibid.*; S/4599, *Off.Rec.S.C.*, 15th yr., Suppl. October–December 1960; S/4651, *ibid.*, 16th yr., Suppl. January–March 1961; S/4779, *ibid.*, 16th yr., Suppl. April–June 1961 : and see generally *ante*, pp. 233–234.

[69] *Ante*, p. 188.

in flagrante delicto. Under the UNEF Agreement (para. 17) the Egyptian authorities may also make a preliminary interrogation. Under both agreements the *Force* authorities may arrest persons for the purpose of dealing with any offence or disturbance in the Forces' premises or at the request of the host State (paras. 15 and 13); and it is provided in the ONUC Agreement that the powers granted do not prejudice its authority to effect an arrest in order to assist in preserving order (para. 13),[70] although, again, such persons had to be delivered to the authorities to whom the individuals were responsible.

The Forces and the local authorities are also obliged to give all assistance in the carrying out of all necessary investigations into offences, and in the production of witnesses and of evidence. They are to notify one another of the disposition of charges in which they are interested (paras. 18 and 14).

All these stipulations, which are reflected in the most recent SOFA, should doubtless be retained (*mutatis mutandis*) in any future United Nations SOFA.

(c) CIVIL JURISDICTION

International law, as it is now reflected in treaty provisions, does not grant a general exemption to members of visiting forces from the civil jurisdiction of the local courts. The NATO SOFA, for instance, recognises that civil actions may be brought against them.[71]

This broadly corresponds to the privileges and immunities of international organisations generally, in that international officials and experts are entitled to immunity from legal process only in respect of words spoken or acts performed by them *in their official capacity*.[72] Procedures are usually established by the Force authorities and the host State in the case of visiting forces for the settlement of civil claims and in practice very few actions are brought, particularly in respect of official acts.[73] Similarly, the agreements

---

[70] It may be recalled that this formed a specific part of the mandate of ONUC: see *ante*, p. 187.

[71] See Articles VIII (5) (g) and (6) (d); and see *Wright v. Cantrell* (1943) 44 S.R. (N.S.W.) 45 where a unanimous Supreme Court of New South Wales held in relation to an action for defamation that members of visiting forces were not, as claimed, absolutely immune from every phase of the jurisdiction of the local courts. In particular the member was not immune from the local civil jurisdiction. However, in the NATO SOFA where the civil liability arises from the performance of his official duties no proceedings for enforcement of a judgment can be taken against the individual (Art. 5 (g)): claims of this kind are usually met with an offer of an *ex gratia* payment by the visiting force and this precludes any further civil action once accepted. Disputes as to the "official" nature of the act may be submitted to arbitration (Art. 6).

[72] See *e.g.*, General Convention, Article V, section 18 (a) and Article VI, section 22 (b) and the Interim Arrangement on Privileges and Immunities of the United Nations concluded with the Swiss Federal Council, 1 U.N.T.S. 163, Article V, section 15 (a) and Article VI, section 19 (b).

[73] See *e.g.*, the provisions of an agreement of 24 December 1958 concluded between New Zealand and the United States: N.Z.T.S. 1958, No. 2; 324 U.N.T.S. 111, which provides for the Office of the Solicitor-General to make recommendations as to settlement.

regulating the privileges and immunities of international organisations establish procedures or require the establishment of procedures for the settlement of disputes where the prospective defendant is entitled to immunity.[74]

In both classes of agreements the underlying approach is functional: indeed, as a matter of principle, how can the organisation or Force continue to operate efficiently whilst refusing the just claims of individuals affected by its action and the actions of its members? Accordingly, if immunity from suit is granted, other methods of satisfying the claims are required.

The UNEF and ONUC Agreements reflect the functional approach. Under the UNEF Agreement members of the Force are immune in respect of official acts (para. 12 (a)); but a procedure for the settlement of claims is set up (para. 38 (b)). In respect of other civil process, *i.e.*, where the liability is not in respect of an " official act," " the Egyptian courts and authorities shall grant members of the Force sufficient opportunity to safeguard their rights "; and if the Commander certifies that a member is unable because of official duties to protect his interests in civil proceedings the matter is to be suspended for a period up to ninety days (para. 12 (b)). The claimant, instead of proceeding in the ordinary courts, may apply to the Claims Commission established to deal with claims in respect of official acts (para. 12 (c)). No property required by a member for the fulfilment of his official duties can be made subject to seizure for the satisfaction of a judgment (para. 12 (b)).

The ONUC Agreement does not accord military members of the Force any civil immunity (it does provide that Secretariat officials are immune from legal process in respect of official acts (para. 9)). However, in respect of matters not covered by the criminal immunity of members of the Force or the immunity of United Nations officials for " official acts," the agreement established certain complex procedures of consultation, good offices and, in certain cases, arbitration *before* any legal proceedings can be taken (para. 10) and in practice these procedures have been substituted for the civil jurisdiction of the Congolese courts. It would seem that this procedure was drafted with the chaotic conditions of the Congo in mind, for in many areas the normal judicial system was simply not operating. Accordingly, the UNEF precedent is probably of more value as a precedent. However, it is particularly necessary to bear in mind the fact that different circumstances will, as these two operations show, call for different answers. So, in the case of Lebanon and Jordan the Observation Group and the Secretary-General's special representative respectively were entitled to full (*i.e.*, diplomatic) immunities from *all* legal process. This points to the desirability of having any standing United Nations Status of Forces Agreement capable of modification.

[74] See *e.g.*, General Convention, Article VIII, section 29 and UN/Swiss Agreement, Article VIII, section 26.

The circumstances will also have some effect on the settlement procedures which are established with the purpose of ensuring that the immunity from suit is not abused. In the case of Lebanon and Jordan, for instance, no claims settlement procedures were established in the relevant agreements: there, however, only a few persons were involved, the operations were likely to be of short duration (as, indeed, they were), the nature of the Group's functions would not bring the members into continual contact with the local populace, and the Group was unarmed, so therefore less capable of causing injury to the local populace. Where those factors are not present, settlement procedures are required and indeed this has been recognised. The UNEF Agreement provides for the establishment of a Claims Commission of three. One member is appointed by the Secretary-General, one by the Egyptian Government, and one by the Secretary-General and the Government jointly or, if they are unable to agree, by the President of the International Court of Justice (para. 38 (b)).[75] This Commission has jurisdiction to deal *inter alia* with claims (1) by an Egyptian citizen made in respect of official acts of members of the Force, and, in the claimant's discretion, non-official acts of members, and (2) by the Egyptian Government against a member of the Force.[76] The Agreement with the Congo has far more rudimentary settlement procedures, and these have been outlined in Chapter 6[77]: basically they differed from the UNEF Agreement in envisaging negotiation, followed if needs be by arbitration, for claims relating to "official acts," and the use of the United Nations' good offices, followed if needs be by arbitration, where the acts were unofficial.[78] Thus, the emphasis was placed on arbitration, which the Special Representative of the Secretary-General could arrange, although there was also a power to establish a Claims Commission if that proved necessary. It is likely that the normal precedent will be the UNEF precedent and not the ONUC precedent.

Clearly, some such Commission should always be established where there is a danger that immunities will lead to injustice and where there is no other appropriate method of settling disputes, and any United Nations Status of Forces Agreement must provide for this.

Two final matters as to settlement of claims should be mentioned. In certain circumstances the volume and amount of claims arising out of a particular form of activity by one party may be roughly equal to similar claims presented by the other party. If so, it is clearly desirable for the two parties to waive all such claims.[79] In fact, the Egyptian Government and the United Nations have concluded a limited agreement of this kind, which with admirable

[75] This formula is open to the criticism—in the light of the *Peace Treaties* case (Second Phase), *I.C.J. Reports*, 1950, 221—that it does not make clear whether a tribunal of only two can operate.
[76] For a full discussion of the settlement procedures in the UNEF Agreement see *ante*, pp. 149–151.
[77] *Ante*, pp. 242–244.   [78] Para. 11.
[79] *e.g.*, NATO SOFA, Article VIII (1), which goes further than this suggestion.

inventiveness is known as a " knock-for-knock " agreement, providing for the waiver of all claims in respect of damage caused by traffic accidents.[80]

In settling the appropriate quantum of damages the United Nations, or its Claims Commissions, will clearly need advice from a local, legally-qualified " assessor." A fractured leg may be worth far less in, say, Gaza, than in New York and any United Nations offer of settlement or award by a Claims Commission should be generous, certainly, but not too far removed from the figure a local court would award in a similar case.

(d) CLAIMS BY THE UNITED NATIONS

It is, of course, clear since the *Reparations for Injuries Case* [81] that the United Nations may prosecute international claims and it has in fact done so, although frequently without success since there have been no formal methods of securing a binding settlement.[82] The UNEF Agreement, as we have already seen, provided in paragraphs 38–40 for the establishment of arbitral tribunals and Claims Commissions which are also competent in respect of claims brought by the United Nations against the host State. The ONUC Agreement must be regarded as exceptional, for in that the only disputes for which a specific means of settlement was envisaged were disputes relating to the interpretation or application of the agreement itself (para. 46). We have earlier suggested [83] that there may have been exceptional reasons for this, and the UNEF Agreement would again seem the better precedent for a standing United Nations Status of Forces Agreement, but supplemented by a specific reference to the use of " knock-for-knock " agreements.

(e) USE OF ARMS AND UNIFORMS

The use to which arms may lawfully be put will depend on the nature of the Force's functions.[84] Prima facie, the host State must be deemed to have agreed to the carriage of arms and the wearing of military uniforms when it consents to the presence of a military force.

To quote Chief Justice Jordan of the New South Wales Supreme Court—

" . . . it is reasonably plain that the local sovereign, *quoad* the visiting force, must be deemed to waive . . . any laws prohibiting the carriage of arms or the wearing of uniforms other than its own." [85]

[80] 388 U.N.T.S. 143. This did not cover claims for death or personal injury, but only damage to vehicles. It also extended to damage to property owned or leased or requisitioned by either Party.
[81] *I.C.J. Reports*, 1949, p. 179.
[82] See Weissberg, *The International Status of the UN* (1961) pp. 182–189.
[83] *Ante*, p. 243. And see *ante*, pp. 242–248, for a general discussion of the position of claims by the United Nations.
[84] See Draper, "The Legal Limitations upon the Employment of Weapons by the United Nations Force in the Congo," (1963) 12 I.C.L.Q. 387.
[85] *Wright* v. *Cantrell* (1943) 44 S.R. (N.S.W.) 45; *Annual Digest* 1943–5, Case No. 37, p. 133.

Accordingly, the agreement relating to UNEF, a military Force with the right of self-defence, stipulates:

"Members of the Force may possess and carry arms while on duty in accordance with their orders. The Commander shall give sympathetic consideration to requests from the Egyptian authorities concerning this matter." (Para. 22.)

The ONUC Agreement, paragraph 39, stated that members of the Force "shall normally wear the uniform prescribed by the Supreme Commander but may wear civilian dress under conditions determined by him. Members of the Force while on duty shall be entitled to possess and carry arms in accordance with the regulations applicable to them." It is probably unwise for any United Nations Status of Forces Agreement to attempt to particularise in any greater detail. What sort of arms should be carried (or, indeed, what kinds of military equipment are needed) can only be determined in the light of the functions of the Force, and the Congo experience suggests that needs for heavier types of arms than originally envisaged may occur.[86] This matter is best left to negotiation between the United Nations and the host State, although, since control of the Force is exclusively with the United Nations, it will normally be for the United Nations to determine what arms are necessary.

(f) USE OF UNITED NATIONS FLAG

By Resolution 167(II) of 20 October 1947 the General Assembly authorised the Secretary-General to issue a Flag Code.[87] The Code issued on 11 September 1952 (this appears to be the most recent) authorised the use of the United Nations flag in relation to military operations only where permitted by the competent organ of the United Nations (Pt. 6). In at least the Lebanon and Jordan cases the Security Council and the General Assembly did not specifically authorise the use of the flag. Presumably in these cases, in view of the delegation to the Secretary-General of general authority to establish the Group, it was considered that he was a competent authority. Equally, so far as is known, there was no express authorisation by either organ in the case of UNEF and ONUC; at least the UNEF SOFA (which includes provisions for the use of the flag) was, however, "approved" by the General Assembly.

Any United Nations Status of Forces Agreement should certainly contain a recognition by the host State of the right of the Force to use the United Nations flag and markings, for without such use there is a constant risk of confusion and obstruction of the Force. The other aspect of this problem, however, is whether this should be the

---

[86] *Ante*, pp. 222, 228.
[87] In Kelsen's view this was illegal: see *Law of the United Nations* (1951) and Supplement (1951) pp. 194, 938–939. The present author disagrees with this view since it ignores the doctrine of implied powers which justified the Resolution.

449

only flag used by the Force, namely, should the use of national flags by national contingents be excluded? This is a matter more appropriately dealt with in the agreements with participating States and the Regulations for the Force. It may be recalled that the Regulations for both UNEF and ONUC prescribed that "other flags or pennants may be displayed only in exceptional cases and in accordance with conditions prescribed by the Commander." This is undoubtedly the right principle, both from the point of view of emphasising the international character of the Force and of avoiding confusion.

(g) LOCALLY RECRUITED PERSONNEL

The right of the United Nations to recruit local personnel and, indeed, the duty of the host State to assist in such recruitment need express recognition in any United Nations SOFA: from this point of view paragraphs 37 and 27 of the UNEF and ONUC Agreements, respectively, were right in principle.[88]

The further question which arises is whether such personnel are entitled to the privileges and immunities of the other members of the Force.

The UNEF Agreement provides that such personnel, unlike their fellow Force members recruited elsewhere than in Egypt, are entitled to immunity for official acts only (para. 24). That restrictive stipulation does not on its face apply to Egyptian nationals recruited outside Egypt.

The ONUC Agreement is not as clear as it might be on this question. It provides that the privileges and immunities set out in the agreement:

". . . shall not be extended to Congolese nationals or other local staff who were subject to Congolese jurisdiction at the time of their recruitment by the United Nations in the Congo. Locally recruited members . . . shall enjoy immunity from legal process in respect of acts performed by them in the course of their official duties . . ." (para. 28).

Reading the first sentence by itself it would seem that *all* nationals are deprived of privileges and immunities. The second sentence, however, indicates that only locally recruited nationals are so deprived (except in the case of official acts). It is suggested that the latter interpretation is to be preferred, and that, as in the case of the UNEF Agreement, *all* personnel recruited outside the host State should enjoy the same privileges and immunities. Locally recruited personnel, in accordance with the precedents, will be entitled to immunity from legal process for official acts only.

[88] Yet the ONUC Agreement was both deficient in not stating the *duty* of the host State to assist in recruitment and yet better in its express rejection of the right of the Congolese authorities to seek to influence local personnel in the performance of their duties.

(h) DEPENDANTS AND CIVILIANS EMPLOYED BY THE UNITED NATIONS

The position of officials has already been considered under the appropriate headings above: generally they are entitled to the privileges and immunities established in the General Convention although in all the agreements these have been increased to a greater or lesser degree. The extent of these modifications appears clearly to depend on all the circumstances: wider privileges and immunities were granted to officials attached to ONUC than to those attached to UNEF, a difference no doubt stemming from the greater degree of internal disorder prevalent in the Congo.

The position of dependants of members of the Force has, so far as is known, been expressly dealt with only in the ONUC Agreement.[89] It provides in paragraph 10 that certain procedures of good offices and arbitration are to be followed in the case of civil claims against dependants before the usual legal processes operate. Otherwise it would seem that dependants are subject to the local jurisdiction.

The extension of any privileges and immunities to dependants will in practice not constitute a problem for an operational Force, for dependants will rarely accompany such a Force: in so far as this is at all likely privileges will be justified only in very exceptional circumstances. The problem becomes much more acute in the agreements relating to bases for a permanent Force, and this is dealt with below.[90]

(i) CUSTOMS AND FISCAL ARRANGEMENTS

Here again the detail contained in the relevant agreements varies according to the size of the Force, the duration of its stay and the nature of its functions. The agreements with Lebanon and Jordan provide quite baldly for freedom of entry without delay or hindrance of property, equipment and spare parts. Only in the UNEF and ONUC Agreements are customs and fiscal matters dealt with in any detail. It is convenient to consider in turn the privileges of the Force, of its members and of Secretariat officials attached to the Force.

The Force as a subsidiary organ of the United Nations is entitled to the privileges of that organisation. Accordingly, as has already been seen, the UNEF Agreement provides that the Force is entitled to the privileges and immunities established by the General Convention. A similar provision was not, of course, appropriate in the case of the

---

[89] Save that the dependants of the Commander of UNEF would, it seems, be entitled under Article V, section 19 of the General Convention to full diplomatic immunity and dependants of officials to the immunities of Article V, section 18: see UNEF, paras. 24 and 25. In fact dependants were allowed with UNEF under an Administrative Instruction: they had roughly the same freedom of movement and a different colour identity card.

[90] *Post,* p. 462.

Republic of the Congo since it had not acceded to the General Convention nor had it declared that it was bound by it. Accordingly, in the ONUC Agreement some of the provisions of the General Convention are set out in detail: similar detail was not necessary in the case of UNEF. The same rules apply to the participating States (para. 23). Those privileges are elaborated in the UNEF and ONUC Agreements to include : —

(1) Exemption from all taxation except where it is in substance remuneration for public utilities [91];

(2) Exemption from customs duties and import restrictions. The agreements ensure that this exemption is not abused by restricting goods imported for service institutes to goods of a consumable nature and other customary small articles. These are not to be resold outside the Force [92];

(3) Exemptions from customs duties, restrictions and prohibitions in respect of United Nations publications [93];

(4) Exemption from sales and similar taxes in the case of important purchases.[94]

Those particular exemptions are by now well established in the relevant instruments and, apart from amplification or modification of detail, they would very likely be appropriate in any future SOFA.

Members of UNEF and ONUC have the following customs and fiscal privileges under the agreements :

(1) Exemption from all personal contributions, direct taxes and personal taxes on the pay received from their government or from the United Nations.[95] It does not seem to have been established as a matter of general State practice that members of a visiting force are exempt from the payment of taxes,[96] but since liability for income tax under municipal law almost invariably depends on domicile, residence, or source of the income and since members of visiting forces are seldom liable under municipal law to pay taxes (and will in any event probably be paying taxes to the sending State) in practice there is probably little difference. Moreover, in the case of salaries paid by the United Nations there are the further considerations that States should not benefit from international funds and that salaries of international civil servants are fixed on the basis that the income tax will not be payable [97];

---

[91] ONUC, para. 16 (a); for UNEF see para. 23 and General Convention, Article II, section 7 (a).

[92] UNEF, para. 23; ONUC, para. 16 (b).

[93] ONUC, para. 16 (c); for UNEF see para. 23 and General Convention, Article II, section 7 (c).

[94] ONUC, para. 17; for UNEF see para. 23 and General Convention, Article II, section 8.

[95] UNEF, para. 26; ONUC, para. 18 (a).

[96] *e.g.,* NATO SOFA, Article X (2).

[97] See an ILO memorandum quoted in Jenks, *op. cit.,* p. 122—although this principle has not yet been universally accepted.

(2) Exemption from other direct taxation except where these are municipal rates for services enjoyed [98];

(3) Exemption from customs duty on personal effects imported on taking up post.[99]

Secretariat officials under the UNEF Agreement are entitled to the privileges listed in the General Convention: exemption from payment of tax on United Nations pay and of import duty on personal effects on first arrival.[1] Again the ONUC Agreement is more generous: officials receive the fiscal privileges accorded to Force members.[2]

These rules, too, appear to be well established in practice and it is likely that they will appear in any future SOFA.

The fact that Egypt generally obtained more favourable terms is also underlined by the fact that the UNEF Agreement contains a term which is not to be found in the ONUC Agreement but which might nevertheless be reproduced in future agreements: it requires the Commander to render all assistance within his power to ensure the observance of the customs and fiscal rules of Egypt (para. 28). The ONUC agreement also specifically requires the United Nations funds to be kept free from local financial controls (para. 20).

(j) CURRENCY ARRANGEMENTS

For many transactions the Force will require local currency [3]; it will wish to make purchases; its members may want their pay in local currency; and finally they may want to take any accumulated pay with them when they leave. Accordingly, both the UNEF and ONUC Agreements require the governments to make available against reimbursement in U.S. dollars, Swiss francs or other acceptable currency local currency at the most favourable rate of exchange (paras. 35, 21), and permit members of the Forces to take accumulated salaries with them when they leave their posts (paras. 27, 23).

The details of such provisions will clearly depend on all the circumstances (the UNEF Agreement, for instance, provides for supplemental agreements) but the considerations mentioned in the first sentence will frequently be relevant, and should be provided for in outline in any United Nations SOFA.

(k) COMMUNICATIONS FACILITIES

If the Force is to function efficiently it must clearly have adequate communications facilities. Both the UNEF and ONUC Agreements

---

[98] UNEF, para. 26; ONUC, para. 18 (a).
[99] UNEF, para. 27; ONUC, para. 18 (b) is slightly wider.
[1] Para. 24 and see General Convention, Article V, section 18 (b) and (g).
[2] *Ante*, p. 238.
[3] It will probably be more convenient for the needs of participating States to be met via the UN, and not by direct transactions with the host State.

provide in some detail for: (1) the same treatment in relation to communications as that accorded to diplomatic missions; (2) prohibition of censorship; (3) use of code and cypher, and couriers who are entitled to appropriate privileges and immunities; (4) use of radio stations; and (5) generally the right of unrestricted communication.[4]

These provisions are clearly essential if the Force is to operate efficiently and should be retained in any future SOFA.

(l) INQUEST AND REMOVAL OF BODIES OF MEMBERS OF THE FORCE

There appears to be no doubt that the host State may hold an inquest into the death of a member of a visiting force, although some Commonwealth legislation during the Second World War provided that no coroner was to hold an inquest in relation to the death of a member of certain visiting forces unless so requested by the authorities of that force or directed by the local executive government respectively.[5]

Equally, however, the force authorities would be permitted by international law to hold their own inquests: this is a legitimate and necessary part of the internal administration of the force.

The UNEF and ONUC Agreements accordingly both provide that the Commander has the right to take charge of and dispose of the body of a member of the Force (paras. 42, 50). It should be noted that the ONUC Agreement does not apply to Secretariat members.

Both agreements empower the Commander to dispose of the deceased's property, but in the case of the UNEF Agreement only after paying any Egyptian debts (para. 42).[6]

(m) DURATION OF AGREEMENTS

The rationale of the stipulations in the SOFA is that the status, privileges and immunities are necessary for the effective functioning of the Force. So long therefore as the Force remains in the host State carrying out its functions there should be no question of withdrawing the privileges and immunities. In other words, the host State should not have any unilateral right of termination of the agreement.[7] There would appear to be no reason why the United Nations should wish to terminate the agreement and it is accordingly suggested that there should be no right to terminate and that the agreement should remain in force until the United Nations operation ceases. In fact both UNEF and ONUC Agreements state that they

---

[4] UNEF, paras. 29–31; ONUC, paras. 33–37 and note the provision in para. 42 of ONUC designed to secure freedom from interference at airports: on the need for this see *ante*, p. 203.

[5] See M'Gechan (1943) 19 N.Z.L.J. 82.

[6] This comparative deference to the Egyptian Government as compared with the Congolese Government is also discernible in, *e.g.*, paras. 26, 29 and 39 of the ONUC Agreement and the corresponding provisions of the UNEF Agreement.

[7] On the question of who determines the completion of the mission of the Force see *ante*, pp. 420–422.

remain in effect until the departure from Egypt and the Congo of the last elements of the Forces and their equipment (paras. 44, 49).

(n) MISCELLANEOUS

Certain miscellaneous provisions not mentioned above are included in the UNEF and ONUC Agreements:

(1) Rules of precedent and ranking of the United Nations Commander (ONUC, para. 19);

(2) Use of ports, roads and bridges, and water, electricity and other public utilities (UNEF, paras. 33, 34; ONUC, paras. 31, 38);

(3) Liaison between the Force and local authorities (UNEF, para. 41; ONUC, paras. 41, 43) [8];

(4) Supplementary agreements (UNEF, para. 43; ONUC, para. 45). It is believed that a considerable number of such supplementary agreements were made by UNEF, particularly with municipal authorities, covering a host of subject-matters.

III. TRANSIT AGREEMENTS

The success of the operations of United Nations Forces, and in some cases even the possibility of such operations, may well depend upon whether Member States are prepared to afford the necessary right of transit through their territory or rights of overflight through their territorial airspace. Every SOFA will, of course, contain provisions relating to access and transit by the Force, and these we have examined in the previous section. However, transit rights may well be needed from States other than the State in which the Force is operating, so that separate agreements to secure these rights have to be envisaged. It may be recalled that this question of the grant of " facilities, including rights of passage "—to use the phrase of Article 43—was one of those upon which the Military Staff Committee could reach no agreement.[9] The question of whether a general guarantee of a right of passage should be furnished in advance, or whether the exercise of any "right" should be left dependent on the consent of the State given only at the time it is needed, has remained a central issue in any approach to the matter made by the United Nations. The more the United Nations has moved away from the centralised system originally envisaged by the framers of the Charter, however, to the consensual approach inherent in the " Uniting for Peace " Resolution and in the way UNEF and ONUC were set up, the more difficult it has become to tackle the problem on a broad scale. Although the Collective Measures Committee established under the " Uniting for Peace " Resolution recommended that Member nations should arrange to provide rights of passage, as well as other assistance, no agreements were made to

---

[8] These are very much more detailed in the case of the ONUC Agreement. For comment on the need for this see *ante*, p. 239.

[9] *Ante*, p. 16.

enable such rights to be exercised immediately and without obtaining the consent of the State concerned on each occasion.

Turning to the *ad hoc* agreements which have been concluded, the Member States which provided contingents for the Unified Command in Korea entered into an agreement with Japan regarding the status of United Nations Forces there.[10]   The Agreement provided in Article IV that United Nations vessels and aircraft should be exempt from payment of tolls or landing charges in respect of agreed ports or airfields, and that they should have freedom of access to the areas where United Nations troops were stationed.   Article V of the Agreement provided that the United Nations Forces should have the use of "facilities" agreed upon by a Joint Board and might enjoy within those facilities all "necessary and appropriate" rights.   Detailed arrangements were made regarding the entry of troops, freedom of access, the use of military scrip, service institutes, and so forth.   In Article VI the Forces were granted the use of public utilities and services under the same conditions as agencies of the Japanese Government.   Two other States also offered to provide bases for the purposes of the United Nations operations in Korea: Costa Rica and Panama both declared their willingness to furnish bases, for use as training areas or otherwise, as the Security Council saw fit although neither offer was taken up.[11]

When UNEF was established, the General Assembly specially requested that all Member States should afford necessary assistance to the United Nations Command, "including arrangements for passage to and from the areas involved." [12]   In response to this appeal, the Italian Government provided transit facilities at Capodichino airport, near Naples, and later at Pisa, including labour for loading planes, storage space and necessary means of communication.[13]   These have been used chiefly as transit points for aircraft converging from North America and Scandinavia, *en route* for Gaza or the Congo, although stores have also been kept there awaiting transport.   In the case of UNEF, a further transit unit has been established at Beirut International Airport, Lebanon.   The Agreement between the United Nations and the Lebanese Government specifies the arrangements to be made regarding the entry of troops and the facilities to be provided at the Airport.[14]

---

[10] U.N.T.S., Vol. 214, No. 2899, p. 51.   [11] S/1645; S/1673.

[12] Resolution 1001 (ES–1), para. 10.

[13] A/3302/Add. 30, *Off.Rec.G.A.*, Agenda item 66, 11th Sess., 1956–1957, Annexes; Report of the Secretary-General, S/3694, *Off.Rec.G.A.*, Agenda item 65, 12th Sess., 1957, Annexes.

[14] U.N.T.S., Vol. 286. No. 4166, p. 189.   United Nations vehicles and aircraft, operating under distinctive identification marks, are exempt from Lebanese registration and licensing regulations.   Troops passing through Beirut are not subject to normal passport and visa control requirements.   Arrangements have also been made for UNEF supplies to be moved from one plane to another, without customs inspection, within the "free zone" area at the Airport.   Office and storage space and technical and maintenance facilities have also been provided by arrangement with the Lebanese Directorate of Civil Aviation.

Arrangements relating to the passage of troops to and from the Congo have for the most part proceeded smoothly. However, after the incident in which a United Arab Republic plane made an unauthorised flight, the Sudanese Government submitted a request to the Secretary-General that in future all flight clearances should be obtained through the United Nations and not by individual governments.[15] At a later stage the Government of Congo (Brazzaville) withdrew permission for flights or landings to be made over or in its territory, in protest against the action by ONUC forces in Katanga.[16] The United Nations, moreover, failed to receive any proper cooperation from the Belgian authorities in Ruanda-Urundi. The Acting Secretary-General found it necessary to draw the attention of the Belgian Government to the fact that: "These authorities have denied transit facilities to United Nations personnel engaged in humanitarian missions, and to United Nations troops being flown into the Congo to help in maintaining law and order for the benefit of Congolese and non-Congolese alike; moreover, they have on a number of occasions molested United Nations personnel and allowed United Nations property, including aircraft, to be damaged."[17] On the other hand, the Italian Government allowed use to be made of the transit facilities at Pisa which had already been placed at the disposal of UNEF. The Nigerian Government, for its part, has provided a staging point and depôt for food and other supplies at Kano, for planes *en route* for the Congo.[18]

In many ways the problems of securing the necessary arrangements with States for transit of a United Nations Force are simply the problems of consent by the host State, but on a smaller scale. In the case of ONUC the position of the United Nations under the Charter was a strong one, for, certainly when an operation was initiated by a *decision* of the Security Council, there was much to be said for the view that Members could, under Article 25, have been placed under an obligation comprising that of giving the necessary transit facilities: nor was the general obligation of Article 2 (5) irrelevant.[19] However, this question was virtually allowed to go by default and, from the time of the Military Staff Committee's deliberations in 1947 onwards, it has tended to be assumed that the grant of such facilities stems not from a pre-existing Charter obligation but only from an agreement under Article 43 or a specific *ad hoc* agreement.

There are thus two alternatives open for the future. The one, which will now be extremely difficult, is to reverse the practice to

[15] Annex, S/4674, *Off.Rec.S.C.*, 16th yr., Suppl. January–March 1961. This appears to have been the standard official procedure. S/4724, *ibid*.
[16] Cable dated 18 December 1961, S/5035, 19 December 1961.
[17] Reply of the Secretary-General dated 16 February 1962, S/5078, 16 February 1962.
[18] First Report of the Secretary-General on the implementation of Security Council Resolution S/4387 of 14 July 1960, paragraph 41, S/4389, *Off.Rec. S.C.*, 15th yr., Suppl. July–September 1960.
[19] This issue is discussed in greater detail *ante*, pp. 417–419.

date by insisting upon the Charter obligations as comprising a general guarantee of facilities. The other, which is the more likely to find acceptance, is for the United Nations to conclude specific agreements in advance with Member States whereby they undertake to provide certain facilities.

IV. BASES AGREEMENTS

In so far as a United Nations Force requires bases within the territory of the host State in which it is operating—operational bases—these will be covered by the Status of Forces Agreement which has already been discussed. The need for a different kind of base and, correspondingly, a different kind of agreement, has to be envisaged for the stage at which the United Nations possesses a permanent Force, whether by way of the attachment of national contingents for a fixed period of years or by means of individual recruitment or by a combination of both methods of raising a Force.[20] Such an agreement will require detailed negotiations with a host State and will far surpass any standing United Nations SOFA in the degree of complexity required in its provisions. These provisions will depend in part upon the geographical situation of the base and the nature of the facilities offered or required there, so that each base agreement will be to some extent *sui generis*: there will be no question of a "standard" agreement to be made immediately applicable as in the case of the United Nations SOFA.

This is not to deny that the fundamental principles required in such an agreement will not be identical for all such agreements: the exclusiveness of United Nations control, freedom of movement, etc., are obvious examples of such principles. Yet the elaboration of these principles will involve certain variations from agreement to agreement. There is, therefore, little point in attempting a comprehensive account of such base agreements in the abstract. What can usefully be attempted is a brief survey of the kind of problems which will have to be dealt with in any base agreement, and in doing this one is able to profit from existing experience with Headquarter Agreements between the United Nations and host States,[21] the Status of Forces Agreements concluded by the United Nations with host States (and reviewed in Section II above) and the now considerable body of treaty law containing agreements between States for the stationing of their forces on each other's territory in time of peace,

---

[20] *Ante*, pp. 334–336.

[21] For example, the UN/U.S.A. Headquarters Agreement (U.N.T.S., 11, p. 11; the UN/Switzerland (U.N.T.S., I, p. 163). A comprehensive collection of such agreements can be found in *Legislative Texts and Treaty Provisions concerning the Legal Status, Privileges and Immunities of International Organisations, UN Legislative Series*, ST/LEG/SER.B/10, Part Two, and ST/LEG/SER.B/11, Part Two.

in particular those agreements which provide for a geographically defined base.[22]

1. *Location of the base*

The location of a permanent United Nations base or bases is a matter for political rather than legal appraisal. The main considerations would be their strategical position, ease of access by sea and by air, the presence of facilities such as a port, air-landing strips,[23] and such other facilities as would make life tolerable for a Force and dependants stationed there for periods up to three years.[24] Moreover, the base area should ideally be large enough to accommodate training areas. To site the base in the territory of a Great Power would probably be unwise, even if a Great Power were prepared to agree. The better plan would be to seek a site in an area like Cyprus, Gaza, Libya, Zanzibar, Ceylon, Singapore, Malta or Aden—assuming that the territory in question will by that time be independent of any Great Power and is not already held as a base by a Great Power.[25] There might be an advantage in situating the base in Suez or Panama on the assumption that, whilst a " foreign " base is not acceptable to the territorial State, the presence of a United Nations Force would be (and would assist in guaranteeing the freedom of passage to all nations). There are, clearly, some " problem " areas in the world in which a " foreign " base is liable to meet with increasing hostility from the territorial State but in which a United Nations base might be acceptable as an alternative and, of course, as a continuing economic benefit to the " host " State. Moreover, the United Nations could take over a base already equipped as such.

2. *The nature of the rights to be acquired by the United Nations*

It has been argued that for such bases the international organisation should acquire sovereignty over the site, so as to make the organisation completely independent from any control by a " host " State.[26] This would no doubt be an ideal solution, long-term, but it is believed that it is not a suitable solution for any arrangement likely to be made in the near future. Setting aside the question whether the

---

[22] For example, U.K./U.S.A. Agreement of 2 September 1940 and 27 March 1941 (L.N.T.S., 203, p. 202 and 204, p. 14); U.S.A./Phillipines Agreement of 14 March 1947 (U.N.T.S., 43, p. 271); U.S.A./Libya Agreement of 9 September 1954 and 24 February 1955 (U.N.T.S., 224, p. 217 and 271, p. 431); U.S.A./Canada Agreement of 28 and 30 April 1952 (U.N.T.S., 235, p. 269 and 317, p. 36); U.K./U.S.A. Agreement of 19 July and 1 August 1950 (U.N.T.S., 88, p. 273); U.K./Malaya Agreement of 12 October 1957 (U.N.T.S., 285, p. 60); and U.K./Cyprus Agreement of 16 August 1960 (U.K. Treaty Series, No. 4 (1961), Cmnd. 1252).

[23] See the discussion by Lord Davies in *The Problem of the Twentieth Century* (1930) pp. 460–472.

[24] A desert area or other desolate place would involve not only an enormous expense in building the facilities but would be likely to have an adverse effect on the morale of a UN Force permanently stationed there.

[25] As is now the case with Cyprus, Aden, Malta, Singapore and Libya.

[26] Lord Davies, *op. cit.*, p. 462.

United Nations has power to acquire sovereignty over territory,[27] the simple fact is that the United Nations is not presently equipped to act as a territorial sovereign, and the problems of equipping the United Nations with the necessary powers and institutions would tend to hinder, in an unnecessary way, the acquisition of these bases. The exercise of complete sovereignty would demand an executive, a legislature and a judicial system of the same degree of sophistication as a national State: the members of the Force, their dependants and civilians attached to the Force simply could not live in a jurisdictional " vacuum." It may be far simpler to leave sovereignty with a " host " State, thus relying upon a complete and existing *lex situs*, with power to adapt, change and apply that law, and concentrate upon ensuring the exclusiveness of the United Nations' administration and control over the base area, by virtue of a long lease— ninety-nine years or perpetuity—granting exclusive possession to the United Nations. Whether this should be for payment will depend in part upon the economic situation of the host State, for such a base will in any event bring considerable economic benefit to the host State. This has so far been a successful solution to the problem of acquiring Headquarters for international organisations and, indeed, to the problem of acquiring *national* bases abroad[28]: there is no compelling reason why it should not be a solution for a United Nations base or bases.

A United Nations base would be best conceived as a defined, geographical area. A modern tendency, forcibly illustrated by the bilateral agreements concluded by the United States under the NATO system, is to conceive of the right to station troops as being a right to station them " at large " in the host State's territory: no defined base area is stipulated and, indeed, the sending State's forces will often use facilities in common with the forces of the receiving State.[29] This pattern, whilst appropriate to a system for collective self-defence, is totally inappropriate to a United Nations base in which the emphasis must be upon the exclusiveness of the United Nations' control and use of the base facilities and its independence from the host State.

3. *The kind of rights to be acquired by the United Nations*

The United Nations will require *exclusive control and authority* over the base area, subject to the provisions allowing for the continued

---

[27] It may be noted that, even in UNTEA, the UN assumed power of administration but not sovereignty (*ante*, p. 260). Nor would the UN in assuming the administration of a trust territory under Art. 81 of the Charter have become sovereign in this sense.

[28] The concept of the " sovereign base-area," as used in the recent U.K./ Cyprus Agreement of 16 August 1960 is now the exception rather than the rule.

[29] U.S./Libya Agreement of 7 September 1954; U.S./Japan Security Treaty of 8 September 1951 (U.S. Treaties, 3, p. 3329); U.S./Spain Defence Agreement of 26 September 1953 (*ibid.*, 4, p. 1895); U.S./Greece Agreement of 12 October 1953 (*ibid.*, 4, p. 2189); U.S./Portugal Agreement of 6 September 1951 (*ibid.*, 5, p. 2263).

application of the local law and the continued jurisdiction of its courts in the matters specifically reserved to the host State in the jurisdictional provisions.[30] It will require power to make regulations operative within the base area necessary for the efficient functioning of the base and of the United Nations Force stationed there, and local laws must be inapplicable to the extent of any inconsistency with such regulations.[31] The base area, the territorial waters of the coast of the base area and the superjacent airspace must be inviolable,[32] and the United Nations must have power to control the entry of all persons, goods, aircraft, vessels or vehicles entering the area. Moreover, the United Nations must itself possess full freedom of access to the area, possibly with rights of transit or overflight across the host State's territory where the geographical situation so demands.

The United Nations may need rights to utilise the public utilities (water supplies, gas, electricity, drainage, etc.) to the extent that the base area is not self-sufficient in these respects.[33] It will certainly need full freedom to establish its independent postal, radio, telecommunications and meteorological services.[34] It will need full freedom to establish or develop all necessary port facilities, landing strips or aerodromes, pipelines, buildings and other installations or facilities necessary for the Force and its personnel and dependants.[35] To this end it will need recognition of the legal personality of the United Nations for the purposes of the local law, including power to acquire land [36] and to contract. It will need recognition of its right to utilise local labour and contractors, either local or foreign, and the State will correspondingly be under duties to assist in the acquisition of lands or the recruitment of local labour.[37]

Rights to the use of the United Nations flag, to the use of arms and military equipment, to the use of specified training areas for manoeuvres and firing ranges,[38] and to the use of military uniforms

---

[30] See UN/U.S.A. Headquarters Agreement, s. 7.

[31] *Ibid.*, s. 8.

[32] *Ibid.*, s. 9. And see U.K./Cyprus Agreement, Annex B, Part II, ss. 2 and 8 (6) for a specification of measures which the U.K. may take to ensure inviolability.

[33] UN/U.S.A. Headquarters Agreement, s. 17.

[34] UN/U.S.A. Headquarters Agreement, s. 4; U.K./Cyprus Agreement, Annex B, Part II, s. 6.

[35] See U.K./Cyprus Agreement, Annex B, Part II, s. 6; U.S./Libya Agreement, Arts. IX, XV, and XVII.

[36] For the situation with UNEF and ONUC over the power to requisition both State-owned and private property see *ante*, pp. 150, 238. Compare the very detailed provisions in the U.K./Cyprus Agreement, Annex B, Part III or the less detailed provisions of the U.S./Libya Agreement, Art. VII. The U.K./Malayan Agreement, Annex IV has a curious, but possibly useful, provision to deal with the situation where a host State does not allow foreign governments to acquire title to land : this provision allows the representatives of service authorities to become " incorporated " under local law and then hold a registered lease for 30 years.

[37] See *ante*, pp. 127, 131, 238, on UNEF and ONUC. And see U.K./Cyprus Agreement, Annex B, Part II, s. 7.

[38] See Part IV of the U.K./Cyprus Agreement, Annex B, specially devoted to the problems of training areas.

and insignia will be required. Exemption from immigration, revenue, customs laws, registration formalities and all fees and charges, save such fees as represent charges for services rendered by the host State will be required, and on a more generous scale than in the UNEF or ONUC Agreements since the needs of a permanent base are greater and wider. The United Nations will need rights to acquire local currency, to issue service scrip. It will need the right to hold inquests, to establish courts-martial or other administrative and judicial bodies necessary to the Force—but, again, subject to the jurisdictional provisions. It will need the right to establish penitentiaries, cemeteries and schools.

It would probably be unwise to regard the base as an area completely isolated from the host State. Members of the Force and their dependants should be accorded rights of entry into the territory of the host State, subject to the wearing of mufti and the absence of arms,[39] and United Nations identification cards or vehicle registrations should be accepted by the host State.[40]

A provision guaranteeing the host State from any intervention in its own domestic affairs would be advisable.[41] And, finally, there would have to be provisions dealing with the possible abandonment of the base, either upon the expiration of the lease or otherwise, and covering such matters as the obligation, if any, to remove installations or the obligation of the host State to pay for "improvements" and title to property within the base area.

This is by no means an exhaustive list. It is intended merely as an indication of the kind of matters which may have to be dealt with and a survey of the many inter-State agreements will no doubt be indispensable before any actual base agreement is drafted, so as to indicate the detailed problems likely to be encountered and the various alternative ways of tackling them. From past experience it may be surmised that some of the most crucial problems will be jurisdictional, so that it is appropriate to give them special mention.

4. *The jurisdictional problems*

(a) CRIMINAL JURISDICTION

The need for complete immunity from the criminal jurisdiction of the host State, which has been regarded as compelling for an operational force, is not nearly so compelling for a United Nations Force stationed in a base pending deployment upon an actual operation. Indeed, such complete immunity is now never accorded under agreements between States and, whilst the fact that a United Nations Force must always be independent of the host State rather than "allied" to it suggests that a greater degree of immunity will be

---

[39] See U.S./Libya Agreement, Art. VII (5).
[40] As in UNEF and ONUC: *ante*, pp. 128, 238.
[41] See the rather general provision in the U.S./Icelandic Agreement of 1 July 1941, paras. 2 and 3 (A.J.I.L. Suppl. 1941, p. 194).

required by a United Nations Force, it is difficult to see the functional justification for such complete immunity. What follows, is, therefore, an attempt to suggest an appropriate distribution of jurisdictional competence.

(i) *Intra-base offences*

For offences committed by members of a United Nations Force or other persons officially attached to the Force—and excluding nationals of the host State recruited locally, members of the United Nations Secretariat and dependants of members of the Force—*within* the base area a *concurrent* jurisdiction might be recognised. However, the *primary* right to exercise jurisdiction should be vested in the United Nations and exercised either, in respect of national contingents, by national courts-martial or by United Nations Courts-Martial in respect of members recruited individually or such contingents as belonged to States accepting the jurisdiction of United Nations Courts-Martial.

The host State could be conceded the primary right to exercise jurisdiction in respect of offences against the security of the host State [42] or against nationals of the host State but not arising out of the official duties of the accused.

Members of the Secretariat not part of the civilian component of the Force itself could perhaps be left with no immunity except for that contained in the General Convention of 1946 for "official acts" —a concept which will rarely cover immunity from the criminal jurisdiction—and locally recruited civilians could be dealt with on the same basis. All other civilians within the base area not officially attached to the Force, including local residents, shopkeepers, etc., and dependants of members of the Force would not require, on the "functional" test, any immunity from the criminal jurisdiction.[43]

(ii) *Extra-base offences*

For offences committed by members of the Force or persons officially attached to it *outside* the base area the solution may be, again, to recognise a concurrent jurisdiction but with the United Nations retaining a *primary* right to exercise jurisdiction over offences committed in the course of official duty [44] and *inter se*

---

[42] This concept would need careful definition: see U.K./Cyprus Agreement, Annex C, s. 8 (2) (c) limiting this to treason, sabotage, espionage or violation of any law relating to official secrets, or secrets relating to national defence; and NATO SOFA, Art. VII (2) (c).

[43] The current trend in inter-State agreements is not to accord immunity to dependants: see the NATO SOFA, Art. VII (1) (b). The same is true of dependants of UN officials under the General Convention of 1946. Dependants would, of course, be covered by the exemption from immigration laws.

[44] Whilst a certificate as to the "official" nature of the act from the Force Commander ought to be regarded as conclusive for any court of the host State, the host State should itself be free to raise this as a dispute before a Joint Liasion Committee established by the UN and the host

offences (*i.e.*, offences solely against the property or the security of the United Nations or against the person or property of another member of the Force, civilian component or dependant). This is by now the general pattern for inter-State agreements dealing with forces " at large " in the receiving State.[45] In all other respects the host State will have the primary right to exercise jurisdiction.

The acceptance of the principle of concurrent jurisdiction, for both *intra* and *extra* base offences implies the necessity for arrangements for arrest of offenders, surrender of offenders, service of process and for protection against an accused being placed in " double jeopardy " (*i.e.*, the possibility of being tried under both jurisdictions for substantially the same offence).[46] It also implies the possibility of waiver of the primary right and, whilst waiver has so far been refused under United Nations SOFA,[47] there is no reason why the United Nations should not contemplate waiver in a bases agreement where this is not likely to affect the efficiency of the Force and would be consonant with the promotion of justice in a matter of particular importance to the host State. However, in the implementation of the inter-State SOFA, the frequency of waivers has often been such as to bring about a distribution of effective jurisdiction quite opposite to that suggested by the treaty provisions[48]; for a United Nations base agreement waiver should be regarded as exceptional rather than normal. Moreover, certain special problems arise in that, so long as the Force remains composed of national contingents, the United Nations Commander could not, without the consent of the participating State, waive any immunity. Experience also suggests the wisdom of specifying that waiver must be express, and should not arise by implication from the United Nations not notifying the host State of its intention to exercise its primary right; and that waiver by the host State should be taken to exclude the possibility of a private prosecution before the courts of the host State where, conversely, the host State waives its primary right.

Where, as is proposed, the United Nations has no jurisdiction over

State or before an arbitration tribunal. The NATO SOFA leaves this matter unclear in criminal matters, as do all the previous UN SOFA, but the U.K./Cyprus Agreement, Annex C, s. 9 (9) wisely provides for arbitration.
[45] This is true even in the Soviet bilateral SOFA which in general concede far greater jurisdiction to the host State: see U.S.S.R./Poland Agreement of 17 December 1956, Art. 9 (2) (U.N.T.S., 266, p. 194).
[46] See the NATO SOFA, Art. VII (8) and U.K./Cyprus Agreement, Annex C, s. 8 (8). On the difficult problem of how far a decision not to prosecute by the authority with the primary right opens up the possibility of prosecution by the authority with a secondary right, despite the double-jeopardy clause, see *Aitchison* v. *Whitly*, Tribunal correctionel de Corbeil, 5 April 1954 (noted in *Ann.Fr.D.I.*, 1 (1955), 579) and before the Cours d'appel de Paris, 16 May 1956 (*ibid.*, III (1957), 721) and reversed by the Cours de Cassation, Chambre criminelle in 1958 (*R.G.D.I.P.*, 63 (1959), 17–18). This problem is discussed at length in Stambuk, *op. cit.*, pp. 96–106.
[47] *Ante*, p. 133.
[48] Stambuk, *op. cit.*, Chap. IV.

local civilians or dependants of members of the Force there are two problems to be faced. First, there is the problem of ensuring that the United Nations, its property, personnel and the base generally are adequately protected against acts detrimental to their security. This can best be met by conferring on the United Nations powers of arrest over *all* persons within the base area, subject to its duty to hand over to the authorities of the host State such persons as are not within the United Nations' jurisdiction. The host State would, on its part, assume a duty to legislate and take such other measures as are necessary to ensure the security of the base and its personnel.[49] Secondly, there is the problem of ensuring that the exercise of jurisdiction by the host State, in particular over dependants (and also over Force members for extra-base offences or where an immunity is waived), shall be in a manner consistent with accepted standards of due process and fair trial. Many of the inter-State agreements contain provisions designed to ensure this which could afford a model for similar provisions in a United Nations base agreement.[50]

One final point needs special emphasis. The whole basis upon which the United Nations could accept the principle of concurrent jurisdiction would be that the Force was *not* an operational force, actually engaged in military operations: it is this which distinguishes the situation from that in which the standard United Nations SOFA, discussed above, would apply. Hence, in the event that the Force came under orders from the competent United Nations organs and had to be placed on an operational footing, ready for embarkation to the area of the world where it was needed, the entirety of the Force should from that moment be accorded complete immunity from the criminal jurisdiction. Indeed, this is precisely the basis upon which many of the inter-State SOFA operate,[51] and provisions to this effect should certainly be inserted in any United Nations base agreement.

(b) CIVIL JURISDICTION

It may be anticipated that the allocation of civil jurisdiction, and the procedures used for settling civil claims, likely to be adopted in a United Nations base agreement will be modelled closely on those

---

[49] For provisions of this kind see the UNEF Agreement, para. 18; U.K./Cyprus Agreement, Art. 2 and Annex B, Part II, ss. 2 and 3; U.K./U.S.A. Agreement of 21 July 1950 (U.N.T.S., 97, p. 194), Art. IV; U.S.A./Phillipines Agreement of 14 March 1947, Art. XV; U.K./Malayan Agreement, Art. 2; U.S.S.R./ Poland Agreement of 17 December 1956, Art. 10.

[50] NATO SOFA, Art. VII (9); U.S./Libya Agreement, Art. XX (5); U.K./Cyprus Agreement, Annex C, s. 8 (9) and note also, in the domain of substantive rather than procedural law, Article 5 whereby the Republic of Cyprus agrees to secure " to anyone within its jurisdiction human rights and fundamental freedoms comparable to those set out in Section I of the European Convention for the Protection of Human Rights and Fundamental Freedoms . . ." The Universal Declaration on Human Rights could perhaps be utilised in the same way.

[51] See NATO SOFA, Art. XV; U.S./U.K. Agreements of 27 March 1941, Art. IV (1) (a) (i).

already adopted in UNEF.[52] Claims between the United Nations (which should represent *all* contingents) and the host State should, failing an amicable settlement, be referred to arbitration. A general and reciprocal waiver—a " knock-for-knock" agreement—would certainly be advisable for damage caused to each other's motor-vehicles.[53]

Claims against members of the Force or its " official" civilian component, brought either by third parties or the host State and arising from the official duties of the defendant would best be dealt with by a Claims Commission, as in UNEF and ONUC.[54] It is the claims for " non-official" acts which pose the greater legal problems and, whilst in principle the jurisdiction of the local courts must be acknowledged, the practice followed in both UNEF and ONUC of offering the claimant the option of going before the same Claims Commission is likely to prove attractive on the basis that only acceptance of an offer of compensation made by the Commission excludes any further claim before the local courts. Similarly, for " non-official" contractual liabilities, the claimant could be put to his option. There are, of course, certain difficulties about relying on Claims Commissions for, as was noted in Chapter 6, dealing with the Congo operations,[55] it is by no means clear what substantive law such Commissions would apply. There is no reason to suppose that the civil law of the host State would be applied inevitably, and from many points of view a permanent United Nations Claims Commission would be desirable if only because it would enable the Commission to develop a body of law, based in part upon " general principles of law," rather in the way the Administrative Tribunals have done.

The United Nations would have to decide, as a matter of principle, whether it would for the sake of good relations stand behind a defendant member of the Force, even for non-official acts. There can be no guarantee, otherwise, that an award of damages will be satisfied, and whilst the assumption of financial responsibility by the United Nations is much more a matter of obligation where the acts

---

[52] *Ante*, pp. 149–151.
[53] See the UN/Egypt Agreement, 388 U.N.T.S. 143. It is doubtful whether this could be extended, in a base agreement, to damage to property leased, requisitioned or otherwise placed in the control of either party since the " balance" would be all on the side of the UN. It is equally doubtful whether this kind of general and reciprocal waiver could be extended to injury or death suffered by military personnel in the course of their official duties, as is often the case in inter-State agreements (see NATO SOFA, Art. VIII (4) and U.K./Cyprus Agreement, Annex C, s. 9 (4)). That arrangement is more appropriate to forces acting together than to an independent UN Force, although it might be useful as an arrangement between participating States with contingents in the base or on actual operations.
[54] Prior reference to the host State, as in some of the inter-State agreements, is a possible alternative. The U.K./Cyprus Agreement, Annex C, s. 9 (6) envisages such a reference, followed by an offer of compensation by the U.K. which, if not accepted, may be followed by arbitration.
[55] *Ante*, pp. 242–244.

are official,[56] it might be argued that the United Nations should assume a general responsibility to meet an award of compensation, leaving the United Nations or the participating State to endeavour to recoup the amount from the salary of the individual defendant.

There is no need to envisage any special immunity for Secretariat officials, who will be either part of the civilian component and therefore covered equally with members of the Force or else covered by the General Convention; nor should there be a need to grant immunity from the civil jurisdiction to dependants.

[56] Note the UNEF Agreement's protection of members from procedures for satisfaction in para. 12. Several inter-State agreements exclude execution or enforcement of a judgment in a matter arising from official duties: NATO SOFA, Art. VIII (6) and U.K./Cyprus Agreement, Annex C. s. 9 (5) (9)

14

Financing of United Nations Military Operations

I. SOURCES OF FUNDS

PRACTICE to date has made it clear that United Nations military operations may be financed from a variety of sources and that an appreciation of those sources is necessary to any understanding of the scope of certain problems such as apportionment and the meaning of the phrase in Article 17 (2) of the Charter " shall be borne by the Members " : these problems may relate to the *net* cost rather than the *total* cost of the operations. In practice the sources used have been the following.

1. *The participating States*

The practice with regard to the financing of the observer groups varied enormously, as did the composition of the groups. Certainly in those like UNSCOB [1] or the Group attached to the Committee of Good Offices in Indonesia,[2] where the observers were appointed by the Member States represented on the Committee and regarded as assistants to their representatives, the United Nations did not assume budgetary responsibility for the major expenses such as salaries, transport to the *locus in quo*, and equipment : the United Nations met the expense of local transportation, salaries of United Nations staff, salaries of local interpreters, etc. A *per diem* allowance, rather than the entire salary, was thought appropriate for such observers, so that the States from which they were drawn bore a good deal of the expense and might be compared with the " participating States " of the truly military operations like UNEF and ONUC. Transportation was often provided by Member States, free of charge.[3] The observer groups like UNTSO and UNOGIL were financed on a much more comprehensive basis. In these cases the government concerned continued to pay the salary and pension contributions required under national legislation, against appropriate reimbursement from the United Nations in respect of any extra costs involved. The United

---

[1] See Report of UNSCOB (A/574): *Off.Rec.G.A.*, 3rd Sess., Suppl. No. 8, para. 19.
[2] *Ante*, p. 62.
[3] *Ante*, p. 71, fn. 48. The UNCOK Group was dealt with on the same financial basis: see Resol. 293 (IV) adopted by the Assembly on 21 October 1949.

Nations itself, however, provided the facilities necessary to enable the observers to perform their task, and also paid a local allowance; in the event of injury or death, compensation was paid to the national authorities for transmission to those eligible under national law. Clearly the more the observers become United Nations officials, on a permanent basis, and less representatives of Member States, the greater will the financial burden on the United Nations be,[4] unless, as with UNTEA and the Yemen Group, there is a prior undertaking by the States affected to finance the entire operation.

In Korea the participating States bore the entire cost of the operations, so that there was never any item on the budget of the Organisation devoted to the cost of the military operations.[5] The reason for this was perhaps more a political reason than a legal one, for, if it is to be argued that this arrangement followed from the fact that the participating States acted voluntarily on the basis of a mere recommendation of the Security Council, this was no less true of UNEF—where States acted on the basis of a recommendation of the Assembly—in which a totally different arrangement was adopted.

In UNEF the costs borne by the participating States represented but a part of the total costs: the actual division of costs has been fully described above in Chapter 4.[6] The practice with ONUC seems to have been based on the UNEF arrangement[7] and, where States voluntarily participate in a peace-keeping operation, this arrangement seems to be a likely precedent for the future. However, there are obvious advantages in setting out the precise terms of this arrangement so that States know, from the outset, the extent of their own financial liabilities. In the formulation of Stand-by Agreements for the future this should be an essential part.

Whether this same arrangement is suitable for operations which assume the character of enforcement action is less clear. The deliberations of the Military Staff Committee were singularly silent on questions of finance[8] and, particularly where a State engages in

---

[4] As in the case of Field Service personnel. In this instance the United Nations has assumed the full cost of training and equipping the persons concerned, whose position differs from that of other United Nations staff members only in respect of the different functions performed.

[5] *Ante*, p. 57.

[6] *Ante*, pp. 139–148.

[7] Secretary-General's Note of 21 January 1963 on the Budgetary and Financial Practices of the UN, A/A.C.113/1, paras. 258–263.

[8] *Ante*, p. 13. The proposals put forward by the Military Staff Committee were based, however, on the idea that self-contained units, together with the necessary supplies, should be provided by Member States, and to that extent therefore it may be argued that it was anticipated that each State would meet its own costs. Whilst this may be the correct assumption as regards any period when units made available were to be kept within home boundaries, as a kind of "latent" force, it is more difficult to suggest that this should have been the rule when units were employed elsewhere in the course of operations on behalf of the United Nations. This distinction between the maintenance of troops and their actual utilisation appears to have been that also adopted by the Collective Measures

such operations as a matter of legal obligation rather than option, there is much to be said for flexibility in determining which costs a particular participating State shall bear. Articles 49 and 50 of the Charter are little more than a recognition of the problem and of the right of a Member State to consult with the Security Council. The most that Committee III/3 at San Francisco could say was that the Organisation should in the future seek to promote a system aiming at the "fairest possible distribution" of expenses incurred as a result of enforcement action.[9] Ideally, this is a matter to be regulated in the Article 43 agreements, and no uniformity is necessarily to be expected. All that can be expected is that, when a binding legal commitment is entered into by a State, towards the Security Council or even the General Assembly, the State should have, in the terms of the agreement, a clear indication of what costs it will be expected to incur directly [10] as a participating State.

The demand for clarity on this question of responsibility for certain costs is appropriate both in an *ad hoc* Force and in a permanent Force based on national contingents provided for a fixed period of time. It only ceases to be appropriate when one envisages a Force raised by direct, individual recruitment, and one advantage of such a system is that it obviates the need for a complicated arrangement, and accounting, as between the United Nations and participating States. However, it is equally clear that, in so far as direct recruitment places the entire cost into the category of "collective" financial responsibilities, the cost will be so much higher.

A distinct issue which deserves notice concerns the local currency needs of the various units. Since it was anticipated that national governments might experience exchange difficulties in providing local currency, the Secretary-General suggested when UNEF was established that the United Nations should make local currency available, against reimbursement in Members' own currencies, at a rate of exchange determined by the Secretary-General in consultation with the government concerned.[11] This suggestion was approved by the

Committee in their proposals relating to the setting up of a body of United Nations volunteers. In its second report the Collective Measures Committee suggested that co-operating States should themselves meet the costs of recruiting, equipping and training the United Nations volunteer reservists, as part of their overall contribution to collective security: *Off.Rec.G.A.*, 7th Sess., 1952, Suppl. No. 17, pp. 12–13.

[9] UNCIO, Documents, Vol. XII, p. 513.

[10] The term "directly" is used as signifying a liability for costs as and when they arise, to be met by the participating State on its own responsibility: there may yet be a further liability on that State as part of its "collective" responsibility, together with all other Members, for the net cost, although in apportioning a share to a participating State the fact that it has borne certain direct costs may serve to reduce the quota required of it.

[11] Report of the Secretary-General on administrative and financial arrangements for the United Nations Emergency Force, A/3383, *Off.Rec.G.A.*, Agenda item 66, 11th Sess., 1956–1957, Annexes.

Advisory Committee on Administrative and Budgetary Questions [12] and by the Fifth Committee.[13] In the exchange of letters with the Egyptian Government relating to the Status of the Force express provision was made for the furnishing of local currency by the Egyptian Government.[14] The Congolese Government agreed to a similar arrangement.[15]

2. *Other Member States by way of voluntary contributions*

The examples of UNTEA [16] and the Observer Group in the Yemen [17] show that in certain cases the *total* cost of the United Nations operations may be borne by States directly interested or involved in the situation giving rise to those operations. This assumption of financial responsibility was voluntary, certainly, but it may be surmised that, without it, the United Nations may not have been prepared to initiate the operations. It is likely, therefore, that certain kinds of United Nations military operations will only be undertaken on this basis, although it is certainly unwise to attempt a definition of the category of operations to which this principle will apply. Given adequate financial resources of its own, in principle the United Nations ought never to make its efforts to deal with a threat to international peace and security conditional upon certain States assuming the obligation to pay the costs—although it might thereafter choose to penalise those States responsible for the situation by way of a heavy apportionment.[18]

In the majority of cases, however, the cost of operations has been reduced rather than totally covered by voluntary contributions of various kinds from States not "participating" in the sense described above in section 1. To the extent that these contributions have taken the form of providing transport and other supplies,[19] these States may be regarded as "contributing" States rather than "participating" States: the distinction has an importance if only because the rule of exclusion of Permanent Members has been confined in its application to "participating" States.

When these services and supplies are provided free of charge they are, in effect, indistinguishable from the other form of voluntary

---

[12] 22nd Report of the Advisory Committee on Administrative and Budgetary Questions, A/3402, *ibid.*
[13] Report of the Fifth Committee, A/3560, *ibid.*
[14] Paragraph 35 of the Secretary-General's letter, A/3526, *ibid.*
[15] Paragraph 21 of the Agreement between the United Nations and the Republic of the Congo relating to the Legal Status, Facilities, Privileges and Immunities of the United Nations Organisation in the Congo, A/4986, S/5004, 27 November 1961.
[16] *Ante*, p. 260.
[17] *Ante*, p. 85.
[18] *Post*, p. 476.
[19] *Ante*, pp. 394–399. Note that Switzerland, a non-Member, provided contributions in this way (*ante*, p. 137), but did so indirectly, so as to avoid being regarded as a "contributing" State.

contribution—the gift of money. It is this other source, the voluntary gift of money, which has also helped to reduce the total cost to a net cost, although, as we have seen in relation to both UNEF and ONUC, the practice has developed of applying the voluntary contributions of money so as to reduce the assessments of the less developed Member States *after* the apportionment stage rather than prior to it.

An important step towards recognising the importance of these voluntary contributions has been taken recently, both in the Assembly's Resolution of 27 June 1963 which affirmed that:

" without prejudice to the principle of collective responsibility, every effort should be made to encourage voluntary contributions from Member States;" [20]

and more particularly in the Resolution of 1 July 1963 on the " Establishment of a Peace Fund." [21]   Under this Resolution the Assembly:

" *Desiring* to make sufficient funds available to the Secretary-General, thus enabling him to discharge, without undue delay, his responsibilities under the Charter in cases of breaches of the peace,
Convinced that the establishment of a peace fund through voluntary contributions from Member States as well as organisations and individuals is worthy of study as a means of furthering this objective
1. *Requests* the Secretary-General to consult all Member States and other interested organisations on the desirability and feasibility of establishing such a peace fund;
2. *Further requests* the Secretary-General to report to the General Assembly at its eighteenth session."

Certainly the availability of a fund established in advance of a particular military operation would be a distinct improvement on the rather frantic, *ad hoc*, attempts to raise large sums of money outside the regular budget which have occurred in UNEF and ONUC. The prospect of enlisting the financial support of individuals and private institutions is a matter which is best left for more detailed examination later in this section.

Where supplies, services or transport are *not* supplied free of charge, these have, of course, no effect on the reduction of the total cost to a net cost. The Charter scheme had envisaged, in Articles 48 and 49, the possibility that this kind of ancillary support might be pledged by way of obligation, either in addition to or in substitution for an obligation to provide armed forces.[22]   In the practice of the United Nations so far, however, no such obligations have been assumed, so that it has been permissible for a State to make its offer of such assistance conditional on payment. There is, however, a certain contradiction in the position which assumes that a participating State must assume certain items of the cost but that a contributing State must not, and this will only be resolved when a

[20] Resol. 1874 (S–IV).
[21] Resol. 1879 (S–IV).
[22] See *ante*, p. 14, on the discussion of this problem in the Military Staff Committee.

comprehensive body of agreements, covering both forms of assistance, is concluded. In the meantime one can only assert two propositions, namely, that no State has a *right* to discharge any part of its collective responsibility for the cost of United Nations military operations by way of the provision of ancillary services but that, so long as these are accepted by the United Nations on a payment basis, a State will have the right to set off its charges against assessments made upon it in respect of the same military operation.[23]

Voluntary contributions of a different kind can be secured by way of loans. Here the effect is not so much to reduce the cost, but to allow the Organisation to spread the cost over a number of years so as to relieve the Organisation from excessive financial burdens at a particular time. An interest-free loan does this and no more: an interest-bearing loan will in fact add to the total cost.[24] There is, of course, nothing novel in an international organisation resorting to a loan.[25] It afforded an obvious, although partial, solution to the problems of financing UNEF and ONUC, and on 20 December 1961 (when the Organisation faced deficits of $59 million and $33 million on ONUC and UNEF respectively) the Assembly by Resolution authorised the sale of $200 million worth of United Nations Bonds for a twenty-five-year period bearing an interest of 2 per cent. per annum.[26] The Secretary-General was authorised to sell these bonds to governments, national banks and approved " non-profit institutions or associations," and repayment of the loan was to be undertaken as part of the annual United Nations Budget. This development was significant not only as an illustration of the potentialities of the loan, but also for the fact that it broke through the principle (which some tend to assume exists) that the United Nations must be financed exclusively by States.

3. All Member States as part of a " collective " responsibility

The Opinion of the International Court of Justice in the *Expenses Case*[27] made clear that the Assembly was entitled to regard as a collective responsibility on the entirety of the membership of the United Nations the expenses of military operations undertaken in pursuance of the principles and purposes of the Charter, and whether undertaken by virtue of a decision or recommendation of either the

---

[23] Such a system presupposes an arrangement whereby these charges are verified and accepted as accurate by the Organisation.

[24] It may be noted that the U.S.S.R. has refused to pay that part of its assessment for the regular budget which represents the interest and capital repayment on the loans raised by the issue of bonds to finance UNEF and ONUC operations: *UN Review*, June 1963, No. 10, p. 6.

[25] For a detailed survey of past practice see Salmon, *Le rôle des organisations internationales en matière de prêts et d'emprunts* (1958).

[26] Resol. 1739 (XVI). The sale of these bonds was authorised by Resol. 1878 (S–IV) of 1 July 1963 to continue until 31 December 1963.

[27] *I.C.J. Reports*, 1962, p. 152; see *ante*, pp. 148, 251–252, 288–290.

Security Council or the General Assembly: this opinion was accepted by the Assembly on 19 December 1962.[28]

The crucial problems have since become those with which the Court did not deal, namely, the problems of apportionment and of the meaning and effect of the phrase in Article 17 (2) " shall be borne by the Members."

(a) APPORTIONMENT

The earlier practice, as we have seen in relation to both UNEF and ONUC,[29] was to adopt the scale of assessments used for the regular budget of the United Nations. In both cases, however, a deviation from this practice occurred in the form of an application of voluntary contributions to relieve the burden on the economically weaker Member States.

The history of the attempt to find a suitable formula—or criteria —by which to apportion the expenses of peace-keeping operations is already a long one,[30] and agreement on this has not yet been reached. However, the Assembly has now been able to adopt " General Principles to serve as Guidelines for the sharing of the costs of future peace-keeping operations involving heavy expenditures" in Resolution 1874(S–IV) of 27 June 1963. This is believed to be a statement of principles important enough to merit citation in full:

" *The General Assembly,*

Noting with appreciation the report of the Working Group on the Examination of the Administrative and Budgetary Procedures of the United Nations,* submitted pursuant to General Assembly Resolution 1854 B (XVII) of 19 December 1962,

Recognising the necessity of sharing equitably the financial burden of peace-keeping operations to the extent not otherwise covered by agreed arrangements,

1. *Affirms* that the following principles, *inter alia*, shall serve as guidelines for the equitable sharing, by assessed or voluntary contributions or a com-

*A/5407 and Corr. 1.

---

[28] Resol. 1854 (XVII). But note that in the Report of the Working Group on Financing of Peace-keeping Operations (A/5407), 29 March 1963, at p. 5, Bulgaria, Mongolia and the U.S.S.R. declared this opinion "incorrect" and suggested that it " does not and cannot create any obligation of any kind for States. Nor does General Assembly Resolution 1854 (XVII) . . . in any way affect the substance of the question."

[29] *Ante*, pp. 144–148, 252–254.

[30] See A/4716 and Add. 1 and 2 (the replies of 50 States to the Secretary-General's inquiries in 1959); A/4971, the Report of the Working Group of 15, 15 November 1961, especially Section F; A/5062, the Report of the Fifth Committee; A/5407, the Report of the Working Group of 21, 29 March 1963; A/5438, the Report of the Fifth Committee. The latest General Assembly Resolution on the financing of ONUC, passed on 18 October 1963, virtually repeats the formula used in the Resolution of 27 June 1963: of the $18·2 million authorised, the Congo is to provide $3·2m., the sum of $3m. is to be apportioned on the regular scale, and for the remaining $12m. the " economically less developed " States are to have their assessments reduced by 45 per cent. The Resolution on UNEF in December 1963 similarly makes no substantial change, and of the $17m., $2m. is apportioned on the regular scale and the rest with a reduction of 42·5 per cent. for the " economically less developed." See *UN London News Summaries*, Releases 37/63 and 45/63.

bination thereof, of the costs of peace-keeping operations involving heavy expenditures that may be initiated in the future :

(*a*) The financing of such operations is the collective responsibility of all Member States of the United Nations;

(*b*) Whereas the economically more developed countries are in a position to make relatively larger contributions, the economically less developed countries have a relatively limited capacity to contribute toward peace-keeping operations involving heavy expenditures;

(*c*) Without prejudice to the principle of collective responsibility, every effort should be made to encourage voluntary contributions from Member States;

(*d*) The special responsibilities of the Permanent Members of the Security Council for the maintenance of peace and security should be borne in mind in connection with their contributions to the financing of peace and security operations;

(*e*) Where circumstances warrant, the General Assembly should give special consideration to the situation of any Member States which are victims of, and those which are otherwise involved in, the events or actions leading to a peace-keeping operation;

2. *Considers* that suitable administrative procedures should be established to ensure that provision for the financing of a peace-keeping operation is made by the General Assembly at the time the operation is authorised.

3. *Requests* the Secretary-General to review in consultation with the Advisory Committee on Administrative and Budgetary Questions, as appropriate, suitable administrative procedures designed to improve the financial procedures to be followed by the General Assembly at the time peace-keeping operations are authorised, and to report to the General Assembly at its eighteenth session on the results of this review and any recommendations he may wish to make regarding procedures to be followed in the future."

This Resolution does no more than mark a general acceptance by the Assembly of the possibility that various criteria might be applied, and of certain special criteria as being, in principle, valid for future operations. The only one so far applied has been that in favour of the economically less developed countries,[31] but the others deserve certain comment.

"The special responsibilities of the Permanent Members of the Security Council" were stressed in the Working Groups [32] and, as may be expected, by the smaller States which, with a certain justification, look to the Permanent Members to make up in financial support for the absence of a military participation in peace-keeping operations.

"Member States which are victims of, and those which are otherwise involved in, the events or actions leading to a peace-keeping operation" is a phrase which in fact includes several criteria.

[31] The Report of the Working Group of 15 (A/4791, para. 35 (e)) indicated that several States felt that a Member's capacity to pay could be deducted from factors such as gross national income, *per capita* income, balance of payments position, and economic and social development needs. In the Report of the Working Group of 21 (A/5407), Canada, at page 6, expressed the view that the regular scale of assessment already took sufficient account of capacity to pay and sufficed for normal operations: only in expenses of over $10m. per annum should a special scale of assessments based upon capacity to pay be adopted, based on national income.

[32] *Ibid.*, A/4971, section F and A/5407, p. 11.

It may, on the one hand, suggest that a "victim" State is to be accorded a lenient assessment [33] or, on the other, it may be thought to reflect the view that States benefiting from the operations should make a proportionally higher contribution: such a view was occasionally advanced over UNEF, when in fact both Egypt and Israel could be regarded as beneficiaries in this sense and, indeed, under the General Assembly's Resolution of 18 October 1963, the Congo is paying $3 million towards the cost of ONUC. However, some of the Working Group of 15 had suggested a different test of benefit directed at States with investments in the area—and benefit being measured in proportion to the value of these investments.[34] The other part of the phrase—"otherwise involved in"—is equally obscure, for that, too, may refer either to States which are participating States, and hence might merit relief on the ground that they are providing troops, or to an "aggressor" State which is regarded as being responsible for the situation and ought therefore to be penalised [35]: the special calls on Belgium were a reflection of this attitude over ONUC financing. Even apart from these ambiguities, it is clear that in any future situation the problems of placing particular States in any one or more of these categories and of determining what assessment shall in fact be made upon the basis of these criteria will remain for an *ad hoc* decision.

It may be noted, finally, that apart from paragraph 2 of the Resolution, which is aimed at ensuring that authorisation of the operation and provision for financing should go hand-in-hand, the Resolution does nothing to fix a ceiling for expenditures on peace-keeping. Some of the States represented in the Working Groups had argued for a predetermined level of expenses in any one year for each operation, which might be apportioned on the regular scale, with expenses above that requiring a special scale, and with extraordinarily high expenses requiring authorisation by the Assembly and special *ad hoc* financial arrangements.[36] Clearly, some Members felt that the situation in which the Security Council might authorise the operation, but the Assembly had to find the money, was an inherently difficult one. A somewhat different concern was expressed by the United Kingdom in proposing that, at a "third stage" of very heavy financial cost, "those relatively few Member States on whom most of the costs would fall could justly expect a

---

[33] A/5407, p. 11 gives the view of 7 States as "including the possibility of total exemption."

[34] A/4971, Section F.

[35] This has been very much the view of the Soviet *bloc*, over both UNEF and ONUC: see the statements by the representatives of the U.S.S.R. in A/C.5/SR.961, pp. 13, 14 and Czechoslovakia in A/C.5/SR.965, p. 14: also A/4971, Section F.; A/5407, p. 5.

[36] A/5407, pp. 7–8 where Canada fixed the limits of the three "stages" at $10m., $10–$75m., $75m. upwards (or more than $125m. for the annual total for peace-keeping operations); and at pp. 14–15 where the U.K. similarly envisaged three stages of expenditures.

greater say in the methods of financing to be adopted." [37]   Hence the concern of the United Kingdom was rather the reverse, namely, that the concurrence of the Permanent Members should be required if expenditures authorised by the Assembly were to rise above a limited ceiling.

(b) EFFECT OF APPORTIONMENT

The general practice in international organisations has been to regard the apportionment of the budgetary expenses amongst the members as creating a legal obligation on the members to pay the assessment.[38]   The position is, of course, different where a particular activity is intended to be financed as a matter of voluntary contribution,[39] but no such intention was evident in the UNEF and ONUC operations where, as we have seen, the Assembly regarded the expenses as being subject to apportionment under Article 17 (2) of the Charter and, basically, on the same scale of assessments as applied to the regular budget.

The International Court of Justice did not directly deal with the effect of apportionment, but the Court did say that "the exercise of the power of apportionment creates the *obligation* . . . of each Member to bear that part of the expenses." [40]   Moreover, it instances the decisions under Article 17 as examples of decisions of the Assembly which have "dispositive force and effect" [41] and referred to its previous opinion [42] to the effect that, once obligations are incurred towards third parties by the Secretary-General on behalf of the Security Council or the Assembly, the Assembly "has no alternative but to honour these engagements." [43]   The Assembly itself seems to have taken this position, certainly in Resolution 1590(XV) of 20 December 1960 where the assessments for the *ad hoc* Congo account were stated to create "binding legal obligations."

Sir Gerald Fitzmaurice, in his separate opinion, dealt at some length with this question, for he took the view that the Court must also deal with this problem of what legal obligations rest upon the Members [44]; and he regarded it as unwise for the Court to assume

---

[37] *Ibid.*, p. 14. The U.K. scheme was that a special Committee could recommend compulsory assessment at this third stage only with the concurring votes of the five Permanent Members: if this concurrence did not exist the special Committee would only be able to recommend expenditure to a limited extent.

[38] See Bowett, *The Law of International Institutions* (1963), pp. 339–340; Chaumont, "La Force d'Urgence des Nations Unies," *Ann.Fr. de D.I.* (1958), pp. 417–420.

[39] As, for example, the programmes of UNICEF, UNRWA and UNKRA: some are part financed in this way, as in the Expanded Programme of Technical Assistance.

[40] *I.C.J. Reports*, 1962, p. 164 (italics added).

[41] *Ibid.*, p. 163.

[42] *Effect of Awards of the UN Administrative Tribunal, I.C.J. Reports*, 1954, p. 59.

[43] *Ibid.*, 1962, p. 170.

[44] *Ibid.*, p. 198.

(as he felt they had) that the *obligation* to pay followed automatically from the determination by the Assembly that expenses were expenses of the Organisation. He regarded the legal obligation as arising from the decision to take a given course of action, and not from the Assembly's apportionment of a Member's share of the expenses.[45] The difficulty was that, whereas this legal obligation rested firmly on Article 25 of the Charter whenever action was taken pursuant to a *decision* of the Security Council, the matter was less obvious in the case of action taken pursuant to a *recommendation* of the Assembly or of the Council. However, Sir Gerald regarded even this latter type of action as creating a legal obligation to meet the expense for *all* Members, for this was the essence of the system of majority voting which had been agreed for the Assembly.[46] The only exception to this would be the case of action which involved either a Resolution consisting solely of the provision of finance,[47] or which initiated a course of action which lay within the province of "permissive" functions of the Organisation as opposed to "mandatory" functions. For Sir Gerald, the expenses of peace-keeping or dispute-settling were obligatory precisely because the functions were mandatory for the Organisation; the "permissive" functions were those relating to social and economic activities.[48] With respect, it is submitted that this distinction is unfounded and highly dangerous for future United Nations activities, and results from an attempt to categorise and distinguish where the Charter really affords no basis for these categories and distinctions. In the present writer's view there is one test, and one only: is the Resolution *intended* as one which will be financed on a voluntary basis? If there is no evidence of such an intention, either in the terms of the Resolution or in the *travaux préparatoires* leading to its adoption, then it is presumed to be a Resolution for which the expenses may be treated by the Assembly as expenses of the Organisation and apportioned in such a way as the Assembly sees fit: and there exists a *legal* obligation to meet an assessment.[49]

This particular principle is vital to peace-keeping operations, and, whilst it may be stated, it must also be acknowledged that several States, particularly the Soviet *bloc*, are far from accepting it. This leads to the further question of the sanctions which may be taken by the Organisation to deal with defaulting States.

The very existence of sanctions for non-payment of arrears

---

[45] *Ibid.*, p. 209.
[46] *Ibid.*, pp. 211–212.
[47] *Ibid.*, p. 213 where he instances the Resolutions calling for "voluntary" contributions to UNICEF, UNKRA, UNWRA and the UN Special Fund as being of this type.
[48] *Ibid.*
[49] It is believed that the San Francisco *travaux préparatoires*, and the practice of the UN to date, support this view (see Document 194 of the dossier supplied by the Secretary-General to the Court, pp. 9–13).

suggests that there *is* a legal obligation to pay the assessments made by the Assembly. Article 19 of the Charter provides that:

" A Member of the United Nations which is in arrears in the payment of its financial contributions to the Organisation shall have no vote in the General Assembly if the amount of its arrears equals or exceeds the amount of the contributions due from it for the preceding two full years. The General Assembly may, nevertheless, permit such a Member to vote if it is satisfied that the failure to pay is due to conditions beyond the control of the Member."

The "arrears" situation had, even by the time of the Court's Opinion, become a very serious one,[50] but at the time of writing no State has fallen two years in arrears. At the beginning of the Fourth Special Session of the Assembly, the Secretary-General notified the President of the Assembly, Sir Zafrulla Khan, that Haiti was in arrears to this extent, and the reply of the President tended to suggest that, had Haiti been present when a vote was taken, he would have regarded that vote as being automatically invalid.[51] The fact that arrears exist not only because of a simple refusal to pay but also because, in the case of States like the Soviet Union, it is denied that there exists a legal obligation to pay, creates an additional complication in applying this sanction. On balance, it is believed that suspension from voting is not an "automatic" sanction,[52] as the President's reply to the Secretary-General tends to

[50] As of 30 April 1962, 63 States owing approximately 43 per cent. of the ONUC assessments had made no payments to the Congo account, and 68 States were in arrears generally (UN Secretariat, Statement on the Collection of Contributions, ST/ADM/SER.B./158, 1962). At the end of 4 years of operations of UNEF, on 31 July 1961, 80 Members owed their full assessments and 3 part of their assessments on UNEF, and the deficit on UNEF was approximately $25m.: A/4857, p. 18 and ST/ADM/SER.B/145, 15 June 1961. By 15 May 1963 a total of 73 States were in arrears: 34 on the regular budget, 56 on the UNEF account, and 67 on the ONUC account: the total deficit of the Organisation had increased from $74.1m. at the end of 1962 to $93.9m. at 31 March 1963: *UN Release 20/63* of 21 May 1963. The gradual growth of the overall budget deficit can be seen in the following table (millions of dollars):

Year	Unpaid obligations	Net Cash	Deficit
1956	24·0	14·7	9·3
1957	38·5	17·3	21·2
1958	43·2	13·9	29·3
1959	44·8	16·3	28·5
1960	89·7	2·8	86·9
1961 (estimated)	114·4	6·9	107·5

Figures are taken from the Secretary-General's statement to the Fifth Committee on 11th December 1961; A/C.5/907.

[51] The exchange of letters of 14 and 15 May 1963 is given in *International Legal Materials*, Vol. 11, No. 4 (July, 1963), p. 797: the President stated: " I would have made an announcement drawing the attention of the Assembly to the loss of voting rights . . . had a formal count of vote taken place in the presence of the representative . . . As no such vote took place, and as the representative of Haiti was not present, this announcement became unnecessary."

[52] For a contrary view see Higgins, "The Politics of UN Finance," *The World Today*, September 1963, p. 387 and Stoessinger, "Financing the United Nations," *International Conciliation*, No. 535 (1961), p. 60. A more reserved view is taken by Hogg, "Peace-keeping costs and Charter obligations,"

suggest, but in all cases a matter for Assembly decision—whether by way of a challenge to the Presidential ruling or by way of a Resolution, if only because any other course would deprive the Assembly of an opportunity to exercise its discretion in the second sentence of Article 19.

The evidence suggests that the Assembly will lean over backwards to avoid taking a firm position on the obligation to pay arrears in respect of the peace-keeping operations at least, and no doubt, in political terms, it is wiser to permit a gradual dissolution of the problem rather than to force an issue which could conceivably result in the withdrawal of certain States from membership or the jeopardising of future peace-keeping operations. Hence in a Resolution of 1 July 1963 on " Payment of arrears in respect of assessed contributions to the United Nations Emergency Force Special Account and the *ad hoc* Account for the United Nations Operation in the Congo," [53] the Assembly:

" 1. *Appeals* to Member States which continue to be in arrears in respect of their assessed contributions . . . to pay their arrears, disregarding other factors, as soon as their respective constitutional and financial arrangements can be processed, and, pending such arrangements, to make an announcement of their intention to do so;

" 2. *Expresses its conviction* that Member States which are in arrears and object on political or juridical grounds to paying their assessments on these accounts will, without prejudice to their respective positions, make a special effort towards solving the financial difficulties of the United Nations by making these payments;

" 3. *Requests* the Secretary-General to consult with those Member States which are in arrears . . . and to work out with them arrangements as to the most appropriate modalities within the letter and spirit of the Charter of the United Nations, including the possibility of payment by instalment, for bringing the payments of these accounts up to date as soon as possible; . . ."

Whether Member States will take advantage of this Resolution of a " face-saving " character remains to be seen, but the expression of hope that payments will be made " without prejudice to their respective positions " is an indication that the Assembly will be reluctant to make this an issue if it can possibly avoid it.

The problems are, therefore, by no means solved, and the Committee of 21 has been instructed to continue its studies,[54] both with regard to an equitable method of apportionment and to " other sources of financing future peace-keeping operations." It is appropriate, therefore, that we refer briefly to the various suggestions which have been made with regard to additional sources of finance and to budgetary improvements generally.

(1962) 62 Columbia L.R. 1259: he also points out that the vote to suspend is uncertain, and it may be regarded either as a simple or a two-thirds majority.

[53] Resol. 1877 (S–IV).
[54] Resol. 1880 (S–IV) of 1 July 1963.

II. PROSPECTS OF FUTURE FINANCING

The search for criteria of apportionment has so far ended with the statement of guiding principles referred to above, and it seems as though specific criteria are likely to be reached *ad hoc* in any future operation. What is clear is that, in accordance with paragraph 2 of Resolution 1874(S–IV), the United Nations will in future be very chary of entering into an operation with an " open-ended commitment "; the lessons of UNEF and ONUC have presumably been digested, and the principal of these is that there is no point in the United Nations undertaking an operation which Members are not prepared to finance, and that in future they are likely to fix far more stringent limits to the finances which may be incurred. One may expect, also, a repetition of the UNTEA and Yemen precedents, so that certain operations will be undertaken either at the financial responsibility of the States directly involved, or not at all.

It would, however, be tragic if Member States were so to fix their priorities of importance that the financing of United Nations military operations became possible only in the most exceptional cases, and within very stringent limits. The entire budget of the United Nations for 1962, covering the regular budget and the UNEF and ONUC accounts, was $214 million : that figure represents 1·4 per cent. of the Soviet Union's defence budget, or 0·4 per cent. of that of the United States or 4·3 per cent. of Britain's annual defence budget or 10 per cent. of the tax received by the British Treasury from the sale of tobacco in the United Kingdom.[55] Put in this light, the *caveats* one is likely to encounter about extravagance on United Nations peace-keeping operations seem a little unreal, and raise very serious questions about the standards applied by States which base their opposition to such operations on the matter of cost.

There is, however, every advantage in suggesting improvements in the system of financing for United Nations military operations. The possible improvements are : —

(1) The establishment of a Reserve Fund which would enable the accumulation of a reserve of capital over the years and avoid the sudden imposition of very heavy assessments. The study which the Assembly has already initiated on the establishment of a " Peace Fund "[56] looks in the right direction.

Such a fund could be financed in various ways[57] :
(a) By setting aside a proportion of the regular budget for each year.

---

[55] Higgins, *loc. cit.*, p. 380.
[56] Resol. 1879 (S–IV) of 1 July 1963.
[57] The major proposals which have been made in recent years can be read in the Report of the Commission to Study the Organisation of Peace, Arthur N. Holcombe, Chairman, *Strengthening the United Nations* (1957); Rosner, *The United Nations Emergency Force* (1963) pp. 183–185; Nichols, *Financing the United Nations, Problems and Prospects*, Center for International Studies, Mass. Institute of Technology, U.S.A. (1961) pp. 23–36; Clark and Sohn, *World Peace Through World Law*, 2nd ed. (revised) (1960), Annex V.

(b) By encouraging voluntary contributions from States, either by gift or loan.[58]

(c) By encouraging voluntary contributions from individuals and institutions. This is not entirely novel, for the United Nations Headquarters is built upon land donated by Rockefeller, but it may meet with objections from States which see in this a possible diminution of their control over United Nations activities in so far as financial dependence on the States diminishes.

(d) By developing public services by the United Nations and the specialised agencies which might be sources of direct revenue, *e.g.*, consultant services to government or private institutions in economic, political or social matters; fees for international radio licensing through the ITU; fees for health certificates through the WHO; fractions of the returns of interest on loans from the International Bank or International Finance Corporation, etc. Here the major obstacle would be to secure the agreement of the specialised agencies which, at the moment, handle the bulk of these services, and may regard this as simply a gift by them to the United Nations.

It may, long-term, be possible to utilise other sources such as income from the usufruct of the ocean beds [59] or Antarctica, a percentage of the defence expenditures of governments, or even taxation of individuals [60]; this last is, in essence, the concept behind the detailed revenue system proposed by Clark and Sohn.[61] Yet, in the immediate future, these bold ideas are, unhappily, less likely to find a general measure of acceptance by States. They might be more acceptable in the long-term era of disarmament.

(2) The conclusion of stand-by agreements with States specifying the assistance, in terms of forces, facilities and supplies to be made available to the United Nations. The advantage of these agreements, from the financial angle, would be that the United Nations could the more accurately estimate in advance what proportion of the support for an operation would be forthcoming from Members direct, and

---

[58] Nichols, *op. cit.*, p. 31 argues strongly for substantial, interest-free loans.
[59] The suggestion that the UN should be given a usufruct of the continental shelf was made by the U.K. Parliamentary Group for World Government, prior to the Geneva Conference of 1958, but the idea met with no support, as the Convention on the Continental Shelf indicates. The "ocean beds" would presumably now have to be the areas beyond the shelf.
[60] Nichols, *loc. cit.*, pp. 23–24; Report of the Commission to Study the Organisation of Peace, *loc. cit.* There is also a suggestion by Bloomfield, *The United Nations and U.S. Foreign Policy* (1960) for directing U.S. military assistance to States entering into stand-by agreements with the UN. This ought to be done as a matter of U.S. policy rather than as part of a UN budgetary device, for it is likely to find strong opposition from the Soviets.
[61] *World Peace through World Law*, 2nd ed. (revised) (1960), Annex V. This scheme is, however, envisaged as appropriate to a stage at which amendment of the Charter and general disarmament are possible: it is not suggested as appropriate at the present time. Of a similar kind are the proposals put forward by the U.K. Parliamentary Group for World Government at the Tokyo Conference in 1963.

therefore what proportion of the total cost would be placed to the general United Nations budget (or Reserve Fund).

The whole of this—and almost every suggestion which is made by other authors—ultimately depends upon the political will of the Member States: the major task remains, therefore, one of developing amongst Member States the necessary will to finance operations and the conviction that such operations constitute a significant step towards the maintenance and preservation of world peace. The argument that the finance is not available is, as such, nonsensical; it means no more than that the *will* to finance the operations is not present.

15

The Application of the Laws of War to Operations by United Nations Forces

---

THE question of the application of the laws of war to operations by military forces operating under the authority and aegis of the United Nations has arisen, almost incidentally, in the operations in Korea and in the operations of UNEF and ONUC.[1] It is a question which does not seem to have been exhaustively examined by the United Nations, and certainly never authoritatively answered in anything more than a very general way. No doubt the inherent difficulties of the question have deterred the United Nations organs from attempting to give an answer, and as yet circumstances have not compelled an answer. Yet, clearly, no study of United Nations Forces could be regarded as complete without attempting to deal with this question.

It is believed that any examination of the areas of the law of war which might be applicable to United Nations Forces, or of the question of the binding force of both customary and conventional rules, or of the practical difficulties in their application to United Nations Forces must follow, and not precede, an examination of two preliminary questions. These are, first, the question of what different functions a United Nations Force may assume; and, second, the question of the different types of command structure which may be adopted for a United Nations Force.

I. CLASSIFICATION OF UNITED NATIONS FORCES IN TERMS OF THEIR FUNCTION

An analysis of the different kinds of functions which have been in the past, and may in the future be, entrusted to United Nations Forces has already been given in Chapter 8 above.[2] That analysis alone will have suggested that the question of the application of the laws of war may be relevant to certain types of functions, but not to others. This question suggests a slightly different categorisation of function to be more useful, namely one directed more to the

---

[1] For Regulations 44 and 43 of UNEF and ONUC respectively, see *ante*, pp. 121, 222.
[2] *Ante*, pp. 267–274.

likelihood of the operations involving armed hostilities under international law. The broad distinction between enforcement functions
and "peace-keeping" operations is clearly important to an understanding of the present question. Moreover, since the second
category of "peace-keeping" operations embraces a variety of sub-
heads, it is believed that a distinction must now be made between
such functions as are entrusted to a United Nations military Force
stricto sensu (*i.e.*, a Force entrusted with arms) and a United Nations
military Force which is military only in the sense that it is composed
of military personnel. It will be seen that, once this distinction is
made, it is only the first sub-category—the *armed* Forces—which are
really relevant to the present inquiry. However, in relation to them
yet a further distinction arises, and this turns on whether the use of
arms is to be by reference to international or municipal law. Thus
the following classification by function emerges:

1. *Enforcement functions*

These, as has been seen,[3] embrace the type of functions to be
entrusted to a Force established under Article 42 of the Charter by
way of a decision of the Security Council, or under Article 39 of the
Charter by way of a recommendation of the Security Council, or
possibly even by the General Assembly by a recommendation under
the Resolution on Uniting for Peace.[4] In any event, the essential
characteristic of such a Force, for purposes of the present inquiry,
is that the Force is designed to take preventive or enforcement
action against a State or other authority.[5] Whilst armed combat
may not be inevitable, it is clear that the mandate of the Force
includes an authorisation to *initiate* hostilities, and these hostilities—
or use of force—whether described as "belligerent action" or
"enforcement measures"[6] are to be taken by reference to
international law and not the municipal law of any State.

2. *"Peace-keeping" functions by United Nations Forces*

(a) BY UNARMED UNITS

It will be recalled that, of the observer groups, only in Indonesia
and in the Yemen have the military personnel forming these groups
been armed.[7] For the rest, being unarmed, the question of the
application of the laws of war is really inapplicable since they have
no capacity for undertaking armed hostilities.[8]

---

[3] *Ante*, pp. 267, 274–278.
[4] *Ante*, pp. 291–293.
[5] The "North Korean authorities" were never regarded as a State by the
United Nations; see *ante*, p. 35, Chap. 3.
[6] *Post*, p. 497.
[7] *Ante*, p. 71.
[8] The view might be taken that such personnel should be entitled to treatment as prisoners of war if captured, but this is believed to be misconceived
for there is no right of capture of UN observer personnel. The most that
might be said is that a State or other authority which, by mistake or even

(b) BY ARMED UNITS

(i) *Units with a mandate capable of authorising armed hostilities under international law*

The armed observer groups, UNEF as an interposition Force, and ONUC as a Force with a variety of "peace-keeping" functions,[9] were all capable of resorting to arms in self-defence and, in the case of ONUC, for preventing civil war and expelling mercenaries. The Congo operations have demonstrated that this limited right to use force, especially when coupled with a right to freedom of movement, may in fact result in hostilities on a not inconsiderable scale.[10] A United Nations Force entrusted with the defence and security of a zone or area under United Nations control would have similar rights of self-defence.

Hence, within this broad category, there is a group of United Nations Forces whose mandates comprehend a "combat possibility," and their operations therefore become relevant to the question of the applicability of the laws of war.

(ii) *Units with a mandate capable only of authorising armed action under municipal law*

It is conceivable that an armed United Nations Force could be entrusted with a mandate which envisaged the use of force by reference to municipal rather than international law. Hence UNTEA included a United Nations Security Force which, whilst no doubt legally capable of defending West New Guinea against an external attack (in which case it would fall under the previous head), was really intended to operate as a militia for the purpose of maintaining internal security and operating on the basis of the existing municipal law or such internal legislation as the United Nations Administrator might promulgate.[11] In such a case, assuming that force had to be used to quell riots or detain civilians, it is believed that it would not be force of a kind to which the laws of war could be held applicable, no more than the internal security forces of a State are subject to those laws in similar situations: the only exception would be where the riotous factions assumed proportions large enough to bring Article 3 of the Geneva Sick and Wounded Convention into operation,[12] or to merit recognition as belligerents.

This classification brings out the limits to the present inquiry and demonstrates that there is no warrant for any general conclusion that the laws of war are, or are not, applicable to United Nations

intentionally, took observer personnel into custody would be bound to accord to them whilst in custody a standard of treatment not less than that accorded to prisoners of war and failure to do so would aggravate the responsibility already incurred.

[9] *Ante*, pp. 186–196.
[10] *Ante*, pp. 169, 171, 173.
[11] *Ante*, p. 257.
[12] *Post*, p. 509.

Forces: much depends on the nature of the functions of the Force. Forces which may be established in the future, to fulfil the various functions listed in Chapter 8 above [13] will, presumably, fall into one or other of the above categories. For example, a United Nations Force designed to fulfil functions under a Disarmament Treaty may well fall into the first category of " enforcement functions "; a Force entrusted with plebiscite functions could fall into 2 (b) (ii)—as a unit capable of using force by reference to municipal law. The importance of this classification has been sufficiently demonstrated to enable us to turn to the next problem of classification, namely that relating to the command structure of the Force.

II. CLASSIFICATION OF UNITED NATIONS FORCES IN TERMS OF THEIR COMMAND STRUCTURE

From what has been said above of the different forms of Command Structure,[14] there are three basic types of structure available to the United Nations. A consideration of these different types will be seen to be extremely relevant to the practical problems of applying the laws of war to a United Nations Force.

1. *Command delegated to a State or group of States by the United Nations*

This was, essentially, the system used in Korea [15] where command was entrusted to the United States as agent for the United Nations. The system can use a single State or a group of States, and the latter method was favoured by the Collective Measures Committee:

". . . upon the determination to adopt measures involving the use of United Nations armed force, the Organisation should authorise a State or group of States to act on its behalf as executive military authority, within the framework of its policies and objectives as expressed through such Resolutions as it may adopt at any stage of the collective action." [16]

It is a system which makes it possible for the Command to be composed of States which are bound as States both by the customary and conventional rules of the law of war; it does not envisage disciplinary control by the Command over national contingents, so that the problems of enforcing their observance remain.

2. *Command entrusted to an individual appointed by and responsible to the United Nations, but lacking disciplinary authority*

This is really the type of structure used in UNEF and ONUC and was apparently the type of structure envisaged by the Military Staff Committee for the United Nations Forces to be established under

[13] *Ante*, pp. 267–274.
[14] *Ante*, pp. 337–352.
[15] *Ante*, p. 40.
[16] A/2215, para. 201 and see *ante*, p. 23.

Chapter VII of the Charter. It has the advantage of subordinating the Commander to the appropriate United Nations political organ, but in terms of the application of the laws of war it has had the disadvantage of raising questions as to whether the United Nations (for command rests with the United Nations, not with States) can benefit by or be bound by the laws of war, and, moreover, it still does not solve the problem of disciplinary control when, as in UNEF and ONUC, this power of discipline rested with the commander of the national contingents and not with the United Nations Commander.[17]

3. *Command entrusted to an individual appointed by and responsible to the United Nations and having disciplinary authority*

This type of Command has not yet existed. We have suggested earlier,[18] that this would be the type of Command preferable for a permanent United Nations Force. The conferment of disciplinary authority could be by agreement with participating States where these provided national contingents, or, where the Force is composed of individuals recruited as such, by the enactment by the Assembly of a code of military discipline applicable to such personnel. With this type of structure the problem of enforcing compliance with the laws of war becomes nearer to that in any national force: but, of course, it does not help to settle the question whether the United Nations, as such, can be bound by, or benefit from, those laws.

III. AREAS OF THE LAW OF WAR RELEVANT TO UNITED NATIONS OPERATIONS

To facilitate the investigation of the applicability of the law of war to United Nations Forces, it is convenient at this juncture to divide that extensive *corpus juris* into groupings based either on the purposes the rules attempt to achieve or on an isolated historical development. Thus, it may be seen that some rules are primarily humanitarian, some are designed to facilitate non-hostile intercourse between belligerents, and others are directed towards circumscribing the participation of third States in the general hostilities. A further category, the laws of war at sea, tends to fall naturally into its own distinct grouping. It is within this broad outline that the various sub-categories of laws pertinent to the operations of United Nations Forces appear:

1. *Laws of a predominantly humanitarian nature*

(a) USE OF WEAPONS—PROHIBITED FORCE

It is a curious but significant reflection on the present state of the laws of war that the rules regulating the conduct of armed combat generally, and the use of weapons particularly, are considered not

---

[17] *Ante,* p. 343.
[18] *Ante,* pp. 337–343.

only the foundation of the humanitarian laws but also the most archaic. The controlling principle of the customary law is expressed in Article 22 of the Regulations appended to Hague Convention No. IV of 1907,—" Belligerents have not got an unlimited right as to the choice of means of injuring the enemy." This rule governs not only the weapons which are " illegal " *per se* (*i.e.*, whose use under any conditions is inhumane) but also the manner in which " legal " weapons may be employed. Thus this rule is applicable to *any* weapon according to the context of the circumstances surrounding its use.[19]

In addition to the general proscription of *all* means that seek inhumanely to kill or wound, or of the use of weapons which needlessly inflict pain or aggravate wounds, there are specific injunctions against the use of poison and poisoned weapons,[20] or treachery.[21] To this category of legal rules also belong the various conventional laws against explosive projectiles,[22] expanding (dum-dum) bullets,[23] projectiles which diffuse gas,[24] and a myriad collection of others.[25] It is not the present intention to do more than simply indicate the type of regulation that this category of the laws of war comprises. It is sufficient at this stage to suggest that regardless of the context of the conflict or the legal identity of the contestants, any use of international armed force must be understood to call into question the application of those laws of war designed to regulate the use of weapons.

(b) USE OF WEAPONS—PROTECTED PERSONS

The customary and conventional laws of war also seek to protect certain classes of persons, in certain situations, against the threat of wounding and killing. This also is an area of the law of war relevant to the activities of United Nations Forces engaged in military activities of an international character. Generally, within the protection of these rules are both civilian populations and non-combatant members of armed forces who do not take part in the actual hostilities.[26] The latter class, like the civilian, is exposed to all injuries indirectly resulting from the lawful operations of war, such as bombardments of cities, etc. In so far as civilians do not take part in combat activities, they are protected from direct attack.[27]

---

[19] Oppenheim-Lauterpacht, *International Law*, Vol. II, 7th ed., pp. 346–352.
[20] Hague Regulations, Article 23.
[21] *Ibid.*, Article 23 (g).
[22] Declaration of St. Petersburg, 11 December 1868.
[23] 1st Hague Conference, 29 July 1899.
[24] *Ibid.*
[25] See Oppenheim-Lauterpacht, *op. cit.*, Vol. II, pp. 341–348.
[26] Oppenheim-Lauterpacht, *op. cit.*, Vol. II, p. 345.
[27] *Ibid.*, p. 346.

(c) CAPTURE, DETENTION AND TREATMENT OF PRISONERS OF WAR

As seen previously, not all armed Forces of the United Nations operate under the control of international law.[28] To the extent that such Forces act under the control and direction of some municipal system, it must be conceded that prisoners taken by the Force in such operations are not entitled to the treatment by their United Nations captors that international law. demands. In the main, however, it is proper to suppose that the great majority of armed United Nations Forces, authorised to employ force, will do so under international law and must necessarily possess the correlative competence to take and detain military prisoners. In this regard the conventional rules of the 1929 and 1949 Geneva Conventions become relevant to the operation of United Nations Forces, depending on the category of protected person into which each respective prisoner falls.

(d) OCCUPATION OF TERRITORY—RELATIONS WITH GOVERNMENT, PERSONS AND PROPERTY

The physical presence of a United Nations armed Force in the territory of either a Member or non-Member State raises additional questions of the relevance of the law of War. As with the example of prisoners of war, it is not to be presumed that all Forces are faced with the issue of adhering in their actions within the territory they occupy to rules of international law. Clearly, a Force operating within a municipal law system is not in " belligerent occupation " as that term is used in international law; neither is that definition relevant in cases where the jurisdiction of a " peace-keeping " Force, for example, is grounded on Status of Forces agreements between the Organisation and the host State.[29] The question of the law controlling the behaviour of United Nations Forces towards the government, inhabitants and property while occupying the territory of a State opposing it does become relevant in instances of " enforcement action " under Chapter VII, or possibly to similar action pursuant to a *recommendation* of the Security Council under Article 39 or the General Assembly under the Uniting for Peace Resolution.

In any of these latter three situations, a United Nations Force may be in actual " belligerent occupation " of territory, or may exercise a civil affairs administration subsequent to hostilities but before the relevant organ has determined that international peace and security is no longer threatened. Under these conditions, the customary and conventional laws of war (Articles 42–56 of the Hague Regulations and the Geneva Convention of 1949 relating to the Protection of Civilian Persons in Time of War being two of the principal sources) are relevant to United Nations Forces.

A short digression is apposite at this point, to indicate that,

[28] *Ante*, p. 486.
[29] *Ante*, p. 432.

irrespective of inherent structural limitations on the application of *all* the laws of war to United Nations Forces, the Charter itself imposes obligations that may stop Member States whose territory the Force is occupying from claiming the treatment of the laws of war. Thus, the provisions of Article 2 (5) enjoining Members to give the United Nations " every assistance in any action " taken pursuant to the Charter, and Article 25 wherein all Members have agreed " to accept and carry out the decisions of the Security Council " can be interpreted as overriding the traditional rules of international law on the relationship between the occupant and the government and public property of the State being occupied. On the other hand, however, as these obligations of the Charter cannot be said to inure to the individual, the fact that it is a United Nations Force in occupation of the territory should not derogate from the standards of treatment of person or property owed to the civilian population.

Parenthetically, it may be remarked that the issue of the application of the laws of belligerent occupation and the conduct of the United Nations Force is distinct from the question of the international responsibility of the Organisation as a whole for the actions of its representatives which result in injury to persons or property. While that subject is outside the present section,[30] it may be stated that the two subjects are not mutually exclusive. The responsibility of an international institution may be engaged as effectively by its military representatives operating in excess of their competence as by any other unarmed mission.

2. Laws designed to facilitate the non-hostile relations of belligerents

Although many of the laws of war designed to achieve a certain degree of peaceful intercourse between belligerents share humanitarian aims, their principal impetus is necessity. This includes the need to safeguard attempts to end the hostilities as well as the necessity of permitting non-hostile relations during the combat itself. Non-hostile relations of this sort can be based on existing rules of international law and on special agreements concluded between the belligerents. In this study it is the former category which is relevant.

It takes little reflection to perceive that the maintenance of avenues of peaceful intercourse with the opponent is an aim as vital to the military Forces of the United Nations as to any other belligerent engaged in armed combat. The reciprocal recognition of safe-conducts and military passports, the traditional adherence to the flag of truce and all the substantial and procedural modalities of a similar nature are relevant to United Nations Forces. For identical reasons the laws and usages respecting the negotiation and execution of capitulations, surrenders, armistices and treaties of peace are

[30] See *ante*, pp. 242–248.

applicable in theory if for no better reason than that if they did not exist as customary or conventional laws of war, the United Nations would have to create them.

3. *Laws intended to regulate the participation of third States in the armed conflict*

Without intending to underestimate the importance of the modern role which the classical concepts of neutrality may yet play, neutrality as a general subject is outside the scope of an investigation of the application of the laws of war to United Nations Forces themselves. However, it is reasonably clear that the relations between the United Nations and "third States" will be governed primarily by the régime of the Charter, not only as between the United Nations and its Members,[31] but possibly between the United Nations and non-Members,[32] and not by the traditional rules applying between belligerent and neutrals.

4. *Laws regulating the conduct of war at sea*

Much of the law of war pertaining to the conduct of warfare at sea had an historical development essentially different from that of land warfare and it shares a common heritage with the laws of neutrality. It is, therefore, not particularly pertinent to the present inquiry. However, inasmuch as a United Nations Force is not limited to land units alone, and is capable of both possessing and using warships, certain of the laws of war at sea, the rules regarding the legality of combatants, both ships and men, and the rules for determining the validity of capture are relevant and will be discussed in a following section concerned with the practical difficulties facing United Nations Forces in applying some laws of war.[33]

IV. EXTENT TO WHICH THE AREAS OF THE LAW OF WAR ARE APPLICABLE TO UNITED NATIONS FORCES

In the light both of the various functions for United Nations Forces and of the types of Forces which may be created to fulfil them, it is now necessary to investigate how far the different segments of the relevant laws of war are applicable to United Nations Forces. This involves a dual inquiry into first, to what extent the law of war, customary or conventional, applies to United Nations Forces as a matter of law, i.e., of its own force, without need of enabling measures of forced rationalisation; and secondly, the problems of practical application which the present state of the law of war presents to the United Nations as such and its military Forces.

[31] Articles 2 (5), 25, 43, 49, 103 and 104 among others. On the obligations of States in the event of UN action see *ante*, pp. 224–230, 417–418.
[32] Article 2 (6); See Oppenheim—Lauterpacht *op. cit.*, Vol. II, pp. 652, 653.
[33] *Post*, p. 515.

1. *As a matter of law*

(a) THEORETICAL COMPATIBILITY OF UNITED NATIONS FORCES WITH THE LAW OF WAR

Since the end of the Second World War, and more particularly since the formation of the United Nations, the leading publicists of the world have exhibited a highly ambivalent attitude towards the law of war.[34] The most fundamental legal problem raised by them was whether *any* of the rules regulating the activities of belligerents *inter se* and towards others apply to United Nations Forces, in the light of the attempts of the community of Nations to limit the *jus ad bellum*—the right to make war.[35] These limitations derive principally from the prohibitions of the Pact of Paris and the Charter of the United Nations which together amount to a surrender by States of not only their ability to embrace war as an instrument of national policy, but also their right to use or threaten the use of armed force in international relations. Action in violation of at least the former of these prohibitions supports criminal prosecution.[36] Upon this foundation rests the allegation that, *vis-à-vis* Forces representing the United Nations, a State which has resorted to the prohibited use of armed force, has, by its original criminality, forfeited the right to be treated according to the dictates of the law of war.

On the theory of the illegality of war, it is sometimes contended that the United Nations Force would be permitted either to disregard the totality of the law of war or, in its discretion, comply with whatever portions of it it feels is commensurate with the mandate given it by the Organisation. In terms of legal doctrine, two propositions are submitted to support the conclusion. The first is the application of the maxim *ex injuria jus non oritur*, which in operation would permit the United Nations Force to "outlaw" the State which breached the treaty obligations inherent in either the Pact of Paris

---

[34] See, among others, H. Lauterpacht, "The limits of the Operation of the Laws of War," (1953) 30 B.Y.I.L. 206; Q. Wright, "The Outlawry of War and the Laws of War," (1953) 47 A.J.I.L. 365; Kunz, "The Chaotic State of the Laws of War," (1951) 45 A.J.I.L. 37; and "The Laws of War," (1956) 50 A.J.I.L. 313.

[35] The initial steps in this movement were directed more at procedural limitation, as in The Hague Convention of 1907 respecting the Limitation of the Employment of Force for the Recovery of Contract Debts; the Hague Convention of 1907 concerning the opening of Hostilities (Article One). The more mature attempts to limit the substantive right to resort to war included a host of treaties following the First World War, collected and discussed in Wasmund, *Die Nachtangriffspakte* (1935), and culminated in 1928 in the General Treaty for the Renunciation of War (Pact of Paris). For a discussion of the relative and conjunctive effect of the Pact of Paris and the Charter on the *jus ad bellum*, see Oppenheim, *op. cit.*, pp. 194–197.

[36] The International Military Tribunal in its judgment, at p. 216, declared aggressive war and war in violation of international treaties to be a crime "differing only from the other war crimes in that it contains within itself the accumulated evil of the whole." In so far as the General Assembly of the United Nations unanimously confirmed and adopted the principles adduced in that judgment (11 December 1946, Resol. 95 (1)) the illegality of aggressive war is to be considered declaratory of international customary law.

or the Charter, or both. Thus, on the basis of an essential illegality, the maxim operates to allow deviation from the fundamental norms of behaviour otherwise compelled by international law.

The second theory would not compel withdrawal of recognition amounting to " outlawry," but rests on the rationale of the law of reprisal. On the basis of the original illegality of the aggressor, the United Nations Force, allegedly, would be justified in adopting methods of combat otherwise unlawful. It is on both the foregoing theories that such advocates of the inapplicability of the law of war as Professor Schwarzenberger base their conclusions that a United Nations Force engaged in hostilities with an aggressor may, in " strict law," disregard the existence of any customary laws which protect either the armed forces or civilian populations, without violating any fundamental principle of international law.[37]

Both of these theories, intended to release from the law of war Forces opposing an aggressor, have been correctly subjected to criticism on humanitarian as well as legal grounds. With regard to the reliance on the maxim *ex injuria jus non oritur*, Lauterpacht has said:

" In relation to the applicability of the rules of warfare to the belligerent engaging in an unlawful war, rigid reliance on that principle would mean in practice that rules of war do not apply at all in a war of this nature. For, unless the aggressor has been defeated from the very outset . . . it is impossible to visualise the conduct of hostilities in which one side would be bound by the rules of warfare without benefiting from them and the other side would benefit from them without being bound by them. Accordingly, any applicability to the actual conduct of war of the principle *ex injuria jus non oritur* would transform the contest into a struggle which may be subject to no regulation at all. The result would be the abandonment of most rules of warfare, including those which are of a humanitarian character." [38]

Thus, on this view, the operative words limiting the application of the maxim are " the actual conduct of war," or the *jus in bello.*

A further argument advanced to illustrate the inapplicability of the maxim to laws promulgated solely for the regulation of armed hostilities relies on examples drawn from international law in which the illegal act, rather than " outlawing" the illegal actor, compels the offended party to respect new legal rights and duties arising directly out of the illegal act.[39] Thus, the illegal act which permits the offended party to retaliate by way of reprisal with an act itself unlawful, simultaneously imposes a new duty on the retaliating party (and correspondingly a new right in the original illegal actor) to respect both the limits of proportionality and the dictates of humanity.[40]

---

[37] Schwarzenberger, " Legal Effects of Illegal War," *Völkerrecht und Rechtliches Welbild. Festschrift Für Alfred Verdross* (1960) pp. 244–245.

[38] H. Lauterpacht *op. cit.,* (1953) 30 B.Y.I.L. at p. 212.

[39] Tucker, *Law of War and Neutrality at Sea* (1957) pp. 6–9, and footnote 14 on p. 9 therein.

[40] *The Naulilaa Arbitration, International Law Reports* (1927–8) Case No. 360; see also Oppenheim-Lauterpacht, *op. cit.,* p. 563; Stone, *Legal Controls of International Conflict* (1959), pp. 354–355.

The very fact that the great mass of the customary law of war which survives to regulate the actual conduct of hostilities evolved in an era when recourse to war was virtually unlimited, tends to indicate the basic ameliorating thrust behind those laws. Scott, in explaining the reasons for the codification of the laws relating to land warfare, said:

" When all offences are punished by excessive or by capital punishment, there is no check upon the criminal who has committed a larger one, because he is not deterred by the punishment which in each case is equally great. If the danger of war and the severity of warfare do not act as a deterrent to war, it is nevertheless humanitarian to free it from suffering as far as possible." [41]

And as more recently argued by Tucker [42] :

" There is strong reason . . . for maintaining that the rules of warfare had both their origin and justification not so much in any indifference to the legal character of war, but in the conviction that whatever the interpretation given to war there must be rules for the regulation, and hence, the mitigation of war's conduct."

It must be remembered that the cornerstone of the theory nullifying the applicability of the laws of war *pendente bello* on the basis of the restrictions on the *jus ad bellum* rests on the positive determination of an aggressor *at the time hostilities are commenced*. With regard to United Nations Forces, this means a decision of the Security Council pursuant to Article 39, requiring unanimity among the Permanent Members (or, at the least, possibly action by the General Assembly under the " Uniting for Peace " Resolution). Recent history has illustrated that it is much more likely that Forces created by the United Nations will operate without an aggressor ever being designated.

A survey of the judicial decisions of international and municipal tribunals which, following the Second World War, were urged by various prosecutors and plaintiffs to adopt either the reprisal or outlawry theories, tends to contradict the idea that an illegal aggressor cannot benefit, nor its opponent be bound, by the law of war during hostilities.[43] The International Military Tribunal at Nuremberg impliedly rejected the argument several times, but most clearly in the cases of Admirals Dönitz and Raeder. In both these cases, in spite of the previous finding of Germany's illegality in waging war, the Tribunal refused to assess guilt on charges of unrestricted submarine warfare against unarmed merchantmen in violation of the customary

[41] Scott, *The Hague Peace Conferences of 1899 and 1907* (1909) Vol. i, p. 524.
[42] Tucker, *op. cit.*, p. 10; See also Castren, *The Present Laws of War and Neutrality* (1954) pp. 57–58.
[43] To this effect, see *List and others* (Hostages Trial) *Law Reports of Trials of War Criminals*, 8 (1949) p. 59; Trial of *Josef Altstotter and others, ibid.*, 6 (1948) 52; *Gold of the National Bank of Albania Arbitration, International Law Reports* (1953) 441, at p. 465, where the Sole Arbitrator relied not on the outlawry theory to refuse to recognise acquisition of property by an aggressor—belligerent, but rather on the belligerent's violation of the law of belligerent occupation. See also, Lauterpacht, *op. cit.*, (1953) 30 B.Y.I.L. 224–233.

laws of war on the ground that the evidence illustrated like conduct by both the British and United States Navies.[44]   It is submitted that the implications of these particular judgments reject the proposition that a belligerent facing an illegal aggressor is not itself bound, *pendente bello*, by the customary law of war. The illegality of the war did not permit the non-aggressor to justify its illegality in actual combat.[45] Similar conclusions can be drawn from one of the most recent of the cases,[46] in which it was argued that an aggressor is not entitled to the benefit of the laws of war.

" In approaching the subject of the applicability of the Hague Regulations I would make the general observations that I do not think there is any ground on which this Court need hesitate to associate itself with the 'dictum' of the Tribunal in *Krupp's* case . . . a 'dictum' which merely confirmed what the International Tribunal had already held, that the doctrine that the provisions of the Hague Convention No. IV and the Regulations attached to it do not apply in 'total' war must be emphatically rejected . . . akin to this view is the conception that even a State waging illegal war is entitled to the benefit of the Hague Regulations, a conception which appears to have been acted upon by European Courts dealing with cases arising out of the Second World War." [47]

It would appear that there exists no rule of international law which, on the basis of the illegality of war or the threat or use of force alone, would compel the finding that the rules of law regulating the actions of belligerents *pendente bello* do not apply to such belligerents to the same effect and with the same force as was traditionally conceived in the law of war. Alternatively, it would appear to be as yet unaccepted that United Nations Forces, absent other legal considerations, are released from the control of the law of war because of the legal status of its opponent.

Continuing with the investigation of the theoretical applicability, as a matter of law, of the law of war to United Nations Forces, there is the basic question of whether a body of law historically evolved to be applied between States alone, and then only within a highly narrow and technical definition of war,[48] can apply even in theory to the Forces of an international organisation in armed conflicts not properly war in the classical sense.

One of the theoretical arguments based on this anomalous character of the United Nations Forces relies in the first instance on the proposition that, whether operating pursuant to a Chapter VII

---

[44] I.M.T., *Judgment*, p. 313.
[45] And see Schwarzenberger, *op. cit.*, who feels that neither the Nuremberg or Tokyo Tribunals "considered that the armed forces or civilian populations of the aggressor State were automatically beyond the pale of international law, or that resort to war without *jus ad bellum* justified the opponents of these aggressors in disregarding the rules of warfare by way of reprisals " at p. 250.
[46] *N.V. de Bataafsche Petroleum et al.* v. *The War Damage Commission, International Law Reports* (1956) p. 810.
[47] *Ibid.*, Whitton, J. at p. 845.
[48] Oppenheim, *op. cit.*, Vol. II, p. 212; for some wider definitions, see Q. Wright, *A Study of War*, Vol. I, p. 8; Stone, *Legal Control of International Conflicts* (1959) p. 304 *et seq.*

decision or recommendation, or the recommendation of the General Assembly, United Nations Forces would not be engaged in war in the sense for which the laws of warfare were created. This view received its most authoritative statement in 1952 in the report of the Committee on the Study of the Legal Problems of the United Nations, an organ of the American Society of International Law.

"The Committee agrees that the use of force by the United Nations to restrain aggression is of a different nature from war-making by a State. The purposes for which the laws of war were instituted are not entirely the same as the purposes of regulating the use of force by the United Nations. This we may decide without deciding whether the United Nations enforcement action is war, police enforcement or *sui generis*. In the present circumstances, then, the proper answer would seem to be, for the time being, that the United Nations should not feel bound by all the laws of war, but should select such of the laws of war as may seem to fit its purposes, . . . adding such others as may be needed and rejecting those which seem incompatible with its purposes. We think it beyond doubt that the United Nations representing practically all the nations of the earth has the right to make such decisions." [49]

While the conclusion inherent in this view, that United Nations Forces may discriminate in combat and use their discretion in the application of the laws of warfare, is essentially the same as in the "outlawry" and reprisal theory, the grounds for the conclusion are distinctly different. Essentially this argument against the general application of the law of war to United Nations Forces depends on the belief that the formal concept of war is not compatible with either the purposes of the Organisation or the authorisation of its Forces. War is conceived as being constituted of different characteristics:

"When force emanates from sources whose validity rests on the common consent of the international community itself, it should be considered not as horizontal and individual but as vertical and collective . . . the state of affairs resulting from the exercises of legal sanctions by a properly constituted international organ . . . could not be considered as an ordinary conflict between States." [50]

It does not appear to be universally accepted that the customary laws of war apply to belligerent States or that only States are capable of being belligerents.[51] There is evidence to support the view that political entities, not otherwise possessing the inherent right to wage war as States, in the traditional definition, have, nevertheless, engaged in armed conflicts to which the customary laws of war have been considered as applicable. Thus, armed conflict between one or more states of a Federal State and the Federal State itself has been considered as *de facto* war, even though the member states have surrendered in the Federal Constitution their legal capacity to wage war on their own. States not possessing the legal capability to

---

[49] 46 *Proceedings A.S.I.L.* (1952) p. 220.
[50] Hsu Mo., "The Sanctions of International Law," (1949) 35 *Grotius Society Transactions*, pp. 8, 9, 10.
[51] Grob, *The Relativity of War and Peace* (1949), containing a collection of historical examples of war in *de facto* existence, without one or both parties being States or without formal declaration of war.

become belligerents within the definition of the law of war, such as neutralised States or States under suzerainty, have, nevertheless, been accorded the privileges and responsibilities of the customary rules of warfare when they have been engaged in actual hostilities. "Whenever a State lacking the legal qualification to make war nevertheless actually makes war, it is a belligerent, the contention is real war, and the rules of International Law respecting warfare apply to it." [52]

In more recent times, war as a juridical concept has undergone extensive changes. Principally, there has been the recognition of a distinction between war "in a formal sense" and war "in a material sense," a recognition which would allow the laws of war regulating the actual hostilities and combat, the *jus in bello*, to be applicable to prolonged armed conflicts of an international character, irrespective of compliance with the formal requisites, or of the incapacities of the participants to be belligerents in "strict law." [53]

"Material war implies a continuous clash of arms conducted by organised armies which engage the responsibility of governments. It does not presume the condition that the belligerents must be States. The existence of war in the material sense is something to be judged by evidence not of intentions but the activities of military forces in the field." [54]

Rather than eliminating, *ab initio*, the United Nations Forces from the responsibilities and privileges of the rules of the law of war based on the supposition that the actions such Forces take do not correspond to the classical legal definition of war, an alternative approach is to investigate when action taken by United Nations Forces amounts to war in a material sense. Thus, not only in terms of what is exigent, but in the light of the historical development of the customary law of war, it appears apposite to consider each individual use of force by the United Nations within the context of the proper purposes for which it was lawfully constituted and the means it must use to accomplish these purposes. In his forceful reply to the previously mentioned report of the Committee of the American Society of International Law, Baxter aptly summarised the major objectives:

"The law governing the conduct of warfare was not framed as a set of rules to permit the playing of a game of ‘war’ between two States, but arises from a much more fundamental humanitarian need. Because it has been recognised that the law of war has a legitimate role to play whenever hostilities exist, its application in the past has not been confined to declared war between States." [55]

[52] Oppenheim, *op. cit.*, Vol. II, p. 249; see also Wehberg, "La Guerre Civile et Le Droit International," (1938) 63 *Hague Recueil* 12.
[53] Guggenheim, *Traité de Droit International Public* (1954) Vol. II, pp. 314; see also Q. Wright, "The Outlawry of War and the Law of War," (1953) A.J.I.L. 365.
[54] Kotzch, *The Concept of War in Contemporary History and International Law* (1956) p. 56; see also Siotis, *Le Droit de la Guerre et Les Conflits Armés d'un Caractaire Non-International* (1958) pp. 18–21.
[55] R. R. Baxter, "The Role of Law in Modern War" (1953) 47 Proceedings A.S.I.L. 90; McDougal and Feliciano, *Law and Minimum World Public Order*, pp. 539–540.

Additionally, the extensive study of the Institut de Droit International [56] into the present state of the law of war adopted the view that a United Nations Force is a belligerent within the definition of and subject to the customary laws of warfare. After recognising the compelling necessity for an overall revision of the law of war, the Institut turned to the extent of the application of the present laws. It concluded that the present law of war took its force from the principle of equality between belligerents during the hostilities and that the overriding necessity for continued adherence to this principle subjects the Forces of the United Nations to the law of war, even in cases where a competent determination of an aggressor had been made.[57] The contributions of these members participating in this study who believed in the advisability of a new code of laws in future to regulate the activities of United Nations Forces, recognised at the same time the compelling necessity to have all military forces regulated by *some* law until then.[58]

(b) THE FUNCTIONS OF UNITED NATIONS FORCES TO WHICH THE LAW OF
    WAR APPLIES AS A MATTER OF LAW

As has been illustrated previously,[59] all Forces representing the United Nations are not engaged in performing functions which would invoke the application of the laws of war. Similarly, it was shown [60] that even those Forces whose mandate comprehends offensive combat or a " combat possibility " may not in all circumstances be called upon to exercise it. This competence possessed by a United Nations Force to engage, to the extent determined by its mandate, in international armed combat may be considered equivalent to " belligerency " (without adopting any other of the legal consequences which

---

[56] 47 *Institut de Droit International Annuaire* (1957) Vol. I, (Session d'Amsterdam).

[57] *Ibid.*, p. 531.

[58] Judge Jessup and M. Yepes represented the view that, *de lege ferenda*, a new code of conduct for hostilities was demanded by the existence of United Nations Forces, similar to the proposal in Jessup, *A Modern Law of Nations* (1958) Chap. 7. But, as regards the *lex lata*, M. Yepes concluded in these words:
    " Ceci ne signifie nullement que les lois de la guerre soient absolument suspendues ou abolies a l'égard de l'agresseur. Car cela serait rendre la guerre plus atroce encore. Une chose est la situation juridique respective de l'agresseur et de la victime, et une bien differente les regles devant être appliqués à la conduite même de la guerre, au traîtement des prisonniers et des blessés, aux bombardements, aux blocus, au respect de la proprieté privée, à la condition de la population civile, à la prohibition d'employer armes causant des souffrances inutiles, etc. Ces règles, fondées sur sentiments humanitaires, doivent être respectées, même dans les cas d'une guerre inégale et même a l'égard de l'agresseur. Le contraire ferait reculer la civilisation à des époques barbares a jamais revolues."
    Op. cit., at pp. 330–331; see also *ibid.*, pp. 332–333 for the similar views of M. Schätzel.

[59] *Ante*, p. 485.

[60] *Ante*, p. 486.

that term of art may connote). Thus "enforcement action" as conceived in Chapter VII necessarily comprehends the assumption of belligerent status by the Forces of the United Nations charged with the responsibility of restoring or maintaining international peace. It would be pure semantic legerdemain not to equate an armed breach of the peace under Article 39 with the existence of a state of war, at least in the material sense. The competence of a Force authorised to maintain or restore peace does not extend, presumably, to that of an army of a State to achieve a total victory, but the character of the hostilities *per se* is equivalent to that which the laws of war were devised to regulate. Indeed, assuming *arguendo* the more limited goals of a United Nations Force, there are compelling reasons why the rules of the law of war intended to mitigate the severity of armed conflict should apply to the actions in which such a Force is engaged.

To a great extent, the experience of the United Nations in Korea substantiates this proposition. It is clear that few, if any, were prepared to designate the action a war in the traditional sense. It is similarly apparent that all interested parties recognised the belligerent status of the Organisation. The universal reliance on the applicability of many of the customary and conventional laws of warfare to the Forces under the Unified Command illustrates strikingly the unique capabilities of those laws in solving the problems which consistently arise in any armed conflict. The consensual adherence to the Geneva Convention Relative to the Treatment of Prisoners of War of 1949 by the People's Republic of China, the Democratic People's Republic of Korea and all of the interested national contingents of the United Nations Command is a forceful example. It is even more persuasive when it is remembered that not one of the major contestants involved had, even by the end of the conflict, completed ratification or adhered to any of the four 1949 Geneva Conventions. In addition, there were the repeated allegations, made by the representatives of the Soviet Union and the Democratic People's Republic of Korea, of atrocities and other violations of the law of war, communicated directly to the United Nations.[61] Further evidence of the reliance on those laws emanates from the record of the persistent attempts at compliance, made by the United Nations Command, with the provisions of the Geneva Prisoner of War Convention regulating the care and treatment of prisoners,[62] as well as in the initial approach to the repatriation problem. Thus, the United Nations Command consistently reported to the Organisation that in choosing sites for prisoners' camps, in communicating the location of camps to the International

---

[61] *Ante*, p. 56.
[62] *UN Yearbook* (1951) pp. 247–248; 16–31 January 1952 (S/2593); *ibid.* (1952) p. 185, wherein is reported the statement of the United States representative in a debate before the First Committee :—"From the very beginning . . . the United Nations Command had observed the provisions of the Geneva Conventions of 1949." See also letter dated 5 July 1951 from Representative Austin of U.S.A. to Secretary-General of UN, 25 *Dept. of State Bull.* 189–90 (1951).

Committee of the Red Cross, in providing intellectual, recreational and educational facilities for prisoners and in promulgating a penal code to govern the conduct of prisoners during detention, it had acted "in accordance with the Geneva Convention of 12 August, 1949, relative to the treatment of prisoners of war." [63]

The United Nations Emergency Force (UNEF) and the Force of the United Nations operation in the Congo (ONUC) were two Forces of the United Nations which were not endowed, *ab initio*, with the competence to attain belligerent status. Both Forces, however, possessed a definite military character, and one of them was eventually involved in armed conflict. The foremost question is whether there is any latent degree of belligerency in such Forces as would ever permit the customary laws of warfare to be applicable to their hostile activities.

Among the principles of the UNEF Force which the Assembly adopted [64] from the Secretary-General's Second and Final Report,[65] for use in future operations, is the following, numbered paragraph 10:

"There is an obvious difference between establishing the Force in order to secure the cessation of hostilities with a withdrawal of forces, and establishing such a Force with a view to enforcing a withdrawal of forces. It follows that while the Force is different in that, as in many other respects, from the observers of Truce Supervision Organisation, it is, although para-military in nature, not a Force with military objectives."

And this in paragraph 12:

"The Force obviously should have no rights other than those necessary for the execution of its functions, in co-operation with local authorities. It would be more than an observer corps, but in no way a military force temporarily controlling the territory in which it is stationed; nor, moreover, should the Force have military functions exceeding those necessary to secure peaceful conditions on the assumption that the parties to the conflict take all necessary steps for compliance with the recommendations of the General Assembly."

In accordance with the expressly limited military functions granted the Force, the jurisdiction of UNEF was essentially consensual, based on an express agreement on the status of the Force concluded between the Organisation and host State, Egypt.[66] In addition to this agreement, the Command and personnel of the Force were entitled to the privileges and immunities granted by Article 105 of the Charter, as supplemented by the Convention on the Privileges and Immunities of the United Nations (to which the host State had acceded on 7 September 1948). Clearly, the combination of (1) strictly limited military authority; (2) consent to the Force's presence in Egypt; and (3) the special jurisdictional immunities of the agreement

---

[63] *UN Yearbook* (1951) p. 248.
[64] Resol. 1001 (ES–1) (A/3354).
[65] A/3302.
[66] *Report of the Secretary-General on Arrangements Concerning the Status of Forces of the United Nations Emergency Force*, 8 February 1957 (A/3526), annexed to which is the exchange of correspondence constituting the basic agreement between the Organisation and the host State.

is inconsistent with the concept of belligerency. The Regulations for the Force, promulgated by the Secretary-General pursuant to a Resolution of the General Assembly [67] recognise this inconsistency. However, the Regulations [68] also recognise that there may exist situations in which the negotiated agreements would not constitute the controlling norm of behaviour for the Force: hence they provide that: " The Force shall observe the principes and spirit of the general international Conventions applicable to the conduct of military personnel." [69]

The necessity for this provision stemmed from the fact that the Force remained entitled to act in self-defence, as the Secretary-General explained:

" . . . in the types of operation with which this report is concerned (UNEF) the use which could be made of the units provided could never include combat activities . . . There will always remain, of course, a certain margin of freedom for judgment, *e.g.*, on the extent and nature of arming of the units and their right of self-defence . . . A problem arises in this context because of the fact that a wide interpretation of the right of self-defence might blur the distinction between operations of the character discussed in this report and combat operations, which would require a decision under Chapter VII of the Charter, and an explicit, more far-reaching delegation of authority to the Secretary-General . . . A reasonable definition seems to have been established in the case of UNEF, where the rule is applied that men engaged in the operation may never take the initiative in the use of armed force, but are entitled to respond with force to an attack with arms, including attempts to use force to make them withdraw from positions which they occupy under orders from the Commander, acting under the authority of the Assembly and within the scope of its Resolutions. The basic element involved is clearly the prohibition against any initiative in the use of armed force." [70]

The position of ONUC was similar, if not identical, if one looks to the Regulations of the Force,[71] the Status Agreement with the Congo, and the original mandate given by the Security Council: the Force was not to be a " belligerent" Force, and self-defence was initially conceived to be the only circumstance in which a combat situation would arise. However, as the mandate was gradually broadened by the Resolutions of 21 February and 24 November 1961, so did the authorisation to use force extend beyond mere self-defence and, consequently, the combat possibilities increase.[72]

Both examples of " peace Forces," non-enforcement action Forces of the United Nations, illustrate the preoccupation of the Organisation with creating a passive " para-military" presence. Both, at least initially, were prohibited from taking military action on their own initiative. In their normal, authorised duties, the actions of the Command and members of each Force were subject to the regulation

[67] Resol. 1001 (ES-1).
[68] ST/SGB/UNEF/1.
[68] *Ibid.*, paragraph 44.
[70] A/3943, paragraphs 178–179.
[71] ONUC Regulation 43.
[72] *Ante*, pp. 191–196, 201–202.

of the agreements between the United Nations and the host States, the agreements between the United Nations and the Members contributing national contingents to the Forces, the general privileges and immunities granted international personnel of the United Nations, and the Regulations for the Force promulgated by the Secretary-General. In its peaceful operations neither the authority granted to the Forces, nor the agreements and rules establishing its jurisdictional presence and regulating its conduct were consistent with even a limited concept of "belligerency" or combat potential. Under peaceful conditions there was no room for the law of war. However, the Organisation reserved to the Forces the inherent right, if only in the last resort, to employ armed forces in order to defend itself, its weapons, its position, and its rights, granted by the agreements, to free movement within the host State. When these reserved rights were directly opposed or attacked by force, it could no longer be maintained that the various agreements and the regulations were the sole standard of conduct for the Forces. It is submitted that under such conditions the consensual agreements on the status of the Force and the agreements with the contributing members could no longer be dispositive of the law for the Forces. The activities of the Force in this "conditional belligerency" were to be regulated by the applicable rules of the law of war, to the extent commensurate with the amount of force necessary to permit effective self-defence or the full execution of its mandate. This view is consistent with the provisions of paragraphs 44 and 43 of the respective Regulations for the two Forces.

It is submitted that the coercive or enforcement action Forces of the United Nations are endowed, *ab initio*, by their authorisation, with the necessary "belligerent" status to subject their use of armed force to the regulation of the law of war. While the activities of United Nations Forces created for "peace-keeping' 'operations are initially not belligerent in nature, the military actions taken by them in self-defence or in the general execution of their mandate are similarly regulable.

(c) THE LAW OF WAR AS BINDING ON NATIONAL CONTINGENTS CONTRIBUTED TO A UNITED NATIONS FORCE

In all but one of the various organisational patterns available to the United Nations, the main body of the Force, whether or not under the direction of a United Nations Command *stricto sensu*, is composed of national contingents contributed by Member States.[73]

It is therefore timely to consider the applicability of the laws of war to national contingents serving under a United Nations mandate before undertaking a similar inquiry involving the United Nations itself.

It is difficult to posit any persuasive theories which would release

[73] *Ante*, p. 314.

a State's military forces from the binding force of the laws of war, *as a matter of law*, simply because they are engaged in fulfilling a United Nations mandate. The only argument upon which that conclusion could rest would be based on the superior legal position occupied by forces opposing an unlawful aggressor; as has been seen earlier, there is strong judicial and other opinion which rejects this theory.[74] Thus, it must be concluded that national contingents in the service of the United Nations are bound, to the same extent and degree, to all those rules of warfare which would obtain if the same forces were engaged in international armed conflict for the State alone.

This conclusion has, in fact, been officially adopted by many States and incorporated by them into the field manuals issued to their armed forces. For example, the United States Army Field Manual adopts the position that the law of war governing the actions of its land forces is applicable to other situations than those involving a formal declaration of war, stating that:

"Instances of armed conflict without declaration of war may include, but are not necessarily limited to, the exercise of armed force pursuant to a *recommendation, decision,* or *call* by the United Nations . . . *or otherwise in conformity* with appropriate provisions of the United Nations Charter." [75]

The emphasis in the above extract (which has been supplied) suggests that the laws of war apply, as a matter of law, not only to individual action by United States military forces pursuant to Articles 51 or 53 of the Charter, but also to United States forces engaged in collective enforcement action as well as " peace-keeping" duties under the direct control of the United Nations. Similar declarations can be found in the United States naval manual,[76] as well as the *British Manual of Military Law*, although the latter is more guarded in its approach.[77]

It is submitted, however, that such statements in official or semi-official government documents are declaratory rather than constitutive, at least as far as the application of the *customary* law of war is concerned. To the extent that various categories of the law of war become relevant in specific United Nations actions, national contingents serving under the United Nations mandate remain bound to conform to those laws, irrespective of the existence or absence of unilateral declarations to that effect. It is further submitted that, even should the United Nations fail to declare its intentions with respect to those laws, the better legal opinion would probably hold that no analogy to pleas of superior orders would exculpate the

---

[74] *Ante,* p. 495.
[75] United States Army Field Manual, *The Law of Land Warfare* (1956) p. 7.
[76] United States Navy, *Law of Naval Warfare* (1955) paragraph 200.
[77] " Although there may be room for argument as to whether hostilities waged for the collective enforcement of international law—in particular under the Charter of the United Nations—constitute a war, both the Hague Rules and the customary rules of warfare are applicable to hostilities of that character." *Part III, The Law of War on Land* (1958) paragraph 7, p. 5.

national contingents from their duty to adhere to all the relevant rules.

Clearly, however, all national contingents are not necessarily equally bound, as a matter of law, by all the conventional laws of war. It is true that most of the pre-Second World War conventions are now considered declaratory of customary law,[78] but in relation to the most recent conventions, being bound depends almost wholly on formal accession by a State, or, at the least, on a declaration to conform. This is of vital import to a United Nations Force composed of national contingents where it is possible that some States will be parties to the conventions while others are not. Not the least important factor is that the more modern conventions represent the greatest efforts to date made to ameliorate the conditions of prisoners of war and sick and wounded combatants. A United Nations Force in which only some of the States contributing national contingents have acceded to the Geneva Conventions of 1949 would very probably be at cross-purposes in its treatment of various classes of protected persons. Of more consequence to the Force itself is the possibility that an opponent engaged in armed conflict with an integrated United Nations Force composed of national units, some adhering to, others not bound by, the Geneva Conventions, might lawfully be entitled to treat the entire Force as not within the reciprocal protection of those laws. The obvious and distressing result could be that combatants whose State, by formal accession, had achieved for them the benefits of the conventional laws of war in all other circumstances, may find themselves unprotected when engaged in United Nations service.

It is for the United Nations itself to avoid such dire consequences. The solution lies in a demand by the United Nations for uniform adherence to all the relevant conventions as a prerequisite to the acceptance of any national contingent or, at the very least, a formal declaration by the State that, for the purposes of service with the United Nations, its contingent and the State itself accept in full the obligations of the conventions in question. Further, the agreements concluded between the organ responsible for the Force and the Member contributing a contingent should provide for the immediate withdrawal from the Force of that contingent should it appear that the conventional laws of war are not applicable to that unit as a matter of law.

The efficacy of such a solution to the problem of lack of uniformity in the application of the laws of war among national contingents serving in United Nations Forces may, however, depend

---

[78] "The rules of land warfare expressed in the Convention undoubtedly represent an advance over existing law at the time of adoption . . . but by 1939 these rules laid down in the Convention were recognised by all civilised nations and were regarded as being declaratory of the laws and customs of war . . ." I.M.T. (Nuremburg), Judgment, p. 65; similarly see I.M.T. (Tokyo) 15 *War Crimes Reports*, pp. 86–87; U.S. Army Field Manual, *The Law of Land Warfare*, (1956); *British Manual of Military Law* (1958) p. 4.

on the extent to which the United Nations, and its command organisation, are bound as a matter of law to both the customary and conventional rules of warfare. Declarations of intentions or formal accession by national contingents will be of little legal or practical significance if the command structure responsible for both strategic direction and disciplinary control of the entire Force is outside the régime of the law of war.

(d) THE LAW OF WAR AS BINDING ON THE UNITED NATIONS AS SUCH

(i) *Customary rules*

Not all the laws of war are relevant to United Nations Forces. So far as the basic distinction between the *jus ad bellum* and the *jus in bello* is concerned, the Charter has made the former inapplicable to United Nations action. The position with the latter is, however, far more difficult. As was seen in an earlier section,[79] many of the rules of warfare obtaining *pendente bello* may be equally irrelevant, *vis-à-vis* a Member of the Organisation. Such was seen to be the case with the treatment of public property in the territory of a Member State in which obligations under the Charter may estop the occupied State from claiming the benefits of the Hague Regulations. And the entire emphasis of the laws of neutrality may be similarly affected.

If the customary law of war is found to be applicable as a matter of law to United Nations Forces, its principal impact is on the regulation of the actual armed combat. This includes all the direct contact between the belligerents; the means adopted for the killing or wounding of the enemy, or the destruction of his resources; the lawful objects of attack, and the treatment of those incapable of further resistance.

As to the actual conduct of armed conflict, the controlling principles of the customary law are expressed in the Hague Regulations. As applied to United Nations Forces, this principle governs not only the weapons with which such Forces may be equipped, but also the way such weapons may be employed.

In addition, customary law [80] would prohibit to the Forces of the United Nations, regardless of the justification for the use of armed force, the use of treachery to wound or kill, the refusal to accept surrender or give quarter, and the inflicting of unnecessary suffering. These and the similar rules of customary law prohibiting individual or collective excesses in combat are applicable in all circumstances of international armed conflict, representing as they do the minimum standards of (in the words of both the 1907 Hague and the 1949 Geneva Conventions) " the usages established among civilised people, the laws of humanity and the dictates of the public conscience."

[79] *Ante,* p. 492.
[80] *Ante,* p. 489.

(ii) *Conventional rules*

It is generally accepted that some of the rules of warfare arising from international agreements are binding as a matter of general international law. These include such treaties as the Hague Convention of 1907 concerning the Laws and Customs of War on Land, and the Regulations attached to it, which, according to the International Military Tribunals and other war crimes tribunals after the Second World War, were declaratory of existing customary law.[81] Similar reasoning was applied to the Geneva Convention, 1929, relative to the Treatment of Prisoners of War,[82] which by its own terms was complementary to Chapter II of the Hague Regulations.[83] In so far as the customary laws of warfare are applicable to United Nations Forces, it is to be concluded that the provisions of these conventions are similarly binding, without requiring accession to them by the United Nations. There are, however, numerous other international agreements embodying laws of war whose provisions are not considered to be binding as a matter of law, without consent to them by States.[84] With respect to the United Nations being bound *as a matter of law* by these conventions, certain difficult questions of law arise. It is doubtful whether these conventions can be acceded to by an international organisation. By their terms they are only binding on *States* which have ratified or acceded to them and have not subsequently denounced them. The additional problem is that almost all of these conventions, with the exception of the 1929 and 1949 Geneva " Red Cross " treaties, are further limited by the employment of " general participation clauses " which provide that the Conventions would be binding only if all belligerents were parties to them. If the United Nations, because it is not a State, is unable to become a party to such Conventions, then the very appearance of a United Nations Force as a belligerent would operate to release from the control of such Conventions any opponent which would otherwise be bound.[85]

Doubtless the United Nations possesses sufficient legal capacity to make or accede to treaties which, while not authorised by specific provisions of the Charter, are authorised by implication from those provisions.[86]

Thus, from the authority given the organisation to create and employ armed Forces can be implied the correlative authority to make treaties on behalf of or for the protection of those Forces. But this can only be possible where, by the terms of the treaty to which the United Nations wishes to become a party, an international organisation is permitted to accede. There is little on which to base

---

[81] I.M.T., Judgment, p. 65; I.M.T. (Tokyo) 15 *War Crimes Trials* at p. 13; *Krupp and Others*, 10 *War Crimes Trials*, p. 133.
[82] *German High Command Trial*, 12 *War Crimes Trials*, pp. 86–87.
[83] Article 89.
[84] For a catalogue of these, see Oppenheim, *op. cit.*, pp. 229–331.
[85] Taubenfield, " International Armed Forces and The Rules of War," (1951) 45 A.J.I.L. 674.
[86] Weissberg, *International Status of the United Nations* (1961), p. 38.

a legal opinion that the United Nations or any international organisation may accede to most of these conventions.

Each of the four Geneva Conventions of 1949 [87] incorporated radical departures from the schemes employed in all prior international agreements respecting the law of war. The question presented by them is whether these changes make it possible for the United Nations to accede to them or to what extent the United Nations may be permitted to declare its intention to respect the conventions and therefore secure for its Forces the reciprocal protection provided by them.

Among the most significant changes adopted by the Geneva Conventions was the acceptance by the High Contracting Parties that the provisions of each of them were to apply without regard to the legality of the resort to war. The Conventions apply " in all circumstances." [88] In addition, and of equal consequence, the Conventions are applicable either to declared war in the classical sense or to an international " armed conflict " in which a state of war is not recognised.[89] The combined effect of both of these common provisions is to recognise the applicability of the rules of war in the Conventions to just such instances of armed conflict in which a United Nations Force would participate.

The position taken by most of the States which are High Contracting Parties and also Members of the United Nations is that their armed forces are bound by the Conventions when participating in an action on behalf of, or pursuant to the authority of, the Organisation.[90] Yet this does not dispose of the question whether the United Nations itself may accede to the Conventions. As has been seen, both the Article 43 Forces of the Charter and the *ad hoc* Forces represented by UNEF and ONUC consist of unified international commands directly responsible to the Organisation and forces made up of unintegrated national contingents. Irrespective of the intention of the national contingents to remain bound by the Conventions, the inability of the Organisation itself to comply with the Conventions will affect the entire Force. Alternatively, the possibility that a national contingent may not be a party to the Convention, could affect both the command and the remainder of the Force. The initial investigation must therefore be into the possible avenues by which the United Nations could attempt to secure for its Forces the rights and duties provided by the Conventions.

[87] Geneva Convention, 1949, for the Amelioration of the Condition of the Wounded and Sick in Armed Forces in the Field; Geneva Convention, 1949, for the Amelioration of the Condition of the Wounded and Sick in Armed Forces at Sea; Geneva Convention, 1949, relative to the treatment of Prisoners of War; and Geneva Convention, 1949, relative to the Protection of Civilian Persons in Time of War; hereafter each respectively referred to as Wounded—Land Convention; Wounded—Sea Convention; Prisoner of War Convention; and Civilian Convention.
[88] Geneva Conventions, 1949, Common Article 1.
[89] *Ibid.*, Common Article 2 (1). [90] *Ante*, p. 504.

The Geneva Conventions were adopted by "High Contracting Parties," all of whom were States. By their express provisions, each is open to accession by "Powers." [91] Disregarding for the moment the ability of the United Nations, its command structure and its Forces generally to comply with the provisions of the Conventions, it would appear that as each convention is open to accession only by "Powers" special provision would be necessary to permit accession by international organisations and commands.[92]

There are two possible alternative methods by which the United Nations could be bound by the Geneva Conventions. The first amounts to little more than an admission that a United Nations Force cannot be bound by the substantive rules of the Conventions. This arises out of the wording of Article 3, common to each of the Conventions, which provides for the reciprocal application by the contending Forces of only the minimum humanitarian safeguards in circumstances "of armed conflict not of an international character occurring in the territory of one of the High Contracting Parties." On its face, this novel and highly salutory provision was introduced into the law of war to regulate, if only tangentially, civil war or insurgency not recognised as belligerency. Notwithstanding, it was during the period of heated combat in Katanga Province that some opinion contended that if the ONUC Force was subject to any part of the Geneva Conventions, only the minimum humanitarian provisions of Article 3 were applicable.[93] There are two difficulties in the way of accepting this view. In the first case it is difficult to see how hostilities in which the United Nations is involved can be regarded as "not of an international character," and in the second the United Nations in the Congo simply did not accept this view.

Although the Republic of the Congo had acceded to the Geneva Conventions,[94] and therefore the ONUC Force was operating in the territory of a "High Contracting Party" according to the definition in Article 3 of the Conventions, both the Regulations for the Force [95] and the communication of the Acting Secretary-General to the President of the International Committee of the Red Cross indicate that the Organisation contemplated that the applicable law of war

---

[91] Wounded—Land Convention, Section 60; Wounded—Sea Convention, Section 59; Prisoner of War Convention, Section 139; and Civilian Convention, section 155.

[92] Baxter, *op. cit.* (1952) 29 B.Y.I.L. 356; Baxter goes on to point out that this problem is not unique to the United Nations but is similar to the legal position of the various defence organisations, NATO, Warsaw Pact, etc., which contain international military commands, integrated in command structure alone; Symposium (1961) 37 *Notre Dame Lawyer* 82.

[93] Draper, (1963) 12 I.C.L.Q. at p. 410.

[94] " In its letter of February 24, 1961, to the Federal Political Department in Berne, the Government of the Republic of the Congo (Leopoldville) confirms that this State would abide by the Geneva Conventions of 1949 as from June 30th, 1960, when it became Independent." *International Review of the Red Cross* (May, 1961) p. 90.

[95] *Ante,* p. 222.

for the Force was that for *international* armed conflicts. The letter states:—

"I am in entire agreement with you in considering that the Geneva Conventions of 1949 constitute the most complete standards according to the human person indispensable guarantees for his protection *in time of war or in the case of armed conflict whatever form it may take.* I also wish to confirm that United Nations insist on its armed Forces in the field applying the principles of the Conventions as scrupulously as possible. . . .
"In so far as UNEF is concerned, a formal provision to this effect has been inscribed in Article 44 of the Regulations . . . a similar provision will apply to the United Nations Forces in the Congo." [96]

The second possible method, at least in theory, is essentially consensual. Article 2 (3), another provision common to each of the Conventions, directs that in instances of armed conflict involving a High Contracting Party of the Conventions and a Power not a Party to them, the former will continue to be bound by all the substantive provisions if the latter " accepts and applies the principles thereof." As a replacement for the " general participation clause " of former international agreements relative to the conduct of war, this section is interpreted not only to compel adherence among High Contracting Parties in conflicts in which a non-party is participating, but also to permit the full application of the treaties between all belligerents if the non-parties, by both words and actions, comply with the Conventions. [97] The Korean experience has illustrated that Article 2 (3) can afford the basis of reciprocal application of the Conventions in situations where neither side has either ratified or acceded to them.

There is an alternative legal construction of Article 2 (3) which would permit only those international political entities which were capable of actual accession to the Conventions to accept the provisions of them when engaged in hostilities with a High Contracting Party. Under this interpretation the " Power" which Article 2 (3) speaks of is taken to be a State. Thus, if the United Nations was found to be incapable of strict accession, it would also be frustrated in its attempts to qualify under Article 2 (3).

The position at present is, therefore, both difficult and obscure, and the better view is that a specific attempt should be made to clarify the position of the United Nations with regard to these Conventions. The solution which would be technically correct, but extremely cumbersome, would be to persuade all the parties to the various Conventions to agree to a Protocol enabling accession by the United Nations. A simpler solution, which in practice might be equally effective, would be for the General Assembly to resolve that

[96] *International Review of the Red Cross* (January 1962) p. 29. (Emphasis supplied.)
[97] Pictet, *Commentaries on the Geneva Conventions of 1949* (1960), Vol. iii, pp. 24–27; Draper, *The Red Cross Conventions* (1952) pp. 12–13.

the Conventions were applicable to United Nations Forces.[98] Certainly, so far as States voting for the Resolution are concerned, this expression of agreement could be regarded as an estoppel, for all future occasions, against such States. Moreover, the Resolution could enjoin States to make the necessary modifications in their municipal law and military manuals.

Thus far, however, we have been concerned simply with the acceptance of the Conventions by the United Nations or a matter of *law*. The question to which we must now turn is whether, as a matter of practice, the United Nations would be in a position to assume the rights or carry out the duties contained in these Conventions.

2. *As a matter of practical application*

A bare declaration by a government or by the United Nations of its willingness to adhere to the customary laws of war has very little effect in law or in fact unless the opponent can depend on an ability to compel the commander and the force to act lawfully. More importantly, the United Nations and its commander must both be responsible for the Force's adherence to the law and capable of ensuring that those individuals who act illegally will be properly disciplined. This is now a recognised principle of the customary law of war. It was codified in 1907 in the Hague Convention Respecting the Laws and Customs of War on Land and the Regulations annexed thereto. Thus, Article 1 of the Convention would require that the United Nations issue " instructions to their armed land Forces which shall be in conformity " with the Regulations. Article 3 requires that the United Nations should be " responsible for all acts committed by persons forming part of its armed Forces." As traditionally conceived this Article referred to a responsibility to pay reparations for breaches of the law of war, but it may be argued that it has now been expanded to include enforcement by trial and punishment of members of the Force who have been guilty of violations. The annexed Regulations, in Article 1, require that in order for any force to be granted the privileges due to belligerents, it " must be commanded by a person responsible for his subordinates." These three articles jointly and severally raise the question of whether the command structure of the United Nations Forces permits compliance with the fundamental principles of the customary laws of warfare. In this respect it is helpful to begin the inquiry by investigating the actual practice of the United Nations.

Due to the anomalous character of the Korean experience, the Forces under the Unified Command, while properly designated United

---

[98] The use of Resolutions to achieve a result which might more correctly have been achieved by a formal act of States parties to a treaty acting as such can be seen in the dissolution of the League and the Permanent Court of International Justice by Resolution of the Assembly of the League in 1946.

Nations Forces, do not qualify as typical "international forces" [99] under an international command structure. Therefore, beyond the precedents which were established concerning the willingness of the United Nations to adhere to the law of war, the Korean action does not help in the investigation of the suitability of the present law to international commands. The only extant examples, and the most likely ones for the future, are the *ad hoc* "peace-keeping" Forces, UNEF and ONUC. It was seen earlier [1] that the Regulations provided by the Secretary-General for each of the Forces made a basic division in command authority between the United Nations Commander and his staff and the commander and staff of the national contingents. It is the division between the Commander's responsibility for good order and the participating State's responsibility for discipline that raises the most serious questions concerning the requisite responsibility along the entire chain of command which the laws of war demand. It would appear that a violation of the rules of warfare by an individual member of the United Nations Force could be protected from punishment by his State, notwithstanding the good intentions of the Organisation or its Commander in the field. If this were the actual fact, declarations by the United Nations of its intention to adhere to the law of war when its Forces are engaged in belligerent activities would be meaningless. The opponent could have little reliance on the efficacy of the bare declaration. The reciprocity of action so necessary to secure the enforcement of the rules of war would vanish.

It is submitted, however, that with particular reference to UNEF and the ONUC Forces, the responsibility to enforce discipline on its own nationals reserved to the participating States was not as discretionary as the Regulations alone would have it appear. The letter from the Secretary-General to the participating States (which, with the official response to it, constitutes an agreement between the United Nations and the participating State, declaring the terms on which the national contingents are to be accepted), explains and modifies the questioned paragraph 13 of the Regulations thus:

" I should appreciate your assurance that the commander of the national contingent provided by your government will be in a position to exercise the necessary disciplinary authority. I should also appreciate your assurance that your government will be prepared to exercise jurisdiction with respect to any crime or offence which might be committed by a member of such national contingent." [2]

If this letter and the response thereto amount to a valid international treaty obligation by the participating State, unconditionally undertaking to enforce against the members of its national contingents all violations of the customary laws of war, then, and to the extent that such an undertaking is legally enforceable, the United

---

[99] Baxter, "Constitutional Forms and Some Legal Problems of International Military Commands," (1952) 29 B.Y.I.L. 335–336; and *ante*, pp. 39–47.

[1] *Ante*, pp. 338–346.

[2] A/3943 Annex I.

Nations Forces are able to comply with the primary responsibility placed on it by the law of war.

Certainly there is already some authority for the view that a State does not lose its capacity to carry out an undertaking to discipline members of its contingent simply because the contingent is placed under a United Nations Command.[3]

There would also be a decided advantage in developing a practice whereby the United Nations would issue to all contingents its own military manual so as to ensure compliance with Article 1 of the 1907 Hague Convention.[4] Indeed, should the United Nations ever proceed to individual recruitment of a Force this would be absolutely essential, together with the requisite machinery of a courts-martial to enforce compliance. The suggestion has been made earlier that even national contingents serving on a fixed-term basis with a permanent Force might, with the agreement of their States, be made subject to the jurisdiction of United Nations Courts-martial.[5]

The present lack of jurisdictional competence in the United Nations has even further repercussions on the problem of the practical application of the laws of war. The Four Geneva Conventions of 1949, for example, were primarily designed to relieve the unnecessary suffering and privation of war victims: sick and wounded combatants and non-combatants, prisoners of war and civilians. Each of the four presuppose that a person protected by one of the Conventions has come under the control of the High Contracting Party as a direct result of the armed conflict in which it is engaged. As it was presumed that each Party to the Conventions would be a State, the Conventions envisaged a code of conduct based on national standards. In order for the United Nations to be

---

[3] See *Jennings* v. *Markley*, 186 Fed.Supp. 611 (S.D. Indiana 1960) wherein Petitioner, in support of the contention that he was being illegally restrained following a conviction by a general court-martial for unpremeditated murder of a Korean boy, while serving with the United States Armed Forces in the Korean action, alleged, *inter alia*, that service with the United Nations Forces directed that he be tried by either the United Nations Military Staff Committee or the International Court of Justice. The District Court denied the petition and held, in part, that:

". . . the United States in supporting the United Nations in its efforts to restore peace and security in Korea was acting as a nation through the use of its armed forces. There is nothing in the Charter of the United Nations from which to conclude that a member of the armed forces of a member nation does not retain his status as a soldier in the army of the respective member nation. As a member of the United States Army, the petitioner, whether being led under the flag of the United States, or the United Nations, nevertheless remained subject to the immediate control and jurisdiction of the United States Army."

Affirmed in 290 F. 2d 892 (1961).

[4] The duty to disseminate information is not confined to this Convention. Each of the four Geneva Conventions contains not only a duty to disseminate the text but also " to include the study thereof in the programmes of military and, if possible, civilian instruction, so that the principles thereof may become known to the entire population, in particular to the armed forces . . ." : Geneva Wounded—Land, Article 47; Prisoner of War, Article 127; Civilian Article 144.

[5] *Ante*, p. 353.

considered a " Power " within the definition of common Article 2 (3) of the Conventions and thus be permitted to " accept and apply the provisions," it seems inescapable that the Organisation must comply with certain fundamental preconditions on which the binding force of the treaties depend.

Apart from the obligation to disseminate the text of the Conventions and promote instruction in them,[6] each Convention requires that a party to it enact legislation " necessary to provide effective penal sanctions for persons committing, or ordering to be committed, any of the grave breaches . . ." [7] which are respectively designated in each text. All of these articles further require that similar legislation be enacted by a party " for the suppression of all acts contrary to the provisions . . ." other than the specified grave breaches, and each party covenants not only to search for violators but to prosecute them " before its own courts." With respect to those prosecutions, all accused persons tried for grave breaches of the Conventions must be accorded certain minimum safeguards of proper trial and defence.[8] In addition to procedural safeguards is the obligation to ensure that the conditions of internment for prisoners who have been convicted are at least equal to those provided for the members of the armed forces of the prosecuting power.[9] Numerous other examples can be found of the requirements of the Conventions with which the United Nations is neither functionally nor legally constituted to comply. A prisoner of war may be punished *only* for acts forbidden by international law or the law of the Detaining Power which must have existed prior to his capture. Trials of accused prisoners (if they are protected persons within the definition of the Convention) must be by the same courts and according to the same procedure as would apply if the prisoner were a member of the armed forces of the Detaining Power.[10] Prisoners of war being prosecuted for war crimes (as opposed to " grave breaches ") committed before capture are similarly prohibited from being tried by *ad hoc* courts.[11] National standards also obtain in the evacuation of prisoners,[12] the conditions for their labour [13] and for their remuneration.[14] In the administration of an occupied area, the relevant provisions permit an " Occupying Power " to promulgate and enforce penal provisions in courts set up by it, and it is necessary for a protected person not only to know who is the " Occupying Power "

---

[6] *Ante*, p. 513, fn. 4.
[7] Geneva Wounded—Land, Article 49; Geneva Prisoner of War, Article 129; Geneva Civilian, Article 146.
[8] *Ibid.*
[9] Geneva Prisoner of War, Article 108; each of the Conventions established that the Prisoner of War Conventions, Article 105 ff, shall be the standard for all " grave breaches " trials.
[10] Geneva Prisoner of War, Articles 82, 84, 99, 102.
[11] *Ibid.*, Articles 85, 99, 102.
[12] *Ibid.*, Article 20.
[13] *Ibid.*, Articles 51–53.
[14] *Ibid.*, Article 60.

but also to be able to appeal convictions to the courts of that Power.[15] From these, and the similar provisions of the Conventions which would require the United Nations to possess legislative and judicial competence which are clearly beyond its powers, there is little doubt that unless the Organisation can ensure that these conditions may be fulfilled, according to the letter and spirit of the Conventions, the rights and responsibilities flowing from the Conventions are inaccessible to the United Nations Forces.

From the foregoing analysis, which is merely illustrative rather than exhaustive, it is seen that in such basic areas of the law of war as the treatment of prisoners of war, the legislative and judicial control of occupied territory, and the treatment of civilian inhabitants and property, the United Nations is presently powerless. But there are other areas beside the conventional laws of war which present similar problems. Foremost among these is the law of war at sea. The use of the United Nations flag on board vessels is not novel, and warships have already operated as part of a United Nations Force.[16] However, unless one presupposes that, for jurisdictional purposes, the vessel remains a national vessel of a Member State, a jurisdictional vacuum is produced in respect of acts on board the vessel. In addition, at the very heart of the laws of sea warfare lies the Prize Court system, permitting the belligerent power to adjudicate the lawful nature of its captures in a municipal court, albeit one to a certain extent applying international as well as municipal law. Clearly the United Nations has neither the courts nor a municipal law.

There are various solutions which could be adopted in an attempt to remedy the practical problems which the United Nations presently faces in applying the law of war. If the political atmosphere of the international community permitted, a protocol of agreement among all the signatories of the Geneva Conventions of 1929 and 1949, as previously mentioned, would be most helpful. Such a protocol could effect an agreement which would " adapt " those Conventions to the special position in international law which the United Nations occupies. A step of that nature does present serious questions arising from the possibly deleterious results of instituting a double standard, one for States and one for United Nations Forces. This could be overcome by permitting the United Nations in each instance to designate the municipal and military law of one of its Member States as the law applicable to the entire Force for purposes of fulfilling all the national standards for the disciplining of prisoners of war, the civil administration of occupied territory and the like. Under this type of arrangement it would be the law of the designated State to which all the rest of the components of the Force would adhere. It might equally be possible for the United Nations to

---

[15] *Ibid.*, Article 106.
[16] *Ante*, pp. 40, 259.

designate one or more Member States providing contingents for the Force to act as its judicial " agents," so as to utilise their existing judicial machinery in the absence of a United Nations machinery.

That the law of war in respect of the special position of the United Nations is in need of reorganisation and fundamental revision is generally conceded. Whether it is possible or even advisable to do more than has been suggested above in the light of the present political realities within the United Nations itself is difficult to assess. But the remarks of Professor Baxter in this regard are highly pertinent :

" Universality of membership in the United Nations, the abolition of the veto now held by the great military Powers, the possibility of international legislation, and the establishment of international police forces would be requisites of any far-reaching changes in the law. It will then be proper to adopt rules governing the conduct of international forces. . . ." [17]

[17] Baxter, *op. cit.*, (1952) 29 B.Y.I.L. 359.

Part Three

16

Disarmament and an International Force

I. THE RELATIONSHIP OF DISARMAMENT TO PEACEKEEPING

ONE of the agreed principles set out in the Joint Statement by the United States and the U.S.S.R. of 20 September 1961 was that:

"Progress in disarmament should be accompanied by measures to strengthen institutions for maintaining peace and the settlement of international disputes by peaceful means. During and after the implementation of the programme of general and complete disarmament, there should be taken in accordance with the principles of the United Nations Charter, the necessary measures to maintain international peace and security, including the obligation of States to place at the disposal of the United Nations agreed manpower necessary for an international peace Force to be equipped with agreed types of armaments. Arrangements for the use of this Force should ensure that the United Nations can effectively deter or suppress any threat or use of arms in violation of the purposes and principles of the United Nations." [1]

In the drafts which followed, submitted by both the United States and the Soviet Union, this principle—which reflects the essential interdependence of proposals for disarmament and proposals for a United Nations Force—was given further amplification.

The "Outline of Basic Provisions of a Treaty on General and Complete Disarmament in a Peaceful World" [2] (hereafter called the "United States Treaty Outline"), presented by the United States to the Geneva Conference of the Eighteen-Nation Committee on Disarmament on 18 April 1962, and endorsed by the other Western Powers at the Conference (Canada, Italy and the United Kingdom), contains proposals not only on disarmament but also on the following subjects:

(1) Reaffirmation of the obligations contained in the Charter of the United Nations concerning the threat or use of force.

(2) Codification and progressive development of rules of international conduct related to disarmament.

---

[1] UN Doc. A/4879, 20 September 1961.
[2] "Blueprint for the Peace Race: Outline of Basic Provisions of a Treaty on General and Complete Disarmament in a Peaceful World," U.S. Arms Control and Disarmament Agency, Publ. 4 (May 1962), hereafter cited as "Blueprint." The same can be seen in the documents of the Geneva Conference as ENDC/30 or in *Further Documents Relating to the Conference of the 18-Nation Committee on Disarmament* (Session 14, March 1962 to 15 June 1962) (1962) Cmnd. 1792, p. 53.

(3) Obligation to refrain from indirect aggression and subversion, and development of methods of assuring States against indirect aggression or subversion.

(4) Peaceful settlement of disputes, both legal and political.

(5) Strengthening the structure, authority and operation of the United Nations.

(6) United Nations Peace Force.

(7) United Nations Peace Observation Corps.[3]

There is a close connection between disarmament and the other arrangements for the maintenance of peace which are listed above. As President Kennedy has stated in his address before the General Assembly of the United Nations on 25 September 1961: "To destroy arms, however, is not enough. We must create even as we destroy— creating worldwide law and law enforcement as we outlaw world-wide war and weapons."[4] In United States official thinking this idea may be traced back to a speech made by Secretary of State Herter on 18 February 1960, where he defined the final goal of disarmament negotiations as follows: "to cut national forces and armaments further and to build up international peacekeeping machinery, to the point where aggression will be deterred by inter-national rather than national force."[5] He pointed out also that to achieve this goal, the following objectives need to be accepted:

"*First*, to create certain universally accepted rules of law which, if followed, would prevent all nations from attacking other nations. Such rules of law should be backed by a world court and by effective means of enforce-ment—that is, by international armed forces.

"*Second*, to reduce national armed forces, under safeguarded and verified arrangements, to the point where no single nation or group of nations could effectively oppose this enforcement of international law by international machinery.

"Unless *both* these objectives are kept firmly in view, an agreement for general disarmament might lead to a world of anarchy. In the absence of effective international peace-keeping machinery, nations might violate the disarmament agreement with impunity and thus seek to gain a decisive head-start in building up their armaments. Moreover, since each State would be allowed to retain internal security forces, populous States would retain quite substantial forces which they might—in the absence of such peace-keeping machinery—use effectively against their smaller neighbours.

"To guard against these dangers, we should, as general disarmament is approached, work towards effective international arrangements which will maintain peace and security and promote justice according to law. We are ready now to take part in appropriate studies to this end. A useful frame-work and considerable body of experience already exists in the United Nations.

"These studies could focus on two types of basic and needed change:

"*First*, the strengthening and development of international instruments to prevent national aggression in a world that has been disarmed, except for internal security forces.

[3] Blueprint, pp. 19–21, 27–28, 33–34.
[4] "Let Us Call a Truce to Terror," U.S. Department of State Publ. 7282 (October 1961), p. 11.
[5] "National Security with Arms Limitation," 42 U.S. *Department of State Bulletin*, p. 354, at p. 356 (7 March 1960).

"*Second*, the strengthening and development of international machinery to insure just and peaceful settlement of disputed issues in a disarmed world.

"Progress along both these basic lines will be needed if the goal of general disarmament is to be fulfilled." [6]

The essential interdependence of disarmament and the development of the United Nations peacekeeping machinery has been stressed repeatedly by the Western Powers.[7] However, whilst accepting this as a general principle, the Soviet Union clearly regarded disarmament as not being dependent upon the establishment of machinery necessary to guarantee, in any absolute sense, a truly "peaceful" world. Mr. Zorin, the Soviet delegate to the Disarmament Conference, opposed the insertion of the phrase "in a peaceful world" in the preamble to the draft treaty, because "we consider it undesirable to make the establishment of a 'peaceful world' a prerequisite for the solution of the problem of general and complete disarmament." [8] Nevertheless, the Soviet Union agreed to the inclusion in that preamble of a paragraph stating the conviction of the parties that "disarmament must be general and complete under strict and effective international control and that such disarmament must be accompanied by the establishment of reliable procedures for the peaceful settlement of disputes and effective arrangements for the maintenance of peace in accordance with the principles of the United Nations Charter." [9]

The Soviet draft "Treaty on General and Complete Disarmament under Strict International Control" (hereafter called "the Soviet Draft Treaty"), first submitted on 15 March 1962, and revised on 24 September 1962, provides for the retention by States, upon completion of general and complete disarmament, of "strictly limited contingents of police (militia) . . . for the discharge of their obligations with regard to the maintenance of international peace and security under the United Nations Charter." [10] This draft contains also a statement of general obligations of States:

" . . .

" (a) to base relations with each other on the principles of peaceful and friendly coexistence and co-operation;

" (b) not to resort to the threat or use of force to settle any international disputes that may arise, but to use for this purpose the procedures provided for in the United Nations Charter;

" (c) to strengthen the United Nations as the principal institution for the maintenance of peace and for the settlement of international disputes by peaceful means." [11]

The draft does not contain any suggestions how these particular obligations should be implemented, though it deals in some detail

[6] *Ibid.,* p. 357.
[7] Statement by U.S. delegate, UN Doc. ENDC/PV.22, p. 6 (17 April 1962); and by the U.K. delegate, UN Doc. ENDC/PV.29, p. 12 (2 May 1962).
[8] UN Doc. ENDC/PV.22, p. 11 (17 April 1962).
[9] UN Doc. ENDC/L.11/Rev.1 (17 April 1962).
[10] UN Doc. ENDC/2 (15 March 1962) p. 2, and A/C.1/867 (24 September 1962) p. 2, also in Cmnd. 1958, p. 12.
[11] UN Doc. A/C.1/867 (24 September 1962) Article 3.

with the question of placing at the disposal of the Security Council of, first, national armed forces and, later, contingents of police (militia).[12]

In the light of these developments, it is possible to conclude that there is a large measure of agreement that disarmament and peace-keeping are inter-dependent. It is generally agreed that disarmament does not necessarily guarantee peace. In the early stages of the disarmament process nations will still have sufficient arms to wage a limited war, and such a war can easily grow into a nuclear war. Even in a completely disarmed world, a nation could use the police or militia forces remaining to it for an attack and, as in ancient days, employ comparatively primitive weapons for a complete destruction of its enemy. It also has to be remembered that knowledge of the new weapons cannot be obliterated and, if a war should start, arms production would be revived, the arms race would be resumed and nuclear weapons would be brought back. It is not sufficient, there-fore, to devise methods for reducing arms and for verifying effectively that nations have disarmed; parallel steps must be taken in other areas to strengthen the institutions for maintaining peace. In par-ticular, it is well known that no inspection system is foolproof [13] and that a determined aggressor can secrete a sizeable number of dangerous weapons without risk of immediate detection. Those nations which have, nevertheless, been asked to abandon almost all their armaments will not consider it possible to take such a step unless disarmament is accompanied by the creation of a strong inter-national peace Force, able to cope with a sudden threat of aggression. Without a stronger United Nations, able to deal severely with an aggressor or, even better, able to stop him at the first sign of danger, a mere agreement on disarmament may become a perilous trap.

This does not mean, however, that peacekeeping measures must accompany all disarmament steps, or should constitute a pre-condition for disarmament. It can certainly be argued that as long as the measures of disarmament proposed for the early stages do not change the present political and military balance in the world, and to the extent that States retain sufficient military forces to protect them-selves against an armed attack or a gross violation of the disarma-ment treaty, no new peacekeeping arrangements are needed. Only in the last stage, when the national forces start falling below a safe minimum, will it be necessary to provide an international guarantee for national security.

However, such an argument rests on the premise that the present peacekeeping arrangements are adequate, and this is a premise which it has been the object of Parts One and Two of the present study to

---

[12] *Ibid.*, Arts. 18, 27, 37.
[13] See the paper entitled "The technical possibility of international control of fissile material production" submitted by the U.K. delegation on 31 August 1962 as a contribution to the Committee's discussion of item 5 (d) of ENDC/1/Add. 3.

deny. To leave the maintenance of international peace and security to the rather delicate balance of military strengths of the States— even supposing that balance can be retained as disarmament progresses—is scarcely, on the historical evidence, a satisfactory way of ensuring world peace. Indeed, the historical survey which Part One of this study has made is clear evidence that there have been occasions on which such a balance proved incapable of maintaining international peace and on which it proved necessary to establish, *ad hoc*, a United Nations peacekeeping operation.

Moreover, the argument rests on the further premise that States will be prepared to sign and implement a treaty on general and complete disarmament without knowing, in advance, whether, in the second and final stages of disarmament, a United Nations peacekeeping machinery equipped with adequate forces can be established and operated. This assumes an act of faith which may simply not be forthcoming. The thesis which this study maintains is quite the reverse, namely that an effective United Nations peacekeeping machinery should be established even prior to disarmament, not only so as to cope with the threats to international peace and security which will, no doubt, continue to arise pending agreement on disarmament but also to demonstrate the possibilities of creating an effective United Nations machinery. Thus States would be able to agree to a disarmament treaty knowing that such a machinery existed, knowing that techniques for its control existed, and knowing that the problems which lay in the future were problems relating to the strengthening of such a machinery and its adaptation to the new problems of disarmament control. Considerable though these problems might be, they are problems of a far lesser order than the establishment of such a machinery *de novo*. Faith would certainly be called for, but not an act of faith of the same, almost blind, character as that called for by a plan which presupposes that no such machinery exists prior to the entry into force of a disarmament treaty.

II. THE RELATIONSHIP OF AN INTERNATIONAL FORCE TO OTHER PEACEKEEPING ARRANGEMENTS

The United States Treaty Outline lumps together all "measures to strengthen arrangements for keeping the peace." [14] There is not only a connection between all these measures, considered collectively, and disarmament, but also there is an intricate system of interdependence between various peacekeeping measures. If a United Nations Peacekeeping Force is established prior to disarmament to exercise the functions appropriate to such a Force (and surveyed in Chapter 8) it would in principle be wrong to establish a separate Force for disarmament functions. Clearly the preferable course

---

[14] Stage I, Section H. Blueprint, pp. 19–21.

would be to expand the existing Force and to entrust to it the additional functions called for under the disarmament agreement. Even if no Force existed prior to disarmament, the creation of a new Force limited to disarmament functions would be nonsensical in a world where the need for a Force to assume a more conventional " peacekeeping " role has been amply demonstrated. The answer must lie in adding additional functions to an existing Force or a new Force, so that it becomes necessary to survey these additional functions which have not hitherto been considered in Chapter 8.[15]

1. *The international Force and peaceful settlement of disputes*

For instance, it is not enough to establish new international tribunals or other means for the pacific settlement of international disputes, or to endow existing institutions with new powers in that area, if no adequate steps are taken at the same time to ensure that the decisions made are properly enforced against States refusing to accept them. For this purpose an international Force is required; it should be able to discharge this task in a disarmed world much better than in the present situation where even weak nations can disobey international orders with impunity.

The United States Treaty Outline provides already in the first stage for the reference to the International Court of Justice of disputes concerning the interpretation or application of the disarmament treaty.[16] It does not contemplate, however, that the decisions of the Court rendered in such disputes should be immediately enforceable by an international Force against the State refusing to perform the obligations incumbent upon it under the Court's judgment. With respect to the international Force, the only provision in Stage I is that an agreement be negotiated to establish a United Nations Peace Force in Stage II.[17] Until such a Force is established, any enforcement of the decisions of the International Court of Justice with respect to disarmament would have to depend either on the exercise by the Security Council of its authority under Article 94 of the Charter to " make recommendations or decide upon measures to be taken to give effect to the judgment," or on direct action by the other parties to the disarmament treaty.

In Stage II, the United States Treaty Outline extends the obligation to refer disputes to the International Court of Justice to all

---

[15] The enforcement of decisions of the I.C.J. has been considered under Chapter 8 but it will be recalled that this particular function cannot with certainty be said to be one which the Charter envisaged for either the Article 43 Forces or for " peacekeeping " Forces, hence it would be desirable in any disarmament treaty to provide specifically for this function and to extend it beyond decisions of the I.C.J. alone.

[16] Stage I, Section H.3.b. *Ibid.*, p. 20. For a detailed analysis of the U.S. proposals, and of the Soviet reactions to any suggestion of compulsory jurisdiction, see Andrew Martin, " Legal Aspects of Disarmament," (1963) I.C.L.Q. Suppl. Publication No. 7, pp. 52–59, 65.

[17] Stage I, Section H.5.c. *Ibid.*, p. 21.

"international legal disputes," without any reservation whatever. Arrangements, not clearly specified, would also be made to assure the just and peaceful settlement of international political disputes.[18] At the same time, the United Nations Peace Force would come into being in the first year of Stage II and would be progressively strengthened during the remainder of that stage.[19] It should be able to enforce the decisions of the International Court of Justice against at least some States, especially if means are devised by that time to enable the United Nations to make the necessary decisions to employ the Force for this purpose.

Finally, in Stage III the United States Treaty Outline would require the parties to the disarmament treaty to "undertake such additional steps and arrangements as were necessary to provide a basis for peaceful change in a disarmed world and to continue the just and peaceful settlement of all international disputes, whether legal or political in nature." [20] Simultaneously, the parties to the disarmament treaty "would progressively strengthen the United Nations Peace Force established in Stage II until it had sufficient armed forces and armaments so that no State could challenge it." [21] No further details are provided on either subject, but it seems clear that the Force to be established under these provisions would have sufficient strength to enforce not only the decisions of the International Court of Justice rendered in legal disputes but also the more controversial decisions ordering peaceful change in various international obligations and situations (revising obsolete treaties, changing unjust territorial settlements, restricting abuse of rights, or removing situations which shock the conscience of mankind) or adjusting international political disputes.

The Soviet Union raised strong objections to this proposal, charging that the West is trying to establish "a police system over States." [22] Indeed the Soviet Union's proposals are singularly lacking in that they contain no reference to the peaceful settlement of disputes or to the desirability of a machinery for peaceful change except in so far as they presuppose the existence of the Charter machinery. Yet that machinery contains no compulsory jurisdiction over legal disputes, and no effective machinery for peaceful change in the sense of a machinery capable of changing the status quo which may be unimpeachable on the basis of the legal rights of the parties but highly unacceptable as the basis upon which friendly relations between States can continue. The elimination of national armaments and the prohibition of the use of force can scarcely appeal to States as principles of action when they are denied the certainty that other States will be bound to accept the jurisdiction of an

---

[18] Stage II, Section G.1. *Ibid.*, p. 27.
[19] Stage II, Section G.3. *Ibid.*, p. 28.
[20] Stage III, Section H.1. *Ibid.*, p. 33.
[21] Stage III, Section H.3. *Ibid.*, p. 33.
[22] UN Doc. ENDC/PV.45, p. 39 (30 May 1962).

international court when a contest over their respective legal rights arises and the certainty that a judgment of such a court will be enforced.

Moreover, given that the status quo may not be synonymous with justice—and this is extremely likely in Asia and Africa where territorial titles and boundaries remain a legacy of a past era in which they ensued as compromises between the European Powers with colonial possessions in those continents—machinery for peaceful change must be provided if the States are expected to forgo the right to change the status quo by force. Otherwise the Soviet notion that " wars of national liberation " are not covered by the prohibition of recourse to force will remain as a highly subjective notion capable of undermining the entire structure.[23]

The issue here, as in many other areas of the conflict between the Western and the Soviet points of view, is whether the international Force should be strong enough to enforce international decisions, or international rules, or disarmament obligations, in a disarmed world or whether the political climate of a disarmed world would be so different that no difficulties would arise with respect to the enforcement of such decisions. The Soviet acceptance of this second approach is facilitated by Soviet insistence that all important decisions should be arrived at by agreement, as it would be easy to give effect to agreed decisions. The Western view is predicated, on the other hand, on the belief that important disputes can seldom be solved by agreement and that acceptance of impartial means of adjudicating such disputes is necessary to ensure peaceful change in a dynamic world society. While it is not expected that there would actually be dangerous cases of refusal to accept the verdict of mankind, the existence of a Force which could ensure the execution of international decisions, if and when necessary, would make such refusals less likely. As long as there is a Force able to execute the decisions of international tribunals, there would be little temptation to disregard them. But if enforcement is doubtful, States may try to avoid fulfilling their obligations under an international decision under some flimsy pretext. As soon as such lack of obedience becomes common and many important States start accumulating grievances against other States which refuse to abide by international decisions, the whole framework of the new order is likely to collapse, including the elaborate disarmament structure. All this could be avoided, however, if a Force were established which could by its very presence, or by a threat of action, or in the ultimate case by the actual taking of enforcement measures, ensure that international decisions are complied with as a matter of routine.

---

[23] See Millis, " The Political Control of an International Police Force " in *Quis Custodiet? Controlling the Police in a Disarmed World*, A Peace Research Institute Report, Washington, April 1963, Vol. II, Appendices, A–46.

2. *Rules of international conduct*

Parallel considerations apply to rules of international conduct. The effective functioning of both international tribunals and an international Force depend on the further development and codification of the basic rules of international law. There is clearly a close connection between international tribunals and world law. Nations are reluctant to submit international disputes to an international court if they do not know what law the court will apply. On the other hand, if nations do not submit cases to the court, it cannot contribute effectively to the clarification of legal principles. This vicious circle must be broken before satisfactory progress is obtained in these two areas.

Similarly, effective functioning of an international Force would depend on the formulation of clear rules of international law needed to govern the Force in its activities. If the Force is authorised to come to the aid of a nation against which aggression has been committed, a careful definition of aggression will be needed. Otherwise, there would be constant danger that the Force would not act when it should assist a nation, or would take unauthorised steps in a situation which does not actually involve aggression. At the same time, there must be strong international courts to which recourse could be had should the Force abuse its authority, and these courts would function much better if they had a clear set of rules to apply.

The United States Treaty Outline provides, in the first place, for the establishment of a subsidiary body of the proposed International Disarmament Organisation (hereafter referred to as " IDO ") to study the question of " the codification and progressive development of rules of international conduct related to disarmament," and the " methods of assuring States against indirect aggression or subversion." [24] In the second place, this Treaty Outline establishes a more effective method for the speedy adoption of new rules, following in this respect the example of such international organisations as the International Labour Organisation, World Health Organisation and the World Meteorological Organisation. The proposed procedure envisages that rules recommended by the special subsidiary body would come for approval before the Control Council of the IDO (a body with limited membership, as distinguished from the General Conference of the IDO in which all parties to the disarmament treaty are to be represented). After approval by that Council the new rules would be circulated to all parties to the disarmament treaty and would become effective three months thereafter unless a majority of the parties to that treaty should signify their disapproval before the expiration of that period. Finally, each party to the disarmament treaty would be bound by the new rules unless, within a year from the effective date (*i.e.*, within fifteen months from their adoption by the Council), it should formally notify the IDO that it did not consider

[24] Stage I, Section H.2. Blueprint, p. 20.

itself bound by the new rules.[25] This procedure does not seem to apply, however, to the arrangements necessary to assure States against indirect aggression and subversion.[26] The proposals of the subsidiary body in that special area would be embodied in a separate international agreement, which would probably be ratified in accordance with ordinary constitutional processes. Such an agreement might provide, however, for its future modification by a process similar to that adopted for the rules of international conduct related to disarmament. Some such rules might have to be adopted in Stage II, in order to enable States to move into Stage III with the assurance that the danger to them resulting from various activities which are not now expressly forbidden by international law would be eliminated. Additional rules might be agreed during Stage III, and the new flexible procedure for their adoption should prove useful also after the actual process of disarmament has been completed. By that time, of course, other procedures, even more effective, might be agreed upon.[27]

A question might be raised about the content of the proposed "rules of international conduct related to disarmament." These rules must be distinguished from the "rules for implementing the terms of the [Disarmament] Treaty," which would be adopted by the Control Council of the IDO and would be binding immediately upon States without need for further approval on their part.[28] While it might be expected that the disarmament treaty would be a long, complicated instrument, with many detailed annexes, it is not possible to foresee all the additional problems which might need to be covered adequately in the future. It is necessary, therefore, to confer on the Control Council the authority to issue supplementary regulations both in cases specifically provided for in the disarmament treaty itself and in cases in which the power to issue them is implied in the treaty. Such regulations cannot, of course, derogate from the provisions of the disarmament treaty and must conform both to its text and to its spirit.

The "rules of international conduct related to disarmament" would deal with entirely different matters. The separate reference to "indirect aggression and subversion" seems to indicate that the basic problem here is to elaborate rules which would ensure that in a disarmed world States would not use means other than military force to achieve domination over other nations. The Charter of the United Nations contains only a few general rules in its Article 2, and from the very beginning various attempts were made to provide a more detailed statement of the basic principles which should govern relations between nations. For example, the International Law Commission of the United Nations was asked to prepare a declaration of

[25] Stage II, Section G.2.a. Blueprint, p. 27.
[26] Stage II, Section G.2.b. Blueprint, p. 27.
[27] Stage III, Section H.2. Blueprint, p. 33.
[28] Stage I, Section G.6.b. Blueprint, p. 18.

rights and duties of States, but the draft presented by it to the General Assembly did not go far beyond the language of the Charter,[29] and the General Assembly decided to postpone final action on it.[30] The Draft Code of Offences Against the Peace and Security of Mankind, prepared by the International Law Commission in 1954 met with a similar fate.[31] Two special committees of the General Assembly struggled with the question of the definition of aggression in 1954 and 1956, and despite elaborate drafts prepared by the Soviet Union they were unable to agree even on the method of approach.[32] More recent proposals by the members of the Soviet *bloc* to codify the principles of peaceful coexistence resulted in the adoption by the General Assembly of a Resolution undertaking to study at its next session "the principles of international law concerning friendly relations and co-operation among States in accordance with the Charter with a view to their progressive development and codification, so as to secure their more effective application." [33] At the conclusion of its eighteenth session in December 1963 the Assembly in fact adopted two Resolutions on the principles of international law concerning friendly relations and co-operation among States: one established a special committee to study progress in the codification of four principles of international law, and the other established a committee to study the establishment of an impartial fact-finding body as a contribution to the peaceful settlement of international disputes.[34] It is evident that, as yet, the work of the Assembly has not developed into the formulation of the more detailed rules envisaged in the proposals of the United States.

One particularly acute problem will be to define the scope and content of the rule of non-intervention. Moreover, study of this problem will require a differentiation between the rule as applied to activities by States and the rule as applied to activities by the United Nations Peace Force, for there is every reason to believe that somewhat different considerations apply. That this problem, in relation to United Nations Forces, admits of no clear, uncontroversial answer has been amply demonstrated in Parts One and Two of the present study.[35] The questions of how far the consent of the territorial State will be necessary to the operations of a United Nations Peace Force, and of how far such consent might permit the Force to assume

---

[29] Report of the International Law Commission, 1949, pp. 7–10. *Off.Rec.G.A.*, 4th Sess., Suppl. 10 (UN Doc. A/925.)

[30] General Assembly, Resol. 375 (IV), 6 December 1949. *Off.Rec.G.A.*, 4th Sess., Resolutions (UN Doc. A/1251), p. 66.

[31] Report of the International Law Commission, 1954, pp. 11–12. *Off.Rec.G.A.*, 9th Sess., Suppl. 9 (UN Doc. A/2693).

[32] *Off.Rec.G.A.*, 9th Sess., Suppl. 11 (UN Doc. A/2638); *idem*, 12th Sess., Suppl. 16 (UN Doc. A/3574).

[33] General Assembly, Resol. 1815 (XVII), 18 December 1962. UN Doc. A/RES/1815 (XVII).

[34] UN Information Centre, London News Summary, Release 45/63, 24 December 1963.

[35] *Ante*, pp. 196–200.

functions which go beyond the necessity of maintaining *international* peace and security require the most careful consideration. By and large, the present writer's view would be that even under disarmament a United Nations Force should not be used to intervene in a purely civil strife, but, clearly, if governments are forced to disarm they will tend to insist on either retaining internal security forces of a size sufficient to maintain their security in the event of internal rebellion or on the United Nations giving a guarantee that it will come to their aid in certain conditions. Would it be proper for the United Nations to give any such guarantee and, if so, under what conditions? It may be that, under disarmament, quite different policy considerations apply to this very difficult situation, but some agreement on policy would seem to be essential as part of the evolution of rules of conduct.[36]

The further, and important, question is for whose guidance are the rules intended? One approach must be to design such rules for the guidance of the organ or organs exercising political control over a Force on the assumption that, save for a limited right to initiate action in its own defence, the Force would have no power to act except where authorised by the political control organ. Such rules would, in effect, fetter the discretion of the States represented on the control organ. The other approach would be to assume that, in accordance with a set of rules, the Force would be able to act automatically to suppress a breach of the rules, and in this event the rules might vary in content and would certainly have to be more specific. There may well be a certain unreality in supposing that such "automaticity" is possible, for in any event a breach of the rules would have to be determined before action was taken, and it can scarcely be argued that the Force would have power both to determine such a breach and to decide to take action. Thus the questions are threefold: what are the rules, which organ determines a breach, and which organ decides that action by the Force shall be taken to suppress the breach?

It might be pointed out that the Soviet proposals contain only a general reference to the duty of States "to base relations with each other on the principles of peaceful and friendly coexistence and co-operation."[37] In the Disarmament Conference, Mr. Zorin, the delegate of the U.S.S.R., based his objections to the United States proposals on this subject chiefly on the ground that they represent an attempt to bypass the United Nations and to weaken that organisation. He pointed out that under the United Nations Charter the function of codifying and developing rules of international law belongs to the General Assembly and to bodies set up by the General Assembly for this purpose, and argued that there is no need to deal with this problem in the disarmament context.[38] But in view of the

---

[36] See Millis, *op. cit.*
[37] Draft Treaty, Article 3, para. 1 (a). UN Doc. A/C.1/867, p. 5.
[38] UN Doc. ENDC/PV. 55, pp. 54–55.

insistence of the Soviet Union in the United Nations and other organisations on the codification of rules relating to aggression or peaceful coexistence, it might agree on the need for codifying certain rules once the disagreements on the nomenclature and the proper forum have been removed. It does not seem to be in the interest of the Soviet Union to leave too much discretion in the hands of an international Force, and the development of basic rules for the guidance of the Force (and of other international organs) should prove helpful in limiting that discretion.

III. THE UNITED NATIONS, THE INTERNATIONAL DISARMAMENT ORGANISATION (IDO) AND AN INTERNATIONAL PEACE FORCE

The United States Treaty Outline would impose upon the parties to the disarmament treaty three distinct obligations with respect to an international Force:

" . . .

" a. Examination of the experience of the United Nations leading to a further strengthening of United Nations Forces for keeping the peace;

" b. Examination of the feasibility of concluding promptly the agreements envisaged in Article 43 of the United Nations Charter;

" c. Conclusion of an agreement for the establishment of a United Nations Peace Force in Stage II, including definitions of its purpose, mission, composition and strength, disposition, command and control, training, logistical support, financing, equipment and armaments." [39]

In later stages the first two obligations are no longer mentioned; the only provisions on this subject deal with the progressive strengthening of the United Nations Peace Force " until it had sufficient armed forces and armaments so that no State could challenge it." [40]

The Soviet Draft Treaty approaches this matter in a more detailed manner, and makes clearer the relationship of the forces to the United Nations. For instance, the following provision is envisaged for Stage I :

" 1. With a view to ensuring that the United Nations is capable of effectively protecting States against threats to or breaches of the peace, all States parties to the Treaty shall, between the signing of the Treaty and its entry into force, conclude agreements with the Security Council by which they undertake to make available to the latter armed forces, assistance and facilities, including rights of passage, as provided in Article 43 of the United Nations Charter.

" 2. The armed forces specified in the said agreements shall form part of the national armed forces of the States concerned and shall be stationed within their territories. They shall be kept up to full strength and shall be fully equipped and prepared for combat. When used under Article 42 of the United Nations Charter, these forces, serving under the command of the military authorities of the States concerned, shall be placed at the disposal of the Security Council." [41]

[39] Stage I, Section H.5. Blueprint, pp. 20–21.
[40] Stage II, Section G.3, and Stage III, Section H.3. Blueprint, pp. 28, 33.
[41] Article 18.

In Stage II, it is provided oniy that the parties to the disarmament treaty should "continue to implement" the measures referred to above.[42] A more elaborate provision is contained, however, in Stage III. Under the Soviet proposal, States would retain in that stage "strictly limited contingents of police (militia), equipped with light firearms," for the dual purpose of maintaining internal order (including the safeguarding of frontiers and the personal security of citizens) and assisting in "the maintenance of peace and security under the United Nations Charter."[43] To accomplish the second of these objectives, the Draft Treaty would impose upon States the following obligations:

" 1. The States parties to the Treaty undertake to place at the disposal of the Security Council, on its request, units from the contingents of police (militia) retained by them, as well as to provide assistance and facilities, including rights of passage. The placing of such units at the disposal of the Security Council shall be carried out in accordance with the provisions of Article 43 of the United Nations Charter. In order to ensure that urgent military measures may be undertaken, the States parties to the Treaty shall maintain in a state of immediate readiness those units of their police (militia) contingents which are intended for joint international enforcement action. The size of the units which the States parties to the Treaty undertake to place at the disposal of the Security Council as well as the areas where such units are to be stationed shall be specified in agreements to be concluded by those States with the Security Council.

" 2. The command of the units referred to in paragraph 1 shall be composed of representatives of the three principal groups of States existing in the world on the basis of equal representation. It shall decide all questions by agreement among its members representing all three groups of States."[44]

In discussing this problem at the Disarmament Conference, the Soviet delegate emphasised that the Soviet Draft Treaty "makes a clear distinction between questions of peace and security, which come within the province of the Security Council, and questions coming within the scope of the implementation of disarmament measures and of control over them, which appertain to the functions of the international disarmament organisation."[45] Accordingly, the Soviet Draft Treaty provides as follows:

"The [International Disarmament] Organisation shall deal with questions pertaining to the supervision of compliance by States with their obligations under the present Treaty. All questions connected with the safeguarding of international peace and security which may arise in the course of the implementation of the present Treaty, including preventive and enforcement measures, shall be decided by the Security Council in conformity with its powers under the United Nations Charter."[46]

On the other hand, the Western Powers, according to Mr. Zorin, "would like to invest the international disarmament organisation not only with the functions of control but also military and political

[42] Article 27.
[43] Article 36.
[44] Article 37.
[45] UN Doc. ENDC/PV.45, p. 37 (30 May 1962).
[46] Article 40.

functions," thus "undermining the United Nations and weakening the Security Council." [47] In particular, "the fact that the creation of armed forces of the United Nations in the United States plan is not based on Article 43 of the Charter of the United Nations shows that the Western Powers have in mind to subordinate these armed forces not to the Security Council, but to some other organ, perhaps the international disarmament organisation." [48] The Soviet proposals thus seem to revert to the position that the Security Council would have a Force monopoly, a position already rejected in United Nations practice, that there would be no truly permanent Force but simply a Force based on the Article 43 agreements and composed of national contingents, and that control would be subject to the double veto of both the Security Council and the " troika " Command.

In defending the Western position, Mr. Dean (United States) pointed out that " Article 43 of the United Nations Charter does not exhaust the means provided in the Charter to ensure the collective security of Members of the United Nations." It is true that Article 43 " provides the means for establishing forces which may be used by the Security Council, but this certainly does not mean that Members of the United Nations may not agree to create institutions such as the United Nations Peace Force which may be necessary in order to safeguard, in a world of general and complete disarmament, their fundamental rights under the United Nations Charter." [49]

Several separate issues are raised by these documents and discussions. In the first place, during the early stages of disarmament both sides would seem to be willing to give another try to the procedure envisaged in Article 43 of the Charter.[50] In the second place, only the Soviet proposals put the international Force squarely within the framework of the United Nations Charter and under the authority of the Security Council. The Western Powers are rather non-committal about that relationship. Instead, in their discussion of the Force, their spokesmen emphasise that the Force must be " strong, impartial and unquestionably effective." [51] Thus the delegate of the United Kingdom has formulated three basic principles which should govern the setting-up of an international Force: (1) " The United Nations peace Force must be strong enough in numbers and equipment to be able to deal rapidly and decisively with any force or opposition with which it may be confronted "; (2) " There is a clear relationship between the adequacy of the peacekeeping machinery in

[47] UN Doc. ENDC/PV.45, p. 37 (30 May 1962).
[48] *Ibid.*, p. 38.
[49] UN Doc. ENDC/PV.55, p. 41 (13 June 1962).
[50] But the U.S. delegate has expressed doubt whether, in the light of past experience, it would be wise to pin all hopes on agreements made pursuant to that Article, as is done in the Soviet Draft Treaty. *Ibid.*, p. 40.
[51] Statement by Mr. Godber (United Kingdom), 12 June 1962. UN Doc. ENDC/ PV.54, p. 15. For criticism of both the Soviet proposals and of the Western proposals—and of the latter on account of their lack of clarity—see Andrew Martin, *loc. cit.*, pp. 64–74.

general, and the peace Force in particular, and the effectiveness of verification machinery"; (3) "the United Nations peace Force must be as far as possible removed from the influence of individual States which have contributed to it, except such influence as may be legitimately exerted through the United Nations." [52] According to the Italian delegate, Mr. Cavaletti, the Soviet proposals subject the use of the international force "to a double veto: first, there is, of course, the veto of the Security Council; then, according to article 37, paragraph 2, of the Soviet plan, there is the veto of any one of the three representatives forming the 'troika' which commands the international troops. It is clear from that article that without the unanimous agreement of the three commanders of the international Force, even a unanimous decision of the Security Council could never be carried out." [53] In his biting reply, the Soviet delegate alleged that the "Western Powers do not desire to afford the Socialist countries and the non-aligned Powers equal possibilities of influencing the use of the international Force. What remains? The Western Powers remain. As far as we know, there are at present no other States in the world. This is how Mr. Godber's principle for the setting up of an international Force outside the influence of individual States looks in practice." [54]

The very title of the proposed international Force, "the United Nations Peace Force," seems to indicate that the Force proposed in the United States Treaty Outline is intended to be a Force under the direction of the United Nations. This Force is supposed to be more effective than that contemplated under Article 43 of the Charter of the United Nations, but there are few indications of how this increase in effectiveness will be achieved. On the other hand, it is quite clear that the Force contemplated by the Soviet proposals would be neither international nor effective. To remedy this situation, it would be necessary to provide for either a limitation of the veto in the Security Council or some other political organ functioning without veto. Such an organ would be available in the Control Council of the IDO, but it might not be desirable to complicate the issue of composition and voting procedure of that Council by vesting in it also the authority over the Force. There are also no grounds for believing that the Soviet Union would look in a different manner upon the question of abolishing the veto merely because the power to direct the international Force would be vested not in the Security Council but in a separate organ. The considerations are not different from those mentioned by the Soviet delegation in connection with a parallel issue, the establishment of the Force by agreement under Article 43 of the Charter or in some other manner. In this respect, Mr. Zorin pointed out that the only reason for avoiding the procedure under Article 43

[52] Statement by Mr. Godber (United Kingdom), 12 June 1962. UN Doc. ENDC/ PV.54, pp. 14–21.
[53] UN Doc. ENDC/PV.51, p. 51 (7 June 1962).
[54] UN Doc. ENDC/PV.55, p. 60 (13 June 1962).

would be " to set up United Nations armed Forces without the agreement of the Permanent Members of the Security Council." He continued : " If you obtain our agreement to the setting up of an armed Force in a certain form this agreement will be in accordance with Article 43 also. . . . If you wish to do this without agreement, you will be acting in opposition to us. But can you conclude a treaty on general and complete disarmament against our opposition? It is quite clear that this is unrealistic." [55] It would seem similarly unrealistic to try to avoid a Soviet veto by putting the primary control of the international Force into the hands of an organ other than the Security Council. If the Soviet Union should be willing to accept veto-free control over the Force, it would not be difficult to devise a method for doing it through the Security Council. The most likely way out of this impasse, which the Soviet Union might be prepared to accept under pressure from world opinion, would be to establish the General Assembly as an organ of secondary control, rather in the way in which, as we have seen in the earlier parts of this study, the General Assembly has emerged as a secondary control organ for the contemporary peace-keeping activities of United Nations Forces.

Though the final decision to use the international Force to ensure compliance with the disarmament treaty would rest with a political body, the Security Council or the General Assembly, the chain of events leading to such use is likely to be triggered by the organs of the IDO. The fact of the violation of the disarmament treaty will usually be discovered by the verification service of the IDO, and the official determination that a violation has occurred will probably be made, under the United States Treaty Outline, by the Administrator, the Chief Executive Officer of the IDO, or by the Control Council of that Organisation.[56] This Treaty Outline is slightly ambiguous on the subject of steps to be taken in case of a violation, and at least one provision seems to envisage direct action by the parties to the disarmament treaty rather than by any organ of the IDO.[57] On the other hand, the Soviet Draft Treaty provides explicitly that the Control Council should promptly notify the Security Council " of any infringements by the States parties to the [Disarmament] Treaty of their disarmament obligations " under that treaty.[58] This provision seems to imply that the Control Council will determine the existence of an infringement, and the Security Council will decide only what action, including possible use of the international Force, should be taken in consequence of it. There is no indication in either proposal

---

[55] UN Doc. ENDC/PV.55, pp. 55–56 (13 June 1962).

[56] Stage I, Sections G.6.e, and G.7.d.

[57] According to Section G.7.b of Stage I, the Administrator should make " available to the Parties to the Treaty data produced by the verification arrangements," thus allowing the parties to draw their conclusions directly from the original data. Blueprint, p. 18.

[58] Article 20, para. 2 (c). UN Doc. A/C.1/867, p. 30. It may be noted, however, that the Soviet Draft Treaty does not expressly provide for an Administrator and centres all functions in the Control Council itself, acting directly or through the " staff of the Organisation."

that in some circumstances any employment of the international Force could take place as a result of a decision of the Control Council of the IDO, without intervention of the Security Council. Neither can it be assumed that the Security Council would be bound in any way by the finding by the IDO that an important violation has occurred; the Security Council might still conclude that the violation in question does not endanger international peace and security and does not require any enforcement action on its part.

The enforcement action by the international Force must be clearly distinguished from the verification function of the IDO, though some non-military enforcement measures might form an integral part of the disarmament process. It is possible, for instance, to envisage the establishment by the IDO of its own guard force and field service, similar to those employed by the United Nations, for the purpose of protecting its buildings at headquarters and in the field and accompanying its inspectors. There might also be some civil police with authority to arrest individuals accused of violations, should the disarmament treaty envisage direct action against individuals rather than governments and States.[59] Finally, the IDO might possess a secret investigation service able to penetrate where uniformed inspectors might not be able to go. A question might arise with respect to assistance to be rendered to these officials of the IDO by the international Force in case of trouble. For example, if an inspector is refused access to a plant in which plutonium might be produced, should he be able to call on the international Force to open the door for him, or must the matter be referred all the way to the Security Council before action could be taken? Or if a member of the secret investigation service should be arrested by a State's police and deprived of evidence of a violation, under what procedures could he be rescued from a national prison? Finally, if a person should resist arrest by the civil police of the IDO, under what circumstances could the international Force step into the picture? It is conceivable that the disarmament treaty might provide, at least in some cases, that the international Force should render provisional assistance to officials of the IDO, subject to the authority of the Security Council to terminate such action at its discretion.

Some of the difficulties listed above might be avoided if a different method of enforcement on individuals were adopted. The United States Treaty Outline requires the parties to the disarmament treaty to " enact national legislation in support of the Treaty imposing legal obligations on individuals and organisations under their jurisdiction

---

[59] Action against individuals might be envisaged, for example, to prevent genocide or war crimes or even the illegal manufacture or possession of arms. Yet to extend such action to this last category could well deny to a people their right of self-determination in situations in which a resort to arms would be the only possible means of overthrowing a totalitarian régime which possessed control of a sizeable militia for internal security purposes.

and providing appropriate penalties for noncompliance." [60] Similarly, the Soviet Draft Treaty contains several specific provisions requiring that parties to the disarmament treaty enact national legislation : ensuring " that no military bases to be used by foreign troops are established in their territory"; prohibiting their citizens " from serving in the armed forces or from engaging in any other activities serving military purposes in foreign States"; " prohibiting nuclear weapons and making any attempt by individuals or organisations to reconstitute such weapons a criminal offence"; and " prohibiting all military training, abolishing military conscription and all other forms of recruiting the armed forces, and discontinuing all military courses for reservists." [61] It is quite probable that the Soviet Union would be willing to accept a more general provision on this subject.[62] The consequence of this approach would be that a discovery by the IDO that an individual has committed a violation of the disarmament treaty would have to be communicated to national authorities which would be responsible for prosecuting the individual. Should the IDO find that the result of national prosecution is unsatisfactory, because of inadequate action of the prosecuting authorities, or biased proceedings, or insufficient penalty, supplementary international proceedings might have to be instituted either against the individual concerned or against the person or government responsible for the denial of justice. The problems involved on this level might be quite different from those arising in direct international proceedings against the original violator. If the case is thus transferred into the intenational arena, the question might arise whether the international Force should be used against a State guilty of gross and constant violation of its duty to punish adequately all violators of the disarmament treaty, whether private individuals or government officials. The decision as to such use would not be in the hands of the IDO but of the political authority in charge of the international Force. It is probable, however, that, if a strong case is presented by the IDO, the political authority would find it difficult to avoid employing the international Force to ensure the integrity of the disarmament treaty.

This whole question of how far enforcement against private individuals should be undertaken by a United Nations Force—as opposed to a system which would delegate that task to States and envisage action only against States either for their own default or for failing to suppress breaches by individuals—is reflected in the uncertainty as to whether a United Nations Force should be a strictly military Force or a " Police " Force. On balance, and taking into account the whole range of functions which a United Nations Force might be called upon to assume, the present writer's view is that a military Force is needed and that it should be designed to operate primarily against States. Its intrusion into the municipal sphere,

[60] Stage II, Section G.5. Blueprint, p. 28.
[61] Articles 9 (3), 10 (3), 22 (3) and 34. UN Doc. A/C.1/867, pp. 10, 11, 18, 24.
[62] This has been suggested by Mr. Lall (India). UN Doc. ENDC/PV.55, p. 24.

assuming functions normally undertaken by the internal police of a State, should be minimal. However, there may be advantages in equipping the IDO with a limited body of police officials who would, in conjunction with the inspectorate and with the municipal police authorities, have certain powers of arrest. Lack of co-operation by the municipal authorities on such a scale as to suggest clear obstruction of the IDO inspectorate, and complicity with the breaches committed by individuals, could then be referred to the political control organ who might then use the United Nations Force directly against the State.

One further connection between the verification machinery of the IDO and the international Force might be mentioned. The existence of an adequate international Force diminishes the value of any hidden armaments and makes the task of the IDO easier. But, as was pointed out by Sir Michael Wright (United Kingdom), if there should be no effective international Force, " there would be a strong incentive to the ambitious, to the unscrupulous or to the bad neighbour to hide arms for selfish or aggressive purposes. In that case the control problem becomes immeasurably more difficult." [63]

There is also another side to this relationship. If the effectiveness of the IDO verification should improve, and the likelihood of hidden stockpiles of weapons should diminish, it should be possible, as Mr. Godber has said, " to bring the United Nations peace Force down to a mere token force." [64] Of course, this would be possible only if there is simultaneous improvement in the general political situation, universal acceptance of basic rules of international conduct and of decisions of international courts interpreting those rules, and smoothly working machinery for peaceful change. Until that time, a strong, impartial and effective Force will be indispensable.

IV. THE CONSTITUTIONAL BASIS OF AN INTERNATIONAL FORCE

An international Force may be established by several methods:

(1) A decision of the Security Council;
(2) A Resolution of the General Assembly;
(3) The treaty on disarmament;
(4) A separate international agreement, independent of Charter amendment or a disarmament treaty;
(5) An amendment to the United Nations Charter.

The first two of these alternatives have been discussed extensively in Chapter 8, and there is no need to repeat here the arguments relating to the power of the Security Council or the General Assembly to establish an international Force without an amendment of the Charter. If, as has been suggested in Part Two of this study, a United Nations Peace-keeping Force were already established by either

[63] UN Doc. ENDC/PV.43, p. 10.
[64] UN Doc. ENDC/P.V.54, p. 15.

organ prior to disarmament there would be obvious advantages in building on that Force and in entrusting to that Force disarmament functions in addition to its existing functions. There would be little point in maintaining two distinct Forces.

The attribution of the new, disarmament, functions would, of course, raise a difficulty in the case of a Force established by the General Assembly for, as we have seen,[65] there is some doubt whether the Assembly can authorise enforcement action against States, and this is pre-eminently the kind of action which would be involved in disarmament enforcement. Thus the attribution of such powers would have to stem not from the present Charter but from the treaty on disarmament, from a separate international agreement, or from an amendment of the Charter. However, even in the case of the Security Council establishing a Force, it is likely that the specific functions involved in disarmament enforcement would have to be spelt out in a separate instrument from the Charter, so that a recourse to one or other of the last three alternatives would be almost inevitable in either case.

The third or fourth alternatives, the treaty on disarmament or a separate international agreement, could therefore be used both to establish a Force if none existed or, preferably, to entrust disarmament functions to an already existing United Nations Force; and, so long as no structural changes were involved in the United Nations itself, no amendment of the Charter would be necessary. The assumption of these additional powers would, given the breadth of the Purposes and Principles of the Charter, be perfectly permissible and all that would be required would be for the United Nations to signify its willingness to assume these powers. This method of increasing the powers of the United Nations was expressly recognised by the Security Council in 1947, when it agreed to accept the special responsibilities conferred upon it by the Italian Peace Treaty with respect to the Free City of Trieste.[66] Similarly, the General Assembly agreed to exercise the powers conferred upon it by Annex XI of that Treaty,[67] with respect to the Italian possessions in Africa.[68] More recently, the General Assembly authorised the Secretary-General to carry out the tasks entrusted to him by the agreement between Indonesia and the Netherlands concerning West New Guinea (West Irian).[69] This practice was approved by the Permanent Court of International Justice in the advisory opinion relating to the Treaty of Lausanne, where the Court declared that " There is nothing to prevent the Parties from accepting obligations and from conferring on the Council powers wider than those resulting from the strict terms

[65] *Ante*, pp. 288–291.
[66] *Off.Rec.S.C.*, 2nd yr. (1947), Nos. 1 and 3, pp. 4–19, 44–61. See also the Memorandum by Mr. Nisot (Belgium), UN Doc. A/AC.18/54 (30 March 1948).
[67] 49 U.N.T.S., p. 214.
[68] UN General Assembly Resol. 289 (IV), 21 November 1949, *Off.Rec.G.A.*, 4th Sess., Resolutions, pp. 10–12.
[69] UN Doc. A/RES/1752 (XVII), 21 September 1962. See *ante*, pp. 255–261.

of Article 15" of the Covenant of the League of Nations.[70] It can
be expected that, if a similar question were presented to the International Court of Justice, the Court would hold that there is nothing
in the Charter of the United Nations to prevent the Member States
from accepting additional obligations and from conferring on the
General Assembly or the Security Council additional powers
exceeding those provided for in the Charter itself.

Any agreement granting new powers to the United Nations might
stipulate that those powers should be exercised by a different voting
arrangement than that specified in the Charter. In the *Treaty of
Lausanne Case*, cited above, the Permanent Court of International
Justice stated that "no one denies that the Council can undertake to
give decisions by a majority in specific cases, if express provision is
made for this power by treaty stipulations," thus departing from the
unanimity rule established by the Covenant of the League of
Nations.[71] Similarly, parties to an agreement establishing an international Force might agree that some decisions with respect to such
a Force should be subject to more lenient or more strict voting
procedures than those provided in the Charter. In this connection,
it may be recalled that the General Assembly recommended in 1949
that these members "seek agreement among themselves upon what
possible decisions by the Security Council they might forbear to
exercise their veto," and suggested twenty-one cases in which the
veto might be abandoned.[72] The United States, in the agreements
relating to aid to Greece and Turkey, waived the exercise of the right
of veto with respect to any decision of the Security Council that
"action taken or assistance rendered by the United Nations makes
the continuance of assistance by the Government of the United States
pursuant to this agreement unnecessary or undesirable." [73] Thus this
separate treaty could embody an agreement on

(1) Complete abolition of the veto *or*

(2) Abolition of the veto in some or all questions of disarmament
enforcement or even more generally in all decisions affecting
the control of the Force *or*

(3) Abolition of the veto by making the concurring votes of all but
one Permanent Member necessary for non-procedural decisions
under Article 27 (3); there would thus have to be two
Permanent Members voting negatively to constitute a veto.

While an agreement on an international Force might be a part
of the disarmament treaty itself or might form an annex to it, the
present United States Treaty Outline does not seem to contemplate

---

[70] P.C.I.J. Publs., Series B, No. 12, p. 27.

[71] *Ibid.*, p. 30.

[72] Resol. 267 (III), 14 April 1949. *Off.Rec.G.A.*, 3rd. Sess., Part II, Resolutions,
pp. 7–10. See also the Report of the Interim Committee, UN Doc. A/578,
15 July 1948, published in *Off.Rec.G.A.*, 3rd Sess., Suppl. No. 10, p. 1, at 16.

[73] Agreement of 20 June 1947, Article 10, and Agreement of 12 July 1947,
Article 6. 7 U.N.T.S., 267, at 274; and 299, at 304.

a simultaneous solution for the problems of disarmament and creating an international Force. It contemplates instead the conclusion of an agreement for the establishment of a United Nations Peace Force during Stage I, *i.e.*, after the coming into force of the disarmament treaty. The disarmament treaty would contain only the obligation of the parties to that treaty to reach such an agreement through " measures within the United Nations," whatever this may mean.[74] The Soviet Draft Treaty, on the other hand, provides that all States parties to the disarmament treaty should, " between the signing of the Treaty and its entry into force, conclude agreements with the Security Council by which they undertake to make available to the latter armed forces, assistance and facilities, including rights of passage, as provided in Article 43 of the United Nations Charter." [75] These agreements would thus be concluded separately from the disarmament treaty, as would the later agreements in Stage III for making contingents of police (militia) available to the Security Council after the completion of the disarmament process.[76] It is not clear whether the coming into force of Stage I is conditioned in the Soviet proposal on the prior conclusion of the first series of agreements for contingents, but it is quite probable that the Soviet Union might not wish to delay Stage I until " all States parties to the Treaty " have concluded these agreements with the Security Council.

The last alternative, amendment of the United Nations Charter, has many attractions in that it would produce a single, comprehensive treaty and thus be " tidier " than a system depending on the supplementing of the existing Charter by other agreements. However, it is possible that the original agreement on disarmament and related matters, while acceptable to the United States and the Soviet Union, will not obtain immediate support from one or more of the other Permanent Members of the Security Council, each of which can block the coming into force of amendments to the Charter.[77] The United States Treaty Outline contemplates that the disarmament treaty would enter into force " upon the signature and ratification of the United States of America, the Union of Soviet Socialist Republics and such other States as might be agreed," and only the beginning of Stage II is conditioned on the accession of " all militarily significant States." [78] Thus, the disarmament treaty itself might come into force without the participation of some Permanent Members of the Security Council, but their accession would probably be required before the commencement of Stage II, as each of them is likely to be considered a militarily significant State. It is important to point out in this connection that the United Nations Peace Force, under the United States proposal, would be established only in

---

[74] Stage I, Section H.5. Blueprint, pp. 20–21.
[75] Article 18.
[76] Article 37.
[77] Articles 108 and 109 of the Charter.
[78] Introduction and Stage I, Section I.l.c. Blueprint, pp. 6–7, 21.

Stage II, and that any Charter amendments which might be deemed necessary to constitutionalise that Force would need to come into force not at the time of the coming into force of the disarmament treaty but only at the end of Stage I, in order to make possible transition to Stage II. It might be possible, therefore, to separate the disarmament treaty and the amendments to the Charter in such a way as to allow the entry into force of the disarmament treaty prior to the entry into force of Charter amendments. The situation is similar here to that envisaged by the Geneva Protocol on the Pacific Settlement of International Disputes, which was approved unanimously on 2 October 1924, by the Assembly of the League of Nations. The signatories to that Protocol undertook " to make every effort in their power to secure the introduction into the Covenant of amendments on the lines of the provisions contained in the following articles." They agreed also that, " as between themselves, these provisions shall be binding as from the coming into force of the present Protocol and that, so far as they are concerned, the Assembly and the Council of the League of Nations shall thenceforth have power to exercise all the rights and perform all the duties conferred upon them by the Protocol." [79] It would seem sufficient for the parties to the disarmament treaty to agree to make every effort during Stage I to introduce into the Charter of the United Nations such amendments as might be needed to enable them to start Stage II. They might even be willing to consider some of these amendments as provisionally binding upon them prior to their official entry into force. Perhaps the real disadvantage of this last alternative of Charter amendment is the somewhat cumbersome machinery provided for in the Charter and the political risk that States may wish to make any amendments necessary for implementing an agreement on disarmament dependent upon other, unrelated amendments to the Charter.

Consequently, it is probable that arrangements for the establishment of an international Force or for entrusting disarmament functions to an existing Force will be made through a special international agreement, supplementary to the disarmament treaty. Such an agreement may provide for amendments of the Charter of the United Nations, but such amendments are not really necessary. The agreement is likely to be negotiated during Stage I of the disarmament process, or even before, but it need not enter into force until the beginning of Stage II. Whether it will be necessary for the international Force to come into being or to assume disarmament functions (if already established) in Stage II, will depend to a large extent on the size and character of the reduction in armaments in Stages I and II. Only if such reduction should bring national armaments near the minimum deterrent level by the end of Stage II,

---

[79] Article 1. 2 Hudson, *International Legislation* (1931) p. 1380. The Protocol did not enter into force.

would it be essential to have the international Force exercising disarmament functions satisfactorily by that time.

V. FINANCIAL ARRANGEMENTS

The cost of the international Force is likely to be considerable. The cost of the United Nations Field Service of 200 men, composed principally of communication technicians and guards was $1,357,000 in 1962, *i.e.*, almost $7,000 per person.[80] The cost of United Nations operations in the Congo (ONUC), involving a military force of some 17,000 officers and men was almost $97,000,000 in 1961, *i.e.*, about $5,700 per person [81]; in addition, however, certain costs of the military personnel supplied to ONUC were borne by the States from which the contingents came.

An international Force composed of highly qualified volunteers is likely to cost more than these two services, and the probable cost per person might be $10,000 per year, including the cost of the necessary equipment and of its maintenance. This expenditure would still be about half of the cost per man of the United States forces, which at present is some $55 billion for a force of over 2,600,000 men. If the figure of $10,000 per person were accepted, it would be necessary to contemplate an expenditure of $3 billion for a force of 300,000 men.

It is not likely that a sum of this size will be available as long as the world has to maintain expensive national forces. But in a disarming world, it might be possible to devote a part of the savings from the reduction of armaments to the international Force. It must be remembered, however, that there will be other competitors for a share in the money previously spent on armaments. On 18 December 1962, the General Assembly of the United Nations adopted unanimously a " Declaration on the conversion to peaceful needs of the resources released by disarmament," in which it noted that " at the present time roughly $120,000 million annually " is spent on armaments, and expressed the belief that " the release of a portion of the savings which would follow upon an agreement on disarmament " would assist in improving the living standards of " countless millions of people in the less developed countries." At the same time economic and social adjustments will be necessary in Member States " which are significantly involved in or affected by current military programmes." [82] No mention is made in the Declaration of the need for reserving a part of the savings resulting from disarmament for the strengthening of the peace-keeping machinery of the United Nations. If this is not done, however, there seems to be only a small chance that adequate financial resources would be made available for an international Force. It might be desirable, there-

---

[80] UN Budget Estimates for the Financial Year 1963, *Off.Rec.G.A.*, 17th Sess., Suppl. No. 5, pp. 110–111.

[81] UN Doc. A/5352 (13 December 1962).

[82] UN Doc. A/RES/1837(XVII), 14 January 1963.

fore, to establish as close a relationship between disarmament savings and an international Force as now exists between disarmament and economic assistance to the developing countries. At present, both the Western and the Soviet disarmament plans are completely silent on the question of the financing of the peace-keeping machinery of the United Nations which is to be strengthened in accordance with these plans.

The cost of equipping the Force could, of course, be reduced by a system which would involve a transfer to the Force of the arms surrendered by the disarming States,[83] although maintenance costs would remain high. Another solution aimed at reducing cost is to restrict the size of the Force and to compensate by giving the Force an overwhelming weapons superiority. This solution, whilst embodying a perfectly sensible principle, requires two qualifications. First, it may well be that in many situations—and especially those situations where a " peace-keeping " role is involved—a United Nations Force could not rely on weapons superiority, for the nature of the operation would preclude such weapons. It would have to rely on a strong, numerical " presence " where the traditional forms of infantry patrols would be of more value than the possession of highly destructive weapons. Secondly, it is sometimes suggested that a United Nations Force should retain the nuclear weapon either to give this weapons superiority or for use by way of reprisals against a State manufacturing and using nuclear weapons illegally. There is sufficient doubt about the legality of the nuclear weapon to render its use, even by way of reprisals, highly questionable; certainly the opinions of many writers are against the equipment of a United Nations Force with the nuclear weapon.[84] However, this view certainly presupposes that the inspection techniques would be adequate to prevent secret manufacture or retention of nuclear weapons by States, and uncertainty as to this may account for the hesitancy of the West to adopt so categorical a view.[85] Whilst the Joint Statement suggested that after general and complete disarmament States should " place at the disposal of the United Nations agreed manpower necessary for an international peace Force to be equipped with agreed types of armaments," [86] later the Soviet Union insisted that this phrase should be revised to limit the equipment of the Force to " agreed types of non-nuclear armaments." [87] At the same time the Soviet Union requested the omission of the provision

[83] See the proposals for a simultaneous reduction of armaments and transfer to the UN in Singer, "The Internal Operations and Organisation of an International Police Force," Appendix D-5 of *Quis Custodiet?* etc., *loc. cit.*, Vol. II.
[84] *Ibid.*, Fisher, "Sequential controls for International Police," Appendix C-4; Singer, *loc. cit.*, D-4.
[85] Andrew Martin, *loc. cit.*, p. 72.
[86] "Joint Statement of Agreed Principles for Disarmament Negotiations," UN Doc. A/4879, p. 5 (20 September 1961).
[87] UN Doc. ENDC/40/Rev. 1, p. 5 (31 May 1962).

that the Force should be equipped with such armaments as are " necessary to ensure, under agreed arrangements, that the United Nations can, in accordance with the purposes and principles of the United Nations Charter, effectively deter or suppress any threat or use of arms." [88] The Soviet Union interpreted the Western proposals as permitting or even requiring that the international Force be equipped with nuclear weapons. It objected to this repeatedly, pointing out, for instance, that the people of the world " do not care whether they perish in a nuclear war occurring between two or three States or in one fought between some State and international armed Forces armed with nuclear weapons." [89]

The Western delegates replied that, in the first place, the question whether the international Force would need weapons in a disarmed world cannot be decided so far in advance and should be left for later determination; and that, in the second place, no verification system has yet been devised which could guarantee that no nation would retain some nuclear weapons in some well-hidden places. It might be necessary to equip the international Force with nuclear weapons as long as there is " the possibility that a given State could possess them and that the peace Force would then find itself unable, through its own insufficiency, to prevent their use." [90]

VI. THE FUNCTIONS OF AN INTERNATIONAL FORCE AND THE PEACE OBSERVATION CORPS

The main functions of the Force should be envisaged as :

(1) The protection of disarmed or disarming States against the unlawful use of force by other States or authorities;

(2) The protection of disarmed or disarming States against forcible and unlawful interference in their internal affairs or, more generally, against breaches of the rules of international conduct related to disarmament [91];

(3) Enforcement of observance of the disarmament treaty;

(4) Other " peace-keeping " functions under the United Nations Charter;

(5) Enforcement of decisions of the Security Council, of the General Assembly and of the International Court of Justice and other organs for pacific settlement whose decisions require

---

[88] *Ibid.* This phrase in the United States proposal for Article 3 of the draft treaty was derived, with some modifications, from the Joint Statement of 20 September 1961, footnote 9, *supra.*

[89] UN Doc. ENDC/PV.51, p. 13 (7 June 1962).

[90] Statement by Mr. Godber (United Kingdom), UN Doc. ENDC/PV.54, pp. 16–17 (12 June 1962).

[91] *Ante,* p. 527. The rules of international conduct related to disarmament, which the international Force might have to enforce, would make more precise the obligation of the Charter of the United Nations with respect to threat or use of force, threats to the peace, acts of aggression and other breaches of the peace, indirect aggression and subversion.

enforcement in the interest of international peace and security [92];

(6) Ancillary functions in the form of plebiscite supervision, protection of international personnel, humanitarian relief work.

Whatever the function, the decision that such a function must be undertaken by a United Nations Force must necessarily be a decision based on adequate information and, presumably, a decision taken by the political organs of the United Nations and not by the Force itself. In the area of disarmament, such information would be provided by the International Disarmament Organisation. In other areas, especially in cases involving alleged breaches of rules of international conduct, such information might be provided by the United Nations Peace Observation Corps. The United States Treaty Outline provides for the establishment of such a corps in the following manner:

"The Parties to the Treaty would agree to support the establishment within the United Nations of a Peace Observation Corps, staffed with a standing cadre of observers who could be despatched promptly to investigate any situation which might constitute a threat to or a breach of the peace. Elements of the Peace Observation Corps could also be stationed as appropriate in selected areas throughout the world." [93]

It may be assumed that this Peace Observation Corps would function in co-operation with, and under the supervision of, the Peace Observation Commission established by the Uniting for Peace Resolution, adopted by the General Assembly on 3 November 1950.[94] The relevant provisions of that Resolution read as follows:

"The General Assembly . . .

"3. Establishes a Peace Observation Commission, which for the calendar years 1951 and 1952 shall be composed of fourteen members, namely: China, Colombia, Czechoslovakia, France, India, Iraq, Israel, New Zealand, Pakistan, Sweden, the Union of Soviet Socialist Republics, the United Kingdom of Great Britain and Northern Ireland, the United States of America and Uruguay, and which could observe and report on the situation in any area where there exists international tension the continuance of which is likely to endanger the maintenance of international peace and security. Upon the invitation or with the consent of the State into whose territory the Commission would go, the General Assembly, or the Interim Committee when the Assembly is not in session, may utilise the Commission if the Security Council is not exercising the functions assigned to it by the Charter with respect to the matter in question. Decisions to utilise the Commission shall be made on the affirmative vote of two-thirds of the members present and voting. The Security Council may also utilise the Commission in accordance with its authority under the Charter;

"4. Decides that the Commission shall have authority in its discretion to appoint sub-commissions and to utilise the services of observers to assist it in the performance of its functions;

[92] For example, an organ created to make decisions on the peaceful change of existing legal rights, as opposed to the I.C.J. which will decide on the basis of existing legal rights (unless the *ex aequo et bono* jurisdiction is used).
[93] Stage I. Section H.6. Blueprint, p. 21.
[94] Resol. 337A(V), Part. B. *Off.Rec.G.A.*, 5th Sess., Suppl. No. 20, pp. 10–12.

" 5. Recommends to all governments and authorities that they co-operate with the Commission and assist it in the performance of its functions;

" 6. Requests the Secretary-General to provide the necessary staff and facilities, utilising, where directed by the Commission, the United Nations Panel of Field Observers envisaged in Resolution 297 B(IV)."

The Commission still exists, though it is not active. Its fourteen members were reappointed in 1952 and 1954; in 1956 Colombia was replaced by Honduras, and the revised membership was reappointed in 1958, 1960 and 1962.

The services of the Commission were utilised only on one occasion. It was requested by the General Assembly to replace the United Nations Special Committee on the Balkans with a Balkan Sub-commission with authority to " dispatch such observers as it may deem necessary to any area of international tension in the Balkans on the request of any State or States concerned, but only to the territory of States consenting thereto." [95] The Sub-commission was actually established by the Peace Observation Commission on 23 January 1952, and at the request of the Greek Government it dispatched observers to the frontier areas of Greece.[96] When the relations between Greece and her neighbours improved, Greece requested that the observer group be discontinued from 1 August 1954, and on 28 May 1954 the Sub-commission agreed to abolish the group.[97] The possibility of using the Peace Observation Commission in another area was raised by Thailand in July 1954, when it was suggested that the Security Council ask the Commission to send a sub-commission to Thailand in order to ensure that the fighting then going on in Indochina did not spread to Thailand. This proposal was vetoed, however, in the Security Council by the Soviet Union, and a further proposal by Thailand that the General Assembly consider the matter was later withdrawn.[98]

The United Nations Panel of Field Observers, mentioned in the Uniting for Peace Resolution, was established by the General Assembly in 1949, together with the United Nations Field Service, as a result of the Secretary-General's more ambitious proposal for a United Nations Guard.[99] The Service, consisting of some 300 persons, provides guards, and transport and communications experts for United Nations missions. The Panel consists merely of a " list of persons qualified to assist United Nations missions in the functions of observation and supervision " to be called into service only " in response to a specific Resolution by a competent organ of the United

[95] Resol. 508 B(VI), 7 December 1951. *Off.Rec.G.A.*, 6th Sess., Suppl. No. 20, p. 9.
[96] UN Doc. A/CN.7/6; *Off.Rec.G.A.*, 7th Sess., Suppl .No. 1, pp. 51–52. For the " Observation Manual for United Nations Military Observers in Greece," see UN Doc. A/CN./7/SC.1 (12 May 1953).
[97] UN Doc. A/CN.7/SC.1/55 (17 May 1954); *Off.Rec.G.A.*, 9th Sess., Suppl. No. 1, p. 29.
[98] *Off.Rec.G.A.*, 10th Sess., Suppl. No. 1, pp. 32–33.
[99] *Ante*, p. 18.

547

Nations." [1] While the Field Service has proved useful, the Panel has not been resorted to, and like the Peace Observation Commission, it exists only on paper.

It has been argued, in Part Two of this study, that a permanent cadre of observers is essential to the capacity of the United Nations to keep the peace, even without disarmament. Hence, as with the Force itself, the ideal situation would be one in which, prior to disarmament, an Observer Corps had been created. This could be done by creating an Observer section within a permanent United Nations Headquarters Military Staff which would take charge of the task of recruiting a volunteer reserve of observers, or of co-ordinating the offers of States to provide a " stand-by " contingent which would include observers. By whatever method this was done, there would be in existence the nucleus of an Observer Corps which could then be expanded to meet the greater needs of a disarmament programme. Moreover, the Corps would emerge as an essential part of the United Nations machinery. This point is an important one for it may be recalled that the relationship to the United Nations of the Corps suggested in the United States Treaty Outline is not entirely clear and the Soviet Union has criticised this proposal as an attempt " to by-pass the Security Council and to prevent it from fulfilling a basic function assigned to it under the Charter." [2] In reply, the British delegate pointed out that, on the contrary, this proposal was intended to strengthen the United Nations, to put more responsibilities on it, which cannot be considered as side-stepping the United Nations. In particular, the Peace Observation Corps would " give confidence that disputes, political or territorial, are nipped in the bud." [3] The Polish delegate found this argument not convincing; he felt that " the heart of the problem is not whether it is sought to set up new bodies within the United Nations or outside it, but whether this is to be done in conformity with, or contrary to, the letter and spirit of the Charter, which lays down the rules for United Nations activities." [4] Nevertheless, the Soviet Union and her allies accepted the Peace Observation Commission in 1950, and they may abandon their objections to the Peace Observation Corps, which is based on a similar idea, particularly if this emerges as an essential part of the United Nations machinery.

Assuming, therefore, that a Peace Observation Corps will be established, either before or as part of the settlement of the disarmament problem, its relation to an international Force needs to be investigated. As proposed in the United States Treaty Outline, the Peace Observation Corps would have two components: certain elements of the Corps would be stationed in selected areas throughout the world, probably in areas where a threat to the peace is

---

[1] Resol. 297(IV), 22 November 1949. *Off.Rec.G.A.*, 4th Sess., Resolutions, pp. 21–22.
[2] UN Doc. ENDC/PV.27, p. 35.
[3] UN Doc. ENDC/PV.43, pp. 10–11.　　　　[4] UN Doc. ENDC/PV.45, p. 24.

likely to arise or where friendly relations among neighbouring nations do not exist or are likely to be impaired; other elements of the Corps would be available at some central point for quick dispatch to any new area where a situation has arisen which might lead to international friction or a danger to peace. Thus the Peace Observation Corps would constitute a new form of United Nations "presence" and could provide quickly information on dangerous events happening in or near the territory in which its elements are stationed. This information would be submitted to both the Security Council of the United Nations and the command of the international Force. Further action would depend on the peace-keeping arrangements which have been agreed upon. If the veto in the Security Council has been abolished with respect to decisions involving employment of the international Force, any action by the Force would require an authorisation of the Security Council.

On the other hand, if a decision of the Security Council in this area remains subject to veto, alternative procedures for the use of the Force might have to be devised in order to ensure that a victim of an armed attack receives adequate protection. The proper alternative lies in utilising the "secondary" responsibility of the General Assembly which could quickly take up the matter under the procedures for summoning an emergency session provided for in the Resolution on Uniting for Peace. Moreover, if, as has been suggested earlier,[5] the Assembly were to establish a committee of limited membership to assume political control over the Force in any circumstance in which the Security Council failed to exercise its own responsibility, there would already be in existence a permanent committee of the Assembly which could assess the situation on the basis of the reports of the Peace Observation Corps even whilst the Security Council debated the item. The Assembly would then meet in the favourable situation of having one of its own committees thoroughly familiar with the developments and possibly prepared to make positive recommendations. The other alternative would be to allow the Force to take immediate action on the basis of the reports of the Observation Corps, so as to take provisional action to assist the victim of an aggression or separate the combatants, or even to give the Secretary-General power to order such provisional action. This last alternative, whilst a possible one, is not one which is likely to command much political support, so that the better solution would lie in improving the General Assembly's capacity to respond.

It may also be noted that the same Observer Corps could be used to report on the actions of the United Nations Force itself, so that the organs of political control could immediately check any excess of authority, or decide to terminate an action when the situation has been remedied. In any decision of the political organs, the reports

[5] *Ante*, pp. 355–356.

of the Peace Observation Corps would be given all due consideration, but would not be treated as conclusive.

The arrangements outlined above are all designed as means of political control over the United Nations Force, to ensure that the Force will be called into action only in proper circumstances. However, there may well be a case for creating certain procedures for judicial control, both over the political organs and over the Force itself. Whilst it cannot be expected that any judicial body will interfere with the political discretion of the political control organs, the Disarmament Treaty may be expected to define the functions of the Force and the powers of the control organs so as to make certain questions arising from the employment of the Force justiciable questions, relating to the interpretation of the Treaty. It might be advisable, therefore, to amend Article 34 of the Statute of the International Court of Justice so as to permit the Court to deal with a contentious issue between a State and either the United Nations or the IDO. Alternatively, though this is a clumsy device, the United Nations might agree in advance that any disputes relating to the use of the international Force would be referred to the Court by means of a request for an advisory opinion.[6] The submission of the case to the Court would not stop automatically any activity of the Force, but the Court might issue a preliminary injunction requiring the Force to cease certain activities. These provisions would probably be analogous to provisions ensuring that the International Disarmament Organisation would not exceed its powers. The United States Treaty Outline deals only with disputes between parties to the disarmament treaty concerning the interpretation and application of that treaty,[7] and does not contain any provisions relating to disputes between a State and the International Disarmament Organisation. Suggestions have been made, however, for the settlement of these disputes which parallel those outlined above.[8]

Control over the Force and its members raises somewhat different considerations and it is likely that this would be best achieved by judicial organs other than the International Court of Justice. The need would be for both a " criminal " and a " civil " jurisdiction, and, as we have suggested in Part Two, there is a clear argument for establishing a permanent system of United Nations Courts-Martial to deal with responsibility of members of the Force for criminal acts and for Claims Commissions to deal with the question of the civil responsibility of the United Nations or members of the Force, either at the suit of States or of individuals. If it were felt necessary to provide an appeal from these Claims Commissions to the International Court of Justice, this could be done by way of an advisory

---

[6] For a similar arrangement, see Section 30 of the Convention on the Privileges and Immunities of the United Nations of 13 February 1946. 1 U.N.T.S., p. 15, at p. 30.

[7] Stage I, Section H.3.b.

[8] Sohn, " Adjudication and Enforcement in Arms Control," in D. G. Brennan, ed., *Arms Control, Disarmament and National Security* (1961), pp. 365–375.

opinion, requested by the United Nations political organs. In this way the International Court of Justice could be used without extending its jurisdiction directly to individuals.[9] All these procedures could, and should, be established for any permanent United Nations Force even prior to disarmament.

Not all the problems relating to an international Force can be solved in advance. The instrument establishing the Force must be sufficiently detailed to provide assurance to States that the Force will function within certain limits and that a system of checks and balances will make it unlikely for the Force to overstep these limits. At the same time, adequate flexibility must be retained to enable the Force, and the political and judicial bodies which will be charged with the control and supervision of the Force, to adapt to new and unforeseen circumstances. The period of actual disarmament, especially Stages II and III, when the power of the Force will not yet be overwhelming, will provide an opportunity to make such adjustments in the structure and functioning of the Force as experience may show desirable. Later changes should also be feasible, and adequate procedures for amending the instrument establishing the international Force need to be provided. The United Nations itself, the International Disarmament Organisation, and any group of ten or more States should be entitled to initiate such amendment procedures. Thus, additional guarantees against abuse of power by the Force could be developed as soon as need for them should become apparent. If there is constant vigilance, the Force can be kept within the strict limits of its authority, and the danger of a " praetorian guard " can easily be avoided.

---

[9] The system could be akin to that used to allow the I.C.J. to deal with appeals against awards by the UN Administrative Tribunal.

Postscript

The United Nations Force in Cyprus (UNFICYP)

THE outbreak of violence between the Greek Cypriot and Turkish Cypriot communities in December 1963 created a situation of civil strife which, from the outset, had implications for international peace and security. These arose from the fact that the Constitution of Cyprus was itself guaranteed by the United Kingdom, Greece and Turkey in the Treaty of Guarantee of 1960 [1] under which the three Powers agreed to take concerted action but, should that not prove possible, each reserved " the right to take action with the sole aim of re-establishing the state of affairs created by the present Treaty " (Art. IV). There thus existed a possibility of military intervention by any one of the three Guarantor Powers.

On 26 December the Cyprus Government accepted an offer from the three Guarantor Powers that their forces already stationed on the island under pre-existing agreements should assist in trying to secure a cease-fire and restore peace. During the two months that followed, the United Kingdom tried unsuccessfully to secure agreement on the replacement of this tripartite (and predominantly British) force by first a NATO force, and then a Commonwealth force. Not until 15 February did the United Kingdom abandon these attempts and request a meeting of the Security Council, proposing that a United Nations peace-keeping force should be established.

I. THE RESOLUTION ADOPTED BY THE SECURITY COUNCIL

On 4 March 1964 the Council unanimously adopted the following Resolution [2]:

" *The Security Council,*

Noting that the present situation with regard to Cyprus is likely to threaten international peace and security and may further deteriorate unless additional measures are promptly taken to maintain peace and to seek out a durable solution,

Considering the positions taken by the parties in relation to the Treaties signed at Nicosia on 16 August 1960,

Having in mind the relevant provisions of the Charter of the United Nations

---

[1] *U.K. Treaty Series,* No. 5 (1961), Cmnd. 1253.

[2] For the debates in the Council, see S/PV.1100, 1101 and 1102 of 2–4 March. The Resolution contained two further paragraphs, 7 and 8, concerning the designation and remuneration of a Mediator, but, since the Mediator was not envisaged as part of UNFICYP, it is not thought necessary to deal with the question of mediation. This Resolution was reaffirmed by the Council on 13 March : *UN Review,* Vol. 11, No. 4, April 1964, pp. 14–15.

and its Article 2, paragraph 4, which reads: ' All Members shall refrain in their international relations from the threat or use of force against the territorial integrity or political independence of any State, or in any other manner inconsistent with the Purposes of the United Nations,'

1. *Calls upon* all Member States, in conformity with their obligations under the Charter of the United Nations, to refrain from any action or threat of action likely to worsen the situation in the sovereign Republic of Cyprus, or to endanger international peace;

2. *Asks* the Government of Cyprus, which has the responsibility for the maintenance and restoration of law and order, to take all additional measures necessary to stop violence and bloodshed in Cyprus;

3. *Calls upon* the communities in Cyprus and their leaders to act with the utmost restraint;

4. *Recommends* the creation, with the consent of the Government of Cyprus, of a United Nations peace-keeping force in Cyprus. The composition and size of the force shall be established by the Secretary-General, in consultation with the Governments of Cyprus, Greece, Turkey and the United Kingdom. The commander of the force shall be appointed by the Secretary-General and report to him. The Secretary-General, who shall keep the Governments providing the force fully informed, shall report periodically to the Security Council on its operation;

5. *Recommends* that the function of the force should be, in the interest of preserving international peace and security, to use its best efforts to prevent a recurrence of fighting and, as necessary, to contribute to the maintenance and restoration of law and order and a return to normal conditions;

6. *Recommends* that the stationing of the force shall be for a period of three months, all costs pertaining to it being met, in a manner to be agreed upon by them, by the Governments providing the contingents and by the Government of Cyprus. The Secretary-General may also accept voluntary contributions for that purpose;
. . .''

The Resolution gives no clear indication of its constitutional basis, but it may be noted that the preamble refers to the situation as " *likely* to threaten international peace and security " and not as an actual threat to international peace and security: this, coupled with the provisions on mediation, suggests that the constitutional basis is to be found in Chapter VI of the Charter, probably Article 36 (1), and not in Chapter VII. Operative paragraph 1, addressed to all Member States, is presumably not a call for provisional measures under Article 40, but more a reminder of their obligations under Article 2 (4).

Paragraph 6, addressed to the crucial problem of financing, is significant in that, following the precedents of UNTEA[3] and UNYOM,[4] the operations were not to be a charge on the budget of the Organisation. The costs were to be met by the four States concerned except to the extent that this was reduced by voluntary contributions from other States.[5] Indeed, it is scarcely to be conceived that the Council would have agreed to the operations upon any other basis. The duration of the operation was optimistically envisaged as three months and this period has already been extended for a further three months, until 27 September 1964.

[3] *Ante*, p. 260.   [4] *Ante*, p. 85.
[5] See S/5682 for the voluntary contribution of £A 50,000 by Australia.

II. THE ROLE OF THE SECRETARY-GENERAL

The extent to which, under paragraph 4, the Secretary-General was entrusted with the composition and the control of the operations is a further striking feature of the Resolution. Certain misgivings could be anticipated after the Congo operations and, indeed, Czechoslovakia, France and the U.S.S.R. abstained on the separate vote on this paragraph. The representative of France said:

"The Security Council is thus divesting itself of responsibilities which are its own . . . The French delegation considers that it is really going very far indeed in the direction of the delegation of powers to grant them in this way to a single individual." [6]

Nonetheless, the Secretary-General proceeded to the composition of the Force, and the Force became operational on 27 March,[7] reaching its planned level of 7,000 by the middle of May. The time taken to constitute the Force, as compared with earlier operations, suggests that the Secretary-General had some difficulty in persuading Member States to participate and, indeed, at one stage there seemed to be some doubt as to whether the Force would ever be constituted. The contingents were eventually drawn from seven States and a clear effort was made, bearing in mind the nature of the mandate, to recruit not only a military force but also a professional, police contingent.[8] It is not known that any special agreement, comparable to the exchange of letters in UNEF,[9] has been made with the participating States. Nor have any Regulations for the Force yet been published.

The arrival of these contingents was, once again, achieved largely by a United States airlift, although charter flights were also used. Logistic support depended heavily on the United Kingdom, but was supplemented by national contingent and United Nations channels.[10] An air component of sixteen aircraft for observation, reconnaissance, liaison and supply was also established.[11]

The Secretary-General placed in command of the United Nations Force General Gyani, who had been on the island as an observer prior to the action by the Security Council, representing the Secretary-General. However, following the Congo precedent rather than that of UNEF, the Secretary-General reported on 29 April that he had

---

[6] S/PV.1102, 4 March.

[7] Report of the Secretary-General, 26 March 1964, S/5593/Add. 3.

[8] See Report of the Secretary-General on the Organisation and Operation of UNFICYP, 8 May 1964, Special Release SPL/43, which gives the following figures: *Military*: Austria, 10; Canada, 1,087; Finland, 1,000; Sweden, 889; Ireland, 636; United Kingdom, 2,719. *Police*: Austria, 28.

In addition he reported the expectation of a Danish contingent of 1,000 by May, of an Austrian field hospital of 54 members, and 70 additional Swedish personnel.

Later arrivals of police from Sweden (40), Australia (40) and New Zealand (20) were reported in Press Releases CYP/58, 59, 72. The intended strength of police is 200.

[9] *Ante*, p. 112.

[10] Report of 8 May 1964, SPL/43, para. 6.

[11] *Ibid.*, para. 7.

decided to strengthen the mission by appointing a special political representative, Dr. Galo Plaza, thus relieving General Gyani of his political responsibilities and allowing him to concentrate on problems of military command.[12]

Apart from his actions in constituting the mission and reporting to the Council, the Secretary-General has also demonstrated a certain degree of personal, political initiative. This can be seen in his appeals to the parties in Cyprus, in particular his " programme of action " outlined on 29 April,[13] and also in his communications with contributing States clarifying the powers of the Force [14] and his conclusion of a Status Agreement with the host State.[15] There has, happily, as yet [16] been no major challenge by any member of the Security Council to his interpretation of the mandate.

III. THE FUNCTIONS OF THE FORCE

These were defined in the original Resolution, with characteristic vagueness, as being " in the interest of preserving international peace and security, to use its best efforts to prevent a recurrence of fighting and, as necessary, to contribute to the maintenance and restoration of law and order and a return to normal conditions."

When, in April, considerable concern was expressed in the British Parliament over the limitations placed upon the Force in the execution of this mandate,[17] the Secretary-General sent an Aide-Mémoire which set out the guiding principles governing the operations of the Force.[18] These included the familiar principles of non-intervention in the political situation, the exclusiveness of United Nations control and command over the Force, and the restriction of the Force to the use of its weapons in self-defence. The principles of self-defence received the most detailed analysis yet seen in any United Nations document. The importance of these principles for all future United Nations peace-keeping operations merits the citation of these principles in full.

" . . .

Principles of self-defence

16. Troops of UNFICYP shall not take the initiative in the use of armed force. The use of armed force is permissible only in self-defence. The expression ' self-defence ' includes :

(a) the defence of United Nations posts, premises and vehicles under armed attack;

(b) the support of other personnel of UNFICYP under armed attack.

17. No action is to be taken by the troops of UNFICYP which is likely to bring them into direct conflict with either community in Cyprus, except in the following circumstances :

[12] Special Release SPL/42, 30 April 1964.
[13] *Ibid.*
[14] *Post*, pp. 555–556.
[15] *Post*, p. 559.
[16] As of the time of writing, 30 June 1964.
[17] *The Times*, 8 April 1964.
[18] *International Legal Materials*, 1964, Vol. III, No. 3.

(a) where members of the Force are compelled to act in self-defence;
(b) where the safety of the Force or of members of it is in jeopardy;
(c) where specific arrangements accepted by both communities have been, or in the opinion of the commander on the spot are about to be, violated, thus risking a recurrence of fighting or endangering law and order.

18. When acting in self-defence, the principle of minimum force shall always be applied, and armed force will be used only when all peaceful means of persuasion have failed. The decision as to when force may be used under these circumstances rests with the commander on the spot whose main concern will be to distinguish between an incident which does not require fire to be opened and those situations in which troops may be authorised to use force. Examples in which troops may be so authorised are:

(a) attempts by force to compel them to withdraw from a position which they occupy under orders from their commanders, or to infiltrate and envelop such positions as are deemed necessary by their commanders for them to hold, thus jeopardising their safety;
(b) attempts by force to disarm them;
(c) attempts by force to prevent them from carrying out their responsibilities as ordered by their commanders;
(d) violation by force of United Nations premises and attempts to arrest or abduct United Nations personnel, civil or military.

19. Should it be necessary to resort to the use of arms, advance warning will be given whenever possible. Automatic weapons are not to be used except in extreme emergency and fire will continue only as long as is necessary to achieve its immediate aim

Protection against individual or organised attack

20. Whenever a threat of attack develops towards a particular area, commanders will endeavour to restore peace to the area. In addition, local commanders should approach the local leaders of both communities. Mobile patrols shall immediately be organised to manifest the presence of UNFICYP in the threatened or disturbed areas in whatever strength is available. All appropriate means will be used to promote calm and restraint.

If all attempts at peaceful settlement fail, unit commanders may recommend to their senior commander that United Nations Force troops be deployed in such threatened areas. On issue of specific instructions to that effect from UNFICYP headquarters, unit commanders will announce that the entry of UNFICYP Force into such areas will be effected, if necessary, in the interests of law and order.

If, despite these warnings, attempts are made to attack, envelop or infiltrate UNFICYP positions, thus jeopardising the safety of troops in the area, they will defend themselves and their positions by resisting and driving off the attackers with minimum force.

Arrangements concerning cease-fire agreements

21. If UNFICYP units arrive at the scene of an actual conflict between members of the two communities, the commanders on the spot will immediately call on the leaders of both communities to break off the conflict and arrange for a cease-fire while terms which are acceptable to both communities are discussed. In certain cases it may be possible to enforce a cease-fire by interposing UNFICYP military posts between those involved, but if this is not acceptable to those involved in the conflict, or if there is doubt about its effectiveness, it should not normally be done, as it may only lead to a direct clash between UNFICYP troops and those involved in the conflict."

It may be noted that, as in the Congo operations,[19] there is little

---

[19] *Ante*, p. 203.

attempt to link the right of self-defence with the right to freedom of movement so as to enlarge the permissible sphere of military action. For example, it is clear that the Force is only to interpose itself between the two sides at the scene of an actual conflict when this is acceptable to the two sides and would be effective. Hence, in the large-scale operations in the Kyrenia mountains which began on 26 April, the Force had to stand helplessly by.[20] Moreover, the dismantling of road-blocks and the restoration of freedom of movement have throughout been conceived as measures to be secured by negotiation rather than by the use of force.[21]

Perhaps the most important limitation of all on the powers of the Force is to be seen in the fact that the Force has no powers of arrest over Cypriots,[22] and no powers to disarm them.

As the Congo experience demonstrated, the chances of a peace-keeping Force restoring law and order when rival armies of armed, and often irresponsible, men are being built up are minimal. Ideally, the solution would have lain in an agreement by both sides to reduce the numbers of armed militia or police under their control to the limits necessary to preserve order in the areas under their control and to place these militia forces under United Nations Command. This could then have been supplemented by undertakings by the Cyprus Government to forbid the carrying of arms by all other citizens, to forbid the importation of arms, and to punish those responsible for a breach of the relevant decrees. The United Nations Force, equipped with powers to disarm and powers to arrest, could then have effectively assisted in maintaining a cease-fire and in ensuring that these decrees and law and order generally were observed. Certainly General Gyani was fully alive to the problem, for on 28 May he stated :

" One of the major obstacles in the way of the United Nations Force is the irresponsible and senseless conduct of armed men of both communities who do not appear to have any discipline or to be responsible to any established authority, but have been acting on their own reckless initiative, regardless of the unfortunate and serious consequences of their acts. Too many unauthorised people in Cyprus are carrying too many weapons . . . It is absolutely essential that these elements of the population, both Greek Cypriot and Turkish Cypriot, should be restrained and disciplined and their weapons removed from them " [23]

However, far from the ideal solution being adopted, the reverse has occurred and Cyprus has become more, not less, of an armed camp. On 9 June the Cyprus Government proceeded to call up Cypriots, other than Turkish Cypriots, to form a newly authorised

---

[20] SPL/42, 30 April 1964.
[21] *Ibid.*, Annex I, the " programme of action " outlined by the Secretary-General. One difference from the Congo operations should be noted, and that is that in Cyprus the road-blocks appear to be directed towards restricting the freedom of movement of the other side and not so much that of UNFICYP.
[22] Save for the limited power to arrest persons on the premises of the Force committing an offence or causing a disturbance there: Article 15 of the Status Agreement.
[23] Special Release SPL/48, 29 May 1964.

National Guard,[24] and this at a stage when it has been estimated that there were already 30,000 regular and irregular Greek Cypriots under arms.[25] There has been increasing evidence of the importation, both official and " clandestine," of arms and ammunition and, to heighten the tension, the practice of taking hostages has continued.

The need for a strengthened mandate for UNFICYP is increasingly being admitted.[26] There are, in principle, only two ways of achieving this. The first is to enlarge the powers of the Force with the agreement of the Cyprus Government: evidence that this is likely is not impressive, for the Secretary-General's " programme of action " which suggested, *inter alia,* that UNFICYP might assist in facilitating and verifying disarming has gone largely unheeded. The only other alternative, given the lack of voluntary co-operation from both sides, is for the Security Council to compel co-operation by assuming mandatory powers under Chapter VII to replace the present powers of mere recommendation under Chapter VI.

That there is sufficient evidence of the existence of a threat to international peace and security, within the meaning of Article 39 of the Charter, can scarcely be doubted. The threat of a Turkish invasion is apparently a real one, and has been invoked by the Cyprus Government in justification for its creation of the National Guard and importation of war materials. What would be required, therefore, would be a unanimous political will within the Security Council to take this step, together with the enlargement of UNFICYP and the concurrence of the participating States. It is by no means clear that, were the Council to determine that a Chapter VII situation had arisen, the Government of Cyprus could terminate its consent to the presence of the Force on the basis that the mandate had been changed.[27]

If the attitude of the parties within Cyprus remains unchanged, and if the Security Council is itself not prepared to strengthen the mandate of the Force, there seems little point in its continued presence except, possibly, as a deterrent to a Turkish invasion.

IV. RELATIONS WITH THE HOST STATE

The presence of UNFICYP was clearly and, since its constitutional basis appears to be Chapter VI, probably necessarily based upon the consent of the host government. Whilst the Turkish Cypriot members of the Cabinet left the Cabinet in December 1963, this has not affected the capacity of the United Nations to deal with the host government, led by President Makarios, as the lawful government of Cyprus. However, the United Nations has, consistently with the

[24] *The Times,* 10 June.
[25] *The Times,* 21 May, article by Humphrey Berkely, M.P., entitled " A Stronger U.N. in Cyprus Needed."
[26] See the report of an agreement between Mr. Inönü, the Turkish Prime Minister, and British Ministers in *The Times,* 30 June 1964.
[27] *Ante,* pp. 414–415.

principle of non-intervention, never associated itself with the view of the government that the Turkish Cypriots constituted a rebellious, unlawful group.[28]

The necessity of placing the relations between the United Nations and the host State on a clear, legal footing led to an early conclusion of the Agreement between the United Nations and the Government of the Republic of Cyprus concerning the Status of the United Nations Peace-keeping Force in Cyprus, 31 March 1964.[29] The speed with which this was negotiated obviated the need for an initial, basic agreement: the general undertaking to act in good faith is contained in the final paragraph of the Agreement itself.

With very slight changes, the Agreement follows the UNEF Agreement[30] more closely than the ONUC Agreement.[31] For example, the provisions[32] on settlement of disputes or claims follow exactly the UNEF pattern, and not the more rudimentary ONUC pattern. There is, however, a more detailed provision on liaison[33] which is more reminiscent of the ONUC Agreement, although not identical to it. Moreover, the freedom of movement clause in paragraph 32 provides for "freedom of movement throughout Cyprus," like the ONUC Agreement and unlike the UNEF Agreement.

How far the host government has fully complied with its obligations under the Agreement is difficult to assess. The road-blocks and restrictions on freedom of movement have been aimed more at the Turkish Cypriots than at UNFICYP, and, whilst various attacks on UNFICYP personnel have occurred, it is difficult to say that the host government has not fulfilled its obligations under paragraph 18 of the Agreement to ensure the prosecution of offenders, for this cannot impose an obligation to use more than due diligence in seeking them out.

The real difficulty has lain more in the political attitude adopted by the host government, in particular its disinclination to reduce the number of armed personnel on the island and to co-operate with the Secretary-General's proposals. To this extent the question is more one of the extent to which the host government has complied with paragraphs 1 and 2 of the initial Resolution than with the Agreement.

In conclusion, the Cyprus operations may, following the Congo operations, raise the whole question of the utility of employing a United Nations Force in a peace-keeping role, to maintain law and order within a State, in circumstances where the United Nations is not receiving the complete co-operation of all parties. It was this

[28] Letter dated 7 May from the Representative of Cyprus to the President of the Security Council, S/5688.
[29] S/5634.
[30] *Ante*, pp. 125–136.
[31] *Ante*, pp. 236–240.
[32] Paras. 38–40.
[33] Para. 41.

co-operation which made UNTEA such an extraordinary, and little published, success. But there, it will be remembered, the United Nations virtually integrated local forces into its own Security Force and assumed direct command over them. It may well be that this ought to be made a condition of United Nations peace-keeping operations of this kind.

Conclusions

NEARLY twenty years have elapsed since the signing of the United Nations Charter. Yet, despite the prominence given to Chapter VII in the Charter, and despite a general agreement that the system of collective security established by the Charter can only operate upon the assumption that the United Nations is given the armed forces necessary to maintain international peace and security, the Charter scheme has not yet been implemented. The history of the attempts to implement this scheme and the alternative scheme which many envisaged could be established under the Resolution on Uniting for Peace of 3 November 1950 has been briefly described in Chapter 2. At the time of writing, however, there is no real "scheme" in existence, and the Cyprus situation [1] has revealed only too clearly the weakness of the United Nations Organisation in dealing with a situation which requires a military force but in which the United Nations is entirely dependent on the voluntary provision of national contingents by those very few States which accept a concept of obligation—albeit at this stage a moral rather than a legal obligation—towards the United Nations and the Purposes and Principles for which it stands.

The extraordinary thing is that the United Nations has been able to establish military forces at all. And yet, since 1948, there has never been a time in which, in one or several parts of the world, a group or Force comprising military personnel was not operating in the name of the United Nations. Whether in the form of observer groups,[2] or of a military Force such as that in Korea,[3] engaged in hostilities indistinguishable from war, or of a "peace-keeping" Force like UNEF in the Middle East[4] or ONUC in the Congo[5]—and whether 200 or 20,000 strong—United Nations Military Forces have in fact played a not insignificant part in maintaining the peace and security of the world. All these military operations have been described in Part One of the present study, and the postscript gives a brief account of the latest military operation, that in Cyprus.

Each and every one of these military operations represented an exercise in improvisation, and, however critical this study may have been at times, the determination and skill of those responsible calls for a special and sincere tribute. Yet the question which must be asked is why the United Nations Organisation, comprising 114 States,

---

[1] See *ante*, pp. 552–560.
[2] *Ante*, Chap. 4.
[3] *Ante*, Chap. 3.
[4] *Ante*, Chap. 5.
[5] *Ante*, Chap. 6.

is content to entrust its responsibilities for the maintenance of international peace and security to a system based on improvisation and chance? Not one of these States would contemplate looking after its own security in so haphazard a manner and yet for nearly twenty years it has remained the basis upon which United Nations military operations have been established. It has not been the intention of this study to answer that question in terms of the reasons behind the policies of Member States, but rather to examine the problems which have been encountered and the principles and practices which have emerged as solutions, complete or partial, to these problems.

However, the conclusion to which the present writer has been forced is that none of these problems can be properly solved except by establishing a permanent United Nations Military Force. The functions which are capable of attribution to a United Nations Force have been outlined in Chapter 8. These, it may be recalled, fell broadly into the two main categories of "enforcement" functions directed against a State or States and "peace-keeping" functions which, whilst possibly including the use of armed force, do not envisage that such force will be used directly against a State. The former, except for the action in Korea, have never been undertaken by the United Nations and Article 42 of the Charter has never been used. The latter have become very much the kind of military operations which the United Nations has been prepared to undertake and it may thus be argued that in initiating a scheme for a permanent Force it is a "peace-keeping" Force which ought first to be aimed at. There are other reasons why it is advisable to concentrate on a Force with peace-keeping functions. These are, first, that such a Force will not need to be of the same order of size as a Force designed for enforcement action [6]; secondly, the doubt over whether the General Assembly could legally authorise enforcement action [7]; thirdly, the likelihood that situations calling for a "peace-keeping" role will be more frequent than situations calling for enforcement action; and, lastly, the likelihood that Member States will find a proposal for a peace-keeping Force both politically and economically more acceptable.

Therefore, on the basis of the experience of the past and in the light of the principles which have emerged, there is every justification for proposing a scheme which would give to the United Nations a permanent military Force for peace-keeping purposes. This will not necessarily mean that the Force could not be used for enforcement action; as we shall see, it could also form the nucleus of a larger Force designed for enforcement action and created by strengthening the permanent nucleus with national contingents from Member States. However, its primary role will be a "peace-keeping" role. Such a scheme or plan can only be introduced gradually, for this is

---

[6] *Ante*, pp. 316–317, 320.
[7] *Ante*, pp. 288–293.

not a moment in time at which great changes can be effected: rather is it a time for the slow evolution of a machinery which can command the trust and confidence of States. The scheme which follows is, in effect, a ten-year scheme to be completed in four stages. The scheme may therefore be set out in the following stages and footnotes will refer the reader to those parts of the study in which the details of the scheme are enlarged upon.

I. STAGE ONE (TO BE COMPLETED WITHIN THREE YEARS)

1. *The United Nations Headquarters Military Staff* [8]

The Security Council or, failing agreement in that organ, the General Assembly, should appoint a United Nations Chief-of-Staff and authorise the Secretary-General to begin the recruitment of a permanent United Nations Headquarters Military Staff of approximately fifty experienced military officers in consultation with the Chief-of-Staff. These would be recruited as individuals for terms of service of, say, five to seven years and would range from a Commander down to experts in communications, transportation, ordnance, intelligence, civil affairs and medical services.[9]

The Military Staff, when constituted, would undertake the following tasks:

(1) A study of the different kinds of peace-keeping operations likely to be undertaken by a United Nations Force composed of national contingents and of the ideal composition and command structure for such a Force in any given type of operation.

(2) A survey of the operational, logistical and administrative problems (including standardisation of equipment and of operational procedures, joint civilian-military operations) encountered in the past and likely to be encountered in the future.[10]

(3) Liaison with the Member States which have declared their willingness in principle to provide contingents for a United Nations Force,[11] such liaison to include a periodic inspection of any such contingents by the United Nations Headquarters Military Staff.

(4) The organisation of joint exercises in which contingents assigned for United Nations duty by several Member States could participate under United Nations Command.

(5) The formulation of plans for a United Nations Staff College and of training schemes to be undertaken by such a College for the instruction of senior officers drawn from the armed forces of States declaring their willingness to provide contingents for the United Nations.

(6) The formulation of model Regulations for the Force,[12] Status

---

[8] *Ante*, pp. 349–352.
[9] See the diagram on p. 350.
[10] *Ante*, Chap. 11.
[11] *Ante*, pp. 330–337.
[12] *Ante*, pp. 334, 336, 372, 376.

of Forces Agreements [13] and Stand-by Agreements [14] for submission to the political organs of the United Nations for discussion and adoption.

(7) The negotiation of contracts and charterparties with public and private associations designed to ensure that the Staff could call on supplies and transport as and when needed.[15]

2. *The political control organs* [16]

Whilst the initiative in carrying out this scheme ought to come from the Security Council (or rather ought to begin there), should this be rejected the General Assembly should assert its secondary responsibility [17] and pass the Resolutions referred to above in connection with the establishment of the Headquarters Military Staff: the budgetary responsibility would in any event be upon the Assembly.

Moreover, whether or not the Security Council assumes the initiative, there would be every advantage in the General Assembly establishing a committee of limited composition, adequately representing the East, the West and the non-aligned States (and with due regard to equitable geographical distribution) which could assume the continuing political control of a United Nations Force in any particular operation which became hamstrung by a veto in the Security Council.[18] Thus the principal burden of political responsibility would be assumed by the Member States and not, as has so often been the case in the past, by the Secretary-General. The practice of vesting continuing political control in the Secretary-General,[19] which has been symptomatic of a shirking of responsibility by Member States, would therefore cease and Member States would be able to devise forms and procedures for exercising this responsibility, whether within the Security Council or the General Assembly (and the committee now proposed).

The political control organ, the Security Council or the General Assembly (according to where the initiative stemmed from)—or even, ideally, a joint committee of both organs [20] in view of the financial implications of the scheme—would also undertake the following:

(1) The consideration and approval of the contracts of service of the members of the United Nations Headquarters Military Staff and of the general plan for the composition of such a Staff submitted by the Secretary-General and the Chief-of-Staff.

(2) The consideration and approval of the plans for a United Nations Staff College.

[13] *Ante,* pp. 432–455.
[14] *Ante,* pp. 371–377.
[15] *Ante,* pp. 405–406.
[16] *Ante,* pp. 353–359.
[17] For the constitutional basis for the Assembly's authority to establish a Force, see *ante,* pp. 285–298.
[18] *Ante,* pp. 355–357.
[19] *Ante,* p. 357.
[20] *Ante,* pp. 354–356, 376.

(3) The consideration and approval of the drafts for Standing Regulations for the United Nations Force,[21] a basic Status of Forces Agreement,[22] and the basic Stand-by Agreements.[23]

(4) A study of the problems involved in establishing and operating a United Nations Force, in particular of such problems as the relevance of consent and of the principle of non-intervention,[24] the application of the laws of war,[25] means of financing the cost of the Force.[26]

(5) The establishment of a system of Claims Commissions to deal with claims arising out of the operations of the Force.[27]

(6) The establishment of the nucleus of an Observer Corps, either by creating an Observer section within the United Nations Head-quarters Military Staff (to be supplemented by a revitalised Panel of Observers, held in reserve) or by extending the basic Stand-by Agreements to include the provision of observers by Member States.[28]

II. STAGE TWO (TO BE COMPLETED WITHIN TWO YEARS)

1. *The United Nations Headquarters Military Staff*

The Military Staff would enter into negotiations with Member States, at the purely military level, in an attempt to reach a provisional understanding on the size and kind of forces a Member State would contribute under a Stand-by Agreement.[29]

It would also draw up plans for the individual recruitment of certain specialised branches of the United Nations Force, for example, a bilingual communications section, vehicle and aircraft maintenance and repair staff, engineers, an observer section,[30] etc.

2. *The political control organs*

These would undertake the following tasks:

(1) The negotiation of Stand-by Agreements with particular States.[31]

(2) The negotiation of Agreements for transit, operational bases, training areas and other facilities to be furnished by States.[32]

(3) Approval of the principle of direct individual recruitment of certain specialised arms of the Force.

[21] *Ante*, pp. 334, 336, 372, 376.
[22] *Ante*, pp. 432–455.
[23] *Ante*, pp. 371–377.
[24] *Ante*, pp. 196–200 and Chap. 12.
[25] *Ante*, Chap. 15.
[26] *Ante*, Chap. 14.
[27] *Ante*, pp. 149–151, 242–248, 375, 383, 447–448.
[28] *Ante*, pp. 315, 330, 548.
[29] *Ante*, pp. 376–377.
[30] For a discussion of the advantages of individual recruitment see *ante*, pp. 334–335.
[31] *Ante*, pp. 376–377.
[32] *Ante*, 405, 455–467.

(4) Consideration of the establishment of an Arms Purchasing Agency, of a United Nations Code of Military Law and of a system of United Nations Courts-Martial.[33]

III. STAGE THREE (TO BE COMPLETED WITHIN TWO YEARS)

1. *The United Nations Headquarters Military Staff*

This would be developed and expanded and a clearer separation made between the Headquarters Staff of the Chief-of-Staff and the Staff of the Commander so as to permit the latter to assume the structure of a true military Command.

An infrastructure appropriate to a multi-purpose Force of 10,000 men would be studied and proposed to the political control organs.

2. *The political control organs*

These would turn to the following tasks:

(1) The devising of a scheme whereby Member States would allocate national contingents to the exclusive control of the United Nations for a fixed period of, say, two years during which they would be placed under exclusive United Nations Command and stationed in bases or training areas made available to the United Nations. Such a scheme would ensure that the size of the Force did not at any one time exceed 10,000 men and would include contingents from States drawn from different areas of the world.[34]

(2) The negotiation and conclusion of a base or bases agreements to provide bases large enough to accommodate the permanent Force of up to 10,000 men.[35]

(3) The consideration of a scheme for individual recruitment of the entire Force, such individuals to be phased in gradually so as to decrease reliance on national contingents.

(4) The establishment of an Arms Purchasing Agency, of a United Nations Code of Military Law and of a system of United Nations Courts-Martial.

IV. STAGE FOUR (TO BE COMPLETED WITHIN THREE YEARS)

1. *The United Nations Headquarters Military Staff*

The Staff would undertake the study of the problems involved in the assumption by the Force of the functions envisaged for the Force in the Disarmament Treaty,[36] and in the light of the results of the study of this problem by the political organs. In particular, it would study the problems involved in augmenting the permanent Force by

---

[33] For argument as to the necessity for these see *ante*, pp. 353, 378, 512–513.
[34] *Ante*, pp. 334, 377–378.
[35] *Ante*, pp. 458–467.
[36] *Ante*, Chap. 16.

contingents of national States in order to constitute a Force of far greater size for enforcement of a Disarmament Treaty.

2. *The political control organs*

These would undertake :

(1) The implementation of the scheme for individual recruitment of the entire Force.

(2) The revision of the Stand-by Agreements with Member States so as to adapt these to the necessity for providing a composite Force for disarmament enforcement, comprising the permanent, individually-recruited nucleus and the supporting national contingents drawn from the Member States.

(3) The consideration, in close co-operation with the Disarmament Conference, of the means whereby the United Nations Force could be assigned to functions envisaged for such a Force in the Disarmament Treaty.

(4) The study of the relationship between the Inspectorate, and any police attached to the Inspectorate,[37] to be established under the Disarmament Treaty and the United Nations Force.

This elaboration of the tasks to be undertaken by the Headquarters Military Staff and the political control organs has not included an assignment of tasks to the Secretary-General. This does not mean, however, that at all stages the political control organs may not delegate to the Secretary-General the general task of co-ordinating the work of the Military Staff with their own work, or of assisting either the political organs or the Military Staff by way of preparing studies and reports, or even of negotiating on behalf of one or the other the various agreements which have to be concluded. These powers of delegation already exist in the Charter and require no special emphasis.

The scheme, in concentrating upon the establishment of a United Nations Force, has also omitted the variety of problems which might ideally be considered in any development of the powers and effectiveness of the United Nations. Thus it may be said that proposals for the alteration of the composition of the Security Council, for the abandonment of the veto on certain questions, and, even more relevantly, for the development of an adequate machinery for peaceful change may all have to be considered at some juncture. This last proposal, for a machinery for peaceful change,[38] is directly relevant in the sense that, without such machinery, a United Nations Force may be tied down to the task of keeping the peace almost indefinitely in a situation in which there is no power in the United Nations to compel, in the last resort, the acceptance of a political solution which will remove the necessity for the presence of a Force. Yet all these proposals are not strictly necessary for the

[37] *Ante*, pp. 531–538.
[38] *Ante*, pp. 525–526.

creation of a United Nations Force. They have been omitted because it is believed that, even without any radical revision of the Charter, there is every point in establishing a United Nations Force and little to be gained by refraining from doing so pending an acceptance of other, allied proposals.

Finally, it may be noted that, whilst the scheme has obvious implications for disarmament [39]—and, indeed, in the Fourth Stage both the Military Staff and the political organs would undertake studies of the problems involved in utilising the Force for disarmament functions—the essential thesis which this study has developed is that the creation of a United Nations Force ought not to be made dependent upon disarmament but should be undertaken *now*. There will thus be created a United Nations Force which can be utilised for present purposes and, when that time comes, adapted and strengthened for any disarmament functions which a Disarmament Treaty may entrust to it. States in entering into a Disarmament Treaty will not be called upon to perform an act of faith by committing themselves to disarmament without any real guarantee that the United Nations Force essential to the whole scheme for disarmament will be created—as is now the case with both the Soviet and the Western proposals on disarmament. The Force will be in existence, there will be several years of experience by the United Nations in the techniques of recruiting, supplying, commanding and, above all, of controlling the Force, and thus the problems of creating a Force for disarmament purposes will be reduced to problems of a totally different order from those which now perplex the disarmament negotiations. All that will be required will be the adaptation and strengthening of an existing institution.

In the immediate future, however, the United Nations will have a Force which will be capable of making a significant contribution to the maintenance of international peace and security. The permanent nucleus will at no stage exceed 10,000 men—or such other limit as the Member States feel disposed to set to it bearing in mind the financial implications of the Force and possible distrust of it. It could, itself, be utilised for no more than a " peace-keeping " operation of limited size. For larger peace-keeping operations or for enforcement action ordered by the Security Council it would have to be enlarged by the national contingents provided by Member States. It is, therefore, a permanent nucleus of which the most important part would be the experienced planning staff, the Headquarters Military Staff, and the network of agreements and arrangements by which the United Nations would be prepared *in advance* to meet a host of different situations. It would put at an end the uneconomical, piecemeal and highly hazardous system which at present operates and would replace it by a system which will afford some guarantee that the United Nations will be able to discharge its responsibility

[39] *Ante*, Chap. 16.

for the maintenance of international peace and security. This is the immediate need, and the scheme set out in these conclusions is no more than an attempt to state how this need can be met. It needs for its implementation some little money,[40] some considerable effort by States and, above all, a modicum of goodwill and sincerity on the part of States to achieve the Purposes and Principles for which they established the United Nations Organisation.

[40] *Ante*, pp. 324–325, 479–481.

INDEX

Advisory Committee, 103–104, 118, 165, 185
  for Congo, 165, 185
  for UNEF, 103–104, 118
Advisory Opinion on Certain Expenses of the United Nations, 20, 33, 34, 95–99, 114, 148, 176, 179, 180, 215, 231, 247n, 250–252, 254, 279, 284, 288–290, 291, 296n, 300–301, 309n, 310, 318, 327, 414–415, 423, 473, 477–479
Advisory Opinion on Effects of Awards of Compensation made by the United Nations Administrative Tribunal, 309n, 310, 477n
Advisory Opinion on Reparation for Injuries, 33, 85, 242, 243n, 308, 310, 448
Advisory Opinion on Reservations to the Genocide Convention, 310
Advisory Opinion on the Interpretation of the Peace Treaties, 310
Advisory Opinion on the Treaty of Lausanne, 539–540
Afro-Asian Powers, 160, 163
Aitchison v. *Whitley*, 464n
Alexander, Maj.-General,
  controversy with Bunche, 189
American Society of International Law, 497
ANC (Armée nationale congolaise), 161–162
  attacks on ONUC personnel, 166, 234
  disarming, question of, 189–190
  threat to law and order by, 161–162
Andrassy, 300n
Armistice agreements, 48–53, 74–77, 78, 80–81
  in Korea, 48–53
  in Palestine, 74–77, 78, 80–81
Assistance and facilities, including rights of passage, 16–17, 136–139, 218, 228–229, 331–332, 417–419
  discussed in Military Staff Committee, 16–17
  for ONUC, 218, 228–229
  for UNEF, 136–139
  And see Logistic support.
Assist-letter scheme, 393–394
Asylum, grant of, by United Nations, 188, 234
Attlee, Earl, 357n

Bases, agreements for, 458–467
  civil jurisdiction, 465–467
  criminal jurisdiction, 462–465
  rights to be acquired, 460–462

Bases, agreements for—*cont.*
  whether sovereignty or lease desirable, 459–460
Baxter, 498, 509n, 512n, 516
Belgium, 153, 154–155, 158, 162–163, 166, 170, 190, 195, 225–227
  intervention in Congo, 153, 162–163, 227
  withdrawal of forces and personnel from Congo, 158, 166, 195, 225–226
Berlin Conference 1954…53
Bloomfield, 482n
Bowman and Fanning, 399n, 403
Boxer rebellion, 6–7
Brownlie, 272n, 304n
Bunche, 155, 189, 217
Bunker, 225, 256
Burns, Lieut.-General, 115, 328–329, 354n
Burns and Heathcote, 426n

Canada, 333, 342, 344, 345, 346, 475n, 476n
  legislation for Commonwealth Forces, 344–345
  offer of stand-by contingent, 333, 345–346
  suggestions on apportionment of expenses, 475n, 476n
  system of command of Forces, 342
Cannon and Jordan, 317, 320, 351
Cease-fires, 48, 73–77, 169, 172
  authority to negotiate, 48
  in Congo, 169, 172
  in Korea, 48
  supervision of, by observer groups, 73–77
Chaumont, 287n, 477n
China, 43–44, 46–47
  intervention in Korea, 43–44, 47
Civil war, 191–194, 424–427, 555–558
  power to prevent,
    in Congo, 191–194
    in Cyprus, 555–558
  propriety of United Nations intervention in, 424–427
Civilian-military operations, 342–343, 347
Civilian relief operations, 58–59, 119, 248–249
  in Congo, 248–249
  in Korea, 58–59
  in UNEF, 119
Claims and Responsibility, 57, 85–86, 149–151, 242–248, 370–371, 374–376, 441–442, 447–448, 466–467, 550–551

Claims and Responsibility—*cont.*
in future, under,
    ad hoc agreements with partici-
        pating States, 370–371
    bases agreements, 466–467
    disarmament, 550–551
    Status of Forces agreements, 441–
        442, 447–448
in past practice,
    Congo, 242–248
    Korea, 57
observer groups, 85–86
UNEF, 149–151
Collective Measures Committee, 21–28,
    47, 294, 337, 419, 455
Command Structure, 40–41, 115–117,
    118–119, 209–212, 337–353, 367–368,
    487–488
for *ad hoc* forces, 337–347
    chain of command, 338–339
    delineation of authority of Sec-
        retary-General and Commander,
        340–343
for permanent forces, 347–353
    appointment of Commander, 347–
        348
    chain of command, 351–352
    delineation of authority of Sec-
        retary-General and Military
        Staff, 352–353
in Congo, 209–212, 339
in future *ad hoc* forces, 367–368
in Korea, 40–41, 338
in UNEF, 115–117, 118–119, 338–339
relevance to application of laws of
    war, 487–488
Commanders-in-chief, 17, 24, 337, 347–
    349
discussed in Military Staff Commit-
    tee, 17
    Collective Measures Committee,
        24, 337
of permanent forces, 347–349
Committee of Sixteen, 42, 368
Congo, United Nations operations in,
    153–254, 271–272, 278
Advisory Committee on, 165
application of laws of war, 222–224
Belgian bases in, 177, 233–234, 444
claims and responsibility arising
    from, 242–248
command structure, 209–212
composition of Force, 205–208
Conciliation Commission, 168, 230
disarming by ONUC, 188–190
financing, 249–254
functions of the Force, 186–196
    assistance in restoring law and
        order, 187–191
    expulsion of foreign personnel
        and mercenaries, 195–196
    maintenance of integrity and poli-
        tical independence of Congo,
        186–187
    prevention of civil war, 191–195
Kitona declaration, 172

Congo, United Nations operations in—
    cont.
logistic support, 218–219
military actions by ONUC, 169,
    171–172, 173–174, 193–194
principles governing operations, 183,
    196–205
    freedom of movement, 203–205
    non-intervention, 196–200
    restriction to self-defence, 200–
        203
relations between United Nations
    and contributing States, 205–224
relations between United Nations
    and Member States, 224–230
    assistance to factions within
        Congo, 227–228
    economic measures to prevent
        secession, 329–330
    expulsion of foreign personnel
        and mercenaries, 225–226
    use of States' territories, 228–229
relations with "host" State, 230–242
    basic agreements with, 232, 429–
        430
    consent to ONUC, 231–232
    exclusive United Nations control
        over ONUC, 233–236
    provincial authorities, 240–242
    Status of Forces agreements, 236–
        240
    withdrawal of Force, 235–236
resolutions of Security Council and
    General Assembly, 154–174
    constitutional basis of, 174–182,
        280
strategic and political control, 212–
    217
withdrawal of contingents, 163, 208–
    209
Consent, 79–80, 124–125, 180, 231–232,
    311–312, 412–427
as constitutional basis for a Force,
    180, 231–232, 311–312
relation to rule of non-intervention,
    422–427
    in enforcement actions, 424
    in peace-keeping operations, 424–
        427
to presence of a Force,
    Cyprus, 558
    observer groups, 79–80, 420
    ONUC, 231–232, 421–422
    UNEF, 124–125, 420–421
    UNTEA, 256
whether legally necessary,
    by aggressor State, 412–413
    by transit State, 417–419
    by victim or host State, 413–417
withdrawal of, 420–422
Constitutional basis for United
    Nations Forces, 32–36, 61–68, 93–
    99, 175–180, 256–257, 274–312,
    538–543, 553
for Congo operations, 175–180, 280

Constitutional basis for United Nations Forces—*cont.*
 for Cyprus Force, 553
 for disarmament force, 538–543
 for Korean action, 32–36
 for observer groups, 61–68
 for UNEF, 93–99
 for UNTEA, 256–257
Crete, action against in 1897...6
Cyprus, United Nations Force in, 552–560
 absence of powers to disarm, 557
 financing of, 553
 functions of, 555–558
 relations with host State, 558–560
 resolutions of the Security Council, 552–553
 constitutional basis of, 553
 role of Secretary-General in, 554–555
 self-defence by, 555–557

Danzig Port and Waterways Board, 4
Davies, Lord, 313, 319, 322n, 459n
Dayal, 162, 233, 400
Dean, Arthur, 533
Disarmament, 519–551
 Amendment of Charter, 541–542
 Force for,
  constitutional basis of, 538–543
  control of, 549–551
   judicial, 550–551
   political, 549–550
  finance of, 543–545
  possession of nuclear weapons by, 544–545
  powers of, 536–538, 545–551
 International Disarmament Organisation, 527–528, 531–538
  powers over individuals, 536–537
  relationship to United Nations and an international force, 531–538
 Peace-Observation Corps, 545–551
 Relationship to other peace-keeping arrangements, 519–523, 523–531
  peaceful settlement of disputes, 524–526
  rules of international conduct, 527–531
   aggression and subversion, 528–529
   rule of non-intervention, 529–530
 Soviet draft treaty, 521–522, 525, 531–532, 534, 535, 537, 541
 United States treaty outline, 519–520, 523, 524–525, 527, 531, 534, 535, 536, 540, 541, 546, 548
 U.S.A./U.S.S.R. joint statement, 519
 Veto, problem of, 534, 535, 540, 549
Discipline, 343–346, 353, 511–512
 relevance to application of laws of war, 511–512
Draper, 178, 203n, 448n, 509n

"Effectiveness" as principle for construction of the Charter, 307–311
Eide and Midgaard, 425n
Enforcement action, 98, 176, 190, 266, 278, 288, 289, 291–293, 316–317, 320, 412–413, 485, 499–503, 536, 545
 application of laws of war in, 485, 499–503. *And see* Laws of War.
 lack of, in Congo, 176, 190, 278
 meaning of, 98, 266, 288, 289, 291
 under disarmament, 536, 545
 whether consent of territorial State required for, 912–913
 whether General Assembly can authorise, 288–289, 291–293
Expenses Case. See under Advisory Opinions.

Financing, 38–39, 85, 139–148, 249–254, 260–261, 324–325, 369, 373–374, 406–411, 468–483, 543–545, 553
 budget deficits, 473, 479–480
  sanctions for, 479–480
 future prospects for, 481–483
 in *ad hoc* agreements, 369
 in stand-by agreements, 373–374
 in permanent Force, 324–325
 of logistic support for United Nations Forces, 406–411
  costs of movement, 408–411
 past practice in,
  Korea, 38–39, 407, 408–409, 469
  observer groups, 85, 411, 468–469
  ONUC, 249–254, 407, 469
  UNEF, 139–148, 407, 469
  UNFICYP, 553
  UNTEA, 260–261, 471
  UNYOM, 85, 471
 resolutions of General Assembly on, 472, 474, 480
 sources of funds, 468–480
  budgetary allocations, 473–480
   apportionment, 474–477
   effect of apportionment, 477–480
  participating States, 468–471
  sale of bonds, 473
  voluntary contributions by States, 471–473
 under disarmament arrangements, 543–545
 And see Advisory Opinion on Certain Expenses
Fisher, 544n
Fitzmaurice, 266n, 417n, 477–478
France,
 amendment to Dunbarton Oaks Proposals by, 418–419
 attitude on Cyprus resolutions, 554
Franck, 420n

Freedom of movement, 79–81, 128,
194, 203–205, 434–436, 559
for observer groups, 79–81
for ONUC, 183, 194, 203–205
for UNEF, 128
for UNFICYP, 559
Frye, 316n, 324–325, 328

General Assembly, 31, 43, 44, 45–46,
47, 50, 52, 68, 91–93, 160–161, 167–
168, 182, 227, 255–257, 270, 285–
298, 355–357, 549
action by,
in Congo, 160–161, 167–168, 182,
227
in Korea, 31, 43, 44, 45–46, 47,
50, 52
in UNEF, 91–93
in UNTEA, 255–257
as organ of political control, 355–
357
need for smaller committee, 355–
357, 549
authority to establish Forces, 285–
298
authority to establish observer
groups, 68
budgetary control. *See* Financing.
emergency sessions. *See* Resolution
on Uniting for Peace.
plan for partition of Palestine, 270
Geneva Conference, 1954...53
Geneva Conventions, 50, 55, 486, 490,
500, 501, 505, 506, 507, 508n, 509,
513–515
And see Laws of War.
Geneva Protocol on Pacific Settlement of Disputes, 542
German High Command Trial, 507n
Gizenga, 168, 172, 185
*Gold of National Bank of Albania
Arbitration*, 495n
Greece, naval blockade against, in 1886
...5
party to Treaty of Guarantee in
Cyprus, 552
Grob, 497n
Gyani, General, 557

Hague Convention No. IV, 489, 490,
506, 507, 511
Halderman, 178, 277n, 311n
Herter, United States Secretary of
State, 520–521
Higgins, 479n, 481n
Higgins, R., 273n, 304n
Hogg, 479n
Holcombe, 481n
Host States, 57–58, 83–84, 110, 125–136,
206–207, 236–240, 260, 374, 428–
455, 558–559
agreements for permanent bases.
See Bases.

Host States—*cont.*
basic agreements with, 428–432
control over composition of Forces,
110, 206–207
past practice in Korea, 57–58
observer groups, 83–84
ONUC, 236–240
UNEF, 125–136
UNFICYP, 558–559
UNTEA, 260, 440
stand-by agreements, 374
status of forces agreements, 432–455
arrest, investigation, 444–445
civil jurisdiction, 445–448
communication and facilities,
453–454
criminal jurisdiction, 436–442
customs and fiscal arrangements,
451–453
dependants and civilians, 451
duration of, 454–455
freedom of movement, 434–436.
And see Freedom of movement.
inquests, 454
local recruits, 450
use of arms and uniforms, 448–
449
use of United Nations Flag, 449–
450
waiver of immunities, 441–442,
464
zone areas, 443–444
And see Consent.
Hostages Trial, 495n
Hsu Mo, 497n

Implied powers to establish United
Nations Force, 307–311
Individual recruitment, 323, 334–336,
352, 353
Institut de droit international, 499
International Committee of the Red
Cross, 501, 509
International Court of Justice,
enforcement of decisions as a func-
tion for a United Nations Force,
267, 524–525
And see Advisory opinions.
International Disarmament Organisa-
tion, 527–528, 531–538
And see Disarmament.
International Law Association, 287n,
318–319
International Law Commission, 529
International Military Tribunal, 493n,
495, 496, 505n
Israel, 90, 106–107, 109
Italy, provision of facilities by, 137

Japan, agreements on Status of Forces,
58, 439
Jenks, 244n, 432, 433

Jennings, 95
Jennings v. Markley, 513n
Jessup, 499n

Kalonji, 162
Kasavubu, 153, 159, 164, 166, 168, 169, 200, 227, 233
Katanga, 155, 157, 166, 169, 171, 174, 228, 229–230, 240
  airstrength, 228
  economic pressure on, 229–230
  gendarmerie, 166, 171
  secession of, 155, 169, 174
  United Nations entry into, 157, 240
Kelsen, 33, 281n, 302n, 307n, 329, 449n
Kennedy, President, 520
Kerley, 67
King Gordon, 153n
Korea, United Nations action in, 29–60
  application of laws of war in, 57–59
  appointment of commander, 40
  armistice and truce negotiations, 47–53
  command structure, 40–41
  constitutional basis for, 32–36
  contributions to the Force, 36–40
  defects of, 60
  establishment of Unified Command, 33
  financing of, 38–39
  logistic supply, 37–38
  nature of, 45–46, 53
  repatriation of prisoners of war, 49–51
  status of forces in, 57–59
  strategic and political control, 41–45
Koretsky, 284
Kunz, 493n

Lauterpacht, E., 273n
Lauterpacht, H., 310n, 417n, 493n, 494
Laws of War, 53–57, 121, 222–224, 245–248, 484–516
  application of to Korean conflict, 53–57, 500, 510
    to ONUC, 222–224, 509–510
    to UNEF, 121
  areas relevant to United Nations operations, 488–492
  effect of command structure on, 487–488
  extent to which applicable to United Nations Forces, 492–516
    as matter of law, 485–487, 493–511
      in enforcement action, 485
      in peace-keeping operations, 485–487
        by armed units, 486–487
        by unarmed units, 485
    as matter of practical application, 511–516

Laws of War—*cont.*
  functions of United Nations Forces to which applicable, 499–503
  laws of sea warfare, 492, 515
  occupation of territory, 490–491
  prisoners of war, 490, 501, 514–515
  responsibility for breaches, 57, 245–248
  self-defence and, 486, 502
  use of weapons, 488–489
  whether binding on national contingents, 503–506
  whether binding on the United Nations as such, 506–516
    conventional rules, 507–511
    customary rules, 506
League Belge pour la défense des droits de l'homme, 244n
Lebanon, 84, 138–139, 439, 440, 456
  agreement with, 84, 439, 440, 456
  facilities for UNEF in, 138–139
  And see under UNOGIL.
Legum, 153n
Logistic support, 14, 17, 37–38, 111, 136–137, 218–219, 387–411
  air-lift, 394–399
  continuing support, 399–403
  communications, 400–401
  equipment, 401–402
  medical services, 402
  procurement system, 402–403
  discussed in Military Staff Committee, 14, 17, 388–389
  finance of. *See* Financing.
  in future *ad hoc* agreements, 368–369
  in Korea, 37–38, 390–391, 392–394
  in observer groups, 389
  in ONUC, 218–219
  in UNEF, 111, 136–137
  proposals for nationalisation of, 403–406
Lumumba, 155, 157, 161, 163, 164, 185, 200
  arrest of, 163, 200
  conflict with Secretary-General, 157
  death of, 164, 185
  dismissal of, 159
  treatment of, 241

MAC (Mixed Armistice Commission), 75, 83
Makarios, President, 338
Martin, 524n, 533n
McArthur, 40, 42–44
McDougal, 305n, 498n
McNair, Lord, 247n, 265, 321n, 358n
Memel Harbour Board, 4
Methods of recruiting United Nations Forces, 330–337
  composite force, 336–337
  national contingents, 330–334
  permanent force, 334–336
Mexico, military action against in 1861...5

Military Staff Committee, 12–18, 23, 361, 379, 388–389, 395, 406, 419, 455, 469–470
Millis, 426n, 526n
Mobutu, 159, 161, 162

NATO,
  attempt to form NATO force in Cyprus, 552
  logistics in, 389
  proposals for integration of forces, 345
  Status of Forces Agreement, 437, 439, 445
Naulilaa Arbitration, 494n
Nichols, 481n
Nkrumah, 190
Non-intervention, 126, 183, 196–200, 282–283, 529–530
  in Congo, 183, 196–200
  in UNEF, 126
  rules for under disarmament, 529–530
  And see Consent.
Norwegian Institute of International Affairs, 337n, 425n
Noyes, 414n
N.V. de Bataafsche Petroleum et al v. *The War Damage Commission*, 496n

O'Brien, 193, 194n, 216, 226
Observer Groups, 61–89, 258, 268
  claims arising from, 85–86
  composition and equipment, 68–71
  constitutional basis of, 61–68
  financing of, 85
  functions, 71–79
    border control, 71–73
    quasi-judicial functions, 78–79
    supervision of cease-fire, etc., 73–77
    supervision of exchange of prisoners of war, 78
    supervision of withdrawal of forces, 77–78
  obligations of States towards, 79–85
    control of civilians, 83
    control of regular and irregular forces, 82–83
    freedom of movement, 79–81
  UNTEA, 258, 260
Ogmore, Lord, 326n
Okumu, 153n
ONUC. *See* Congo.
Oslo Conference on United Nations Security Forces, 321, 335n, 425n

Pakistan proposal, 317
Palestine, 62–63, 69, 71, 73, 74–77, 80–81, 82, 83, 270, 308n
Para-military, appropriateness of term, 328–329

Paris Peace Conference, 7
Parliamentary Group for World Government, 274, 482n
Participating States, 37–39, 111–115, 131, 205–224, 259, 358, 361–371
  ad hoc agreements with, 361–371
  agreements over UNEF, 111–115, 364–365
  contributions to finances of United Nations Forces, 468–471
  demand for political control of United Nations Forces, 358
  in Congo, 205–224
  in Korea, 37–39, 362, 363–364
  in UNTEA, 259
  matters for inclusion in future *ad hoc* agreements, 365–371
  powers of, 114
  privileges and immunities of, 131
Peace Fund. *See* Financing.
Peace-keeping operations, 267–274, 317–322, 413–417, 485–487, 499–503, 519–523, 545
  application of laws of war to, 485–487, 499–503. *And see* Laws of War.
  as functions of composite force, 320–322
  as functions of permanent force, 317–319
  assistance in national disasters, 273
  defence of United Nations zones or areas, 270–271
  frontier control, 269
  interpositionary functions, 269–270
  maintenance of law and order in a State, 271–273
  observation of cease-fires, etc., 268
  plebiscite supervision, 273
  prevention of international crimes, 274
  under disarmament, 519–523, 545
  whether consent of host State required for, 413–417
Peace-observation Commission, 355–356, 546–547
  And see Resolution on Uniting for Peace.
Peace Observation Corps, 545–551
Peaceful co-existence, 529, 530
Pearson, 91, 315–316, 328, 333
Permanent Force, 322–327, 377–378, 531–538, 543–544, 562
  agreements for, 377–378
  necessity for, 562
  pros and cons of, 322–327
  under disarmament, 531–538
  cost of, 543–544
Permanent Members, 110–111, 332, 349, 371–372, 475
  exclusion from UNEF, 110–111
  from permanent force, 349
  from stand-by agreements, 371–372

Permanent Members—*cont.*
 special responsibilities for finance,
  475
Plebiscites, 7–11, 258–259, 273, 546
 envisaged in W. Irian, 258–259
 envisaged under disarmament, 546
 supervision of by international
  forces, 7–11, 273
Poirier, 329n
Political control of United Nations
  Forces, 24–25, 41–45, 326, 353–360,
  531–538
 defects of in Korean action, 41–45
 discussed in Collective Measures
  Committee, 24–25
 organs of control, 353–360
  General Assembly, 355–357
  Secretary-General, 357–359
  Security Council, 354–355
 problems with a permanent force,
  326, 353–359
 techniques of, 359
 under disarmament, 531–538
Prisoners of War, 49–51, 490, 500–501,
  514–515
 repatriation problems in Korea, 49–
  51
 And see Laws of War.
Privileges and immunities. *See* Host
  States, agreements with.
Provisional measures, 177–178, 280–
  283, 444

Regional arrangements,
 as constitutional basis for United
  Nations Forces, 305–306, 362
Regulations, 102–103, 112, 119–121,
  219–222
 for ONUC, 219–222
 for UNEF, 102–103, 112, 119–121
Resolution on Uniting for Peace, 21,
  90, 98, 290–298, 304, 318, 355, 391,
  455, 546–547
Responsibility. *See* Claims and Re-
  sponsibility.
Robertson, Lord, 321, 327n
Rosner, 90n, 481n
Royal Institute of International
  Affairs, 314
Ruanda-Urundi, 163, 228
Russell, Ruth, 108

Saar, plebiscite in, 10–11
Salmon, 473n
San Francisco Conference, 418
Sanitary Police at Alexandria, Con-
  stantinople and Tangiers, 4
Scandinavian joint force, 345–346
Schachter, 175, 177, 267n, 278n, 279n,
  281n, 308n
Schwarzenberger, 279n, 295n, 300n,
  318–319, 322n, 494, 496n
Schwebel, 20n, 301n
Scutari, occupation of in 1913...7

Secretary-General, 18–21, 25–26, 41,
  65–66, 99–104, 155–156, 169, 183–
  186, 212–217, 229, 299–301, 320,
  323–324, 357–359, 554–555
 appeal for economic pressure on
  Katanganese authorities, 229
 as source of political control over
  permanent Force, 357–359
 authority to establish observer
  groups, 65–66
 authority to establish United
  Nations Force, 299–301
 death of Hammarskjoeld, 169
 interpretation of Congo mandate,
  155–156
 proposals for a United Nations
  Guard, 18–21, 320, 324
  for Committee for Korea, 41
  for Volunteer Reserve, 25–26
 role in Congo, 183–186, 212–217
  in Cyprus, 554–555
  in UNEF, 99–104
 views on permanent force, 323–324
Security Council, 14–18, 30–36, 76–77,
  175–182, 274–285, 331–332, 354–
  355, 531–538, 540–542, 549, 552–
  553
 action in Congo, 175–182
  in Cyprus, 552–553
  in Korea, 30–36
  in Palestine, 76–77
 as organ of political control over
  United Nations Force, 354–355
 constitutional authority to establish
  United Nations Force, 274–285
 discussion of Report of Military
  Staff Committee, 14–18
 possibility of renewal of attempts
  to conclude agreements under
  Article 43 of Charter by, 331–332
 role under disarmament, 531–538,
  540–542, 549
Self-defence, 17, 23, 34, 108, 183, 194,
  200–203, 293, 302–305, 486, 502,
  555–557
 as basis for Korean action, 34
 for United Nations Force, 302–305
 as justification for independent use
  of forces made available to the
  United Nations, 17, 23, 293
 principle of, as applied in Congo,
  183, 194, 200–203
  in Cyprus, 555–557
  in UNEF, 108
 relevance to application of laws of
  war, 486, 502
Seyersted, 243n, 245n, 277n, 296n,
  308n, 309n, 327, 329, 417n
Shanghai, International Settlement of,
  4–5
 Volunteer Corps, 5
Singer, 335n, 544n
Sohn, 277n, 280n, 286n, 296n, 300n,
  313, 317, 335n, 345n, 416n, 481n,
  482, 550n

Soviet Union, 15–18, 20, 35–36, 44, 93–
94, 154, 160, 164, 184, 207, 213–
214, 227, 276, 284–285, 288, 291,
294, 295n, 331–332, 348, 356, 357,
474n, 476, 479, 534, 554
attack on Secretary-General, 164,
184, 213–214
attitude on Congo, 154, 160, 207,
227, 284–285
on Cyprus, 554
on financing of United Nations
Forces, 476n, 479
on Korean action, 35–36, 44
on Opinion in *Expenses Case*,
474n
on UNEF, 93–94
position in Military Staff Committee, 15–18, 331–332
proposal for " troika," 348, 356, 534
reaction to Secretary-General's proposals for United Nations Guard,
20
system of military command in,
341
views on constitutional basis for
United Nations Forces, 276, 284–
285, 288, 291, 294, 295n, 357
views on disarmament. *See* Disarmament.
Stambuck, 437n, 464n
Stand-by agreements, 315, 320, 332–
333, 371–377, 439, 565
contents of, 371–377
alternative functions of Force,
372–373
finance, 373
logistics, 373
negotiation by United Nations,
332–333, 376, 565
Stand-by forces offered by States, 333,
345–346
Status of Forces Agreements. *See*
Host States, agreements with.
Stoessinger, 479n
Stone, 33, 34, 280n, 281n, 287n, 296n,
302n, 303, 304, 306n, 496n
Strategic control of United Nations
Forces, 41–45, 117–118, 212–217,
359–360
in Congo, 212–217
in Korea, 41–45
in permanent force, 359–360
in UNEF, 117–118
Switzerland, assistance to UNEF, 137

Tangier, international settlement of,
5
Taubenfeld, 507n
Transit agreements, 136–139, 455–458
Transit rights,
whether dependent on consent, 417–
419
Transport, 394–400, 408–411
Tshombé, 155, 157, 173, 189, 240–241

Tucker, 495
Tunkin, 295n, 326n
Turkey, 552, 558
Types of Force, 313–330
composite force, 319–322
national contingents, 315–316
permanent force, 316–319, 322–327
arguments against, 323–330
arguments for, 322–333

Union-Minière, 199n, 229
United Kingdom, 94, 170, 172, 190,
193n, 199n, 228–229, 247, 295, 309,
401, 476–477, 552
attempts to form Force for Cyprus,
552
attitude to Congo, 170, 172, 190,
193n, 199n, 228–229
to disarmament Force, 533–534,
548
to financing of United Nations
Force, 476–477
to UNEF, 94, 309
contemplation of claims by, 247
opposition to use of Uniting for
Peace Resolution, 295
refusal to supply bombs to ONUC,
401
United Nations Commission for the
Unification and Rehabilitation of
Korea (UNCURK), 59, 64
United Nations Commission on Korea
(UNCOK), 29–30, 64, 77
United Nations Courts-martial, desirability of, 353, 442, 463, 513, 550
UNEF, 90–151, 270, 289–290, 295–296,
429
administrative arrangements for,
118–119
agreements with participating
States, 111–114
character as an international force,
121–124
command structure, 115–117
composition and recruitment, 109–
111
constitutional basis of, 93–99, 289–
290, 295–296
establishment of, 90–93
failure to establish civil administration in Gaza, 107–108
financing of, 139–148
functions of, 105–109
relations between United Nations
and Member States, 136–139
Status agreement, 125–136, 429
strategic and political control, 117–
118
UNFICYP. *See* Cyprus.
United Nations Field Service, 19–20,
299, 402–403
United Nations Guard, 18–19, 268, 299,
320
proposals for, 18–19

United Nations Headquarters Military
Staff, 320–321, 325, 326, 330, 336,
349, 359–360, 376–377, 405–406,
548
appointment of, 349
cost of, 325
need for observer section in, 548
role in logistics planning, 405–406
in negotiation of stand-by agree-
ments, 376–377
in strategic direction of United
Nations Force, 359–360
structure of, 350–351
And see Conclusions.
United Nations Korea Reconstruction
Agency (UNKRA), 59
UNMOGIP, 63–64, 69
United Nations Neutral Nations Supervisory Commission, 49
UNOGIL, 64–65, 69, 73, 77, 81, 82,
269, 297
United Nations Panel of Field Observers, 19–20, 547–548
United Nations Panel of Military
Experts, 23
UNSCOB, 61–62, 68, 71, 79
United Nations Security Force. *See*
UNTEA.
UNTEA, 65, 69, 71, 74, 77, 81, 255–
261, 268, 271
composition of, 259–260
constitutional basis of, 256
establishment by General Assembly,
255–257
financing of, 260–261
functions of, 257–259
privileges and immunities, 260
UNTSO, 63, 74–77, 83, 105, 268
UNYOM, 65–66, 70–71, 74, 268
United States of America, 15–17, 29–
30, 32, 36–47, 52, 57–58, 60, 88,
136–137, 218, 395–398, 504

United States of America—*cont.*
action in Korea, 29–30, 32, 36–47, 52,
57–58, 60
in Lebanon, 88
air-lift for United Nations Force,
136–137, 218, 395–398
Army Field Manual, 504
position on disarmament. *See* Disarmament.
position on Military Staff Committee, 15–17

Venezuela, blockade of in 1902...6

Wehberg, 313
Weissberg, 54n, 420n, 507n
West Irian. *See* UNTEA.
West New Guinea. *See* UNTEA.
Withdrawal of United Nations Forces,
235, 259, 375, 379–386
in Congo, 235
in W. Irian, 259
of consent to presence of Force.
See Consent.
of national contingents,
under *ad hoc* agreements, 379–
385
under stand-by agreements, 375,
385–386
World Veterans Federation, 321
Wright, 493n, 496n
Wright v. *Cantrell*, 445n, 448n
Wyndham Place Trust, 314

Yepes, 499n

Zafrulla Khan, 479
Zorin, 521, 530, 534